Everyday Encounters with the Lord

EVERYDAY ENCOUNTERS WITH THE LORD

Meeting God and Hearing His Word
in Everyday Experiences

A year of daily devotional thoughts

Tony Elder

ELM HILL

A Division of
HarperCollins Christian Publishing

www.elmhillbooks.com

Everyday Encounters with the Lord
Meeting God and Hearing His Word
in Everyday Experiences

Published in Nashville, Tennessee, by Elm Hill, an imprint of Thomas Nelson. Elm Hill and Thomas Nelson are registered trademarks of HarperCollins Christian Publishing, Inc.

Elm Hill titles may be purchased in bulk for educational, business, fund-raising, or sales promotional use. For information, please e-mail SpecialMarkets@ ThomasNelson.com.

All Scripture quotations, unless otherwise indicated, are taken from the New King James Version®. © 1982 by Thomas Nelson. Used by permission. All rights reserved.

Library of Congress Cataloging-in-Publication Data

Library of Congress Control Number: 2018946843

ISBN 978-1-595557957 (Paperback)
ISBN 978-1-595557872 (Hardbound)
ISBN 978-1-595557995 (eBook)

I dedicate this devotional to all those encouragers over the years who told me how they were blessed through my writings and that I should compile them into a book.

PREFACE

Isn't it amazing that the Lord of heaven and earth wants to fellowship with us? He desires to reveal more about Himself to us, as well as truths about ourselves, the world we live in, and His will for our lives. Likewise, He wants us to respond to Him with our praises, our concerns, our hopes, our requests, our love, and our obedience. Yes, there is a God who loves us and wants to meet with us.

But we don't just have to go to a church building on a particular day in order to encounter Him. Hopefully we meet Him there, but we can fellowship with Him at other times too. I'm a strong proponent of the benefit of spending special time every day seeking such fellowship with the Lord, so it makes sense that I would compile some of my writings into a daily devotional book. Hopefully it will enhance your personal quiet times of Bible study and prayer.

However, God can be found outside those specified devotional times as well. He can speak to us in the common experiences of life. Many of the articles in this book spring from everyday occurrences—from a conversation with a grandchild to an encounter with nature to a holiday event. God is there. Biblical truths can be seen. We can hear from Him if we'll just tune in to His frequency.

It's my prayer that these devotions will be a help and blessing to you. I hope you'll encounter God as you read them. I trust you will respond by hearing, receiving, submitting to, and applying whatever God shows you. And maybe it will even result in helping you encounter God and hear His voice in your own everyday experiences.

Tony Elder

ACKNOWLEDGMENTS

First of all, I would like to thank my chief encourager and proofreader, my wife of thirty-seven years, Cheryl. She has been there with me through all of these journeys. I greatly appreciate the support of all of my family, including my parents, my children, and my grandchildren. I especially want to thank them for being partners in this endeavor, as they have willingly and gladly allowed me to share about some incidents from their own lives as a means of illustrating certain truths.

I am thankful for a supportive church family to whom I have had the privilege of ministering for many years. They have encouraged these types of ministry endeavors which have reached beyond the membership of our local congregation without any complaints that it took my attention away from them.

I would especially like to express my gratitude to *The Rockdale/ Newton Citizen* for giving me the opportunity to write a weekly newspaper column. Those articles provided the majority of the material included in this book.

I would like to thank the kind and patient people at Elm Hill Publishing who have been so helpful and skillful in guiding me through this new adventure.

Most of all, I am grateful for a God who lovingly condescends to reach down to meet with us and reveal to us His eternal truths. I am thankful that He still reigns as Lord, His Word still holds true, and He still calls us to be a holy people. It is only due to His grace and enablement that this book could be written.

Take on a New Challenge This Year

"I press on, that I may lay hold of that for which Christ Jesus has also laid hold of me"

– Philippians 3:12

Recently one of my grandsons came over to our house with a specific purpose in mind—to be able to ride his bicycle without the use of training wheels. Due to the limited space around his own home for practicing, he hadn't been able to take the final steps toward his goal. But since we live on a cul-de-sac, it was a perfect spot for working to achieve this childhood milestone.

As soon as we started practicing, I could tell he was so close to getting it. He only needed a few pointers and a lot of encouragement. Whenever he felt the bike start to tilt, he would put his foot down on the ground to catch himself rather than lean the other way to try to compensate and maintain his balance. He simply needed to build up a little confidence and be willing to trust himself to keep from falling.

After working on it for a while, he made significant improvement. Finally I asked him if he wanted to try riding down our driveway. After a brief hesitation, he said he was ready. When he successfully maneuvered the length of our driveway, circled around, and came all the way back to the top without stopping, I knew he had officially become a bike rider. And by the grin on his face, he knew it as well.

Most of us learned how to ride a bicycle a long time ago, but maybe we're facing some adult challenges today which are just as daunting as bike-riding can be to a kid. We're not very confident about our ability to do it. We're afraid of falling. We keep putting our foot down to catch ourselves rather than risking letting go and trusting God.

As a new year begins, maybe some of us need to be encouraged to take the plunge to tackle that new challenge or opportunity. It's time to remove the training wheels, put ourselves out there, and go for it. It's time to quit merely talking about it and start doing something.

For some of us, it may apply to our relationship with the Lord. We need to stop holding back, surrender ourselves completely to God, and let Him lead us along the road to spiritual maturity. For others, it may apply to some specific task or opportunity for service which God has for us. It may not be easy. It might take a significant commitment of our time and effort. But if this is what the Lord wants us to do, He will enable us to do it. And it will be worth any sacrifice we might have to make.

However there's another side to this truth too. Maybe there are some folks around us who need us to be their encouragers. They're the ones who are trying to ride without the training wheels. And they need someone like you to run along beside them, to give them bits of advice when needed, to lend a hand of support, and to provide uplifting words of encouragement. They need you to cheer them on. They need someone to be there to pick them up and soothe their hurts when they stumble and fall. And they need someone to be there to help them celebrate their moments of achievement and success.

So let's be willing to take the plunge ourselves this year to reach for new milestones in our walk with God and our service to Him. And at the same time let's be a help and encouragement to the people around us who are doing likewise.

What new challenge does God want you to pursue?

MAINTAIN A REGULAR AND BALANCED SPIRITUAL DIET

"All Scripture is given by inspiration of God, and is profitable for doctrine, for reproof, for correction, for instruction in righteousness"
— II TIMOTHY 3:16

I often encourage people to make a daily practice of reading the Bible. It's strange—you usually don't have to prod anyone to eat dinner every day, but many of us have to be reminded to feed regularly on that which nourishes and strengthens our souls.

At the beginning of a new year, when some people especially focus on changes they can make to improve their lives, a fresh commitment to reading and studying God's Word is commendable. There are numerous reading schedules and suggestions available for those who are serious about that worthwhile pursuit. I particularly like the ones that take you on the journey of reading through the whole Bible in a year's time.

However, I realize that some people may not feel that they can read three or four chapters every day, as many of those programs require. Yet they still want to develop that daily habit of Bible reading. It would be a big step forward for them simply to read one chapter faithfully each day. Or there are others who want to focus on smaller portions of scripture, spending time at more in-depth study. With that in mind, I recently came up with a tool for the folks in my church (see Appendix A). I'm calling it the Bible Highlights Reading Schedule. It's a compilation of 366 chapters from the Bible—one for each day of the year. I tried to select chapters that would cover the main narratives or convey the primary truths taught in God's Word.

Surprisingly I found this to be one of the most difficult tasks I had undertaken in quite a while. After all, what chapters in God's written revelation to mankind do you skip over? Which ones do you dare to judge to be less important than others? I hadn't progressed far in this exercise before I found a fresh appreciation for the warning in the Bible not to subtract from any of its words. I was reminded of the fact that all portions of God's Word are significant.

Do you tend to spend most of your time reading in the New Testament? Let's not forget that those Old Testament narratives are a history of God's dealings with mankind too. The stories of those characters are not irrelevant to us as they serve as examples of how we should live and relate to God, and in some cases, how we shouldn't. Even those tedious genealogies, the instructions about building the tabernacle, and other less inspirational passages serve a purpose that we would do well not to ignore.

Maybe some of us need to seek a more balanced spiritual diet this year. It's possible to get so focused on one portion of scripture or one subject, as important as they are, and neglect others that would benefit us in different ways. How long has it been since you've read the account of Abraham and been challenged by his faith? How many of us need to observe and follow Joseph's example and flee from sexual temptation? Who doesn't need to be reminded that we serve a God who is great enough to part waters, slay giants, and save His people from floods, Pharaohs, and fiery furnaces? But then there are others who may enjoy the stories, but fail to dig deep into the spiritual concepts taught by Jesus and by the Apostle Paul in the New Testament.

Parts of the Bible may need to be emphasized more than others. However, none of it is worthy of our neglect. Will you commit yourself this year to a daily and more balanced diet of the spiritually nourishing Word of God?

Determine with God's help to read His Word more regularly.

ENDEAVORING TO SEE
MORE CLEARLY THIS YEAR

"Show me your ways, O Lord; teach me Your paths. Lead me in Your truth and teach me."

– PSALM 25:4–5

One of my first tasks in this new year will be to get a new pair of eyeglasses. When I had my annual eye exam, I had a difficult time reading small print with my current prescription. However, it's not due to the fact that my eyesight has worsened. I've already been wearing progressive bifocals for about a decade now. It seems that this problem has to do with the glasses themselves. The area on the lens intended to aid me in seeing objects that are close up is so unusually small that I have a hard time finding it. No matter how I tilted my head or moved the printed card while wearing my glasses, the lettering remained somewhat of a blur.

As we begin another year, it might be a good idea for all of us to make clearer sight one of our goals and priorities. No, I'm not trying to drum up business for my wonderful ophthalmologist. I'm referring primarily to our seeing God's will and understanding better His direction for our lives.

Unfortunately, many of us would have to admit that we tend to see His will better at a distance than we do up close. In other words, it's easier to discern what God wants to do in other people's lives than it is to grasp what He's saying to us or what changes He may want to make in our conduct and attitude. It's reminiscent of Jesus words in the Sermon on the

Mount. We have little problem in spying the splinter in our companion's eye, but we can't see the two-by-four that's stuck in our own eye.

And that can be a problem, especially as we make resolutions or seek guidance about what improvements we can make in our lives this year. If we don't see the real issues, we can focus our time and efforts on the wrong areas, or at least on secondary things.

Sometimes we sing songs like the one in the church hymnal that says, "Open my eyes that I may see...." We pray for enlightenment—that God would show us His will or give us clear guidance. And it's true that we need God's help in order to see. But too often the main problem isn't the lack of revelation from God, but rather an unwillingness on our part to see and acknowledge the truths God is trying to show us. That especially holds true when the Lord is dealing with those close-up and personal issues in our lives. It can be humbling to acknowledge our need to change. And it can be painful to submit ourselves to the divine touch as God surgically deals with those issues in our lives.

We may not need more spectacular signs from God or greater revelation as to what His will is for us. It may be that we simply need to receive and submit to what He has already shown us or has been saying to us. Instead of praying for God to open our eyes, it could be that we need to quit purposely closing them to whatever it is that God wants us to see.

So as we pray, read the Bible, and seek God's will, let's make this part of our prayer: "Lord, open my eyes to the truth. And help me to keep my eyes open, even when You're showing me those up-close aspects of my own life that you want to change and improve. I'm willing to see whatever You show me, and to submit to Your will for me."

I hope to see more clearly in more ways than one this year. How about you?

Is there something God has been showing you, but which you've refused to acknowledge?

A Great God Is in the Driver's Seat

"And the Lord said to Abraham, 'Why did Sarah laugh, saying, "Shall I surely bear a child since I am old?" Is anything too hard for the Lord?"'

– Genesis 18:13–14

I know someone who recently revealed the good news that she is expecting her first child. While that is commonly an occasion for joyful celebration, it is especially so in this situation. It has been one of those cases where the desire to bear children has failed to be fulfilled for a period of years. There have been many prayers, along with all the medical tests and usages of modern technology, to try to assist in the conception of a child. So it's a special blessing to see those many years of disappointments and frustrations melt away in the light of the news of this new life God has given.

It's interesting how often a similar scenario is recorded for us in the Bible. There are a number of stories about those who were barren who eventually gave birth. Such a list would include the likes of Sarah, Rachel, Hannah, Samson's mother, and Elisabeth. One reason for those stories is because they show a common longing in the human heart, along with an emphasis on the importance of childbearing in that particular culture. But another purpose in those biblical accounts is to remind us of some truths about God.

For one thing, they help us remember that God is in control. We often stray into the mistaken notion that we are the masters of our own destiny.

We plan everything out, thinking we know exactly how all the pieces of the puzzle will fall into place in our lives. Sometimes that includes figuring out the specific number of children we're going to have and the perfect time to bring each one into the world. Maybe we see the right time being whenever we get more financially secure, or whenever we move into a bigger house. Or for others, the right time may seem to be now. But so often those well-laid plans don't work out as we had hoped.

Sometimes we're guilty of being one of those the Bible describes who declares his detailed plans for tomorrow when he doesn't really know what the next day may hold. We're reminded that we should say, "If the Lord wills, we shall live and do this or that" (see James 4:15). Whether it's the barrenness of a womb, the unexpected conception of a child, a sudden sickness or death, a car accident, the loss of a job, or countless other unplanned events in our lives, we're often reminded that we're not in the driver's seat as much as we like to think we are.

Another truth those biblical accounts reveal has to do with the power of God. They remind us that God can do what we can't do. They show us that when we come to our wit's end, and even when modern technology has done all it can do to no avail, there is a great God who can still accomplish what may seem impossible to man.

It was within the context of the angel of the Lord revealing to Abraham that Sarah was going to bear a child that this question is asked: "Is anything too hard for the Lord?" It was a question with an obvious answer—an answer we need to keep in mind in our situations. However difficult things may look, there is a great God who still hears our prayers and can do what seems inconceivable to us.

So whatever challenge we're facing, let's remember these truths from those biblical childbearing stories. God is in control, working out what He knows is best for us according to His time and purpose. We need to keep praying, believing, and submitting to His will, not ours. And let's never lose faith in the right answer to the question, "Is anything too hard for the Lord?"

Be assured that your situation is not too difficult for God.

What If a Calendar Documented Our Growth?

"But grow in the grace and knowledge of our Lord and Savior Jesus Christ."

– II Peter 3:18

Many of us have probably either purchased calendars recently or received one as a gift. Someone gave me one which has beautiful scenes from nature for each month of the year, along with quotations from the Psalms. It is now decorating the wall of my office at the church. There are calendars produced for almost anyone, displaying everything from generic photographs to pictures of specialized interests. For example, dog lovers can find one for virtually any breed of canine, like the one I received and enjoyed a few years ago exclusively about basset hounds.

However, my favorite calendar has to be the one our daughter gave us one year. It didn't have preprinted pictures for each month. Instead, there was an empty place to insert a photograph as each page was turned. January had a recent snapshot of our grandson already included. Then throughout the year, at the beginning of each month, our daughter gave us an updated photo of our little pride and joy. In March, he was donning a St. Patrick's Day hat. In July, he was wearing red, white, and blue. In the October picture, he was showing off his Halloween costume.

On New Year's Day, as we removed that calendar from its twelve-month residence on our refrigerator, I enjoyed looking through all those photographs again and reliving some memories. However, the most obvious truth those pictures revealed was how much our grandson has grown over the past year. He looked like such a baby in January but as the months went by, you could see him progressing more and more into becoming the "big little boy" which he was by December.

I wonder…if our Heavenly Father had kept such a photo calendar of us over the past year, what would it have looked like? I'm not thinking about pictures of how we've changed physically—those calendars are cute for kids, but they might be rather pathetic or discouraging for some of us adults if they showed us progressing in grey hairs, wrinkles, and other signs of aging. No, I'm referring to God taking pictures of our heart, our character, our soul. Would it show that we've grown over the past year? Would there be more of God's love lighting up our faces? Would there be more godly wisdom showing in our eyes? Would we look more like Jesus in character and conduct than we did a year earlier? Would our hearts be more passionate for God and more full of His purity and grace?

My grandson didn't have to put forth effort to grow. It happened naturally, but only because there were people in his life who intentionally made sure he ate well and maintained good health. We have to accept that responsibility for ourselves regarding our spiritual growth. We can't make ourselves grow, but we can maintain a close, healthy relationship with the Lord. We can seek to know Him better and to love Him more. We can feed regularly upon His Word. We can guard against anything that would hinder our spiritual growth and let the Holy Spirit cleanse us of any impurities which would infect our hearts with disease. The Lord promises that if we will intentionally draw close to Him, He, in turn, will draw close to us. And such a relationship will inevitably lead to growth.

As we continue into this new year, let's make sure that our Heavenly Father's calendar will record significant spiritual growth and progress in our lives, too.

In what ways do you hope to have changed and progressed spiritually by this time next year?

It's the Little Things that Can Make a Difference

"But lay up for yourselves treasures in heaven, where neither moth nor rust destroys and where thieves do not break in and steal."
— Matthew 6:20

Like many people, including the guy in a current insurance commercial, I have a longstanding habit of putting my loose change in a jar when I empty my pockets at the end of the day. I think it was a little over a year ago when someone gifted me with a special container for that purpose. I suppose you could call it a "smart jar"—if we can use that description for phones, then maybe it's appropriate for other inanimate objects. This container not only collects my coins, but it counts them as I make my deposits. I think it gains this intelligence from the size of the coins as they are forced through the slot.

So now I don't have to guess how much money I've collected over a period of time. My jar provides me with a running total. I hadn't paid much attention to that number for a while, so I was pleasantly surprised recently to discover that I had amassed over $130 since I had last emptied the jar. Therefore it's definitely time to roll some coins and head to the bank.

It's interesting how such small amounts of pennies, nickels, dimes, and quarters can grow into a significant number over time, often with us giving little thought to it and considering such change as our leftovers. We rightly pay more attention to those weekly paychecks or to other occasional bigger financial windfalls which come our way. But let's not lose sight of how the little things can add up and make a difference too.

The same holds true in other areas of our lives. Jesus instructed us to "lay up for yourselves treasures in heaven" (Matthew 6:20). As we consider what constitutes our fulfilling that command, we might tend to think of some of the bigger, less-frequent opportunities which come our way. Maybe we think about the time we were able to share our testimony before a large group of people. Or we think about an occasion when God allowed us to be in the right place at the right time in His harvest field to help lead someone to Christ. Or maybe we remember the time we received an extra-big financial blessing and was able to pass it along by giving a significant donation to some charitable organization. Those are wonderful opportunities for doing something which may have lasting, eternal value.

However, let's not overlook the little daily ways we can store up such treasures as well. You may not get to speak before large crowds very often, but most days you have conversations with individuals whose lives you can impact. A kind or encouraging word, a brief testimony, or an acknowledgement of God's goodness and blessings might be just what that person needs to hear. You might not get to reap the harvest of a lost soul very often, but you can daily sow seeds that God may use to eventually bring people to faith in Him. It may be rare for you to have the means to make a donation that would put your name on an organization's list of top donors, but your regular tithe and offering to your church, or a few dollars here and there to other charitable causes can still make a difference.

Like our loose change in a jar, those small, daily acts of love, those little nuggets of truth, those regular acts of faithfulness to serve God and minister to others will add up over time. We may tend to think of them as not being very significant, but God notices. Keep depositing those "little things" each day. They will probably make up the majority of our treasure in heaven.

Look for little ways in which the Lord can use you to make a difference today.

OUR CONDUCT SHOULD MATCH
WHAT WE SAY WE BELIEVE

"Now then, we are ambassadors for Christ...."

– II CORINTHIANS 5:20

Did you hear about the man who robbed a store while wearing a shirt emblazoned on the front with the message "Jesus Loves You"? Authorities think he may have worn the item of clothing specifically in order to gain trust and deflect suspicion before carrying out his act of theft. It's despicable when someone uses the Christian faith as a cover for his ungodly actions. However, we do encounter such charlatans on occasion. Maybe you've received one of those emails calling you "dearly beloved in Christ" as someone tries to scam you out of some money. And unfortunately there have always been a few so-called ministers around who are only putting on a show of following Christ in order to take advantage of their flocks for their own personal gain.

While we have to be on guard against such folks who put up a false front of being a follower of Christ, thankfully most of us don't fall into that category. Our more common problem tends to be unintentionally not living up to what we outwardly profess. Maybe we wear our T-shirt with some kind of thought-provoking Christian adage or verse of scripture printed on it, only to lose our temper, act unlovingly, or in some other way display conduct that isn't in keeping with the message we're so prominently exhibiting on our clothing. Or we drive vehicles with a bumper sticker proclaiming some biblical truth or with one of those license plates declaring "In God We

Trust," but then we drive without regard for the law or display a discourteous or even hostile attitude toward others on the road.

We're not like that thief who was intentionally trying to fool people. We really do love Jesus, believe the Bible, and are putting our trust in God. However, we have to admit that we don't always represent our Lord and our faith as faithfully as we should.

The easy thing to do in light of this situation is simply to make excuses for ourselves—"I'm only human"—"We all makes mistakes"—"No one is perfect." While those may be true, we shouldn't settle for being less than what God calls us to be. We are to be "ambassadors for Christ" (II Corinthians 5:20). We represent Him in this world. Our lives should be a testimony to who Jesus is and what He can do in people who allow Him to come into their hearts.

Even if we're not wearing a Christian shirt, a cross necklace, or anything else that proclaims our faith to those around us, we should still hope to be such a Christlike example that people will see Jesus in us. We may not have a fish symbol on our car or display one of those "In God We Trust" tags, but we should still treat other drivers and the laws of the road with the respect and courtesy due them.

Yes, we're going to falter at times. There will be moments when we embarrass ourselves and will be ashamed that our conduct didn't match up with our profession of faith. But we can seek God's forgiveness and ask Him to help us not do the same thing again. He can change our hearts and attitudes, enabling us to be better representatives of Him and of what we say we believe.

Don't be afraid to wear those Christian shirts or otherwise proclaim your faith. However, let's be sure to seek God's help in living up to any Christian message we choose to have on display. We should always aim to be good ambassadors for Christ whether we're wearing such apparel or not.

Live each moment as if everyone around you knows you're a follower of Jesus.

OUR ULTIMATE LOYALTY
ALWAYS BELONGS TO GOD

"No servant can serve two masters; for either he will hate the one and love the other, or else he will be loyal to the one and despise the other."

– LUKE 16:13

There are times when a sports fan's loyalty to his favorite team is put to the test. We just completed another season of college bowl games and now the NFL playoffs are in full swing. These occasions can sometimes result in teams which rarely compete against one another facing off in an important game. No doubt some people find themselves in a quandary when two teams they like, two teams they have cheered for all season, two teams to which they have some degree of connection and loyalty take the field on opposite sides of the ball.

The problem is that you can't really pull for both teams to win. It would be about as confusing as trying to play yourself in a game of table tennis. I suppose you could hope both teams play well. You might cheer for certain players to perform at their best level. You might applaud each team when it makes a big play. You might wish for a close game. But if it came down to one final play at the end of the game to decide the contest, you would have to make a choice as to whether you wanted one team to score or the other team to stop them. Do you really want that runner to get into the end zone? Do you want to see that football get kicked through the uprights? Or do you hope it falls short? With which team does your ultimate loyalty lie?

When it comes to our loyalty to the Lord, sometimes there is little problem in recognizing the enemy and choosing to be on God's side. But other times conflicts arise between good things in our lives and what God wants us to do. Most of the time we probably find our families, work situations, church obligations, personal desires and plans on the same team as the Lord. But what about when we suddenly find one of those other areas competing against God's will for us? What about when God is pointing us toward one fork in the road when our ambition wants us to take the other way? What if God is directing us to go someplace that would require putting more distance between us and beloved family? Whom do we choose to win in our lives when one of our favorite things collides with the plans of the One whom we call "Lord"?

I can only imagine how difficult it was for Abraham the time God told him to offer up his son as a sacrifice. He suddenly found his family, his affection, and his plans for the future, along with God's own promises about that son, on the other side of the ball from what God was telling him to do. But Abraham showed both his faith and his loyalty to God by being willing to obey that command (although, if you know the story, God stopped him from actually going through with the deed).

Jesus warned us that following Him would sometimes put us in conflict with our own families and friends. There would be times when we would have to choose between good things and Him. We would even find our own selves on the other team at times, having to pray as He did, "Not my will, but Yours be done."

The bottom line is simply that we can't serve two masters. At some point we have to choose with whom our loyalty truly lies. Are we going to do what God says and be on His team, or not? Whatever choices we face, let's always be loyal to our one and only Master.

Is there any area of your life you're not submitting to the lordship of Jesus?

BE CAREFUL OF DEVELOPING SPIRITUAL NUMBNESS

"You should no longer walk as the rest of the Gentiles walk…who, being past feeling, have given themselves over to lewdness, to work all uncleanness with greediness"

– EPHESIANS 4:17–19

I've got a shiner. It's not bad—just a little bruising under my left eye. I jokingly told my congregation that it was not from my wife punching me in the eye, at least not this time. However with what has reportedly transpired in the relationships between some ministers and their spouses over the years, I suppose I should be careful even joking about such matters. Anyway, mine is just a slight bruise. If my wife had done it, I'm sure it would have been much worse.

You'll be glad to know that my particular contusion is the result of a medical procedure, not the aftereffect of a fight. Unfortunately I'm going to have to return to that doctor's office for a second round of minor surgery next week, in order to take care of the rest of the problem. That means I'll once again get to sit uncomfortably tilted back in a chair in such a way that it reminds me of getting stuck hanging upside down on a Ferris wheel. The procedure itself isn't so bad. It's just the preparation for it that is painful. I appreciate medicines that can numb an area which is going to face a surgeon's knife, but wouldn't it be nice if they could find a way to make painless the shot which injects that medicine? I find that a needle implanted near a sensitive area such as the eyelid is especially excruciating.

Numbness can be a good thing when it comes to medical procedures, but the lack of feeling isn't so good when it comes to spiritual matters. In Ephesians 4:18, when the Apostle Paul was describing the condition of people who had not received new life in Christ, he commented not only on the fact that their understanding was darkened and their hearts blind, but also that they were "past feeling." That phrase would seem to indicate an emotional, moral, and spiritual numbness. It might describe someone who feels little or no compassion for the people around them. It might indicate someone who is unmoved when others, even God, express love and care for them. But it may also refer to a numbness to the pain of guilt, shame, and condemnation that comes from personal wrongdoing. We are in a sad condition when we have so hardened our hearts against God or others that we no longer possess those natural feelings.

However, I believe those who do know Christ also need to guard against experiencing some degree of spiritual numbness. When the Holy Spirit reveals sin in our lives and we choose to ignore it or not to act upon it appropriately with confession and repentance, we may start losing some of our feeling. Such conviction can be painful. When God's Word shows us our faults, it can be like a sharp sword piercing deep within our hearts (Hebrews 4:12). But sometimes we need to feel that pain in order to recognize that we have a problem which needs God's forgiveness and cleansing.

Granted, some people may be oversensitive about such matters and constantly beat themselves up over their unworthiness. But I believe the far greater and more common problem is a lack of sensitivity to sin in our lives. We live in a world that will inject us full of soothing anesthetics, assuring us that such behavior or attitudes are not wrong, they are natural, everyone does it, and God will accept us anyway. And if we're not careful, we will end up being numb to the voice of God and the conviction of the Holy Spirit. Let's be willing to feel the pain so that we can receive the God-given remedy.

Have you grown numb to something God has been speaking to you about?

18

GOD DOESN'T RESTRICT
THE GIVING OF HIS GRACE

"Behold, now is the accepted time; behold, now is the day of salvation."

– II CORINTHIANS 6:2

It's time again. I hear that the Girl Scouts in our area are starting to take orders for their cookies this weekend. One of the leaders of the troop which meets at our church gave me advanced warning that it was coming. With that, I've been able to spend the past week dreaming about which cookies I wanted and how many to buy. I've got to have a couple of boxes of my favorite—the Do-si-dos. And of course my wife will likewise need a box or two of those Samoas to which she is so partial. And you can't buy Girl Scout cookies without getting some Thin Mints. They're even good after a few months in the freezer. The problem is all the cookies are so tasty that it's hard to eliminate any of the varieties from my list. However, my wallet insists that I exercise some degree of restraint.

It wouldn't be so difficult if you could pick up those specialty cookies any time you wanted them, but the Girl Scout authorities are exceptionally strict about when the various troops and regions can take orders and distribute those delicious treats. If I get a craving for an Oreo or a Nutter Butter, I can easily find a store with that product on the shelf waiting to satisfy my urge, but if I get a taste for a Do-si-do, unless I've got a box stashed away somewhere, I may have a long wait until I can get another.

I'm glad that God doesn't have any such restrictions on the distribution of His grace, especially His gift of salvation. We don't have to wait for special occasions, such as religious holidays, to respond to His invitations. If I sensed a deadness in my soul today, I wouldn't want to have to wait until Easter to experience a resurrection to new life. I would want to get that important matter taken care of as soon as possible. And what if here in January you were forced to delay receiving Jesus into your heart until the celebration of His coming into the world at Christmas the following December? Imagine going eleven months knowing that your heart wasn't right with the Lord, but unable to do anything about it until December 25th rolled around.

The good news is that we don't even have to wait until Sunday to respond to God. Neither do we have to do it within the walls of a church building. Many years ago when I came to that point of recognizing my need for forgiveness and asked Jesus to come into my heart, it took place on a weekday evening in the living room of my own home. While I've known many people who have received God's saving grace while kneeling at a church altar, I'm aware of others who experienced that pivotal moment while driving in a car, enjoying the beauty of nature, or quietly contemplating in the privacy of their own bedroom. I seem to recall the Apostle Paul encountering Christ in the middle of a road.

We don't have to wait for a particular time, season, or place before receiving God's grace. He invites us to come to Him today. Whenever we sense our need and hear His call, that's the time to act.

Even though I'm placing my cookie order this weekend, I'm going to have to wait several weeks for the shipment to arrive before my taste buds will finally be satisfied. But you don't have to wait another moment to have the longing in your soul satisfied. You can stop reading right now and seek to receive God's forgiveness, cleansing, and saving grace.

God's grace is available to you right now. Go ahead and receive it.

BE SOMEONE WITH A DIFFERENT KIND OF SPIRIT

"But My servant Caleb...has a different spirit in him and has fol-lowed Me fully...."

– NUMBERS 14:24

Is it just me, or does it seem like more people these days are expressing negative attitudes about life in general, and especially a pessimistic out-look concerning the future? We may have some valid reasons for concern as we see certain economic, political, and spiritual trends in the world, but we need to be careful that we don't fall into the trap of becoming dis-couraged, hopeless, and complaining people.

I remember hearing a few years ago that the Consumer Confidence Index (CCI) was at its lowest level ever. That figure would seem to indi-cate that many people weren't feeling very good about what was ahead for our nation economically. Apparently a great number among us were still concerned about the possibility of job losses, home foreclosures, and higher prices.

However, I would like to suggest that there's another CCI which shouldn't have changed. I would call it the Christian Confidence Index. What has changed regarding God and His promises that should cause us to lose our confidence as followers of Christ? Is God no longer around or available to help us? Is His Word no longer valid? There's an old say-ing—"The future is as bright as the promises of God." Have the promises of God somehow changed resulting in the future not being as bright as it has been in the past? I don't believe so. As long as God and His Word are the same, we have reason to look ahead to tomorrow with faith, assurance, hope, and encouragement.

I didn't open up my Bible this morning to find that it had been supernaturally altered so that some of God's promises were missing or changed. Jesus still promises to be with us always. And Paul still assures us that God will supply all of our need according to His riches in glory. Even though our society is changing and some of our personal circumstances are different, the promises of God are the same. We can still count on them today.

In Numbers 14:24, Caleb is described as having a different spirit from the rest of the Israelites. In verses 26–29 of that chapter, the attitude of the majority is shown to be a negative, complaining, and pessimistic one. When they reached the border of the land God had promised to give them, they refused to go in. Based on the reports of giants and fortified cities in that land, they thought the endeavor was hopeless. The people complained about why God had brought them there to die. Although Caleb saw the same thing as the other spies, he reached a different conclusion. He declared, "Let's go up right now and take possession of the land. We are well able to overcome it."

Will we face our circumstances like the majority of the Israelites did—if the road ahead looks uncertain, or difficult, then we'll complain and turn back? Or will we face them with a different spirit—one that has confidence that if God has led us here and is telling us to move forward, then we are able to do it with His help?

Yes, there may be some problems, giants, and challenges ahead, but we don't have to let the prospect of those things mold us into pessimistic, complaining people. Apart from God and His Word, the future can look bleak. But when we take into account God's presence and His promises, we can be people of faith, hope, and optimism. The future is still bright for those who put their trust in Him. So no matter what kind of negative outlook others around you may possess, you be a Caleb—be someone with a different spirit.

As you face challenges today, show a spirit of faith in God.

Is a New Challenge
Worth the Risk?

"By faith Abraham obeyed when he was called to go out to the place which he would receive as an inheritance."

– Hebrews 11:8

Last weekend I was reminded of the mixed feelings I can experience on those rare occasions in our neck of the woods when the possibility of frozen precipitation is in the weather forecast. There's a part of me that with childlike anticipation always hopes for it to happen. There's a unique beauty in the snowflakes floating to the ground, as well as in the resulting soft, white blanket which drapes over the landscape. I enjoy watching it and even getting out in it to some extent. And if my grandkids happen to come by, I would probably be enticed to join them in playing more extensively than I should in such a winter wonderland.

However, at the same time another part of me almost dreads the same event or hopes that it might pass us by. After all, it would disrupt my planned activities. Sometimes that might be a welcome change, but other times it might hinder me from doing something I was really looking forward to. Such winter weather events can result in other inconveniences, such as not being able to travel or losing electricity and heat. It can even escalate to something beyond inconvenience—it can become risky and dangerous with tree limbs falling and slippery conditions on the roads. Thus I'm often torn between wanting to experience the unparalleled beauty and enjoyment of a snowfall, but at the same time dreading the possibility of the disruptions, risks, and dangers it could pose for myself or others.

We sometimes experience similar circumstances as we make our journey with Christ through life. We see a fresh challenge or opportunity the Lord seems to be bringing our way and we have mixed feelings about it. We recognize how it could be something beautiful which would bring glory to the Lord. At the same time we realize it will come with its share of changes and inconveniences. It might not only disrupt what we're accustomed to doing, but it presents some potential risks and dangers. Underneath the beauty can be some slippery spots.

I was reminded of this in connection with what our church is currently doing. We have combined our Sunday morning worship service with another congregation. Our two groups are very likeminded doctrinally and spiritually, but we're very different in other ways—ways which sometimes tend to lead to division and separation in society. There is potential for great beauty when believers of different races, cultures, and customs come together in a spirit of unity to worship their one Lord. It can be a wonderful witness to the world and a foretaste of our fellowship in heaven. However, it also comes with changes, inconveniences, and even some dangers. Is it worth the risk?

Maybe you ask the same question as you face some challenge or opportunity in your life. You can see the potential beauty. You dream of what God might do through such a situation. But you also see those slippery slopes on which you could fall. And it's certainly going to disrupt your life to some extent. Is it worth it?

If God is leading, it certainly is worth the risk. There may be some inconveniences to endure. We may slip, slide, or even fall down at times. However the beauty and joy of what God creates as we obediently follow His guidance will far outweigh any downside.

In order to enjoy a good snowfall, I'll make a few adjustments and endure some hardships. Let's do the same in connection with those new opportunities God brings our way.

Step out in faith to follow wherever God is leading you.

UTILIZE THE ARMOR GOD HAS PROVIDED FOR YOU

"Put on the whole armor of God, that you may be able to stand against the wiles of the devil."

— EPHESIANS 6:11

Making use of a Christmas gift from one of our children, my wife and I recently stepped back in time for a few hours. We visited a venue in our area where you can enter the world of castles, royalty, knights, and other medieval personages and practices. We enjoyed a delicious feast in which your only eating utensils were your fingers, although they did provide you with a moist towelette at the conclusion of the meal. I doubt if that feature was characteristic of the time period, but we still appreciated it.

There were performances by beautiful, well-trained horses, along with contests and battles between knights. I think my wife even came close to swooning when she caught a carnation tossed to her by the congenial combatant who was supported by our section of the audience.

While those knights wore their armor to protect them as they did battle, there were numerous other impressive suits of armor out in the lobby on display. A nearby sign informed the patrons that those suits were available for purchase. The price wasn't shown, but based on how much their T-shirts cost, I'm sure I couldn't have afforded a whole suit of armor. And even if I could buy one, I don't think such an item would quite fit in with the decor of the rest of our house, although it might make for an interesting conversation piece.

The Bible tells us that our King has provided a suit of armor for His followers. If you need to be reminded of the details, check out Ephesians 6:10–18. However, we need to keep in mind that this armor is not meant simply to be on display in our lives as a museum piece. God didn't give it to us just so we can look at it, talk about it, and show it off to others. He intends for us to wear it and to use it.

In that passage in Ephesians, we're told to "take up" and "put on" the whole armor of God. It's not enough to possess it. We're to wear it. And we don't do so simply in order to model it before our friends or to try to impress people. The Bible instructs us to wear it in order "that you may be able to stand against the wiles of the devil" and "that you may be able to withstand in the evil day, and having done all, to stand." This armor is a vital tool to protect us as we do battle against evil and sin.

I'm afraid there are too many of us who don't put up much of a fight against temptation and Satan. We've found it easier just to give in to their attacks and seductions, knowing that forgiveness, healing, and restoration are available to us afterwards. But that's not how our King expects us to live. He calls us to resist the devil and to flee from temptation. He wants us to discover that He can not only pick us up when we get knocked down, but He can also enable us not to fall in the first place. We can be more than forgiven losers: we can be victorious conquerors through Christ.

Let's not leave our armor sitting on the shelf or in the display case. Let's be valiant knights for Jesus. Take up that armor of truth, righteousness, faith, prayer, the word of God, and all the rest. Those aren't museum pieces for us to enjoy. They are weapons for us to employ in our daily battle against evil. So don't just sit back and admire your God-given armor—use it.

Are there any pieces of your armor which you've been neglecting to use?

MAKE SURE YOUR "SORRY" IS SINCERE

"For godly sorrow produces repentance leading to salvation, not to be regretted."

— II CORINTHIANS 7:10

Do you remember the old board game called "Sorry"? Recently I played an updated version of it. It has all the old elements of the game, but with a few added features. For example, there is an "ice" marker which can get assigned to a game piece, freezing it from being able to move until someone else gets stuck with it. As with other old things which get updated, I'm not sure I appreciate all of those new features.

However, the general idea of the game remains the same, including the classic feature of being able to draw a card which enables you to take a game piece out of start and use it to knock off one of your opponent's men while declaring, "Sorrrrryyyyy!" The first time my granddaughter received the opportunity to make that move, from the look on her sweet face you could tell that she truly regretted having to send someone else back to their starting line. However, when my little grandson was told that he could do it, with a smirk on his face he instantly targeted one of my men. His "sorry" didn't sound very sincere. I think he rather enjoyed knocking off his Papaw.

How sincere are our expressions of being sorry? I'm not talking about in playing a game, but in real life, concerning real failings, and in real relationships. I'm afraid there are times when we use that word "sorry" rather flippantly. There's not much sincere regret behind it. We can tend to use it as a quick means of excusing our wrongdoing or attempting to smooth over some difficult situation. It's easy to say "sorry" without truly meaning it. Maybe some of us need to be more careful in the casual use of that word, as well as ask God to help us truly feel the regret we ought to possess in certain situations.

We especially need to guard against misusing that word in relation to God. We've all sinned. We all have our faults. And therefore we all rightly have times when we need to come to God and say, "Sorry." It's important that we admit our wrongdoings before God in order to receive His gracious forgiveness. However, let's guard against a few possible attitudes as we do so.

First of all, let's not express a "sorry" to God that is void of sincere regrets. Don't just say the word because you think you're supposed to or because you know that's what God wants to hear. Take any sin in your life seriously. Think about God's love for you, the price Christ paid for you through His death on the cross, the pain your sin has caused the Lord, and other such truths which should stir up real regret for what you've done.

Secondly, let's make sure we don't just regret the fact that we got caught or are having to face the consequences of our deed, but that we truly regret what we did.

Finally, let's go beyond simply being "sorry" to being repentant. Sometimes we can regret what we do without any intention of changing our behavior or attitude. Or we can tell God we're sorry, knowing that we're likely to do the same thing the next time we're facing that situation. The Bible says that godly sorrow leads to repentance (II Corinthians 7:10). Let's be sorry enough that we're willing to change and go a different direction. Regret your sin to the point that you are determined with God's help not to repeat your action.

Unless you're playing the board game, saying "sorry" isn't much fun. However it's often needed. So when it is, let's do so sincerely and completely.

Think about it the next time you say "I'm sorry"—do you really mean it?

LET'S FOCUS LESS ON OUR DIFFERENCES

"There is neither Jew nor Greek, there is neither slave nor free, there is neither male nor female, for you are all one in Christ Jesus."
– GALATIANS 3:28

We were able to enjoy a rare snow event in our area earlier this week. For some of us that involves sledding, snowball fights, and building snowmen. For others of us, there's contentment with simply looking out the window at the beautiful scenery from the warmth of our houses. I was mainly one of the latter participants, although I did traipse through the snow a few times, using my dog's need to go outside as an excuse. And I confess that I did throw one snowball at my wife—hitting my target, I might add.

Part of the splendor of a blanket of snow is how it covers and "evens out" everything. Imperfections are hidden and distinctions are lost underneath that layer of white. For example, it can be difficult, if not impossible, to determine exactly where a cement driveway ends and an asphalt roadway begins—or where the edge of the pavement gives way to the regular ground. The bare spots in the yard, the grassy areas, and the pine islands all look the same under the cover of several inches of snow. My weed-infested lawn suddenly looked as good as the well-manicured lawn of a neighbor.

Wouldn't it be nice if more of us could view the world in a similar way? My analogy of the snow breaks down somewhat at this point, because I don't believe uniformity—all of us looking, acting, or thinking the same—is the answer. Not only do our distinguishing features add variety to life, but our God-given differences are purposeful and can be positive aspects for us and for the world. But too often we emphasize our distinctions and let them divide us, rather than focusing on the commonalities that should unite us.

It seems to me that this was part of the dream expressed by Dr. Martin Luther King, Jr. It was not the dream of a world in which there was only one race or one social class. It was the dream of a world where those differences among people were not the focal point by which individuals were judged. All persons would be recognized as being equally valuable human beings created in the image of God. And in our nation, those differences among us could be acknowledged and celebrated while at the same time taking a backseat when necessary to the fact that we are all united as Americans.

Long before Dr. King, the Apostle Paul expressed a similar truth about the Church. "There is neither Jew nor Greek, there is neither slave nor free, there is neither male nor female, for you are all one in Christ Jesus" (Galatians 3:28). Paul referred to conditions in his day that could sharply divide people and factors which society used as a basis for radically different treatment of people. He reminds us that our common faith in Christ overshadows all those distinctions. In the midst of our diversity—whether in race, social class, or denominations—the Church is one body in Christ. However this doesn't mean that the Church is to tolerate sin among its members. The Church is still called to be a holy people, however diverse those believers may be otherwise.

I suppose neither the world nor the Church needs to be blanketed in a snow that makes everyone look the same. Rather maybe it's our attitude or outlook that needs some revision. How would our community or our local churches be different if we focused less on the distinctions and imperfections which divide us and more on the important factors which unite us?

Lord, help me to focus more on that which binds me together with my fellow believers.

LET'S NOT MAKE EXCUSES
FOR OUR WRONGDOING

"Therefore do not let sin reign in your mortal body, that you should obey it in its lusts."

– ROMANS 6:12

As I was watching the local news on TV, there was an all-too-common report about a man being carjacked in the parking lot of a metro Atlanta grocery store. And in this case, even though the victim willingly handed over his keys, the perpetrators still shot him.

However what gained my attention even more were the comments of the other customers whom the reporter interviewed about this incident. One man stated that he thought what the carjackers had done was "a little excessive." Another guy offered the opinion, "It's hard times. I guess people gotta do what they gotta do. But it's unfortunate."

Really? Have we become so accustomed to crime that we're ready to excuse people for committing such acts? Yes, it was unnecessary and "excessive" to have shot the victim, but trying to steal his vehicle in the first place was "excessive" too. And did these individuals "gotta do" what they did? I don't think so. No matter how hard the times and how tough a spot we might find ourselves in, we have a choice in how we respond to those difficulties. In most if not all cases, there are better options than resorting to criminal activity.

Such attitudes in our society toward those who break the law should disturb us. But we should also guard against developing a similar mentality when it comes to our own acts of wrongdoing. I'm not just referring to actions which could result in our being arrested and jailed. I'm talking about anything that God would classify as sin—anything in word, thought, or deed that runs counter to what we know to be God's will for us.

Too often we seem to think *People gotta do what they gotta do* when it comes to sin and temptation. For example, it might be suggested that adultery was understandable under those circumstances—after all, the person was in an unhappy marriage and his needs weren't getting met. Or another person was in a tough spot in which she felt like she had to cheat or lie in order to avoid some negative consequences. We tend to focus on the fact that "we're only human," we're weak, and we're susceptible to temptation. We may not come out and say it, but we often feel like we have no choice but to sin.

However that's not the way the Bible pictures the life of a follower of Christ. On the one hand, we won't live sinless lives. "If anyone sins, we have an Advocate with the Father, Jesus Christ" (I John 2:1). And "if we confess our sins, He is faithful and just to forgive us our sins" (I John 1:9). But squeezed between those statements is another truth: "these things I write to you so that you may not sin" (I John 2:1).

God's Word teaches that as believers we are no longer slaves to sin— we don't "gotta" give in to sin's attraction or obey its directives. Romans 6:14 declares, "Sin shall not have dominion over you." We've been set free from sin and are able, with God's help, to do what the Lord wants us to do.

Temptations can be strong and we can be weak. But the God whose Spirit lives in us is greater and more powerful. And we always have a choice to do the right thing. "God is faithful, who will not allow you to be tempted beyond what you are able, but with the temptation will also make the way of escape, that you may be able to bear it" (I Corinthians 10:13).

Don't fall for the lie that you "gotta" sin. You can choose to do God's will. And He will help you follow that better pathway.

When temptation comes, resist it rather than making excuses for giving in to it.

Don't Be Part of the Gospel-Lite Crowd

"I marvel that you are turning away so soon from Him who called you in the grace of Christ, to a different gospel...."

– Galatians 1:6

One day I was cleaning out a drawer in my file cabinet when I found a calendar I had saved from the year 1988. It was one of those specialized flip-calendars with a different cartoon for each day. This particular version was made specifically for pastors. So it included humorous depictions of church life and other subjects which ministers would especially appreciate.

As I perused its pages, I soon realized that many ideas which were considered funny back then for being so uncommon, extreme, or ridiculous had now become fairly commonplace. For example, there was a cartoon of a church with an ATM outside its door promoting 24-hour tithing. And "The Church of the Air" was depicted which advertised a different celebrity minister leading each service by way of video. And there was the cartoon of a pastor who was said to be "overdoing the casual approach" because he was preaching while sitting in his easy chair with a cup of coffee in hand. Then there was the church which called itself "The Lite Church"—home of the 7.5% tithe, 15-minute sermons, and 45-minute worship services. Its sign declared "We only have eight commandments—your choice." Its motto was "Everything you've wanted in a church...and less!"

Yes, many of those cartoons brought a smile to my face. But others were actually more sad than funny—to see that over the course of time the church has become the cartoon caricature of itself from several decades ago. I'm not suggesting that every church fits that picture, but those serving up some form of "church-lite" are becoming more of the rule than the exception.

More ministers and churches appear to be proclaiming a message of the inherent goodness of man and the idea that everyone will end up in heaven one day. There seems to be less preaching on sin—not wanting anyone in our churches to feel guilty or uncomfortable. Many preachers are determined not to offend anyone—except maybe those old-fashioned religious people. Some seem to take pleasure in using such worldly, crude, even profane language in the pulpit that makes the saints squirm in their seats.

We promote attendance without commitment, or loyalty to an organization over commitment to Christ. We offer short, superficial, well-orchestrated entertainment as our acts of worship. We try to do as that church on the calendar—give people what they want…and less. Many who do so would point to Jesus' example—His compassion, openness, acceptance, and message of love. But Jesus wasn't afraid to talk about sin. He came preaching a gospel of repentance. And Jesus spoke more about the prospect of everlasting punishment than about heaven. Neither was Jesus afraid of offending people—and not just those religious Pharisees. He said some things which made many of the common people, the seek-ers of His day, so uncomfortable that they quit following Him. And Jesus called people to commitment—to put the kingdom of God first and to be willing to leave everything in order to follow Him.

I don't know where the church will be decades from now. Maybe things we think of as ridiculous and extreme today will be the norm at that time. But we don't have to go there. We can be the exception. We can still proclaim and live the full gospel, the hard gospel, the true gospel that calls for repentance and total commitment to Christ. Insist on something more than gospel-lite for you and your church.

Is there any area in which you are compromising on the one true gospel?

TAKE THE MESSAGE OF
GOD'S WORD PERSONALLY

"But the word is very near you, in your mouth and in your heart,
that you may do it."

– DEUTERONOMY 30:14

Last weekend when I first saw a news report about a missing husband and wife, I thought it was an unfortunate and potentially tragic situation. But when I realized I actually knew the couple—that we had been fellow church members with this nice lady many years ago—the story really hit home. So I kept checking the news throughout the day to receive updates on the search for these missing persons.

Isn't that the way it often goes? We may hear about certain people, their situations and predicaments. We may respond with some degree of slight interest to genuine concern. But when it involves somebody we know, our own family, or ourselves, it really gets our attention and has a bigger impact on us.

It reminds me of the time the prophet Nathan told King David about a man who had a great number of flocks and herds. But this rich guy took the one and only pet lamb from a poor man in order to slaughter it to feed one of his guests. David became angry over this incident. But then the prophet revealed to the king, "You are the man." He was pointing out how David was guilty of a similar sin by having committed adultery and arranging for the husband's death in order to cover up his act of indiscretion. Once David realized this story was about him, it deeply affected him, leading to heartfelt confession and repentance.

Maybe there are some stories, facts, and truths in the Bible which we need to take more personally than we do. The general statements may affect us to some degree, but not as much as they should. In many cases we need to realize it's talking about me and you.

When the Bible declares that God so loved the world that He sent His Son, we should take it personally. God loves you. God cared enough about you to take such action. You are the one.

And when we encounter the fact that Jesus came and died as the sacrifice for our sins, realize He did it for you. You are the reason He needed to pay that price. It was your sins which nailed Him to the cross. And it's your sins which can be forgiven. You are the one.

When God says He doesn't want anyone to perish, but all to come to repentance, He means you. And when He states that whoever believes in Jesus will have eternal life, He is saying it's possible for you to receive such a wonderful gift.

When God's Word calls believers to love others and be holy, He's talking to you. When He commissions His followers to be His witnesses, to be lights in a dark world, and to share the gospel, He is sending you. You are the one.

Granted, not every story or statement in the Bible applies directly to us personally. But we need to recognize those which do. Don't just read those accounts as history. Don't simply consider them as truth or general statements of fact. Don't just think about how it applies to the world, or your spouse, or children, or neighbor. Don't focus on how much your fellow church member needs to hear that truth. Take it personally. Look and listen for God's message to you.

If God's Word isn't moving us and affecting us very deeply, maybe it's because we're looking at it as more of a textbook to be studied rather than as a personal letter to be received. Read the Bible, see yourself in its truths, and seek to hear what God wants to say to you.

Read God's Word today and listen for His personal message to you.

BEWARE OF THE CONSTANT
WARNING SIGNAL

"And in vain they worship Me, teaching as doctrines the command-ments of men."

– MATTHEW 15:9

My wife's former car was equipped with one of those signals which lights up when the tire pressure gets low. Such a device can be helpful for those of us who have a hard time judging whether or not a tire is adequately inflated just by eyeballing it. However, in cold weather this particular gauge didn't function as well. It tended to light up and stay on even when the tire pressure wasn't low. As such it was more both-ersome than helpful. Every time I saw that light, I wondered if it was a false reading from the cold temperatures or if one of the tires might truly need some air. So every once in a while I would go ahead and check the pressure just to be sure, even though it almost always turned out to be unnecessary.

Sometimes we have to guard against an oversensitive warning system when it comes to our walk with God. Granted, the opposite situation is the more common problem for most people. They don't pay attention to the warning signs from their conscience, from the Holy Spirit, or from God's Word when something is malfunctioning spiritually. But there are others who live under a constant cloud of guilt. The warning light is always on in their lives. They are continuously examining themselves and beating themselves up over their perceived failures to measure up to the standards they've set for themselves.

Notice that I'm talking about "their" standards, not God's standards. We should certainly be seeking to live the way God wants us to live. And we can trust Him to enable us to do so. But as high as God's standards are, we sometimes raise the bar even higher by adding our own lists of "dos and don'ts" to the mix. We are overcome with guilt when we realize we forgot to say a blessing before our meal. "Oh no, maybe the Lord won't bless this food to strengthen me, but instead He'll let it make me sick!" Or we are rattled with guilt over the fact that we were too ill to attend church last Sunday. Or we feel like we need to do penance because we didn't read our daily devotional this morning.

If we're not careful we can end up fitting the description Jesus gave of the scribes and Pharisees of His day. They added their own traditions and regulations to God's commands, making following God more of a burden than a joy for themselves as well as for others. Jesus said that they were "teaching as doctrines the commandments of men" (Matthew 15:9). He also pointed out how they emphasized the little, secondary matters, while neglecting the more important issues. He suggested they were those "who strain out a gnat and swallow a camel" (Matthew 23:24).

Don't get me wrong: God is concerned about the little things in our lives too. He wants us to obey Him in everything, big and small. But sometimes we can get so focused on the little things and let them weigh us down that we neglect the more important and clearer teachings about God's will for our lives.

Let's be sure to differentiate between man's ideas and God's commands. And let's distinguish between the workings of an oversensitive conscience and the guidance of the Holy Spirit. Sometimes we have good reason to feel guilty. But God doesn't want us to live in a constant state of flogging ourselves over our perceived shortcomings. He wants us to rejoice in His forgiveness and cleansing, and to be able to live our lives with the assurance that all is well with our souls.

Take a look at the standards you're aiming for—are they yours or God's?

Don't Forget to Turn Your Light On

"You are the light of the world. A city that is set on a hill cannot be hidden."

– Matthew 5:14

One night recently, I was driving down a local interstate highway when something caught my attention in the rearview mirror. Amidst the various headlights of the cars traveling behind me, I noticed a strange, dark spot. As I focused more intently on it, I realized it wasn't simply an empty section of the road—it was actually a vehicle going along without its lights on. Needless to say, due to the potential danger I kept a close watch on that car until it had passed me and driven out of sight.

That encounter led my wife and me to comment on how we had both been witnessing a greater number of such incidents in recent times. Most of the time it occurs around dusk rather than in the dark of night. I suppose people think they can still see the road sufficiently, hence they don't believe they need their headlights. However, drivers should realize that the main issue isn't about them being able to see where they're going: it's about others being able to see them.

Sometimes we forget about a similar truth in connection with our journey of faith. It's not just about us receiving the light we need in order to successfully make our way to Jesus and eventually to heaven. It's also about letting others see the light.

That's what Jesus indicated in His familiar words in the Sermon on the

Mount. He suggested that we are not to keep our light to ourselves. Rather He commanded, "Let your light so shine before men, that they may see your good works and glorify your Father in heaven" (Matthew 5:16).

It's all too easy for individual believers or entire churches to get so focused on themselves and their personal journeys that they lose sight of the need to shine their lights outward so others can benefit from it. The Bible declares, "For by grace you have been saved through faith" (Ephesians 2:8), but that's not the end of the road. It goes on to say that we are "created in Christ Jesus for good works." And the "good works" which result from our relationship with Christ can point others to Him and bring glory to Him.

But what about Jesus' later condemnatory words in that same Sermon on the Mount about people who did their charitable deeds and other good works in order to be seen by men (Matthew 6:1)? Wasn't Jesus teaching that we ought to do our good deeds in secret? In those cases, Jesus wasn't referring to believers who were letting His light shine through them. He was referring to religious people who did their good works in order to draw attention to themselves and to receive the praise of men. One of the main differences is between doing good works in order for us to be seen and glorified, or doing good works in order for the light of Christ to be seen and for God to be glorified.

Letting our lights shine doesn't mean being showy. We can do good works with a humble spirit, not seeking recognition for ourselves but for the Lord. Much of it comes down to our motives. Are we seeking to be the star, standing on stage in the spotlight, and receiving the applause of other people? Or are we seeking to let the light shine on Christ and He be the recipient of the praise?

So as you continue your journey on the road of following Jesus, don't neglect to turn your lights on. People don't necessarily need to see you, but they do need to see Jesus shining through you.

Let's put into practice those familiar words, "This little light of mine, I'm gonna let it shine."

We Can't Earn God's Free Gift of Salvation

"For by grace you have been saved through faith...it is the gift of God"

– Ephesians 2:8

One of the TV commercials for a certain restaurant chain has stood out to me recently. For one thing it simply makes me drool. It begins by asking the question, "What's better than pie?" while showing pictures of a variety of such delicious-looking pastries. What's your favorite kind of pie? I enjoy all kinds—cherry, pecan, pumpkin, chocolate, peanut butter. As a matter of fact, I can't think of a type of pie that I don't like. However, if I had to choose a favorite, it might be a warm slice of apple pie topped with a scoop of vanilla ice cream. I'm getting hungry just thinking about it.

But something else about that commercial got my attention too. It asked, "What's better than pie? Free pie." It seems that if you go to this restaurant on Wednesdays and order a meal, they'll give you a free slice of the dessert. Sounds pretty good to me.

Let me ask a similar question about a different subject. What's better than salvation? Think about all the different wonderful aspects of what it means to be saved. What's better than having the assurance that your sins have been forgiven? What's better than knowing that all is well with your soul and that you're at peace with God? What's better than enjoying close fellowship with Jesus? What's better than knowing you've got heaven to look forward to once this life is over? Think of all the marvelous slices of the pie of salvation—joy, hope, love, fellowship with other believers, and so much more. What could be better than salvation? How about free salvation?

In a classic passage of scripture, Ephesian 2:4–10, it indicates that our salvation is free. While it doesn't use that specific word, it describes our being saved in terms of God's mercy and love. It also says it's a "gift" of God. When someone gave you a gift for Christmas last month, did that person come up to you afterwards holding out a receipt saying, "This is what you owe me for the present I gave you"? I don't think so. It was a gift—it was free. If you had tried to pay for it, the person probably would've been offended.

Likewise salvation is God's free gift to us. Not only do we not have to pay for it—we can't. God refuses to accept any efforts on our part to try to buy or earn our salvation. We have to receive it by faith as a gracious gift from a loving and merciful God.

The problem is that we tend to want to try to earn that gift. Some people spend their whole lives attempting to be good enough to be worthy of salvation. They hope they can do enough good works to counteract all the bad things they've done over the course of their lives so that God will allow them to go to heaven.

But none of us can ever be good enough. However, the good news is that Jesus was good enough to pay the price for our salvation, making it free for us. Maybe some of us need to get off the futile treadmill of trying to be good enough and simply receive God's free gift of salvation through faith in Jesus and His sacrificial death.

You might want to go over to that restaurant some Wednesday and enjoy a free slice of pie. And as you're eating it, you can also rejoice in the fact that while salvation is great, free salvation is even more wonderful. Hmmmm…I wonder if they serve warm apple pie topped with vanilla ice cream. Maybe I'll see you there.

Spend some time thinking about how wonderful salvation is and thanking God for His great gift to us.

CAN YOU COUNT ON GOD TO GIVE YOU WHAT YOU WANT?

"Delight yourself also in the Lord, and He shall give you the desires of your heart."

— PSALM 37:4

My granddaughter got her wish. She had been praying that it would snow on her birthday. And it did. It certainly wasn't the blizzard other parts of the country experienced from this same weather system. It wasn't even enough to make a snowman. But at least she was able to see the flakes fall and wake up the next morning to a dusting of the frozen precipitation scattered across the ground.

However, my granddaughter didn't receive her more specific request. Her full desire was for it to start snowing after her birthday party began so that all her friends would get snowed-in at her house. So she didn't get everything she had dreamed of, probably to the relief of her parents, but at least she received a good taste of it.

To what extent can we count on God to give us those things we want and pray for—whether it's snow, money, healing, or countless other items which might be found not only on people's wish lists but also on their prayer lists?

Many of us have heard and maybe even quoted the Bible verse which states that the Lord "shall give you the desires of your heart" (Psalm 37:4). This statement has become a favorite for many individuals, preachers, and sectors of the church. However, we need to be sure we consider the whole passage in order to avoid a serious misinterpretation of the promise.

Don't leave out the first part of the verse. The whole sentence reads, "Delight yourself also in the Lord, and He shall give you the desires of your heart." This promise is made specifically to those who delight in God. I don't believe "delight" simply refers to someone enjoying God or taking pleasure in His blessings. In the surrounding verses, the Psalmist is referring to someone who is trusting the Lord and committing his way to God. Therefore, the ones who can truly count on God giving them the desires of their hearts are those who want what He wants, who are surrendered to His will, and who are trusting Him to do what is best.

Obviously we shouldn't expect God to help us fulfill some kind of sinful desire. But maybe some of our other longings, although not sinful as such, are not as centered on God's will, pleasure, and purpose as much as they could be. We're still wanting to interject what we would prefer and think is best, in spite of our limited understanding, instead of focusing more on what God in His infinite wisdom desires and knows is best. We want what we want rather than really seeking and surrendering to what God wants.

Some people quote that verse in connection with the desire to have more money, bigger homes, and nicer cars. We might even assure God that if He gives us more money, we'll use it for ministry and for helping others. If God does choose to bless us financially, we certainly should use it to be a blessing to others. However, the Bible warns us about loving money, coveting what others have, and putting too much emphasis on our worldly possessions. Are we really seeking what God wants, or just trying to make our own wishes for worldly gain appear to be more spiritual than they really are?

God wants us to bring our needs and wants to Him in prayer. Let's just keep a close eye on our hearts and make sure that our desires stay in line with what He desires. And when they do differ, let's always yield our wills and wants to His.

Are you praying with the understanding "not my will but Yours be done"?

Our Lives Should Match Our Message

"For our gospel did not come to you in word only, but also in power, and in the Holy Spirit and in much assurance, as you know what kind of men we were among you for your sake."

– I Thessalonians 1:5

I remember when I first started toying with a webcam with the idea of trying to create some kind of video blog. As the camera was displaying my image on the screen, I was reminded to take note of what could be seen in the background behind me. Was there anything visible that could be a distraction or a hindrance to the message I would be sharing?

I suppose I could stage my home office each time I shot a video so that there would be particular items included in the picture—an inspirational quote, a family photo, a well-worn Bible. However, my inclination is to leave my office in its usual condition. What can be seen behind me? My grandfather's antique mantle clock. A shelf filled with old books. A framed picture of our beloved basset hound who died some years ago. And a couple of homemade cards from my grandchildren. Those images reflect certain aspects of who I am without detracting from the message.

Could you imagine if I filmed a video of a gospel message with an anti-Christian slogan visible in the background? Or a statue of Buddha? Or some lewd photo, magazine, or DVD? Or even if the background just revealed a cluttered mess? Any of those things would seem to be a contradiction, or at least a hindrance, to the message being given.

We need to keep this in mind as we share the gospel in all settings. The kind of life we live is always present as a backdrop to whatever message we may be proclaiming to those around us. Our actions, attitudes, and character displayed will either enhance our witness for Christ or will detract from it.

In some cases, people might try to keep the background of their lives out of focus or hidden, so that no one can see what's really there. Other people might attempt to stage what's visible in their lives—put on the appearance of godliness and purity when they know others are looking. But as people get to know us or take a closer look, they're eventually going to see the kind of life we lead, what's important to us, and the type of persons we are. Will that reality coincide with our gospel message or will it contradict it?

When the Apostle Paul was reminding some believers about his previous ministry among them, he referred not only to how he preached the word to them, but also "what kind of men we were among you for your sake" (I Thessalonians 1:5). Paul was faithful to proclaim the truth to those folks, but the manner in which he and his companions conducted themselves while they were among them confirmed their testimony.

You may be skilled at effectively being able to voice the words and accurately share the truths of the gospel, but you need to make sure your conduct and character isn't diminishing the impact of your witness. We've all probably been disappointed by people who could "talk the talk" of Christianity but didn't "walk the walk."

Certainly none of us are perfect in our behavior. However with God's help, we can be better people. So let's seek to be individuals whose verbal testimony for the Lord is confirmed by the kind of life we live.

Make sure your walk matches your talk.

THE LORD IS ABLE TO KEEP US FROM FALLING

"Now to Him who is able to keep you from stumbling...."

– JUDE 24

You never know what you might hear when you receive public prayer requests during a church service. That's one reason, along with time restraints, why many congregations no longer include that opportunity as part of their time of worship. It's much safer and quicker to only mention a few requests which have been submitted and screened beforehand.

But at the church I serve, we still regularly give the opportunity for the spontaneous sharing of such requests. Last Sunday it was interesting to hear an unusual theme that developed during our prayer time. It seemed that several people within our small congregation, or their relatives, had fallen over the past week. One came through the experience apparently unscathed, another with minor injuries, and yet another having to be hospitalized. Thus as we prepared to pray, I lightheartedly suggested that maybe we need to be more earnest in claiming the assurance given to us in the Bible that the Lord is the One who can keep us from falling (see Jude 24).

Interestingly enough, later that day I heard that a well-known TV personality had also taken a fall and had been hospitalized. Physical falls can result in some significant injuries, especially for folks as they get older.

But of even greater consequence is when someone stumbles and falls spiritually. And of course that's what the Bible is referring to when it talks about the Lord being able to keep us from falling. On the one hand, it's wonderful to know that God is the loving Father who will pick us up, dust us off, and help us get back on our feet again after we've taken a tumble in our walk with Him. But let's not forget that He's also the mighty God whose strong hand can hold us up and keep us from falling in the first place.

Many of us gratefully rely on the Lord for forgiveness and second chances, but let's not sell Him short in the fact that He can also so strengthen us and help us that we don't have to seek His forgiveness quite as often or have to be given so many second chances. One of the themes throughout the Psalms is that God is the One who can set our feet upon a rock and establish our steps (Psalm 40:2). He's the One who "does not allow our feet to be moved" (66:9). And in one place the Psalmist testified, "You have delivered…my feet from falling" (116:8).

In the New Testament, Paul warns us about falling. But then he adds, "No temptation has overtaken you except such as is common to man; but God is faithful, who will not allow you to be tempted beyond what you are able, but with the temptation will also make the way of escape, that you may be able to bear it" (I Corinthians 10:13). In other words, we can fall but we don't have to.

So if we do stumble, does that mean God let us down? No, it probably means that we didn't rely on God to uphold us and maybe even fought against His attempts to do so. Maybe we didn't seek the way of escape which He provided, or we willfully ignored it or chose to go our own way instead. God can keep us from falling, but He's not going to force us to stand if we insist on doing otherwise.

Hopefully there won't be any more physical falls to report among my congregation this week. And let's all seek to cooperate with the God who can keep our spiritual feet on solid ground too.

When temptation comes today, rely on the One who can keep you from falling.

GOD WILL ALWAYS REMEMBER
HIS PROMISES TO HIS CHILDREN

"For He Himself has said, 'I will never leave you nor forsake you.'"
— HEBREWS 13:5

Recently some of the female members of our family took a little trip up to Cleveland, Georgia, to Babyland General Hospital. In case you're not familiar with that particular institution, don't plan on going there to be treated for any medical need. In spite of its name, it's not a place to go in order to give birth to a child or for specialized pediatric care.

Babyland General is the home of Cabbage Patch dolls—those cute characters with the uniquely puckered faces looking somewhat as if they've just tasted a lemon. The main purpose of the excursion was for our granddaughter to enjoy this experience, although I think the other participants in this "girl's trip" derived just as much pleasure from it.

During their visit, they witnessed the "births" of a few Cabbage Patch babies. And my granddaughter was given the opportunity to adopt one of the dolls of her choosing. Later I saw the cute video of her raising her hand while solemnly repeating the words of a promise to take care of her new baby forever and ever.

I can tell you that she has taken that vow seriously. Besides feeding the baby and changing its diaper, she takes it with her everywhere. At a local restaurant, she placed her baby in its own high chair. And during a dental appointment, a kindhearted dentist fulfilled her request to check her baby's mouth too.

We can be confident that God takes even more seriously His promises to care for His beloved children. The Bible assures us that God cannot lie and He is faithful to do whatever He says He will do. And the experiences of many of us over the years testify to this truth. He has made certain promises to watch over, provide for, and be with those whom He has adopted into His family.

He has promised never to leave us or forsake us (Hebrews 13:5). He has promised to supply all our needs (Philippians 4:19). He has assured us that He will provide us with the necessities of life if we will seek first His kingdom and His righteousness (Matthew 6:33).

God's Word assures us that He will direct our steps, give us strength, bestow wisdom on us, and bless us with peace. The Bible pictures God as a shepherd taking care of His sheep, as a mother bird watching over her chicks, and as a strong fortress protecting its inhabitants. He promises to make His home with us now, and to allow us to make our home with Him for eternity.

You don't have to be a fan of the *Toy Story* series of movies to recognize that eventually some other toy may replace that doll as the center of my granddaughter's affection. Or one day she'll be so busy with other things in life that her pucker-faced baby will likely spend most of her time sitting on a shelf or in the back of a closet. The promise she made as an almost three-year-old at Babyland General will gradually fade in her memory.

But that's not the case with God. He will never shelve us or throw us aside as a forgotten plaything of the past. We will always be able to depend on God to love us and fulfill His promises to us. When we put our trust in Christ as Savior, the Creator of the universe vowed to be our Father, to love us, and to care for us forever and ever.

Let's not ever doubt that truth or forget it. God never will.

Rest in the assurance that God will be faithful to fulfill all His promises.

Don't Let Good Things
Become Objects of Worship

"You shall have no other gods before Me."
– Exodus 20:3

A couple of months ago, I pursued my penchant for old books by pick-ing up a few interesting-looking volumes at the annual big sale at the local library. After having read some of my other purchases from that occasion, I'm now making my way through a novel set during the times of the early church. The book is entitled *The Silver Chalice*, referring to the cup Jesus drank from on that memorable last evening with His dis-ciples. Some familiar biblical characters appear in the account, such as Joseph of Arimathea, Luke the beloved physician, and the Apostle Paul. The story follows the adventures of a young artist who is commissioned with sculpting a suitable frame within which to encase that sacred relic.

While I find the book enjoyable, there is one aspect of the story that bothers me whenever I encounter it, whether in fiction or in real life. It's the excessive reverence given to any object, even one as legendary as that particular vessel. In the novel, people go so far as almost to worship the cup. Additionally, the author seems to empower that relic with a some-what magical quality.

I can understand having strong feelings about certain objects, espe-cially those connected to people we love or admire. One of my treasured possessions is a mantle clock that had belonged to my grandfather. It may not be very valuable monetarily, but it has great worth to me. So obviously some object so closely connected to Jesus would naturally be treasured by His followers. But that doesn't mean we should go so far as to worship it or to view it as some kind of magic charm.

Do you remember the bronze serpent that God instructed Moses to make (Numbers 21)? It was an object used by God to bring healing to His people. Yet the Bible tells us that many years later the people had turned that image into an idol which they worshiped (II Kings 18:4). Although God had commanded its creation for a good purpose, He later had to destroy it due to the people's excessive reverence of it.

There are many physical objects that aid us in our faith. Many of them deserve a certain degree of reverence on our part. However, let's be careful not to cross the line into actually worshiping those objects or viewing them more with superstition than with faith.

For example, a cross can be a vivid reminder to us of God's love and a symbol of the price Christ was willing to pay for our salvation. But it's not a magic charm that we ought to try to use to ward off evil or to make our wishes come true. Likewise a church building can be a sacred place for worship, but let's be careful not to fall into the trap of exalting the place that has come to mean so much to us instead of the Person whose presence makes it special.

Even something as important as the Bible can be treated more like a book of magic rather than a book of divine revelation. People may try to use it to manipulate God and to help them get what they want rather than to let God use it to transform them and to show them what He wants. The Bible isn't a volume of incantations for us to recite and believe. It's a book intended to cause us to believe in and become personally acquainted with its Author.

Let's be thankful for God giving us things that are helpful to our faith and worthy of our admiration, but let's not exalt them into objects of the worship that is due only to Him.

Is there anything (or anyone) in your life to which you are giving excessive reverence?

WHICH CANDIDATE DO YOU CHOOSE AS YOUR LEADER?

"Do you not know that to whom you present yourselves to obey, you are that one's slaves whom you obey...."

– ROMANS 6:16

During an election year, one of the main questions we end up answering is who will be leading our country as its president for the next four years. As we go through that lengthy process, it's usually interesting to see the various candidates rise and fall in the polls, often in conjunction with either accusations about their personal lives or their performances in debates. But when the day actually arrives for the primaries or the general election, it's the voters who get the opportunity to make their choice.

The decision as to who will next serve in the Oval Office may be a very important one for the future of our country, but there's another choice that each one of us must make that has an even more profound and long-lasting significance for us. It's the decision as to who we're going to allow to be president, leader, master, or ruler over our own lives. Let's take a look at several of the candidates.

First of all, there is self. He's the candidate with which we tend to be the most comfortable. However, we must admit that his track record isn't very praiseworthy. He has limited knowledge about the situations we face. And he tends not to act very wisely when left to himself. Even when he knows what needs to be done, he often doesn't have the power or ability to accomplish it. Self is the ultimate flip-flopper, being too easily swayed by the opinions of others, too easily attracted to whatever glitters the most, and too easily deceived by the draw of momentary pleasures. At the root of self's difficulties is a sin-tainted heart that is bent toward doing wrong.

Another candidate vying to take a position of leadership in our lives is Satan. Some might consider him to be the epitome of a politician with his propensity to lie and to tell us whatever we want to hear. He will run negative campaign ads against everything that is good and decent in our lives. He will promote a broad range of issues from apathy to blatant immorality to self-righteous hypocrisy. He will often team up with self to pursue their common goals.

It's important to remember that this devilish candidate isn't looking out for what's best for us. He has his own agenda that includes trying to hinder God's work in our lives and ultimately seeking to ruin us. Satan is the candidate of the defeatist party. Although we may choose to follow His leadership in our lives at the moment, ultimately it will be revealed that he has lost to Christ in a landslide.

The other major candidate on our ballot is God. He's the only one worthy of the office. He is infinitely knowledgeable and is capable of doing whatever is needed. Not only is He dependable, but it is impossible for Him to lie. His wisdom is out of this world. And His character is beyond reproach. And best of all, He truly cares about us and is seeking after our best interests.

When you compare the different candidates, there is really no contest when it comes to whom we should choose to be master of our lives. But the Bible reminds us that we cast our vote not primarily by whom we proclaim to be our leader, but by whom we actually follow. So whose leadership are we following? To whom are we yielding our allegiance and service? The answer to those questions will reveal the true candidate of our choice.

Which candidate has your loyalty and obedience? Do you need to change masters?

Don't Try to Control
the Spirit of God

"He who believes in Me, as the Scripture has said, out of his heart will flow rivers of living water.' But this He spoke concerning the Spirit...."

– John 7:38–39

One year, a strange bit of news came from the annual big boat show in Atlanta. It seems that the event had to delay its opening by a few hours. Why? It was because of water. That's right—water shut down the boat show. That would be akin to subfreezing temperatures shutting down an ice cream factory. The two are supposed to go together. Boats are meant to be operated on water. So what was the problem?

From what I heard, apparently a demonstration pool got out of control, tipping over and inundating one area with thousands of gallons of water. It wasn't so much that the boats couldn't handle the situation. They would have survived in water without any problem. However, those in charge of the show didn't think their customers would be pleased about having to wade through puddles in order to see the vessels they had on display. Hence, workers frantically strove to squeegee up all the spilled water so that the show could operate as planned.

Something else that naturally goes together is the church and the presence of the Lord. Jesus promised that "where two or three are gathered together in My name, I am there in the midst of them" (Matthew 18:20). Or another way of looking at it is that believers and the Holy Spirit share such a close connection. The Bible assures those who put their trust in Jesus that "you are the temple of God and that the Spirit of God dwells in you" (I Corinthians 3:16).

However, I'm afraid that if the presence of the Lord really manifested itself in some of our gatherings, we wouldn't know how to handle it. It might rock our boat and make us rather uncomfortable. If the Holy Spirit was poured out on us in His fullness and power, we might be tempted to shut things down. He might take us in directions we hadn't planned on going. We might have to change our order of worship or toss our bulletins out the window. It might not fit in with our preferred style of worship. Things might get excessively noisy or a little too quiet for our liking.

It's not that we have anything against the Spirit of God. We like to talk about His presence and even evoke His coming to be with us in our prayers and in some of our songs, but we tend to like to keep him in our little demonstration pool, where we think we have Him under control. We can point to Him being there and let Him out in small amounts, but we don't want Him spilling out and having free run of the place. If the Holy Spirit really manifested Himself among us, some of us might be running around trying to squeegee Him out of the way so that we could proceed with our religious activities as usual.

The Bible sometimes uses water as a picture of the Spirit of God—as living, life-giving water. Let's not hinder His flowing into our lives and our churches. God's Word provides similar instructions when it tells us not to quench the Spirit (I Thessalonians 5:19). Listen to His voice. Follow His guidance. Don't try to restrict His activity in your life or in your church. We're not supposed to try to control Him—we should be allowing Him to control us.

So don't be afraid to let the living water of the Holy Spirit float your boat. He'll take you exactly where you need to be.

How would your life be different if you let the Holy Spirit have full control?

DON'T BE DISCOURAGED
BY HARD TIMES

"But we also glory in our tribulations, knowing that tribulation produces perseverance; and perseverance, character; and character, hope."

– ROMANS 5:3–4

"It could be worse." So I was told by the young man from the cleanup service who was sent out to our church by the insurance company. His comment came over the noise of commercial fans and dehumidifiers which were working tirelessly to try to erase the effects of an incident with the plumbing that had left our building virtually flooded. Behind him I could see where walls had been torn out about eighteen inches above the floor in order to remove wet insulation. I didn't even want to think about the small kitchen in which the vinyl floor had to be ripped out, along with cabinets being moved in order to reach all of the flooring.

It was a mess. We weren't able to hold church services there one Sunday. But yes, I had to agree that it could've been worse. Just considering the fact that on the day I discovered the problem, I almost didn't go to the church due to a full day of meetings elsewhere. If I hadn't decided (or been providentially led) to drop by the church for a few minutes early that morning, the water may have run for another day and done much more damage before being stopped.

Sometimes when we're facing difficulties and trials, we do try to console ourselves with the idea that it could be worse. Recently one of my friends at a nursing home was dealing with a rather painful physical condition. During the course of our conversation, she detailed a number of the aches and pains she has to endure at this point in life. But then she commented on how she looks around at some of the other people in her place of residence and she realized that it could be worse.

As I've heard others voice similar sentiments in the face of hard times, I've wondered to what extent the Bible supports such a point of view. If you think of any examples, let me know. One that came to my mind is from the book of Hebrews in the context of referring to Christ's suffering. "For consider Him who endured such hostility from sinners against Himself, lest you become weary and discouraged in your souls. You have not yet resisted to bloodshed, striving against sin" (Hebrews 12:3–4). In other words, you may be suffering, but it could be worse.

However, God's Word takes this subject matter to an even higher level. It's not just the idea that our circumstances could be worse. We can also have an assurance that God is working even through the difficulties to bring about good things in our lives. In that same chapter of Hebrews, it goes on to refer to how God can use some of those painful experiences in life to make us better, more godly people. Elsewhere the scriptures indicate that we can glory in our tribulations because we know that they produce such good qualities in us as perseverance, character, and hope (Romans 5:3–4).

No, we weren't able to hold worship services in our building that Sunday. But we had a wonderful time of intimate worship and warm fellowship at one of our member's homes. Yes, our building was a mess. But our furnishings survived the ordeal in good condition. And when everything got restored, it was in better shape than it was before.

Whatever difficulties you're facing today, don't be discouraged. Remember things could be worse. But also go a step further and look for God to use these trials to bring good things into your life and character.

Look for God's plan and purposes in the trials you're facing today. And if you don't see it yet, trust Him anyway.

Comfort Food for the Soul

"Therefore comfort one another with these words."

– I Thessalonians 4:18

It wasn't how I had expected to spend my weekend. Like many people, I was figuring on a relatively uneventful couple of days while hopefully catching a little football on TV. However, the death of a cousin quickly changed those plans, especially since she had requested that I be one of the ministers officiating over her funeral service. That occasion reminded me that while many of us are going about our usual activities, there are those among us who are experiencing grief, pain, and loss. And in those situations, there is the need for comfort.

Certain places, people, and things can provide us with some measure of comfort. The place we call home, that well-worn recliner, the pillow that we take with us on trips, the beloved members of our family—those are some of things that we view as comforting. We even have particular edible items that we refer to as "comfort foods." My wife has a favorite restaurant and a favorite meal that she orders there. If she's had a rough day, it's not unusual for her to call me up and say, "I think I need Frontera tonight."

I'm thankful that we have some truths from God's Word that can bring us comfort during those difficult times in life. Just like my wife doesn't tire of going to that same restaurant to get her favorite food when she needs it, we shouldn't tire of hearing these familiar truths from the Bible when we're grieving or hurting. We need that reminder. We need the comfort that those truths bring to us.

So if you're one of those experiencing some grief or loss today, take a moment to chew on some comfort food for your soul.

"And God will wipe away every tear from their eyes; there shall be no more death, nor sorrow, nor crying. There shall be no more pain, for the former things have passed away" (Revelation 21:4). If we're following Christ, once this life is over we can have assurance of a new home. And it will be free from all the things that cause pain and sorrow in this life, including sickness and death.

"Let not your heart be troubled; you believe in God, believe also in Me...I go to prepare a place for you. And if I go and prepare a place for you, I will come again and receive you to Myself; that where I am, there you may be also" (John 14:1–3). Jesus is preparing a place where we can go and be with Him for eternity.

"In the world you will have tribulation; but be of good cheer, I have overcome the world" (John 16:33). In this life, we're going to experience some hard times. We may have to deal with sickness, loss, relationship problems, and everything else that could fall under that heading of tribulation. But we can be comforted knowing that Jesus has overcome the world and all its tribulation, including death itself. He rose to new life, giving us assurance that we will live too.

"Yea, though I walk through the valley of the shadow of death, I will fear no evil; for You are with me; Your rod and Your staff, they comfort me" (Psalm 23:4). What comforts us as we're forced to walk through the valleys? It's the knowledge that the Lord our Shepherd who loves us and can protect us is right there with us.

Maybe God wants to give you the gift of comfort today. If so, unwrap it with faith in Him and with trust in His promises. Let not your heart be troubled—believe in Jesus and in the timeless truths of His Word.

Which promises of God do you need to trust for comfort today?

LET'S NOT FORGET

TO BE GENTLE

"Take My yoke upon you and learn from Me, for I am gentle and lowly in heart."

– MATTHEW 11:29

I remember when our first granddaughter arrived in the world. While Mom and Dad were busy at the hospital, we took charge of our two rambunctious little grandsons. As I watched them run around our living room with seemingly limitless energy playing with each other, I recognized what would need to be an oft-heard phrase in their home in the days ahead—"Be gentle." Those boys would have to be reminded that they can't play with their baby sister in the same tornadolike fashion in which they often relate to one another. They can't pull on her tender arms or grab her in a rough manner. They have to be careful when running and jumping around not to land on top of their fragile baby sister or not to accidentally hit her with one of their toys. For a while I often heard myself and their parents voice the same command to them several times—"Be gentle."

Sometimes we also need to hear that reminder from our Heavenly Father. Gentleness is a Christlike characteristic that can be easy for us to overlook. Yet it's listed as one of the fruits of the Spirit—one of those qualities that should be increasingly evident in our lives as the Holy Spirit transforms us into more godly people (Galatians 5:22–23). And in one of Jesus' rare descriptions of his own character, He stated, "I am gentle and lowly in heart" (Matthew 11:29).

Jesus could certainly be rough, as when He threw the moneychangers out of the temple, but He could also be gentle, as when He welcomed little children to come to Him to be blessed. He could be harsh in His condemnation of the religious leaders, calling them snakes and hypocrites, but He could also show tender compassion and forgiveness for an adulteress who was being publicly shamed and condemned by her critics simply in an effort to entrap Jesus.

So why is it that we tend to neglect cultivating this important characteristic in our lives at times? Maybe it's due partly to the fact that we live in a world in which we've had to develop some fairly tough and thick skin ourselves. As we've taken hits of pain, persecution, and disappointments, we expect others to be equally tough and deal with such harsh realities themselves. Or possibly we are so wrapped up in the battles we are fighting in this world as soldiers of Christ that we don't see much room for what might be considered being soft. We see the necessity of being bold and assertive, while sometimes equating gentleness with weakness and timidity. In a world full of deception and lies, we see the need for being straightforward with the truth, even if it comes across harsh or hurtful. Even in dealing with our brothers and sisters in Christ, we get used to heated debates over biblical issues or treating each other with strict, tough love.

We need to keep in mind that there are fragile souls and hurting people who may need to be handled with a more gentle touch. There are lost lambs who may need to hear the painful truth, but with less "in-your-face," harsh tactics and more with a gentle, loving spirit. There are baby Christians with whom we may need to interact with more patience and tenderness due simply to their spiritual immaturity.

Our grandsons got the message and did a pretty good job of being gentle with their new baby sister. Likewise let's pay attention to our Father when He reveals our need to exhibit that quality in certain situations or with particular individuals. Let's allow the Holy Spirit to infuse us with more of that Christlike spirit of gentleness.

In what areas of your life do you need better to exhibit that quality of gentleness?

OTHER ROADS TO GOD
LEAD TO DEAD ENDS

"I am the way, the truth, and the life, No one comes to the Father
except through Me."

– JOHN 14:6

A few years back, before GPS was so common, one of the members of my church accompanied me on a quick trip into Tennessee for a meeting with a few other pastors and laymen. As I found our destination on a map, it looked like the easiest and quickest route to get there would allow us to stay on familiar interstate highways all the way. But then I noticed another road that appeared to be a way to cut off a corner and avoid getting near a large city. Although it wasn't an interstate, the map did indicate it to be a limited-access highway. But as I looked more closely, I noticed that the line representing that road had a few gaps in it, possibly communicating the fact that the road wasn't yet completed. With the temptation of saving a little time and a few miles dangling in front of us, my passenger and I debated on whether to take a chance on exploring that different route. Could it be that this highway had been finished since my map was published? We finally decided to stick to the original road which we were certain would get us to our destination.

On the return trip, we happened to stop to eat at a place near where that other road crossed the interstate. My passenger asked one of the restaurant's workers about that route. We were told that the highway was not completed and only local traffic should go that direction. If we had tried to follow that way, we would've eventually hit a dead end.

I'm thankful that there is a sure way for us to reach our destination— to find God, eternal life, and heaven. Jesus came to provide that route, and from an old rugged cross He declared that it was finished. Jesus didn't fail to complete His mission or leave any gaps. Although the road of following Him by faith is not always the easiest route, it will not lead us to a disappointing dead end where we will find ourselves having to backtrack or to find some other way to reach the goal. Jesus truly is the way to God and no one comes to the Father except through Him.

Unfortunately many people are attempting to bypass that tried-and-true way to reach that destination, and are spending their days experimenting with other roads. They may be trying to cut a corner because they don't like part of Jesus' message or they're seeking to avoid the implications of a full commitment to Christ. Some might be searching for an easier road or one that is more acceptable to the world in which we live today. Or maybe they think they know better about spiritual matters than an old outdated map book that was written thousands of years ago. Many roads look inviting. They may appear to lead in the right direction. They can hold promises of peace, joy, and a right relationship with the Creator. And some of those roads may seem to deliver on those promises for a while. But eventually they all lead to a dead end. None of them can complete the journey to a reconciled relationship with God and everlasting life with Him in heaven.

New roads or old roads with new names are constantly popping up on the spiritual map, but don't be deceived into thinking that they're going to get you to God and to heaven apart from Christ. Upon close examination, none of them can help you complete that journey. The way of grace and salvation that Jesus provided through His life, death, and resurrection is still the only road leading to that glorious destination.

Watch out for attractive detours and side roads. Stay on the one road which leads to God.

MAKING EVERY SUNDAY
A SUPER ONE

"But the hour is coming, and now is, when the true worshipers will worship the Father in spirit and truth; for the Father is seeking such to worship Him."

– JOHN 4:23

It should be about time for Super Sunday again. No doubt there are some of you who have no interest whatsoever in football or the special festivities associated with this day on which the NFL decides its champion. Others, like myself, will probably tune in to watch at least part of the game, along with the celebrated, but usually overrated, commercials. But then there are those who really get wrapped up in the whole aura surrounding the Super Bowl. It doesn't matter whether their favorite team is playing or not. For them, the event itself has become a cultural experience filled with traditions. They faithfully tune in to the pregame show that seems to drag on forever while giving them every viewpoint and every bit of trivia they could imagine about the participating teams and players. Additionally, some people are as insistent about the particular food they prepare to eat on this evening as they are about what they consume on Thanksgiving Day. But instead of turkey, cranberry sauce, and green bean casserole, it may be chicken wings, chips and dip, or a variety of other options. And then there's the social aspect. Many use it as an occasion to gather with family or friends around the TV set to cheer their team, criticize the officiating, and have good-natured disagreements over opposing viewpoints about the ballgame, the advertisements, or the halftime show. Regardless of the degree to which you may or may not be a Super Bowl aficionado, we should realize that there are those for whom Super Sunday is a day that is planned for and looked ahead to with great expectancy.

What if we approached every Sunday with a similar spirit, in connection with it being a day to gather for public worship? Some of us might have to admit that our attitude toward that day of the week isn't one of joyful anticipation. Do we honestly look forward to that opportunity to go to church or do we dread it as some kind of a necessary burden when we'd rather be somewhere else involved in other activities?

May I offer a few suggestions? Prepare for the big day ahead of time. During the week, ask God to bless those upcoming services. Don't wait until Sunday to start thinking about God and getting right with Him. Pray, confess, read God's Word, and submit to His will before you go to church. Study your Sunday School or small group lesson prior to attending class.

Also, be faithful to tune in. Wherever you go to church, be a regular participant. And be committed not just to being there but also to getting involved. Tune in to what's being said or sung—don't lose the battle of a wandering mind. Ask God to make you more passionate for Him and His work, so that you will get more excited when His team scores a victory.

Approach Sunday with expectancy. Expect to be fed by God, regardless of how good or poorly a sermon is preached or what style of music is used. Look for the Lord's message to you. And at the same time, anticipate that God might want to use you to feed someone else. Your presence, testimony, or kind words might be just the food another person needs. Remember the social aspect of the day—you aren't there just for yourself, but in order to encourage, build up, and help your brothers and sisters in Christ.

So let's try to learn some things from the Super Bowl fans among us. Having more of their spirit of preparation and excited expectancy regarding our times of public worship might make every Sunday a little more super.

How can you better prepare yourself for those weekly worship services?

JESUS DIED FOR US ONCE AND IT WAS ENOUGH

"With His own blood He entered the Most Holy Place once for all, having obtained eternal redemption."

– HEBREWS 9:12

Yesterday was Groundhog Day. Due to a well-known movie by that title, in many people's minds the occasion isn't just associated with whether or not Punxsutawney Phil sees his shadow, but it has also become forever tied to the concept of somebody inescapably having to relive the same day over and over again, as Bill Murray's character was forced to do in that film.

A certain scripture reminded me of that idea recently. It talks about how Jesus' sacrifice for our sins is so much better than those animal sacrifices under the old covenant. It points out that if Jesus' sacrifice was of the same value as those Old Testament offerings, "He then would have had to suffer often since the foundation of the world" (Hebrews 9:26).

Imagine that with me for a moment. What if Jesus had to go through all He endured in suffering and dying for our sins over and over again? Wouldn't it be terrible if He had to relive that day regularly? What if Jesus had to suffer that scourging which tore into His flesh over and over and over—to have those nails driven into His hands and feet again and again—to carry the weight of our sins day after day? How awful if Jesus would have needed to endure that event multiple times. But thankfully it wasn't necessary. That passage in Hebrews lets us know that Jesus only had to do it once. His sacrifice was far superior to those offerings of goats and bulls. In Christ's case, once was enough. His offering of Himself for our sins accomplished what was needed and it never had to be repeated.

One of the truths we can take away from that fact is nothing else can do what Jesus' sacrifice accomplished. Nothing else can bring us into favor with God. Nothing else can save us from our sins. Nothing else can get us to heaven. As the old song declares, "What can wash away my sin? Nothing but the blood of Jesus."

If we're trying to mend our broken relationship with God by means of anything other than faith in the Lamb of God who died for us, we're not going to succeed. None of us are likely to be trying to do it by making animal sacrifices, however we sometimes try to accomplish it in other ways. One of the most common practices is by trying to be good enough. We think if we can just do enough good deeds, we'll be able to earn God's favor or offset all the bad things we've done. However, the Bible makes it clear that such attempts won't work. It's not possible for our good works to save us—they aren't enough.

We can attend church every time the doors are open, faithfully give our tithe and other offerings, and win the "Citizen of the Year" award for our tireless volunteer efforts to help people in our community. But it still wouldn't be enough.

The only thing that was enough is what Jesus did for us. Maybe some of us need to quit trying to be good enough and instead humble ourselves before God with the admission that we're sinners who aren't good enough. We need simply to put our trust in the Lamb of God who did the one thing that was good enough to save us from our sins.

Groundhog Day is past, unless you're still reliving it today. And Jesus died once to save us from our sins. Thankfully that one time was all we needed. Put your trust in the fact that it was enough.

Rejoice in the truth that what Jesus did for you on the cross was enough.

Is Something Not Smelling Right in Your Life?

"Search me, O God, and know my heart; try me, and know my anxieties; and see if there is any wicked way in me, and lead me in the way everlasting."

– Psalm 139:23

"Church stinks!" No, that wasn't the disparaging comment of some atheist. Neither was it the declaration of a church member who had been disappointed or frustrated by the pastor or by the petty behavior of some people in the congregation. It wasn't even the outburst from a teenager who was told by his parents that he would have to attend the worship service that day instead of going to the ballgame with his friends. It was the thought that ran through my own mind when I walked through the door of our church one day. I wasn't upset, frustrated, or discouraged. I was simply making an observation. My nose was informing me that something inside our church building really did stink. There was a strange, unpleasant odor wafting its way down our hallway.

Naturally I tried to pinpoint the source of the stench, but to no avail. Knowing from past experience that my sense of smell isn't the greatest, I enlisted a couple of other people to help sniff out the problem. The consensus was that it didn't smell like leaking gas; it seemed to be more like the reeking of something dead. Continued searches didn't turn up any deceased carcass of a squirrel or other creature in the attic. The only possible point of origin which we discovered was a dirty diaper which had been overlooked for an indefinite period of time by those disposing of the garbage. And if you've had any experience dealing with those items, you know that they can put out quite a nasty odor. So we proceeded to cover the unwanted scent with an abundant application of air freshener while we waited to see if the problem had been remedied by getting rid of that diaper.

What do we do when we suddenly notice that something doesn't quite smell right in our own lives? We catch a faint scent of some filth that we've allowed to enter the doors of our minds. We get a whiff of deadness, the odor that always accompanies sin. The sweet aroma of a fresh relationship with God has been slowly replaced by a stale atmosphere, the result of complacency, lack of growth, or simply going through the motions of religious activity. We can't pinpoint the exact cause, but we know that something isn't as it should be. What do we do?

Some people try to ignore the smell, either denying it until it gets unbearable or until they get used to the stench. Others will try to hide it or cover over it with all kinds of air fresheners, such as busyness, church involvement, community service, or sacrificial giving. What we need to do is to allow God to search our hearts and show us the real source of the problem. We need to enlist His help in making a thorough inspection of our premises. Sometimes we may not like what we find. It may be a decaying carcass we've got hidden in a closet, or some filth from our past which we've never gotten resolved. It may be out in the open where it's easy to see or it may be buried behind walls of denial. We should look to the Lord as the One who can reveal our need and can cleanse us of that impurity as we repent and seek forgiveness.

In that recent episode, we didn't want to just cover over the unpleasant odor in our church building. We wanted to make sure we discovered the source and got rid of it. Let's do the same thing regarding any foul-smelling attitude, spirit, or action that we've allowed entrance into our lives.

Lord, make me sensitive to anything in my life that isn't pleasing to You.

ENCOUNTERING THOSE IN NEED OF FINANCIAL ASSISTANCE

"Inasmuch as you did it to one of the least of these My brethren, you did it to Me."

— MATTHEW 25:40

One of the great joys and blessings of Christian ministry involves opportunities to meet and assist people who are going through tough times and are in need of financial help. One of the great discouragements and curses of Christian ministry involves opportunities to meet and assist people who are going through tough times and are in need of financial help. If you deal with those situations very often, you probably know exactly what I mean by those statements.

Some of the people you encounter in those circumstances possess lives and stories that are inspirational. They've endured unbearable hardships, overcome tremendous challenges, and are still pressing ahead with faith and persistent effort. I recall one family our church helped with some groceries. Not only did they seem sincerely grateful for the assistance, but they also appeared to be doing everything they could to get out from under their need for such dependence. Although the house they lived in was far from large, they were making arrangements to downsize and move into another place that would be more affordable. Additionally, the husband, while working one job, was learning new skills that would hopefully lead to a better job in the future.

It's a joy to play a small role in God's plan to provide for the needs of such people. You come away experiencing the truth of the words of scripture that "it is more blessed to give than to receive." You give with the hope of providing help and encouragement to someone else, yet you end up being encouraged and strengthened by them.

But then there are the other people you encounter—the ones who suck the joy right out of giving—the ones who cause you to question whether you should ever take the risk of reaching out to someone in those circumstances in the future. It's not just the people who are deceptive about the extent of their need, or who make a living preying on the generosity of others, but it's also the ones who accept help without gratitude—and those who seem to think they're entitled to such assistance. I think of someone I encountered who received help, but then kept asking for more and more. It seemed that all his energy went toward maintaining his lifestyle that was dependent on the help of others rather than trying to get out from under it. When he was informed that he had received all the help that was available, a spirit of anger, resentment, and entitlement quickly rose to the surface.

Let's remember that it's not just the pastors, churches, and other charitable organizations who are responsible to deal with those situations. One day we will all be held accountable for how we responded to those around us who were lacking in food, clothing, and other basics of life (Matthew 25:31–46). While we pray for a good economy and for provision for those in need, maybe we also need to pray for ourselves to respond properly to these situations. Would you join me in such a prayer?

"Heavenly Father, never let us lose a heart of compassion for people around us who are in need. Give us the courage to reach out and to give. At the same time, give us the wisdom we need to be responsible stewards of the resources with which you have placed under our care. May we be generous but not careless. May we look for the best way to help people, not simply the easiest way. Give us the grace to do what we can do ourselves for those in need, and the humility to point them to others who can do more than we can or who can do it better. May we always embody Your spirit of love, care, and generosity. Amen."

Honestly examine your attitude toward those in need—is it Christlike?

GOD'S MASSIVE RECALL
AFFECTS YOU

"For all have sinned and fall short of the glory of God."

– ROMANS 3:23

Since we had a couple of Toyotas in our family of vehicles at the time, some years ago I watched with more than just casual interest the information about the recall of a large number of their cars. As you might remember, there had been reported instances of accelerators sticking on certain models. The problem was pointed to as a possible cause for a number of accidents and even a few deaths. For a while Toyota admitted to a problem but was not able to offer a solution. It was rather unnerving for some people to have to drive around in a car that you believe could accelerate uncontrollably at any moment. I know, because I've been there.

One time we owned a car that occasionally manifested a similar problem which was finally diagnosed as being related to a nonfactory cruise control that a previous owner had installed on the vehicle. I know how it feels to be driving down the interstate with a stuck accelerator and the difficulty of maintaining enough composure and control to get the car stopped. Thankfully, Toyota eventually came up with an apparent fix for their problem.

While Toyota's recall was huge, covering several million vehicles, we're all involved in an even more massive recall from our Manufacturer. There was nothing wrong with our Creator's design and skill. After He made mankind, He looked us over and rightfully declared us to be very good. Unfortunately, man exercised his freedom to mess up God's original creation, not only making the first model flawed, but passing that defect of sin along to all subsequent models. So now we're all under recall. The one who made us can no longer look at us and say "very good." Instead, He declares that we're all defective—we're all sinners who need to be restored.

There are some people who choose to ignore the problem or who deny the existence of any serious moral or spiritual defect in humanity. Others recognize the defect, but don't believe anything can be done about it. Some try to tinker with their vehicle themselves, thinking that they can resolve the issue and make themselves good enough to meet the original standards of the Creator. But all such efforts inevitably fail. The truth is that we're driving a defective vehicle that is accelerating uncontrollably down a road leading toward destruction. Without a solution, at some unknown point in time we will plummet into an abyss of spiritual death for eternity.

The good news is that our Creator came up with an adequate fix for our problem. It was costly—much more than the expense Toyota incurred from their recall. It cost God the life of His own Son.

God's solution doesn't restore us to the same perfect condition as the original model, at least not in this life, but it gets us off the road leading to destruction and onto the narrow pathway of eternal life. It forgives us of the damage we've done along the way. And it so transforms our vehicles that we can stay on that right road and find ourselves being increasingly cleansed from sin and unrighteousness. Every day we can look more like the holy creation God intended for us to be.

Have you received your recall notice yet? It's been sent to you. Maybe you've just overlooked it or neglected to answer. Throughout the pages of the Bible, our Designer has called us all to come to Him and receive the fix for this self-inflicted flaw. Let's respond to that call and be freed from the fear, shame, and guilt associated with our spiritual defect.

Have you let your Creator fix your sin defect?

WHEN WE FALL, IT'S SERIOUS BUSINESS

"For the wages of sin is death, but the gift of God is eternal life in Christ Jesus our Lord."

– ROMANS 6:23

On these cold winter days, it has been tempting to spend more of my leisure time in our warm house curled up in a comfortable chair with a good book. One winter I worked my way through seventeenth century Englishman John Milton's epic poem, *Paradise Lost*. From the Old English language, as well as the form of the prose, it was a challenge. *If thou canst imagin' trying to reed this page in sech a fourme as this one centence is, thou mayesdt gain some notion of the difficulte it canst bee.*

If you're not familiar with Milton's poem, it expands upon the biblical account of Adam and Eve in the Garden of Eden, especially focusing on the fall of man. While much of its content is purely speculation, the poem vividly conveys the seriousness of sin and its consequences. It helps us picture the intensity of the purity, innocence, and pleasantness in life that was forfeited by Adam and Eve's disobedience of God. And it reminds us that their foolish choice not only drastically affected them and their futures, but it had a long-reaching impact upon all their descendants and the world as a whole.

When any of us make a similar choice to deliberately act contrary to what we know to be God's will, in a sense it may not carry the same weight as that act by our first ancestors. However, we need to guard against an attitude of taking that personal sin too lightly. Afterwards we may be able to find forgiveness through Christ, but that doesn't mean we don't still lose something every time we choose our way over God's way.

When we sin, we erect a barrier that stands between us and God. We lose some degree of our close relationship and fellowship with our Heavenly Father. Our hearts may grow a little more callous, making it harder for us to find that spirit of true repentance so necessary in restoring our intimacy with God. And we have no idea what opportunities for spiritual growth and service we may have lost through our taking the wrong pathway. Sometimes we can't retrace our footsteps—that foolish choice, although forgiven, has forever altered our course in life.

And although our choosing to disobey God will not affect as many people as Adam and Eve's sin did, we do need to realize that our actions will have an impact on others. We try to convince ourselves that our little sin is a personal matter that won't hurt anyone else, but how many spouses have been affected and marriages ruined over the so-called little indiscretions of their partner? How much are our children and grandchildren impacted by whether or not we're walking close to God? If we allow sin to come between us and the Lord, how many people around us will miss out on the more positive influence we might have had on their lives otherwise?

We may not have Paradise to lose when we choose to disobey God, but we do still lose something. Innocence is lost and guilt is gained. Purity is lost and shame is found. What is best for us is sacrificed for a lesser alternative. And the light of Christ that is meant to shine brightly through us grows a little dimmer.

So let's take sin seriously and choose to follow God's will for our lives.

Is there any sin you've been allowing to gain a foothold in your life? Think about what it may be costing you. Seek God's help to give you cleansing and victory over that sin today.

BE CAREFUL ABOUT MAKING CLOSE TIES WITH UNBELIEVERS

"Do not be unequally yoked together with unbelievers."

– II CORINTHIANS 6:14

One day, I noticed a slight error on one of the electronic message boards above the interstate as you head from our area into Atlanta. This is one of those messages which encourages safe driving by reminding us of the number of fatalities on Georgia roadways so far this year. However, on this particular sign a few lightbulbs are out or some other glitch in the electronics has resulted in a missing letter. So instead of "fatalities," the sign warns us about "fatal ties."

I have to admit that I had a little fun by letting my imagination run in some odd directions when I first spotted that mistaken message. Are there killer neckties in our midst? After all, there have been times when I've worn such items and felt like they were slowly choking me to death. Could I unknowingly have been dealing with one of those fatal ties? Maybe the SyFy channel needs to come up with a movie about "The Attack of the Killer Ties." They could run it after showing *Sharknado*. I don't want to be charged with being a conspiracy theorist, but could these fatal ties have something to do with so many pastors no longer wearing ties while they preach? Did they hear the rumor that some terrorist organization had sent in these sinister fashion accessories to wipe out some of our Christian leaders?

Putting such lighthearted speculations aside, the Bible does actually warn us about certain ties or bonds which could be harmful, even fatal, to believers. The Apostle Paul sounds the warning: "Do not be unequally yoked together with unbelievers. For what fellowship has righteousness with lawlessness? And what communion has light with darkness? And what accord has Christ with Belial (or Satan)? Or what part has a believer with an unbeliever?" (II Corinthians 6:14–15).

We need to be careful about entering into too tight of a bond with anyone who isn't a believer or with anything that is contrary to Christ. Such a relationship could end up pulling us in the wrong direction, hindering our spiritual growth, and even resulting in us turning away from our faith. It could truly become a fatal tie.

On the one hand, Jesus made it clear that we are not to isolate ourselves from this ungodly world. We are to be in this world, interacting with our fellow sojourners, being the salt and light which positively impacts the people around us, and fulfilling our mission to be witnesses of the gospel. Therefore, we should be seeking to have enough of a connection to this world and unbelievers that we can relate to them and effectively minister to them.

However, on the other hand, we have to guard against creating such a bond that it gets in the way of our relationship with the Lord or otherwise drags us down spiritually. There can be a time and purpose for strengthening connections with unbelievers in the hopes of winning them to the Lord, but there is also a time and purpose for adhering to Paul's subsequent command, "Come out from among them and be separate, says the Lord" (II Corinthians 6:17).

So be careful about entering into too deep of a union with anyone who doesn't share your faith or with anything that doesn't enhance your walk with Christ, whether in marriage, business, or friendship. No matter how strong your faith, such ties could harm your soul.

And in the meantime, you might also want to keep an eye out for any sinister-looking neckties hanging around.

Are you getting too close to something or someone ungodly?

Develop Godly Habits Which Will Help You Stay the Course

"Take heed to yourself and to the doctrine. Continue in them...."
– I Timothy 4:16

I've been reminded once again how we can be such creatures of habit. A section of the main road between my house and our church has been shut down due to work being done on a bridge. Signs had been posted for weeks warning drivers of this upcoming closure, so I've had time to get used to this idea. I know in my mind that I cannot travel that way now and need to take an alternate route.

However, this is the highway I have traversed on a daily basis, and sometimes several times a day, for many years. So during the brief time since this change has been introduced, I've already found myself on several occasions turning onto that familiar road rather than heading toward the little detour which has become a necessity. Traveling the usual way is so engrained in me that I automatically go that direction unless I stay focused and consciously think about the fact that I shouldn't do it.

Habits are like that. And this is why it's helpful for us to establish good patterns of behavior in our lives.

On the one hand, we shouldn't want to be people who are journeying along our particular pathway in life simply because that's the way we've always gone. We rightly disapprove of the idea of doing certain things just "out of habit." For example, as believers we don't want to be guilty of merely going through the motions of worship, prayer, Bible reading, visiting shut-ins, and other actions related to our faith. We should seek to focus on what we're doing, thinking about the words we're saying, and serving others with the right spirit and motivation. What Jesus said about worship could be applied to many areas of our lives—it should be done "in spirit and truth" (John 4:24), and not just as an unthinking, automatic reflex.

However, on the other hand, getting into the habit of following good pathways in life can be a positive thing. There may be times when we do lose focus for a while or when we aren't thinking and end up cruising on autopilot for a period of time. But isn't it better that we're still following the habit of gathering for worship, of reading our Bibles, of saying our prayers, and other such practices at those times rather than straying off into other directions which could do us more spiritual harm? If we keep turning onto those roads of the spiritual practices which have become engrained in us, it's more likely that God can use those means to get through to us and show us our need to refocus.

So getting into the habit of doing a good thing isn't bad. Let's just keep an eye on our hearts and motives. Let's try to make sure those actions aren't being done simply as a habit void of the engagement of our minds and souls.

I understand this highway I frequently travel is predicted to be shut down until the end of the year. Hopefully over time I'll get to the point where I quit making that habitual turn in its direction. Who knows maybe a year from now, after that route is reopened, I'll be writing about how difficult it is to get accustomed to going that way again because I've developed the habit of traveling the other route. In the meantime, whenever I make that wrong turn, maybe it can serve as a reminder of these truths about habits.

So what habits are you developing in your life? Make sure they are good and godly ones that will help steer you in the right direction.

Examine and evaluate the habits in your life—be honest with yourself.

LET'S SHOW OUR LOVE FOR JESUS IN THE BEST WAY

"If you love Me, keep My commandments."
– JOHN 14:15

How do you show your love to that special someone on Valentine's Day? Many of us probably do it in the traditional manner—with a nice card, flowers, a box of candy, and dinner at a favorite restaurant. But sometimes people get a little more creative and go beyond those normal expressions of affection. Those may involve us putting forth more time and effort than money.

For example, a guy might cook a meal for his beloved rather than take her out—if he can do it without subjecting her to food poisoning. Or a person could write a poem or create his or her own card, rather than purchasing the Hallmark version. Anything that brings back special memories or shows that we put some thought into what the other person truly enjoys is often greatly appreciated. Don't get me wrong—I'm not Mr. Romantic. Just ask my wife. Simply because I know what might be creative or more meaningful doesn't mean that I always do it. Like many others, I could stand improvement in the area of expressing my love.

How do we show our love for Jesus? There are the more common ways. We could send Him a card, in a sense, by lifting up a prayer which says, "I love You." We could offer to Him the flowers and candy of our worship and praise—actions which the Bible describe as being a sweet smell or taste which He enjoys. We could spend time dining with Jesus, enjoying fellowship with Him in prayer and in His Word. Those can be good expressions of love, but are they the best ones?

We might think of more creative or extravagant ways to show our devotion to Jesus, like the woman in the Bible who poured expensive oil on Him out of her deep sense of love. We could become more loud and expressive in our public worship. We could join a monastery where we could spend more time alone with Jesus. We could pour ourselves out in service to Him, maybe even as a missionary to a foreign land. Although some of His followers might do some of those things, they aren't the answer Jesus gave to the question. Jesus clearly told His disciples that the best way to express our love for Him isn't with flowers, candy, cards, better worship, greater offerings, sacrificial service, or even a 55-gallon drum of expensive perfume poured out on Him. He said, "If you love Me, you will keep My commandments" (see John 14:15, 21–24). The greatest way we can show our love for the Lord is simply to obey His Word.

We need to realize that such obedience isn't just a nice way to express our love for Him occasionally, like giving someone flowers. It's the main evidence as to whether or not we truly love Him. If we're not keeping His words on a regular basis, it may be a sign that our love for Him is lacking. Love for Jesus is more than a warm feeling of worship and gratitude. It's a commitment that expresses itself in submission to Him and in obedience to His commandments.

Do you love Jesus today? Probably most of us reading this would quickly respond in the affirmative. But are we expressing that love by obeying Him and His Word? Our love for the Lord should show not just through our saying it, singing it, and feeling it, but also through our submitting to His will for our lives.

Show the Lord that you love Him today. Fully submit to His will and His Word.

GOD SHOWS US WHAT LOVE IS

"He who does not love does not know God, for God is love."

– I JOHN 4:8

When you search for Valentine cards, do you notice any of those that began "Love is…"? They often try to briefly define or describe that important concept in a different, funny, romantic, or catchy way. One of my least favorite attempts at such a definition is the one that came from a movie—"Love is never having to say you're sorry." If you take that description to heart, it could be a recipe for disaster in a relationship.

It would be nice if the Bible defined love for us. It gives us quite a detailed description of the subject in I Corinthians 13, but the closest the Bible seems to come to defining love is not some passage where it says, "Love is…," but rather in a scripture where it reads, "God is…." I John 4:8 tells us that God is love. So if we look at God, His character and actions, what do we learn about love?

For one thing, we come to realize that love is commitment. It's a determination to stick with someone through thick and thin. All through the Bible God promises not to leave or forsake His people. Even when man sinned, God didn't give up on him but sent His own Son to provide a way for salvation. Do we love God that way? If so, it means that we keep trusting Him when we go through valleys of sickness or financial hardships. It means that we don't give up on Him when it seems like our prayers are going unanswered.

Does commitment describe our love for others? Such love means sticking with people through tough times. It means not giving up on a spouse, child, or friend when they falter. It means being there when others have turned their backs on those people.

When we look at God, we also recognize that love is forgiveness. Think about how often God had to forgive the Israelites during their tumultuous journey through the wilderness after being freed from slavery in Egypt. Remember how Jesus, even as He hung on the cross, asked His Father to forgive those who had put Him there. Think about how graciously God has forgiven you and me.

We've all needed to be forgiven by others. Likewise, we've all needed to forgive someone else. It's the lack of forgiveness that breaks apart so many relationships—marriages, children and parents, friendships, and churches. And sometimes it's over little things that don't really matter. However, pride keeps us from offering forgiveness. It's not easy to forgive when we've been wronged. But if Jesus could forgive us, can't we show such love and forgive others?

God also shows us that love is unselfishness. God wasn't thinking about Himself, but about us when He sent His Son into this world. He sent Him so that we wouldn't perish but could have eternal life. Jesus exhibited such love when He lived out His statement that "greater love has no one than this, than to lay down one's life for his friends."

We're not loving the way God does unless we're giving consideration to the interests and needs of others. Selfishness quenches the fire of love when we've got to have things our way, when we're too busy doing what we want to do, and when we're unwilling to sacrifice for the good of the other person. But even a stubborn problem like selfishness can be overcome through the power of God working in our lives.

Loving others as God loves us. It may not be very funny or catchy, but that's what love really is.

In what ways does your love need to be more like God and His love?

God's Odd Way
of Showing His Love

"In this is love…that He loved us and sent His Son to be the propitiation for our sins."

– I John 4:10

At our church's annual Valentine Banquet, our romantic, creative natures were put to the test. Each person was given a list of eight words from which they were to formulate sentiments appropriate for Valentine's Day. The challenge lay in the fact that these particular words were not the kind you would normally think of as being romantic or that you would commonly find in a Hallmark card for the occasion. There were no words like "rose" or "devotion" or "beautiful" included on the roster of choices. Instead, the participants had to create their expressions of love by using words such as "broccoli," "thunderstorm," and "algebra." And they were given only ten minutes in which to complete the task.

As you might imagine, some people struggled with this exercise. However, by the time it was over, we discovered that there were a number of creative romantics in our midst. So if you're someone who forgot to get your sweetheart a Valentine card and are going to be writing your own at the last minute, here are a couple of ideas from our banquet that you might want to include. "Your love is healthier for me than eating broccoli." "Our love for one another is more electrifying than the most powerful thunderstorm." Then again, maybe you've still got time to run to the store and pick up a good card.

There are some words and concepts that we just don't associate with love. It's difficult to imagine how they could go together. Sometimes we can force them into compatibility, as we did at our banquet. Other times, they fit together because of our unique circumstances. For example, someone might actually associate "algebra" with love because he first met his soul mate in a classroom where they studied that subject together.

Before Jesus came into the world, it would have been equally difficult for anyone to imagine how God's love could be associated with certain words such as "manger" or "crucifixion." Remember that a manger was a feeding trough for animals. How could that be connected to divine love? Yet now we do know the connection. It has become all too commonplace in many of our minds. God showed His love for us in that He sent His Son into the world in flesh and blood to be born in such humble circumstances that His first makeshift crib was a manger. Imagine that—God willingly relegating Himself to a feeding trough out of devotion to our welfare.

I imagine it would have been even more confounding for an individual to come up with some way to associate the idea of "crucifixion" with love. Maybe something like this: "If you didn't love me, it would be more excruciating than the pains of crucifixion." However, now we see that cruel form of criminal execution as one of the main symbols of how much Jesus loves us. His everlasting Valentine to us says, "I loved you so much that I was willing to suffer the agony of crucifixion so that you could be saved from spiritual death, be reconciled with your Heavenly Father, and receive the gift of eternal life." What amazing love!

God used some rather odd ways to show His love for us. But nothing Hallmark could put out could better express this greatest of all loves. Maybe we had better stick with "heart" and "roses" instead of "broccoli" and "thunderstorm" when conveying our love for each other, but nothing could ever replace the manger, the crucifixion, and other such unusual expressions of God's great love for us.

Spend some time meditating on how God has shown His great love for you.

DON'T JUST SEEK TO LOVE MORE
BUT TO LOVE BETTER

"And may the Lord make you increase and abound in love to one another and to all...."

– I THESSALONIANS 3:12

Maybe at some point you have found yourself in one of those feigned arguments with someone dear to you—a spouse, a child, or a grandchild—as you debate the issue of who loves whom more. A child might stretch her little arms as far apart as she can while declaring, "I love you this much." Someone might suggest that he loves you to the moon and back. After several back-and-forth attempts to express the height, depth, and length of his or her love, one person will often try to put an end to the contest by making reference to infinity or maybe infinity times infinity.

Hopefully we all recognize how important love is. The Bible lifts it up as the preeminent characteristic in the lives of followers of Christ. But at the same time, we have to admit that our love doesn't always measure up to what it should be. Why is that? Is the problem the fact that we don't love people enough? Certainly it could be. In one letter Paul told some believers, "And may the Lord make you increase and abound in love to one another and to all, just as we do to you" (I Thessalonians 3:12). Sometimes we do need to possess more love for others.

But in some cases the issue may not be that we need a greater amount of love. It's hard to imagine how we could love some people more than we already do. Even now we love that wife, that husband, those children with all our heart. We already love them to infinity times infinity. How can you improve on that?

But maybe we need to think of it less in terms of quantity and more in terms of quality. It could be that we don't need to love them more, but we do need to love them better. Most of us would have to agree that no matter how much we love those precious folks, it's true that our love for them could be of a better quality. We could love them with a more Christlike love, as well as express our love in more meaningful ways.

This world and those who don't know Christ talk a lot about love and experience a degree of love, but it often falls way short of the type of love the Bible indicates we can have. Many in our world today don't know the pure, holy, selfless kind of love the Bible advocates. They only experience a shadow of it—one that too often gets intermingled with unkindness, jealousy, wrath, suspicion, lack of trust, physical violence and abuse, neglect, unfaithfulness, and abandonment.

Even as believers we often fall short in the quality of our love for others. We need to keep growing in love—not just in trying to love more, but in seeking to love better. What does such love look like? It looks a lot like Jesus and His sacrificial love for us. But beyond His example, the Bible also gives a description of such love: "Love suffers long and is kind; love does not envy; love does not parade itself, is not puffed up; does not behave rudely, does not seek its own, is not provoked, thinks no evil; does not rejoice in iniquity, but rejoices in the truth; bears all things, believes all things, hopes all things, endures all things" (I Corinthians 13:4-7).

So think about the individuals around you, carefully consider these characteristics of godly love, and let's ask the Lord to show us how we can start loving those people better.

Lord, help my love for others to increase in both quantity and quality.

WILL YOU LET HIM
BE YOUR VALENTINE?

"We love Him because He first loved us."

– I JOHN 4:19

Here we are at another Valentine's Day. Have you eaten any of those little candy hearts yet—the ones with brief, affectionate messages printed on them? I've always preferred chocolate treats myself (a hint for my wife), but apparently those hard candies are popular for many people, especially children. They convey such messages as "Luv Ya," "Hugs & Kisses," "Cutie," and a variety of other terms of endearment. The most common sentiment I recall being written on those hearts was the plea, "Be Mine." It expresses the desire for someone to make a commitment of love to you.

It reminds me of the classic comic strip character, Charlie Brown. He was always disappointed when it came to Valentine's Day. He would anxiously wait at his mailbox, looking for cards, but never receiving any. Even his dog, Snoopy, would get Valentines in the mail, but not poor ole Charlie Brown.

Whether or not you have a special person with whom to celebrate this day, there is Someone who wants you to know how much He loves you. God has sent you a Valentine. He has given you His heart with His desire written on it—"Be Mine." Does it seem strange to think of God in terms of being your Valentine? Maybe it's because we connect the idea too closely with physical attraction and affection. But when you think of it in terms of relationship, love, and commitment, you can find the concept all through the Bible.

God's great desire is for you to be His. That's why the very first of the Ten Commandments is "You shall have no other gods before Me" (Exodus 20:3). God wants to have the same kind of committed, exclusive relationship with you as is associated with a married couple. Jesus proclaimed that the greatest commandment is "You shall love the Lord your God with all your heart, with all your soul, with all your mind, and with all your strength" (Mark 12:30). He loves you and wants you to love Him above all else.

Think of some of the words and phrases God uses to describe His followers—His chosen ones, His special treasure, those who are precious to Him, His beloved. God uses what could be described as mushy, romantic language to show how much we mean to Him.

And let's not forget that Valentine's Day often means expressing one's love with gifts beyond cards—flowers, candy, or dinner. And God has shown His love to us by giving us the gift of eternal life. "In this the love of God was manifested toward us, that God has sent His only begotten Son into the world, that we might live through Him" (I John 4:9).

That's the greatest expression of love—Jesus giving Himself as the sacrifice for our sins. "Greater love has no one than this, than to lay down one's life for his friends" (John 15:13). God has given us the most costly of presents—more valuable than diamonds or gold.

God is like a suitor who has done everything He can to woo us to Himself. He has sent us clear messages that He loves us and wants us to have a special relationship with Him. He has showered us with blessings and gifts. And He has exhibited the extent of His love by giving Himself for our sakes.

The only question is our response to God's plea to "Be Mine." Let's not leave Him waiting at His mailbox with disappointment. Let's be as committed to loving Him as He is to loving us. Let Him be your Valentine.

Have you opened your heart to receive God's great love for you?

FEBRUARY 15

THE PROBLEM MAY BE IN OUR OWN HEARTS

"For I acknowledge my transgressions, and my sin is always before me."

– PSALM 51:3

I'll confess that I'm writing from the perspective of a peanut butter lover. I regularly enjoy that spread sandwiched between two saltine crackers. For Valentine's Day, my thoughtful wife, who is very familiar with my tastes, gave me a heart-shaped box full of Reese's candies. When I eat certain kinds of soup on a cold winter day, nothing sets it off quite like half a peanut butter sandwich cut diagonally, just the way my mother did it when I was a kid. So it wasn't any great surprise that when I first heard the news about a recall of that product, its smell could be found fresh on my breath. Although the brand name and the numbers on the lid of the near-empty jar in my cabinet matched those that were being recalled, I figured ours was safe since I had been eating on it for a couple of weeks without any stomach problems. Apparently some other people weren't so fortunate.

However, I was also aware that there had been a stomach virus going around, even among those who hadn't eaten any peanut butter. It wouldn't have surprised me if some people who were simply suffering from the flu bug might have tried to blame their ailment on the manufacturers of that food product—especially if it might have meant being able to get some money out of it in a lawsuit. Granted, those businesses should be held accountable if their product was the source of illness for certain people. And I suppose if I had been sick, I would have wondered if that spread on my crackers had been the cause. But I can see how the manufacturers could easily become the scapegoat for others who prefer to blame someone else for their problems rather than admit that it might just be the common stomach bug within them.

It's not unlike the way we tend to look for opportunities to blame others for certain problems in our lives which may actually be the result of the disease of sin and selfishness residing in our hearts. We may try to make ourselves look like the victim when, in reality, we are the perpetrators who knowingly rebelled against God's will or made a poor choice based on our own selfish desires.

We find examples of it all through the Bible. When Aaron was confronted about having made that infamous golden calf in the wilderness, he tried to say that the people made him do it. When Samuel rebuked King Saul for failing to destroy all the livestock of the conquered Amalekites, Saul also tried to shift the blame to the people who "took the plunder." Both failed to own up to the source of the contamination and poison that was found in their own hearts.

Let's not be guilty of the same thing. Sure, there are times when we truly suffer as the result of the actions of others, just as some people may have been legitimately sickened by contaminated peanut butter, but there are other occasions when we need to recognize our responsibility for what we're experiencing and the part our own fallen nature may have played in it. Rather than deny it and shift the blame, we need to confess it. And we serve a God who, rather than recalling us and destroying us, can work in us to cleanse us of that spiritually poisonous disease.

I didn't forsake peanut butter. I just switched brands for a while. But let's pray that the Lord will help us to forsake the attitude that tends to play the victim. When needed, let's recognize, confess, and seek cleansing from the inner sin and selfishness that causes many of our problems.

Lord, help me to own up to my sins and not shift the blame elsewhere.

There Is a Redemption Island for You

"For the wages of sin is death, but the gift of God is eternal life in Christ Jesus our Lord."

– Romans 6:23

I remember when a particular edition of the reality show, *Survivor*, was given the interesting subtitle "Redemption Island." From what I could tell in the previews, it seems that they were adding a new twist to the game. Up until then, whenever a contestant was voted out by the tribe, his or her torch was snuffed out, marking the end of the road for that individual. But in this season the participants would get a second chance. It was illustrated in the previews by host Jeff Probst putting out the fire in someone's torch only to have the flame flare back up again. When someone was voted out, he was sent to "redemption island" where he would do battle with another contestant for the opportunity to get back in the game.

Redemption is a wonderful concept. It offers the possibility of restoration to those who have fallen. It provides hope for those who thought all was lost. And it's an idea that God put in place long before any TV writers decided to use it to spruce up some longtime reality show.

Due to our original parents, Adam and Eve, being outlasted, outwitted, and outplayed by Satan, we inherited a sinful disposition that takes us down the path toward spiritual death and destruction. As a result, every one of us fails to pass the test at some point when confronted with the choice of doing what's right and pleasing to God or going a different way.

Experience confirms the truth that the Bible declares—"All have sinned and fall short of the glory of God" (Romans 3:23). And the consequences of that fact are nothing short of devastating. "For the wages of sin is death…" (Romans 6:23). There's no way around it. According to the rules of the game, if we've sinned, that's it. We deserve to die, physically, spiritually, and eternally. Our lives are snuffed out and we end up feeling like torches in a place where "the fire shall never be quenched" (Mark 9:43).

It would be a sad and hopeless condition, if not for that marvelous concept of redemption. However, even then, we're not good enough to deserve a second chance. And we're not strong enough to defeat our opponent in order to gain that opportunity. We don't have to try to battle our way back into God's favor, and we could never achieve victory by doing so. That fight has already been won by someone else—by God Himself in the person of His Son, Jesus Christ. He fought and died and arose as Conqueror in order to redeem us and to give us another chance.

Redemption means that the first part of Romans 6:23 isn't the end of the story. There's more. "For the wages of sin is death, but the gift of God is eternal life in Christ Jesus our Lord." Even though we deserve to be separated from God and from all that's good for eternity, God gives us another chance to avoid those consequences and to live for eternity with Him instead.

The only battle we have to fight is with ourselves—the battle to overcome our pride and self-will that wants to try to earn its place, that balks at repentance and confession, and that bristles at the thought of submitting our will to God's. The only way to be a spiritual survivor is through faith—trusting Jesus as our Redeemer.

We've all fallen, but God's giving us another chance. Let Him kindle that fire of life in your soul.

Thank the Lord for His wonderful redemption which graciously gives you another chance.

DON'T TRY TO WIN
AN OSCAR FROM GOD

"Do not be like the hypocrites...."
– MATTHEW 6:16

"And the Oscar goes to...." It's getting close to that time of year again as the entertainment industry hands out its annual honors known as the Academy Awards. I'll admit that I'm not a big modern movie buff. I usually prefer the older flicks like the ones shown on Turner Classic Movies. But most likely I'll still tune in for at least part of the Academy Awards Show, just to see who wins.

And I usually don't hold actors and actresses in very high esteem. What I have witnessed and heard about the behavior and lifestyle of many entertainers is not only foreign to me, but isn't what I would consider admirable. However, I do have to admire the skill of many actors who can not only memorize lines of dialogue, but who can so believably portray characters, even when those roles are very different from the real life and personality of the performer.

However, it's important for us to remember that true Christianity isn't about acting. Jesus leveled some of His harshest criticism at those He termed "hypocrites"—a word whose roots come from the theater and the playacting of its participants. Faith in Jesus isn't about knowing the right words to say or giving a convincing portrayal of a person who is religious. I cringe whenever I hear words like "performance," "audience," and other theatrical-related words used in connection with worship services.

Christianity is less about what we try to appear to be and more about who we really are.

Unfortunately, the Church could give out some Oscars too. The following is a short list of some possible nominees.

Best Musical Number: the singer, choir, or praise team who is only concerned about hitting the right notes and receiving the applause of the "audience" rather than focusing on the words and seeking to please God.

Best Director: the church administrator who is so worried about the order of service and that everything be done exactly as planned and with such excellence that no room is allowed for the Holy Spirit to work in a different or unexpected way.

Best Supporting Actor: the church member who shows up periodically to make a big production of putting his offerings into the plate or making his pledges. Or the one who only gives if he gets public credit for it, such as a plaque with his name engraved on it.

Best Producer: the pastor who draws people in with his winsome personality while avoiding or compromising truths of the gospel that might make people feel uncomfortable. Or the minister who skillfully preaches inspiring sermons while secretly living an immoral life.

Best Actor and Actress: the numerous laymen and ministers who recite the historic creeds from memory, sing the songs, pray beautiful prayers, regularly attend church, and actively serve, but who don't have a real relationship with God through faith in Christ.

Maybe we should leave the acting to those in Hollywood who do it best. We should seek to be genuine in our faith, even though such openness may reveal our shortcomings and show that we still have miles to travel in our spiritual journey.

Let's always remember that the goal in our lives is not to win an Oscar for the best portrayal of a Christian, but to actually let the Lord transform us into the godly person He wants us to be.

Is your Christianity just in appearance or is it truly in your heart?

Our Fruit Reveals
What Is in Our Hearts

"You will know them by their fruits. Do men gather grapes from thorn-bushes...."

– Matthew 7:16

Today is my wife's birthday. One year more emphasis than usual was placed on this event due to it being one of those milestones in which she turned an age whose number ends in zero. Although she has not been shy about acknowledging how old she is, I think it would be wise for me to leave it up to her to share that news rather than to state it here for widespread publication.

My wife received some nice gifts and cards for the occasion, but of course some of us had to give her a hard time about the situation too. One person at our church brought her a bouquet in a vase. From a distance it appeared to be an arrangement of greenery with dark flowers, or what my wife first thought were dead roses. But upon close examination, one could see that the objects at the end of the stems were not flowers at all, dead or alive. They were prunes which had been affixed to those stems. My wife was jokingly told by her benefactor that she might need the "help" those prunes can provide for people her age.

You should have seen the puzzled expressions on the faces of our young grandchildren as they examined that gift. They realized how odd and unnatural it was to see those shriveled prunes where they would normally expect to see beautiful flowers.

It reminds me of some ridiculous pictures put forth in the Bible in order to illustrate a certain truth. In Matthew 7:16, Jesus asked, "Do men gather grapes from thornbushes or figs from thistles?" A similar question is raised in James 3:12—"Can a fig tree, my brethren, bear olives, or a grapevine bear figs?" The obvious answer to both of those questions is "No." You don't find olives on fig trees, and neither do you see figs growing on grapevines or thistles. And you don't normally see prunes stuck on the end of flower stems.

The truth being conveyed is that we can know a tree by its fruit. Jesus was saying that we can recognize false prophets by their deeds and doctrine. James was suggesting that people's words, or the fruit of their mouths, reveals what they really are in their hearts and character.

There are times when we find ourselves puzzled and disappointed at the fruit being borne in the lives of people or the fruit coming out of their mouths. It doesn't fit with what we thought that person was or with what they professed to be as a follower of Christ. Granted, we are all susceptible to occasional stumbling in our actions and to allowing some hurtful or corrupt words burst from our lips on the spur of the moment. But if we witness that kind of fruit consistently in someone's life, the Bible suggests it is an indication of what that person is truly like on the inside.

What should really disturb us is if we see such fruit frequently coming out in our own lives. If so, we should take it as an indication that something isn't right with our tree. Jesus doesn't just want to forgive us for yielding bad fruit—He wants to change us into a tree that bears godly fruit, such as love, joy, peace, longsuffering, kindness, goodness, faithfulness, gentleness, and self-control (Galatians 5:22–23).

The Lord doesn't intend for us to be prune bouquets. Let's be trees bearing good fruit to the glory of God.

What kind of fruit is springing forth in your life? What does that suggest about your relationship with the Lord?

Warning: The Bible Can Be Dangerous to Your Health?

"Desire the pure milk of the word, that you may grow thereby."
— I Peter 2:2

It seems that we're constantly receiving warnings about foods and other items that could pose a threat to our health. I remember a few years ago when such a scare had to do with orange juice. We were being told that some of that product being brought in from other countries contained a degree of certain chemicals and pesticides which some would consider to be unsafe. I heard one woman on the news declaring that she hadn't purchased any orange juice ever since that report came out.

I have to confess that I continued to drink my glass of OJ every morning. After all, my mother told me that I need the vitamin C. And who are you going to believe—your mother or some scientific study? Don't get me wrong—I'm actually very grateful for those who watch out for the health and safety of consumers. But I don't easily alter my lifestyle for every little negative news report that comes out about a product. If I did, I probably wouldn't be able to eat or drink anything. And that would definitely pose a threat to my health.

Apparently, even the Bible is a risk to our health. It used to be that whenever you had to spend some time in a hospital, you could count on a couple of things. One was staff telling you that you need to rest, while they kept you awake all night with their incessant checking of your vital signs. The other was having a Gideon Bible nearby to be able to read in between those nurses' visits.

However, many hospitals no longer allow those Bibles to stay in patients' rooms. It's not that they're anti-Christian. It's simply a health issue. They completely clean up a room when one patient is discharged and before another takes up residence in that location. Everything is either cleaned or disposed of, which means that Bibles as potential germ carriers can't stick around from one patient to another. It's understandable. And I'm grateful for their concern. But I'm even more grateful that there are those who still seek the spiritual health of people along with their physical health. For example, at one of our local hospitals, the Gideons still graciously offer to supply the facility with Bibles to be made available to those who request them. It might not be as convenient as having that sacred book already present on the table right next to you, but at least it's available upon request.

It's strange to think of the Bible as a health risk. It's one of our greatest sources for spiritual sustenance. When He was being tempted in the wilderness, Jesus noted, "Man shall not live by bread alone, but by every word that proceeds from the mouth of God" (Matthew 4:4). Peter encouraged believers to "desire the pure milk of the word, that you may grow thereby" (I Peter 2:2). The Bible actually promotes health and growth in the lives of those who feed on it.

What really puts a person at risk is to neglect God's Word. To do so puts one in danger of being deceived by lies and half-truths. It puts one at risk of becoming weak in the faith and susceptible to temptation. It can stunt one's growth and hinder a person's effectiveness in serving the Lord. I'm less concerned about the germs I may receive from sharing a copy of the Bible and more grateful that its truths can help me ward off evil and sin in my life.

So whatever you may decide to do about any food warnings which are issued, make sure you don't risk your health and well-being due to neglecting to read and obey God's Word.

Faithfully take time to feed on God's Word each day.

Looking Back Can Help Us Appreciate Where We Are Today

"And you He made alive, who were dead in trespasses and sins, in which you once walked according to the course of this world...."

– EPHESIANS 2:1–2

One time when the work was just beginning on painting the inside of our church building, I was somewhat uncertain about the color that had been chosen for the sanctuary. We weren't aiming for a drastic change, just a slightly darker hue from what we presently had. When I first saw the new color, it had only been applied to the edges of the wall. And in contrast to the old color that still covered the rest of the wall, the new one looked like a much darker shade, more so than I had expected.

But based on past experiences with paint, I decided to reserve judgment until the whole room was completed. Sure enough, when the job was finished the color looked great. Some people commented that it looked to be almost the same color we had before. To my eyes it also seemed very similar at that point. However, in my mind I could still see the stark difference that was present when the two colors had appeared side by side.

Similarly there are times when we look at our present lives, attitudes, and relationship with the Lord with a degree of disappointment and frustration. It doesn't seem like we're making the progress we ought to be. We're still struggling with various issues. We are too aware of our weaknesses and shortcomings. And we know that we have a long way to go in many areas of our lives before we come close to being like Jesus.

That's why it can be helpful at times to look back. When we remember where we used to be and how far we've come, the contrast often becomes more evident to us. When we put them side by side in our minds, like those two colors of paint, we can better see the difference.

We should keep in mind that there are some pitfalls to avoid when looking behind us. We don't want to glorify our past sinful lives or revel in those ungodly actions. Neither do we want to stir up guilt and condemnation over past wrongs for which we have already been forgiven.

However, there can be value in remembering the old life from which our Savior has delivered us. It can stir up gratitude and love for His grace toward us. And it can remind us of how far we have traveled on our journey since that time.

In his letter to the Ephesians, Paul often pointed out the contrast between what those believers used to be and what they were now. They were dead in trespasses and sins, but now they were alive in Christ (2:1–5). They used to "walk according to the course of this world" and conducted themselves in the lusts of their flesh, but now they were "created in Christ Jesus for good works" (2:2–10). They were once "strangers," but now were "fellow citizens with the saints and members of the household of God" (2:19). And now, instead of being in darkness, they lived like children of light (5:8).

We all have a long way to go in our journey toward Christlikeness, but most likely we've come many miles from where we first began. Think back—do some comparing—and see if it isn't so. Give God thanks for what He's done for you. And be committed to letting Him continue that work in you until it's completed.

With gratitude think about where Jesus brought you from and where you are today.

DOES GOD NEED TO RESIGN?

"The Creator of the ends of the earth, neither faints nor is weary."
— ISAIAH 40:28

I remember when Pope Benedict XVI announced that he was going to resign. It was an especially noteworthy occurrence since it bucked the longstanding trend of popes serving in their position until death. I understand that the last time a pontiff resigned, it was almost 600 years ago. To put it in proper perspective, that previous resignation took place prior to George Washington, John Wesley, Martin Luther, Christopher Columbus, and even Betty White.

Pope Benedict specifically cited health reasons for his decision. Due to his advanced age, he didn't believe he had the strength in mind and body to continue to adequately fulfill his duties, particularly in a world that is changing so rapidly.

Whether or not you view the pope to be the head of the church on earth, many of us will acknowledge that the ultimate authority and ruler over the church is God Himself. And I imagine there are some people around who think it's about time for Him to resign too.

After all, He's also getting on up there in age. He not only goes back before Christopher Columbus, but before Julius Caesar, Alexander the Great, Moses, Noah, Adam, and infinitely beyond the beginning of time. Even when the prophet Daniel had a vision of God over 2,500 years ago, He already was pictured with white hair and was referred to as the Ancient of Days (Daniel 7:9). That would make Him superancient now.

Some might suggest that God needs to step aside because He is having a hard time keeping up with the changes in our modern world. He still promotes those old-fashioned ideas about sin and atonement, the devil and hell, absolute truth, holiness and purity, along with other ideas that don't fit in with society's way of thinking today. If He would just resign and let someone who's more progressive take over, it would make His way considerably more attractive to a lot of people.

Others might think that God may simply be getting tired in His old age and unable to do what He used to do. After all, have you seen any Red Seas being parted lately? Have any of you been resurrected from the dead? Some might wonder if maybe God is just too old and weary to perform those great miracles anymore.

Fortunately the Bible puts such speculation about God to rest. It clearly reveals Him to be a Divine being who doesn't age and grow tired as we do. He never changes, and never will.

Likewise, His truths do not become outdated. His ideas do not need to be discarded or revised as society changes. His Word still stands today, and it is still as true as ever. If our world is no longer recognizing and conforming to God's Word, it's a sign of the deterioration of our society, not the deterioration of God.

And if we're not seeing any miracles in our day, it's not God's fault. There are many people around who will testify to how God is doing great things in their lives. He is still answering prayer. There are miracles taking place around us if we'll just open our eyes and recognize the hand of God in those events. The Bible declares that "the Creator of the ends of the earth neither faints nor is weary" (Isaiah 40:28). God is no less powerful and no less capable today than He was when He parted the Red Sea for the Israelites.

So God doesn't need to resign. We just need to do a better job of following His leadership and trusting Him to show His power in our lives today.

How should it affect your life to know that God and His Word never changes?

Depend on the Lord
to Keep You from Falling

"Therefore let him who thinks he stands take heed lest he fall."
– I Corinthians 10:12

One of my church members was recuperating from a stroke. He had been undergoing a period of intense therapy in the rehabilitation section at one of the area hospitals. When I first visited him in his room set up for patients with his type of medical issue, a unique feature stood out to me. Above the bed were some words painted on the ceiling tile in such a way as to be easily read by the patient who reclined in that spot. In bright, bold lettering it read, "Call nurse. Do not fall."

That message was intended to remind a patient not to try to get out of bed on his own. One of the problems is that individuals in those circumstances often can either forget about their condition or simply think they can do more than they're able to do, and end up falling and hurting themselves even worse. From what I've been told, the staff in that department is very firm about warning patients from trying to do too much too soon. In various ways they reaffirm the message of seeking assistance rather than risking the setback of experiencing a fall.

It reminds me of what Paul wrote in relation to our spiritual well-being: "Therefore let him who thinks he stands take heed lest he fall" (I Corinthians 10:12). We can run into problems spiritually when we lose sight of our complete dependence on the Lord. We begin to think we're strong enough to stand on our own two feet against the problems we face and the challenges which pop up on our pathways. So we fail to seek God's guidance before making an important decision. Or we don't pray for God's help but step out to battle the enemy in our own strength. We start trying to walk the pathway of following Christ with self-confidence rather than God-confidence. And in doing so, we put ourselves at great risk of taking a tumble—one which might not only hurt us and result in a setback from which it might take some time to recover, but which also might adversely affect others.

But Paul didn't stop with that word of warning. He continued, "No temptation has overtaken you except such as is common to man; but God is faithful, who will not allow you to be tempted beyond what you are able, but with the temptation will also make the way of escape, that you may be able to bear it" (I Corinthians 10:13). In other words, we don't have to fall. God is able to uphold us through times of temptation and trial. He has provided the means for us to be able to stand in spite of the difficulty of the challenge and in spite of our own weaknesses. There is a way to escape falling. We just have to look for it. And we need to call on the Lord and depend on Him to be there to help us find it and to lead us through it.

As this scripture says we can count on God—He is faithful. He hasn't left us alone to fight the battle. He wants us to look to Him for help. He wants to be there to support us and to keep us from falling.

So let's not forget that the ultimate Helper is available to us. And let's not ever deceive ourselves into thinking that we're strong enough to walk without Him.

It's a message we might not have clearly painted on our ceilings or walls, but we can try to keep it in the forefront of our minds: "Call on the Lord. Do not fall."

When temptation comes today, pray and depend on the Lord to help you resist it.

BELIEVERS ARE UNDERDOGS, YET WINNERS

"And God has chosen the weak things of the world to put to shame the things which are mighty."

– I CORINTHIANS 1:27

The Olympics often bring with them a number of interesting stories. There are the heartwarming ones having to do with close family relationships. There are the inspirational accounts of athletes who have overcome tremendous obstacles to reach their goals. The games themselves often write another chapter in the script of many of those stories. High-profile competitors at the top of their respective sports come to the Olympics with high hopes. Some complete their journey as expected with dominating, gold-medal performances, while others falter and suffer the heartbreak of disappointment.

In most Olympics there is often another kind of story that emerges—the ones about the underdogs. Inevitably there are at least a few cases in which little-known athletes or unheralded teams unexpectedly turn in the performance of a lifetime, resulting in their receiving one of those coveted medals. I'll confess that those tend to be some of my favorite Olympic outcomes—I like to pull for the underdog.

As followers of Christ, we will often find ourselves viewed as the underdogs by many in this world. In other words, we won't be looked upon as being the smartest or the strongest or most successful. We won't be voted the most likely to succeed in this world. We won't enjoy much respect at times. The world doesn't expect us to win.

But such a view shouldn't surprise us. Jesus faced similar circumstances. Isaiah prophesied of Christ: "And when we see Him, there is no beauty that we should desire Him. He is despised and rejected by men.... He was despised, and we did not esteem Him" (Isaiah 53:2–3). As a humiliated Jesus went to the Cross, many looked at Him as being a failure and loser.

Jesus warned His disciples that they would be treated the same way. The Apostle Paul also observed "that not many wise according to the flesh, not many mighty, not many noble, are called. But God has chosen the foolish things of the world...and God has chosen the weak things of the world...and the things which are despised God has chosen" (I Corinthians 1:26–28). God likes to use those whom the world considers underdogs. Why? So that we won't be able to claim any glory for ourselves, but rather give it all to the Lord. We recognize that He's the One who deserves the gold medal for anything we accomplish.

A few years ago there was a TV commercial which incorporated the catchy tune from the old cartoon show, *Underdog*, as it advertised running shoes. Part of that song refers to "speed of lightning, roar of thunder." It reminds me of the picture the Bible gives us of God's awesome glory and presence. It's often described in such terms as thunder and lightning. It should remind us that whatever good we accomplish as Christ's followers and as underdogs, it's not due to our own power and strength. It's only because of the presence and power of God in our lives. The thunder and lightning comes from the Holy Spirit living in us and working through us.

Although Jesus was seen as an underdog, He rose victoriously from the grave. And one day He'll return to this earth in all His glory as King and Judge. And while this world may not think very highly of us at times, we are more than conquerors through Christ. God uses the foolish, the weak, and the despised to accomplish His will in the world.

The world may view you as an underdog, but if you're faithfully following the Lord, always remember that you're a winner.

Accept the "underdog" title and rejoice in the victory that is still yours through Christ.

What Do We Need to Turn Over to the Lord?

"By faith Abraham, when he was tested, offered up Isaac, and he who had received the promises offered up his only begotten son...."
— Hebrews 11:17

When my granddaughter was little, she loved to sing, especially as she rode along in the car. It brought joy to my heart to hear her sweet voice melodically declaring "Our God is an awesome God," along with other tunes she had learned at church.

However, her repertoire wasn't limited to spiritual music. She sang about the wheels on the bus going 'round and 'round, along with other common children's songs. And after watching what was the latest Disney animated feature at the time, she got stuck on one song in particular. And I do mean stuck. Over and over and over she would sing "Let it go, let it go." And those three words are the only part of the song she sang. Her mom, tired of hearing the same phrase repeatedly, tried to teach her the lyrics to the rest of the song. But for a while our granddaughter just kept belting out "Let it go" like a broken record.

Those same words are not unusual for us to hear from the Holy Spirit too. Often God needs to instruct us to "let it go." In some cases, we will hear that command as we deal with conviction of sin and God's call for us to repent. There may be some particular "pet sin" which we have a hard time forsaking. There is something about it that makes it attractive to us, in spite of the harm it does and the roadblock it presents between us and a right relationship with the Lord. But if we're truly serious about our spiritual need, it's going to have to be dealt with. And until we do, we're liable to hear that small divine voice telling us over and over, "Let it go, let it go."

We may also hear similar instructions concerning aspects of our lives that aren't necessarily sinful, but which haven't been surrendered to the Lord. Christ doesn't just want to be a part of our lives—He demands to be Lord over our lives. At some point we will come face-to-face with the call to put ourselves and everything we have under His control. We have to take our hands off the steering wheel, climb out of the driver's seat, and let Jesus be in charge.

However, again there are often one or more areas in our lives in which we tend to struggle with surrendering to the Lord. We want to call the shots regarding that matter. We want to still have veto power if the Lord starts taking us in a direction we don't want to go. We want Jesus and eternal life, but we think we know better how to run certain aspects of our lives. But God says to us very clearly, "Let it go." The Bible says that we need to present ourselves as a living sacrifice to God (Romans 12:1)—that includes our whole being and all that we possess.

Abraham had to be willing to let go of his beloved son Isaac when God told him to do so. And God greatly blessed him as a result. In contrast, the young ruler who encountered Jesus was unwilling to let go of his many possessions in this world. So he walked away from Christ sad and spiritually lost.

How do we respond when we hear those words from the Lord? Do we hang on even tighter to whatever it is, or do we loosen our grip and turn it over to the One who can handle it so much better than we can?

When God tells us to "let it go," let's be sure to listen and obey.

What is God calling you to surrender to Him? Let it go!

It's Hard to Stop
Once You Start

*"But you, O man of God, flee these things and pursue
righteousness...."*

– I Timothy 6:11

Winter weather often spawns a flurry of pictures and videos chronicling people's experiences as they deal with the frigid temperatures and frozen precipitation. They range from people down south getting excited over seeing a few snowflakes to northern residents trying to dig out from mounds of the white stuff. You've probably seen some of those images showing drivers losing control of their cars while traveling on icy roads.

I watched one such video in which a vehicle topped a hill onto an ice-covered street. When the car reached a certain point, the person controlling the camera could be heard to say, "That's it"—in other words, there was no turning back from or stopping what was inevitably going to happen next. Sure enough, in spite of the valiant efforts of the driver to halt any further progress, the car slowly slid sideways down the sloped road, eventually crashing into a couple of other vehicles which had previously followed the same course. And the impact from this newest victim caused them all to slide even further down the hill.

Life can be full of slippery slopes. We can take one wrong turn or one misstep and suddenly find ourselves in a situation that is spiraling out of control. As hard as we try, we can't avoid the consequences of that initial action. In some cases, we can't seem to right ourselves and get back on track again. We want to put on the brakes, but it seems we just keep sliding further and further toward an eventual crash.

Don't get me wrong. I'm not one who puts much stock in that saying, "The devil made me do it." Neither do I give much weight to the excuse, "I couldn't help it." I believe God gave human beings free will. In any situation or when facing any temptation, we have a choice. We can do what's right and pleasing to God or we can decide to go a different direction, which often means doing what we want to do instead.

However, sometimes we find after taking a step in a certain direction that it becomes more difficult to turn around or to stop. One lie tends to lead to another. Giving in to a certain temptation not only makes it easier to do so the next time we face it, but also tends to lead us into deeper sins. We still have a choice, but the further we slide, it gets tougher and tougher to make the right choices.

Maybe we see the slippery spot and think we're strong enough or wise enough to drive right over it without any problem. But even four-wheel-drive vehicles can lose control when roads are completely iced over. No matter how spiritually mature we may be, if we're not careful we could find ourselves involved in a spinout. It might just be a minor incident that hinders our spiritual progress or it could end up causing us to crash, damaging our character, our witness, and maybe hurting others around us.

So what do we do? Watch out for those icy roads in your life. As the ancient philosopher suggested, "Know thyself." Know your weaknesses and where you tend to be tempted. Avoid those areas. Don't take that first step in the wrong direction, thinking it won't hurt to go just a little distance down that road or thinking you'll be strong enough to stop. And always look to the Lord as the One who can help you do the right thing in those situations.

So let's not even start down that wrong pathway—it could be a slippery slope from which it will be hard to recover.

Are you flirting with any "slippery slopes" in your life? Don't take another step in that direction.

TOTAL ABSTINENCE
OR MODERATION?

"Therefore let us not judge one another anymore, but rather resolve this, not to put a stumbling block or a cause to fall in our brother's way."

– ROMANS 14:13

At a gathering where refreshments were being served, I approached someone who was eating some of the hard, sticky candy being offered. I commented that I was going to have to stay away from that sweet snack due to the fact of having had a temporary crown put on one of my teeth only a few days before. Therefore, in accordance with my dentist's instructions, I wasn't going to take the risk of eating something which might break or pull off that vulnerable piece of dental work. To my surprise, this person responded that she also had just been fitted with a similar device. However, her approach was to go ahead and eat the tempting candy, only making certain she chewed on the opposite side of her mouth from where the crown was located.

Was one of us right and the other wrong? I don't think so—not as long as we both were able to carry out our plans. I chose not to take any chances that I might accidentally chew some of the hard stuff on the wrong side of my mouth in spite of my best efforts and good intentions. The other person was willing to take that risk in order to enjoy this sweet treat, confident she could avoid crossing the boundary which would put her crown in jeopardy.

Sometimes we face similar moral and spiritual issues. We might call these "gray areas"—practices concerning which God hasn't given clear-cut commands. Don't get me wrong—there are plenty of black-and-white areas in our lives. Let's not start relegating our actions to the "gray area" simply because we don't like that divine prohibition and we really want to continue that particular practice. There is right and wrong. There are certain things we are commanded to avoid altogether. However, we should also recognize there are other areas in which believers may differ in their personal convictions and individual practices.

In New Testament times, a couple of such issues were the eating of meats offered to idols and the observance of certain holy days. The Apostle Paul addressed these subjects in some of his letters, concluding in one instance, "Therefore let us not judge one another anymore, but rather resolve this, not to put a stumbling block or a cause to fall in our brother's way" (Romans 14:13). In our day, some might place in this category such issues as Christians drinking alcoholic beverages or playing the lottery.

Some of us believe the best course of action in these matters is total abstinence. If you don't delve into those practices at all, you won't ever find yourself going too far and crossing over the lines to the extent where it does become sinful or harmful, such as into drunkenness which the Bible clearly condemns. Others see no harm in enjoying such practices as long as they can keep them within the lines of moderation.

Here are a few questions we might want to ask ourselves about such matters. Am I truly seeking what God wants me to do above what I want? Is my confidence in myself or in God to keep me from going too far? Will my engaging in this practice have a negative influence or impact upon anyone else? Does it fit within my overarching aim of glorifying God?

Let's be careful about harshly judging others in these matters. Everyone has to prayerfully draw his own conclusions and be held accountable before God. But at the same time we, as children of the King, should be cautious when it comes to doing anything that might potentially put our crown at risk.

What gray areas do you struggle over? Ask the aforementioned questions about those issues.

CLOTHE YOURSELF WITH GOD'S PROTECTIVE GEAR

"Therefore take up the whole armor of God, that you may be able to withstand in the evil day...."

– EPHESIANS 6:13

One day I was in the presence of some people carrying on a conversation about the recent death of a police officer who was shot in the line of duty, a tragic circumstance occurring all too frequently in our day. At one point it was noted that the deceased officer wasn't wearing a bulletproof vest at the time of the fatal incident. One of the participants in this discussion was a person who likewise serves in law enforcement. She declared that she never walks out of her house in uniform without wearing her protective vest.

The conversation proceeded to talk about the type of vest she wears, making sure it fits properly, and guarding against there being any gaps through which a bullet could enter. One person recounted the case of another officer who had a small gap in the side of his vest. A bullet made its way through that one little crack in his protective gear and proved to be fatal.

It's understandable that law enforcement officials have to take precautions for their safety. Not only does their duty place them in dangerous situations at times, but simply wearing the uniform which identifies their occupation can put a target on their backs. There are individuals around who see such officers as the enemy and seek to do them harm.

Shouldn't we, as followers of Christ, be just as diligent in making certain we're wearing the protective gear God has provided for us? Do we dare risk going through the day without some part of our spiritual armor?

We have a target on our backs too. When we let our lights shine for Christ, some people are attracted to that light, but others despise it. If certain people know you're a believer, there will be times when you will be pierced by their hate-filled looks, bruised by their disparaging remarks, and suffer varying degrees of discrimination or persecution. However, they're not the main adversary. The Bible informs us that we have a spiritual enemy who has us in his crosshairs. He is intent not only on tempting us, hindering us, and getting us off track, but his ultimate goal is our destruction (see I Peter 5:8). In Ephesians 6 we are warned that "we do not wrestle against flesh and blood," but against spiritual evil powers.

Thankfully God has not left us without the protection and weapons we need to stand up against those forces. This passage of scripture details the various pieces of armor God has provided for us, including truth, righteousness, salvation, faith, the word of God, and prayer. Let's make sure we possess and use these effective instruments as we both defend ourselves and press forward with the work of God's kingdom.

Let's not overlook the fact that we are instructed to "take up the whole armor of God" (v.13). Every piece is important. Neglecting any part of our protection could open us up for attack. Don't leave any gaps or cracks through which one of Satan's bullets could sneak. Keep clothed in truth when others around you are compromising on it. Lift up your shield of faith in the face of every new difficulty that tempts you to doubt God. Become more skilled in the knowledge and use of the sword of God's Word.

It's tragic when a believer falls when encountering one of the devil's attacks. However, it doesn't have to happen. God has given us the means not only to survive, but also for victory. Therefore, let's be as diligent in wearing our spiritual armor as a police officer might be in wearing a protective vest.

Reexamine that list of armor in Ephesians 6. Are there any gaps in your protection?

Let's Make Sure We're Not Causing Our Own Problems

"Get up! Why do you lie on your face? Israel has sinned...."

– Joshua 7:10

Many of us have viewed our share of cute animal videos on the internet. We've probably all seen some in which dogs howled or pets reacted in other comical ways to people playing musical instruments. Admittedly, after having watched several such videos, I now usually skip right past anything that looks to be of that genre. However, one such clip got my attention recently. The initial reason for my interest was that the canine involved appeared to be at least part basset hound, the same kind of dog we used to have in our family. But in addition to that connection, this video had a slightly different twist to it: it was the animal itself that was playing the instrument. The dog was raised up with its paws resting on the keyboard of a piano. When he moved his paws the piano sounded, no doubt irritating his sensitive ears and causing him to howl. Subsequently every time he moved his paws, the scenario repeated itself. The silly dog didn't seem to realize that he was the one causing the irritation that he kept howling about.

We may tend to chalk up such actions to the cute ignorance of an animal friend, but aren't we intelligent human beings guilty of similar silliness at times? We complain and howl about things which irritate us while the source of those irritants can directly or indirectly be traced back to our own actions.

We complain about the condition of our society today while we keep electing leaders and supporting policies which result in those conditions. We howl about what's going on in our nation while failing to pray for our leaders as the Bible encourages us to do. We complain about our communities while refusing to take the time to get involved in ways that might bring about its improvement.

How many of us howl about our own personal difficulties and problems when they're the result of our own bad decisions and poor choices? We complain about a certain physical ailment, but we keep practicing the bad habits that contributed to that condition. We grumble about our financial difficulties while continuing our undisciplined spending or while maintaining the same kind of poor work habits which has caused us to lose jobs in the past.

And what about our relationship with God? Have you ever complained about how God doesn't seem to be working in your life like He does in other people's lives? Where are the miracles and the answers to prayer? Have we cried out about the need for personal revival? Why doesn't God pour out His Spirit on us as He has done with others?

There may be other reasons involved, but let's make sure we aren't part of the problem ourselves. In some cases, maybe we aren't experiencing these things because we aren't asking and praying about them. Or maybe God isn't working in our lives because we've allowed some barriers to come up between us and Him. Sin, insisting on our way instead of God's way, or lack of submission to God's Word and will—those are all hindrances to our fellowship with God. The Lord promises to draw near to those who draw near to Him (James 4:8). Are we just complaining about God not being near us or are we taking strides ourselves in the meantime to draw closer to Him?

I don't believe the Lord minds us crying out about our concerns and problems. However, let's make sure that as we're howling about these matters, we don't have our own paws pressing down on the piano keys.

What problems are you facing? Are you doing anything to contribute to those difficulties?

LEARNING FROM DIFFERENT TRADITIONS

"Let all things be done decently and in order." "Serve in the newness of the Spirit...."

– II CORINTHIANS 14:40; ROMANS 7:6

Friends, liturgists, and nonliturgists, "Lent" me your ears!

As I've heard other Christians speak about their various observances of the season of Lent which the church enters around this time of year, I've been reminded of my own nonliturgical background and tendencies. If your church emphasizes the various seasons of the Christian calendar, carrying out certain rituals related to those special times of the year, then you are probably from a more liturgical tradition than I am. Many who would fall into that category also follow the lectionary with its prescribed scriptures to be read or to be preached from on particular Sundays. Some of us might feel uncomfortable and confined with such a regiment of worship, while others would experience a sense of loss if they strayed away from it. I believe we of different traditions can appreciate certain aspects of one another's worship while also learning some things.

People like me who may not emphasize every season or special day on the Christian calendar should not be ignorant of those occasions and their significance. I should know that Lent doesn't have anything to do with cleaning out the filter of my clothes dryer or of allowing people to borrow money from me. And Advent is not some convention that gathers at the local convention center every December for those who are in the advertising business. And hopefully I know that Epiphany is not the shot you're given to ward off an allergic reaction. We should know something about these events and be open to how God might want to make use of them in our personal lives and ministries.

Additionally, we nonliturgical folks should recognize the value of orderliness and of a systematic approach to worship that guards against us getting stuck in ruts, constantly preaching the same thing, and unintentionally slighting certain truths or portions of scripture. Sometimes I'm afraid we try to hide lack of preparation, poor quality, and confusion behind the guise of being Spirit-led. Liturgical worship can also remind us of the fact that certain rituals can drive home truths through their rich symbolism in a way that words alone cannot accomplish.

On the other hand, those who are more liturgical have to guard against getting so tied down to order and ritual that there isn't any openness to spontaneity and the leadership of the Holy Spirit. They have to be careful about the tendency to focus so much on the form of worship or the symbolic act itself that the spirit and meaning of the action gets lost in the background.

Those who adhere closely to the Christian calendar also need to remember that those truths being focused upon at that point are valid all the time. For example, self-denial isn't just a principle to put into practice during Lent. It may be emphasized during that season, but it should characterize our lives as Christians throughout the year. And certainly abuses should be avoided, such as the concept some people have of Fat Tuesday or Mardi gras as a last opportunity to revel in extravagant self-indulgence before entering that penitential time of Lent.

So let's not be too critical about those who may be more or less liturgical than we are. There are some positive aspects we can take away from both, as well as some pitfalls to avoid. Who knows, next year when Ash Wednesday rolls around, maybe I'll observe it by doing something more spiritual than just cleaning out my fireplace.

What do you need to learn from the religious traditions of others?

ARE YOU LIKE A LION OR LIKE A LAMB?

"Behold, the Lion of the tribe of Judah...in the midst of the elders,
stood a Lamb as though it had been slain."

– REVELATION 5:5–6

Can you believe that the month of March is here already? So what's the weather like today? There's the old saying that if March comes in like a lion, it will go out like a lamb, and vice versa. So if it's stormy or windy on this first day of March, then it will supposedly be calm and pleasant at the end of the month. From what I understand this proverb doesn't have a very good record for accuracy, but it can be an interesting idea to observe and check out this time each year.

I don't know who came up with the specific members of the animal kingdom to use in describing this presumptive weather phenomenon, but they certainly present a picture of polar opposites. We think of a lion as being ferocious, bold, and courageous, while a lamb is gentle, meek, and timid. They just don't fit together...except in the Bible.

On a couple of occasions, Christ is referred to as a lion—the Lion of the tribe of Judah (Genesis 49:9; Revelation 5:5). However, He is more commonly described as a lamb. John the Baptist proclaimed that Jesus was "the Lamb of God who takes away the sin of the world" (John 1:29). He is also pictured as "a Lamb as though it had been slain" (Revelation 5:6).

In one sense these two aspects of Christ can be separated. He came into this world primarily as the sacrificial lamb who gave His life in order to provide for our salvation. And when He comes again, He will do so mainly as the lion who will bring judgment and who will reign forever.

But in another sense we can see both characteristics of the lion and the lamb embodied in Jesus at the same time. He was the lion who spoke with the authority of God. He acted boldly, such as when He cleansed the temple of the moneychangers. He moved courageously toward His destiny of dying on the cross.

Yet we also see the lamb in Jesus. He was loving and gentle, welcoming the sick, the needy and the little children to come to Him. He meekly allowed Himself to be treated unfairly. He was willing to suffer and sacrifice for the good of others. Jesus didn't just quietly enter like a lamb at His first coming and will be going out exclusively like a lion at the end of time. He has, and always will be, both the lion and the lamb.

And maybe that says something about how Jesus' followers should be too. After all, we're supposed to be becoming more and more like Jesus ourselves, aren't we? Some of us have the lion part down, but where's the lamb? We stand boldly and courageously for God and the truth. We're ready to rip into the enemies of the Lord like a lion attacking its prey, but is the love, compassion, and gentleness of the lamb present as well?

Others of us do well in possessing the lamblike qualities, but we're lacking the lionlike ones. We love people and seek to meet their needs. We're willing to turn the other cheek and wash the feet of others. We strive to be peacemakers and value unity, but are we willing to bravely confront sin and take a stand for God and for what's right?

In nature lions and lambs simply don't go together. But in God's order they do. Jesus was a bold and courageous lion as well as a gentle and self-sacrificing lamb. We need to let Him mold us into that same image too.

Do you need to be more like a Christlike lion or a Christlike lamb?

BE SOMEONE WHO LEANS TOWARD THE LIGHT

"But he who does the truth comes to the light...."
– JOHN 3:21

My wife received a pot of blooming tulips as one of her birthday presents recently. We enjoyed the beautiful flowers in our house for a short time until they eventually got replanted in our yard. After they had been sitting on the kitchen table for a couple of days, there was a very noticeable change in their appearance. The long, flowering stems which had been almost vertical in appearance were now tilted markedly to one side. My first thought was simply that the plants were beginning to wither or to slump under the weight of the blooms. But then I realized that the stems still looked healthy and strong. They weren't faltering. They were purposefully slanting in a certain direction for a reason. In a sense, they were reaching toward something. They were leaning toward the source of light.

Isn't that a great description of what we should be as followers of Christ? We are people who should be leaning toward the light. First of all, this characterization should picture our devotion to Christ Himself. Jesus said that He is the Light. We should be those who are drawn to Him, pursuing Him, and reaching toward Him.

However, it should also be a fitting description for how we respond to the light of revelation and truth which the Lord shines upon our lives. Jesus reminded us that there are those who are actually resistant to and repelled by His light. He said, "The light has come into the world, and men loved darkness rather than light, because their deeds were evil. For everyone practicing evil hates the light and does not come to the light, lest his deeds should be exposed" (John 3:19–20). Maybe these folks could be compared to some of the slimy creatures which hide under rocks or the roaches which scatter to find a safe place in a dark crevice as soon as a light is turned on.

However, Jesus went on in the next verse to describe those with a different reaction to the same light. He said, "But he who does the truth comes to the light, that his deeds may be clearly seen, that they have been done in God." It's not just that we don't run from the light or don't despise it. It's not even that we don't mind it or tolerate its presence. It's the idea that we should actually welcome that light when it shines upon us. We pursue it and embrace it.

This doesn't mean that we as believers never have anything in our lives of which to be ashamed or which we might not like to be revealed. Sometimes the light of truth will shine on our lives or into our hearts revealing a wrong deed, a selfish attitude, or an impure motive. Other times it might uncover some area that needs improvement or a greater degree of Christlikeness.

At those moments we may be tempted to throw up our arms to try to shield ourselves from that painful light. We might consider making excuses for ourselves or maybe even try to scurry off into some darker corner in order to avoid the close scrutiny of the light.

However those are the moments when we need to remind ourselves that the light is a good thing. It helps bring us to repentance. It prods us toward needed change and improvement. It keeps us from blindly living in the darkness of sin or drifting away into spiritual unhealthiness.

So let's be those who keep leaning toward the light even when its rays pierce and sting, knowing that it is the precious source that will cause us to grow and blossom.

What light is the Lord shining upon your life? Are you shying away from it or welcoming it?

Never Too Old for a New Relationship

"They shall still bear fruit in old age; they shall be fresh and flourishing...."

– Psalm 92:13–14

I caught a story one time about a couple who met through one of those internet matchmaking sites. They got acquainted, dated for a while, and apparently fell in love. It wasn't long before the man proposed and the woman accepted. They are now reportedly happily married. It sounds like a story you might see on a TV commercial for one of those web sites. However, this particular couple is somewhat unusual. He is eighty-seven years old and she is eighty-five. Maybe that's one reason they figured it might be best not to have a long engagement.

From what I understand, both of these individuals had been previously married and both of those relationships had endured for over sixty years. But then their spouses died and they were left alone. However, these two senior members of society decided that they weren't ready for widowhood to mark the end of their lives. They chose not to settle for loneliness in their remaining years. They sought out companionship and found it with a little help from modern technology.

It's an interesting story. You can't help but admire people who, even when they're older, muster up the courage to venture into a new relationship. We tend to think of people who are older as being set in their ways and either unable or unwilling to make any significant changes in their lives. We excuse ourselves and others by quoting that old saying, "You can't teach old dogs new tricks." But it's refreshing to see older people who are willing to try new things, who want to continue to learn and grow, and who are even willing to reach out in a new relationship.

Do you know what is even more admirable? It's to see someone in his or her latter years who ventures out by faith into a new relationship with God. It tends to be unusual, but it happens. And what a wonderful thing it is. I'm not talking primarily about a deathbed conversion, but simply about someone in his seventies, eighties, or beyond who invites Christ into his heart and receives the gift of eternal life.

Statistics tell us how much better it is to reach out to people with the gospel when they're young. Not only are they more likely to be open to receiving it, but they also can then live their whole lives in service to God. The older people get, the less likely it is that they will receive God's free gift of salvation. But let's not take those statistics as an excuse for neglecting to minister to and witness to those of the older generation. Our God is powerful enough to soften the hardest of hearts and to overcome years of spiritual neglect or apathy. He hasn't given up on that person yet, and neither should we.

While we're at it, let's check our own attitude. Some of us may not be in our seventies and eighties, but we may possess that stubborn, unadventurous spirit that would keep us from moving forward in our relationship with God. We can get stuck in our same old ruts and find it hard not only to get out but to even want to get out. We make excuses for not drawing closer to the Lord or for not venturing out in some new area of ministry. We pray for revival, but in our hearts we're hoping we can experience it without having to make any major changes in our lives.

Let's receive a little inspiration from a couple of eighty-somethings who took the plunge into a new relationship. No matter how old we may be, let's be willing to pursue a closer walk with God.

How open are you to venturing into something new and fresh in your relationship with the Lord today or in your service for Him?

Guard Against Rash Actions

"Then the men of Israel took some of their provisions; but they did not ask counsel of the Lord."

– JOSHUA 9:14

One day as my basset hound and I returned home after a walk through the neighborhood, we encountered an interesting situation. When we headed into our backyard, my dog suddenly stopped with a serious stare on her face that I recognized as her stalking pose. I followed her gaze and spotted a white cat near the edge of our property. I grabbed a tighter grip on the leash just in time as she lunged toward her intended prey. As you might imagine, the cat immediately took off into the nearby brush.

But then another movement caught my attention. I suddenly realized that there was another guest in our yard, having gone unseen due to it being so closely camouflaged with the pine straw, as well as my focus having been on the cat. A brown rabbit, startled by the sudden retreat of the cat, also went into a sprint. Only it came running directly at my dog and me. I was surprised at how close it got to us before finally veering off and taking refuge underneath our deck. Fear had made it run, but in its hurry to avoid the cat it ran right toward a type of dog that had been bred for hunting rabbits. I guess that's what some would call "leaping out of the frying pan and into the fire."

Meanwhile my poor basset hound didn't know what to do. She seemed to stand there in amazement as well, not sure which creature to pursue. And I think she may have been confused seeing a rabbit running toward her rather than scurrying off in the opposite direction.

That rabbit may have been fast, but its rash choice of direction almost proved costly for it. Rash decisions and actions on our part also often prove unwise. Fear, impatience, or even enthusiasm might cause us to run ahead without thinking things out, without looking at where that path may lead, and without consulting God for His guidance.

There are times when we do need to act quickly. Certainly when we know that God is saying to go and to do it now, we need to trust Him and move ahead. But in those circumstances where we haven't discerned God's will but rather are being pressured by other forces or by our own feelings, we need to be careful about acting rashly.

Many rash actions in the Bible led to problems and heartache for those involved. Esau later grieved over the fact that he had acted so impetuously out of a little hunger that he gave up his birthright to his younger brother. Joshua made an unwise treaty with the Gibeonites because he acted quickly instead of taking time to seek counsel from God. A man named Jephthah made a rash vow that cost his daughter her life (Judges 11:29–40). And we can't forget about the disciple of Jesus who has come to be so closely associated with this characteristic. On one occasion, Peter rashly reacted to Jesus' predictions about His suffering and death by daring to rebuke the One he had just proclaimed to be the Son of the Living God. He thought he was running in the right direction, but he ran right into the enemy of his soul, allowing Satan to use him.

Let's be careful about allowing our circumstances, fears, or zeal to cause us to act too rashly. In most instances, we can take the time to pray and to reflect on any guidance the Bible may give us about the situation. We can look down the road at the long-range consequences. We can let calm thinking direct us more than our emotions.

Don't be like a rabbit running toward a basset hound. Think and pray before you act.

Commit yourself to guarding against rash actions—pause, think, and pray.

Is There Anybody We Can Trust or Believe?

"Jesus said to him, 'I am the way, the truth, and the life.'"

– John 14:6

The concept of "fake news" has become very prominent in our society in recent times. It's an idea which suggests that certain stories made public are actually fabricated, exaggerated, or misleading. People on both sides of the political spectrum have accused their adversaries of this practice. It used to be easier to recognize such stories and to easily dismiss them as not being credible. However, as trust in both leadership and media outlets deteriorate, it often gets more and more difficult to try to discern who or what to believe.

Sometimes such "fake news" seems to result from someone speaking rashly without adequately checking out their sources. Other times the stories appear to be intentional efforts to mislead people in order to propagate a certain viewpoint. The ability to rightly discern the truth in it all is being made more difficult by skilled professionals who know how to omit certain facts, twist the truth, choose the right soundbite, or even edit the video in such a way as to make things appear the way they want them to look. It used to be that "seeing is believing," but even our own eyesight can't be trusted in this age in which many people have become so savvy in how to project distorted images of reality.

It's not my purpose today to try to tell you whom to trust in this environment, at least not when it comes to government leaders and the media. I would simply encourage you not to blindly accept anyone's version of the truth, but rather to check out those matters for yourself as much as possible.

However, it is my purpose to remind us all that there is still Someone in whom we can confidently trust and believe. In a day when truth seems to be all too vague and elusive, Jesus still declares that He is the truth (John 14:6). In a time when it's hard to know who may be lying to us and who isn't, the Bible points us to the fact that God cannot lie (Titus 1:2). Among a vast array of contradicting stories all claiming to be reality, we can still be assured of the reliability of Scripture. The Bible is the result of holy men of God speaking as they were moved by the Holy Spirit (II Peter 1:21). We are also told that "all Scripture is given by inspiration of God" (II Timothy 3:16). So when the lines between truth and fiction are blurred, we can still count on God and on His Word.

However as we do, let's guard against being guilty of following some of those same practices we're witnessing in the world around us. Don't edit out the portions of the Bible which you don't like. Don't pick out your favorite soundbites of what Jesus said while ignoring some of His tougher statements or the ones which might make you less popular with today's society.

Don't just present the side of the Bible that fits your opinions or preferences. Let's not create our own version of "fake news" when it comes to what God says. Remember that all of Scripture is inspired by God, not just the parts which affirm our personal views and feelings.

As you probably know, the word "gospel" means "good news." Let's be thankful that it's not only good news, but it's real news—it's not fake. It's truth which we can depend on. And it comes from a faithful God in whom we can trust. So if today's confusing environment ever causes you to doubt whether or not you can trust anyone or believe anything, remember the Lord and His Word.

Be thankful that you can always trust in God and believe His Word.

WE SHOULD STILL BE BECOMING MORE LIKE JESUS

"For whom He foreknew, He also predestined to be conformed to the image of His Son."

– ROMANS 8:29

As I was riding our stationary bike one day recently, I turned on the television to help keep my mind off my straining muscles and the seemingly slow-moving clock. I ended up tuning into an old movie I hadn't seen before. Now I know some of you might think of films in the 1980s as being old, but I'm referring to classic black-and-white movies—this particular one having been filmed in the 1940s.

As I watched, an actress came on the screen for what would be described as a "bit part." She was there only for a moment, delivered a few sentences of dialogue, and she was gone, not to be seen again throughout the rest of the picture. But as I watched and listened to this actress, I asked, "Is that who I think it is?" I'm thankful such questions no longer have to run around in my mind for days, tormenting me until I either discover an answer or forget about them. Now I can simply "google it" and find out the information almost immediately. Sometimes I'm wrong, but in this case I was right. It was Irene Ryan, the actress who would later become famous to many of us by portraying Granny on *The Beverly Hillbillies* TV show.

As far as I know I had never seen this actress in her younger days. I could only picture her as the elderly matriarch of the Clampett clan. So I was fascinated to see what she looked like decades before taking on her most well-known role. She looked very different, but her facial expressions, mannerisms, and voice still betrayed her identity.

When we've known people in only one season of their lives, it's sometimes hard to imagine them as being anything else. I suppose it was difficult for those who became acquainted with Peter after Pentecost to think of him as someone who would have been so frightened that he would deny Christ to a servant girl. Or others who came to know the great missionary, Paul, might not have been able to picture him as the infamous persecutor of the early Church. People who only know me as a preacher and pastor might have a difficult time seeing me as the extremely shy teenager who would go to great lengths to avoid ever having to do any kind of public speaking. However, people change. And the power of Christ is especially effective in transforming lives.

As the years go by our physical appearance changes, although for some it's less noticeable than it is with others. Our inner self and character should also be changing. Through the transforming power of Christ, we shouldn't be the same people we were before we put our faith in Jesus. And we should continue to experience growth and progress throughout our years here on earth. One of God's main purposes for us is to conform us to the image of His Son (Romans 8:29). Therefore we ought to be becoming more like Jesus as time goes by.

As you look back at pictures of yourself from twenty or thirty years ago, you can probably see a big difference. As you think back to the type of person you were at that time, can you also see growth in your character and in possessing more Christlike qualities in your life? And if you're still here a couple of decades from now, how do you hope to be different from what you are today?

Let's allow the effective, transforming power of God to keep working in us and making us more like Jesus as long as we have life and breath.

Give thanks for how the Lord has changed you over the years. In what specific ways do you still need to be more like Him?

You Can Be a Fisher of Men

"Then He said to them, 'Follow Me, and I will make you fishers of men.'"

– Matthew 4:19

When I was a child, we didn't live far from Lake Lanier. Consequently it was not unusual for our family to go fishing occasionally. However, my older sister seemed to be incompatible with the whole fishing experience. It seemed like every time we went she would have an accident, encounter some problem, or unintentionally cause a disruption.

For example, there was the time we were fishing late into the evening when she knocked the lantern over into the water. Or there was the memorable moment when she walked behind someone who was casting a line and got the hook caught in her nose. Fortunately I think she was able to yell out and grab the line attached to the hook in order to avoid a more serious injury.

Whatever could go wrong tended to go wrong when my sister got around the lake where fishing was taking place. This propensity for committing such a comedy of errors in relation to this particular activity resulted in my sister despising the whole idea of fishing for many years. We still laughingly give her a hard time about it.

Maybe some of us feel the same way when it comes to fishing for men. I'm referring to the activity Jesus referred to when He recruited some of His disciples. You may remember that a few of them were actual fishermen. When Jesus called two of them, Peter and Andrew, to leave their profession in order to accompany Him on a full-time basis, He said,

"Follow Me, and I will make you fishers of men" (Matthew 4:19). They were going to quit catching fish for a living and instead start focusing more on seeking lost souls.

I don't believe Jesus' statement was meant to be applied only to Peter and Andrew. I think it shows something Jesus expects of all believers. If we're going to follow Jesus, we have a responsibility to reach out and minister to the people around us who need Him. He calls us all, to some degree, to be fishers of men.

While many of us may have a concern for people who don't know the Lord, I'm afraid some of us don't really believe what Jesus says—that He can make us fishers of men. Maybe we even feel like my sister did about regular fishing. It just doesn't seem like we're very good at reaching out to people. Every time we make an attempt at it, something seems to go wrong. We try to share our faith but we stumble all over our words and it doesn't come out right. We try to let our lights shine, but then we kick the lantern into the water. It seems like we say the wrong thing or our actions get misunderstood. Instead of catching any souls, we're afraid that our well-intended but faulty efforts end up chasing some people away.

But Jesus says if we follow Him, He will make us fishers of men. Do you believe that? No matter how we may have struggled over such efforts in the past and regardless of how unsuccessful we may have been, Jesus can enable us to do our part in reaching out to the lost.

My sister ended up living at a lake for a number of years. Although she never became an avid fisherman, she got to where she could enjoy fishing and not experience any of those previous adversities when she did.

Similarly let's follow Jesus, put those past experiences behind us, and trust Him to use us to make a difference in the lives of people who need Him. Trust Jesus to make you a fisher of men.

What have been some of your frustrations in witnessing for Christ? Trust Jesus to help you overcome your fears and weaknesses while helping you effectively reach out to those who need Him.

JESUS IS MORE THAN OUR SPIRITUAL SAFETY NET

"Shall we continue in sin that grace may abound? Certainly not!"
— ROMANS 6:1–2

A few years ago, one group was reporting an undesirable milestone for the Golden Gate Bridge in San Francisco. The previous year marked its deadliest annual period in connection with the number of people who committed suicide by jumping off the structure. This report seemed to be stirring up support for a longtime proposal—the construction of some kind of safety net to thwart the efforts of such jumpers. The main impediment to the fulfillment of this idea had been the cost, which some said would exceed sixty million dollars at the time.

On the one hand I suppose such a net might eliminate an easy way to carry out such an act, deterring those who may take that horrible step on the spur of the moment. But on the other hand if someone is serious about ending his or her life, a safety net under one bridge will not stop that person. The individual will simply find some other way to carry out the deed. I'm certainly no expert on the subject, but it seems like our primary focus should be on the reasons people want to commit suicide in the first place—helping people deal with the issues which get them to that place of jumping off a bridge. Spending millions of dollars on a safety net may be a secondary solution, but it seems to be an example of treating the symptom rather than curing the disease.

It reminds me of the way some people view what Jesus has

accomplished for us. They see Him as simply having constructed a safety net for people—a means by which individuals can avoid the consequences of their sins. Rightfully they recognize that Jesus died on the cross as the sacrifice for our sins in order for a holy God to be able to graciously bestow forgiveness on otherwise hopelessly lost sinners like us. Jesus paid a high price in order to spare us from having to face the results we deserve for having stepped off the pathway of obedience to God's will. The Bible clearly declares that the wages of sin is death (Romans 6:23). Spiritual and eternal death is what we all deserve. God's Word suggests that hell may not have been designed for us, but rather for the devil and his angels. However because of our sin, we do deserve such a fate. But those who put their faith in Jesus are saved from taking that plunge into the depths of the fiery pit. So yes, through Jesus thankfully we do have a safety net to catch us.

But if Jesus had stopped there, He too would have been guilty of only treating the symptom rather than curing the disease. Jesus doesn't just save us from the consequences of our sinful choices. He also changes us and saves us from our sinful selves. Salvation doesn't just mean we can keep jumping off the bridge of disobedience to God, assured that Jesus will keep us from spiritual ruin. Salvation means Jesus can transform our hearts to such an extent that we don't want to keep living in sin. We can find power and grace to start living more in harmony with God's will and plan for our lives. The Bible declares that we are no longer to continue in sin but are to walk in newness of life (Romans 6:1–4).

I'm glad that Jesus catches us when we fall, but I'm also grateful that He so works in our lives that He can keep us from falling in the first place. Let's quit testing God's safety net so often and instead experience the daily victory of not even wanting to take the plunge.

Seek God's power to keep you from falling into sin.

ALWAYS STAY VIGILANT
FOR YOUR ADVERSARY

"Be sober, be vigilant; because your adversary the devil walks about like a roaring lion, seeking whom he may devour."
– I Peter 5:8

One time I witnessed a violent attack in the town in which I live. It was surprising to see this life-and-death struggle taking place in broad daylight on Main Street right in front of the courthouse. No, it wasn't one of those criminal acts which seems all too often to get this once sleepy little community in the news.

As I was driving along, a short distance ahead of me a hawk suddenly came swooping low across the road. It seemed to be struggling to fly, flopping its wings in an odd fashion until it actually plopped down in the middle of Main Street. Then I saw the problem. In its sharp talons it was trying to carry off a pigeon—one that was almost as big as the hawk itself. As my vehicle approached the feuding fowls, the hawk flew off empty-handed. It all happened so fast I didn't have time to stop and was afraid I was running over the pigeon. But apparently it managed to escape in the opposite direction.

I realize that such acts in nature occur all the time. That's what hawks do. But rarely do I get to witness one. And I certainly didn't expect to see it play out on a busy street between a line of stores and the county courthouse.

The Bible reminds us that we have an adversary who is preying on our souls. He's not described as a hawk, but rather as a lion. "Be sober, be vigilant; because your adversary the devil walks about like a roaring lion, seeking whom he may devour" (I Peter 5:8).

There are times when we almost expect the devil to show up with his arsenal of deceptions, lies, and temptations. For example, when we find ourselves traveling through one of the wildernesses or valleys of life, we can usually count on our adversary trying to take advantage of our weakened state with attempts to discourage us, to lead us off the right path, or to get us to doubt God.

But one of the reasons we have to "be vigilant," as that scripture indicates, is because the devil will also attack us at unexpected moments or in surprising places. When we've just experienced some great event or victory in our lives and we're celebrating on the mountaintop, we need to be watchful for Satan to show up. He may tempt us on such occasions with the pride of thinking too highly of ourselves or with the idea that we're capable in ourselves and don't need God as much anymore. While traveling the smooth and easy paths of life, he may attack us in such areas as becoming complacent, lazy, or losing our passion.

And the predator of our souls doesn't just show up at wild parties or on dark street corners at midnight. He may swoop down into our thoughts and hearts as we're sitting in church, or trying to pray, or seeking to give counsel to someone who is hurting.

We shouldn't be surprised when the devil shows up, because that's what he does. Just like that hawk hunting for prey, he is looking for souls to tempt and destroy. Thankfully the Bible tells us that we can resist him through the power of Christ. We don't have to be carried off by his temptations and deceptions. There is always a way to escape his clutches if we'll look for it.

So don't let down your guard. You never know when or where the devil might show up. Don't let yourself be one of the pigeons he carries away.

Watch out for Satan at unexpected times and places.

Don't Let Envy and Discontentment Swallow You Up

"They and all those with them went alive into the pit; the earth closed over them."

– Numbers 16:33

Talk about a rude awakening! I guess you heard about the poor guy in Florida a few years ago who was asleep in bed when a sinkhole opened up, swallowing him, his bed, and practically the whole room. The nightmarish facts make it sound like a scene from some Hollywood disaster movie. I understand that the man was screaming for help as he was plunged twenty or thirty feet and as the ground closed back in over him.

It's hard to imagine such a horrible fate. If I lived in one of those areas of Florida where such sinkholes are prevalent, after hearing this story I might be tempted to sleep with a rope tied around my leg with the other end anchored to the ceiling fan.

This incident reminds me of a time when God used similar means to bring judgment on a group of Israelites. Let me make it clear: I have no reason to believe this tragic event in Florida had anything to do with God's wrath being poured out on this particular man who died in such an awful manner. Some such events are simply natural disasters that adversely affect the godly and the ungodly alike.

The biblical incident to which I referred took place during the time of Moses. A group of men from the tribe of Levi rose up in rebellion against

Moses and Aaron. They had become envious of the two top leaders of the Israelites and dissatisfied with the position and sacred responsibilities God had entrusted to them—the care of the tabernacle. They wanted to be priests too, even though God had not chosen them for that high office.

This account ends up with God's judgment falling on that group in a unique way. The earth opened and swallowed them up, along with their families and possessions. The Bible says, "They and all those with them went alive into the pit; the earth closed over them, and they perished from among the assembly" (Numbers 16:33).

This incident should serve as a reminder to all of us not to take lightly the position God has put us in and the responsibilities for which He has equipped us. It's tempting to enviously look at others who are gifted differently from us and wish we could be like them. We may even go so far as to turn away from what God has called us to be in order to seek to be like someone else.

Don't get me wrong. We need to be open to new avenues God may open up for us as we go through life. And some of those will stretch us and get us out of our comfort zones. But let's not seek greener pastures simply because we're discontented with who we are, how God has made us, and with the gifts He's given us. Let's not try to become something we're not and that God doesn't intend for us to be.

For example, I enjoy music and admire those who inspire others with their singing. But anyone who has ever heard me sing will agree that it would be ridiculous for me to try to become a soloist.

Moses reminded those men that what God had called them to do in serving in the tabernacle was not a small thing. And wherever God puts us and whatever role He wants us to play in life, it's not a small thing either.

Be grateful for how God has created you and for the position He has put you in to serve Him. Rest assured that it is no small thing. But if you insist on thinking otherwise, you might want to consider sleeping with a rope tied to your leg.

Give God thanks for your gifts, abilities, and opportunities for serving Him.

MARCH 11

GOD USES CHRISTIAN MUSIC TO CHANGE OUR LIVES

"Speaking to one another in psalms and hymns and spiritual songs."
– EPHESIANS 5:19

On a couple of occasions recently, I found myself at places where 70s music was being played. For many people, the tunes of that particular decade may not be very highly regarded—for example, think disco. However, that was the decade that encompassed my teen years. And it seems to me that the music which was popular whenever we were teenagers tends to hold a special place in our hearts and memories. We may laugh or cringe as we sing along with some of it now, but we do still sing those familiar lyrics as evidence of the long-lasting connection between youth and their music.

As I listened to some of those songs, my mind conjured up ancient but very vivid memories of a time before there were CDs, MTV, and iPods: sitting in a pizza restaurant listening to the jukebox; shooting hoops in my backyard on a hot summer afternoon while a nearby radio is blaring; driving my first car with the 8-track tapes playing; gliding around the roller skating rink trying to keep time with the disco music. Admittedly some of those memories get skewed over the years. Actually I wasn't a very good skater and spent most of my time clinging to the rail or awkwardly making my way around the rink trying not to fall down.

Christian music can also evoke some strong emotions and stir up precious memories. Some of it may be based primarily on sentiment as those songs remind us of departed loved ones, former places of worship, special events, or simply those seemingly better times from our past. But for many of us there are probably also Christian songs which hold a special place in our hearts due to them having been used by God to touch our lives in some manner.

For some, there may be an invitational hymn that was being sung and that the Holy Spirit used to draw us to God as we came to put our trust in Jesus as our Savior. Or maybe there are hymns, popular Christian music, or praise songs which the Lord has used to minister to us in a time of need or crisis. Remember any of these from my list? "Through it all, through it all, I've learned to trust in Jesus, I've learned to trust in God." "And whatever it takes to draw closer to you, Lord, that's what I'll be willing to do." "Turn your eyes upon Jesus, look full in His wonderful face; and the things of earth will grow strangely dim in the light of His glory and grace."

Christian music can be a wonderful and effective means by which God speaks to us. Paul advocated "speaking to one another in psalms and hymns and spiritual songs, singing and making melody in your heart to the Lord" (Ephesians 5:19).

While we sing our new songs of praise, it can be helpful to remember the old songs too. We have a history with them. Singing them can do far more than take us on a sentimental journey. It can remind us of how God has worked in our lives in the past. It can instill gratitude in our hearts to the Lord for what He has done. But it can also cause us to examine our current relationship with the Lord in light of those past experiences. It can raise questions, such as "Am I still walking close to the Lord today?"

Let's be thankful for how God uses music to minister to us. And let's be open to what He may want to say to us and how He may want to change our lives through those songs we sing today.

Listen to some Christian music today and let it minister to you. Read an old favorite hymn. What is God saying to you through the words of that song?

One Day All Things Will Be Made Right

"Do not be deceived, God is not mocked; for whatever a man sows, that he will also reap."

– Galatians 6:7

There was a TV commercial that depicted a variety of situations in which people are treated unjustly. Then it suggested that a certain law firm will help you get what's fair. It was an effective ad because it plays off something most people have sensed and struggled with all their lives—the idea that life should be fair.

As kids we whined over the lack of fairness—when parents disciplined us for something we didn't do—when teachers punished the whole class for the bad behavior of one student—when the other kid got to play the better position on the team not because of his skill or effort, but simply because of his parents' relationship with the coach.

As we've moved on to adulthood, the circumstances have changed but we still witness a lack of equity in many aspects of life. Maybe it has to do with bosses and work situations, with romantic or family relationships, with our treatment by people in government or by the laws that regulate our lives. We even see such unfairness when natural disasters strike or health issues surface—matters over which we find it hard to blame anyone except maybe God Himself.

In the face of such harsh realities, some people give up on the concept of fairness altogether. They often become hardhearted and cynical, living according to some form of the philosophy that "life stinks." Others try to hold to a belief that some force like karma will come into play or that a just God will make sure people reap what they sow while here on this earth. They expect that people's bad deeds will one day come back to bite them and that the good deeds of others will be rewarded at some point down the road in life.

The Bible does indeed promise that we will all reap what we sow—that those who do wrong will be punished, and that those who do what's right will be rewarded. The problem or misconception is the idea that such settling of accounts will take place here and now, or at least during our lifespan. Some rewards and punishments may come to fruition in this life, but God doesn't guarantee such.

We shouldn't give up on the concept of fairness—we just shouldn't count on receiving it while here on earth. Jesus talked about good people suffering and being persecuted, but then went on to declare that they would receive a great reward "in heaven" (Matthew 5:12). On the other hand, Jesus pictured evil people who would grow and flourish in this world like tares in a field of wheat, but at the "end of this age" would face the punishment of everlasting fire where "there will be wailing and gnashing of teeth" (Matthew 13:24–30, 37–43).

That promise of a future judgment day is essential in satisfying our sense of fairness. Life often isn't fair, but God is. And one day He will punish the wicked and reward the righteous.

So in light of that truth, let's not allow ourselves to get too frustrated over the seeming inequities of life. At times good people are going to suffer and the ungodly are going to flourish. The efforts of good people to do right and to help others may go unnoticed or be unappreciated by many, but there is a day of reckoning coming.

Maybe there are competent lawyers who can help you get what's fair in some areas of life. But more importantly, we can depend on the fact that there is a God who sees and knows everything. And one day He will make all things right.

What lack of fairness in life tends to frustrate you? Remind yourself of a future day coming when God will reward and punish appropriately.

MARCH 13

LET'S LOOK BEFORE WE LEAP

"Let every man be swift to hear, slow to speak, slow to wrath."

– JAMES 1:19

As I pulled my car into a parking spot at an assisted living home, I noticed a cat sitting on the rail of the porch. It was intently looking up toward the eaves of the roof as if it spied some small creature there that it wanted to attack. Suddenly the feline acrobatically hopped several feet upward onto a crooked section of the drain pipe near the roof hoping to get within reach of its prey. It continued to focus its gaze at something over its head, although I never caught a glimpse of its objective. I can only assume that if something was really present other than a cat's active imagination, it was probably a small lizard of some kind.

A little while later when I exited the building, I noticed the cat was still sitting there. It didn't seem to be hunting anymore but rather assessing its situation. It looked like it may have regretted its rash decision to jump onto that lofty perch and wasn't quite sure about the best way to get down again.

It reminded me of a couple of cats that had been members of our family over the years. I can remember them getting all excited and in the heat of that moment climbing a tree. But once they got up there, they suddenly weren't sure about getting back down. They often had to be coaxed to work up the courage to try to scoot down that trunk and get their paws back on solid ground.

It's not just cats who sometimes plunge into a situation and then find it hard to get back out again. We've all probably done it at some point.

A moment of passion, anger, excitement, or simply curiosity resulted in us rashly doing or saying something that we soon regretted. We wish we could rewind the tape of our action or take back the words, but it's too late. We're stuck there now, berating ourselves for our foolish action and wondering how to get out of our predicament.

The Bible provides us with a number of examples of such impetuous acts. There was Esau who in a moment of exhaustion rashly traded his birthright for a bowl of stew. There was David who in a moment of lust hopped into bed with another man's wife, only to find frustration and roadblocks as he attempted to cover up his deed. And there was Peter who in a moment of zeal dared to rebuke the Son of God for predicting His own suffering and death. They each took a leap in the emotional heat of the moment, probably thinking that they were pursuing a good course at the time. But when the moment passed, they were left with regret, fear, and the reality of the consequences of their actions.

On the positive side, we can be assured that we can find forgiveness for our rash deeds through heartfelt repentance and faith. But unfortunately there are aspects of such actions that aren't easily undone. We may be forgiven but still find ourselves having to clean up a mess or live with the ongoing consequences.

The old adage "Look before you leap" may not be a biblical quotation, but it is good advice. That doesn't mean there isn't room in our lives for spontaneity or for being open to some Spirit-led impulse. But we do need to guard against emotion-driven rashness. We would often benefit from looking, thinking, and praying before we take a plunge.

I bet that cat will think twice before taking such a leap next time. And I hope we will too.

Guard against rash actions or words. Take time to consider the consequences, to think about God's will, and to pray about it.

Lying Isn't So Bad, Is It?

"Therefore, putting away lying, 'Let each one of you speak truth with his neighbor....'"

– Ephesians 4:25

A little news story caught my eye a while back. It was about a man whose pants had caught fire. This wasn't someone who was firing up his grill for a cookout, burning debris in his yard, or even filling up his car at a gas pump. This was a lawyer who was arguing a case before a jury in a courtroom at the time of the incident. Considering the reputation of lawyers, I wonder if anyone present was tempted to yell the childish chant, "Liar, liar, pants on fire!"

The defense attorney was reportedly fiddling around in his pocket when the smoke started rising from his trousers. He later blamed it on a faulty e-cigarette battery. However, interestingly enough, at the time it happened he was arguing that his client's car had not been intentionally set on fire but rather had spontaneously combusted. Therefore some wonder if this may have been a staged production by the defense that went wrong. Maybe that lawyer had best be careful what he claims about the incident, because if he isn't being entirely truthful he might just find his pants catching on fire again.

Lying is one of those practices which has become more acceptable to our society, or at least it's overlooked as not being a very serious offense. Some people even admire those who have become so skillful in its usage. At the very least we tend to see it as a "little sin," a harmless deception, a convenient means of avoiding a difficulty, or maybe even a compassionate act used to keep from hurting someone's feelings.

However the Bible indicates that God views it quite differently. Among a list of six things which God hates is "a lying tongue" (Proverbs 6:17). Believers are encouraged to put away lying (Ephesians 4:25). And in the book of Revelation liars are specifically singled out as among those who will not enter heaven's gates (21:27) but rather will "have their part in the lake of fire which burns with fire and brimstone, which is the second death" (21:8). In light of those and other similar passages of scripture, lying doesn't seem so innocent or harmless.

Some people will argue that when the Bible condemns lying it's referring primarily to what is called "bearing false witness"—lying which specifically besmirches the reputation of others or falsely accuses them of wrongdoing. However, "a false witness who speaks lies" is listed separately in that passage in Proverbs 6 as one of the six things which God hates. And in the Ephesians reference, when it exhorts believers to put away lying, the practice it recommends in its place is not simply being a truthful witness but truth-telling in general—"Let each one of you speak truth with his neighbor."

The Old Testament declared about people who made certain vows, "He shall not break his word; he shall do according to all that proceeds out of his mouth" (Numbers 30:2). In the New Testament we are encouraged to be people who don't have to swear or take oaths—our simple yes or no should be sufficient. In other words, we should be people whose words can be depended on as reliable and truthful.

Sometimes lying will seem to be the easy way out. We may falter at times in this area, giving in to the momentary pressure not to be truthful. But let's seek to be people of integrity both in our conduct and our words. Don't fall into the trap of taking lying lightly. If you do, if those passages in Revelation are any indication, you may one day find more than just your pants on fire.

Lord, help me be someone who values truth and who always tries to be truthful.

Don't Overlook
the Simple Truths

*"But I fear…your minds may be corrupted from the simplicity that
is in Christ."*

– II Corinthians 11:3

One day some of our family stopped by my parents' home for a brief
visit. Although our young grandchildren were unable to join us, my
mom had blown up a couple of balloons for them to play with just in case
they had shown up.

As we adults sat in the living room, it wasn't long before someone
had picked up those two balloons and started batting them into the air.
Suddenly the room was filled with shouts and laughter as adults ranging
in age from their twenties to their eighties were enthusiastically swatting
and kicking these colorful floating spheres back and forth. My daughter-
in-law videoed a few moments of the action, posting it on Facebook. She
included a comment about multigenerational entertainment and how it
doesn't take much.

Please don't misunderstand about my family. We can enjoy interaction in numerous ways, including some meaningful conversation and
playing more strategic or complex games. However, it's interesting how a
broad range of generations can gravitate toward a simple activity generally
associated with children such as knocking around a couple of balloons.

Maybe this is something we should keep in mind as we interact with
others concerning the message of the gospel. There are times when it is
appropriate, necessary, and helpful to enter into deep conversations with

people about the complexities of our Christian faith. We need to be ready to answer the tough questions some people will bring up about evil, suffering, the existence of God, and the reliability of the Bible.

However, let's not overlook the simple truths which both young and old can understand—basic elements of our faith toward which everyone tends to gravitate. For example, there's a song we tend to relegate to children. It says simply, "Jesus loves me! This I know, for the Bible tells me so." The idea that "Jesus loves me" is something that can resonate with people of all ages. And it doesn't take a seminary degree to comprehend. The words of this song also communicate a foundational faith in the Bible as the authoritative Word of God. It doesn't defend the Bible but simply accepts it as being God's sacred and reliable revelation.

Even the youngest among us can understand to some extent the fact that Jesus loved us so much that He was willing to die for us so we could live. Likewise even the oldest and hardest hearts can often still be touched by this truth that someone loves them as much as Jesus does.

We don't always have to engage in strategic games of chess or complicated video games of debating with those who need Christ in their lives. Sometimes we just need to swat a balloon reminding them that Jesus loves them and how He manifested that love through dying on the cross for their sins.

As we go through this season leading up to Easter, we may hear some complex arguments about various theories of atonement, evidences to support the biblical account of Jesus' death, or all the proofs for believing Jesus truly rose from the grave. These can be important points to emphasize.

However, let's not neglect to proclaim the simple truths which God has used over the centuries to draw people to Himself: Jesus loves you. The Bible says so. Jesus loved you so much He died on the cross for you. "Greater love has no one than this, than to lay down one's life for his friends" (John 15:13).

Knock that balloon around and you may be surprised at who will readily respond to it.

Remind yourself of the basic truths of the gospel and share them with someone today.

Church Is a Place for Those Who Need Spiritual Help

"Not that I have already attained, or am already perfect; but I press on...."

– Philippians 3:12

There was a local news story one time about three young men who got into a fight. Unfortunately such an incident normally wouldn't be considered very unusual or especially noteworthy. But in this case, the circumstances and the location of the altercation is what makes it stand out. The headline said it all—"Three men get into fight outside an anger management class."

Since two of the participants were reportedly heading into this class, I guess we now know why they needed to be there. Maybe the third person who was involved ought to join them for the next session. We're told that when other members of the class saw what was going on, they jumped in—no, not to join in the fisticuffs, but to break it up. So at least some of the folks in that class seemed to be learning something.

When we read such an account we probably don't think, *It simply goes to show you that those people who attend anger management class are just a bunch of hypocrites!* No, actually it testifies to the fact that they need help in that area of their lives. And we should be somewhat relieved they are seeking, or more likely being forced to seek, help to overcome those issues. In other words, anger management class would seem to be the appropriate place for them to be.

However, many people often express a different view about people who attend church. If churchgoers do something wrong or reveal a bad attitude, one common response is, "I'm not going to church or having anything to do with those people there, because they're just a bunch of hypocrites!"

Maybe we should look at it differently. Maybe we should recognize that those people may be right where they need to be—seeking spiritual help and strength to overcome those faults and sins in their lives.

One problem is that people don't always make the distinction in churchgoers between those who are unbelievers and those who have put their faith in Christ. Not everyone who goes to church has found that life-changing experience of receiving Jesus as Savior.

But another problem is that even among believers there can sometimes be the perception that such folks have "arrived" spiritually. However, the truth is that all of us still have a lot of growing to do. We still have our faults and shortcomings. God is still working on us. We are not yet a completed project, and we won't be as long as we are here on this earth.

Don't get me wrong. That doesn't give us an excuse for continuing to commit sin or for not seeking to gain victory over bad habits or poor attitudes. While we aren't picture-perfect imitations of Christ yet, we should continually be seeking to move in that direction. And what better place to help us make progress in that quest than to be at church where we can feed on God's Word and be uplifted by the worship and fellowship with other seekers of that goal.

Maybe we should look at church and those who go there more like that anger management class. We are people who are dealing with a sin problem and with spiritual issues in our lives. But we recognize our need and are seeking the help of our Lord to overcome those matters. We may still stumble both within the walls of the church building and when we're outside its doors, but at least we're seeking help from the right Person in the right place.

Be thankful that God is still working on you, while at the same time remembering that He is also still working on the people around you.

WE NEED TO ANSWER
GOD'S SUMMONS

*"Now the word of the Lord came to Jonah...But Jonah arose to flee
to Tarshish from the presence of the Lord."*

– JONAH 1:1–3

One day as I was walking down the driveway perusing the contents I had just retrieved from my mailbox, one item in particular drew my attention. When I got a glimpse of the return address, I thought I knew what it was. Then as my eyes went further down the notice, I saw the statement in red letters confirming my suspicions—"Important: Jury Summons Enclosed."

I immediately realized this was not a letter I could simply toss in the trash or add to the stack of neglected mail on the kitchen table. As I opened it up, it contained the declaration: "Your attendance is required by law." It also warned, "Failure to respond will result in further court action." That last cautionary note was also emphasized by being printed in the color red. I don't think those words carry the same weight as Jesus' words printed in red in the Bible, but they certainly shouldn't be ignored.

I will make sure I respond to this summons to jury duty. And I do plan to be present to serve in that capacity on the designated day. I'll do so not only because of the forewarned consequences if I don't, but also because of the privilege of carrying out my responsibilities as a citizen.

Do we pay such attention to God when He speaks to us? When we receive a summons from Him—a command to do something or a call to service—do we try to ignore it, toss it aside to be dealt with at some indefinite time in the future, make excuses for not fulfilling it, or even rebelliously refuse to respond and run away from it? A summons from the Lord should not be taken lightly.

Jonah, along with many others of us since his time, found out there are consequences to ignoring God's call. Although he tried to run the other way, he couldn't outrun God. It took a divinely-sent storm and a big fish to get Jonah to the place of submitting to God's will for him.

Many years ago when I received a very clear calling from God to preach, I tried to get away from it. As much as I attempted to ignore it, God kept bringing it up over and over. It seemed that every Bible verse I read or every sermon I heard would remind me of that summons I was neglecting to answer. I believe God allowed a few storms in my life to try to redirect my course. Thankfully I didn't end up in the belly of a fish before I finally said yes to God's will for me.

But answering God's call is more than just fulfilling our duty or trying to avoid the negative consequences of our failure to act. We should also come to realize what a privilege it is for us to serve the Lord in whatever way He is directing us. And we should also remember that it will be the best path in life that we could take. Receiving and responding to God's summons will bring us a sense of fulfillment and joy that nothing else could supply. God is wanting not only to fulfill His plan, but also to do what's good for us.

What summons are you hearing from God? Is it the call to come to Him for salvation? Or maybe it's a call to go and serve Him in some way. Whatever it is, take it seriously. It is an important notice. Failure to respond will have its consequences, including the fact that you'll be missing out on a great blessing.

Answer God's call today. You dare not ignore it.

AVOID A MESS:
ASK GOD FOR HELP

"Yet you do not have because you do not ask."
– JAMES 4:2

I was out and about with two of my grandsons when we stopped for lunch at a fast-food restaurant. As I was placing our order, they were each busy procuring the necessary accompaniments to our meal, which I soon discovered consisted mainly of a handful of ketchup packets. After we were seated, I had to send one of them back to retrieve the less important items as far as young boys are concerned, such as napkins and plastic eating utensils.

When the younger of my two grandsons started to try to tear open his ketchup packet, I cringed, recognizing the potential risk involved. However, I let him make several futile attempts at the task before finally asking if he wanted my help. In response to my offer to assist him, my grandson got a determined look on his face. He answered dogmatically, "No, I'll bite it open"—no doubt mimicking the actions of some adults in the family who had used that method to deal with such stubborn containers in the past.

I can report that he was successful in opening the packet. However as he did, ketchup squirted out onto his shirt, onto the table, and primarily in a large swath across his face. At that point I was glad we had gone back to get the napkins.

A spirit of independence and of wanting "to do it myself" can be a good thing at times. I wouldn't want to hamper the development of that attitude in my grandchildren, especially when so many people today are more than willing to depend on others to take care of their needs rather than taking that responsibility themselves.

But sometimes we do need to recognize our dependence, especially when it comes to God. The Bible condemns those who possess a self-sufficient spirit that proclaims, "I have need of nothing" (Revelation 3:17). And it commends individuals who realize their own faults and limitations but who lean upon God to overcome those shortcomings.

It's wisdom, not weakness, to look to God for help. And we have a Heavenly Father who wants us to come to Him with our needs and concerns. He's provided us with an effective tool to seek His assistance—prayer. He says, "Ask, and it will be given to you" (Luke 11:9). He even tells us that there are some things we don't have simply because we haven't asked for them (James 4:2).

Yet how often do we stubbornly act like my grandson did at the restaurant? We know God is available to help. We are well aware of the vehicle of prayer which is at our disposal. We may even hear His invitation to assist us. But we become even more determined to try to do it ourselves, often with a similar result of making a mess of the whole matter.

What tough situation are you dealing with these days? There's a time and place for dogged determination that keeps on trying. But there's also a place for handing matters over to Someone who is much more capable of taking care of the situation than we are. As a matter of fact, even as we're doing everything we can do, we need to be prayerfully depending on God to help us and to do what we can't do. Sometimes it's not a question of either doing or praying—it's both at the same time.

So let's recognize our dependence on God and seek His help before we bite the ketchup packet. It's much easier to let God do it the right way than to have to clean up the mess we make from trying to do it solely on our own.

What is there today for which you need to pray and seek God's help? Do it!

LET THE STORY OF THE CROSS TOUCH YOU AGAIN

"I am the good shepherd. The good shepherd gives His life for the sheep."

– JOHN 10:11

Some stories always touch our hearts no matter how often we hear them. For example, can anybody watch the movie *Old Yeller* without being moved by it? I remember as a child having tears in my eyes as I left the theater after my first encounter with that Disney film. And I confess that it still gets to me. That's why I intentionally avoided that movie for a period of time after our beloved basset hound died. I'm afraid it would have affected me even more in light of that event.

Why does it get to us? It's because it's primarily a story about love—the love between a boy and his dog. It's heart-wrenching to see that youngster have to make the tough, adult decision to shoot his pet after it comes down with rabies. But do you remember how Old Yeller contracted that disease in the first place? He got it from defending his family from an infected wolf. It was the dog's love for his family that caused him to suffer and die the way that he did.

While the account of Jesus and His crucifixion is on a whole different level from that of Old Yeller, there is a similarity. Jesus was motivated by love as well. He suffered and died out of love for us. Jesus described Himself as the Good Shepherd who gave His life for the sheep (John 10:11). Out of love, He was protecting us from the rabid wolves of Satan and sin. Another time Jesus proclaimed in reference to His upcoming actions at the cross, "Greater love has no one than this, than to lay down one's life for his friends" (John 15:13). That's what Jesus' death was all about. He loved us and laid down His life for us.

It's important to remember that Jesus wasn't just fulfilling a duty by dying for our sins. He wasn't simply doing a job that His Heavenly Father had given Him to do in redeeming us and saving us. Neither was He acting from any other lesser motivation. Jesus was willing to endure the cross out of love for you and me.

No doubt many of us will be coming into contact once again with the familiar account of Jesus' crucifixion as we approach Easter again this year. Maybe you'll hear a sermon on the subject, read the story in the Bible, or watch the event portrayed in a movie or in a passion play. For some of us it may be a story we've heard countless times since we were children. But it should still touch our hearts today. If it doesn't, then maybe we're not focusing enough on what's happening and why.

We shouldn't just read the account of Jesus' suffering and death as history. We shouldn't simply view it as a noble story, an inspiring story, or a sad story. We should keep in mind that above all the account of Jesus at the cross is a love story—a love story that involves you personally. It's all about Jesus' love for you.

So as you hear the story again or watch the portrayals of Jesus being mocked, beaten, and dying, remember why He did it. Force yourself to think about the truth that He did it all out of love for you, as painful as it may be to contemplate that fact.

If "Old Yeller" can still bring a tear to our eyes, then surely that precious old story about what Jesus did for us at the cross should touch us even more.

Lord, give me a fresh appreciation for what Jesus did on the cross for me, as well as for why He did it. May it move me to give my all for the One who gave His life for me.

LET'S BE SURE TO
PAY ATTENTION TO THE
RIGHT THINGS

"Watch, stand fast in the faith...."
– I CORINTHIANS 16:13

It was the first game of the season when my grandson was five years old and playing on a baseball team. As we sat in the bleachers, my daughter explained that one of the biggest challenges the coaches and parents face at this age is simply getting the kids to pay attention while they're out in the field. Apparently there tends to be a lot of twirling around, hat tossing, and other such activities that reveal young minds which are occupied elsewhere rather than on the game at hand. My daughter expressed her pride at how well my grandson's team seemed to be doing in that area on this opening day, especially compared to how they had been acting in practice. Regardless of what else happened in the game, she saw their attentiveness as a major accomplishment to be celebrated.

An example of that issue surfaced at one point when a ball was hit toward a player on the opposing team. He was bent over busily running his fingers through the dirt and grass, not even aware that he was in the middle of the action, in spite of the efforts of the crowd and the coaches to get his attention. Several players ran past him to retrieve the ball before he finally looked up from his preoccupation with the ground and realized his missed opportunity.

Likewise I imagine there are times when God would consider it a victory if He could just get His children to pay attention. We tend to get wrapped up in our own affairs and get easily distracted from being about our Father's business. We become entranced in the temporary things of earth and fail to keep our upward focus on the heavenly perspective of life. We look at "the things which are seen" rather than "the things which are not seen" (II Corinthians 4:18) and lose sight of the important battle for souls taking place around us.

Throughout the Bible there are exhortations from God for us to watch, pay attention, and stay focused. If we would listen today, I believe we would still hear God calling us to do so.

He would tell us to watch and pay attention to what's going on in the world and in our culture. Notice the signs of the times of which Jesus spoke. See the direction that society is heading and the changing attitudes toward the Christian faith. Watch so that you'll be ready for the challenges, tribulations, persecution, and the inevitable return of Christ one day.

Furthermore I believe God would tell us to watch and be alert so that we'll be prepared to face any attacks from the enemy. Pay attention so that you can avoid those temptations or so you can seek God's help to overcome them. Watch so that you can exercise the faith required to deflect those fiery darts of the wicked one that he hurls in your direction. Pay attention so that you can recognize the enemy and not fall prey to his deceptive tactics.

I believe God would also encourage us to watch in order that we not miss any important opportunities. We need to pay attention so that a chance to serve Him doesn't bounce right past us unnoticed. We need to watch for opportunities to show God's love to others, to help those in need, and to be a ready witness for Christ.

We all got a good laugh from watching that inattentive little ballplayer on the field, but I don't think God finds His children's lack of attention amusing. We're involved in something much more significant than a Little League baseball contest. Therefore let's make sure we keep our minds in the game.

In what area is the Lord reminding you to watch and pay better attention?

God Can Still Do
Great Things for Those
Who Trust Him

"Talk of all His wondrous works!"
– Psalm 105:2

As Christians, we need to be careful not to neglect the great responsibility and joy of sharing with others about the great things God has done. That's what the Bible says the disciples of Jesus were doing on the day of Pentecost after being filled with the Spirit. The crowd testified, "We hear them speaking in our own tongues the wonderful works of God" (Acts 2:11).

Such declarations on our part shouldn't be confined to the amazing acts of God in the past—whether the parting of the Red Sea for the Israelites, the miracles of Jesus, or something God did in our lives twenty years ago. We should see God's hand in our present world and give Him glory for the fresh ways in which He reveals His love, power, and majesty. May I share a couple of such stories with you today?

A man in our church received word from his boss that he was going to be laid off from his job. He had worked for this large company for thirty-four years. Becoming unemployed at age sixty in our current economy was not a pleasant prospect. Over the course of the next couple of days as word of his situation spread, fellow Christians prayed and a rather big corporate customer who worked with this man expressed strong displeasure about his departure. In a very unusual, if not unprecedented, move for this company, they reversed their position and offered him the opportunity to remain at his same job.

Some might give most of the credit to the powerful customer who stood up for this man whose skills they valued. And no doubt that was a huge factor. But I believe there was Someone even greater who was intervening and answering prayer in connection with this matter. God did something that seemed highly unlikely, if not impossible. He deserves the glory for it.

Then there was another incident that culminated around the same time. This story goes back several years with a couple unsuccessfully trying to have a baby. They resorted to some of the amazing ways the medical community can assist in conception. After many disappointments, including a miscarriage, they gave birth to a healthy baby boy. However, they decided not to go through that process again, and the mother was informed that she would be unable to get pregnant without those artificial means. But about nine months ago, this couple conceived another child. And just recently this "miracle baby" was born.

Why is it important that we share such stories? First of all, it's because God is worthy of receiving the praise and glory for His wonderful works. It's only right that we acknowledge with thankful hearts what God has done. But secondly, we all face various challenges, difficulties, and seeming impossibilities in life. And we need the reminder that there's a God who can do great things in behalf of those who trust Him.

When word got around that the man in our church had been restored to his job, he received a message from someone stating simply, "He lives!" Our church member responded by quoting a verse of that song—"I serve a risen Savior, He's in the world today; I know that He is living, whatever men may say."

Let's remember that the Lord is alive and active in our world today. He's not just the God who used to do great things. He still does them today. Trust Him to do wonderful works in your life. And when He does, be sure to tell others about it.

What great things has God done in your life? Maybe it was years ago—maybe it was today. Tell others about it!

Some of Us May Need to Reconnect with the Lord

"Draw near to God and He will draw near to you."

– James 4:8

I recall the time my oldest daughter went back to work after having been on leave for a while due to giving birth to our first granddaughter. Her return meant that we would also be back to babysitting a couple of days each week. On that first day of having our grandkids with us again, I spent some time reconnecting with my younger grandson. At one point he seemed so attached to me that some family members were calling him Papaw's boy. But in recent times those feelings had seemed to cool considerably. Maybe it was due to the fact that we hadn't been able to spend much fun time together—just seeing each other at church or when we went out to eat as a family. And when we were together, occasionally I found myself being the "bad guy" needing to tell him no about something, a word that he especially doesn't like to hear.

So when our babysitting duties renewed, I intentionally took time simply to hang around with my grandson. We read books, played with toys, and sat together watching *Sesame Street*. I even gave a few horsy rides on my poor, aching back. And as the day wore on, based on my grandson's attitude and actions, I think some needed rebonding took place.

Do some of us need to reconnect with the Lord in a similar way? Maybe you can think back to a time when you were especially close to

Him—enthused about going to church, loving to spend time reading the Bible, and looking for opportunities to tell others about Jesus. But something has happened to cool that relationship.

Possibly our circumstances have changed in such a way as to make it more difficult to find time for close fellowship with the Lord. Perhaps we've allowed other things to crowd Him out of a prominent place in our lives. Maybe we've been guilty of having done some things that we know weren't pleasing to the Lord. So it seems like whenever we get close to Him that all we hear is "No" or "Thou shalt not" or feel a strong, convicting sense of condemnation.

If that's the case, what do we do? It will probably require some intentional action on our part to strengthen that fading relationship. It won't just happen by itself. The Lord is certainly ready and willing to draw closer to us, but we may need to remove some barriers that are keeping us apart.

Try carving out some special time in your schedule just to hang out with the Lord. I'm not talking about Sunday mornings at church or your regular devotional times. Give up something else in your routine and spend some time in fellowship with God. Think about His great love for you and the various ways He has shown that love to you over the years. We may need to hear His words of correction, but let's also hear His words of comfort and encouragement.

Read His Word, not simply to get your quota of chapters in for the day, but to seek to hear some message directly from God to you. Go to church with an expectation of meeting God there and with a heart set on worshiping Him. Focus less on the formalities and the fallible human beings involved in those services and instead focus on the Person who should be the center of our attention and praise.

If your relationship with the Lord isn't as close as it used to be, don't let it keep going in that direction. What will you do today to try to strengthen your bond with your Heavenly Father?

Take a specific step today to try to better connect with the Lord.

Let's Trust God to Take
Care of Our Situation

"Trust in the Lord with all your heart, and lean not on your own understanding."

– Proverbs 3:5

I remember the year I thought I had done a good job of preparing for the time change that weekend. None of us like to wake up an hour behind schedule, but it would be especially problematic for a pastor to be running an hour late on Sunday morning. So I reminded myself several times throughout the day on Saturday about setting my clocks before going to bed that night. I remembered which way I was supposed to turn them— "spring forward." I even went ahead and changed the time on the clocks at the church that day while I was in more appropriate attire for climbing a ladder. And then later that night as bedtime approached and my mental sharpness tends to diminish, I'm proud to report that I still didn't forget about that important task. I went through our house and made the necessary changes before crawling into bed with the peaceful assurance that I would wake up at the appropriate time.

When my radio came on Sunday morning as my wake-up call, I realized that the program being aired wasn't the one I usually heard at that time. After a few news headlines were given and the weather forecast reported, the announcer stated the time. It was a full hour earlier than what my clock read, a whole sixty minutes sooner than I had intended to get up. My first irrational thought was that the radio station had forgotten to change their time. But when I got out of bed and checked my watch and several other clocks in the house, they all confirmed the time announced on the radio. What had happened to my bedside clock radio? Had I accidentally set it ahead two hours instead of one? I was sure I hadn't made such a foolish mistake. Then it struck me: this was a fairly new clock radio. I hadn't gone through a time change with it before. I vaguely remembered reading something in the instructions that came with it that this smart electronic contraption would automatically change itself when Daylight Savings Time began. So I had manually moved it ahead an hour, then the clock moved itself ahead another hour. That's how I ended up losing two hours of sleep that night of the time change instead of the usual one hour.

That situation reminds me of how we sometimes jump ahead of God. Like my new clock radio was programmed to know when Daylight Savings Time would begin and adjust for it, the Lord knows exactly what's coming into our lives. Not only is He aware of it but He's prepared for it and has it covered. He's got it under control. However, we often lose sight of that truth and want to try to take care of it ourselves. We interject our own faulty wisdom and efforts into the situation, usually with the result of messing things up. If we had only waited, prayed, and trusted God, we would've been in much better shape.

I should have paid closer attention to those instructions that accompanied my new radio, or at least made a better mental note about that one significant feature which came into play that weekend. And we should pay close attention to what God has revealed about Himself. He truly is a great God who can handle the problems and challenges that come our way. He's wiser and more powerful than we are. He has given us some great promises on which we can rely. So let's quit rushing ahead trying to do it all ourselves and instead look prayerfully for God's direction and help, mindful of our dependence on Him. To do otherwise is to risk losing much more than simply an hour of sleep.

What situation in your life do you to entrust to God and to His care?

Are We Experiencing a Spiritual Resurrection?

"Just as Christ was raised from the dead by the glory of the Father, even so we also should walk in newness of life."

– ROMANS 6:4

When my grandson was little, I remember enjoying watching him make progress in his ability to speak. He was learning to pronounce an increasing number of words and was gradually becoming more understandable each day. However, there were still times when he rattled off a sentence as if I should know exactly what he meant, yet I didn't have a clue as to what he said. Sometimes I would try to get him to repeat it, hoping that I could make some sense of the gibberish the second time around. But if I wasn't successful at that point, I often simply nodded my head in agreement, hoping not to let on that I was completely in the dark while at the same time encouraging him to keep trying.

There were times when I think the disciples must have been like that as Jesus spoke to them. Only in their case it wasn't due to Jesus' lack of communication skills but rather to their own inability to understand. It seems like the disciples had an especially tough time comprehending what Jesus tried to tell them about His upcoming death and resurrection. I can see them listening to those prophetic words with glassy eyes and nods of agreement while not understanding a word Jesus meant. Maybe it was the combination of their own misguided expectations about Jesus being an earthly king and the fact that they didn't have the Holy Spirit yet in His fullness to enlighten them about the truth. Whatever the reason, in spite of Jesus' plain words foretelling his resurrection, His followers seemed to be totally surprised by its occurrence.

With the advantage of hindsight, it's easy for us to be critical of the disciples for not comprehending such an important concept Jesus so distinctly shared with them. However, I'm afraid some of us are just as guilty of missing the truth about another resurrection clearly taught in God's Word. We may believe in the scriptural testimony and historical evidence of Jesus' resurrection, we may be looking forward with assurance to our own resurrection one day, but do we understand the extent to which we can experience a spiritual resurrection in our lives right now?

The Bible teaches that "just as Christ was raised from the dead by the glory of the Father, even so we also should walk in newness of life" (Romans 6:4). It talks about a real change which can take place in believers, freeing them from sin's dominion and empowering them to live for God. The Bible teaches not only that we are forgiven for the wrongs we have done, but that we are spiritually resurrected and enabled by the Holy Spirit to live a new life of loving God and walking in obedience to His will.

How do we miss that truth? Why do some people insist that we can't help but be slaves to sin every day? Maybe, like the disciples, we have some misguided expectations which are hindering us from comprehending what the Lord is saying. Some of us may be giving the power of sin too much credit, while others may simply be looking for an excuse for their own lack of holy living. We don't experience greater victory over sin because we're not expecting it or seeking it.

The Bible declares that the same great divine power which raised Jesus from the dead is at work in us. Let's not underestimate the power of God to change us, to deliver us from wrong attitudes and lifestyles, and to raise us up to godly living.

Acknowledge the biblical teaching about the possibility of living victoriously over sin. Then trust the Lord to help you experience it more fully.

MARCH 25

BE WILLING TO RECEIVE
GOD'S FREE GIFT

"For by grace you have been saved through faith, and that not of yourselves; it is the gift of God...."

– EPHESIANS 2:8

Who doesn't like freebies? One week I was told about a couple of eating establishments which were offering free food. One day my favorite place to go for ice cream was offering a free cone for anyone who stopped by—and as you might imagine, I did. The very next day another restaurant was giving away free breakfast biscuits to its patrons.

When free stuff like that is being offered, we tend to take advantage of it. Bigger crowds usually flock to those businesses on occasions when they're providing such perks. Sometimes we grab those freebies even if we don't need them or aren't especially interested in them. Some people in our area attend the local Cherry Blossom Festival every year around this time. Many who will be checking out the festivities will probably fill their bags with free gifts being distributed from various booths. After being sorted through and more closely examined later, some of those items may be found to be needed and useful, but others will probably get thrown in a junk drawer or tossed in the garbage. Yet we eagerly reached out for it or accepted it initially simply because it was free.

It makes you wonder why more people don't reach out to accept the free gift Jesus offers to them. Why don't crowds flock to those churches which are faithful to preach the gospel? The heart of their message is the good news that God is wanting to give us something for free—something needed and valuable. He wants to give us a gift which when unwrapped provides peace, forgiveness, hope, life, a home for eternity, and much more. And it's all free!

Back in the Old Testament, God issued an invitation through the prophet Isaiah, "Everyone who thirsts, come to the waters; and you who have no money, come, buy and eat. Yes, come buy wine and milk without money and without price" (Isaiah 55:1). That offer is reiterated in the New Testament where it declares that the salvation which quenches our thirst and satisfies our souls is strictly by God's grace and is His free gift to those who will receive it by faith in Christ.

So why don't more people pursue this spiritual freebie? There may be numerous reasons, but here are a few possibilities. Some people don't believe the offer is legitimate. They treat it like that phone call claiming you just won a free cruise to the Bahamas. You know there's a catch to it, so you hang up the phone. There are those who don't take God's free offer seriously. They don't believe in Him or they don't believe in the possibility of what He's offering them. So they just hang up on God without pursuing it further.

Other people may believe God is offering the gift, but they refuse to accept it. While the blessings of the gift sound good, they know it will result in some changes in their lives—changes which they aren't willing to make. They want to hang on to the practices and lifestyle to which they're accustomed, not making room for the new and better things God would give them even though it's free.

Then there are others who just have a hard time accepting what God offers as a gift. They believe it's something which must be earned. So instead of receiving the freebie, they choose to spend their days trying to be good enough to merit those favors from God.

Is anything holding you back from accepting God's gift of salvation? His offer is real. The gift is extremely valuable. And best of all, it's free. So open your heart and receive it.

Have you received God's free gift? Are you letting others know about it?

A Simple Obituary: I Am Alive

"I am He who lives, and was dead, and behold, I am alive forever-more. Amen."

<small>– Revelation 1:18</small>

I suppose it's a sign of getting older: you notice yourself paying greater attention to the obituaries in the newspaper. You recognize more names there. More of your contemporaries seem to be passing away. As I view those notices, I see where some families use that opportunity to write virtually a small book about their deceased loved one's life and accomplishments.

However, maybe you heard about the ninety-two-year-old man in Sweden who went the opposite direction when he died a few years ago. He had asked his family to publish a simple three-word obituary upon his death. It read, "I am dead."

What if you were given the task of writing Jesus' obituary? Where would you even start? You could go back to eternity past such as in John's Gospel—"In the beginning was the Word...." But even if you began at His birth, it would take more than a sentence or two to try to explain the fact that He was born to Mary and supposedly to Joseph. And what would you say about what Jesus did in His life? Which miracles would you include and which would you omit? There would be so much to say you could end up declaring as John did at the end of His Gospel: "And there are also many other things that Jesus did, which if they were written one by one, I suppose that even the world itself could not contain the books that would be written" (John 21:25).

But if you took a page from the book of that Swedish man, you could actually keep Jesus' obituary rather simple. It could be taken from what Jesus said of Himself in Revelation 1:18—"I am He who lives, and was dead, and behold, I am alive forevermore." The three words in Jesus' obituary could be, "I am alive." Yes, Jesus really did die. He was real flesh and blood, not just some ghostly apparition. He actually suffered the pain and agony recorded in scripture. He was crucified and died for our sins. But that wasn't the end of the story. A short time later His tomb was found to be empty. Angels testified to the fact that He had risen. Jesus Himself showed up providing evidence for the assertion—"I am alive."

Notice the other significant truth Jesus adds to His "obituary" in Revelation 1:18—"and behold, I am alive forevermore." Jesus didn't just come back to life in order to die again. He was raised to live forevermore. Jesus still lives today. He is our living High Priest who is interceding on our behalf before His Heavenly Father. As one of our Easter songs declares, "He lives, salvation to impart; you ask me how I know He lives— He lives within my heart." Jesus is the living Savior who can still save us and give us eternal life today.

Although I like the simplicity of it, I wouldn't want my obituary to read, "I am dead." I would have to add a little something to it—maybe "I am dead, yet I live." Such a statement would express the reality of life after death and especially life in heaven with the Lord for those who know Him. Maybe a better way of putting such an obituary would be, "I am with the Lord." That says it all: "I'm dead. I'm gone from this world. But that doesn't mean I'm no longer existing. I'm living on in a better place and in the presence of the Lord."

Let's thank God that Jesus lives. He died, but now He lives forevermore. And if He lives in our hearts, we can be assured of living forevermore as well.

Rejoice today in the knowledge that your Savior lives and in the assurance it gives that you will live forever too.

Life Is Short, So Make Today Count for Eternity

"As for man, his days are like grass; as a flower of the field, so he flourishes. For the wind passes over it, and it is gone...."

– Psalm 103:15–16

This is the one time of year when my yard might get noticed for a positive reason. Most of the time the landscape on our property is fairly forgettable. I don't have one of those lush well-manicured lawns with sculptured flowering shrubbery—the kind that gets its picture in the newspaper as yard of the month. My lawn consists of more weeds and bare spots than grass. And although we do have some azaleas and gardenias scattered around, they're not as abundant and beautiful as those in neighboring yards.

But about this time each year our front yard bursts with beauty due to the blossoms on our two cherry trees. And when our neighbor's Bradford Pear decides to put forth its blooms at the same time just across our driveway, it adds to the scene. It looks beautiful, but only for a very short time. Often it only lasts about a week, depending on how the wind blows and the rain falls. Very quickly those blossoms will fade and fall off, revealing the green leaves which will endure until the fall season. My yard then returns to its normal drab condition, along with a plethora of dying cherry blossoms strewn on the ground.

The Bible reminds us that our time here on earth is similar. "As for man, his days are as grass; as a flower of the field, so he flourishes. For the wind passes over it, and it is gone" (Psalm 103:15). While some might consider this a rather somber thought, it can serve as a needed reality check for many of us. It's helpful for us to remember that life is short. Our time to blossom and flourish comes and goes all too quickly. Without that perspective we can deceive ourselves into wasting or misusing what we do possess of this precious commodity we call time.

Therefore there are those who will trumpet the call of *carpe diem*— "seize the day." Both within and without the context of Christianity, people tell us to make the most of today's opportunities—grab all the gusto you can get. And there's certainly some truth in those statements. Life is short, so don't procrastinate and don't miss out on all the good you can do and enjoy today. Make that phone call, send that note, carry out that act of kindness, tell that person how much you care about him, share that truth—do whatever it is you really need to do while you still have opportunity to do so.

However let's not mistake this truth as simply inspiration to hurry up and do whatever will bring us pleasure. The shortness of life should remind us that we need to be giving priority to those things which will matter most in the long run, especially those which will make a difference for eternity. Jesus stated that we need to lay up for ourselves treasures in heaven (Matthew 6:20). So while we're blossoming, let's invest our time in people, in influencing them in positive ways and in ways that will help prepare them for eternity. Let's give ourselves to doing what pleases God, not just what pleases ourselves. Let's cultivate a closer and deeper relationship with Jesus. Let's seek to let our lights shine as brightly and as impactfully as we can for this short time while we're here.

I think I'll go out and take a picture of my yard today, before all those cherry blossoms disappear. Maybe I should post that snapshot somewhere where I'll see it every day as a reminder that time is short and to make the most of today.

Lord, help me to number my days, to remember that life is short, and to make the most of this time while I am blossoming. Help me to be busy with that which will matter for eternity.

LET'S PRAY FOR JESUS TO ENABLE US TO LOVE OUR ENEMIES

"Love your enemies, bless those who curse you, do good to those who hate you, and pray for those who spitefully use you and persecute you."

– MATTHEW 5:44

I remember when one of my daughters added another pet to their household. It was one of those tiny crossbreed dogs called a chiweenie—a cross between a chihuahua and a dachshund. She was a cute little thing—quite energetic and playful. One day when I was visiting she was constantly wanting me to engage in a game of tug-of-war with her and her chew toy, or she would be crawling all over me looking for protruding fingers, shoelaces, or other interesting items on which to nibble.

I also noticed on that occasion the tense relationship between this new member of the family and the cat who resided in the house. We know all about the tendency for those two species not to get along very well. These two were no exception. The cat wasn't hostile to the point of attacking this little canine it towered over in size, but it obviously considered it a pest to be avoided. Whenever the chiweenie came up towards the cat to yap at it or try to grab its tail, the feline would back off and offer a clear hiss of warning.

But one morning when my daughter opened the door to let the dog out of its crate where it stays the night, not only did the dog emerge but so did the cat. Apparently it had been snoozing unnoticed in the back of the crate when the dog was put in for the night, and they got locked in together. The good news is they survived the ordeal. The only sign of conflict was a small spot on the dog's nose where the cat may have swatted at him at some point. I don't know if that nightmare experience traumatized either pet or if it might have opened the door to a more cordial relationship between the two.

Imagine getting locked in close quarters with some person you don't get along with well. What if you got stuck in an elevator for several hours with that annoying person at work? Or what if, in one of those winter storms we experienced this year, you had gotten snowed-in for several days with someone who considers you to be an enemy? Similar happenings have occurred where two conflicting individuals have been forced to spend time together—sometimes resulting in them almost driving each other crazy, and other times actually bettering that relationship.

There are going to be people with whom we don't have a natural affinity. Due to personality differences or other issues, we may be like cats and dogs. However, Jesus told us to love our enemies, to bless those who curse us, to do good to those who hate us, and to pray for those who spitefully use us and persecute us (Matthew 5:44). In other words, we still need to try to get along with those people and even seek to have a loving and gracious attitude toward them—the same kind of love and grace God shows to all people, including us.

I don't think the answer is for Jesus to lock us up in a cage together. What is needed is a change in heart. And no, not just a change in the other person's heart—but a change in my heart. I need the Lord to fill me with more of His spirit of love and kindness. I need to realize how good God has been to me in spite of all my faults, sins, and annoyances to Him. And I should pray for Him to help me possess and manifest that same spirit toward those big cats who keep hissing at me, as well as toward those little yappy chiweenies in my life.

Who might consider you an enemy? How can you show love to that person?

THE RESURRECTION OF JESUS IS A REALITY

"All who are in the graves will hear His voice and come forth."

– JOHN 5:28–29

"It just can't be."

"What can't be?"

"Well, you can't be. You're gone."

"I was gone, but I came back."

"But you can't come back…not after you're gone. It just ain't decent."

The preceding dialogue was taken from an early episode of *The Andy Griffith Show*. Sheriff Andy Taylor had been surprised by a visit from a former resident of Mayberry, a man named Tom Silby. The reason this encounter was especially unnerving to the small town sheriff is because, as he remarked, he hadn't seen Tom in a long time, not since his funeral. Now that you know the context of their conversation, maybe it makes a little more sense.

As the two men continued to talk, the whole story came to light. It seemed that Tom had left his wife a couple of years earlier. However, unbeknownst to him, she had been too proud to admit that fact to anyone. Instead, she concocted some tale about Tom having gone out of town where he supposedly had been run over and killed by a taxi. She had proceeded to have a nice funeral for him and had been pretending to be a grieving widow ever since.

I guess it would be startling to run into someone whose funeral you had attended. After all, as Andy said, when you're gone you can't come back. Of course, as it turned out, Tom had never left this world in the first place. But there is Someone else who actually did leave and come back. And that's what we celebrate here at Easter.

I wonder if anyone had a similar conversation with Jesus after His resurrection. I can imagine someone confronting the resurrected Christ with the declaration, "It just can't be." Maybe it was someone who had witnessed His crucifixion, seeing the bruised and bleeding Jesus take his last breath. Or maybe it was someone who had seen His body wrapped up and laid in the tomb. They knew without a shadow of a doubt that He was dead. But here He was—He had come back.

The resurrection of Jesus was a unique event. It testified to the fact that Jesus Himself was Someone unique—the very Son of God. Normally this was an occurrence that couldn't be. It wasn't possible. Dead people don't come back. But Jesus wasn't a normal person. His death wasn't just another death. He died as the sacrifice for our sins and then rose again as the victorious Savior of the world.

And to top it off, His resurrection gives us the assurance that we're going to come back too. We're not going to pop up in this world again after we die, but one day we are going to be resurrected. Jesus said, "All who are in the graves will hear His voice and come forth—those who have done good to the resurrection of life, and those who have done evil, to the resurrection of condemnation" (John 5:28–29).

I know there are still people today who would say "It just can't be" concerning the resurrection of Jesus. But the evidence for it is overwhelming. And you can experience the most convincing evidence of all by putting your trust in the living Christ as your Savior.

If Jesus is knocking on the door of your heart, let Him in. And you'll discover that it can be—He really did come back from the grave.

Do you have the assurance that the living Christ is living in your heart?

THERE IS SOMEONE WHO KNOWS WHAT YOU ARE GOING THROUGH

"For we do not have a High Priest who cannot sympathize with our weaknesses, but was in all points tempted as we are, yet without sin."

– HEBREWS 4:15

Do you remember the shooting at the US Capitol building in July of 1998? It resulted in the deaths of a couple of Capitol police officers, drawing a lot of attention in that pre-9/11 era. My family and I in particular found ourselves sensing a special connection to that tragic event. Why? It was due to the fact that we had just been there a few days before the shooting took place.

As the reporters described the locations involved, we could picture exactly where it had happened. We had stood in some of the very spots shown on the video footage on the news. And we sympathized with the innocent people who were forced to face the violence and fear, realizing how close we came to being part of that group.

Similarly, I remember an occasion in which we all felt compassion for the Haitians whose land was devastated by an earthquake. However, there were those in our communities who carried a special burden for that place because they had been there on mission trips or for other reasons. They could identify not only with the location but also with people whom they personally knew who were suffering as a result of this natural disaster.

It makes a difference when we've been there—not just in a physical location but also in personal experience. If you've experienced what someone else is going through, it often results in a greater ability on your part to identify with and feel for that person.

Sometimes we may feel like no one else knows what we're going through. We feel like the wealthy in our society have a hard time identifying with the average person who struggles to make ends meet. We feel like the politician within the beltway of Washington DC has a hard time understanding the concerns of common folks like us. Maybe we even wonder at times if God—the wise, all-powerful Lord of heaven and earth—really understands what it's like to be in our shoes. Does He truly know how bad we can feel physically, how hard it is to stay encouraged in tough times, or how strong the pull can be to give in to certain temptations?

We can be assured that God does know, because He's been there. In the person of Christ, He came into this world, lived as a man, and faced all the experiences that we encounter. The Bible says that Jesus is our great High Priest who can sympathize with our weaknesses. He was tempted in all points as we are, yet without sin (Hebrews 4:15).

Are you physically exhausted? Christ has been there—remember His falling asleep in a boat in the middle of a storm? Do you have so much to do and too little time to get it all done? Jesus has been there—just look in the Gospels at some of the busy days He experienced. Are you living in unstable times, facing uncertainties and concerns about the future? Jesus lived in similar times. Are you suffering being discriminated against or ridiculed for your faith? Jesus can sympathize with you. He suffered far more than any of us have to this point. Are you tempted to get discouraged, to give up, and to find an easier path to walk than the one that follows God's way? Think of Jesus' struggle in the Garden of Gethsemane. He has been there.

We can be comforted in the assurance that Jesus knows what it's like to be in our shoes. And because He walked that path victoriously, He can give us the wisdom, grace, and strength we need to be faithful in our circumstances and to overcome our temptations too. Whatever you're going through today, Jesus has been there and He can help you through it.

What are you facing today? Jesus has been there. Jesus can help you.

IN HIS BIG MOMENT, JESUS THOUGHT OF YOU

"But God demonstrates His own love toward us, in that while we were still sinners, Christ died for us."

– ROMANS 5:8

Those who are suffering from that annual malady called March Madness are usually at their peak about this time. One year the frenzy was even more noticeable in our area since the big event itself, the Final Four in the NCAA basketball tournament, was being held right here. For the players on those teams as they vied for a chance at the national championship, it would be the biggest game of their lives.

Imagine one of those games going down to the wire. The guard is expertly dribbling the ball down the court with time running out and his team trailing by one point. He's being hounded by his opponent who is trying to steal the ball. The player is having to keep his eye on the clock to make sure time doesn't run out before a shot can be launched. He's watching his teammates who are running around attempting to get open in order to receive a pass. The coach is yelling instructions—the crowd is roaring—and the final five seconds are ticking off the clock. Suddenly that guard does the unthinkable. He turns and peers into the crowd to the one spot where he knows his dad is standing. This is the dad who taught him how to play basketball, instilling in him a love for the game. This is the man who spent countless evenings shooting hoops with him in the driveway. This is the faithful supporter who has sat and watched him play every game from the time he was in the county league, through high school, and now in college. With five, four, three seconds on the clock, this player locks eyes with his dad, gives him a thumbs-up sign, and proceeds to hit a three-pointer to win the game as the buzzer sounds.

Honestly, I don't think you're going to see that happen in the tournament. If a player were to let himself get distracted and look off into the crowd, especially at such an important moment, I would hate to think what his coach would do to him. That dad probably wouldn't be very happy about it either. However, after reflecting on it, he might be impressed and moved by the actions of his son. To think that at such a critical moment in the most important game of one's life, his son thought about him. It may not have been a wise move under the circumstances, but it was an expression of love revealing how much his dad meant to him.

This season in particular, we are remembering Jesus' big moment as He suffered and died for the sins of mankind. It was a moment that would alter eternal destinies. It was the critical time when Jesus carried the weight of the world on His shoulders. At that pivotal hour, He wasn't just thinking about the big picture of the world that He loved and came to save. The Gospel accounts reveal that He also took time to focus on individuals—Peter who had denied Him—Mary, his mother, who needed someone to take care of her—a thief on a cross next to him who needed to be forgiven and welcomed into God's kingdom. And if Jesus thought about them, I believe there's a good chance that He thought about you and me as well. As Jesus went for the winning shot that would bring victory over sin and death, He looked through the crowded ages of history and focused on you. He suffered and died out of love for you. Such an act should move us to return that love and to open our arms to the One who cared that much about each and every one of us.

How does it affect you to consider that Jesus didn't just die for the world in general, but He died specifically for you?

Watch Out for the Weeds

"For if you live according to the flesh you will die; but if by the Spirit you put to death the deeds of the body, you will live."

– Romans 8:13

A couple of us in our church spent part of a day clearing out the weeds from around the shrubbery which surrounds our building. We hadn't given those areas much attention so far that spring, so they were beginning to be overrun by some unwanted intruders. Why don't roses or azaleas or other beautiful flowering plants pop up on their own and become predominant when the ground is left uncultivated? Theologically, I suppose we can trace it back to the fall of man in the Garden of Eden. Part of the curse as a result of sin was the ground bringing forth thorns and thistles. Thanks a lot, Adam!

I was reminded of this as my wife and I were watching one of our favorite TV shows. There's not much on television these days I can recommend, but if you haven't checked out *When Calls the Heart* on the Hallmark Channel, you ought to give it try. It's one of the rare programs these days that promote wholesome values and faith. It doesn't just portray people who attend church or acknowledge God, but whose faith actually affects the way they live and how they deal with the challenges they face in life. In this recent episode, a certain saying was quoted at least twice—"Bad things happen if good people do nothing." Much like weeds take over if we don't take steps to stop them, bad things will crop up if we don't stand against them.

We often think of this concept in relation to what is taking place in our nation or our communities, and rightly so. If good people just stand by and do nothing in the face of injustice and other social vices, evil will take over. However, let's not overlook the fact that this principle also holds true in our own personal lives. If we aren't paying attention to or dealing with the little intruders into our hearts and minds which tend to keep us from a close relationship with the Lord, those things will tend to grow, become more prominent, and eventually choke out the godly aspects of our lives.

The Bible says, "For if you live according to the flesh you will die; but if by the Spirit you put to death the deeds of the body, you will live" (Romans 8:13). This verse indicates that we have an important role to play in keeping our lives free of those things which would drag us down spiritually and interfere with our walk with God. There is a cooperative aspect to it. It is "by the Spirit"—we need His guidance and only He can cleanse us. However, we need to be actively involved in standing against those hostile intruders. By the Spirit we need to recognize those "weeds" in our lives as harmful invaders and we need to be willing to have them expelled. We don't allow them to coexist with the godly, fruitful, flowering parts of our lives, because they will eventually negatively affect them. We have to pull them out of the soil of our lives, pulling them up by the roots, and put them to death.

Weeding is an ongoing process—it's a constant battle. We may have pulled some weeds a while back, but if we aren't continually cultivating a close relationship with God, they will tend to return. Have we allowed some of those weeds to come in? Doing nothing about them isn't a viable option. If left to themselves, they will eventually take over. Let's acknowledge them for what they are and seek God's help in getting them out of our lives.

What "weeds" have cropped up in your life lately? What are you going to do about them?

GET ON THE TEAM WITH
THE UNDEFEATED ONE

"If God is for us, who can be against us?"
– ROMANS 8:31

I remember when one of the big sports stories was from the women's college basketball tournament. A team which had won 111 straight games finally lost. We all knew they were going to have to lose a game at some point. No one remains perpetually undefeated. Or do they?

Has God ever been defeated? If so, I'd like to know who managed to accomplish it. We human beings may deprive ourselves of experiencing all the good things God wants to do in our lives, but His ultimate plans and purposes continue to move forward, with or without us.

Has Christ been defeated? The devil certainly tried to do so. He attempted to have Jesus killed at birth. He enticed Jesus with various temptations to try to sway Him from His mission. Satan stirred up violent opposition to Jesus, trying to bring about His death prematurely. I wonder if the devil thought He had finally ended Christ's long undefeated streak when He was nailed to the cross. Maybe immediately following that event Satan was celebrating, cutting down the net, boasting of his victory. Yet a short time later he came to realize that what he thought was Christ's defeat was actually His greatest triumph of all. Satan thought the final buzzer had sounded. But it hadn't. There was one last shot—and Christ nailed it with a slam dunk in an empty tomb.

If God and Christ are undefeated, then we should pay even more attention to a couple of verses from scripture. Romans 8:31 asks, "If God is for us, who can be against us?" In another passage it declares, "I can do all things through Christ who strengthens me" (Philippians 4:13). If the undefeatable God is for you, what does it matter who's against you? If the ever-victorious Christ is strengthening you, what is it that you can't do?

This concept takes me back to my days in junior high school taking PE classes. We had a coach who occasionally would join one of our teams as we played some sport. This guy wasn't very tall, but he was muscular and solid as a rock. If you got him on your team no matter what you were playing, you had it made. If the coach was on your team, who could defeat you? Nobody.

Similarly, if God is on your team, you're not going to be defeated no matter who or what comes against you. Disease may rob you of physical strength and ability. The boss may take away your job. The economy may force you to have to sacrifice and do without certain things. Death may take away someone close to you and will eventually put your own body in the grave. The devil may throw all kinds of tests and temptations your way. But if God is for you, you're going to come through it all triumphantly. Those things that are against you can certainly impact your life, but they can't defeat you unless you let them.

"If God is for us"—that's an important "if." However, it's not about us trying to persuade God to come and be on our team. It's about us making sure we are on His team. We need to make sure we're walking with Him, seeking His will, and doing what He wants us to do. If we're trusting Jesus and are in line with His will and way, we can be assured of ultimate victory.

None of us are undefeated. But we can get on board with Someone who is. And that will make all the difference.

Are you on God's team? In what area do you need to rely on the fact that God is with you and His purposes cannot be defeated?

APRIL 3

Heaven Will Feel Like Home

"These...confessed that they were strangers and pilgrims on the earth. For those who say such things declare plainly that they seek a homeland."

– Hebrews 11:13–14

I was riding along with a husband and wife from my church to a small town in east Tennessee for the burial of the man's mother. As we drove into the area, the man commented that whenever he arrived at this place, he always felt as if he were coming home. Strangely enough, he has never lived in that town. He has spent plenty of time visiting there, since it was his father's hometown and relatives resided there. But with its strong family connection, it seems more like home to him than other places where he has lived for a long time.

Many of us have certain places in our lives which provide us with a similar sensation. It may be where we grew up as a child, or where we raised our families, or where we are presently living. It's a locale with which we possess some kind of meaningful connection. We feel like we belong there. It feels like home.

For those who know Christ as their Savior, we have such a place to look forward to. We've never lived there before. As a matter of fact, we've never visited the place or even seen pictures of it. Oh, we may have seen some depictions of what an artist or filmmaker might imagine it to be like, but none of those do justice to the reality of the glory of heaven. We do have some descriptions from the Bible of that place, but they are filled with such symbolic images and describe something so beyond our limited minds that we're still left with a rather cryptic picture.

Yet when we arrive at that future destination, it will feel like home. Why? Because we have such a strong connection to it. Jesus will be there. Family, friends, and others who trusted Christ as their Savior will be our fellow residents. It will be a place that Jesus has been preparing just for us. It may not be exactly what we imagined beforehand, but it will be even better.

The Bible compares us to some of the Old Testament patriarchs who were looking for God to fulfill His promises to them of a homeland. It says they "confessed that they were strangers and pilgrims on the earth" and "now they desire a better, that is, a heavenly country" (Hebrews 11:13–16).

This scripture reminds us about the other side of this truth. The more heaven feels like home to us, the less this world seems to fit that description. I don't know about you, but this world seems less and less like home to me these days. Some of it comes from getting older. As our bodies wear down and as our friends die, this world seems less attractive to us.

However, it goes beyond just the factors accompanying aging. I feel less and less at home in a world whose values are veering farther and farther away from God's Word. I find myself at odds with so many popular views, political opinions, and lifestyle practices of my contemporaries. I feel less at home in a place where terrorism is on the rise, oftentimes in connection with a growing opposition to Christianity.

There are aspects of this life I still enjoy and treasure—my family, my wife's lasagna, grandchildren, Dairy Queen ice cream, my church family, old movies, and much more. But there are many reminders around that we are "strangers and pilgrims on this earth." Let's look forward to the time when we'll arrive in a new and glorious place. And when we get there, we'll experience that special sensation of knowing we're home.

Where is it that feels like home to you? How can you cultivate that same sensation concerning heaven?

Let the Holy Spirit Flow through Your Life

"He who believes in Me, as the Scripture has said, out of his heart will flow rivers of living water."

– John 7:38

One time, my wife and I were enjoying a couple of days at a state park in Tennessee as participants in a retreat sponsored by our church association. One of the attractions of this particular park is the three notable waterfalls within its boundaries. Having visited this location before, I was looking forward to gazing once again upon those beautiful wonders of nature.

However when we arrived at the most well-known of those waterfalls, the one the park itself was named after, I was a little disappointed. It was still a spectacular view, but there was less water cascading down its precipice than I had witnessed previously. I was later told that the flow had been diminished due to a dam upstream where the capacity was being regulated. So even though this landmark is billed as one of the highest waterfalls in the eastern United States, it wasn't as awe-inspiring to me as I had remembered.

I actually was more impressed on this occasion by the other less-noteworthy falls in the park which we subsequently visited. They weren't as tall or famous as the main one, but they had a much greater stream of water flowing over them, providing a more spectacular sight and sound.

This incident reminds me of what Jesus said about His followers. He declared, "He who believes in Me, as the Scripture has said, out of his heart will flow rivers of living water" (John 7:38). John's Gospel goes on to explain that Jesus was making reference to the Holy Spirit which would be poured out on His disciples after His resurrection and ascension.

It's not always the believers who receive more notoriety or are given greater prominence who are the most effective, inspiring, or influential. It's not always those who seem to stand the tallest in many people's estimation who are actually receiving and overflowing with the greatest degree of the presence and power of God. Sometimes it's the "lesser" among us in man's view who are experiencing more of the inflow of God's Spirit into their hearts, as well as impacting others as the Spirit pours out of them those rivers of living water.

None of us should want to be a tall waterfall with a great reputation who just has a small measure of God's Spirit trickling through our heart and life. Regardless of how big or small we might be in the eyes of others, let's seek to be those who are filled to overflowing with the refreshing waters of the Holy Spirit.

And the good news is that any of us can experience what Jesus was talking about. If we've put our trust in Jesus as our Savior, we have His Spirit living within us. The more we surrender ourselves to Him, the more He can fill us with His power, purity, and love. And the greater that divine presence grows in our hearts, the more it can overflow to positively impact the lives of those around us. The Bible assures those who hunger and thirst after righteousness that they will be filled. So let's thirst for more of the living water in our lives. Let's open every corner of our hearts to the lordship of Jesus, allowing Him to have complete control. And let's pray for His Holy Spirit to fill us to capacity and to flow through us to touch the lives of others.

Don't settle for being a channel containing only a trickle of living water. Keep seeking, praying, and yielding to God until you experience rivers of the Holy Spirit gushing forth from your life.

Lord, fill me to overflowing with your Spirit today!

THE CROSS: REPULSIVE OR BEAUTIFUL?

"For the message of the cross is foolishness to those who are perishing, but to us who are being saved it is the power of God."

– I CORINTHIANS 1:18

"That's a stanky tree!" Such was the loud declaration of our two-year-old grandson in his already-thick Southern accent. He was referring to a Bradford pear tree situated near where he was playing at the time. If you've only admired those particular plants from a distance, you might not know what our grandson was referring to. When those pear trees put forth their beautiful white blossoms in the early spring, they also emit a rather unattractive, pungent odor for a brief time. To put it bluntly—they stink.

When our grandchildren had first noticed this unpleasantness in the air, we had quietly pointed out the source. And a week later our grandson had not forgotten it. Whenever he got near that tree, he would repeatedly trumpet his announcement about that "stanky" tree for all the world to hear. Although his characterization of the tree was rather humorous, I hoped we hadn't inadvertently caused him to see just the negative aspect of Bradford pears. I would hope he could still appreciate the beauty of the blossoms and not just focus on the unpleasant odor.

Especially around Good Friday, but other times as well, our attention focuses on a very different kind of tree—the cross on which Christ died. This wooden structure also comes with a mixed bag of qualities. There are some people who find it repulsive because of the smell of death surrounding it. It wreaks of suffering, torture, pain, injustice, and bloodshed. How can people who claim to be compassionate and religious look favorably toward an instrument of execution? How can they treasure the horrible stench of someone agonizingly dying on a cross? How can they sing songs which express gratitude for the blood of Christ?

Others of us might recognize the purpose of Jesus' suffering and death, but still have to admit to a certain degree of unpleasantness associated with the cross. It reminds us that we are sinners. It reveals the seriousness of our sin. It reflects the wrath of a holy God. And it shows us just how awful our sin must be if it resulted in such a high price having to be paid by Jesus. There is a foul odor emanating from the cross—the awful, combined smell of sin, suffering, shame, and death.

However as believers in Christ, we also recognize the beauty of the cross. We see in it the blossoms of hope and redemption. We see the beauty of God's love in sending His Son to be our Savior. We recognize the wonder of Christ's love in His willingness to suffer and die in our place. We smell the fragrant scent of forgiveness, grace, cleansing, and eternal life bursting forth from the awful scene of crucifixion. We don't just see a horrible execution. We see a glorious, loving act of self-sacrifice. We don't just see the goriness of the blood. We see the power of that blood to wash away our sins.

The cross has always had this dual effect. The Apostle Paul wrote, "For the message of the cross is foolishness to those who are perishing, but to us who are being saved it is the power of God" (I Corinthians 1:18). To some the cross appears to be foolish or even repulsive. To others it displays the wisdom, love, and power of God. For believers, the beauty of the blossoms on the cross overcome the stench of suffering and sin.

Don't make the mistake of viewing the cross only as a "stanky tree." What stinks is our sin—our sin which made the cross necessary. Put your faith in Jesus and experience the beauty of that cross—the beauty of love, forgiveness, and salvation.

Be thankful for the beautiful aspects of the cross.

MAKE THE MOST OF YOUR
NEW LIFE IN CHRIST

"I will give you a new heart and put a new spirit within you."
— EZEKIEL 36:26

M aybe you heard about the young man who died in a car crash as
he was fleeing from the police. A short time before this violent
conclusion, he had reportedly attempted an armed robbery and carjacked
a vehicle. His life ended when he lost control of the car, smashing it into
the signpost of a bank.

Afterwards it came to light that the young man had received a heart
transplant two years ago. Early reports indicated that at first the hospital denied his application for this procedure due to his juvenile criminal
record and their concerns that he would not adequately follow the suggested guidelines for taking care of this valuable gift if it was offered to
him. But reportedly after being pressured to do otherwise, the hospital
consented to the transplant. The recipient assured everyone that he would
straighten out his life and make good use of this second chance he was
being given. Tragically, it doesn't appear as if he followed through on
those original good intentions.

Likewise some of us have been given an invaluable gift. We often even
refer to it in terms of a new heart. We don't actually receive a different
blood-pumping physical organ. However, we do experience a dramatic
change within us. Jesus talked about it as being a new birth. The Apostle

Paul declared, "If anyone is in Christ, he is a new creation" (II Corinthians 5:17).

What a wonderful opportunity it is when we receive Christ as our Savior. In spite of all the bad things we've done in the past, we've been given another chance. We have our sins forgiven, our hearts cleansed, and the Holy Spirit living within us to help us live for the Lord. So are we making good use of this precious gift? Let's not waste this opportunity.

Too many people start out on this road with every intention of being a faithful follower of Jesus, only to falter and fall back into the old way of life. Their initial intense love for Christ is allowed to grow cold. The attractive lures of the world pull them away from living in obedience to the Lord. They go back to doing what they want instead of what God wants. And sometimes they keep straying until they're driving out of control and heading toward a dangerous crash.

Consider the biblical example of King Saul. When God's prophet anointed Saul to be king, it was said that "God gave him another heart" (I Samuel 10:9) and the Spirit of God came upon him. However, it wasn't long until Saul started traveling down a habitual pathway of disobedience to God. Eventually he reached the awful point where God rejected him as king and the Spirit of the Lord departed from him (I Samuel 16:14).

There was so much potential in Saul and in what God could do through him as king of Israel. But he gave in to selfishness, jealousy, and pride, allowing himself to be overcome by a violent and unstable spirit. His life got out of control and he crashed, dying as a tragic figure to be pitied.

Don't let that happen to you. If you're a believer in Christ, you have been given another chance and a great opportunity. Although we all will stumble at times, as we humbly confess and repent God will pick us up and help us get back on track. It's when we keep insisting on going our own way that we dig ourselves a hole that's hard to get out of.

As a believer, you have great potential to live for Christ and to serve Him. Don't squander this new heart and new life Jesus has given to you.

Lord, help me make the most of the new life I have in You.

Deal with Whatever Is Holding You Back Spiritually

"Let us lay aside every weight, and the sin which so easily ensnares us."

– Hebrews 12:1

One day I pulled out my chainsaw to tackle the long-overdue task of cutting up some fallen and leaning trees in my yard. For a long time I wouldn't use one of those powerful instruments at all, mainly due to the tales my wife told me about chainsaw-related injuries she had dealt with back when she was an ER nurse. So although I now use that tool occasionally, I do so with great respect and caution.

On this occasion, the job went well for a while. But as I tried to tackle one last tree, I wasn't quite careful enough and wise enough in how I was cutting. I managed to get the blade bound in the tree and had a hard time getting it free. In the process, my chain quit turning and the saw began to smoke. I was afraid I was burning up the motor or the clutch.

Later I discovered the problem: the brake had come on. I don't know if it automatically engaged when the saw got stuck or if I may have grabbed the brake lever in my attempts to pull the tool free. At any rate the smoke was coming from the fact that I was giving it gas at the same time the brake was trying to keep the chain from turning.

It's kind of like stepping on the accelerator of the car while firmly holding the brake pedal down. The engine might rev up loudly, but the vehicle is being held back from going anywhere.

Let's make sure we're not doing something similar in our relationship with the Lord. Maybe we're revving up our spiritual engine, but it doesn't seem like we're making any progress. We're going to church more often, reading our Bibles regularly, praying, and generally taking the steps which normally lead to moving forward in our walk with God.

That's good, but let's make sure that we aren't guilty of applying our brakes at the same time. Willful disobedience to God can hold us back from making progress in our spiritual journey. No matter how much we stomp on the accelerator through participating in public worship, attending Bible studies, or even fasting a meal or two in order to spend time in prayer, known sin in our lives will hinder us from making the headway we desire. Therefore, it needs to be dealt with. Stepping even harder on the gas isn't going to help. We have to get before God with a repentant heart and receive His forgiveness and cleansing concerning that issue. Until we do, it's going to hold us back or significantly slow us down.

In one place the Bible compares it to weights hindering a runner. It instructs us to "lay aside every weight, and the sin which so easily ensnares us, and let us run with endurance the race that is set before us" (Hebrews 12:1). In another verse it says the specific sin of pride causes God to resist us—in other words, it puts on the brakes in our relationship with Him.

What's holding you back from being all God wants you to be? Is your spiritual life smoking with frustration because you're trying to pursue God while at the same time hanging on to something you know He isn't pleased with? You're going to have to look to the Lord to help you lay aside that weight if you want to get back on track.

It's time to take off the brake, start moving forward, and become a more effective and powerful tool in the hands of the Master.

Does it seem like you're spinning your wheels spiritually? Ask God to help you identify the source of the problem. Then with His guidance and enablement, lay it aside.

Don't Die or You Might Get Arrested

"Jesus Christ, who has abolished death and brought life and immortality to light through the gospel."

– II Timothy 1:10

Did you hear about the action taken by the mayor of a small village in southern Italy? He made it illegal for anyone within his jurisdiction to die. That's right. So if you live in Falciano del Massico and proceed to die there, you're guilty of breaking the law.

Apparently this strange decree came about due to the village not having a cemetery in which to bury its dead. And it was involved in some kind of dispute with the nearby town which does have a burial ground—the one they had previously been allowed to use. So the mayor, only half-seriously from what I understand, issued this ordinance forbidding the residents of his village from dying.

I wonder what the penalty would be for breaking that law. You couldn't exactly sentence the person to death. We all know that this is a ridiculous law because death is inevitable. No matter how much someone may not want to die and may attempt to avoid it, there comes a time when there's nothing anyone can do about it. As a matter of fact, shortly after making this declaration, the mayor of this village admitted that a couple of his elderly residents had already disobeyed his decree.

The Bible tells us that Jesus "has abolished death and brought life and immortality to light through the gospel" (II Timothy 1:10). He accomplished this through His coming into this world, living a sinless life, going to the Cross as the sacrifice for our sins, and being resurrected as our living Lord.

This doesn't mean that Jesus outlawed death like that mayor in Italy did. He did far more than pass a law that no one could keep. Neither does it mean that after Jesus' resurrection no one ever died again. To this day we are still making visits to the funeral homes as friends and loved ones continue to face the inevitable end of life.

So what did Jesus do? For one thing, He showed definitively that there is life beyond the grave. These bodies may perish but our souls or spirits continue to live. Jesus revealed that death is not the end of the road for anyone, but simply the passageway into a different state of existence. He also gave us the assurance of a resurrection one day similar to His own, when our bodies will be raised and transformed into something new, better, and fit for eternity.

But most of all, Jesus conquered death. After the nails were driven into His hands and feet at His crucifixion, Jesus arose to drive the nails into death's coffin. Although that longstanding enemy is still presently exercising its power over humanity, because of Jesus it is certain that one day death will be no more. One of the great promises of scripture is of a time when "there shall be no more death, nor sorrow, nor crying" (Revelation 21:4).

Additionally, those who are trusting Jesus as their Savior can be secure in the knowledge that they will not have to experience what the Bible refers to as "the second death"—facing separation from God for eternity in the lake of fire. Interestingly enough, death itself, along with hell and the devil, will be cast into that awful place (Revelation 20:10, 14).

Mayors, presidents, and kings can pass all the laws they want against death, but it won't change a thing. However through His resurrection, Jesus has changed everything. He has sealed death's fate and has assured His faithful followers of a glorious life in heaven with Him for eternity.

Give thanks today for Jesus' victory over death and the assurance of your own resurrection.

OTHER PEOPLE CAN HELP
KEEP YOUR LIGHT SHINING

*"Open rebuke is better than love carefully concealed. Faithful are
the wounds of a friend."*

– PROVERBS 27:5–6

I recently had to change a couple of lightbulbs on my car. One was for
the headlight. I had discovered that deficiency myself when I started
up my car one morning and noticed the lack of brightness being reflected
off the garage wall. I got out to check and, sure enough, one of the bulbs
was burned out.

However, the other problem had gone undetected by me. It was one of
the brake lights on the rear of my car. Because of its location, I obviously
would have a harder time seeing that malfunction—especially if I have to
be inside the vehicle stepping on the brake pedal for it to manifest itself.
But fortunately someone else noticed it and informed me of the situation.

How do we know when there's a problem with our relationship with
the Lord? Sometimes there are indicators that we should be able to recognize ourselves if we're paying attention. When we observe that we
are reflecting less of Christ's character and more of the darkness of this
world, we may need to do some soul-searching. When spiritual vitality
and strength seem to be lacking, we ought to check our connection to the
Source of power. When we see little evidence that we're being the light of
the world that Jesus calls us to be, we should stop and ask why.

But other times the problem may be difficult for us to see. It may take someone else to bring those issues to our attention. Thankfully the Holy Spirit is always faithful to convict us of sin and to reveal any areas of our lives in which we're lacking. But in addition to His guidance, we sometimes need to listen to the people around us. They may notice deficiencies that we can't see.

When someone close to you starts asking about what's bothering you or expresses concerns about a change in your demeanor or behavior, it should raise some red flags. Maybe they're totally misreading you, but could it be that they're seeing something that you've failed to realize or something you're refusing to admit?

None of us need a bunch of self-appointed critics looking over our shoulders, passing harsh judgment on our every deed. But the Bible makes it clear that we can benefit from the caring observations of others. Correction and rebuke can be a sign of love, while ignoring someone's faulty ways can do them great harm. I didn't get upset when someone told me that my brake light was out. I was thankful to find out about it so that I could correct the problem before it resulted in an accident. Similarly we need some people close to us who will hold us accountable. It's an asset to have those around us who care enough to point out a problem in our lives when they see it.

Once I knew about the issue with my car, I didn't wait long to get those bulbs replaced. Not only did I not want to get a ticket, but I also wanted to get the car working properly again for the safety of myself and others.

When we realize that something isn't right in our relationship with the Lord, let's not put off dealing with it. It's not simply a matter of getting it taken care of before we die and face God. We need to resolve it immediately so that we can function to our fullest potential now in the way God intended. We were meant to be lights in this dark world. For our sake and for the sake of others, let's get rid of anything that would hinder us from shining brightly.

Do you take it to heart and seriously consider what they're saying when friends, family, or fellow believers point out areas of concern in your life?

APRIL 10

LET'S SERVE GOD WITH THE SAME ZEAL WE DO OTHER THINGS

"Be...fervent in spirit, serving the Lord."
– ROMANS 12:11

I remember one Sunday following the morning worship service I was talking with some of the parishioners when my four-year-old grandson went zooming past like a rocket. In spite of his having been told not to run in church, a few minutes later he came flying by again. I suppose he was letting out energy after having been cooped up in the nursery for an hour. As several of us commented about our desire to have such vigor, my mind went back to the previous day.

That same grandson was playing soccer for the first time that spring. Although his team was doing quite well, Joshua hadn't fully gotten into the game yet. He was improving, getting in a few kicks during the last contest. He ran around and followed the action for the most part, but he didn't move very fast. He seemed to shuffle around on the field, especially compared to the way he was zipping through the church building after our service. I thought that maybe the next time he was out on the soccer field I should have hollered out, *Joshua, run like you were in church!*

I wonder if God sometimes views our actions similarly, albeit in the opposite direction. He sees how much zeal we express as we cheer for our favorite basketball team in the Final Four or as we urge the Braves to have a banner year. But then we get to church and are afraid to say "Amen" or to sing loudly enough to be heard. Maybe God wants to holler out at us, "Be enthusiastic, as if you were at a ballgame!"

If we would listen, maybe we would hear several such admonitions from the Lord. "Exercise your soul to health and godliness, like you regularly exercise your body." "Give time and energy to serve Me in some way, like you do when involved in your hobby!" "Be as quick and consistent to talk to Me as you are in calling up your best friend." Or "make sure to read My Word each day as faithfully as you watch your favorite TV show."

The prophet Haggai had a similar word from the Lord for the people of Israel. After they returned from their captivity in Babylon, the temple lay in ruins. Original intentions to rebuild it had been forsaken and neglected for various reasons over time. In the meantime the people were busy rebuilding their own homes, sometimes extravagantly. Finally God spoke through Haggai about the need to get back to the important project of reconstructing the temple. He said, more or less, "Rebuild My house, like you were rebuilding your houses! Use that same time, energy, and resources to do My work!" Fortunately the people listened and renewed their work on God's house.

Is God trying to get across a similar message to us today? If so, we should realize that it goes deeper than our actions. Our actions reflect what's in our hearts. It's about what we consider important, what we desire, and whom we love. What's more important to us—the winning of a ballgame or the winning of souls into the kingdom of God? What do we want more—to try to know as much as we can about our favorite celebrity or to try to know all we can about God and His will for us? And whom do we love most? Do we love the Lord with all our heart and soul?

When it comes to our relationship with God, let's love Him like we love our spouse. Let's worship Him with more zeal than we have for anything else in this world. Let's serve Him with the best of our time and energy, not with our leftovers.

As we walk with God, let's run as if we were an energetic little boy in church.

Lord, renew my passion for You and my zeal in serving You.

Meet the Challenges That Come with Spiritual Growth

"Every branch that bears fruit He prunes, that it may bear more fruit."

– John 15:2

I had avoided it as long as I could. I finally had to fire up the lawn mower and reacquaint myself with the task of cutting my yard. It's not that I dislike the work—I actually enjoy being outside and getting some needed exercise, except during the hottest part of the summer. What I don't care for are the effects from my allergies that can make me rather miserable not only for that day but also for several days after mowing.

So I appreciate the break from this job that the winter months provide. But I also know that when spring comes around, I don't want the vegetation in my yard to remain dormant and dead. You'll notice that for the sake of truthfulness, I'm careful about the terminology I use to describe what is in my yard. It consists of far more weeds than it does grass. But I still prefer, for the sake of a better appearance, for whatever is out there to be green and growing during this season of the year.

I'll admit that I don't do much to encourage the growth of the greenery in my yard. With adequate rain and warmer temperatures, it just happens—at least for the weeds. But the growth does need to be managed. And that's where my work comes in.

Similarly we don't want to hinder spiritual growth in ourselves or in others. There are things we can do to cultivate such growth, but ultimately it springs from a close, vital relationship with Christ. If our hearts are warm with love for Him, and if our souls are being fed by His Word and refreshed by a constant flow of the living water of the Holy Spirit, growth will happen.

We don't want to be dormant and dead spiritually, but at the same time we need to be prepared for the fact that growth presents some challenges. It will require some tending on our part and on God's part to keep us from being overrun by some common problems.

Paul dealt with growing Christians in growing churches in some of his letters. And at times he had to crank up his mower to help them manage their growth. He had to encourage the Corinthians to cut back on their spiritual pride, where they were getting a little too cocky about how much they were growing. He also had to help them maintain a balance in connection with their spiritual gifts, so that one type of person or ministry didn't flourish to the point of choking out other equally valuable ministries. Paul also had to prune back some wild shoots that were in danger of spreading beyond the boundaries of God's desire for things to be done in orderly and understandable ways that would allow for maximum benefit for all. Additionally, in many of the churches, Paul had to weed out false doctrines and teachers that were popping up and trying to take over.

As we grow in our walk with God, we also need to keep our eye on such matters while listening closely for the guidance of the Holy Spirit. Are we maintaining a humble spirit as we see the great things God is doing in our lives? Are we getting out of balance, going to extremes, focusing on one aspect of our faith while neglecting other areas of equal importance? Are we being careful to know the truth of God's Word ourselves, so that we can check out what others say about it and can recognize false teaching when we encounter it?

Let's be sure to keep growing. But let's also do the weeding and mowing necessary to manage those challenges that can accompany such growth.

Are you experiencing spiritual growth? In what areas does God need to do some pruning so that you can grow even more?

GOD IS WITH YOU
AS YOU LEARN TO FLY

"Be strong and of good courage...the Lord, He is the One who goes before you."

— DEUTERONOMY 31:7–8

I was sitting in my living room when I noticed some unusually frequent and nearby chirping of birds coming from outside the window. Moments later I spotted one of those beautifully brilliant red cardinals perched on the bannister of our front porch. It isn't uncommon to see that species of fowl in our yard, but this one got my attention as it kept turning its head as if it were trying to see something up toward the ceiling of the porch. I slowly and carefully made my way over to the window so as not to spook the bird. When I was able to look up inside the porch, I saw the object of the cardinal's concern. It was a young bird clinging to the small ledge along the inside of the porch. I assumed it must be the offspring of this daddy cardinal, even though it showed no signs of the signature red coloring at its young age. Apparently it had only recently emerged from its nest and was learning to fly under the watchful tutelage of its father (I concluded it was the father because I understand it's the male of this species that sports the brighter red color).

As I continued watching to see how this situation would get resolved, daddy and child often tweeted back and forth—in the original practice by that name, of course, the one not requiring modern electronics. A couple of times the dad actually flew up into the porch skillfully fluttering for a few seconds in an almost stationary position in front of his youngster. I don't know if his purpose was to get a better look at his offspring or to let the young bird see him with the assurance that its father was right there.

Finally the young bird took the brave leap over toward our window. After momentarily clinging to the screen, it took off awkwardly fluttering in a low trajectory across our driveway and into our neighbor's yard with daddy following closely behind.

We're all still learning to fly in life and in our journey with God, aren't we? As we aim for the skies, we may have moments when we soar like an eagle, but too often we still flutter along a little too close to this world. As we do so, sometimes we find ourselves in precarious situations. Maybe from taking some wrong turns or as a result of circumstances beyond our control, we suddenly find ourselves out on a ledge—not sure where to go, what to do, and afraid to move. But if we're children of God through faith in Christ, we have the assurance that we're not alone. Our Heavenly Father is nearby. We can call out to Him and He will answer us. His voice rings out from scripture to assure us of His promises to guide us, strengthen us, and provide what we need to get through this situation. He encourages us to hang in there, to keep trusting Him, and to step out in faith to bravely follow Him. And every so often, just when we need it most, in various ways He rises up to reveal His presence to us, reminding us that we are not forsaken.

If you're perched on one of life's ledges today, take to heart the words spoken to Joshua as he was preparing to leave the nest to take over as the newly appointed leader of Israel: "Be strong and of good courage...the Lord, He is the One who goes before you. He will be with you, He will not leave you or forsake you; do not fear nor be dismayed" (Deuteronomy 31:7-8).

Know that God is near—look to Him for the guidance and help you need today.

BE READY FOR HARD TIMES BEFORE CHRIST RETURNS

"Therefore you also be ready, for the Son of Man is coming at an hour you do not expect."

– MATTHEW 24:44

Do you remember those *Home Alone* movies? The original one has become part of the usual lineup of films aired during the Christmas season. It's about a young boy who mistakenly gets left behind when his family goes away on a trip. And while he is at home by himself, a couple of thieves decide to target his house for a burglary. When this little kid realizes what is about to happen, he makes all kinds of preparations to thwart their efforts. He concocts traps to hinder those burglars from their criminal purposes, such as slippery spots on which they slide and fall down, and heavy items rigged to conk them on the head. He creates all sorts of havoc and pain for these thieves trying to burglarize his home. It was all because he was watching and ready. Those intruders quickly discovered they were messing with the wrong person.

It reminds me of Jesus' admonitions to us in connection with His Second Coming. He instructed His followers, "Watch, therefore, for you do not know what hour your Lord is coming. But know this, that if the master of the house had known what hour the thief would come, he would have watched and not allowed his house to be broken into. Therefore you also be ready, for the Son of Man is coming at an hour you do not expect" (Matthew 24:42–44).

Let's not mistake this idea of watching as simply the passive act of looking out the window ready to run out and welcome Jesus when we see Him coming. Jesus suggested that the homeowner needed to watch in order to be ready to protect his home from an intruder, much like the little kid in *Home Alone*. It's more like the watchfulness of a soldier on guard duty, including a readiness to warn others and to do battle.

Of course, I'm not saying that we need to be prepared to do battle against Jesus. However, we do need to be prepared to do spiritual battle in light of all the hardships and attacks we may have to face leading up to Christ's return. As I read through the book of Revelation again recently, I was struck by its portrayal of God's people having to face some tough times as the return of Christ draws nearer. Followers of Christ will be targeted. The book of Revelation pictures martyrs—those who will be killed because of their faith. It talks about evil forces making war with the people of God and overcoming them. It shows that believers will have final victory—they are shown in glory in heaven later. However here on earth, they are going to be persecuted and killed. I believe we're living in times in which we can very easily see that scenario becoming more and more of a reality, both in other parts of the world and right here in our own nation.

So let's not think of Christ's return solely in terms of being watchful and ready for Jesus to come and whisk us out of this world. In recent years I've come to see less biblical support for the common idea of a rapture of the Church prior to the tribulations of the last days. Instead of expecting to escape those hardships, we may need to make sure we have our spiritual armor on in order to endure those trials we might have to face as believers as the end draws near.

We may need a little of that *Home Alone* attitude, but in our case we know we won't really be alone. The Lord will be with us to help us through and to see us home.

What do you need to do to better prepare yourself for facing hard times as Christ's return approaches?

TAKE THE FIRST STEP OF
RECEIVING GOD'S REVELATION

"Do you not yet perceive nor understand? Is your heart still hardened?"

– MARK: 8:17

As the annual deadline draws near for filing income taxes, let me encourage everyone to make every effort to get your paperwork correct. If the IRS even suspects you of making an error, it can be quite an ordeal trying to get the matter resolved. If you can avoid it, don't mess with the IRS.

My wife and I were embroiled for months in an effort to straighten out a matter that was questioned on one of our previous returns. But the problem we experienced at the beginning wasn't over the issue itself, but simply in trying to get the right department of the IRS to receive and acknowledge our written explanation and supporting documents. We mailed them, faxed them, had an IRS employee fax them—every time with our being instructed to wait a month for it to be processed and then we should hear something back. But in each case, the only thing we heard back is that they didn't have a record of ever having received our communications.

It's frustrating when you keep sending something, using a variety of methods, and the intended recipient still doesn't acknowledge receiving it. How can you take the next step in resolving an issue if you can't even communicate?

I wonder if God gets frustrated over our refusal to receive His attempts at communicating with us. My hours of waiting on the phone and sitting in an IRS office are miniscule compared to the thousands of years God has been trying to get through to mankind.

Think of all the various ways He's tried to get His message to us. He's revealed Himself through nature. Creation itself shouts to mankind that there is an intelligent and powerful God who formed it. Yet man has been guilty not only of not accepting that revelation but also of going so far as to worship the creation rather than its Creator.

Then God has spoken through his prophets and other messengers. Think of the powerful lives, preaching, and even miracles associated with the likes of Moses, Elijah, Isaiah, and others. However many of them found themselves rejected, persecuted, and even killed.

Additionally, He has given us His written Word—an inspired, reliable, authoritative communication from Him. Although the Bible has traditionally been a best-selling book, how many of its copies today lie on shelves untouched most of the time? And many people are willing only to accept the parts of the Bible which they find most palatable and harmonious with their own lifestyles and views.

And ultimately He gave us the living Word, Jesus Himself, who is the supreme revelation of God, what He is like, and what He has to say to mankind. But many refused to accept the testimony of who Jesus was. He ended up being crucified like a criminal.

God has also given us the Holy Spirit to speak to our hearts. He is faithful to show us the truth, yet so many harden their hearts and don't listen to His still, small voice as He convicts of sin and tries to draw us to God.

Sometimes in scripture I can sense the Divine frustration coming through. "Because when I called, you did not answer; when I spoke, you did not hear (Isaiah 65:12). "Do you not yet perceive nor understand? Is your heart still hardened? Having eyes, do you not see? And having ears, do you not hear?" (Mark 8:17–18)

Let's open up our hearts to God's revelation in all the ways He's endeavored to communicate it to us. Because only then can we truly move toward a right relationship with Him.

Be open to what God is trying to tell you.

THE CROWDED WAY IS NOT NECESSARILY THE BEST WAY

"Wide is the gate and broad is the way that leads to destruction, and there are many who go in by it."

– MATTHEW 7:13

Some weekends I make it a point to steer clear of downtown Atlanta. It's whenever I hear that there will be huge crowds in the area due to major sporting events, big conferences, or other special events. It's not that I normally venture into our nearby capital, but I do at least travel that way at times, if nothing else simply to get to the other side of town to visit my parents.

Some people enjoy being part of such big crowds. It's exciting to be where the action is or to witness firsthand popular events which people will be talking about. It's nice to be able to say, "I was there" rather than simply "I watched it on TV." It can be invigorating to sense and to participate in the atmosphere surrounding those activities. It's just not the same when you're sitting by yourself in your own home viewing the festivities.

However as I've gotten older, the prospect of big crowds tends to make an event less attractive to me instead of more inviting. I don't care for all the hassle that can go along with attending those events, such as heavy traffic, expensive or hard-to-find parking, rude people, unpredictable weather, and ear-shattering noise. My idea of a prime seat has transformed from the front row of the arena to my comfortable living room recliner.

Jesus reminded us that in the more important areas of our lives, the way of the crowd is not always the best way. He told His followers, "Enter by the narrow gate, for wide is the gate and broad is the way that leads to destruction, and there are many who go in by it. Because narrow is the gate and difficult is the way which leads to life, and there are few who find it" (Matthew 7:13–14).

So according to Jesus, going along with the crowd is not the most reliable way to find the right pathway toward life—spiritual life, a life lived in right relationship with Him, and eventually life in heaven. Following what's popular is not likely to lead you to that desired destination.

We sometimes talk about a person's willingness to "brave the crowds"—indicating that it takes courage to face the difficulties associated with being among a large group of people. But I would suggest that it often requires more courage to refuse to be part of the crowd. As Jesus indicated, it can be difficult to walk on that less-traveled pathway which leads to life. It's not easy at times to choose the unpopular stance. If you've ever been in a crowd in which most people are moving one direction while you're trying to go the opposite way, you know how hard and even bruising such a course can be. You can expect to receive harsh looks, to be ridiculed, and to get shoved around if you dare to go against the tide of popular thinking.

Other times the difficulty is in the fact that we find ourselves walking that road alone, except of course for the promised presence of the Lord with us. Faithfully standing up for Jesus and for the truth of His Word is increasingly becoming a lonely path for someone to choose to follow in today's world.

Maybe you enjoy crowds. And that's fine when it comes to ballgames, concerts, and other special events. But concerning our walk with the Lord, remember that the practice of following the crowd is liable to lead you astray. Let's keep our eyes on Jesus and make sure we follow Him, no matter how few people accompany us. It may not be the popular pathway, but it's definitely the best one.

Are you willing to go against the crowd in order to stay true to the Lord?

WATCH OUT FOR WHAT IS
BEAUTIFUL BUT HARMFUL

"Charm is deceitful and beauty is passing."
– PROVERBS 31:30

Recently as I've driven around, I've noticed the patches of wisteria dotting the landscape along certain stretches of the road. The presence of that plant is especially evident this time of year due to the seasonal blooming of its colorful clusters of flowers. Those violet hangings often brighten up otherwise drab and plain scenery.

I can imagine my young granddaughter, whose favorite colors are pink and purple, sighting those plants and proclaiming their beauty. She might wish that she had some of those purplish flowers hanging in the trees and bushes around her yard. And that would be understandable, because as a youngster all you see is the attractiveness of such an object.

But what my granddaughter wouldn't realize is how invasive, damaging, and deadly that plant can be as well. It may look pretty in the spring, but if you don't watch it and properly prune it, it can get out of control. And although it may display outward beauty, underneath it might be strangling the life out of other plants and small trees. I understand that its vines can even damage weak fences, shutters, or other objects on which it's allowed to climb.

The Bible warns us against judging strictly by the outward appearance of an object or person (I Samuel 16:7). It reminds us that beauty and charm can be deceitful (Proverbs 31:30). Jesus described the religious leaders of His day as being like "whitewashed tombs which indeed appear beautiful outwardly, but inside are full of dead men's bones and all uncleanness" (Matthew 23:27).

Additionally, outward attractiveness is often a major contributor to a person being tempted to do wrong. In humanity's first sin, one of the factors which persuaded Eve to take the forbidden fruit was that "it was pleasant to the eyes" (Genesis 3:6). Could it be that the fruit just happened to be in Eve's favorite color?

When Achan sinned by taking some of the spoil from the overthrow of Jericho for himself, he confessed to having seen and coveted a "beautiful Babylonian garment" (Joshua 7:21). And when David was tempted to follow a path that led to adultery and murder, it began with the recognition that his neighbor's wife "was very beautiful to behold" (II Samuel 11:2).

Don't get me wrong. Beauty is a wonderful gift which God has given us to enjoy. He has created our world, as well as the universe, with some magnificent displays of masterful artistry. God recognizes and appreciates beauty. And I believe He wants us to do so as well. When God was giving Moses instructions about the priesthood, He told him to make the garments of the high priest "for glory and beauty" (Exodus 28:2). God didn't just want the clothing to fit properly and to be practical, but also to look nice.

The problem isn't beauty itself. It's the fact that we tend to be blinded and persuaded by what's outwardly attractive to us. We focus on the cluster of pretty flowers and don't look deeper to see the strong vine that is doing great damage. We reach out for the beautiful rose and don't realize the danger until we get stuck by its thorny stem.

Let's not allow the outward attractiveness of an object, a person, or an activity blind us to its true nature. Let's not be deceived by something that's beautiful, but which would damage our relationship with God or bring death to our souls.

Wisteria is a beautiful plant, but one that has to be kept under control. Don't let anything beautiful but deadly invade your life, get out of control, and strangle the spiritual life out of you.

Have you been giving in to something attractive yet spiritually harmful?

LET'S BE REFLECTORS OF THE LIGHT OF CHRIST

"For you were once darkness, but now you are light in the Lord. Walk as children of light."

– EPHESIANS 5:8

I remember when many of us were saddened to hear of the death of artist Thomas Kinkade. His inspiring works were popular among the general population of the world and especially in the Christian community. A copy of one of his paintings which was given to me and my wife some years ago adorns a wall in our living room. It's the depiction of a cross situated on a rocky hill with the sun rising in the background as its rays begin to lighten the misty landscape.

Light was the signature component of Mr. Kinkade's art. It wasn't just the light from the sun but the radiance emanating from the windows of cottages, churches, and other quaint structures that he painted which caught our eyes. Some have referred to this artist as a messenger or warrior of light, always reminding us of the hope and warmth of light in the midst of the darkness.

I'll admit that there was a time when I thought the works of Mr. Kinkade were being somewhat overpromoted. Not only did you find them in wall hangings, calendars, and puzzles, but on the faces of cups, coasters, and almost any knickknack imaginable. But from what I understand that abundance of availability wasn't primarily the result of a moneymaking motivation as it was from the desire of the artist to share his pictures with as many people as possible.

Similarly all followers of Christ are called to be bearers of the light. The Bible refers to us as "children of light" (Ephesians 5:8). We are instructed to "walk in the light as He is in the light" (I John 1:7). We are also described as those who should seek to be "without fault in the midst of a crooked and perverse generation, among whom you shine as lights in the world" (Philippians 2:15).

Probably the most familiar reference to this concept comes from Jesus' Sermon on the Mount where he plainly declares to His followers, "You are the light of the world. A city that is set on hill cannot be hidden. Nor do they light a lamp and put it under a basket, but on a lampstand, and it gives light to all who are in the house. Let your light so shine before men, that they may see your good works and glorify your Father in heaven" (Matthew 5:14–16).

It wasn't just Thomas Kinkade's mission to communicate light to this world. It's also the job of all believers. We might not do so through the medium of painting pictures, but we do it in those unique ways in which God has gifted each of us. We bear the light through the lives we lead, the words we say, and the good works we do to help others.

Instead of painting a house or a church with lights in the windows, we can be the ones who are illuminating those places through the power and presence of Christ being reflected in our lives. Rather than depicting a sunrise on canvas, we can be the source of light in the dark shadows of this world. We can be the ones who bring warmth, truth, love, and hope to people and places where those qualities might otherwise be lacking.

The world may have lost one valiant warrior of light when Mr. Kinkade died, but we can all now step up to make sure that we're doing our part to continue that mission. We should want as many people as possible to see the light of Christ while their hearts and lives can still be transformed by its rays. Today let's commit ourselves afresh to being the light of the world.

How can you reflect the light of Christ today?

God Can Do What We Can't Do

"Call to Me, and I will answer you, and show you great and mighty things, which you do not know."

– Jeremiah 33:3

One day I revved up my chainsaw to cut down a few small dead trees in my yard. However, there was one such target that I decided to forego. It was a somewhat bigger pine with a large section already partially snapped and leaning against another tree. And it was looming right over our fence. I debated several options in my mind as to how I might try to get it down without hitting the enclosure, but they all seemed likely to result in the need for fence repairs. So finally I decided to hold off on that particular risky job until I recruited some assistance or felt a little braver.

As it turned out, I waited long enough that I received help from a different source. A storm that hit during the nighttime hours took aim at my dilemma. When I went outside the next morning, not only did I have a yard full of sticks, small limbs, and pinecones to clean up, but I also discovered that my dead tree was down. And the fence was still standing undamaged. Upon closer examination, I saw that the tree had broken into three pieces. Two short sections fell as expected toward the fence, but the longer section somehow inexplicably reversed direction and went away from the fence. It couldn't have been placed on the ground more perfectly. I told several people that God did what I couldn't do. It was a puzzle I couldn't solve, but God knew how to take care of it.

Maybe we have some other situations like that in our lives. We see the problem and the potential danger, but we just don't know how to tackle it. We're afraid that whatever we do might cause things to fall apart and result in us making an even bigger mess of everything. It's an enigma for which we have no promising answers.

But thankfully we know Someone who can guide us and provide us with help. He's the One who spoke through the prophet Jeremiah saying, "Call to Me, and I will answer you, and show you great and mighty things, which you do not know" (Jeremiah 33:3). As we pray and trust in the Lord, He can show us what we need to do or He can bypass us and do what we can't. "Trust in the Lord with all your heart, and lean not on your own understanding; in all your ways acknowledge Him, and He shall direct your paths" (Proverbs 3:5–6).

The Bible is full of examples of how God can do what we can't. When our backs are up against a wall, He can part the waters. When we're marching against an impregnable fortress, He can cause the walls to fall down. When the opposition outnumbers us, He can send them running off in a panic. God can help us today with whatever constitutes our Red Sea, Jericho, or Midianites.

We periodically need such reminders about who God is and what He can do, not just from past episodes in the Bible but also from seeing Him work in our present circumstances. Maybe another strong wind will knock a tree over on that same fence—I don't know. But on this occasion, God used a storm and a fallen tree to remind me that I can trust Him to take care of the difficult situations in my life. I may not always know what to do, but He does. And He is able to do whatever is needed.

What tough situation are you facing? Take it to God in prayer. Look for Him to direct you in what you should do. But also trust Him to do what you can't do about it.

GOD AND PERRY MASON— THEY BOTH ULTIMATELY WIN

"The Lord reigns; let the earth rejoice"
– PSALM 97:1

How many of you remember watching the old *Perry Mason* TV series? I don't know that I was around to view the first airings of those shows, but I certainly saw the reruns when they were shown frequently some years later. For anyone who may not know, Perry Mason was a brilliant defense lawyer who seemed to always successfully defend his client, usually against the charge of murder. No matter how bad the situation looked for that client, you could always be assured that when all was said and done, Perry Mason would win the case.

Or should I say "almost" always? You might imagine how upset some people got on one occasion when this great fictional lawyer actually lost a case. As I recall, this particular show began with a guilty verdict being returned against the defendant he represented. However, the fact that the episode began with that trial's unprecedented conclusion was a clue that it might not end that way. After Perry continued to investigate the murder throughout the appeals process, he was able to clear his client. So although he technically had lost the case, he demonstrated that his client was innocent and he hadn't truly been defeated. He still emerged as the great Perry Mason.

How would you feel if you thought God had been defeated? What if it appeared to you that the all-powerful Creator of the universe, the all-wise

Defender of His people, and the God for whom nothing is impossible had lost a case? It might be rather disturbing news. God, like Perry Mason, simply isn't supposed to lose.

Maybe there are times when that thought has crossed your mind, such as when a particular situation in your life didn't turn out the way you thought it should. Or possibly it was when a prayer seemed to go unanswered. Maybe you saw it as a defeat for God when your candidate, whose stand on the issues seemed to be more in line with what God says, lost an election. Or maybe it was after some cataclysmic event which resulted in many people suffering or in a great loss of life. The headlines scrawled across the page of your mind—"God Suffered a Defeat!"

Whenever those situations arise, we need to remind ourselves that whatever happened didn't occur because God lacked power or ability. It didn't take place due to God not being as great as we thought. It wasn't a case of the devil or some other force getting the best of Him. We may not understand why something happened. We may not see God's plan and purpose. However, we can be sure that God is still the Almighty, that He is yet in control, and that in the end His promises will ring true.

We should also keep in mind that on some occasions when it appeared that God was defeated, He may not have been fighting the battle in the first place. Could it be that we had allowed some sin to enter the picture as a barrier between us and the Lord? We lost not because God wasn't able, but because our hearts weren't in the right condition for Him to represent us and fight for us. While that may not always be the case, we should at least check to see if the fault may lie with us.

So let's be careful about jumping to any conclusions about God having suffered a defeat. We can be assured that He will always come out the victor in the end. Let's just make sure that there's nothing in our lives hindering Him from being on our side in the battle.

In what area of your life do you need to be reminded that God is still victorious and is in control?

Giving Can Be a Test of Our Love

"So let each one give as he purposes in his heart, not grudgingly or of necessity; for God loves a cheerful giver."

– II Corinthians 9:7

One day our youngest grandson burst into our house to excitedly tell us about his preschool Easter egg hunt and party. He had several toylike items in hand to show us, along with one piece of candy he seemed especially glad to have received. It was an Easter version of a popular candy bar. I wanted to affirm his enthusiasm for that treat, so I told him how good it tasted and that it was one of my favorites too.

Immediately my grandson's expression turned more serious as he looked down at that prized treat. Without hesitation he suggested that he could break the candy in half and give me part of it. I quickly declined his offer, assuring him that I would rather he enjoy it all. However, I was touched by how readily he was willing to share something he so prized with his papaw. I don't think he would have so easily made that offer to just anyone. It was an indication of his love for me.

Our willingness to give, to share, and to sacrifice can often reveal the extent of our love and compassion for others. How quickly and readily are we willing to give up something we value for the sake of another person? Many of us would have to confess that too often, even when we were willing to share, we have given grudgingly or with less than stellar motives.

Our attitude in this matter can also expose the extent of our love for

God. Remember Abraham? He had a prize egg in his basket. It was his son, Isaac—the miracle-child God had given him in his old age—the one who was going to fulfill God's promises about blessing Abraham and his descendants. Yet at one point God gave Abraham the strange instructions, "Take now your son, your only son Isaac, whom you love, and go to the land of Moriah, and offer him there as a burnt offering on one of the mountains of which I shall tell you" (Genesis 22:2). God didn't downplay what Isaac meant to Abraham. He even reminded Abraham that this is the son "whom you love." He didn't try to make this seem like an insignificant action. Nevertheless God was basically saying, "Give him up. Give him to Me." Did Abraham love God enough to make such a sacrifice?

Many of us assume how Abraham must have struggled over this matter. However, the scripture doesn't record any hesitation on his part. He didn't wrestle with it for days and weeks. The Bible simply says that the next morning—and it even says "early" the next morning—he got up and prepared to do what God had told him. How could Abraham have responded so readily? It was a sign of both his faith and his love for God. After God stopped him from carrying out this deed, God said the fact that Abraham had not withheld his son from Him was a sign of his attitude and spirit toward God.

What is our attitude and response when God leads us to give, to share, or to sacrifice? What about when it involves things or people whom we so greatly value? Maybe we like to think we love God, but those situations tend to reveal the true nature of our devotion to Him.

God shared His greatest gift with us—His Son. If He so loved us, we should be prepared and willing to offer up ourselves and whatever we prize in life to Him. When God says "Give," let's be ready to do so gladly and with love in our hearts.

What is God asking you to give to Him or to share with someone else? Do so with a heart of love.

APRIL 21

Some Guidance for When We're Feeling Frustrated

"How long, O Lord?... But I have trusted in Your mercy."
— Psalm 13:1, 5

I can remember a few occasions as a kid when I came upon a bug crawling along the ground and decided to play a little game with it. I would place a stick, rock, or other object in its way to block its path. When the bug turned to head another direction or maneuvered around the obstacle, I would pick up the object and put it down in front of the tiny creature again. I might continue to hinder the bug's journey and keep it crawling around in circles until finally finding something else to do for my amusement.

Sometimes we can feel like that little bug. We refer to it as frustration. We're prevented from achieving some goal or desire because something keeps blocking our way. It's keeping us from getting where we want to be or maybe even where we believe God wants to us be. Poor health, our inabilities, financial issues, people, or other factors beyond our control keep popping up and hindering us. Just when we think we've overcome one challenge and are finally headed in the right direction, another stick gets thrown in our path. When that happens, it isn't a very fun game for us, is it? Frustration often results in anger and discouragement.

Does the Bible have anything to say to help us when we're frustrated? God's Word doesn't appear to speak directly about this common problem. However if you read the Psalms, you can hear frustration coming out at times as the Psalmist is pouring out his heart to God. From looking at those various psalms, I gleaned a few truths for us to remember, as well as several actions we can take when we're feeling frustrated.

First, keep in mind that God knows what's going on. The Psalmist would ask, "God, where are You?" But later in faith he would affirm, "Lord, I know You're looking on and see what's happening." Don't fall for the lie that God has forgotten you. He sees your struggles. He hears your prayers. He's there.

Secondly, remember that God is a great God. Those obstacles may look as intimidating to us as a rock might appear to a bug, but no challenge we face is bigger than our God. We may not be able to do anything about those hindrances, but He can.

It's also important to remember that God is holy and just. He's not like a little kid placing obstacles in our way simply to amuse Himself or to try to make it tough on us. There's a reason for it being there. It may be to take us in a different and better direction, or it may be strengthening us to face another difficulty further down the road. Often we may not know the reason, but we can be sure God's actions are based on His love and righteousness. God isn't intentionally seeking to frustrate us.

As far as actions to take—first, let's commit our ways to the Lord. Commit that road you're traveling on to Him. Make sure it's the path God wants you on. If it is, depend on the Lord to get you to your destination.

Trust the Lord. Trust Him to take care of this matter in His time and in His way. Don't just keep banging your head against a wall that's not going anywhere. Watch, wait, and look for God's direction and help.

Finally, hope in the Lord. Believe that sooner or later God's going to deliver you, open the door, or show you a different road to take.

Don't let frustration overcome you. Let your faith overcome your frustration.

What's frustrating you? What truth about God do you need to remember? What action listed above do you need to take?

God Doesn't Protect Us from All Our Bad Choices

*"I call heaven and earth as witnesses today against you, that I have
set before you life and death, blessing and cursing; therefore choose
life, that both you and your descendants may live."*

– Deuteronomy 30:19

In a comic strip, an elderly man returns home from shopping with an injured foot. He explains to his wife that he was in the parking lot of the grocery store when he gave in to a sudden urge to step up on the back of the shopping cart to ride it down a small slope, as some of us may have done in our younger days. His wife responds with a sentiment sometimes offered to provide comfort and hope in the face of an unexplainable misfortune: "Well, everything happens for a reason." However this wise woman then adds, "Sometimes the reason is you're a numbskull."

This humorous account should remind us of an important truth. While we acknowledge the existence and intervention of a gracious God in our world, we should also keep in mind that He has given us the power of choice. God is sovereign. He is ultimately in control over what takes place in the universe, in the world, and in our own lives. He is working out His will and purposes, and no one is able to keep His plans from being fulfilled. However, God has created us with a free will that allows us to make choices which can greatly affect our lives and futures. Sometimes adverse events occur in our lives not necessarily because they were part of some grand, unalterable divine plan, but simply because we were guilty of making a foolish decision.

I usually pay attention to the messages on church signs as I'm driving past them. Sometimes they inform me as to what events are taking place in other churches. Other times those messages remind me of some truth, inspiring me or challenging me. Occasionally what's communicated on those signs confuses me or raises questions in my mind as to their validity. I saw one such message which declared that God will wreck our plans when He sees that our plans are about to wreck us.

Certainly there's a degree of truth in that statement. No doubt there have been occasions in all of our lives when God in His mercy has spared us from going down a road that would have led to great harm to ourselves or to others. We may have looked back later and thanked God that He wrecked those particular plans. And there are probably numerous other such instances of which we're not even aware when God graciously kept us from making a mess of things.

However, we need to be careful about presuming upon God's mercy. Whether it was intended this way or not, this particular message makes it sound as if we can count on God to keep us from making the bad choices that would get us into trouble. I don't believe we have any guarantee that God will always intervene to spare us from the consequences of our foolish decisions and actions.

If you decide to hop on the back of a shopping cart, to drive while intoxicated, to pursue an adulterous affair, or to act immorally, God may not stop you. He may allow you to have what you want, along with its results. Thankfully for those who love God, He can take even our wrecks in life and work them together for good (Romans 8:28). But that doesn't mean He's automatically going to spare us from experiencing those wrecks if we're choosing to go there. If we're determined to act like a numbskull, He may let us.

Yes, God is merciful and He can protect us as He often does, but He also gives us the power to choose. So let's be sure we choose wisely.

Remember that your choices have consequences. So make wise choices today.

TRUST JESUS TO HELP
YOU FACE THE FIGHT

"Yes, and all who desire to live godly in Christ Jesus will suffer persecution."

– II TIMOTHY 3:12

I have a penchant for old books. Occasionally I'll visit the used-book sale at our local library and pick up such antiquated copies of some of the classics. I've been reading one such volume recently, Stephen Crane's *The Red Badge of Courage*. While some of these works of literature have been on my "always-heard-about-but-never-read" list, this one had been part of my assigned reading way back in high school. It was one of those I read hurriedly at the time simply to complete the assignment. But now I can take my time, read it for my own pleasure, and better appreciate its meaning.

One of the main issues in the book is the main character's worries about how he, as a new young soldier, is going to handle fighting a battle when he finds himself in that situation. Will he fight bravely and with honor, or will he run away in fear or otherwise act in some kind of shameful manner?

Maybe we have similar curiosity about how we would handle certain battles in life. We witness acquaintances who are being forced to deal with the diagnosis of a serious disease, along with its tough treatments. We wonder if we would have the courage to valiantly fight such a foe or give up in despair. Would we lean more heavily upon God at those moments, or would we turn our backs on Him in anger and doubt?

We see others who have to face unbearable loss as they grieve over the deaths of loved ones. How would we handle it if it was our child who died in that crash? How would we deal with undergoing persecution that some believers face in other parts of the world? Would we stand firm in our faith, or would we deny Christ in some way? Or what if a certain temptation came my way—could I find the strength to say no to it?

The bottom line is that in many cases we don't know how we will react to a given situation until we actually encounter it. We hope that we will face it honorably and in a way that will glorify God, but at the same time we are all too familiar with our weaknesses, fears, and sinful tendencies.

But I'm even more concerned about those folks who believe if they're godly people, their faith somehow keeps them from having to experience any of those hard battles in life. In their theology, they equate godliness with smooth sailing. Or in their eschatology, they see themselves as escaping this world before having to face any serious persecution or tribulation. If you don't think you're going to have to fight the battle, when it comes you can find yourself woefully unprepared.

The Bible declares that "all who desire to live godly in Christ Jesus will suffer persecution" (II Timothy 3:12). And Jesus told His followers, "In the world you will have tribulation; but be of good cheer, I have overcome the world" (John 16:33).

We are going to have to fight some battles in this life. Some of them will greatly test us, but Christ has overcome all those enemies, including disease, persecution, and death. And we simply need to trust Him to give us the grace, wisdom, strength, and courage we need to stand against those foes when they do rise up against us.

We can experience peace of mind knowing that one way or another, there is victory in Jesus.

Know that you'll face some battles today. Trust the Lord to help you overcome.

APRIL 24

LET GOD BE THE
UMPIRE OF OUR LIVES

"In those days there was no king in Israel; everyone did what was right in his own eyes."

– JUDGES 21:25

I remember enjoying watching Little League baseball games one spring as two of my grandsons participated in that pastime. However one game wasn't as pleasant, primarily due to the actions of the officiating umpire. No, I'm not complaining about the way he called balls or strikes, or about his ruling a player out on the base path when he looked to be safe. What I'm referring to goes much deeper than making erroneous judgment calls.

This particular umpire was a young man who seemed unwilling to accept his role as the one who was arbiter of the rules of the game. He failed to make firm decisions and seemed to be unduly swayed by the opinions of those around him. He quickly lost control, allowing coaches and fans to dictate to him his rulings on the field. It seemed that he simply tried to appease whoever complained the most or the loudest. Either he didn't know the rules very well or he was afraid to take a firm stand concerning what those rules stated.

The result of his actions was chaos. It was a game full of uncertainty and confusion, numerous lengthy discussions among the coaches and umpire, and growing unrest among the vociferous fans. Meanwhile the five and six year olds were just trying to have fun playing a game of baseball.

I believe our society is heading down the road to such chaos. We're trying to ignore the eternal truths given to us by our Creator and instead make ourselves the umpires of the game of life. In our case, it's not God's fault. He hasn't lost His backbone to exercise His authority as the supreme arbiter of the universe. Neither has He changed His mind about what's right or wrong simply because a growing number of people seem to be loudly disagreeing with His standards.

We're the problem. We think we know better than God. Many people aren't paying attention to how God rules on issues, or think His opinions can be altered by what the majority believe or by whoever protests the loudest.

It reminds me of the time in Israel's history recorded for us in the book of Judges. That era was fittingly described in the Bible by these words: "In those days there was no king in Israel; everyone did what was right in his own eyes" (Judges 21:25). How did such an attitude work out for that society? Just read through the book of Judges and see for yourself. It was a time of terrible violence, unrestrained sexual immorality, and general moral chaos.

Yet here we are again in our day suggesting that we have no "king" or umpire to dictate what is right and wrong in our lives. We think we can make those calls ourselves. We believe everyone can do whatever they think is right and it's okay. But if we continue to travel that road, we're going to find it leading to the same place it did for Israel—to a destination of moral confusion and messed-up lives. As a matter of fact, I believe we're already experiencing ample results of our trek down that pathway.

But doesn't God want us to enjoy life? If by that we mean getting to do whatever we want to do—no. Our heavenly Father knows that what will bring His children the greatest joy and blessing is living in accordance with His wise standards.

So whether it's a Little League game or life itself, ignoring the one true umpire while we all try to fill that role for ourselves will only lead to a chaotic and unpleasant experience. So let the umpire be the umpire. And let God be God.

Remind yourself that you're not God and that you need to listen to and obey the One who is.

Don't Hide from the God Who Loves You

"The Lord is gracious and full of compassion, slow to anger and great in mercy."

– Psalm 145:8

I recall when one of our daughters received a new member into her family. No, not a baby. The addition to which I'm referring was a little eight-week-old kitten that they adopted.

Our grandchildren had been all excited about the prospect of this new pet. Our granddaughter who was two-years-old at the time in particular spoke so affectionately about the "kitty" and demonstrated how she was going to smother it with kisses.

However when they brought the kitten home and let it out in the house, it immediately scampered off and hid. It found refuge for hours under sofas, behind entertainment tables, and in other tight, dark places. There were times when the family wasn't even sure where the new resident of the house had concealed herself. Probably as a result of a combination of the trauma of the car trip, fear of strangers, and the uncertainty of being in a different place, the cat was missing out on all the joy and affection that the family wanted to bestow on it. But finally she came out of her refuge and allowed the kids to love on her and play with her. Apparently she discovered that her hesitation and fears were unfounded—that she was with people who would care for her.

It reminds me of the way some people look at God. Out of fear, lack of understanding, uncertainty, or other reasons they run away and try to hide from Someone who loves them and who greatly desires to shower them with affection, care, and blessings. Certainly God can be rather intimidating. His greatness is beyond our ability to comprehend. He is powerful, wise, and mysterious. And possibly most unsettling of all is the fact that He is perfectly holy and pure—a stark contrast to the fallen nature of humanity with all of our moral faults and weaknesses.

When we get a good look at God we rightly tend to say with the prophet Isaiah, "Woe is me, for I am undone!" (Isaiah 6:5). Or as when Peter realized the greatness of Jesus, we join him in declaring, "Depart from me, for I am a sinful man, O Lord!" (Luke 5:8). We want to run and hide from this awe-inspiring God who is so much bigger and better than we are.

If we could only see the fuller picture of God, we would realize that while He truly is the all-powerful Creator and Judge who could zap us out of existence in a blink of an eye, He is also Someone who yearns to have a close, loving relationship with us. If we would dare to draw near to Him, we would discover that He is only seeking that which is for our good.

God's primary desire is not to see people suffer and be punished, but rather to see them saved and blessed. When He convicts us of sin or disciplines us, it's because He wants us to find the remedy for that malady which has infected our souls and brings such pain into our lives.

Too many people are shying away from a God they consider to be angry and fearsome, when in reality He longs to smother them with His kisses of goodness and grace. We owe Him proper respect and honor, but we can also enter into a relationship with Him in which He sees us as His beloved children.

So if you've been running and hiding from God, it's time to draw close to Him and trust that He is Someone who truly loves you and wants to bless you.

Is there some reason you are hesitant about drawing closer to God? Think about His great love for you. How does that affect your attitude toward Him?

SEEK THE SECRET TO
EVERLASTING LIFE

*"But the water that I shall give him will become in him a fountain
of water springing up into everlasting life."*

– JOHN 4:14

I was one of those who grew up when *American Bandstand* was a regular
feature on TV. Actually it was my older sister who liked to watch the
show. However, that was back in the time when most of us just had the
one television set located in the living room of the house. So whatever
one person watched the rest of us viewed as well, unless we decided to
go elsewhere. As I recall it was not unusual for us to experience quite a
few sibling battles over the decision as to which channel to watch. One
of those common squabbles revolved around the fact that I preferred
Saturday sports over that weekly music and dancing show.

The death of Dick Clark, the iconic host of *American Bandstand*,
brought those days back to mind. For so many years as the rest of us aged
and changed, it seemed that Dick Clark had discovered the fountain of
youth. It wasn't until the last decade or so before his death that the years
finally appeared to catch up with him, especially after he suffered a stroke.
In those last years, it was both inspiring and painful to watch his courageous struggle to continue to host his annual New Year's Eve celebration.

Many people wish they could duplicate Dick Clark's longevity of a
youthful appearance. They search for that elusive secret of the fountain of
youth. Today there are those who use chemicals and medical procedures

to try to achieve that goal. Some are successful for a time. Others can end up looking like a different person or like something more artificial than human. I guess there's nothing wrong with wanting to look young. However at some point we all need to come to terms with the fact that everyone is aging, life here on earth is not going to continue forever, and one day we're all going to go the way of death, just as this one who was called "America's oldest teenager."

Maybe we would be better off being less obsessed with seeking a secret to youth and long life in this world and being more concerned with discovering the secret to eternal life—a glorious existence in heaven that will endure forever. What if we spent as much time being concerned about our souls and preparing them for what's to come as we spend on trying to get our bodies to look good and to last for as long as possible?

There may not be a fountain of youth, but Jesus spoke about "living water" that He could provide for those who put their faith in Him. When we drink of this water, not only does it satisfy that deep-seated thirst in our souls for a close relationship with God, but it also "will become in him a fountain of water springing up into everlasting life" (John 4:14). Although we're going to grow old and die one day, we can have the assurance of a glorious existence once this life is over. These bodies will wear out and return to dust, but our souls can live forever. And there God promises us a new body—a spiritual one that will be incorruptible.

There's an old gospel song that refers to heaven as "a land where we'll never grow old." Let's make sure that we're prepared to go to such a place—a place where we'll all discover the secret to not aging—a place where we'll all be a little more like Dick Clark.

How are you preparing for eternal life?

DOES HONESTY REALLY PAY OFF?

"Those who deal truthfully are His delight."
– PROVERBS 12:22

One year a little-known Englishman, Brian Davis, was battling for his first win on the PGA Tour in Hilton Head, South Carolina. I happened to catch the final couple of holes of regulation play on TV, watching Davis end up in a tie with fellow-golfer Jim Furyk. At that point I had to head out to church for our evening Bible study, so I only got to read about the incident that occurred on their first playoff hole.

It seems that Davis hit his ball into a hazard area, ending up in some sand and tall grass near the water. I understand that he actually hit a very good shot from that precarious position, but immediately consulted with an official and called a penalty on himself. He believed he had broken a rule by disturbing some reeds on his backswing, a suspicion that was confirmed by the TV replay. Davis' honesty resulted in a two-stroke penalty and cost him any chance of obtaining that coveted prize of his first tournament victory.

If this had been a movie on the Hallmark channel or a Disney fantasy, we might have expected a fairy tale ending. Somehow the honest golfer would have made a miraculous shot to win the tournament and experience an immediate reward for his integrity. But this wasn't Hallmark or Disney. This was real life. And many of us know that such honesty isn't always rewarded in this world in which we live.

You might be honest about a mistake you made at work and end up getting chewed out by your boss, or maybe even getting fired. A teenager might confess some hidden transgression to his parents only to face a severe tongue-lashing or a harsh penalty. You might be honest about some tax matter and end up having to pay more as a result. Being honest doesn't always mean that we will experience the reward of a storybook ending.

However, honesty is still the best policy. I know that's not a biblical quote, but the principles of honesty, integrity, truthfulness, and confession are clearly taught in God's Word. In our relationships with other people it's best to be honest, even if they may not appreciate it or if we suffer some negative consequences. It's important that we be honest with ourselves about our actions, attitudes, and the condition of our hearts. Otherwise we will tend toward self-deception, often falling into the pitfall of either having too high or too low an opinion of ourselves. And honesty with God is one of the first steps in getting on good terms with Him. We must recognize our spiritual need and confess our sins in order to receive the forgiveness that is made available through Jesus Christ.

Since I'm not a huge golf fan, I didn't know Brian Davis before that incident. But I didn't quickly forget his name. I knew if I saw him in a tournament in the future, I would tend to pull for him. Not because of His skill or ability at golf—but because, on at least this occasion, he showed himself to be honest and a person of integrity. And in comparison to some other pro golfers who have been in the news for less stellar reasons, that's something I admire. I might be awed at another athlete's greater skill, but I pull for someone I like—someone who exhibits signs of good character.

And if we'll pursue that virtue of honesty in our own lives, not only might others admire us, but most importantly God will be pleased and will be pulling for us.

Lord, help me to be honest and truthful in my dealings with others today, no matter the consequences.

COUNT THE COST OF
FOLLOWING JESUS

"For which of you, intending to build a tower, does not sit down first and count the cost.... So likewise, whoever of you does not forsake all that he has cannot be My disciple."

– LUKE 14:28, 33

I always consider it a privilege to be invited to have a role in a marriage ceremony. However, I also view it as a responsibility. I don't preside over a wedding until I have first spent some time with the bride and groom—sharing a few important concepts and words of advice, exploring their view of marriage, and making sure that they have talked over certain issues with each other prior to taking this significant step in their lives. Usually I give them a list of questions to discuss which covers a wide range of topics including the number of children they want, how well they get along with their future spouse's family, their tendencies regarding saving and spending money, and the part religion will play in their lives.

I believe it's helpful for couples to talk about such issues before they take their vows, rather than discovering to their surprise at a later time that they have serious, if not irreconcilable, disagreements about some major aspects of their life together. Most of the prospective marriage partners I counsel enjoy the opportunity to participate in those discussions and find that it strengthens their relationship.

The Bible compares a person's relationship with the Lord to a marriage. Maybe people need to give more consideration to what that commitment to Him involves before taking that step. Jesus spoke about the value of "counting the cost" before venturing out in a major endeavor (Luke 14:25–33). In that scripture, He seems to be suggesting that the cost of following Him will include putting Him first in our lives, bearing our cross, and being willing to forsake everything that would hinder our walk with Him.

It's not unlike those marriage vows in which a person pledges to "forsake all others and keep yourself only unto him/her, so long as you both shall live." God expects the same kind of faithfulness from us. I'm afraid that too many people try to serve God without giving up all the other gods in their lives. They want the benefits of forgiveness and heaven, but without exercising the degree of love and loyalty to the Lord that He requires.

Let's be clear what committing ourselves to a saving relationship with Jesus Christ is going to mean. He doesn't just want a part of our heart. He calls us to love Him with all of our hearts. He doesn't desire token obedience or just doing enough to get by. He calls us to a life of total surrender to His will. And He's not going to settle for being a guest in one room of your heart. He is going to insist on being the sole Master of the house.

If we haven't already done so, let's take time to "count the cost" of a relationship with Christ. We might need to spend some time in His Word and in prayer pondering such questions as, "Am I willing to let Jesus be first in my life? Is there something I'm not willing to give up for the Lord? Am I ready to love and obey God with all of my heart?"

Marriage calls for a deep commitment of love and faithfulness to one person above all others. And so does our relationship with Christ.

Have you counted the cost of following Jesus? How would you rate your level of commitment to Him?

GOD IS MORE ABOUT
BELIEVING THAN FEELING

"That if you confess with your mouth the Lord Jesus and believe in your heart that God has raised Him from the dead, you will be saved."

– ROMANS 10:9

One time I heard a rather well-known and influential celebrity say some interesting things about God and religion. She pointed back to an experience she had a number of years ago when she embarked on a search for "something more than doctrine." As a result of her quest, she had concluded that "God is a feeling experience, not a believing experience." She made the claim that "if your religion is a believing experience, if God for you is still about a belief, then it's not truly God."

As is the case with many deceptive statements, her remarks contained a certain measure of truth. Christianity is more than simply following a bunch of rules. It involves more than knowing facts about God or adherence to a set of beliefs. The Christian faith is about a personal relationship with God. However that doesn't mean that doctrine and beliefs are not important. We shouldn't jump to the conclusion that it doesn't matter what you believe, as long as you get in touch with God and feel His presence.

I find especially interesting the emphasis this celebrity and others place on feeling—this idea that God is a feeling experience, not a believing experience. If that's the case then there are quite a few Bible verses we need to go back and revise. Romans 10:9 doesn't state that if you confess with your mouth the Lord Jesus and feel Him in your heart that you will be saved. It reads, "that if you confess with your mouth the Lord Jesus and believe in your heart...." It even goes on to talk about belief in a specific fact or doctrinal statement—believing that God has raised Jesus from the dead. This is just one example. In a concordance I only found nine references to some form of the word "feeling" in the King James Version of the Bible, but over 300 references to some form of the word "believing."

Although the Christian life is about a personal relationship with God, it's a relationship based on truth. It's grounded in what God has revealed to us about Himself and His will. It's not simply about what feels right, but what God says is right. But this other way of thinking is so attractive to people. It fits right in with the popular philosophy of our day that goes something like this: "How can something that feels so right be wrong?" That is the basis many are using to judge right and wrong—does it feel right? To them it doesn't matter what God says—the truth is whatever feels right for that person at that time.

We have to be careful of falling into that trap of walking by feeling rather than by faith. Although it's wonderful to sense God's presence and to feel His touch, we need to guard against seeking a feeling rather than seeking God Himself. The Bible doesn't say, "Be still and feel that I am God"—it says, "Be still and know that I am God." I don't just sit still, wipe my mind blank, and wait for a warm feeling. I can be still and meditate on who God says He is, what He has done, His promises, and I can know that He is God.

We shouldn't base our relationship with God simply on feeling. There is truth and revelation which we need to believe. It will involve having faith in God and trusting Him. It will also mean obeying His commands, regardless of how we feel. Let's not give in to these deceptive philosophies that will try to steer us away from the truth. We need to live primarily by faith, not by feeling.

Are there any ways in which you're allowing your feelings to guide you more than your faith? Meditate on what you know about God. How should that affect what you feel?

God Enables Us to Make the Tough Journey

"As His divine power has given to us all things that pertain to life and godliness."

– II Peter 1:3

One Saturday, a group from our church took an excursion to national battlefield. Having grown up in that area, I was very familiar with the site. But for many of the folks who accompanied us, it was a new experience. They found it interesting to tour the visitor's center and learn about the historical significance of that location. And the weather cooperated magnificently for us to enjoy a picnic lunch and to hike up the trail to the top of the mountain.

I'm not sure how many years it had been since I had last made that trek. I have fond memories of making my way up those familiar trails as a youngster with my family and with my church youth group. As we walked it again on this occasion, I recognized the various twists and turns of the pathway, almost like getting reacquainted with an old friend after many years of separation. However as we progressed on our journey, one difference began to emerge. Somehow that trail had gotten considerably steeper since my last visit. I didn't remember it being quite so difficult to make that climb. It didn't look any different, but what other explanation could there be?

Don't try to tell me that it has anything to do with me being ten or fifteen years older than the last time I made that hike. Don't remind me that I'm a grandfather now. The trails must have become steeper due to erosion over that period of time. No, the reality is that I'm not quite as young and strong as I used to be. Don't get me wrong—I'm not over the hill yet. This experience just reminds me that it takes me longer to get to the top of some hills.

Does it seem like the path God calls us to walk on as Christians these days is a lot steeper than it used to be? Our society has changed. Christian values are not so popular. Temptations abound and have easier access to us. Godly role models are few and far between. Ministry seems tougher. People appear to be less open to the truth and less responsive to Christ's call to be a disciple. That narrow path that leads to life seems to be steadily morphing into more of an uphill, painful, precarious climb.

However true those observations may be, let's remember that there are Christians today and throughout history who were called to travel tougher roads than the ones we traverse. Additionally, let's make sure that weakness on our part isn't a major component in the problem. Let's not be guilty of making excuses for our lack of godliness or spiritual progress by blaming a steeper path. Could it be that we're simply not as strong as we could be? The Bible says that God has given us everything we need to live for Him and to live godly lives (II Peter 1:3). No matter how steep the path, He can enable us to walk with Him and make the climb.

Are we making good use of the grace He's given us to strengthen us for the journey? We can daily feed on His Word. We can lean on the everlasting arms of God through prayer. We can experience the fullness and power of the Holy Spirit in our lives. That narrow road may be difficult—Jesus warned us that it would be—but He has given us what we need to reach our glorious destination.

Are you making good use of all the resources God has made available for you to help you live the way He wants you to live? Trust the Lord to give you strength to face the tough challenges of our day.

AFFIRM GOD'S FORGIVENESS
OF PAST SINS

"There is therefore now no condemnation to those who are in Christ Jesus."

– ROMANS 8:1

As I recollect, my first exposure to the writings of Edgar Allan Poe came as a reading assignment at school. It was his short story, "The Tell-Tale Heart." Do you remember that one? It was about someone who committed a murder, hid the body, and was ultimately overcome by the guilt of his horrible deed. The perpetrator of the crime believed he could hear the heartbeat of his victim growing louder and louder in the presence of investigators. That deafening noise in his mind finally became so intolerable that it drove the man to a dramatic confession of the murder.

One of the truths this story illustrates is the tremendous power of guilt. It can not only make a person miserable, but can even play mind tricks on its host. We may not hear the sound of a dead person's heartbeat, but we're certain that other people can see right through us and are aware of the awful things we've done.

Guilt, although never pleasurable, can be a good thing. It can help us recognize our sins and how terrible they are. God can use guilt in our lives to bring us to repentance and confession, vital steps in our journey toward faith and salvation. Without a sense of guilt, we can become insensitive to wrongdoing and hardened in our hearts toward God. If we aren't made aware of our need for forgiveness and cleansing, we won't reach out for God's gracious remedy.

However, many of us are well aware that the devil can likewise use guilt in our lives for his purposes. He can keep bringing up those sins from our past, beating us over the heads with them. Even though we have long ago repented of those wrongs, confessed them to God, and received His forgiveness, their shame and guilt sometimes resurface. We hear a voice planting doubts in our minds, *How can God love somebody who did something so awful? You're just fooling yourself if you think God would forgive you of such a terrible thing. You can't serve God and live for Him—He can't use somebody who's done what you've done.*

Certainly there will be times when we will look back at our past with regret. We may be reminded of some of the consequences of our former wrongs—how they have adversely affected our own lives or the lives of other people. Nevertheless those regrets should not lead to a false sense of guilt or undue condemnation. If God has granted us forgiveness for those sins, we need to accept it, affirm it, and not let the devil rob us of that assurance.

When we are tempted to let guilt from the past overcome us, steal our peace, or hinder us from moving forward in our walk with God, let's remind ourselves of God's promises. "If we confess our sins, He is faithful and just to forgive us our sins and to cleanse us from all unrighteousness" (I John 1:9). "There is therefore now no condemnation to those who are in Christ Jesus" (Romans 8:1).

Don't let the devil play mind tricks with you about your past which has been covered by the blood of Christ. When he tries to revive that heartbeat of guilt and condemnation, refuse to listen. Know that it's not true. Remind the devil and yourself that your former ways have been put to death and you are now alive in Christ. God knows about those skeletons in your closet and has forgiven you.

Instead of feeling false guilt about old sins, reaffirm your gratitude to a wonderful God who has shown you forgiveness. Do that enough times and the devil might quit bringing up the subject.

Feeling guilty? Confess and repent. If you've done so, affirm that you've received God's forgiveness and be thankful for it.

ARE WE LOOKING MORE LIKE JESUS?

"But we all…are being transformed into the same image from glory to glory"

– II CORINTHIANS 3:18

A re you familiar with the story written by early American author, Nathanial Hawthorne, entitled "The Great Stone Face"? The title refers to a mountain with a natural formation on one side of it which looked like a man's face. There was a legend among the residents of the nearby valley that one day someone from their valley would become a great person and he would look like that face on the mountain.

One little boy who grew up being told about the legend spent much time gazing on this unique formation, studying its features, and hoping to witness the rise of the great person who would exhibit its admirable qualities. Several times throughout his life, his hopes rose as certain individuals became great and successful people. But whenever he met them, he came away disappointed, realizing that they lacked certain key features exhibited in the stone face.

Finally in his later years, someone recognized the fact that this man himself had come to look exactly like the face on the mountain he had so contemplated and revered. He had become well-known for his wisdom, goodness, kindness, and integrity. He had gradually taken on those great character qualities he had seen revealed on the stone face, so that now its image could be seen in his own face.

What a great picture that is of the Christian's transformation into the image of Christ. The Bible says, "But we all, with unveiled face, beholding as in a mirror the glory of the Lord, are being transformed into the same image from glory to glory, just as by the Spirit of the Lord" (II Corinthians 3:18). This reminds us that being a believer isn't only about experiencing the forgiveness of our sins and having the assurance of going to heaven one day. It's also about an ongoing change in our character—becoming more and more like our Lord Jesus Christ.

This process begins when we put our trust in Jesus as our Savior and continues throughout our lifetimes. As we behold the glory of the Lord, gaze upon Jesus in His Word, fellowship with Him, listen to Him, obey Him, and seek to be the kind of people He wants us to be, God transforms us and instills more of those Christlike qualities in us. But this scripture reminds us that it is "as by the Spirit of the Lord." It's not something we accomplish on our own by seeking to be better people or simply trying to imitate Jesus. It requires the Holy Spirit changing our hearts and minds. But we need to seek such a change and cooperate with the Holy Spirit as He works on us.

One day in his later years, Salvation Army Officer Samuel Logan Brengle was visiting in a home. When he left, the little girl who lived there asked her mother, "Would Jesus have looked like Brother Brengle if He had lived to be seventy-five?" This little girl saw the image of Jesus in that old, godly Salvation Army officer.

Would anyone ever wonder that about us? Are we exhibiting such qualities in our lives that people see Jesus' attitude and spirit in us? Do they look at you and think, *Jesus must have been a lot like that person*?

No matter how Christlike you look today, there is still plenty of room for those godly qualities to expand and grow in your life. We've still got a long way to go. The important thing is for us to continue on the journey. Let's allow the Holy Spirit to keep chiseling away at us to make us more like Jesus.

What does the Spirit need to chisel from you in order to make you look more like Jesus? Will you let Him do it?

Seek Out the Kindred Spirits Around You

"But now indeed there are many members, yet one body."

– I Corinthians 12:20

I remember when many of us were saddened to hear about the death of actor Jonathan Crombie, best known for playing the beloved character Gilbert Blythe in the classic television production of *Anne of Green Gables*. The female members of my family were especially touched by the news concerning this handsome actor. You might say, in Anne's words, that they were in the depths of despair.

Our family has always enjoyed and held in high esteem this TV version of the Anne stories. It was one of the first video gifts I ever purchased for my wife. If she or one of our daughters was stuck at home sick for the day, it was not unusual for them to spend their recuperation time watching their own *Anne of Green Gables* marathon.

Some of you may remember that Anne was always on the lookout for what she termed as "kindred spirits." Sometimes she would recognize such a connection with someone immediately, as with her best friend, Diana. However, other times it might surprise her that someone who at first seemed not to fit that description in the least would end up changing or revealing themselves to be such a kindred spirit after all.

As followers of Christ, we are privileged to have a special connection with other believers. One of the great joys in life is meeting people for the first time and immediately sensing the mutual bond of being part of the same family of God. It's wonderful to encounter kindred spirits who share your love for Christ, along with the values and priorities that accompany a relationship with Him.

Because of that real spiritual connection, some people feel closer to their church family and to fellow believers than they do to their own blood relatives who don't share that mutual relationship with Christ.

However, let's not forget that everyone is a potential kindred spirit. We may more easily recognize that fact about some individuals than we do about others. Some people may seem so hard-hearted or hostile toward spiritual matters that we tend to write them off as hopeless cases. But sometimes such people aren't as cold as they appear on the surface. Or through our persistent showing of love and sharing of the truth, the icy hearts of those folks might start melting and eventually be transformed by the power of Christ. God's grace is still able to change hostile Sauls into Apostle Pauls.

Anne Shirley (and please note for fans of this series that I am careful to spell Anne with an "e") didn't just find other people with a kindred spirit, she actually influenced them to become such spirits. Her own spirit was infectious. She made those around her better. She brought out the positive qualities in those whom she encountered.

Surely we should be seeking to have a similar impact on the people we come in contact with each day. Let's pray that the Spirit of Christ will so shine through us that others will want to possess that spirit too.

So be thankful for and enjoy those around you who are kindred spirits in Christ. But also recognize the potential in others to be part of that connection as well. You may not be able to reach large numbers of people, but there may be one or two valuable souls on whom you can have a significant impact. Live in such a way that others will want to be kindred spirits with you.

Be thankful for the "kindred spirits" in your life. Make an effort to reach out to someone today, making a positive impact on that person.

Seek to Draw Closer to God

"Let us draw near with a true heart in full assurance of faith."

– Hebrews 10:22

A few years ago, my wife and I took a trip of a lifetime. For the first time, and most likely the only time, we vacationed in Hawaii. We flew into Honolulu where we boarded a cruise ship to sail around various islands for a week.

As you can imagine, along the way we experienced numerous beautiful sights and spectacular scenery. There were majestic mountains, many of which were adorned by waterfalls. There were lush green valleys and flowering tropical plants. At one point we sailed along the magnificent Na Pali coast. We viewed breathtaking bays and beaches. We even got to see a little flame and lava bubbling up from a volcano.

One of the highlights of our trip was taking a helicopter ride over the "garden island" of Kauai. It's one thing to view all these scenes I've described from a distance. It's totally different to get up close as the helicopter allowed us to do. We were even able to go to a few places that weren't accessible by any other means.

It reminds me of how we can approach the awesome God who is holy, all-powerful, and in many ways beyond what our finite minds can fathom. Some people choose to simply observe Him from a distance. They recognize His might and majesty, but for various reasons don't want to get too close. They are satisfied with Him being "the Man upstairs" to whom they can holler out when they get in trouble or have an especially difficult problem and need some divine assistance.

However when we keep God at arm's length, we're missing out on so much. He doesn't want just to be admired from a distance. The Bible shows us over and over again that God is accessible and wants to dwell right in the midst of His people. And through His Holy Spirit He can even live in our hearts. God's Word encourages us to "draw near with a true heart in full assurance of faith" (Hebrews 10:22). It also promises, "Draw near to God and He will draw near to you" (James 4:8).

It can be inspiring to see the person and power of our Creator from a distance, but it's even better to get to know Him personally and up close. Will you dare to take the adventure of a lifetime and explore how closely you can get to God?

More carefully examine the majestic character of our great God. You may never reach the summit of that mountain, but keep climbing in your knowledge and awe of who God is. Bathe under the waterfalls of His abundant grace and love. Let Him pour out His mercies on you fresh and new each day.

Discover the calm, serene beaches of knowing that your heart is at peace with God and of relying on Him day-by-day. Experience the growth in your life as you walk through the lush valleys with your Creator. You can even draw close to His volcanic, fiery wrath, knowing that you have nothing to fear if your heart is right with Him. It can remind you of how seriously God views sin, as well as give you a fresh burden for those who are going to face His wrath unless they repent and put their faith in Him.

God is so great and so wonderful. We could spend the rest of our lives exploring Him and still only touch the surface. Don't settle for a distant view of this spectacular God. Commit yourself to drawing nearer to the majestic God who wants to draw close to you.

Commit yourself to taking greater steps to drawing closer to God. What is the first step you can take today?

LAY ASIDE THOSE BURDENS
THAT WEIGH YOU DOWN

"Let us lay aside every weight, and the sin which so easily ensnares us"

– HEBREWS 12:1

There was a time when one of our daughters used our home for the purpose of holding a two-day garage sale. She considered it to be a better location for such an event than her residence. So we were glad to help her out, along with giving us an opportunity to participate by trying to sell a few items ourselves. We were especially interested in getting rid of several larger pieces of furniture which we no longer used.

A few of those items were snatched up quickly by the early morning bargain hunters who ventured by. But at the end of the first day, two of our largest offerings in the sale still remained. And I really, really wanted someone to take those particular items. I could claim that my motivation was primarily a noble one of wishing to help someone find something they could use. But honesty compels me to deny that claim. Neither was monetary compensation the principal motivation. I have to admit that the main reason behind my desire to see those furnishings sold was simply not wanting to have to carry those heavy loads back down into my basement. It was a combination of their backbreaking weight and the amount of space they occupied that led me to whisper a prayer for someone to come and purchase them. As time went by, we were willing to considerably reduce the amount of money we would accept for those two items.

Thankfully my prayer was answered and they were both taken before the sale was over.

The Bible encourages us to "lay aside every weight, and the sin which so easily ensnares us, and let us run with endurance the race that is set before us" (Hebrews 12:1). Sometimes we're guilty of allowing things in our lives that weigh us down. They hinder us from effectively running the race and living a victorious life in Christ. They take up time and space in our lives that could be used for better things. But too often, like garage sale items, we hang on to them out of some fondness for them, some connection to our past, or just not wanting to go through the effort of cleaning out our spiritual house. It's easier and more comfortable to hang on to them, rather than get rid of them.

But we need to recognize those bad habits, hurtful attitudes, or other such baggage as burdens that are holding us back. We need to do as the scripture says and lay them aside. Let's make whatever sacrifices we must in order to let go of those things.

For unbelievers there is an even greater burden weighing down on them. John Bunyan, in his literary masterpiece *Pilgrim's Progress*, famously depicted the heavy burden of sin and guilt which weighs down every traveler through life. It's a load from which we are incapable of freeing ourselves. It is only when the pilgrim reaches the cross that he finds freedom from that ponderous burden.

If we've experienced such deliverance, let's never forget it or take it for granted. Let's be grateful for a Savior who died to set us free. But if you're still lugging around the weight of guilt and sin today, know that Christ can lift that burden off you as well. Put your trust in the One who loved you enough to take your burden of sin upon Himself.

If you're tired of holding onto and carrying some such heavy load in your heart, have a spiritual garage sale. Lay that burden aside. Jesus has already paid the price for it. Trust Him to come and haul it off.

Is there some sin weighing you down which you need to lay aside? Trust the grace and power of Christ to free you from that burden.

Don't Let Infighting Hinder Your Journey Upward

"They were all with one accord in one place."
– Acts 2:1

Did you hear about the fight that broke out on Mount Everest a few years ago? When you think about climbers trying to reach the peak of that famous mountain, you think about a group of people focused on one particular goal. And in order to achieve that lofty goal, it usually takes teamwork. People on such an expedition have to work together as they battle the frigid temperatures, strong winds, the effects of high altitude, and their own inner struggles over giving up. They can't afford to start fighting each other or it will keep them from reaching that summit for which they are aiming.

However, on this particular occasion that unity of purpose was disrupted by a conflict between three European climbers and their guides—the Sherpa, a people who are native to the area. It seems that the guides had instructed the climbers to wait while they laid down some ropes, but those climbers went ahead anyway. And as they did, they knocked some ice down on the Sherpa. Reportedly a fight ensued, including punches, kicks, and rock-throwing. Supposedly there were even threats made that the climbers would be killed if they didn't leave.

I don't know if they ever settled the debate as to who was primarily responsible for the conflict—the climbers or the Sherpa—but whoever was at fault, it certainly disrupted the unity and teamwork normally associated with such an expedition.

As believers in Christ, we're on our own adventurous expedition. We're constantly journeying toward greater spiritual heights, including the Everest of Christlikeness and ultimately heaven itself. And we've got our enemies and obstacles to battle as well. We have to climb in the frigid spiritual atmosphere of a society that is turning away from God. We've got a strong wind of opposition blowing against us, trying to hinder us from being faithful followers of the Lord. Additionally, the enemy of our souls will tempt us along the way, doing everything he can to hinder our journey upward.

We also have our own inward battles to fight. We must guard our hearts and desires from leading us off in wrong directions. And we need to keep our eyes focused on the Lord and His promises so that we don't get discouraged and give up.

In this journey, we need a similar spirit of unity and single-minded purpose with other believers. We need to work together, help each other, support one another, and stand together against those mutual enemies in order to reach the spiritual summit for which we're aiming.

One of the phrases we find several times in reference to the believers in the book of Acts is that they were "with one accord" (Acts 1:14; 2:1; 4:24). Not only were they physically together in one place, but they were united in purpose—praying for the same thing and seeking a common goal. In such an atmosphere of spiritual unity, God did some marvelous things in the life of the Church. I believe God can still do great things today, both in the individual lives of His followers and in His Church as a whole. But we need to work together and pray together in order to reach those heights to which God wants to take us.

It's a shame when an expedition toward a mountaintop allows infighting to hinder it from reaching its goal. As believers, we've got even greater heights to aspire to than Everest. Our Guide is well able to get us there. Let's seek to be "with one accord" so that we all can complete our journey to the summit.

Is anything hindering you from being "with one accord" with a fellow believer? What can you do about it?

SERVE GOD WITH
A LOVING SPIRIT

"Serve the Lord with gladness."
– PSALM 100:2

A s I babysat my then two-year-old granddaughter one evening, our playtime was interrupted by a buzzing sound from another room reminding me of an unfinished earlier task. So I asked Julianne if she wanted to help Papaw get his clothes out of the dryer and hang them up. She responded enthusiastically positive, like little children often do until they get old enough to recognize such tasks as being work.

As I unloaded the dryer, my helper was only able to carry one pair of my pants in her little arms, leaving me to tote the rest of the large burden of laundry. We took the clothes into the bedroom, piled them on the bed, and proceeded to hang them up. My granddaughter would bring an article of clothing over to me and I would place it on a hanger. During that process, I had to repeat instructions to her several times about what specifically I wanted her to bring to me. Sometimes she would run to get another shirt and be holding it out to me before I was ready for it. Most of the time she came across the room with half of the shirt or pair of pants dragging along on the carpeted floor—certainly not the best procedure for dealing with clean clothes.

Did I admonish her? Did I send her away, knowing that I could probably do that job quicker and better by myself? No. The zeal of my granddaughter in wanting to help me was far more valuable than doing the task in what I might have considered to be "the right way." Her love and enthusiasm transformed a common household chore into one of the joyful highlights of the evening.

I have to believe that our heavenly Father looks at us and our efforts to serve Him in a similar fashion. And I'm so thankful that He does.

Sometimes we may feel like we have our hands full with the task we've been given or the burden we've been called upon to bear. But let's remember that our Father is always carrying the heavier portion of that load. Let's maintain a grateful attitude for His help, along with a constant sense of reliance on Him and on the power of prayer.

Let's be thankful for the patience of God—that He is willing to repeat His instructions to us over and over when we don't understand or when we simply didn't pay attention to Him as we should.

And we have to confess that there are times when we try to run ahead of God and He has to teach us the discipline of waiting on Him.

No doubt all of our feeble efforts fall short of the perfection with which God could do the job. We drag things across the floor, dirty them up, or in other ways falter in the performance aspect of our service to the Lord.

But I don't think God minds. He may gently try to teach us better ways to do things, but I believe He's pleased with our service to Him if we're doing it out of a heart of love for Him.

I could imagine that ten years or so from that day, my granddaughter might do that same task with the sour attitude and rolling eyes that teens are famous for. At that age she could do it all herself and might hang those clothes more neatly than I do. But I wouldn't appreciate it as much because of the difference in attitude.

Let's serve God with the best of our abilities, striving for excellence. But most of all, let's do it with a childlike spirit of enthusiasm and love that means even more to our heavenly Father.

What is your attitude and spirit towards serving the Lord? How can it be improved?

BE GRATEFUL FOR A MOTHER'S PROTECTIVE LOVE

"And in the shadow of Your wings I will make my refuge."

– PSALM 57:1

One day I was out in my yard hooking up a hose to the outside spigot and pulling it around to where I needed to spray some water. However in the process of that task, I suddenly became aware of an unusual degree of noise coming from the area in front of my house where I had just been working.

The ruckus was being made by a couple of birds, cardinals to be specific. They weren't providing the pleasant, melodic chirping that we often enjoy hearing from our feathered friends. This was a louder and harsher sound—what I can only describe as fussing. They didn't seem very happy about something. I quickly put two and two together, recognizing that it was springtime, that we had seen cardinals in the bushes in front of our house, and surmised that they were unhappy with my presence because they had a nest nearby.

About the time that thought entered my mind, I spied a very young bird standing on our walkway, right next to the hose. It quickly hopped back toward the shrubbery with mom and dad fluttering nearby. So when I went back later to turn off the water, I tried to move slowly and quietly so as not to disturb that family of cardinals too much. But the whole time I was doing it, the mother bird was flying nearby squawking at me. I can't blame her. I later discovered their nest in the bush right beside the water spigot. That mother was just doing what moms do—caring for and protecting her offspring.

As another Mother's Day approaches, let's be thankful for moms who love, watch out for, and protect their children. While someone has warned us about the fury of "a woman scorned," I'm not sure she could hold a candle to the mother who thinks someone is trying to hurt her kids. A mother's love will go to great lengths to try to keep her children from serious harm.

So I find it interesting that throughout most of the Bible, God has chosen to reveal Himself to us in terms of a Heavenly Father. Yet there are a few instances when He compares Himself to a mother, especially in relation to the loving protection that a mom provides. The picture we're given several times of God safeguarding us is that of a mother bird covering its offspring with its wings.

Certainly there are other vivid analogies used in the Bible to convey the same concept—God being our fortress, our refuge, our strong tower, our high rock, and our shield. Those ideas also express protection, especially showing how strong and impregnable a fortress God can be when we take refuge in Him. However, those pictures are lacking something. They show great power to defend, but in a cold battlefield sort of way. They don't express the love and the care that is the motive for such protection, the kind that can be seen in the comparison to a mother bird.

God isn't just a hard stone wall standing between us and danger. He's also like a mom who loves us. We may have to face the storms, literally as some have experienced in recent days, or figuratively in the form of other difficulties that come into our lives. But as we do, we know that God is near, He cares, and He is watching over us. As the winds of adversity blow, we can find a peaceful shelter under His wings.

Let's be thankful for moms who have lovingly watched over us. And let's remember that we have a God who loves us even more and who is even better able to protect His children.

Give thanks for loving and protective moms, as well as for a God who is like them.

Let's Bow Before
God in Submission

"Now do not be stiff-necked, as your fathers were, but yield your-selves to the Lord."

– II Chronicles 30:8

If you don't suffer from neck or back problems, you should consider yourself blessed. I know some people who have a terrible time with such ailments. In the last few years, I've found myself becoming suscep-tible to lower back pain. I have to be careful about bending over, how I lift objects, and even how long I stay in a standing or sitting position. However, I have to admit that I find it hard to refuse when my little grand-son smiles at me and asks, "Papaw, back?" Giving him a ride on my back usually results in a couple of days of discomfort, but the joy and laughter it brings to him is well worth the price.

A term that is found fairly often in the Old Testament to refer to the people of Israel is sometimes translated "stiff-necked." I understand that the Hebrew word refers to the back of the neck or the back itself as being stiff. God first used that description for the Israelites when they turned so quickly from Him to worship a golden calf in the short time Moses was up on the mountain receiving the Ten Commandments. What does that term mean? Many of us have been taught that it refers to the people being stubborn or hard-hearted, but how does the concept of a stiff neck or back convey that idea?

One of the things I learned in the little bit of Hebrew language I studied in seminary was that it uses a lot of word pictures and imagery. It stands in contrast to the concise, logical, abstract concepts in the Greek language of the New Testament. For example, the Greek might simply say "joy," while the Hebrew will try to picture it in some way—and I'll just make one up—like a smiling face. So in the Hebrew mind, what is being pictured by that term "stiff-necked"?

If your neck or back is stiff and rigid, I suppose that could picture being firm, resolute, or with your head looking straight forward with determination and stubbornness. But as I thought about it, another idea came to mind. I don't know if it's right or not. Keep in mind that I'm like the seminary student who took one semester of Greek and began to use it in his sermons in ways that were total misinterpretations. One of his professors commented that the student knew just enough Greek to be dangerous. So remember that I know just enough Hebrew to be dangerous.

But it seems if your back or neck is stiff and rigid, then what is it that you either cannot do or are refusing to do? You're refusing to bow—you're showing your unwillingness to submit. The Israelites were a stiff-necked people because they often showed themselves to be unwilling to bow to God. They refused to submit to His will and words.

In II Chronicles 30:8, the people are exhorted not to be stiff-necked, but rather to yield themselves to the Lord. That tells us what the opposite of being stiff-necked is—to yield, bow, or submit ourselves to God and His will for us.

Some of us may not have any physical problems with our necks or backs, but we suffer from a similar spiritual malady that the Israelites had. We have a tough time bowing in submission to God. It may be concerning life in general, or it may only be in one specific area. Let's not just bow before God in worship and adoration. Let's loosen those stiff backs and also bow before Him with a yielded heart.

Is there some specific area in your life in which you're being "stiff-necked"? Submit to God and to His will concerning that issue.

THERE IS NO UTOPIA
THIS SIDE OF HEAVEN

"That we may lead a quiet and peaceable life in all godliness and reverence."

– I TIMOTHY 2:2

Did you hear the startling news? Thelma Lou was robbed in Mayberry! Well, it wasn't exactly Thelma Lou, but rather the actress who portrayed that character on *The Andy Griffith Show*. And it didn't actually happen in Mayberry either. The incident occurred some years ago in the small town of Mount Airy, North Carolina—the location that was the inspiration for that beloved fictional town where Andy, Opie, Barney, and the rest of the TV gang lived.

It seems that the eighty-three-year-old actress at the time, Betty Lynn, had moved to Mount Airy a couple of years earlier in order to escape the crime in Los Angeles. My guess is that she often traveled to that southern town anyway to appear in their various events in which they commemorate the show that is still a fan favorite. But on this occasion, Betty had her wallet stolen while shopping in one of Mount Airy's stores. Where is Deputy Barney Fife when you need him?

Who would have done such a thing? Surely not Otis Campbell. He may have liked his moonshine, but when he wasn't drunk Otis was quite a nice guy. Some people might suspect Ernest T. Bass. Although he was an ornery and strange character—or as Barney would say, "He's a nut"— about the worst thing Ernest T. would do is break a few windows by throwing rocks at them. My guess is that the perpetrator was the stranger whom the townsfolk randomly chose and honored as their special guest for Founder's Day, even though unbeknownst to them, he was a skillful pickpocket. Whoever it was, I heard that they caught him.

I guess it just goes to show that no place is as utopian as we might like to think—not even Mayberry. Betty Lynn was trying to avoid being a victim of crime in the big city, only to find that even in a sleepy hamlet that many picture as a model of safety and quiet living, there are still those who do wrong and break laws. It's a reminder that there is no perfect paradise this side of heaven. As long as people—human beings with fallen natures—are around, there will be some degree of sin, wrongdoing, and crime.

If you think you are living, or ever have lived, in a sinless utopia, you're fooling yourself. Some places are quieter and safer than others, some communities are filled with friendly people who generally watch out for one another and respect the law, but even Mayberry had its town drunk, occasional bank robbery attempts, family violence, and of course, rampant jaywalking.

However, the reality of sinful humanity doesn't mean that we simply surrender our communities to crime and evil. We can still work toward making our less-than-perfect localities better places to live. We can elect good officials and pray for those who serve. We can support our local law enforcement. We can make our voices heard in public matters that affect the welfare of our community.

But most of all, we can strive to be the kind of people ourselves who will make our community a good place to live. We can seek to be people who love God, love our neighbor, and treat others as we would like them to treat us. We can be law-abiding citizens. We can be friendly and helpful to others. We can be the light that will hopefully spread to those around us.

We don't live in heaven yet, nor should we expect to do so on this earth. But in spite of living in a world of sin and evil, let's keep trying to make our communities good places to live. It may not be heaven, it may not even be Mayberry, but you can contribute to making it a better place than it would be without you.

What can you do to make your community a better place in which to live?

LET GOD TREAT THE DISEASE, NOT JUST THE SYMPTOMS

"Create in me a clean heart, O God."
– PSALM 51:10

Ugh! I hate being sick. I'm still recovering from a few days that included at some point a sore throat, runny nose, coughing, and fever. While I still managed to fulfill some of my responsibilities during that time, I also was forced to forego other pleasures, such as spending part of Mothers' Day with my mom.

Some of us have become quite adept at managing our symptoms when we're sick. We keep a box of tissues close by at all times. We mask the pain of a sore throat with lozenges. We take certain medications to suppress coughs or reduce fevers. We get extra rest. However, most of the time we can't do much about the cause or the illness itself. We either have to go to the doctor for expert help or simply let the sickness run its course over time.

As human beings, we also have to contend with a spiritual malady in our hearts and souls. Many of us have developed certain skills in dealing with the symptoms of this problem too. We've learned how to cover it up so other people can't see it so readily. We make excuses for it, not only to others but also in our own minds. We suppress the guilt and the shame which accompanies this sickness of the soul. We even lash out at those who acknowledge our problem or who dare suggest that we need to change. We often condemn those who try to point us in the direction of spiritual health as being unloving and intolerant.

Over the course of our lives and with having to deal with this issue so often, we have learned how to live with sin and how to manage its symptoms. Hide it. Ignore it. Excuse it. Blame somebody else. However, the Bible indicates that the proper way to deal with this problem is to acknowledge it, confess it, and seek God's forgiveness. "If we say we have no sin, we deceive ourselves, and the truth is not in us. If we confess our sins, He is faithful and just to forgive us our sins and to cleanse us from all unrighteousness" (I John 1:8–9).

But even if we rightfully acknowledge this sickness of the soul, we have to be careful that we don't use the means of seeking forgiveness as just another way to manage those symptoms. God's will isn't for us to continue in sin while constantly coming to Him asking for His forgiveness for the same matter over and over again. Don't overlook the last part of that passage of scripture. God will not only forgive us, but He will cleanse us. He doesn't just deal with the symptoms—He's the great Physician of our soul who can heal us of the disease itself.

When David wrote Psalm 51 after committing his sin concerning Bathsheba, he not only acknowledged his sin and sought forgiveness, but he also asked for God to "wash me thoroughly," "cleanse me," and "create in me a clean heart, O God." He knew he needed more than to escape God's condemnation for what he had done in the past. He needed God's cleansing power to help him live the right way as he moved forward.

Let's not become satisfied with living with a sin-sick heart and simply managing its symptoms. Let's look to the Lord as the One who can also cleanse our hearts and make us whole. He can empower us to gain greater victory over sin and can help us enjoy a life of better spiritual health.

If there is some sin in your life you've been trying to "manage," it's time to take it to the Lord and let Him cleanse you of it.

MAY 12

WE SHOULD LOOK TO THE CREATOR FOR OUR VALUES

"Woe to those who call evil good, and good evil."
– ISAIAH 5:20

Maybe you heard about the error made at one of those popular roadshows where they evaluate antiques. A man brought in what was described as a "grotesque jug" which the experts thought may have been an object from the late nineteenth century. They suggested its value could be as high as $50,000. Later it was discovered that this presumed rare work of art was actually someone's high school project from the 1970s. The creator came forward with an old photo of her and her creation. As it turned out the object wasn't worthless, nevertheless it wasn't anywhere near as valuable as first thought.

Everyone makes mistakes, even the so-called experts. This wasn't an intentional effort to deceive anyone, but it can still make a big difference whether something is looked upon as a valued antique or simply as a worthless piece of junk. This particular jug might have continued to be misevaluated if the original artist had not come forward.

Our society is constantly making value judgments. Many issues over which cultural battles are fought have many facets which can make it no simple matter to find acceptable solutions. However as a presidential spokesman said one time about one such controversial subject, "It comes down to values." The same could be said about a number of such issues over which struggles are taking place.

In some cases there are those who are intentionally trying to change the longstanding values of our society. In other instances people are just going along with the popular view or are basing their evaluation on other subjective factors, such as whatever feels right. In the meantime the lines are not only being blurred between right and wrong, or good and evil—but those values are being turned upside-down.

The Bible warns, "Woe to those who call evil good, and good evil; who put darkness for light, and light for darkness; who put bitter for sweet, and sweet for bitter" (Isaiah 5:20). However, someone will raise the objection, "But how can we really know what is good, what is true, and what is right?" This is where we have to go back to the original artist, the Creator. He comes forward in the midst of our society of experts who are debating these issues and reminds us of His original and unchanging designs, purposes, and will. If we forsake His evaluation of these matters, we have nothing certain on which to base our beliefs.

Concerning the host of issues being debated today, we need to pay attention to the Word of God, along with the confirming testimony of nature, logic, and common sense. Our society is not just in the process of forsaking Christian values, but values of morality and decency which have stood the test of time in various cultures. It has been proven that for a society to ignore or turn away from such values is to its detriment.

So what do we do? We make sure we know what God says about these matters—not just what others claim He says. We hold firm to His evaluation of these current matters, as well as others that will arise over the horizon as we move forward. And we had better prepare ourselves for not being very popular, and even facing opposition and attacks.

Some will claim that we are on the wrong side of history when it comes to these matters—that eventually they will be valued as good and acceptable. However, I don't mind being on the wrong side of human history—as long as I am on the right side of the eternal God.

Think about where your values come from. Why do you believe what you do about certain issues? Are you giving priority to what the Bible says about them?

BE A REAL CHRISTIAN, NOT JUST A PRETENDER

"Therefore, if anyone is in Christ, he is a new creation."

– II CORINTHIANS 5:17

When one of our grandsons celebrated his third birthday, his party guests included not only the usual group of family and friends but also a visit from several firemen in a fire truck. This was quite a treat for a little guy who got excited whenever he spotted one of those big red vehicles and who would sometimes run around pretending to be putting out fires.

So on this special occasion, he was thrilled to get to sit in the truck, wear a fireman's hat, and assist in holding a hose as water sprayed out of it. Now did all this make my grandson a fireman? Of course not. And it wasn't just the age factor involved. If some of us adults had joined in those same activities, we still wouldn't have been a member of that respected group who help protect us and our property. Without the proper training and authorization, we would be just as much pretenders as my little grandson.

That fact seems so obvious when it comes to firefighters and other professions. Yet we seem to be so easily deceived about a similar truth when it comes to being a Christian. Simply looking like, talking like, and acting like a follower of Christ doesn't make us one.

We can faithfully sit in a church service every Sunday and still not be a Christian. We can wear whatever garb we may associate with follow-ers of Christ, whether long dresses, T-shirts with a Bible verse printed on them, or a shirt displaying the name of a church and still not be a

Christian. We can even use the same equipment a faithful believer might employ—such as reading a Bible, saying a prayer, or doing a kind deed to help someone. We can imitate all the actions we've seen in Christians while still falling short of being one ourselves.

So what does it take to be a Christian? The Bible describes it in a number of ways: believing in Jesus (John 3:16); loving the Lord your God with all your heart, soul, and mind (Matthew 22:37); being born again (John 3:3); and repenting and being converted (Acts 3:19). In another place it says, "If you confess with your mouth the Lord Jesus and believe in your heart that God has raised Him from the dead, you will be saved" (Romans 10:9).

In other words, it's all about a relationship with God through faith in Jesus Christ. It's not about wearing a particular hat or performing certain actions. It's about receiving God's love and grace He's shown to us through sending His Son to die on the cross for our sins. It's primarily a change in our hearts—a transformation accomplished by God.

As a result of that inward change, we will start doing some of those things Christians do. But they spring from our relationship with Christ, not the other way around.

It's cute for a young child to pretend to be a fireman. However, let's make sure that we're more than simply pretenders when it comes to being a Christian. It's not a bad thing for individuals to seek to imitate Christ and His followers, but don't mistake such action as being what makes one a Christian.

I would be proud if my grandson grew up and chose to go through all the training and proper channels to truly become a fireman one day. And any of us can become true followers of Christ, but we need to move beyond pretending and mere imitation and start seeking a real personal relationship with the Lord.

Are you just "doing" Christian things, or do you have a personal relationship with Jesus which you are cultivating?

ARE WE GIVING WHAT WE
HAVE FOR THE LORD'S WORK?

"Silver and gold I do not have, but what I do have I give you."
– ACTS 3:6

I once read an excerpt from George Washington's journal on the day he left Mount Vernon to assume his duties as our first president. On that significant occasion, he penned these words: "At 10:00 I bid adieu to Mount Vernon…with the best disposition to render service to my country in obedience to its call, but with less hopes of answering its expectations." It seems Washington was ready, willing, and enthused about answering the call to serve as president, but I find it interesting that he was concerned he might not meet the nation's expectations of him.

Maybe some of us can relate to that in connection with serving the Lord. We want to serve Him, we're enthused about the possibilities, but we're afraid we're not going to measure up and be able to do what He expects of us.

If that's the case, there are a couple of principles from an incident in Acts 3 which should encourage us. This was the time Peter and John met a lame man at the gate of the temple and healed him. Do you remember what Peter told the man? "Silver and gold I do not have, but what I do have I give you; in the name of Jesus Christ of Nazareth, rise up and walk" (Acts 3:6). One principle that can help us with our concerns about meeting God's expectations as we serve Him is: the Lord doesn't expect us to give what we don't have to give. Peter didn't think, *God can't use me to do anything for this poor man because I have no money to offer him.*

Sometimes we're tempted to think, *God can't use me because I don't possess this particular talent or ability.* Or *If only I had the money to help this person out.* Or *If only I had the resources to begin that ministry.*

Let's not allow discouragement over what we don't have keep us from serving the Lord. Some of us need to quit beating ourselves up over what we can't do or don't have the resources to do. God doesn't expect us to serve in those ways if we don't have those things to give. Don't get me wrong. This isn't an excuse not to serve. If God calls us to do something, He will give us the abilities and resources to do it. But this principle reminds us that there are some things we may not be gifted to do and therefore certain ways we may not be expected to serve Him.

But there's a second important principle here: the Lord does expect us to give what we do have to give. The Lord used Peter as he gave what he had to give. Peter gave something much more valuable than money to the lame man—the gift of being able to walk through the healing power of Jesus Christ.

You may not have the skills to construct a church building in South America, but what skills and abilities do you possess? Are you giving those to the Lord to be used in some way to serve Him and to help others? We may not have the abundant talent and resources others enjoy, but let's give what we've got, like the widow who threw a fraction of a penny into the temple treasury. Jesus may value and use our small gift in greater ways than those who are giving out of their abundance.

So as we encounter the hurting, needy, and lost people of this world, let's focus less on what we can't give and more on what we do have to give. Let's give what we have and trust God to use us to touch those people's lives.

What do you possess in the way of talents and resources that God wants you to give to Him for His service?

MAY 15

KEEP YOUR SPOTLIGHT ON CHRIST AND THE CROSS

"For I determined not to know anything among you except Jesus Christ and Him crucified."

– I CORINTHIANS 2:2

If you had driven by our church on this particular morning, you might have seen the unusual sight of myself and another member of our congregation perched on the roof of our building. No, we weren't literally trying to get closer to God or to climb to greater spiritual heights—although crawling around precariously on a steep roof can certainly encourage someone to do some serious praying.

On this occasion we had ventured up there to check out a malfunctioning steeple light. We had hoped it would simply be a matter of changing a burned-out bulb, but as it turned out we needed to replace the entire fixture. When we did, we tried to situate it in such a way as to make sure the spotlight would shine all the way up the structure. We especially wanted to be certain that it would reach high enough to illuminate the cross which rested at the very top of the steeple.

The Apostle Paul was concerned that he, fellow believers, and the Church as a whole always shine the spotlight on Christ and the cross. When Paul preached, he wasn't trying to impress people with his dynamic personality, his speaking skills, or his great knowledge. He stated to one church, "For I determined not to know anything among you except Jesus Christ and Him crucified" (I Corinthians 2:2). He also encouraged those same people not to boast in themselves and their accomplishments, but told them instead, "He who glories, let him glory in the Lord" (1:31).

It can be tempting for a church to turn the spotlight on things other than Christ and the cross. Some may do so intentionally, out of a desire to be more accepting of others and less offensive to certain people. They want to focus on more positive messages rather than talking about sin, atonement, and a sacrificial death. But when we do that, we are turning away from the very heart of the good news God has for people.

Other churches may stray from that emphasis unintentionally. We want people to know about the wonderful pastor we have who does such a good job of feeding his flock with God's Word. We want to encourage people to attend our church by highlighting the inspiring musicians or the effective children's ministry. And that's fine. But while we promote and emphasize these other positive aspects of the church, let's never let the main spotlight stray away from Christ and the cross. No individual, regardless of how greatly gifted and used of God, should be allowed to eclipse our Savior Himself. And no program or ministry should ever outshine that greatest of events—when Christ died for our sins.

Likewise as individual believers, we need to be careful to keep the spotlight focused on Jesus. There may be times when we will receive compliments and praise, maybe even for our service to the Lord and to the church. While we might be grateful for such acknowledgement, let's always remember that any gifts we possess and any good we do is all because of Jesus and the cross. Let's be sure to pass such praise and glory on to Him, not only in our own minds but also voicing that acknowledgement in the presence of others. Don't let others start shining the light more on you than on your Lord.

Although that steeple light on our church is reaching up to the cross, I may still have to make some adjustments to cause it to shine even brighter in that direction. Similarly let's make any necessary adjustments in our actions and attitudes in order to keep the spotlight shining as brightly as possible on Christ and the cross.

The next time you receive praise, turn the spotlight to Jesus.

DON'T BE BLIND TO THE TRUTH

"Whose minds the god of this age has blinded, who do not believe, lest the light of the gospel of the glory of Christ, who is the image of God, should shine on them."

– II CORINTHIAN 4:4

Getting reacquainted with the world of Little League baseball one spring a few years ago was a joy…for the most part. However, I was also reminded of the one perennial smudge on this otherwise pleasant experience—the parents and other adult onlookers. It's wonderful watching the kids have fun playing ball. But while doing so, you often have to endure parents yelling at coaches, arguing with umpires, and even berating poor scorekeepers who wait longer than a millisecond to update the scoreboard.

One thing I especially noticed about those adults sitting in the bleachers is how their bias toward their child's team blinds them to the reality of what is taking place on the field. I know it happens to some degree in every sport on any level, but it seems to be especially pronounced among the parents of Little Leaguers. They holler in protest at the umpire who dares to make a call against their child or his team, even if the play was not even close enough to be debatable. At one game I heard a lady swear up and down that the opposing team already had two outs in the inning, despite the umpire, official scorer, the other onlookers, and the rest of the free world assuring her that they only had one out. I wouldn't be surprised if she still believes her skewed version of reality to this day as she tells others how her son's team was treated unfairly.

I suppose we all are guilty of viewing the world around us through a lens that is affected by certain biases. It may be understandable, and even somewhat humorous, to see someone's enthusiasm for her child's team cause her to be so blind to obvious realities on a ball field. But it's a much more serious matter when we pit ourselves against God in our refusal to believe and accept the truth.

The Bible says that the gospel is "veiled" to those who are perishing, "whose minds the god of this age has blinded, who do not believe, lest the light of the glory of Christ…should shine on them" (II Corinthians 4:3–4).

Some people refuse to even believe that there is a God who has created us and who loves us. They don't believe the field exists on which the game of life is being played out where souls hang in the balance between eternal life and everlasting punishment. They are unwilling to accept what the scoreboard says—that left to ourselves we're going to lose—that it's only through Christ's sacrifice on the cross and His home run of a resurrection that we can come out a winner—and that time is running out for us to put our faith in Him.

Others may believe in God but don't like the way He coaches. They're so intent on doing things their way that they only hear from Him what they want to hear. They will even twist His words or explain away what He says in order to justify their actions. And when He starts umpiring and calling certain actions or attitudes sin, some folks will argue with Him until they're blue in the face.

Let's always seek to be open and receptive to whatever God says in His Word, regardless of how it may run counter to our own ideas, preferences, or traditions. Let's not be blind to what's really going on this world.

"Lord, help me not to be so affected by my biases that I refuse to see what You've made so plain or refuse to hear what You've spoken so clearly. And also, Lord, please improve the vision of the umpire who I still think missed that call at second base."

Do you have any bias that is hindering you from seeing and receiving some truth from God?

God Judges by the Love in Our Hearts

"You shall love the Lord your God with all your heart, with all your soul, and with all your mind. This is the first and great commandment."

– Matthew 22:37–38

One weekday I was in the sanctuary of our church when I discovered a Sunday school craft that one of my grandsons had left behind. Although I knew its return could easily wait until the next time I would normally see those members of the family, I decided to use the opportunity to drop by my daughter's house to deliver the lost item and say hi to my grandkids.

When I arrived it was around lunchtime, and the children were chowing down on peanut butter sandwiches. After a brief visit, I said my goodbyes. As I did, the kids wanted to give me a hug and a kiss. They reached out without even thinking about wiping their hands and mouths that were covered with the brown gooey stuff they were consuming. Realizing that I was heading out from there to visit some people at the nursing home, I graciously declined the kisses, explaining why. However, I did gratefully but carefully accept the hugs.

I think I came through the experience without any noticeable smears of peanut butter on me. However, even if my grandkids had kissed me and gotten me all messy, I really wouldn't have minded, even if it had meant going home to wash up and change clothes. I knew it was simply them wanting to express their love for me. It would bother me more if they didn't want to hug me.

Similarly, I don't believe God minds when our actions that stem from a lack of understanding or poor abilities come across a little messy at times, as long as they spring from hearts of love. Sometimes we get the idea that a holy God expects absolute perfection from His children—a standard impossible for us to live up to. But what He's looking for first and foremost are people who love Him with all their heart, soul, mind, and strength.

John Wesley, the founder of Methodism, talked about perfection in the Christian experience, but he expressed it in terms of "perfect love." It's a perfection that allows for human weaknesses, ignorance, and mistakes. It isn't about always behaving perfectly, but about our thoughts, words, and actions flowing from a heart filled with love for God and love for our neighbor.

Such a concept doesn't excuse wrong behavior or provide a loophole for us to knowingly disobey God while claiming that we love Him, but it makes room for the fact that we as limited human beings may not always adequately express outwardly our love relationship with God or the motive of love that's in our hearts.

Just because I may passionately sing a song of praise and worship to God doesn't mean it will be in key or be pleasant for others to hear. I may not sing it perfectly, but God values it as coming from a heart devoted to Him. Or your effort to help someone in need might fail because of your lack of knowledge about the situation, even though you were motivated by love.

We're always going to have a little peanut butter on our fingers as we try to hug God and express our love for Him. We will often find our outward expressions of love to others being misunderstood or falling short of the intended results, but that's okay. Let's keep striving to make our actions line up better with what's in our hearts. But when they don't God understands, as long as we're doing it out of devotion to Him.

Keep an eye on your motives. You're going to mess up at times, but the main thing is that your actions are springing from a heart of love for God.

Let's Treat Temptation like Spam

"Watch and pray, lest you enter into temptation."

– Matthew 26:41

It seems as if I've been receiving more spam through my e-mail account lately. Those unsolicited and unwanted messages at the very least can be annoying and at worst can be harmful to your computer if you open up the wrong one. In some cases those mass mailings come from people who are simply trying to sell you their product. However, others are generated by scoundrels who are out to perpetrate a scam. And there are even those that contain viruses intended to disable your computer.

But isn't it interesting how these messages are portrayed in their subject lines? There are those that make it sound like you won a lottery or that some generous soul wants to give you a big donation. Others scream out in big bold letters accompanied by exclamation points that they contain some urgent message that needs your immediate attention. Some try to sneak in with vague messages intended to rouse your curiosity just enough for you to open it up. And then there are the ones that try to sweet-talk their way into your computer with tag lines such as "dearest," "beloved," and "with great respect." Some go so far as to add a religious note—"My dearest in the Lord." Is it just preachers who get those pious-sounding ones, or do some of the rest of you receive such messages?

It reminds me of how our adversary often approaches us with temptation. At the beginning he doesn't show us the whole picture of what he's really trying to sell us, the harmful consequences down the road, and the destruction to which it will eventually lead. Instead, he puts a nice-sounding subject line on it in order to pique our interest and get us to take the first step in that direction. He will make it sound like we would win the lottery in wealth, power, pleasure, or some other personal benefit if we'll simply pursue that particular path. But he fails to point out the price that we'll pay in other ways—in our own peace of mind, in our relationships with other people, and in our relationship with God.

Other temptations pressure us with their call of urgency—"You've got to act now—this may be your only chance." They try to get us to act impulsively, rashly, and emotionally rather than taking time to wait on the Lord, to think, to pray, and to seek God's guidance.

On other occasions, the enemy of our soul will show us just enough to get us curious. We're not sure if it's bad or wrong, but it looks interesting enough for us to check out. And if we're not careful we can find ourselves sliding down a slippery slope from which it can be hard to regain our footing.

And the devil is not beyond using a little sweetness in his tone, even with a touch of piety. The Bible warns us that he can appear to be an angel of light. We have to look beyond appearances and ask the Lord to help us discern the true nature of the situations that are before us.

We need to treat those temptations in the same way we ought to deal with spam. I don't even open them up. I don't leave them hanging around on my computer. I delete them as soon as they show up. I don't allow myself to be gullible, curious, or pressured by those taglines. And neither should we toy around with temptation nor take that first step in the direction in which it entices us. Treat temptation like spam—recognize it, avoid it, and get rid of it.

And if you ever send me an e-mail, don't title it "dearest in the Lord" or I'll probably never open it.

Lord, help me to recognize any temptation that comes my way today and to avoid it.

Let's Be Willing to Take the Next Step toward Maturity

"Walk as children of light."
– Ephesians 5:8

I remember when one of my grandsons was getting ready to celebrate his first birthday. He was at that stage where he was almost ready to start walking. He would easily pull himself up and walk around furniture while holding onto it. He liked to take steps while firmly grasping the steadying hand of a familiar adult. Physically, his little legs seemed to be strong enough for this milestone task. However, mentally, I don't think he was quite ready to take the plunge. Or maybe that was the problem. He was a little too scared of those times when he would inevitably take a misstep and plunge toward the floor.

When we encouraged him to try to walk, there were times when he would bravely take two or three steps before faltering. But other times it appeared as if he didn't even want to try. He would allow his legs to hang limp or he would immediately plop to the floor to crawl to his desired destination. At that point he seemed to lack the confidence required to venture out in this new direction. When he watched his big brother running around, you could see in his eyes that he knew such activity was his destiny as well, and he was anxious to join him in doing it. But at the same time, he knew that it would mean leaving the safety of being close to the floor on hands and knees and instead wobbling unsteadily in an upright position that could result in falls, bumps, and bruises.

We can be similarly hesitant when it comes to taking steps toward spiritual maturity. It's interesting that the Bible describes our relationship with God as being a "walk." Some of us probably pray regularly for a closer walk with the Lord. We know that it's God's intention for us to keep making progress in that journey toward Christlikeness. We are challenged when we see others around us who have deeper prayer lives, greater knowledge of the Bible, more evidence of the fruit of the Spirit, and whose lights shine brighter for Jesus. They seem to run circles around us when it comes to nearness to God.

We want to be like them. We want to join them on that journey to spiritual maturity, but at the same time we're afraid to leave the safety of our current condition. We've gotten used to crawling and aren't too sure that we want to take the risk that would accompany making a major step forward in our journey with God.

We need greater confidence—not in ourselves but in the Lord. The Bible emphasizes that this walk with Him is one of faith. It's going to require leaving behind some old ways in which we've gotten settled and comfortable. It will mean taking steps into uncertain situations or down pathways in which our view ahead is limited. We may wobble, stumble, and take some falls, but we can be confident that the Lord will be with us to guide us, to catch us, or to soothe our hurts and help us back up again.

I didn't blame my grandson for his hesitation. I was just excited about him taking that next step, literally, in his maturity and for him to enter that adventurous stage of being a toddler. And I believe that's how the Lord looks at us. He's not expecting us to walk perfectly at this point. But He wants us to keep moving forward toward becoming the godly persons He's called us to be. He knows that we can do so much more if we would be willing to trust Him as He leads us in our spiritual journey.

So let's go. Let's take that next step in pursuing a closer walk with God.

What step toward greater spiritual growth will you take today?

CHRIST CAN SET US FREE

"He also brought me up out of a horrible pit, out of the miry clay,
and set my feel upon a rock, and established my steps."

– PSALM 40:2

One time my daughter found trapped in our garage a disoriented young cardinal—not one of the church officials by that title but the bird. Although we had seen and heard evidence of the presence of their nest in our yard, we had only spied the mother and father of the brood until now. In spite of the garage door being open and the bird having matured to the point of being able to fly, its inexperience led to repeated and futile efforts to escape by flying above the door into a dead end. My sympathetic daughter tried to help guide it to the path of freedom, only to have the creature end up crashing into a window several times. It finally found a place of momentary rest where one of those windows had been left ajar at the top for ventilation purposes. However, the young bird then fell between the window and the screen, finding itself even more confined than before.

As the fledgling fluttered down to the bottom of the window, it became covered with cobwebs, dead bugs, and living ants. It was trapped in an awful predicament with seemingly no way to escape without outside assistance. Meanwhile, my daughter noticed something that brought tears to her eyes. As the trapped bird chirped in despair, outside that same window in the bushes sat a couple of its brothers or sisters tweeting in response. I can only imagine what they were saying—asking him what he was doing in there, cheering him on in his efforts to escape, or maybe berating him for his stupidity, if they're anything like some brothers and sisters I know. The father bird was also seen flying by to see if he could do anything to help his wandering child.

I'm glad to report that the story has a happy ending. It took some effort, since that window is rarely used, but my daughter was able to raise it up to allow the bird to escape from its imprisonment. It found its way out of the garage this time, where the rest of its family immediately joined it in flight, celebrating its restored freedom.

If a young bird being in such peril tends to touch our hearts, how much more should we be moved by the predicament of people who have not received deliverance through Christ. And we've all been there at some point. Disoriented and uncertain when it comes to spiritual matters and in finding one's way to the right path. Trapped in the condition of having offended a holy God, yet not able to make things right with Him. Covered to some degree by the filthiness and cobwebs of our sin. Trapped in a place where death always seems to win out.

Sadly some of us don't even realize that we are in such a dangerous condition. Others are fluttering around, vainly trying to crash through windows of false hope or to lift themselves up to where they'll be good enough for God's approval. Yet we're helpless to escape on our own. We must be willing to accept the help of our rescuer, Jesus. He wants to open the window, deliver us from death, brush off the filth, and free us to soar to the heights for which He created us.

I hope your story has had a happy ending of finding that freedom in the Lord. And for those around us who are still trapped, let's be like the cardinal's family outside the window. While we can't perform the rescue ourselves, we can pray, we can encourage, and we can point out the way to freedom.

Have you let Christ set you free? For whom do you need to praying and encouraging to find their way to freedom?

Doing Whatever You Want Leads to Chaos

"Everyone did what was right in his own eyes."
– Judges 21:25

It would be a while before I would complain again about the traffic in my area. One time I found myself where I had determined never to return—driving in the middle of New York City. One wrong turn on our way to Long Island and there we were. Additionally, the roads we needed to turn onto in order to most easily get back on course were all blocked off. And from observing the educational attire being worn by some of the pedestrians, we concluded there was some kind of graduation activity going on which was making the area even more crowded than usual.

What makes the traffic so bad in the Big Apple is that drivers seem to do whatever they want regardless of the rules of the road. In our neck of the woods there are certainly some crazy drivers, but most of the time there is some semblance of orderliness to our traffic jams. However, in New York City the idea of lanes of vehicles quickly disappears as everyone converges from various directions. And if someone decides to move over into your "lane," don't kid yourself into believing that they're going to wait for you to let them over. They're coming and you had better get out of the way. Oh, I haven't even mentioned the numerous bicycle riders weaving in and out of the traffic. The word I would use to best describe the mess of cars, trucks, bicyclists, and pedestrians in which we were entangled for over two hours that afternoon is "chaos."

Such is what you inevitably get when everyone is doing his own thing. When society ignores law, rebels against authority, and shuns God-given values, the result is chaos. I believe we are experiencing an increasing degree of it in our day and in our nation. We're not staying within the well-defined lanes which civil societies have tended to follow. Some might call such movement freedom, but it can easily degenerate into lawlessness and confusion.

The Bible describes how the people of Israel fell into such a condition. It repeatedly notes that during a certain time period "everyone did what was right in his own eyes" (Judges 21:25). Their society became a mixed-up world of immorality, barbarism, and idolatry. And they were regularly facing God's judgment as He tried to steer them back onto a better course.

However, it's not just society as a whole that suffers when this kind of attitude prevails. Individual lives also become chaotic as a result of ignoring God's will and ways. What a mess people have made of their lives as a result of rebelling against God's authority or simply ignoring His commands and principles. Imagine how confused the kids of today will be in their adult years if they grow up in this kind of an environment that is taking away moral absolutes and leaving them with a very subjective view of what may be right or wrong.

Many people today are determined to veer out of the proper lane and go their own way regardless of what God says about it. And often if they insist on doing what is right in their own eyes, God will eventually step aside to let them have their way. The good news is that even in the midst of God's judgment there is mercy, if we'll turn back to Him and submit to His ways.

So let's pray for this chaotic world we're living in. And no matter what our society does, let's be sure to be individuals who aren't just doing whatever we want but what we believe God wants us to do.

Pray for our rebellious society and for God's mercy on us. Is there any way in which you're doing your own thing instead of seeking and following what God says to do?

JESUS WALKS WHERE WE WALK

"And the Word became flesh and dwelt among us."
– JOHN 1:14

One of my daughters and her husband went on a trip to Israel. They were part of a group taking a tour of what many refer to as the Holy Land. While I've never made that journey myself, I imagine it is quite inspirational to visit many of the sites mentioned in the Bible—to walk through the streets of Jerusalem, to ride in a boat on the Sea of Galilee, and to participate in baptisms in the Jordan River. I'm sure it makes the Scriptures come alive when a person stands at spots where significant events are purported to have occurred, such as Jesus' birthplace, the hill on which He was crucified, and the empty tomb.

Some of these tours use the promotional phrase, "Walk where Jesus walked." As helpful as such a pilgrimage as that can be, and as happy as I am for those who get to experience it, I'm even more grateful that Jesus chose to walk where we walk. He came to us. He took on flesh and blood and made the humbling journey to enter this world as a human being. We should never lose our sense of wonder and awe at the fact of Christ's incarnation—"And the Word became flesh and dwelt among us, and we beheld His glory, the glory as of the only begotten of the Father, full of grace and truth" (John 1:14).

Even today Jesus continues to choose to walk where we walk. His Spirit lives in the hearts of those who put their faith in Him. He makes His home with us. The Spirit of Jesus accompanies us through the high points of our lives, through the dark valleys, and through all the multitudinous daily mundane experiences in between. He goes with us to our workplace, to school, to the ballpark, and in our homes. He walks where we walk.

While the truth of Jesus' abiding presence should give us a great measure of comfort and joy, it should also challenge us. It should remind us of our calling, our mission, and our need to follow in His footsteps. We should also seek to be incarnational in a sense. In other words, we need to walk where others walk.

We shouldn't isolate ourselves from a lost world. We need to be careful not to retreat into the Holy Land of our church buildings waiting for people to come to us. We shouldn't reserve the good news of salvation in Christ for the few people who choose to make the pilgrimage to where we are. We need to be going out into their world, walking where they walk, and letting the glory of Christ, full of grace and truth, shine through us.

This doesn't mean that we take part in the sins of others or that we compromise biblical principles. Although Jesus became human with all its weaknesses, He remained sinless. "For we do not have a High Priest who cannot sympathize with our weaknesses, but was in all points tempted as we are, yet without sin" (Hebrews 4:15). Like Jesus, we can walk where others walk and still be godly people.

A trip to the Holy Land is a wonderful opportunity, but I'm glad we don't have to go to Israel to find Jesus. He walks where we walk. And likewise let's not force others to make the arduous journey to come to us in order to find Him. Let's walk where they walk and let's allow them to see Jesus in us.

Look for opportunities today to be incarnational—to take Jesus to others by walking where they walk.

WE HAVE THE POWER
TO OVERCOME EVIL

"Behold, I give you the authority to trample on serpents and scor-
pions, and over all the power of the enemy."

– LUKE 10:19

"**O**uch! Ow!" That was my reaction when I experienced my first sting by a scorpion. I've encountered such creatures numerous times, but when I've seen one I've always treated it with careful respect as I subsequently disposed of it. The problem on this occasion was that I didn't spy the culprit until after he had inflicted his attack on my finger.

I think I have come away from this experience with a better appreciation for why Jesus would associate scorpions with Satan and the powers of evil. It was when a group of Christ's followers were rejoicing over the fact that they had been able to cast out demons in the name of Jesus. He told them, "Behold, I give you the authority to trample on serpents and scorpions, and over all the power of the enemy, and nothing shall by any means hurt you" (Luke 10:19). Although this particular scorpion did hurt me, I am pleased to report that I quickly took the authority to trample on it until it was dead.

There are various thoughts as to the extent to which believers have been given the authority Jesus spoke of in that verse. Some relegate such power only to those early followers of Christ. Others interpret this passage to mean that Christians today should be boldly exercising such authority over all the evils and demons in our world.

Regardless of your view of that particular passage, hopefully we can all agree that believers do have the ability through Christ to resist and overcome evil. We aren't helpless victims of Satan and sin. The Bible clearly instructs us to "resist the devil and he will flee from you" (James 4:7). In the classic passage from Ephesians 6, it warns us about the wiles of the devil, the fiery darts of the wicked one, and spiritual hosts of wickedness. But it tells us that we can be strong in the Lord in the face of those enemies. It reminds us we have God-given spiritual armor which can cause us to withstand those evil forces. We do wrestle against such powers, but we can emerge from that experience victorious through Christ.

But as we think about the authority to overcome evil, let's not just picture exorcisms performed over the demon-possessed, or laying hands on the sick for divine healing, or bold prayers commanding Satan to pack his bags and leave our home, school, or community. Let's recognize that we can experience such victories in our own battles with temptation. Through Christ we can overcome the personal demons of addiction, sexual immorality, impure thoughts, malicious verbal assaults, pride, selfishness, and all other means the enemy uses to attack our souls. We don't have to be victims who are constantly trying to recover from another spiritual beating and defeat. We have been given the authority to withstand those attacks.

And don't forget we can do more than simply resist evil. The Bible says, "Do not be overcome by evil, but overcome evil with good" (Romans 12:21). We can conquer evil by doing good. We can replace evil thoughts with a mind focused on godly things. We can overcome sexual immorality by lavishing Christlike love upon our wives and husbands. We can replace selfishness with unselfish acts of helping others. Don't cast out evil and leave a vacuum in its place. Fill your life with good.

But one word of warning: don't try to trample those scorpions with your barefooted self-effort. You'll only get hurt. Be sure to put on the boot of Christ. Only through Him can we have the power and ability to overcome evil.

Take authority in Christ over the evil that oppresses you. How can you overcome it with good?

A Serious Disease Requires a Strong Remedy

"For he who has died has been freed from sin."
– Romans 6:7

I have a couple of acquaintances who are currently battling cancer. Each of them has been recently undergoing the grueling experience of the combination of chemotherapy and radiation treatment. Those sessions often result in patients dealing with extreme fatigue, hair loss, bad nausea, and other difficult side effects. But those brave warriors who are forced to fight this battle know that those are challenges which must be endured in order for the disease to be treated. As one of them expressed to me, "It's like they almost have to kill the body in order to kill the cancer."

We face a similar battle when it comes to dealing with the cancer in our souls. This deadly spiritual disease isn't one that just affects a few. We've all been infected by it. We could simply call it "sin," but don't think of it in terms of any particular action. Those acts of sin are simply the symptoms of the disease which lies deep within us. It's a selfishness, a willfulness, a tendency toward rebellion, and a bent toward ungodliness that pulls against any of our desires and efforts to follow God.

We could trace virtually all of our spiritual failings to this disease in our soul. It's what causes us to insist on having our own way. It's what makes us unwilling to submit to God. It's what instills in us a desire to pursue the wrong things rather than pursuing godliness. Those various sinful acts we may commit are rooted in the condition of our heart, the thoughts in our minds, and the desires of our soul.

So what can we do about this spiritual malady? Some simply ignore it or give in to it, suggesting that it can't be overcome. They might adhere to the philosophy that it's okay to let this cancer rule in your life, as long as you seek forgiveness for every incident when it springs to the surface.

Others might try to appease this spiritual disease, to cover up its symptoms with bandages, or to try to treat it with mild remedies. But that would be like trying to treat cancer by taking cough medicine or a couple of aspirin. The cancer in our souls won't be overcome by a frequent dose of church attendance, an occasional prayer, or through giving some money to that homeless guy holding up a sign at the interstate exit.

A serious disease requires a strong treatment. The Bible suggests that in order to truly be free from this condition, we must die to our self-centered nature. "Knowing this, that our old man was crucified with Him (Christ), that the body of sin might be done away with, that we should no longer be slaves to sin. For he who has died has been freed from sin" (Romans 6:6–7). We have to come to the point of completely surrendering our wills to the Lord's will, letting His desires take priority over our own. Then we will be able to testify, "I have been crucified with Christ; it is no longer I who live, but Christ lives in me; and the life which I now live in the flesh I live by faith in the Son of God, who loved me and gave Himself for me" (Galatians 2:20).

It can be painful to let the Great Physician treat our spiritual cancer. It may feel like part of our very being is being ripped out. But we can't afford to deal with this condition gently. Only as we die to sin and self-centeredness can we find fullness of life in Christ.

Have you completely surrendered your will to the Lord's will? Be willing to face the pain in order to experience the remedy.

BE WILLING TO BE A SACRIFICIAL SOLDIER FOR CHRIST

"You therefore must endure hardship as a good soldier of Jesus Christ."

– II TIMOTHY 2:3

For more than twenty-five years our church has conducted a monthly worship service at a local nursing home. I can remember when my children, who at the time were about the same age as my grandchildren are now, would join with a few other kids from our congregation to form a makeshift junior choir for the occasion. Those elderly residents especially seemed to enjoy it when the children enthusiastically sang, along with all the motions, "I'm in the Lord's Army."

Associating our faith with military concepts is frowned upon by many people these days. They don't like terms such as crusades, soldiers, and warfare to be used in connection with Christianity. Some have revised or removed well-known songs from hymnals because of their strong militaristic language.

However, it was God in His Word who originally made such a comparison. The Bible makes reference to believers putting on the armor of God (Ephesians 6:11), enduring hardship as good soldiers of Christ (II Timothy 2:3), and being engaged in warfare (II Timothy 2:4). Certainly those militaristic ideas can be taken too far or abused. We need to be clear about the kind of warfare we're talking about and avoid misunderstandings which would cause people to place us in the same category as terrorists or suicide bombers. But if God sees some value in making this connection between our faith and the military, let's not "throw out the baby with the bath water." While avoiding extremes, let's affirm the truths within those comparisons from which we can learn and benefit.

As Memorial Day approaches when we remember and honor those who gave their lives in serving our country, I believe it can be helpful for us to remember that we are soldiers too. As the song suggests, we are in the Lord's army. And the kind of spirit we recognize in those who died in military service should be similar to the spirit we possess as followers of Christ. Those soldiers loved our country enough to be willing to make the ultimate sacrifice for it. Do we love our Lord to that degree? Those fallen heroes were committed to carrying out their duty even when it put their lives at risk. Are we so committed to the cause of Christ?

This is one of the values I see in the military comparisons. It lends balance to some of the other pictures we connect with our faith. It helps us avoid thinking the Christian life is always going to be an easy, pleasurable pathway. It keeps us from falling into that consumer mindset of Christianity being all about me and my needs getting met. It helps us to see that following Jesus isn't just about warm and fuzzy moments of joining hands singing "Kumbaya."

There are enemies to encounter, hard roads to climb, sacrifices to be made, and responsibilities to be fulfilled—even to the point of putting our own wishes, plans, and very lives at risk. Jesus said, "If anyone desires to come after Me, let him deny himself, and take up his cross, and follow Me" (Matthew 16:24). Too many of us want to follow Christ without it costing us anything. When it comes time to deny self and take up our cross, we make excuses or refuse to take that route.

Let's seek to have the same kind of spirit and commitment in our faith as those fallen soldiers we honor. Love the Lord and be so committed to Him that you'll be willing to risk anything in His service, even your own life. After all, we're not merely civilians or tourists in this world—we're in the Lord's army.

How would it change your attitude and behavior if you thought of yourself as a soldier of Christ?

LET'S KEEP LEARNING
AND GROWING

"Not that I have already attained, or am already perfected; but I press on...."

– PHILIPPIANS 3:12

It wasn't referred to as a graduation. They called it a "Moving On Celebration." That seemed to be a fitting title for this class of fine young people as they came to the end of their school year. They were leaving behind one important stage in their journey and preparing to move forward to...kindergarten. That's right. This particular ceremony which I was attending was for the pre-k class of one of my grandsons.

When you think about the many years of formal education ahead for that group of kids, they've got a lot of "moving on" yet to do. However, the same can be said for all who will be celebrating graduations this year. For many leaving high school, they will be pursuing further studies at various universities and colleges. Others of them, along with those obtaining their college degrees, will begin receiving a different kind of education as they enter into their chosen fields of employment.

The truth is we should never stop moving forward in our education, whether in formal ways or in simply learning from our life experiences. I'm proud of my wife for adding another degree to her credentials a few years ago, completing her courses with a 4.0 average. We all need to keep growing in knowledge and improving our skills throughout the years of our lives.

And the same holds true in our journey with Christ. We should always be seeking to move on to the next level. Some of us may not be much more than newborn babies in the faith who need to learn those basic ABCs of following Jesus. Others of us may be battle-tested veterans who have traveled this way for many years. But no matter what our current status, we all have greater heights to which to aspire.

There is always more that we can learn about God—this infinite Being who is so far beyond us in His majesty, power, holiness, and love. There is more that we can learn about the Bible, I don't care how long you may have preached or taught a Sunday School class. And there is more that we can let the Lord teach us about ourselves—helping us set aside our rose-colored glasses we tend to wear when we look into our own hearts and instead enabling us to see ourselves more as He does.

We can also keep learning more of the skills to be successful in our walk with God. We may know what we ought to do, but we all could use some improvement in living up to that knowledge. Do you really think your prayer life is as good as it can be? Aren't there ways we could better show God's love to those around us? Couldn't our lights shine even brighter in this dark world? We all have areas in our lives in which we need to keep experiencing spiritual growth.

Let's maintain the attitude of the Apostle Paul. He declared, "Not that I have already attained, or am already perfected; but I press on, that I may lay hold of that for which Christ Jesus has laid hold of me. Brethren, I do not count myself to have apprehended; but one thing I do, forgetting those things which are behind and reaching forward to those things which are ahead, I press toward the goal for the prize of the upward call of God in Christ Jesus" (Philippians 3:12–14).

As believers, let's stay committed to moving forward in our relationship with Christ. Let's keep growing, right up until the day we're called home to heaven. Then that occasion will truly be a "Moving On Celebration."

What step can you take to learn more about God or to improve some skill for use in His service?

Be a Treasure Hunter

"Therefore every scribe instructed concerning the kingdom of heaven is like a householder who brings out of his treasure things new and old."

– MATTHEW 13:52

I thought of Jesus' words to His disciples quoted above on an occasion in which I was feeling very much like that householder of whom Christ spoke. My wife and I were cleaning out some cabinets and sorting through the contents of boxes in preparation for a little remodeling work being done in a couple of rooms in our house. In the process, along with the junk we discarded we discovered a number of long-forgotten treasures.

Some were newer, like the tablecloths from the church which had been discovered missing as we were preparing for our Homecoming dinner. Apparently at some point we had brought them home to be washed, where they had gotten lost under a stack of other items.

But most of the treasures we pulled out were older. I doubt that any of the items we found are worth anything monetarily—not even the autograph of former heavyweight champ, Evander Holyfield. But some of them did hold sentimental value for us, especially those which were connected to our children when they were little. We came upon Girl Scout sashes, Little League baseball uniforms, and several pictures, such as the one of my son when he met the Power Rangers. Even my grandchildren were impressed by that photo.

God has provided an even greater treasury for us to explore—the Bible. As we read God's Word we discover all kinds of valuable truths.

Some of them are old. We may rediscover a few of those stories we were taught as children in Sunday School. We might be reminded of verses that God used to help us through some tough times in our lives. We may be reunited with truths which once helped us put our faith in Christ and assisted in our growth in grace.

But we also might find some new treasures in those familiar pages. No matter how many times I read the Bible, I often see something that I hadn't noticed previously. And those truths of God's Word are truly timeless and relevant today. God may use one of those old, familiar promises to assure you or comfort you regarding a current situation you're facing. The stories, principles, and truths haven't changed—and by the way, they never will. But the Spirit of God can make them alive and new to us. God can use His Word to touch our lives in fresh ways—to bring conviction of sin, to strengthen our faith, to soothe us with His love or in whatever way we may need it.

If you haven't been regularly reading God's Word, you're missing out on the opportunity to find some valuable treasures for your life. It's great if we can try to read through the whole Bible. Not only does it help us see the bigger picture, but sometimes we'll find the most helpful tidbits of truth in the most unlikely places. But if nothing else, read a few verses or a chapter each day with your heart set on hearing something from God. Keep reading until God reveals one of those valuable nuggets of gold for your life.

Let's also remember that those treasures from the Bible aren't meant simply to stir up old memories or to bring us pleasure. God wants to use them to do a remodeling job on us, as He continues to make us more into the image of His Son.

So let's recommit ourselves today to being treasure hunters in God's Word.

Are you regularly reading God's Word? Start writing down one nugget of truth God shows you from your Bible reading each day.

LET THE CHARACTER OF CHRIST SHINE THROUGH YOU

"Till we all come…to the measure of the stature of the fullness of Christ."

– EPHESIANS 4:13

I've grown accustomed to seeing various creatures around the porch of our church building. My most frequent encounters are with the various types of lizards that have taken up residence in the area underneath the shrubbery. I usually just get glimpses of them scurrying back into the brush as I approach. However one day I was surprised by one falling off the top of the door as I opened it up. Fortunately it landed on the pavement beside me instead of on top of my head. And depending on the season of the year, it's not unusual to find centipedes, spiders, ants, and other such bugs in the area.

So as I was unlocking the church door one morning, I hardly paid attention to a small bug crawling up the side of the wall. But as the realization dawned on me as to what it was, I did a double take. As I turned back to look more closely, I saw that it truly was what I had thought. Although it couldn't have been more than an inch long, the distinctive features revealed without any doubt that it was a praying mantis. I've seen those interesting creatures around the church before, but usually about four or five times the size of this one. Although it was the tiniest one I could recall ever encountering, it's shape, movement, and other characteristics allowed me to positively identify it as one of those piously-named insects.

I wonder if people can so readily identify us as followers of Christ? Although we are not actually smaller versions of the one-and-only Son of God, we should be reflections of His character and should share those qualities that are so distinct in Him. To some degree people ought to be able to recognize Jesus in us.

What are some of those distinctive characteristics that made Jesus stand out from the crowd? One was His purity. He was the sinless Son of God. While none of us in this life will ever attain to that same kind of sinless perfection, there should be growing evidence that we are continually gaining greater victory over sin in our lives. We can have hearts purified by faith (Acts 15:9) and resulting lives that bear the fruit of holiness (Romans 6:22).

Jesus was also different because of His compassion. In contrast to the religious leaders of His day who were harsh toward sinners, Jesus offered mercy and grace. He reached out in love to those whom others ignored. The Bible indicates that love should be one of the most distinctive qualities people see in us as Christians (John 13:35). The kind of compassion that reaches out to help the needy, that speaks up to share the gospel with the lost, and that offers forgiveness and hope to those who have done wrong will mark us as followers of Christ.

Jesus was also noted for the authority with which He spoke. We carry similar authority, not when we simply share our opinions or current popular ideas, but when we stay true to God's Word and speak from it what God has clearly revealed to be His will.

Let's use the words of an old chorus as our prayer today: "Let the beauty of Jesus be seen in me; all His wonderful passion and purity. O, thou Spirit Divine, all my nature refine, till the beauty of Jesus be seen in me." As I recognized that miniature version of a praying mantis, may others recognize the glorious character of Christ in our small, human frames.

Do people see characteristics of Jesus in you? How can you cultivate some of those Christlike qualities in which you're lacking?

ARE OUR DAILY LIVES CONSISTENT WITH OUR FAITH?

"And such were some of you. But you were washed, but you were sanctified."

– I CORINTHIANS 6:11

I was standing in line at a community event when I overheard the group of people in front of me begin to talk about their church. Due to their close proximity and the loudness of their voices, I probably could not have helped but listen in. But admittedly that subject naturally garnered my attention. I didn't hear the name of the church or the names of any specific persons, and I'm rather glad that I didn't.

The conversation was about several individuals in that congregation who led Bible studies or otherwise faithfully served the church. The people speaking had thought highly of these individuals as Christians and church leaders based on what they had witnessed on Sundays. But when they went to the Facebook pages of those persons, they saw pictures and read posts that seemed blatantly inconsistent with their Sunday saintliness. One person described it as a "disconnect" with their faith.

If the truth were told, that conversation could probably have been about some people in most of our churches. Sometimes they are individuals who regularly attend worship services but who have never experienced a personal relationship with Jesus Christ. In other cases, it may be Christians who are newly converted and still immature in their faith. If our church is doing its job of reaching out to the lost, there should be representatives of those groups in our congregations. And in those situations it's understandable that there might be such a contradiction in behavior, at least for a while.

However what should disturb us, as it seemed to bother the group discussing these matters on this occasion, is when such a disconnect exists in those who appear to be the mature saints and leaders of a congregation. And such persons don't seem to see it or realize it. It raises questions about the very validity, or at least the depth, of their relationship with Christ. Such disparity is evidence that something is wrong when the lifestyle of a Christian is not consistent with his profession of faith. We know in our hearts that one's faith should make a difference in how we live throughout the week, not just in what we do and how we behave on Sundays.

The Bible says that if we are "in Christ," then we are new creations (II Corinthians 5:17). We don't just act differently; we are different. Salvation is not simply a behavior modification program. It changes who we are. It reaches to the depth of our minds and hearts. It transforms our desires, values, and priorities.

God's Word speaks of Christians not just as those who no longer commit certain sins, but as those who were adulterers, thieves, drunkards, and the like, but are no longer. We have been "washed" and are new and different now (I Corinthians 6:9–11). And that profound difference should show wherever we are, whether sitting in a pew or in our living room recliner.

Maybe those folks standing in line weren't talking about someone in your church or mine, but people who exhibit such a disconnect between their faith and their daily lives is a problem that doesn't seem to be uncommon. Let's make sure that we're not one of them. That disconnect might not show up on our Facebook page but might be evident on our job, at school, or in the privacy of our home.

Let's remember that being a Christian isn't just about what we do on Sunday. It's about what we do and who we are and what's in our hearts every day.

Does anything in your private life, including your posts on social media, reveal a "disconnect" with your faith?

Should We Remember
or Forget?

"Forgetting those things which are behind."
– Philippians 3:13

Memorial Day is a time for pausing to give thanks for those individuals who were willing to sacrifice their lives in service to our country. It's a time to remember. Remembering can be a tricky thing—not just in our ability or inability to recall events from years gone by, although the failure of my memory to function as sharply has become more noticeable to me in recent years. I'm discovering more and more of those *Jeopardy* questions that I know but can't quite bring to the forefront of my mind quickly enough. Some of us as we get older are also finding it disturbing that we can clearly recall the details of certain events twenty years ago but can't remember why we just walked into the kitchen. By the way, have I written about this before? At the moment, I can't remember.

Remembering can also be a rather tricky question biblically. Are we to forget the past or remember it? On the one hand, the Bible talks about "forgetting those things which are behind and reaching forward to those things which are ahead" (Philippians 3:13). But in other instances, God's Word commends remembering the wonderful works of God, along with specific events such as the Israelites' deliverance from Egyptian slavery, Christ's death, and even the tragic fate of Lot's wife.

I'm not sure that trying to wipe particular past occurrences from our memories is the answer being recommended in that passage in

Philippians. We may wish we could forget some of the things we've done or witnessed, or things that were done to us. Yet those images remain, and their consequences may still affect us. Maybe the "forgetting" stands in contrast to the idea of "reaching forward." Could it be that God is instructing us not to reach toward what's behind us? We may still remember what took place but we can refuse to dwell on it, try to recapture it, or allow it to cling to us as an albatross around our necks.

There can be great benefit in recalling the positive happenings of previous years. We can rejoice in God's goodness. We can remind ourselves and others of the power and love of the Lord. We can gain confidence that the God who has helped in the past will be there to provide whatever we need in the future. However when we nostalgically hold onto those past victories, trying to relive them and refusing to move forward, it can become a hindrance to us.

We can also profit from remembering some of our negative experiences in life. We can learn from our mistakes or from those of others. We can see where God has brought us from and how His grace is sufficient to overcome our weaknesses. But when we allow those past events to get us mired down in regrets, bitterness, and hopelessness, we are letting them hold us back from the present and future God has for us.

Regardless of what has happened in the past, whether wonderful or horrible, God can help us to move forward from where we are. He can even use some of those events which we view as negative to make us better people and to give us an opportunity to help others who may be experiencing similar situations.

So let's remember…with smiles and tears. Let's remember…but not cling to the past. Let's remember…with faith and hope. Let's remember… while we keep reaching forward to the things which are ahead of us.

Is there something from the past you're allowing to hold you back? Is there something from the past you need to remember, learn from, or give thanks for?

Relish Your Uniqueness
in God's Family

"Now you are the body of Christ, and members individually."
– I Corinthians 12:27

Before our second grandchild arrived in the world, we were informed to expect another boy. My mind pictured a carbon copy of his brother, especially with the full head of white hair that has been the distinguishing feature of our first grandson. However, Jaycen (no, that's not a spelling error) has proven to be his own little man. His hair was darker—a light brown with a reddish tint to it, which has only gotten redder as he's matured. He was also lacking the dimpled chin of his brother and father. Some people were suggesting that he seemed to have more of the physical characteristics of his mother. And personality differences also quickly emerged, even as an infant. Whereas our first grandson relished lying in a stretched-out position, this child seemed to prefer sleeping curled up.

Granted, those were initial observations based on the first few days of this child's life. As he grew, there were many similarities to note between him and his brother. But Jaycen is still making it clear that he is a unique individual within this family, not a replica of anyone else.

That can also be a helpful truth to keep in mind for members of the family of God. Sometimes we get the idea that our Heavenly Father wants us to be exactly like some other Christian we know and admire. We may try to imitate them in certain ways, which isn't necessarily a bad practice. Paul instructed some of his brothers and sisters in Christ to imitate him

(I Corinthians 4:16). However, in doing so, we need to be careful that we don't start looking upon some of our distinguishing qualities as liabilities when in fact they may be assets, both to us and to God.

The Bible makes it clear that our Creator has made each one of us to be unique individuals. He has purposefully formed us a certain way. We are also told that His Spirit doesn't give every Christian the same gifts. As Paul explains, we are all part of the one body of Christ, but we are individual members with abilities and other qualities peculiar to us (I Corinthians 12:27). And God wants it that way. He wants His toolbox to have a variety of useful instruments, not simply be full of all hammers or all screwdrivers.

Within His family of those who have received Christ into their hearts, the main goal is not conformity to one another as much as it is for us to be transformed into the image of Christ. And that image is going to look a little different in each person because of our distinctive personalities, appearances, and abilities. If we are Christians, we have Christ living in us. But "Christ in me" is going to express itself in some ways that will differ from how "Christ in you" is manifested.

Surely there will be, and ought to be, some family traits which we will share. We should manifest such characteristics of our Father as love, purity, mercy, justice, and many others. But the manner in which we reflect those qualities will vary from person to person. Our primary aim isn't to be a clone of a fellow Christian, but rather to allow Christ to show Himself through us with all of our distinct features in body, mind, and spirit.

So instead of letting your uniqueness be a source of frustration, celebrate it. Let God shape you more into the Christlike image that only you can fulfill. The Lord has a slot in His toolbox in which only you will fit and a work that only someone like you can do.

What are your unique qualities? How can they be positive attributes as you reflect the image of Christ and serve Him?

GOD IS ALWAYS WORKING
BEHIND THE SCENES

*"Then the Lord opened the eyes of the young man, and he saw.
And behold, the mountain was full of horses and chariots of fire all
around Elisha."*

– II KINGS 6:17

My wife and I recently enjoyed a vacation in the Caribbean on one of the largest cruise ships on the seas. One morning we participated in what was called an "All Access Tour," giving us a behind-the-scenes look at parts of the ship the passengers normally don't get to see. We toured the galley, where all the abundant and delicious food is prepared. We saw the laundry facilities, the storage areas, the control room, and even made it up to the bridge where the captain steers the ship.

It was interesting to see this whole other world that was hidden beneath the surface of the public dining, entertainment, and shopping areas. It was enlightening to realize all the activity that takes place out of sight in order to facilitate a good experience for the guests. The technology, skill, hard work, and efficiency required is amazing. It made me appreciate even more the amenities which we can so easily take for granted, everything from a hot meal to a clean towel. And I certainly appreciated all the precautions taken to ensure a safe voyage for all who are on board.

Let's not forget that the world we live in is a lot like that cruise ship. What we see is only the tip of the iceberg—well, maybe that's not a good analogy to use when talking about ships—but you know what I mean.

There is a whole other world of activity going on which we normally can't see. We experience the results of it. We reap the benefits of it. But much of it is veiled behind a curtain that we can only access through the eyes of faith.

There have been rare occasions when the veil has been lifted to give people a glimpse of the other world. There was the time when the Syrian army had surrounded the prophet Elisha. When his servant panicked, Elisha prayed for God to open his eyes to see this unseen realm. Suddenly the servant could see a vast spiritual army prepared to fight on their behalf. Likewise the shepherds were allowed to see the heavenly host praising God at the birth of Jesus. And Stephen was permitted to look into heaven itself to see Jesus standing at the right hand of God.

However, those are the exceptions. Generally we aren't granted such access. The important thing is that we not forget about the reality of what's going on behind the curtain. It's easy to focus on our visible world and lose sight of the invisible one. The Bible reminds us that "we do not look at the things which are seen, but at the things which are not seen" (II Corinthians 4:18). While this may be referring primarily to our future reward, we also need to keep in mind the spiritual realities of the moment.

Although we don't always know where life is taking us, we are aware that God, our captain, is at the helm keeping us on the proper course. When problems arise, we know that our Lord is sitting in the control room, aware of the issues, and able to handle whatever comes up. We may not see it, but there is a crew of angels constantly ministering to our needs, protecting us, and battling in our behalf. Such a perspective can cause us to better appreciate what God is doing and the blessings we receive as a result of His unseen actions.

So as we cruise through this life, let's remember that there's so much more going on than what our eyes can see. Be thankful for that essential divine activity which is hidden from our view. Without it our world would be a sinking ship.

In what situation that you're facing would it be helpful to remember that there is divine activity going on which you cannot see?

MAKE SURE YOU'RE
A FAN OF JESUS

"Now in giving these instructions I do not praise you, since you come together not for the better but for the worse."

– I CORINTHIANS 11:17

I remember an occasion when I made it a point to watch every moment of an Atlanta Braves' baseball game on TV. I even recorded the program, so if I had to leave the room for a few moments, I could go back and quickly review whatever I had missed. I bet you didn't know I was such an avid fan. Or am I?

I do normally keep up with what the Braves are doing. As a kid, I faithfully listened to their games on the radio, pulling for the likes of Hank Aaron, Rico Carty, and Felipe Alou. These days I will sometimes watch part of their games, or at least turn to that channel occasionally to see what the score is. However, it's rare for me to sit and watch a whole game or even a majority of such a contest. On this particular occasion, I wasn't tuning in primarily to watch the Braves play. The main reason for my intense interest in this specific event was not the ballgame itself, but the fact that my daughter and her family were in attendance. I was primarily watching to see if they showed my grandchildren on TV. After all, they do sometimes focus the camera on cute kids, and what children could be cuter than my grandkids?

We need to be aware of similar possibilities when it comes to our participation in worship services or other church-related activities. Just because we're in attendance or "tuned in" doesn't necessarily make us avid followers of Jesus. Are we there for the right reason? Are we worshiping the Lord in spirit and in truth, as Jesus advocated? Sometimes our motives can be deceptive or we can be guilty of focusing on something other than the main event or purpose of the gathering.

Maybe we came there more intent on seeing our friends than on meeting Jesus. Or in some cases we might be more focused on being seen, giving a performance, or some other self-exalting reason rather than being focused on honoring the Lord. Maybe we're there more to enjoy the uplifting musicians or the dynamic speaker than to delight in the fellowship with God. In some cases we might simply be following tradition instead of pursuing a relationship with the Lord. There's a ballgame going on—a contest for souls—an opportunity to worship the Almighty God—a chance to hear the Lord's message for us—but we're focused on some secondary matter instead.

The Apostle Paul addressed such an issue in the church at Corinth. The people were coming together faithfully to participate in the Lord's Supper. However, some of them were gathering only to selfishly overindulge in the food and drink. As a result, some who were hungry among them were being neglected, as well as the sacred commemoration of Christ's death being observed in an unworthy manner (see I Corinthians 11:17–34). An uninformed observer might have concluded that those participants were wonderful Christians. However, Paul saw their practice as a reason for rebuke rather than praise.

Don't get me wrong. It's good to be in church to participate in worship services and ministry opportunities. Let's just keep an eye on our motives. Let's make sure we're focusing on the main reason for being there. It's not just about enjoying all the secondary aspects of the experience. Let's not just be fans of church, religion, tradition, or good friends—let's be devoted fans of Jesus.

Check your motives. Why do you go to church?

ACCEPT JESUS' OFFER
TO PAY YOUR BILL

"Knowing that you were not redeemed with corruptible things...
but with the precious blood of Christ."

– I PETER 1:18–19

It was an unexpected blessing. My wife and I were eating lunch at one of our local restaurants recently, not simply one of the fast-food joints but a nicer sit-down establishment. After enjoying a delicious meal, we were looking for our server to come by with our check. As we were starting to make our preparations to pay the bill, our server informed us that the check had already been taken care of. We weren't certain we had heard or understood her correctly, but she went on to assure us that we didn't owe anything for our meal that day.

We still don't know the source or reason for this unusual occurrence. In spite of what the server described as "confused" looks on our faces, she offered no further explanation about the situation. We quickly looked around the restaurant to see if we might spy some familiar face who would have offered such an act of kindness, but to no avail. So we just gratefully accepted this gracious gift, giving thanks to the One from whom all blessings ultimately flow.

Jesus has done something very similar for each of us. He has paid our debt. However there's a huge difference in this case: this debt is one that is impossible for us to pay ourselves. It's the debt which has resulted because of our sin. Jesus took care of it for us by going to the cross and giving Himself as the sacrifice for our sins. He paid a great price in order for us to receive this benefit. In 1 Peter 1:18–19, it reminds us that we "were not redeemed with corruptible things, like silver or gold…but with the precious blood of Christ." As a result, God's Word comes to us with the good news—"Someone has paid your bill; your debt is canceled; you don't owe anything."

Unfortunately some of us have a difficult time accepting this wonderful gift. We think we must earn it in some way. We have a hard time getting past our tendency to do it ourselves and to be self-made individuals. There are some people who spend their entire lives trying to do good deeds with the hope that it will be enough to pay their debt with God. They have no real assurance of salvation, just the wishful thought, *I hope I've been good enough.*

Thankfully we don't have to rely on our own insufficient righteousness. We just need to put our faith in the One who has paid our bill. And then we can show our love and gratitude to Him by seeking to live the way that would bring honor and glory to His name.

I suppose my wife and I could have attempted to refuse to accept this gracious gift of a free meal which was offered to us that day. We could have grilled the server to try to find out more details about who had done this and why. Maybe there are a few people around who would've gotten angry or offended at such an offer, but I dare say that most people would have been like us and gladly received this act of kindness and grace.

Why can't we be equally open to this gracious act of Jesus on our behalf? Why do we allow our sinful pride to keep us from humbly admitting our sinfulness and our inability to save ourselves? The offer still stands today. You can have your debt paid and know that your account with God is free and clear. Accept Jesus' loving and gracious gift—He really has paid your bill.

Are you still trying to rely on your own works to find acceptance with God? With thankfulness, accept what Jesus has done for you. Rejoice in the truth that He has paid your bill.

Guard Against Becoming Blind to Your Faults

"He will guide you into all truth."
– John 16:13

One day I walked through our church building trying to look at each room with fresh eyes. I had been reminded of how accustomed we get to those settings we view on a regular basis. It's easy for us to overlook aspects of those surroundings which might strike someone seeing it for the first time in a negative way.

So as I examined each room, I made a list of such items which needed our attention. However even then, I was very surprised when I came through a second time and spied some obvious needs I had failed to note the first time around. It just confirmed to me how blind we can be to such matters which are so familiar to us.

This exercise resulted in some of us spending one morning straightening up, getting rid of clutter, and touching up scuff marks on walls. Trash and other unusable items were thrown away, while other unwanted items were donated to a local charity.

Likewise it can be helpful for us at times to try to look at ourselves, our hearts, our lives, our relationship with God, and our relationships with others with fresh eyes. We are so familiar with who we are and what we do that it's easy to overlook certain weaknesses and faults. We can quickly see the speck in someone else's eye, but we're blind to the plank in our own eye (see Matthew 7:1–3).

When we examine ourselves in this way, we need to be brutally honest with ourselves. We don't need to beat ourselves up, but neither should we gloss over those areas that need improvement and attention. Sometimes it might be helpful to ask someone we trust to point out any negative aspects in us which they see. And we can spend time in God's Word, letting it shine the light of truth on our character and conduct. It will remind us of God's standards and can give us unchanging principles by which to measure ourselves.

We can also depend on the Holy Spirit to show us areas in our lives which need to be addressed. He will guide us into truth and is faithful to convict us of sin, righteousness, and judgment (see John 16:5–15).

Each of us is a work in progress. There's always more growing to experience and more improvement to make. The problem is when we become blind to our faults and quit making any headway toward Christlikeness. We get used to the filth we've allowed to slowly build up in our lives. We no longer see the scuff marks of sin on our hearts. We allow secondary things to so clutter our lives that they get in the way of what God wants us to be doing. Or maybe that clutter is hindering our witness for the Lord before others—our light for Christ is getting blocked out by a lot of other unnecessary junk we've allowed to accumulate in our lives.

So let's ask the Lord to open our eyes to any blind spots in our view of ourselves. Let's guard against getting complacent about those familiar areas of our lives. Let's keep making headway in that ongoing process of being cleansed from sin, having hindrances to our walk with God removed, and being molded into the image of Christ.

"Search me, O God, and know my heart...see if there is any wicked way in me, and lead me in the way everlasting" (Psalm 139:23–24).

Ask someone you trust about the weak spots in your life. Use those as the basis for some prayerful reflection. Ask the Holy Spirit to help you see yourself in a more truthful light, as well as seek His help for cleansing and correction.

JUNE 5

PAY ATTENTION TO THE
SMALL VOICE OF GOD

"But the Lord was not in the fire; and after the fire a still small voice."

– I KINGS 19:12

I was sitting and praying in the quietness of the church sanctuary on a weekday morning when I heard something. No, it wasn't a voice from heaven. It was a very faint little tap on the ceiling above my head. About ten or fifteen seconds later I heard it again. It seemed to come at that same regular interval, almost like a very slow drip from a faucet.

Although I was tempted to ignore this almost inaudible sound, the image of water dripping caused me to conclude that I should go up in the attic to check things out. As I explored the area above where I had been sitting, I heard nothing and saw no sign of anything which might have caused the noise. But as I made my way back to the stairs, I did discover a problem. The pipe which carries condensation from the use of our air conditioning had come loose. So the pan surrounding the furnace was full of water and beginning to overflow onto the attic floor.

This wasn't a difficult issue to fix, but if it had gone unnoticed much longer, it probably would have caused damage to our ceiling. But this leak wasn't anywhere near where I had heard the noise in the sanctuary. And I saw no sign that the water had traveled anywhere close to that area. Could the sound of the dripping have radiated that far? Or could it be what I've suggested to a few people—maybe the Holy Spirit tapped on the ceiling just to get me to go up in the attic so I would find this hidden problem?

It reminds me of how God's Spirit often seeks to communicate with us. His voice can frequently be heard more as a whisper than a clap of thunder. Remember the prophet Elijah's experience when God met him on a mountain (I Kings 19:11–12). There was strong wind, followed by an earthquake, and finally a fire. But the Bible states that God was not in any of those powerful manifestations. But then there was a still, small voice. And that's when Elijah heard from the Lord.

Often God speaks to us in ways we'll miss if we're not tuned in to Him. It may be the initial prick of our conscience when we start to do something which we know is not in line with God's will for us. It might be a soft tap on the shoulder of our heart as we struggle over some decision. It may be a verse of scripture which comes to mind at just the right moment.

Often we look for neon lights scrolling a divine message across the sky or listen for a thunderous voice that knocks us over with its great force, but God often chooses to communicate to us in softer and gentler ways. We just have to pay attention.

I never would've heard that tap on the ceiling of the sanctuary on a Sunday morning with people chatting and music playing. But in the quietness it could be heard. We often need to quieten our hearts before God and simply listen. We need to get away from all the competing voices and all the distractions. It's nice when we can physically get alone in a quiet place. But sometimes that may not be possible. We may just have to tune other things out and focus our hearts on God wherever we happen to be.

Let's not ignore God's voice. He may be trying to tell us something important that will help us avoid a big mess in our lives down the road. What is that still, small voice wanting to say to you today?

Get alone in a quiet place or try to focus more fully on the Lord wherever you are. Listen for His still, small voice speaking to you.

JUNE 6

LET GOOD OVERCOME
EVIL IN YOUR LIFE

"Do not be overcome by evil, but overcome evil with good."

– ROMANS 12:21

Did you hear about the special deal offered by a well-known chain of nurseries? And I'm referring to the type of place that raises and sells plants, not the kind that takes care of small children. At all of their store locations, they were giving away packets of ladybugs. I understand that each bag contained about 150 of those helpful insects, with the expectation that more than half a million of the bugs would be distributed over the two-day period.

Those nurseries were promoting ladybugs as a beneficial creature that can help keep one's garden healthy. How does it do that? By preying on the so-called "bad bugs" which can do damage to the plants. Of course there are other ways to get rid of pests, but some of those methods will kill off good insects too. Using the ladybugs is a more natural form of pest control.

With my limited knowledge of such matters, I assumed that 150 ladybugs would be sufficient for an entire small garden. However, I heard an expert suggest that one of those packets was about the right amount to cover merely two plants. I guess it's the principle that if you inundate the bad with the good, the bad will get wiped out.

As I thought about it, that seems to be a biblical principle as well. Whether you're talking about the evil in the world around us or the sin

315

which too easily shows up in the gardens of our own hearts, one way to conquer the bad is by cultivating the good. The Apostle Paul put it this way—"Do not be overcome by evil, but overcome evil with good" (Romans 12:21). He warned against using the deadly pesticide of personal vengeance against one's enemy. It might hurt the other person, but it will also do damage to our own hearts. Instead, we should do good—"If your enemy is hungry, feed him; if he is thirsty, give him drink" (12:20).

Rather than simply focusing on ridding ourselves of the bad things, we would do well to try to fill our lives with the good. Paul instructed his young coworker, Timothy, to flee such evils as youthful lusts and the love of money. But at the same time, he encouraged him to pursue righteousness, godliness, faith, and love.

The more we fill our lives with godly, pure attitudes and actions, the less room there will be for any kind of ungodliness or impurity. If we inundate our daily circumstances with a spirit of steadfast faith, it's less likely that doubt and fear will have an opportunity to take root and grow. If we allow the Lord to fill our hearts with love for others, it will eat up any hatred, envy, bitterness or other unloving attitudes we might be harboring. If we're overflowing with devotion to God, what chance is there for anything else to usurp His rightful top spot in our hearts?

On the one hand, we do need to identify the harmful pests in our souls and seek God's cleansing. But at the same time, let's be filling that space with the beneficial qualities that will assist with the removal of the bad.

Think about some particular "bad bug" that keeps showing up in your life, spoiling the good fruit which God desires to grow in your garden. What positive quality do you need to pursue in its place to keep your soul healthy? Instead of expending all our energy on trying to wipe out the bad, let's be sure to spend just as much time cultivating the good.

What good thing do you need to cultivate in your life as a means of overcoming something negative?

JUNE 7

Let's Listen to
Our Conscience

*"Now the Spirit expressly says that in latter times some will depart
from the faith...having their own conscience seared with a hot iron."*
– I Timothy 4:1–2

Do any of you remember Larry Mondello, a friend of Theodore "Beaver" Cleaver on the old TV show, *Leave It to Beaver*? Larry was a pudgy, red-headed (I suppose—after all, it was black-and-white programming), freckled-faced boy who didn't seem to possess much will-power when it came to resisting doing something wrong or foolish.

In one episode I viewed on a channel that specializes in such classic shows, Beaver and Larry found a wallet in the gutter next to the road. It contained a significant amount of money, but no identification for the owner. Larry immediately spoke excitedly about the two boys splitting the cash between them. But Beaver said that he was going to turn it in at the police station, reminding his friend that it was the right thing to do. Larry agreed, but then made a rather cute and interesting comment. As I recall it was something like, "Wouldn't it be great if we had just come to earth from the planet Mars and didn't know that it was the right thing to do?" In other words, if that was the case they could keep the money, not know it was wrong, and not feel bad about it. I guess that was a young-ster's way of recognizing how a guilty conscience works and of wishing that sometimes it wasn't so effective.

Maybe there have been times when we've thought it would be nice to be able to plead ignorance as to what was right or wrong in a given situation, or when we've wished that our consciences weren't quite so sensitive. If only we could take that action or indulge in that momentary pleasure without feeling guilty about it afterwards. Sometimes the Larry Mondello within us needs to be reminded of the value of knowing right from wrong and the important role our conscience plays in keeping us on the right track.

In the first chapter of Romans, the Bible gives us a picture of those who "suppress the truth in unrighteousness" and who do "not like to retain God in their knowledge" (1:18–32). These are people who ignore God's standards of right and wrong, and who have refused to listen to their conscience to the point that they've rendered it ineffective. They travel so far in their moral downward spiral that God gives them up to their "uncleanness," to "the lusts of their hearts," and to a "debased mind." They become filled with all kinds of unrighteousness as they plunge toward spiritual and eternal death.

In another place, the Bible declares that in the last times there will be those who depart from the faith, "having their own conscience seared with a hot iron" (I Timothy 4:1–2)—in other words, a conscience that has become hardened, tough, and unfeeling. A sensitive conscience is not something to lament, but rather something for which to be thankful. It can protect us and keep us from the painful consequences of foolish choices in life if we'll just listen to it.

Unfortunately we live in a day when what is right and wrong is not as clearly taught or recognized. Many are suppressing the truth and hardening their consciences. In one sense, we find ourselves living among those Martians who don't know the right thing to do.

But let's not be one of them. Along with listening to God's Word and the Holy Spirit, let's cultivate the moral protection God has built within us of a conscience. Be thankful for that inner voice and pay attention to its guidance.

What is your conscience saying to you? Have you been listening to it or ignoring it?

Make Sure You're Plugged-in to God

"For without Me you can do nothing."
– John 15:5

During a regular checkup with the dentist, my hygienist apologetically had to abandon me for a few minutes. She was summoned out of the room in order to try to fix a problem with one of the dental machines in another part of the office. I'm not sure what that particular implement was used for, but like so many mechanical instruments in our world today, it relied on computer technology. So she and my dentist were working from the assumption that it was a problem with the computer or the software program, probably based on their past experiences with the contraption. But their efforts at the computer to get the machine working properly continued to fail. That's when someone made a humbling discovery: the realization that the machine had never been turned on that morning.

My dentist, being a good Methodist, has certain routines he likes to follow. But that morning when he had first entered the building, something had distracted him from making his usual trip around the office to turn on all the various pieces of equipment. And somehow along the way this one had gotten overlooked. So while searching for all the possible answers to the problem, the most basic and obvious solution hadn't even been considered—the machine had no power. It had been easy to assume that it was plugged in and turned on.

When our lives seem to be malfunctioning and problems mount up, as we seek guidance and solutions let's not neglect one of the most basic and important factors. Is our connection with God intact? Are we in proper relation to our great source of help, strength, and power?

Don't get me wrong. I'm not suggesting that if we're "plugged in" to God, our lives will be problem-free. However if our relationship with God is lacking, it will assuredly have a negative impact on so many other areas of our lives. It will result in us failing to function in the way God intended.

Too often we look everywhere else for the answers to our struggles and don't examine the most vital component to successful living. We check our relationships with our families and friends; we look at our physical health as to whether we're eating right, exercising, and getting enough rest; we examine our environments at work and at home. As a result we spend time and money consulting doctors, counselors, lifestyle experts, and various other resources.

Again, don't misunderstand me. At times we may need to look at those areas and seek help from those skilled professionals, just like someone occasionally may need to resolve software issues in that dental machine. But sometimes, as in the case of that instrument on that day, the main issue may be more fundamental. We may be having many of these other problems primarily as a result of our connection with God being broken.

We may need medication for certain conditions in our bodies, but no pills are going to take away our guilt of sin or the emptiness of a soul estranged from its Maker. We may need marital or family counseling, but no advice is going to cleanse us of the selfishness that keeps us from getting along with others. We may need help in changing certain aspects of our lifestyle, but only God can change our hearts.

So when life seems to be falling apart, don't overlook the obvious. Make sure that your relationship with God is right. If it is it won't solve all your issues, but you'll have a divine Resource who promises to be there to give you the wisdom, power, and grace you need to successfully deal with whatever problems you do experience.

Having problems? Is your lack of connection with God contributing to it?

WE CAN GO WHEREVER
GOD LEADS

"He who calls you is faithful, who also will do it."
— I THESSALONIANS 5:24

A while back I noticed a problem with a couple of our local traffic signals. No, I'm not referring to the ones in a busy shopping area that get so out of sync that during peak traffic times, only two or three vehicles can make it through on the green light. I'm thinking of a couple of signals with a much different, and more amusing, issue. It was especially pronounced at one location. When the green arrow appeared directing you to make a left turn, it wasn't in the normal horizontal position. It was twisted quite markedly so that the arrow actually directed traffic to the upper left, as if we were somehow supposed to get our cars airborne.

I like to be a good citizen and adhere to the law, but I was unsuccessful in my attempts to obey those directions. It didn't work when I tried going faster as I made my turn, like an airplane gaining speed for takeoff. I didn't find a button on my car that would allow it to sprout wings or a helicopter rotor as if I were James Bond. Lifting myself off of the seat with my hands raised didn't do much, except to scare the driver in the lane next to me. Even singing "Chitty Chitty Bang Bang" failed to inspire my vehicle to rise from the pavement. I concluded that my only hope to obey that signal was to make sure that I was approaching that intersection as the rapture occurred.

Some impossible demands placed upon us are laughable. However, others can be downright frustrating. Have you ever felt like God was directing you to do something that simply wasn't possible? You want to be a faithful follower—you don't wish to defy God's guidance—but what He's asking of you seems to be beyond your capability to fulfill. He's pointing upward when you're stuck driving a land-bound vehicle.

However there's a major difference in that scenario. For one thing, we are talking about a great God with whom nothing is impossible. He could make a car fly if He wanted to do so. Secondly, we're dealing with a loving God who would not frustrate us by asking us to do something that we weren't capable of doing. We may not be able to go that direction on our own, but as we draw upon His resources of strength and grace, we find that it is possible.

Where is God's arrow pointing in your life? Is it to overcome some temptation or sin that has held you in its firm grasp for years? Remember that "God is faithful, who will not allow you to be tempted beyond what you are able, but with the temptation will also make a way of escape, that you may be able to bear it" (I Corinthians 10:13).

Are you hearing God's call to a holy life and a closer relationship with Him? Right after the Bible declares that God can sanctify us completely, it says, "He who calls you is faithful, who also will do it" (I Thessalonians 5:24).

If God is guiding you into some new area of service, your obedience will result in you being able to say with Paul, "I thank Christ Jesus our Lord who has enabled me, because He counted me faithful, putting me into the ministry" (I Timothy 1:12).

There will be times when we will need to make sure it's God whom we're hearing. But when we are certain that it is His arrow pointing the way as our lives intersect some challenge or opportunity, we can be assured that He will enable us to go that direction. No matter how difficult it may look, we know that "I can do all things through Christ who strengthens me" (Philippians 4:13).

Follow God's calling and direction today with confidence that He can enable you for the task.

Don't Get Caught
in Satan's Trap

"And do not lead us into temptation, but deliver us from the evil one."

– Matthew 6:13

'Tis the season. Have you been bugged by any of those pesky fruit flies which tend to find their way into our homes this time of year? They can be irritating, not just from their hovering around us but also from their penchant to alight on our food as we're preparing it or trying to eat it. Unless you don't mind the extra protein in your meal, it can be an ordeal attempting to keep those pests at bay.

When those little critters started showing up in my house this time as the weather got hotter, I decided to try out one of the suggestions I had found after researching the subject. I put a little apple cider vinegar in a small cup along with a few drops of dish detergent. The theory is that the flies will be attracted to the sweet liquid, but the detergent makes it slippery and causes them not to be able to fly away. Instead they sink and drown in the concoction. Some suggest that you heat up the vinegar to make it more pungent. However if you do, be careful not to get it too hot. It might cause a minor combustion and make a mess in your micro-wave—don't ask me how I know that to be true.

Well, I'm glad to report that after a somewhat slow start, this trap has proven to be very successful at my house. Every time I walk into the kitchen, I check the cup and give my wife an up-to-date count of victims.

If we know how to bait traps for fruit flies, it shouldn't come as any surprise to us that the master deceiver and tempter is well-aware of how to create effective traps for us. Yes, there is an evil spiritual being around who is out to get us. We do have to guard against his efforts to hinder us in our walk with God. His ultimately goal is very simple—to destroy us. While our own affections play a big role in our temptations, we should remember that we not only have to battle ourselves but also an outside force who is trying to play off those desires.

Satan often uses similar tactics to what I've described in catching those fruit flies. He puts something enticing in front of us. It may not be apple cider vinegar in our case, but it might be something comparable that we humans tend to find attractive. It could be something that whets one of our physical appetites, appeals to our pride, or captivates our minds.

We're drawn to it, possibly not seeing the risk, or sometimes in spite of recognizing the potential danger. We flitter all around it. We see how close we can get to it—telling ourselves that we're doing it just in order to take a look and to be better informed about such matters.

Unfortunately the devil often adds his own form of dish detergent to that temptation. If we get close enough, we find ourselves on a slippery slope from which it's hard to pull away. Thankfully God is greater than the devil. He can provide ways of escape in times of temptation and give us strength to get away from those traps. However, we shouldn't keep putting God's grace and power to the test. If we persist in giving in to the devil's bait, God may allow us to have our way and face the consequences of our poor choice.

So if you're having fruit fly issues, you may want to try this simple trap. And let it serve as a reminder not to allow yourself to be a victim of Satan's snares.

When temptation comes your way, run from it, resist it, and look for God's way for you to escape.

JUNE 11

A Relationship with Christ Changes Our Behavior

"And whatever you do, do it heartily, as to the Lord and not to men."
                                        – Colossians 3:23

Today is my oldest grandchild's birthday. On the eventful Sunday morning when he entered the world, I was rushing back and forth from waiting with family at the hospital to leading the worship service at our church. It changed our lives as we became grandparents for the first time. And I quickly discovered that becoming a grandfather transformed me in some ways. It wasn't long before I was being told that I acted differently, strangely, even rather goofy at times. If my grandson was sitting next to me in a restaurant, you might have caught me making funny faces. In his presence, there were times when I made animal sounds or exaggerated my actions. I received a rug burn on my knee from crawling on the carpet in hot pursuit of my giggling grandson. Before he came along I didn't act that way, at least not since my children were very young.

Why did I act differently from before? Did my grandson force me to do it? Would he not love me if I failed to act in those ways? Was I trying to earn his affection by being funny or making him laugh? No. I simply had a desire in my heart to do things that please him. It had to do with loving him and relating to him. I actually enjoyed acting in such a manner, even if others may have thought it strange, simply because it built and strengthened the bond between my grandson and myself.

When we come to know Christ as our Savior, there's a change that takes place within us. And there should be a resulting difference in both our conduct and our character. We seek to live a holy life and to behave in ways that are pleasing to God. Some people who knew us previously might think such behavior to be odd. They wonder—why would anyone want to spend part of their precious time on the weekend attending church? And surely anyone who takes time every day to read his Bible must be some kind of fanatic. Why would someone become so consumed with doing the right thing, even when no one is around to know about it or when there's no chance of getting caught? Isn't it strange that this person is more concerned about helping others than about his own needs? People don't easily understand when a person who receives Christ begins to act differently, refusing to do some of the things he used to do.

Why do we do it? Is God forcing us to act that way? Are we trying to earn God's favor through such conduct? No. We do it because we want to do it. We have the desire in our hearts to please God. We have new priorities, valuing our relationship with the Lord above all else. Much like with my grandson, it's about loving and relating to someone important to us. Nothing compared to knowing that I put a smile on my grandson's face. And likewise there's nothing comparable to knowing that my attitude and actions are pleasing to my Heavenly Father.

We're different from we were before we knew Jesus. And that change should show up in our behavior in many ways. I didn't really care if other people laughed at me over my antics with my grandson. Neither should it bother us if others don't understand our conduct as followers of Christ. What matters is knowing that He is pleased with us.

How is your conduct different because of your relationship with Christ? Seek to please God in all that you do today.

JUNE 12

BE A BLESSING TO YOUR SPOUSE

"An excellent wife is the crown of her husband, but she who causes shame is like rottenness in his bones."

– PROVERBS 12:4

Since June has historically been known as a prime time for getting married, there are a number of us who will be celebrating wedding anniversaries this month. The Bible says, "He who finds a wife finds a good thing, and obtains favor from the Lord" (Proverbs 18:22). Based on what is written in the rest of the book of Proverbs, I don't think this can be taken as a blanket statement covering all wives. I believe the implication is that if you find a "good" wife, you have found a good thing. I'm happy to be able to say that as of today I will have obtained such favor from the Lord for many years. If you know my wife, you know I'm not just saying that.

Another fitting proverb reads, "An excellent wife is the crown of her husband" (12:4). Now wives, don't misread that. This isn't giving you biblical sanction to crown your husband, as in beating him over the head—even though he may deserve it at times. Rather it's suggesting that your relationship with your husband is one that should be a positive thing in his life, bringing him honor. After all these years, I'm still honored to be married to my wife. She is certainly a blessing and a crown in my life.

However, the book of Proverbs doesn't just paint the rosy side of marriage. Remember who wrote many of these pithy sayings. It was King Solomon. And if you know anything about his history, you realize that he had plenty of experience with all kinds of wives. So he knew about both the good ones and the bad ones.

While Solomon extolled the virtue of an excellent wife, in the same verse he also noted, "She who causes shame is like rottenness in his bones." Think about the constant irritation and aching associated with bone cancer, arthritis, or other joint pain. Every time you move, you're reminded of your malady. A bad marital relationship can be a similar source of continual discomfort.

Solomon also denounced a "contentious" wife as being like a "continual dripping" (19:13). Those who habitually stir up strife, find something wrong, are negative, and nag are like water dripping from a faucet—a constant annoyance. Solomon suggested that it's better to confine yourself to a small corner of a housetop than to live in a large house with a contentious woman (21:9). In other words, life with such a person is not a pleasant experience.

Whether husbands or wives, let's examine our own attitudes and actions towards our spouses. Let's make sure that we're not the kind of person who makes life hard, unbearable, or unpleasant for our marriage partner. It's so easy to fall into such negative ways of thinking and relating to others, especially after many years of being together.

Solomon said that "a good woman builds her house, but the foolish pulls it down with her hands" (14:1). Let's be the kind of people who build our marriages, families, and homes—not those who tear them down through selfishness and negativity. Let's seek to be a blessing, not a burden.

It also says in Proverbs that "a prudent wife is from the Lord" (19:14). So don't take her for granted. If you've got a good, wise wife or husband for that matter, consider it a gift from God. Give Him thanks for that person. I know I do.

Happy anniversary, dear.

If you're married, give thanks for your spouse. Find some special way to be a blessing to that person today.

Enjoy Spending Time with God

"In Your presence is fullness of joy; at Your right hand are pleasures forevermore."

– Psalm 16:11

One year I received a nice homemade Father's Day picture from my grandchildren. It portrayed each of them as little monkeys clinging to a vine. Above the drawing was the following sentiment: "We love hangin' with you, Papaw!" While I could easily focus on the appropriateness of comparing those kids to wild monkeys at certain times, instead let me comment on the caption accompanying the picture. I hope it's true. It's nice when your kids or grandkids simply like to be around you. It reveals that their devotion to you isn't just about the presents you give them, the special places you take them, or the activities you do with them. If they enjoy just hanging out with you in a variety of settings and situations because of who you are, that's gratifying evidence of a close, loving relationship.

Do we love to hang out with our Heavenly Father? Certainly we appreciate all that He does for us—providing for our needs, helping us through tough times, protecting us from various dangers, and preparing a wonderful home in heaven for us. But is our relationship with Him based on more than just what He does for us and the promises of the special place to which He's going to take us when this life is over? Do we enjoy simply spending time with God?

I like the way the Psalmist expressed it: "In Your presence is fullness of joy" (Psalm 16:11). He found joy in just being with God. In another psalm it declares, "How lovely is Your tabernacle, O Lord of hosts! My soul longs, yes, even faints, for the courts of the Lord; my heart and my flesh cry out for the living God" (Psalm 84:1–2). The tabernacle and courts of the Lord represented places where God had especially promised to be present. This person was expressing a deep desire in his heart to have fellowship with God.

As we consider this concept, we should realize that in one sense we are never outside of God's presence. He is the omnipresent Spirit who is there wherever we find ourselves. We could not escape His presence even if we wanted to do so.

But we should also have a desire in our hearts just to hang out with God at times, in the sense of being aware of His presence and fellowshipping with Him as we share our hearts with Him and listen for what He might want to say to us. For example, do we look forward to going to church in order to meet God, to worship Him, and to hear His message for us? Of course God's presence isn't limited to a modern-day tabernacle. While public worship is beneficial as a special opportunity to be in God's presence with other believers, we can meet with Him at other times in the privacy of our own homes, or wherever we are in the solitude of our own hearts and souls. Do we look forward to reading our Bibles and discovering what God may want to say to us today? Do we enjoy spending time in prayer, talking things over with God as we might do with a close friend? Or do we see church attendance, Bible reading, and prayer as burdensome acts which we dread?

Let's try to appreciate God more for who He is, not just for what He does for us. Recognize how much He loves you and enjoy His presence as you go through your day. Let's seek to find joy in just hanging out with our Father who cares so much for us. The desire to do so is a sign of the loving, close relationship we should be having with Him.

Enjoy your time with God today.

AVOID THE BAD BY
FOCUSING ON THE GOOD

"Whatever things are true, whatever things are noble, whatever things are just, whatever things are pure, whatever things are lovely...meditate on these things."

– PHILIPPIANS 4:8

When I was a young teen, my dad and I started trying to play golf. "Trying" is the key word. Although we enjoyed those father-son excursions onto a local public course, we never developed into very good players. We definitely weren't part of the country club set. We used inexpensive equipment and hit balls that we found during regular walks along the side of a road skirting another little par-three course. And I learned to play not by taking lessons from a pro but primarily from reading the volumes of *Golf Digest* given to me by my uncle, an avid golfer.

One of the greatest challenges we found while playing was the water holes. If there was water on the course, our balls inevitably found it. That was especially true of my dad (at least that's the way I remember it). Even the smallest of ponds would attract his balls like a magnet. It was always a victory to be celebrated if we managed to play through a hole with a water hazard without creating a splash.

We knew that the problem was primarily in our heads. We would see the water and focus so hard on trying to avoid it that it ended up looming even larger in our minds. The more we attempted to stay away from the hazard, the more likely it seemed we would be to drown our ball in the watery grave.

I believe we sometimes suffer from a similar malady when it comes to other things we seek to avoid in life. God puts His firm finger on something in our behavior, attitude, or spirit that is posing a hazard to our relationship with Him or that is hindering us from receiving all the blessings He desires for us to have. So we steadfastly focus on steering clear of that action, breaking that bad habit, or improving our attitude. But it seems the harder we try to avoid it, the more it gets into our heads. We may be thinking about not doing it, but we're still thinking about it—maybe more than ever. And more often than not, it results in us finding ourselves being drawn to it like a magnet.

I'm told that in golf it can be helpful to ignore the water hazard and focus more on the fairway or green where you want your ball to land. Concentrate on the positive picture of where you want your ball to go rather than on the negative place you're trying to avoid.

That can be helpful for us to do in these other areas of our lives too. Instead of thinking about what we shouldn't do, let's focus more on the positive actions and attitudes that we're seeking to have. Let's follow the instructions Paul gave when he wrote the following: "Finally, brethren, whatever things are true, whatever things are noble, whatever things are just, whatever things are pure, whatever things are lovely, whatever things are of good report, if there is any virtue and if there is anything praiseworthy—meditate on these things" (Philippians 4:8).

Maybe we need to quit trying so hard not to do the wrong things, and give our attention more fully to doing the good things. If we fill our minds and hearts with what's pleasing to God, there won't be room for the bad stuff.

So let's all focus less on the water hazards in life and look more at reaching those green fairways where God wants us to live and thrive.

But I still think if I ever take up golf again, it might be best for me to look for a course without any ponds.

Think more about the good you should be doing today rather than the bad you need to avoid.

JUNE 15

UNLOCKING THE MAIN MYSTERY
OF THE ORIGIN OF THE UNIVERSE

"In the beginning God created the heavens and the earth."

– GENESIS 1:1

Are some of you dads hoping to receive a new electronic gadget for Father's Day this year? Maybe you're thinking large, as in a big screen HDTV, or one bigger than what you already have. How about one with 3-D capabilities? Or maybe you would want the latest iPhone or tablet. Or are you simply hoping for a new game to play on your video system?

Admittedly much of that technology is foreign to me, but I know there are some folks who like to have the latest, greatest gadgets available. If so, do you have an Alpha Magnetic Spectrometer-2 (AMS) among your high-tech devices? Probably not—especially since I understand that one costs nearly two billion dollars.

The AMS was an experiment that one of the Space Shuttle crews took with them to the International Space Station. It sounds complicated, but from what I've gathered, it was some kind of state-of-the-art particle detector. It is able to collect and measure cosmic rays to an extent previously not possible.

What was the purpose of this costly experiment? Although it was hoped that it would lead to a better understanding of cosmic radiation, I kept hearing about another possible objective as well: that it would help us understand the origin of the universe. There are those who claim that this instrument may unlock some of the mysteries and answer some lingering questions about how the universe began.

I never did hear anything about if this experiment eventually revealed anything about that subject, and what conclusions were reached by the scientists interpreting its data. However, I don't have to spend two billion dollars or travel into space to find out the greatest truth about the origin of the universe. I just have to open up the Bible to its very first verse. "In the beginning God created the heavens and the earth" (Genesis 1:1). The most important truth about creation is the fact that God did it.

Technological instruments like the AMS may reveal some of the details of the how, what, and when of creation. Those specifics may help us better understand the general account the Bible gives us of that event. But whatever else it reveals, it will not detract from the certainty of the "who" of creation. Maybe like so many other scientific discoveries, it will only corroborate that there is a great Designer behind it all.

Why is that truth so significant? For one thing, it lays the foundation for all other truths God has revealed about Himself, letting us know who He is and what kind of God He is. Secondly, it affirms that there is reason and purpose in our existence. The universe is not an accident, and neither are you. Also, the fact that God could create such a vast and complex universe shows us how powerful He is and what He can do in our lives today. As the prophet Jeremiah declared, "Ah, Lord God! Behold, You have made the heavens and the earth by Your great power and outstretched arm. There is nothing too hard for You" (Jeremiah 32:17).

Maybe there are some questions about the origin of the universe that the AMS will help answer. But let's not ignore the vital truth that has already been revealed to us. God is the Creator of the heavens and the earth. And He is your Maker. And He has made you for a purpose. So let's seek His will for us and trust Him to enable us to do it—with or without a new electronic gadget for Father's Day.

How does the fact that God created the universe affect your view of what He can do in your life?

SOMETIMES THE LITTLE CHALLENGES CAUSE US TO STUMBLE

"Catch us the foxes, the little foxes that spoil the vines."
— SONG OF SOLOMON 2:15

A few years ago on Father's Day weekend, my dad was pulling extra duty around his house. The added responsibilities came from the fact that my mom was nursing a broken arm. It would be exciting to describe how my "young at heart" grey-haired mother managed to suffer this injury by skiing down a mountain slope, skydiving out of an airplane, or skateboarding through the neighborhood. However, she wasn't engaged in any behavior that we'd normally think of as being risky.

It wasn't like the other time she broke her arm many years ago. At that time she was unwisely running through a parking lot racing my sister and me to the car when she slipped on a small oil slick. I was wearing my own cast at the time, having lost my balance and fallen about twelve feet to the ground while building a tree house two weeks earlier. But on this occasion my mom wasn't doing anything you would think of as being a possible health hazard. She was simply walking in her living room when she dragged her foot on the carpet, lost her balance, and took a fall, resulting in a couple of broken bones in her left forearm that required some surgery.

Sometimes we know that we're putting ourselves at risk and tell ourselves to be more cautious. For example, around that same time I was very careful when I climbed up on the roof of my house to clean out my gutters. I didn't want a repeat of history with my mom and I both in a cast at the same time. But I don't normally think about the possibility of stumbling or falling when I'm walking on solid ground.

It's not always the risky behavior that results in us taking a tumble, whether physically or spiritually. We can be extra cautious when facing a situation in which we know we'll be confronted by a temptation, and rightfully so. Likewise we might prepare ourselves for a difficult situation that we know will challenge our faith. But sometimes it's the common circumstances that sneak up on us and cause us to fall.

Think about King David in the Bible. He didn't stumble in his faith when he encountered the obvious giant obstacle named Goliath. He didn't falter while King Saul was hunting him down as a fugitive. But one run-of-the-mill day as he took a leisurely evening stroll around home, he unintentionally got an eyeful of another man's wife, pursued his impure desires, and ended up not only becoming guilty of adultery but afterwards conspiring to commit murder as well. David wasn't doing anything spiritually risky at the time—but that's when he fell.

We can't ever afford to let down our defenses against sin, temptation, and Satan. We can bravely declare that the battle is the Lord's as we sling our stones at the giants blocking our way. We can walk close to God as we face the clear perils of financial hardships, relationship problems, battles with disease or sickness, and other such trials. We can find shelter under the protective hand of God when we see struggles with doubt, fear, and ungodly desires springing up. But sometimes it's in the everyday normal stuff of life that we get caught off guard and stumble. An unexpected moment leads to giving in to passion, becoming uncontrollably angry, saying hurtful words, or cowering in fear.

Fortunately, as David found out, when we do stumble there is forgiveness and cleansing available to the repentant of heart. But we still need to guard against falling in the first place.

Let's not ever get careless in our relationship with God. Don't let the little things trip you up.

Watch out for the little things today that might cause you to stumble spiritually.

SOME GREAT PEOPLE YOU
WOULD NEVER KNOW

*"See, I have called by name Bezalel, the son of Uri...And I have
filled him with the Spirit of God, in wisdom, in understanding, in
knowledge, and in all manner of workmanship"*

– EXODUS 31:2–3

Imagine attending a red carpet event in Hollywood where you've managed to procure a prime view of the guests as they get out of their limos
and walk down the decorated entranceway. You expect to see all kinds of
big-name movie stars and celebrities, but as the people exit their fancy
vehicles, you discover that you don't know most of them. Someone with
a microphone calls out their names and uses the word "great" to describe
these guests, but you've never heard of them. Out of the couple of hundred people you watch arrive and be introduced as great people, you end
up only recognizing one or two of them as being famous celebrities.

It wouldn't surprise me if heaven were somewhat like that. We sometimes express our anticipation of seeing and talking to great people like
Abraham, Moses, and Paul. But I imagine that those biblical celebrities
are going to be few and far between. There are going to be many people
there whom we don't know, yet whom God announces to be great.

For example, if God put down the red carpet for the great people
from the book of Exodus, Moses, Aaron, and their sister Miriam would
probably step out of the first limo, and rightly so. But I think the occu-
pants of the next limo could surprise us. Two guys might get out of that

vehicle, provoking us to ask, "Who are they?" Once you get past the Egyptian plagues, the parting of the Red Sea, and the giving of the Ten Commandments, there are still fifteen chapters left in Exodus. They deal with the building of the Tabernacle—an important event in which two men named Bezalel and Aholiab played a vital role (Exodus 31:1–6).

What stands out to me about these two men is that they weren't the preacher, prophet, or Sunday school teacher. They didn't hold a position that you would automatically associate with spiritual leadership. They were blue-collar kind of guys who worked with their hands to create things. They carved wood, built furniture, and molded metals into useful vessels and beautiful decorative items. These were men who walked around with sawdust on their sandals, dirt under their fingernails, and splotches of dried, molten metal on their work clothes.

But I believe they were two of the greatest guys you would never know. The Bible says that Bezalel was filled with the Spirit of God. It says that the Lord put wisdom and understanding in their hearts, giving them the ability to be skillful craftsmen. Moses may have received the vision and instructions for the Tabernacle from God, but it was Bezalel and Aholiab whom God used to turn that vision into reality.

Do you think you can't be great in God's sight because you don't possess the right kind of gifts or talents, the kind that makes you more prominent in worship services or other church activities? I think we're going to find many great people in heaven who weren't preachers, evangelists, or Sunday School teachers. They were people who bagged groceries, answered phones, paved parking lots, and did a host of other jobs. But they were Spirit-filled people who did those things for God's glory and who made themselves available for God to use whatever abilities they did have.

Greatness in God's sight isn't based so much on possessing certain gifts, but yielding what gifts we do have to Him and letting Him use us. Heaven's going to be made up mostly of lesser-known people like Bezalel and Aholiab—people God sees as great. Will you be one of them?

Are you using what you have and what you do for the glory of God?

Let's Make Use of the Weapon of Prayer

"Praying always with all prayer and supplication in the Spirit."
– Ephesians 6:18

I walked into the church sanctuary one Tuesday morning and was surprised to find a strange object sitting on the altar. It was a sword. Did somebody mistakenly think we were singing about the cavalry instead of "At Calvary" that previous Sunday? No, upon closer examination I saw that this wasn't a real sword but a toy version of that weapon. I immediately recognized it as belonging to my grandson. It was a souvenir gift to him from one of the men in my church who had recently returned from visiting Mount Vernon, the famous home of George Washington. During his after-church wanderings while waiting on Papaw to lock up the building, my grandson had undoubtedly put down his new toy on the altar and then forgot about it.

I suppose that the sight of a sword on the altar could bring to mind several truths. For example, someone might think of an act of consecration or surrender—the laying down of one's weapon as a sign of peace—the proverbial beating of the sword into a plowshare. We sometimes talk about "laying something on the altar" as an indication of giving it over to the Lord. However, my thoughts headed in a different direction, probably stemming from the idea of the altar being a great place for meeting with God and talking to Him. That image of the sword and the altar reminded me that prayer is where the real battle needs to take place.

We often forget that truth, at least I do. As we face problems and challenges, we dig in to do battle. We make our plans, form our strategies, and then take the necessary action. We fight for what we believe is right, while taking aim at those people or ideologies that we view as being the enemy. And there's nothing wrong with that. But sometimes we have to be careful or we start depending more on ourselves and our skill to win the battle instead of relying on the Lord to give us the victory.

The image of warfare is not uncommon in the Bible. God's Word reminds us that we face spiritual enemies who are trying to deceive, hinder, discourage, and destroy us. However, it also states that "though we walk in the flesh, we do not war according to the flesh" (II Corinthians 10:3). We do battle differently from the way this world does it. We refuse to swing the swords of slander, dishonesty, vengeance, and other common tactics. In contrast, our arsenal includes things like faith, truth, righteousness, love, and of course prayer. And the Bible suggests that the weapons we use are not only different, but are more powerful than the ones used by this world. They are "mighty in God for pulling down strongholds" (II Corinthians 10:4).

The weapons of the world are like plastic toy swords when compared to the mighty power of prayer. Prayer brings the Spirit of God into the conflict. He can do things we can't. He can change people's hearts and minds. He can do battle against the real enemy—the invisible spiritual forces working behind the people and circumstances which our eyes see. He can also work in us to enable and strengthen us for the battle.

Prayer isn't the only thing we need to do. We can still plan, strategize, and take action. But if we're not praying, we're failing to make use of one of the most important and powerful weapons we possess.

What battles are you facing today? Don't try to handle them all by yourself. Unleash that secret weapon of prayer and let God do what you can't do.

Take your battles to the Lord in prayer.

JUNE 19

God Can Rebuild
Broken Lives

"Weeping may endure for a night, but joy comes in the morning."

– Psalm 30:5

Years ago I was privileged to attend a conference at a church in Bayou La Batre, Alabama. By the way, you'll discover from the locals that when you pronounce the name of that place, don't try to sound out two strong syllables in that word "bayou." Instead, run it together so that it almost sounds like you're walking out the door telling someone "bye." That little coastal community was put on the map for many folks through the movie *Forrest Gump*. But a few years ago, hurricane Katrina almost wiped it off again. Much of the town was severely flooded, including the building this particular church occupied at the time.

You can imagine the devastating effect this event had on the congregation. It is epitomized in the story of one elderly church member whom I knew. After the storm, when she walked through the door of her home right next to the church and saw the destruction, it was such a shock that her memory was never the same. It must have been heartbreaking to see their church in such a mess. Although they received much assistance in the subsequent cleanup, they never returned to that beloved facility. They ended up selling it to another congregation, while they relocated a few miles further inland.

Although there was still some construction work to be done, this particular conference was the first official event to be held in their new sanctuary. It was larger than the one at their former location, and it was going to look beautiful when the project was completed. It was a joy to be able to celebrate with this congregation in what God had done to allow them to rebuild.

God specializes in rebuilding—not just churches, but individual lives. That fact is helpful to remember because we all are subject to facing personal storms that can drastically alter our lives. Sometimes they can be the result of circumstances over which we had no control. We may find ourselves the victims of forces of nature or the actions of other people, but then there are other situations in which the devastation may be partially, if not totally, the result of our own bad choices or behavior.

In either case, we shouldn't lose hope. God can help us rebuild our lives. In situations in which we carried part of the responsibility for what happened, we may need to go down that road of repentance. And when we do, we must be willing to forgive ourselves as well as receive God's gracious pardon. But that process of rebuilding can be a long and difficult road.

As in the case with that church in Bayou La Batre, God may not restore us to the exact same place where we were before. And it may difficult leaving some of that past behind us. But the Lord can use that event which we saw only as a heartbreaking tragedy and turn it into something good. He can bring us to a different place in our lives—one that may end up being bigger and more beautiful than the one we left behind.

I don't know what hurricanes or floods have hit your life, turning it upside-down. But don't throw in the towel. Trust God to bring you through and to complete a rebuilding project that is greater than you could ever imagine. As the Psalmist declared, "Weeping may endure for a night, but joy comes in the morning" (Psalm 30:5). I'm glad I was there to share in that church's joyful morning after a long night. Keep looking ahead to the morning that God has in store for you.

Don't lose hope over past tragedies or failures in your life. God can do a rebuilding project and help you get through the night to that morning of joy.

BE A PERSON OF INTEGRITY IN DEALING WITH OTHERS

"And just as you want men to do to you, you also do to them likewise."

– LUKE 6:31

I was traveling home after speaking at a church conference when my stomach started informing me it was lunchtime. As I weighed my options which were displayed at the upcoming interstate exit, I decided to stop at one of my favorite fast-food restaurants for one of their chicken sandwiches. After placing my order, paying for my meal, and receiving my food, I found a seat in their busy dining area.

However almost immediately I questioned in my mind whether or not I had received my several dollars of change back from my payment. It didn't seem like I had, but I'm getting where I don't trust my memory as well as when I was younger. I sat down mulling over the possibility, even checking my wallet to see if I could determine the facts by the bills I possessed. Still uncertain, I decided it was probably too late to check into it anyway. Just as I had reconciled myself to the possibility of having made an unintentional extra donation to that restaurant, along came the young lady who had taken my order. She had hunted me down to ask if she had neglected to give me my change. She thought she had failed to do so, graciously apologized, and proceeded to take the steps to correct her mistake.

The actions of that employee illustrate just another reason why this is one of my favorite restaurant chains. It would have been easy for her to dismiss the idea that she had made a mistake, especially since I had already walked away. She wouldn't have had to confess her error or go to the trouble of making it right, but how she handled the situation revealed traits of honesty and integrity, which I greatly appreciate.

We need to remember the importance of how we treat other people. It not only reveals our character, but it also reflects our relationship with the Lord. The Bible condemns those who take unfair advantage of others or who are unjust in their business practices. Jesus gave us the "Golden Rule"—"And just as you want men to do to you, you also do to them likewise" (Luke 6:31). He also affirmed that we're not only to love the Lord our God with all our heart, but we're to love our neighbors as ourselves.

Admittedly we're all going to make mistakes in our dealings with others. We might forget to return someone's change. We might unintentionally hurt or offend someone. We might say a harsh word, lash out in anger, act selfishly, or otherwise not behave very lovingly or in accord with the Golden Rule. While we need to seek God's help to avoid such actions, we also need to respond properly when we're guilty of that kind of behavior. Don't just sweep it under the rug and forget about it. It might be easier to ignore our mistake and not take responsibility for it. In some cases, it may seem like nobody would ever know about it—except for the Lord.

Jesus reminded us of the importance of getting wrongs settled with others before we come to worship God (Matthew 5:23–24). Is there someone you need to go to in order to confess, apologize, or make restitution? Maybe you're not sure if you hurt the person or not. Under those circumstances, it would be easy to let it go. But if there's any doubt or if you sense the Holy Spirit tugging at your heart about it, you probably need to hunt down that person and check into it anyway. Hopefully that person will appreciate your integrity—and I know God will.

Is there a wrong, or perceived wrong, against someone that you need to take the first step in making right? Don't put it off. Take care of it today.

Let's Seek to Be
a Better Church

"I know your works, love, service, faith, and your patience.... Nevertheless I have a few things against you."

– Revelation 2:19–20

Some years ago I heard about a car crash in Atlanta that injured a couple of children while also damaging part of a church building. As I watched the reports of this incident on the news, I noticed the name of the church. It was called "The Perfect Church." While I don't like to be critical of what local congregations call themselves, even without knowing anything else about this group I'm fairly certain this church didn't live up to its name.

While some people seem to be searching for the perfect church, many of us have concluded that such an entity does not exist. And even if it did, as soon as we with all our faults walked through the doors, it would no longer be perfect.

We may love our local churches. I hope you do. We can be thankful for its many good qualities, for its caring pastor who faithfully preaches the gospel, for its ministries in the community, and for the wonderful fellowship we enjoy there with other believers. But very few of us would consider our churches to be perfect.

It's kind of like when LeBron James once referred to himself as the greatest basketball player in the world. Whether he is or not, it was rather arrogant of him to make that claim about himself. And it seems not only arrogant but also somewhat self-deceptive for a church to claim to be perfect. May I suggest that if there ever is a perfect church, it would not advertise itself as such. If it did, it would no longer be perfect.

I don't see any perfect churches in the Bible. Paul could refer to the church at Corinth as sanctified and gifted, but he also had to deal with some serious issues within that body of believers, such as division and sexual immorality. Most churches mentioned in scripture had some good qualities for which to be grateful, but also some faults to be addressed. In the midst of handing out accolades to these congregations, there is almost always a "nevertheless" included to bring them back down to earth. They may have been good churches, but they weren't perfect.

There can be good reasons at times for leaving a local congregation to seek to worship elsewhere. But maybe some of us need to quit our unrealistic search for a perfect church and instead seek to make the church where we worship the best it can be. And in many cases that may mean letting God change us in some ways and deal with our own faults and sins.

Let's seek to be churches that love God with all our hearts and love our neighbors as ourselves. According to the Bible, that's about as close to perfection as you're going to get. Be a church that faithfully shares the gospel and the unchanging truths of the Word of God. Let's be true to our mission of making disciples. Let's reach out to a lost world with compassion and love. Let's be united with fellow believers in purpose and spirit. Let's seek to keep ourselves pure and holy in the midst of an unholy world. Let's be the light shining in the darkness.

There are no perfect churches, but let's seek to be good churches, faithful churches, churches busy fulfilling the mission Christ has given us. We may not be perfect, but we can seek to glorify the Lord in all we do. And we can humbly look to Him for the help we need to become even better churches.

What can you do to make your church better?

GOD RIGHTLY IDENTIFIES US ALL AS SINNERS

"For all have sinned and fall short of the glory of God."

– ROMANS 3:23

In addition to being a fan of old movies in general, I have always enjoyed in particular some of those films directed by Alfred Hitchcock. Maybe that seems strange for a pastor since Hitchcock's movies aren't exactly the type of inspirational and uplifting material you might view on the Hallmark Channel. I think it's his method of generating suspense which appeals to me, along with his being able to mix a little light humor into those otherwise dark situations.

Recently I watched one of those Hitchcock flicks which I hadn't seen before—*The Wrong Man*. It's about someone who is mistakenly accused of being a robber. This theme of mistaken identity was a favorite subject for Hitchcock. He liked to show how an innocent person could suffer all kinds of trouble simply from being misidentified or falsely accused.

Most of us have likely found ourselves being "the wrong person" at some point. Maybe as a child we were punished for something one of our siblings did. Or in our adult years we got a phone call or knock on the door from a bill collector looking for someone with the same name as ours. It's not always easy to prove our innocence, and sometimes we may end up suffering unjustly.

However when God identifies us as being lost sinners, along with all the rest of humanity, we would do well not to claim that He has the wrong man or woman. God's Word has clearly declared that all have sinned (Romans 3:23). Our tendency is to want to deny that accusation. We try to make excuses for our behavior or blame someone else. We compare ourselves to others and point out how much better we are than those contemptible people. We list all of our good qualities, along with some of the admirable, even religious, things we do. We're kind to animals. We don't steal. We haven't murdered anyone. We go to church. We pray at times. Maybe we even read daily devotional books like this one.

However none of us have gone through life without sinning against a holy God. The Bible states, "If we say that we have no sin, we deceive ourselves, and the truth is not in us" (I John 1:8). We're fooling ourselves if we think we're good enough to please God and get to heaven based on our own goodness and innocence. We all need forgiveness. And the pathway to finding it isn't by denying our sin. On the contrary, the Bible goes on to say, "If we confess our sins, He is faithful and just to forgive us our sins and to cleanse us from all unrighteousness" (I John 1:9). Admitting our need and our guilt is the way to experience God's forgiving grace.

If anyone knows what it means to be "the wrong man," it's Jesus. He's the only one who has ever lived on this earth who could claim complete innocence and purity. Yet He was falsely accused, was forced to undergo great suffering, and was executed. He was the wrong man. We were the ones who deserved to suffer for our sins.

But thankfully Jesus was also the right man. He was the only one who could take our punishment upon Himself and be the unblemished sacrifice for our sins. No one else could have provided forgiveness and salvation for us.

So when God says we're sinners or points out some specific sin in our lives, let's not claim He's got the wrong man. Let's own up to our guilt. And as we do, let's put our trust in the right Man for the forgiveness and cleansing we need.

When God shows you something sinful in your life, how do you react? Confess your sin and depend on Jesus for forgiveness and cleansing.

A Narrow Focus Can Make Us Spiritually Blind

"Hearing you will hear and shall not understand, and seeing you will see and not perceive."

– Matthew 13:14

One day I received quite a shock as I exited a local grocery store. When I walked over toward the area where I thought I had left my car, it wasn't there. Afraid that I was experiencing one of those "senior moments," I considered the possibility I may have parked elsewhere. But the more I thought about it, the more certain I was I had parked in that part of the lot.

Additionally, there weren't a great many other cars around since it was early in the morning. So I was quickly able to scan the rest of the lot and realize my vehicle was nowhere to be seen. My heart began to race as I felt a sense of panic. *Was it stolen? I had only gone into the store for a few minutes to pick up a couple of items. Would someone have taken it so quickly?*

As I stood there looking over the parking lot questioning my sanity and thinking what I should do next, another customer who had just left the store walked by. Realizing how strange I must have looked, I commented to her that apparently I had lost my car. She quipped that she had a similar experience a while back until she became aware she was looking for the wrong car. As soon as those words left her mouth, the realization hit me like a ton of bricks. I had driven my wife's car to the store. And sure enough there it was, only a few feet from where I was standing. I had been so focused on looking for my car that I hadn't even noticed our other vehicle right in front of my face. So yes, I did experience a "senior moment" after all.

I'm still amazed at how blind I was that day. But maybe it helps to explain the spiritual blindness from which we can suffer. The Bible refers to those who have eyes but can't see. Sometimes we can miss what's right in front of us due to our being so focused on how we think things should be or how we want them to be.

Some people refuse to believe in God or simply don't want to believe. They are blind to the evidence of His existence that is all around them. However at the same time they will accept alternate ideas which have less credibility and which require more faith than the belief in the Creator.

Others of us refuse to see our own faults and sins which the Lord tries to reveal to us. We can clearly see them in other people. But when it comes to our own wrongs, we tend to ignore them, deny them, take them lightly, or make excuses for them.

Some of us are blind to certain truths in God's Word. That particular idea or doctrine is not what we were taught or it's not what we want to believe. Therefore we overlook distinct evidence in the Bible which contradicts our long-held notions. For example, I believe many Christians are so set in their ideas about how things are going to play out in "the last days" that they aren't open to some clear teachings in the Bible which might suggest an alternate scenario. In that and other areas, we're often guilty of looking for our car—what we want the Bible to say—rather than seeing the real vehicle of truth that is right before our eyes.

We all need to guard against spiritual blindness. Let's not have any "senior moments" when it comes to seeing the truth God is trying to show us.

Ask the Lord to show you any spiritual blindspots in your life.

JUNE 24

HAVE THE COURAGE TO BE A
VOICE IN THE WILDERNESS

"The voice of one crying in the wilderness: 'Prepare the way of the Lord'"

– ISAIAH 40:3

Did you realize that today is a holiday? Now don't go panicking thinking that you forgot to send a card, buy your wife a bouquet of flowers, or acknowledge this special day to all your Facebook friends. June 24 really is a holiday, but not one that is celebrated in our country. In Quebec, Canada, this is St. Jean Baptiste Day. That's right—it's a holiday in commemoration of John the Baptist.

While we might consider this biblical forerunner of Christ a worthy person to be honored, we could probably think of other biblical figures whom we would be more likely to dignify by naming a holiday after them. Abraham, Moses, and David are just a few who come to mind. Yet when we look at what the Bible declares about John the Baptist, it's hard to deny that he should be near the top of the list when it comes to great individuals. Jesus said that no one greater than John had ever been born (Matthew 11:11). Now that's a hard testimony to refute. Who could be more deserving of a holiday than the man Jesus proclaimed to be the greatest ever born?

What made John such a great man in God's sight? We could point out several notable characteristics of this man of God, but let's focus on just one—his courage. It was the courage to be different, to stand alone when necessary, and to confront sin wherever it was found and no matter whose toes got stepped on in the process.

Do you remember the prophetic phrase that was used to describe John? Isaiah, looking ahead to John's ministry, referred to him as "the voice of one crying in the wilderness." Those words not only indicate that John was out in the desert proclaiming God's word, but I believe it also refers to his courage to be a voice for God in the spiritual wilderness of his day. He was willing to speak for God when others weren't. His was a lone voice in a time of spiritual dryness and deadness.

John came calling people to repent. He pointed out their sin and encouraged them to turn back to God. He didn't alter his message based on the latest opinion poll or on what might be considered politically acceptable. He wasn't afraid to deliver his message to the more prominent and powerful in society, which ended up getting him imprisoned and ultimately beheaded.

Such courage to speak God's word without compromising the truth was one of the qualities that made John great in God's sight. He called sin what it was. He didn't just deliver the easy message of love and acceptance, but also the tough, unpopular message of repentance.

We need great people today who will likewise stand up for what's right and true. We need to be such voices in the wilderness. At a time when many are ignoring or changing God's Word to make it more pleasing and acceptable, we need to have the courage to proclaim what God really says. Are we willing to be voices in the wilderness, to stand alone if necessary in order to speak for God? Let's pray that we'll have more of John's kind of courage.

Even though we don't live in Quebec, maybe we should choose to remember and celebrate the life of John the Baptist today. Anybody want to come over and munch on some locusts and wild honey? No takers? Then maybe a better way for us to honor John would be to remember his example and to ask God to help us be more like this courageous and great man.

Lord, give us courage today to speak for You, even if it means standing alone or facing ridicule for doing so.

Let's Make Sure We Are
Not Just Playing the Role
of a Christian

"You shall not be like the hypocrites."
– Matthew 6:5

One day I was sitting in a park observing Alice and the White Rabbit. No, I wasn't dreaming. Neither had I ventured through a looking glass. My family and I had made the trek to Orlando, Florida, where we were visiting Disney World on that particular day. I had found a place to sit to rest my weary feet for a few minutes while my grandchildren stood in line to meet the aforementioned storybook characters.

I watched as the young lady dressed up as Alice interacted with the various children who excitedly greeted her. I thought she did a wonderful job portraying the animated Disney character which she represented. Both her verbal expressions and her mannerisms, including her hand motions as she expressed surprise or glee, expertly mimicked Alice in Wonderland.

Her professionalism showed as the actress had her picture taken over and over with each new guest or group. Regardless of the differing circumstances, she was able to strike the same pose, duplicate a slight tilting of her head, and generate the same bright smile each time. As we encountered other such characters in the park that day, many of them were equally talented in portraying their various roles.

I'm afraid that some of us can become rather adept at imitation and role-playing too. We know what a Christian should look like and act like, so we tend to play the part. We even know the right words to say to make ourselves appear spiritual in a given situation. "Praise the Lord!" "I'll be praying for you." "All things work together for good." "God bless you."

Similarly we can duplicate the mannerisms of devotion—a bowed head, carrying a Bible, a gaze upward with a finger pointing toward the heavens, or countless other outward expressions which often are manifested by people of faith. Certainly such actions can be genuine demonstrations of a person's relationship with God, but those same gestures can just as easily be portrayed by pretenders who are merely playing a role.

We need to be sure that we possess the reality of Christianity and aren't simply being actors who knowingly, or maybe even without realizing it, are living out a fantasy. We shouldn't just be acting like followers of Christ; our behavior should be a reflection of who we truly are. It should be the fruit growing out of a heart that knows Christ as Savior. Those outward godly mannerisms should reflect the inward holiness that we possess due to the Spirit of God residing within.

Around the same time as our trip, one of the workers who was helping remodel our kitchen commented a couple of times about how I was always smiling. I appreciated her observation, along with the knowledge that I appeared to be a happy, pleasant person, but it also made me wonder how much of my smiling was simply a reflex action that I've come to wear on my face or how much of it is truly a reflection of the peace and joy that I have in my heart through Christ. I don't want to be like Alice, with a fake perpetual smile on my face. I want it to be a genuine expression of who I truly am. And I hope that it is.

On the one hand, as believers we need to always seek to do the right thing and have a godly spirit no matter what our circumstances or whether we feel like it or not. But on the other hand, let's be careful that we don't fall into the trap of simply playing the role of a Christian. Let's not be a make-believe character out of Christian world. Let's be the real thing—a true, devoted follower of Jesus Christ.

Reflect on your good actions—are they genuine?

GOD WILL SEE US THROUGH LIFE'S PAINFUL EXPERIENCES

"My grace is sufficient for you, for My strength is made perfect in weakness."

– II CORINTHIANS 12:9

Ow! Sorry, but I just sat back in my desk chair again and felt another prick of pain. Those common concepts of "sit back and relax" and "lie down and rest" aren't very fitting for me at the moment. It's nothing major. I just had another mole removed from my back. It was one of those that came back from being biopsied showing enough suspicious qualities that the dermatologist thought it best to perform further surgery to make sure none of it remained. Therefore I've got a number of stitches in my lower back at the moment. I keep telling myself the pain will be gone in a few more days—that's when I'm scheduled to get the stitches out. But in the meantime those little stabs of pain from my skin being poked are rather irritating and are especially making for some restless nights.

Even though I know it was a good thing to have the mole taken off in order to avoid it developing into something more serious, and although I realize those stitches are performing a valuable service in keeping my skin pulled together so it can heal properly, it still doesn't lessen the discomfort they create.

Many of us have other things in our lives comparable to that—a situation or circumstance that brings us some degree of pain and heartache, disturbing our peace of mind. In some cases, it may be something we know is for our own good—such as the chastening from our Heavenly Father which is referred to by the writer of Hebrews. He declared, "No chastening seems to be joyful for the present, but painful; nevertheless, afterward it yields the peaceable fruit of righteousness to those who have been trained by it" (Hebrews 12:11). Some such painful experiences are designed by God to help us grow in Christlike character and conduct.

But then there are other sources of distress in our lives for which we have no understanding or explanation as to their purpose. All we know is that they're difficult and painful to endure. It reminds me of the Apostle Paul's "thorn in the flesh" (see II Corinthians 12:7–10). I'll leave it to others to speculate as to the exact nature of that source of suffering, but whatever it was Paul didn't see anything positive about it. He even referred to it as a "messenger of Satan." Yet when he pleaded with God three times to remove it, the Lord chose not to do so. Apparently there was some purpose in it. Paul concluded that it was intended, if nothing else, to keep him humble. God's response to the apostle's request was simply the assurance His grace would be sufficient for Paul to put up with that so-called thorn. We can claim that same promise for ourselves and our painful situations. If God chooses not to remove it from our lives, He will certainly give us the grace we need to endure it. But in the meantime, it still hurts.

I can look forward to those stinging pricks from my stitches ending in a few days. And we can all look ahead to a time when whatever is bringing us pain in this life will be only a memory. It may be soon, or it may be many years from now. But one day God promises all pain will be behind us. Until then, let's trust that He will enable us to endure our thorns—His grace truly is sufficient for each of us, no matter what we're facing.

For what painful situation do you need to hold to the promise of God's grace being sufficient for you?

JUNE 27

Our Final Years Get
Us Ready for Heaven

"Remember now your Creator in the days of your youth, before the difficult days come."

– Ecclesiastes 12:1

Those who have read my writings or heard my sermons over any length of time are familiar with our basset hound, Dorothy. Through the years, she and her antics have provided me with a rich resource of memorable illustrations of certain truths. Some have shared with me how they enjoy and remember various "Dorothy stories." It was definitely a sad time when our beloved pet passed away.

Dorothy was quite old for her breed of dog. And over those last months her health had deteriorated significantly. She had become unable to eat very much, including the treats that she used to love so much that she had been willing to "shake hands" or twirl around in order to receive one. She eventually became too feeble to take her usual walks through the neighborhood where her sensitive nose would excitedly busy itself sniffing out the latest trails of other creatures that had passed that way.

Old age and poor health had robbed Dorothy of most of her passion for life. That became obvious in her final days when she hardly glanced at a nearby rabbit in the yard and when she failed to get stirred up by a rumble of thunder. The look in her eyes made it clear that she was tired of living and was ready to go.

I've seen a similar look in the eyes of some elderly people I've known, or have heard them express those sentiments verbally. If we live long enough to experience our bodies wearing out, life tends to lose much of its attraction. The writer of the book of Ecclesiastes refers to that stage of life as "the difficult days" and uses some rather creative word pictures to describe a person's physical deterioration (12:1–5). Poor eyesight is represented by the sun and moon being darkened. "Strong men bowing down" may refer to the legs and knees giving out. "Music being brought low" seems to describe the failing sense of hearing. "Grinders ceasing" is probably symbolic of our teeth not allowing us to chew our food as well as in past years. There are also references to the fear of heights or how one has to be careful not to fall. That passage ends with the summary statement that "desire fails."

Many elderly people can relate to that condition. Their declining health, along with the fact that the names of many of their friends and acquaintances are frequently showing up in the obituaries, also causes them to be less active socially. All of this combined with a lack of mobility and forfeiture of independence often results in a profound sense of loss.

In a way I believe God uses all those factors to prepare us for leaving this life. Earthly things just don't hold the attraction that they once did. They lose their luster and heaven looks better and better as each day goes by for those who are trusting Jesus and are spiritually prepared. We tire of the pain, discomfort, and loneliness—finding it harder and harder to put forth the effort required to keep living. We're ready to go.

However, it's important to remember that our lives are in God's hands. As long as He gives us breath, there's still a purpose in our being here. We still have things to do and other lives to touch. So even when our bodies ache and our passions wane, we need to hang in here seeking to fulfill God's will for us until He decides that it's time to call us home.

And when my time comes to go, I think it would make that home even a little brighter if I were to find a certain hound there to greet me.

Are you experiencing some of the "difficult days" related to aging? Hang in there till God calls you home.

A Good Testimony
at Life's End

"I have fought the good fight, I have finished the race, I have kept the faith."

– II Timothy 4:7

It was a rather short and simple e-mail that I received one time. It quoted the words of the Apostle Paul from II Timothy 4:7—"I have fought the good fight, I have finished the race, I have kept the faith." Then there was a person's name and the dates of his birth and death. And that was all. It was this family's way of announcing that their loved one had passed away after battling cancer for over a year. We had heard a few days earlier that he had gone into hospice care, so this news wasn't totally unexpected. The unusual aspect was that this young man was only thirty-one years of age.

Some deaths are harder to understand and more difficult to deal with than others. But whatever the circumstances, it makes such a difference when we know that the person involved knows the Lord and can be tied to those timeless words in the Bible. It gives us peace and joy, even in the middle of our own pain, grief, and sense of loss. That e-mail caused me to take a closer look at those familiar claims of Paul.

"I have fought the good fight." This sentiment was especially appropriate for this particular individual. In spite of unfavorable reports from medical tests and doctors, he did not give up in his struggle to overcome this disease. He had sought out all kinds of treatments, both conventional and otherwise. He came to the end knowing he had done all he could do.

We all face battles with various challenges and problems in life. It's honorable when we can look back with the assurance that we tackled those difficulties rather than running from them or choosing the easier path. That's especially true in the battle with sin and evil. Let's do all we can to fulfill God's purposes for us and do it with faith and integrity

"I have finished the race." This isn't just talking about coming to the end of life's road. It also refers to our having followed the course that God has set out for us. Too many people blaze their own trails and follow the path they've planned rather than seeking and following God's will for their lives. When our lives are over, we should be able to do more than sing along with Frank Sinatra that "I did it my way." We should be able to look back with the testimony that we did it God's way.

"I have kept the faith." This is probably the most significant of the three statements—to reach the end of life and be able to say that we've kept the faith. There is so much that we encounter during our lifetimes that can hinder us from remaining on that narrow road of faith in Christ. Storms of various kinds can blow us off course. Successes can tempt us to trust in ourselves rather than in God. Obstacles can cause us to fear and to falter. The pleasures of sin can lure us into their deceptively attractive traps. Nice-sounding, convincing oratory can pull us away from the truth. Sometimes even those final days of dealing with suffering and death can test us.

If we can endure all that life throws at us and come to the finish line still trusting Jesus, still walking with God, still loving Him and seeking to obey Him, then by the grace of God we've truly got a wonderful testimony.

Let's pray that Paul's claims will be equally true for each one of us.

Are you staying on course as to be able to have a clear and inspiring testimony at life's end?

God Has a Purpose
for Our Struggles

"For whom He foreknew, He also predestined to be conformed to the image of His Son."

– Romans 8:29

I remember when a couple of three-year-old boys in our church took their first swimming lessons. From what I heard, it sounded like it went well and that the youngsters had a good time. However, early in the week, when the instructor tried to get the boys to stick their faces into the water to blow bubbles, they didn't want to do it. No matter how much she encouraged them, they wouldn't take that important step. So what did the instructor do? She dunked them!

From my secondhand information I'm not clear on whether or not she physically forced their heads into the water. I was told that at one point she played a game that, in a roundabout way, got the boys to put their heads under the surface of the pool. And they were fine with it. Before that session was finished, those boys were plunging under the water to retrieve toys from the bottom of the pool.

Someone might think, *Well, that was cruel, or rude, or deceptive, to dunk those little boys or to trick them into putting their faces in the water when they didn't want to do it.* But if they hadn't learned to take that step, they weren't going to be able to learn to swim. And that was the goal of the instructor, even if it meant some momentary discomfort or unhappiness on the part of those kids.

What is God's goal for us? It's not just to provide for our needs or to make us happy. It's not simply to hold us close and love on us, or to be our friend. His goal is to help us grow and become more like Christ (Romans 8:29). And that explains why He brings or allows certain things into our lives. Some of them may be difficult, uncomfortable, and even painful for us. But the Lord often uses those circumstances to train us to become better, stronger, more mature disciples.

Most of us probably experience times when we're floundering in the water. We're struggling with hurts and hard times. We may wonder where God is and why He's letting us go through these difficult circumstances. In those moments we need to remember that He hasn't forsaken us. If we could see the whole picture of the pool, we'd realize that He's right there within reach of us, watching us, and making sure that we don't drown. Nevertheless He may be letting us struggle for a time, because He knows it will make us stronger, will make us grow, and will make us more like Him.

Think about Job. This godly man thought God had dunked him and he couldn't understand why. Did God not care about him? Had he done something wrong? Job wasn't aware of having done anything to make God mad at him, yet he had lost his possessions, his children, and his health. Although Job was floundering, God had not forsaken him. His Almighty arms were ready to keep Job from going under for the final time. In the end, this experience made Job stronger and gave him a better understanding of the greatness of God and of his relationship with the Creator.

Although God may not be shielding us from certain hardships or discomfort at the moment, it doesn't mean that He doesn't care. The disciplining, testing, or whatever it may be is actually an indication of His love for us. He cares enough to train us and to help us grow.

Let's trust our Heavenly Father through those tough times. When it seems like He's dunked you, keep in mind that He's just trying to teach you how to swim.

Keep trusting God through your tough times. Let Him do His work of making you more like Jesus.

Staying Connected to Christ Keeps Us Consistent

"Abide in Me, and I in you."
– John 15:4

Garage doors are heavier than they look. There was a time when I had been having to pull one down by hand due to the sporadic nature of our electronic opener. It would work fine for a few days, but then suddenly it wouldn't operate properly. And reaching high to tug on that door takes its toll on a grandfather's elbow joints and back. The problem was with the safety sensors—one of those gadgets situated just above the ground that shoots a beam of light across to make sure that nothing gets squashed by that heavy door as it rumbles shut. Those devices are helpful; over the years ours may have spared one of the nine lives of a couple of cats I know. But in this case, it seems that the connection refused to remain tight. An electrician friend who took a look at it said that the sensor itself needed to be replaced. The connector in it was so worn out or corroded that the wire just wouldn't stay in it very well. The movement of the garage door, or simply time itself, would cause it to work loose very easily.

Loose connections sometimes plague our relationship with God as well. They can result in what we could refer to as sporadic spirituality. One minute we can be standing firm in our commitment to God and the next we find ourselves giving in to temptation. Right after talking to someone about God and our faith, we end up talking to someone else about the latest office gossip. Peace of mind is suddenly interrupted by extreme anxiety. We express love to a person in the morning, but later that afternoon we unnecessarily rake that person over the coals. We help somebody today, but tomorrow we willfully turn our backs on an opportunity to relieve someone's suffering. What's wrong with us? One minute we seem to be working fine, with actions and attitudes that reflect Christ. The next minute our faith seems to be completely "out of order."

Consistency comes with maturity. And in this life we will never be free from that susceptibility to spiritual failure. But if we're "consistently inconsistent," maybe we need to check our connections with God. Are we staying close to Him? He doesn't pull away from us. As a matter of fact, we possess some great promises which assure us that nothing from outside ourselves can ever disconnect us from the Lord and His love. However, sometimes we're guilty of pulling ourselves away from Him. Or we allow other things to come in and disrupt our fellowship with God.

It's kind of like that garage door. Sometimes the movement of that door going up and down would loosen that electrical connection. And there are circumstances that come up in our lives which can test our commitment and shake our faith. We've got to be determined to hold firmly by faith to the Lord during those times.

Time itself can also be a factor in having a loose connection. Over the years, we can experience a lessening of that fervor that keeps us close to God. That journey with God can grow familiar and old. However, that doesn't have to be the case. If we seek to hold tight to God, He can keep things fresh and new in our relationship with Him. Instead of it growing older, it can, as one song suggests, grow sweeter every day.

So let's keep an eye on our connection with the Lord. If we let it get loose, we may find ourselves all too often not functioning like a Christian ought to be.

Are you seeing too much inconsistency in your life? Check your connections with the Lord.

Is There Hope for Our Country's Future?

"If the foundations are destroyed, what can the righteous do?"

– Psalm 11:3

As another Independence Day draws near, are you optimistic or pessimistic about our country and its future? No doubt in some of our churches this Sunday there will be patriotic services and positive messages about the greatness of America, how God has favored our nation over the course of its history, and how that bodes well for its future. In other cases, there will likely be a "doom and gloom" atmosphere with the various faults and sins of our country being pointed out and condemned, while sounding the warning of God's impending wrath and judgment.

Is one of those attitudes more realistic and appropriate than the other? Or could it be that there is reason for both optimism and pessimism as we evaluate where we are as a nation and what may lie in store for us in the days ahead?

Certainly we can count our blessings and rejoice over the heritage we have received as Americans, as well as the freedoms we still enjoy. We can be grateful for the Christian foundation upon which our country was built. However, we need to recognize that such a solid foundation does not guarantee God's favor, blessing, and protection as we move forward. Foundations can crumble or can be forsaken by a society. The Bible indicates such a possibility when it asks in Psalm 11:3, "If the foundations are destroyed, what can the righteous do?"

Therefore we should certainly have some grave concerns about the present state of our country and its future. As God is being ignored and His Word is being reinterpreted or rejected by a significant portion of our society, we can expect to lose favor with God and to face not only the consequences of our sins but the judgment of a holy God.

Does that leave us without any hope? I'm not sure how optimistic we can be about the future of our nation. Such hope can only be based upon a combination of God's mercy and the people's willingness to humble themselves before Him, repent of their sins, and submit to His will. Without a turning back to God, there isn't much grounds for optimism for the future of the nation. But neither do we have to sink into the mire of despondency and pessimism. As believers we always have reasons to be positive about the future. No matter what happens, God will be with His faithful followers. We can count on Him to continue to guide us, strengthen us, protect us, and enable us to face whatever situations we encounter. And when all is said and done, we have a better country to look forward to when we leave this one.

So let's return to the question posed by the Psalmist. What can the righteous do when the foundations are destroyed? We can pray. We can pray for our nation and its leaders. We can pray for a revival of true faith. We can pray for God's mercy in the midst of His judgment. We can also stand firm in upholding the truth of God's Word. We can refuse to give in to the pressure to conform to standards which oppose the teachings of the Bible. We can continue to live the kind of life that will be an example and witness to the people around us. We can choose to love instead of becoming consumed with anger, bitterness, and resentment over the condition of our society. We can stand on that foundation whether our nation chooses to do so or not.

So let's not get fooled by an unfounded optimism nor get weighed down by an overwhelming pessimism. There's reason for concern about our nation, but there's always hope for the future in Christ.

On what are you basing your view of the future of the nation? What more could you be doing under these circumstances we find ourselves in?

Let's Be as Brave as Our Founding Fathers

"Only be strong and of good courage."
– Joshua 1:18

When I was in first and second grade I attended an elementary school named after one of Georgia's signers of the Declaration of Independence. Do you remember who those three gentlemen were? Georgians today probably associate their names more with counties than anything else—Lyman Hall, Button Gwinnett, and George Walton.

When we think of all those who put their "John Hancock" on that significant historical document, maybe we think of them similarly to the charter members of an organization. We remember them and honor them as being the founding fathers, some of the first ones to commit themselves to the forming of our nation as an independent body.

But let's not lose sight of the great risk these signers were taking. They weren't just the lucky winners who were chosen to have the honor of representing their states and going down in history as being present for this ceremonial occasion. These men were putting their lives on the line by signing this declaration. They had the courage to be personally identified as rebels against the greatest power in the world at that time. It has been called one of the boldest acts in the records of time. If the colonies had failed in this struggle, these signers were dooming themselves to the fate of being executed by hanging. Yes, there's a good reason we've honored those men by placing their names on counties, schools, and other entities.

We've been blessed to live in a nation in which it hasn't required much courage to be identified as a Christian. That's not the case in other parts of the world. And times are changing in our own country.

What if you knew that if you signed on to follow Christ you would be discriminated against in the workplace? What if you knew the IRS might target you for audits? What if you knew it would cause many in society to view you as a dangerous person and as an intolerant hater of certain people due to your antiquated biblical views? Keep in mind, these are just hypothetical situations. Or are they?

Will we have the courage to openly identify with Christ—to sign our names to the fact that we are aligning ourselves primarily with Him and His Word? By doing so, we will be declaring that if the mighty power of our government ever tries to force us to do something against the principles of scripture, we will have to obey God rather than men. We will be stating clearly that we believe in and intend to adhere to the eternal truths of God's Word in spite of society's changing morals and standards.

We will be declaring our independence not only from sin, but also from the dictates of political correctness and from the pressures of this world to get us to conform to its unbiblical views and lifestyles. Do we have the courage to take such a stand?

Too many people who have signed on as Christians are buckling under the current pressures to compromise their beliefs and their loyalty to the Savior. We need some spiritual Lyman Halls, Button Gwinnetts, and George Waltons. We need believers who are willing to sign their names on the dotted line to let this world know that they are dedicated to Jesus and they are going to stay true to His Word no matter what others say about them or do to them.

May God give us Christians today the same kind of courage those signers of the Declaration of Independence possessed.

Lord, help us to be more courageous when we face ridicule and opposition due to our faith.

Independence from God Is Nothing to Celebrate

"I can do all things through Christ who strengthens me."

– Philippians 4:13

I recall a time when we were able to enjoy a little vacation time at the beach with our grandchildren. On one occasion as we ventured out into the ocean, the waves were a little rough, at least for my then five-year-old grandson. At first, he held tightly to either his daddy or me as the swells of water passed by. Nevertheless, as time went on, he got a little braver. He would let go for a moment, wanting to stand on his own. But as soon as he saw a big wave heading toward him, he would look to grab one of us to help support him or to lift him up high enough so that it wouldn't splash over his head.

Along the way, we tried to teach him how to be a little more independent out in the ocean. We tried to help him learn to watch for the waves and how to time his jumping to ride the swells successfully. He learned to turn sideways to the wave to minimize the impact or to turn his head away from it in order to keep it from splashing in his face. The goal was to try to make him more confident and less dependent on us. And he certainly made progress to that end in the time we were out there.

While God has chosen to reveal Himself to be like a father and we His children in many ways, let's be careful not to think that His goal for us is to get us to stand on our own two feet apart from Him. As we take time to celebrate the anniversary of the birth of our nation this week, we tend to extol the concept of independence. And it is something to value and to seek to achieve in many aspects of our lives. But not when it comes to our relationship with the Lord.

Too many of us try to stand on our own strength and wisdom in the ocean of life. We like to have God close by—so that we can cry out to Him or grab hold of Him when it looks like some especially big wave is in danger of overwhelming us. But as long as we can keep our heads above water, we're more content on our own rather than relying on God.

That is not God's intention for us. In some ways, He doesn't want us to stay like little children. He intends for us to grow in wisdom, knowledge, skill, and grace. But at the same time, He desires for us always to recognize our dependence on Him. He wants us to trust Him, rely on Him, and draw our wisdom, strength, and our very life from Him. It's not His goal for us to ever let go of His hand and to stand on our own apart from Him.

Yes, the Bible says that I can do all things. But don't leave out the rest of the sentence—"through Christ who strengthens me" (Philippians 4:13). It is only because I'm holding on to Christ that I have the strength to do what's needed. Jesus portrayed this relationship of dependence on Him very clearly in John 15. "I am the vine, you are the branches. He who abides in Me, and I in him, bears much fruit; for without Me you can do nothing" (verse 5). It is only as we stay connected to Christ that we can do anything worthwhile. Without depending on Him, we can do nothing. But when we're relying on Him, we can do "all things." What a difference!

So let's make sure we're holding on to the great God who can uphold us through all the rough waves of life. And let's celebrate our dependence.

Are there any areas of your life in which you're losing that spirit of dependence on the Lord?

WE HAVE A RESPONSIBILITY TO PRAY FOR OUR LEADERS

"I exhort first of all that supplications, prayers, intercessions, and giving of thanks be made for all men, for kings and all who are in authority."

– I TIMOTHY 4:1–2

One time I was asked to give the invocation and lead the Pledge of Allegiance at a local Board of Commissioners meeting. I was honored by the invitation and gladly accepted the opportunity to serve in this way. It was interesting to be part of the proceedings that I usually only get a glimpse of on the local government access channel on cable TV or read about afterwards in the newspaper. I enjoyed watching our government leaders carry out their duties and observing the interested citizens who came out to share their concerns.

This experience reminded me to be thankful for the freedom we have to assemble in such a manner to take care of the business of the community. We still have a voice in what our government does and we can let that voice be heard. It also served as a reminder of an admittedly oft-neglected duty to pray for those who serve in such positions of leadership. This is a biblical mandate as expressed in I Timothy 2:1–4: "Therefore I exhort first of all that supplications, prayers, intercessions, and giving of thanks be made for all men, for kings, and all who are in authority, that we may lead a quiet and peaceable life in all godliness and reverence. For this is good and acceptable in the sight of God our Savior, who desires all men to be saved and to come to the knowledge of the truth."

Although the Bible instructs us to pray "for kings, and all who are in authority," it doesn't tell us exactly how to pray for them. What requests do we need to make in behalf of our government leaders? The question becomes even more complicated when we find ourselves faced with leaders whose views we oppose and with whose actions we often strongly disagree.

First of all, that scripture in I Timothy does tell us one way to pray—to give thanks. We can give thanks for individuals who are willing to serve in these positions. In a day when all public figures are subject to such close scrutiny, harsh criticism, and frivolous lawsuits, it's a wonder that anyone would be willing to put himself or herself in that position. Let's be grateful for those who do, and especially for those who serve well.

Then we can pray for wisdom for our leaders—that they might know what's right to do and what's best for those whom they serve. We may need to pray that some leaders would become more open to God's guidance and to the wisdom He can give.

We can then pray that God would give those decision-makers the courage to do the right thing, regardless of whether it's popular or not, and regardless of the personal political consequences. We need leaders who will be brave enough to do what's good for the community or the country, even if it hurts their chances for reelection.

Although that scripture doesn't tell us how to pray, it shows us the goal or the end result of such intercession—"that we may lead a quiet and peaceable life in all godliness and reverence." If our communities aren't as quiet, peaceable, godly, and reverent as we would like, maybe we're not praying enough for our leaders. The decisions they make go a long way in determining what kind of community we live in.

So on this Fourth of July, let this holiday be a reminder to us of our God-given duty to pray for those in leadership positions in our community, state, and nation. They need our prayers, whether or not we happen to like their politics. And if we'll be faithful to do so, we know on the authority of the Bible that we're doing what is "good and acceptable in the sight of God."

Pray for our leaders today. Make a commitment to do so more regularly.

GOD AND HIS WAYS ARE STILL BEYOND OUR UNDERSTANDING

"My wrath is aroused against you...for you have not spoken of Me what is right."

– JOB 42:7

I thought I had this particular weather event figured out. I had just seen a picture of the local radar showing a big blob of precipitation headed in our direction. It looked like once it hit we would be sopped in for the rest of the afternoon. Knowing I needed to pick up a few items at the grocery store, I thought I could do so before the rain arrived. However between it taking me longer than expected to get started and the slowness of service at the store, after checkout I was greeted at the door with a pouring rain.

I decided to wait a couple of minutes to see if there might be a break in the downpour, giving me a window of opportunity to get my groceries in the car without getting soaked. So when the precipitation lightened, I took off for my vehicle. However just as I was finishing loading the last bags in the trunk, the bottom fell out of the sky. Although I was caught in it for only seconds, I got drenched. To add insult to injury, this turned out to be the worst part of the afternoon weather. Not only did the rain let up a short while later, but the sun even peeked out. So much for my figuring out the weather.

Similarly we need to be careful if we ever begin to think we've got God completely figured out. We may see what He tends to do based on history and our own experiences with Him. We might study His Word and have a good concept of the picture He reveals about Himself. But just about the time we think we've got a solid grasp of His will and His ways, He does something to remind us that He is still far beyond what our finite minds can comprehend. He lets us know that no image we carve in our minds can fully depict Him and no box we construct can contain Him.

Job's friends thought they had a clear image of God in view on their radar. They had witnessed how He moved. They were certain that the hardships and losses in this life were always a sign of God's judgment, while physical and financial prosperity were clear indications of His pleasure. Yet they ended up having to humble themselves before both God and Job because of their mistaken notions.

There are some today still propagating similar false ideas about God and prosperity. However, they're not the only ones who need to guard against thinking they have God all figured out. No matter how deep our understanding of Him, we need to keep in mind what He has told us—"My thoughts are not your thoughts, nor are your ways My ways.... For as the heavens are higher than the earth, so are My ways higher than your ways, and My thoughts than your thoughts" (Isaiah 55:8–9).

Granted, there are certain ways in which God is predictable. He will always be faithful to His character. He will always be good, loving, true, righteous, and holy. We can be certain that He will fulfill His promises and will act in harmony with His Word. However, we also need to remember that He sees the bigger picture and is far wiser than we are. He may do some surprising things that might appear to conflict with our image of Him simply because of our limited view.

So be careful. Just when you think you've got the Almighty and His ways mastered, you might get drenched with a reminder that He's still greater than we are and more complex than we can imagine.

Keep seeking to know more about God and His ways. There is always more to learn.

THE LORD CAN HEAR
YOUR CRY FOR HELP

"In my distress I called upon the Lord, and cried out to my God; He heard my voice."

– PSALM 18:6

My wife enjoys telling folks about the occasional incidents over the years when I have awakened her during the night because I was mumbling in my sleep, sometimes actually rising to a level where I would holler out. It hasn't happened often, but enough to provide my wife with ammunition for giving me a hard time about it.

Since I either wake myself up when I yell out or my wife tries to wake me, I usually remember the reason for my outburst. It's normally due to a dream of some kind in which I'm in trouble and am attempting to call out for help. The predicament may vary from sinking in floodwaters to some bad person pursuing me. But whatever the problem, I try to call out for help but nothing comes out of my throat. I keep struggling to do so until I finally emerge from my dream to actually voice the cry out loud. When I wake up, I can still feel the frustration of attempting to yell out for assistance and being unable to do so.

Maybe some of us feel that way at times in our waking moments too. In some cases, problems pour out on us like a flood threatening to overcome us. On other occasions, the things we fear most in life appear to be approaching. And many times the evil in the world seems to be surrounding us. We sense the danger and know that we're going to need help to make it through. Sometimes our cries for help get muffled by our own sense of hopelessness and despair. Sometimes we may not know whom to reach out to and may sense that we're all alone. On other occasions, we may feel like our cries are simply falling on deaf ears. Frustration sets in as we try unsuccessfully to call out for help or feel the inability to do so.

The good news is that we can awake from that state of mind to a better reality. There is Someone we can reach out to for help—Someone who does hear and respond to our cries—Someone who has the power to help us. All through scripture we can find invitations to call out to God and look to Him for help in our time of need. "Call to Me, and I will answer you" (Jeremiah 33:3). "Ask, and it will be given to you; seek, and you will find; knock, and it will be opened to you (Matthew 7:7).

The Psalmist declared how God was there for him when he needed Him: "In my distress I called upon the Lord, and cried out to my God; He heard my voice from His temple, and my cry came before Him, even to His ears" (Psalm 18:6). And probably one of the most well-known affirmations of faith in God's availability to assist us is this one: "I will lift up my eyes to the hills—from whence comes my help? My help comes from the Lord, who made heaven and earth" (Psalm 121:1–2).

In our times of trouble and distress, the Lord wants us to look to Him for help. And at those times when we don't know what to say or can't find the voice to say it, we can be assured that the Lord knows our thoughts and can hear the very cries of our hearts.

So don't let frustration overcome you. Keep casting your cares upon the Lord—the One who cares for you. Remind yourself that the One who made heaven and earth is able to help you in your situation today.

What is troubling you today? Take that concern to the Lord in prayer, knowing He hears the cry of your heart.

In Contentious Circumstances, Pray and Trust the Lord

"Behold, how good and how pleasant it is for brethren to dwell together in unity!"

– PSALM 133:1

My wife and I sometimes watch some of these TV shows in which houses are renovated. One of those programs involves two brothers who help people find less expensive houses which need some work done on them. Then they proceed to renovate those "fixer-uppers" into the types of residences those homeowners dream of. At one time during the summer, a version of that show aired called "Brother vs. Brother." In this case, each brother picked a house, renovated it in stages, and invited certain people to judge which one had done the better job. It was a friendly competition, usually with some kind of agreed-upon embarrassing consequences for whomever lost that week's challenge.

Such a brotherly competition can be lighthearted and entertaining, but it can be a different story when we face "brother vs. brother" within the realm of the church. If we've been in a fellowship of believers for any length of time, we've all probably witnessed it or experienced it firsthand at some point. Why? Because even within the unity of the body of Christ, there is diversity. Even though we may be unified in the main aspects of our faith, there will be various secondary matters in which we share differing opinions and preferences. In many cases, we can maintain our one-mindedness in Christ in spite of those differences. We can find areas of compromise or simply agree to disagree on less important matters as we continue to fellowship and serve the Lord together.

But what about when those differences do start to hinder our unity? In his first letter to the Corinthians, the Apostle Paul declared that such contentions can be a sign of carnality—an unspiritual attitude or spirit—on the part of one or more of those involved (see I Corinthians 3:3). So whenever we find ourselves involved in a contention, it's good for us to examine our own hearts, minds, motives, and actions to make sure there is nothing unspiritual on our part which is helping to fuel the fire.

However, carnality may not always be a factor. Paul and Barnabas were two Spirit-filled men who had a sharp contention as recorded in Acts 15. While some try to figure out who was at fault, this disagreement may have resulted simply over what each godly man felt was more important. Neither may have been unspiritual, but their focus was different. We need to remember that sometimes contentions aren't about someone being unspiritual, but just about different viewpoints which are strongly believed and felt.

Here's another truth to keep in mind: as much as we may dislike contentions, sometimes they are needed for the purposes of correction or cleansing. There are situations in which ignoring a problem would be wrong. Sometimes situations need to be addressed and people need to be confronted.

Additionally, God can use contentions to fulfill His plans and purposes. No doubt Satan has used such circumstances to hurt people, destroy churches, and hinder the work of God's kingdom, but I believe God can bring something good out of those painful circumstances as well. The end result of Paul and Barnabas' conflict was the formation of two missionary teams instead of just one. Can we dare believe that God can transform our contentious situations into a blessing?

So when you're facing a "brother vs. brother" experience, commit yourself to praying—for yourself, for others involved, and for God to fulfill His will and purposes.

What is the cause of your contentious situation? What might God be wanting to accomplish?

JULY 8

God Wants to Bless
You Abundantly

"Surely goodness and mercy shall follow me all the days of my life."
– Psalm 23:6

One day when my wife and I were babysitting our grandchildren at their house, we had to keep an eye out for the newest member of their family at the time—an energetic, playful kitten. At times it would like to find something to stalk, with its favorite prey being human feet. So we had to be vigilant in order either to avoid or prepare for these attacks. We might be innocently walking along or dangling our feet off a chair when this little cat would sneak up and pounce on its target.

Of course the actions of that kitten were considered cute and harmless, except for startling someone who wasn't expecting it. But we usually think of the idea of stalking in a much more negative light. We picture a wild beast zeroing in on its victim just before violently attacking it. Or we associate this idea with obsessed fans who follow celebrities around, or individuals who pursue other people with an intent to do them harm.

Biblically we might connect the practice of stalking with Satan, whom God's Word describes as being like a roaring lion going around seeking people to devour. But have you ever associated this concept with God? Is there a sense, a positive sense, in which God is similar to a stalker?

In one of the most well-known portions of scripture, Psalm 23, the Lord is described as our shepherd who takes care of us. In the closing verse of that psalm, it states, "Surely goodness and mercy shall follow me all the days of my life." The word translated "follow" can be used to refer to an animal pursuing or stalking its prey. Think about that. If we are in a right relationship with God, His goodness and mercy are constantly stalking us as we go through our time here on earth. The Lord is looking for ways to pour out His grace upon us. He is wanting to pounce on us, not to do us harm but to do us good. He is always pursuing us in order to seek to bless us.

This is one of those truths that is so easy for us to overlook or forget. We can sometimes feel like we're having to beg and plead to a hesitant God to help us. Or we feel like we're having to reach out and tug on the arm of an unwilling God to let a few crumbs of goodness and mercy fall our way. But that's not the case.

Go back to the previous verse in that psalm where it says, "My cup runs over." God is like a generous host. He doesn't just give us a small drink of blessing out of His infinite resources, but rather He pours out His grace to us until it's more than we can hold. God wants to bless us and bless us abundantly.

All of us experience God's goodness and mercy to some degree in our lives. But if we're not receiving an abundance of His blessings, the problem isn't with God. We need to look for any ways we may be hindering Him from being able to bless us to the extent He desires to do so. Are we running from Him as He pursues us? Are we holding our hand over our cup, not allowing Him to pour His goodness into it?

Our Shepherd wants to take care of us and bless us if we'll let Him. His goodness and mercy are just looking for an opportunity to pounce on you today. Don't hinder Him from filling your cup to overflowing.

Lord, show me any way in which I'm hindering your desire to abundantly bless me.

LET'S NOT FORGET TO
EXPRESS OUR GRATITUDE

"Enter into His gates with thanksgiving, and into His courts with praise. Be thankful to Him, and bless His name."

– PSALM 100:4

I remember when a road maintenance crew came through the stretch of state highway in front of our church. They did one of the most thorough jobs of clearing off the right-of-way that I had witnessed in the many years we had been in that location. They didn't just mow a few feet on either side of the road, as other such workers had often done. These guys had the courage to tackle our despised patch of kudzu, actually making a significant dent in it—although I was sure it would make a quick recovery, as that infamous plant is known to do. This crew also cut down all the weeds along the bank above the road. Only three or four plants—I guess you could actually call them small trees which were too big for their weed-eaters—remained, and I quickly committed myself to going out and cutting those down while they were accessible. However before I could follow through on that plan, the next day I discovered the workers had returned and had removed even those objects from the landscape.

I was so impressed by the job that was done I decided to call the state department of transportation to compliment them on the work. I was pleasantly surprised to get a real human being on the other end of the line who, after a couple of attempts, got me in touch with the appropriate person. Immediately he wanted to know what county I was calling about. As he continued to ask for further information, it was obvious he was preparing to receive what he assumed was either a complaint or request. I stopped him and told him I simply wanted to compliment the crew for doing such a great job on that stretch of road. The person I spoke with expressed his great surprise as this was not the type of call he was accustomed to receiving.

I must confess that in spite of my actions on this occasion, I'm often not as conscientious about passing along compliments and expressing gratitude. Many of us could do a better job of saying thanks to people or commending them for what they've done. Think about how encouraging it is to us when someone takes the time to show their appreciation for us or our work.

And what about when it comes to calling up the Lord on His heavenly hotline of prayer? Would He be shocked for us to talk to Him primarily for the reason of thanking Him for something He's done in our lives? Is He more accustomed to hearing our complaints about something bad happening to us? Would He be surprised if we just lifted up our voices to praise Him rather than to ask for some divine favor?

I guess nothing really surprises God since He knows everything. And I know the Bible says He wants us to bring our needs and concerns to Him. But it also says to let our requests be made known to God with thanksgiving (Philippians 4:6). I believe it pleases Him when we take time to acknowledge His greatness, love, and holiness. I think it puts a smile on His face when we remember to express our gratitude for previous blessings instead of just always seeking His present and future assistance.

Take a few moments today to glorify God for who He is and to thank Him for His goodness to you. And let's all try to be more mindful to compliment and thank other people too.

Maybe I should start right now—I really do appreciate all of you who just took the time to read these words and to take them to heart.

Express thanks to those whom you encounter today. Take a few moments to pray without making any requests—just offer your thanksgiving and praise to God.

JULY 10

LET'S EXAMINE OUR
SPIRITUAL FEEDING HABITS

"For everyone who partakes only of milk is unskilled in the word of righteousness, for he is a babe. But solid food belongs to those who are of full age."

– HEBREWS 5:13–14

During a vacation at the beach, I noticed the differences in the way various species of birds went about the task of finding food. There was one that stood with its feet planted at the edge of the water, watching and waiting for its food to come within reach. Another kind of bird kept busily running back and forth with the ebb and flow of the waves, as if it didn't want to get its feet wet as it searched for something to eat.

There was another species that had an interesting method. It flew low and parallel to the shore along the area where the water was only inches deep. It opened its mouth, allowing its bottom beak to skim the surface of the water as it flew along, hoping to come away with some small morsels of nourishment.

Then there were the birds that hunted their prey a little farther away from the shore. One would fly overhead until it spotted its objective, and then actually dive into the water in an attempt to retrieve its dinner. Finally there were the ones who stayed out in the deeper water, floating along and sometimes plunging into the water to obtain something to satisfy their hunger.

My observations of those beach fowl reminded me of the various ways some of us go about in search of nourishment for our souls. There are those who make little effort to find such spiritual food. They simply stand at the edge—not going to church or reading the Bible—possibly grabbing hold of an occasional nugget of inspiration that happens to pass their way.

Others vacillate back and forth with the ebb and flow of life. They will occasionally open up a Bible, attend a worship service, or tune in to a religious broadcast, but they don't ever stay long enough to get their feet wet in the ocean of God's revelation. They taste and run—move forward, then retreat—no consistency in their efforts or results.

Then you have those who just like to skim the surface of the things of God. They want to receive just enough to get by on. They may be afraid of going deeper, not wanting to risk being thought of as some kind of religious fanatic. All of these folks we've mentioned so far like to stay close to shore—wanting to get some spiritual food while still maintaining close ties with the world apart from God.

However, others are willing to dive into the deeper water of regularly reading God's Word and getting involved in worship and group Bible studies. But even then, some are hit-and-run feeders who take that plunge for a while but suddenly fly off and disappear for months or years at a time.

I guess I like the idea of being like those birds that stay out in the deep water for long periods of time. Those are the folks who enjoy spending time seeking God and hearing from Him. They're not afraid to get away from the shore of worldliness and are not ashamed to be known as a seeker of God's will. They're willing to commit to Bible reading, regular worship, the accountability of a church family, and personal involvement in ministry. They can appreciate those basic truths on the surface and feed on them as if it were their first time. But they can also dive deep and explore the more challenging truths of God. They are in it for the long haul and through all kinds of weather. They are not easily deterred from receiving their spiritual food.

Let's take a look at our own practices when it comes to seeking nourishment for our souls. What kind of bird are you?

In what ways might you need to change and improve your spiritual feeding habits?

GIVE GOD COMPLETE CONTROL

"I beseech you therefore, brethren, by the mercies of God, that you present your bodies a living sacrifice, holy, acceptable to God, which is your reasonable service."

– ROMANS 12:1

One time I encountered an issue in which I had to seek technical support for the security program which protects my home computer. In the process of receiving assistance with the problem, at one point I allowed the technician to have remote access to my computer. I have to admit that I was hesitant to take this step. I've resisted scammers who have desired such access when they called me claiming to be legitimately concerned about some problem with my computer. I knew that in the hands of the wrong person, such control could lead to viruses, identity theft, and other harmful consequences. However, in this situation I knew that I had been the one to initiate the contact. I had some degree of faith that I could trust this person. But it was still somewhat unnerving to sit there in front of my monitor watching some stranger moving the curser around and controlling such a significant piece of equipment in my life, along with having access to all of its files and information.

If it's difficult and scary to yield control of a computer to someone, how much more intimidating can it be to think about surrendering control of our very lives to someone else—yes, even to God. We may like the idea of God being part our lives. We are grateful to be able to go to Him for help when we get into trouble. We may even enjoy times of fellowship with Him and with His followers. We might invite Him into our lives and grant Him access up to a certain point. However, we still like to be the one in control. If God tries to lead us in a direction we don't like or if He tells us to do something that's hard or goes against our preferences, we want to be able to pull the plug on that plan or to shut it down. We're willing to accept God as a trusted advisor, but we aren't willing to give Him total control. We still want to have the final say, just in case.

It's wonderful to invite Jesus into your heart, but God's will extends even beyond that momentous milestone. He also calls His followers to completely yield themselves to Him as Lord of their lives. In Romans 6, Paul likens it to being slaves to God as we willingly submit to Him as our Master. Later in the same epistle he implores, "I beseech you therefore, brethren, by the mercies of God, that you present your bodies a living sacrifice, holy, acceptable to God, which is your reasonable service" (Romans 12:1).

It's reasonable for us to give control of our lives over to God. Why? Because we can trust Him. He knows what He's doing. He can see the bigger picture that we can't see. He knows what is best for us. And He loves us more than anyone else does or could. It would not be reasonable to turn over the control of our life to just anyone. It would be foolish to put such power in the hands of most people. However, it's the wisest move possible to give God such access. He will always take us down the pathway that will prove to be the right one and the best one.

Would you be willing to take that step today? "Lord, I'm going to take my hands off and let You call the shots from now on. Wherever you lead, I will follow. Whatever you want me to do, I'll obey. I'm yours, completely and without reservation."

Trust God enough to let Him have full control.

Pray a prayer of complete surrender to God and let Him take full control of your life.

Look to God for Guidance

"Then the men of Israel took some of their provisions; but they did not ask counsel of the Lord."

– Joshua 9:14

O ne day I called in a request to have the utilities marked on a section of our church property. A couple of our men were going to be digging some small post holes in preparation for displaying a banner. Knowing that a gas line and water line were situated in that same general area, we thought it best to have the exact locations of those underground utilities marked so that we could avoid any unnecessary problems.

It has been made quite simple to submit such a request. All you have to do is call the number 811. And the service is free. I suppose the utility companies would much rather take a little time to spray-paint a few colored ribbons along the ground rather than have to deal with the major headache and cost involved if someone were to accidentally hit one of their lines. You've probably witnessed the aftermath of such events, resulting in gas leaks or water leaks causing evacuations, traffic rerouting, or a fountain of water spewing high into the air.

Similarly, many of us could avoid a great deal of trouble and pain if we would simply check with the Lord before rushing into action. He would much rather give us guidance to help us avoid making a mess, rather than having to deal with the cleanup and repair work afterwards. It's not that the aftermath causes any more of a headache for the Almighty God or that it uses up more of His infinite power. Unlike the utility companies, He isn't thinking about the inconvenience, extra effort, or additional resources that such a scenario would cost Him. No, He's thinking more about us. He wants what's best for us. And He's aware of how our moving forward without looking to Him for direction can result in some bad consequences for our lives. This is another sense in which the words of that old song ring true: "O what needless pain we bear, all because we do not carry everything to God in prayer."

Joshua was a great and godly leader of the people of Israel. The only negative aspect about Joshua the Bible recounts was an incident when he and the other leaders acted without asking counsel of the Lord (see Joshua 9). This rash decision caused the Israelites to have to deal with a group of people who became a thorn in their side for years to come.

Too many of us not only overlook asking God's guidance, but we are so determined to do what we want to do that we intentionally don't seek out His direction. We think we know best and would prefer not knowing if God says something contrary to our wishes on the matter. Or we may see the line He's drawn on the ground warning us of the hazard of digging in that spot, yet we decide to risk it anyway. We might think, *Maybe that's an old marking. It may be outdated and irrelevant now. We know better today. The majority of society, experts, and even some government officials say that it's okay to dig into that spot.* So we go ahead and as a result we, along with people around us, suffer the negative consequences.

We should always be concerned about following God's will and direction. In some cases, it will be obvious and won't require much thought or prayer. But other times we may need to earnestly search His Word and spend much time in prayer about a matter.

Call on God before you dig. And pay attention to His guiding markers. By doing so, you can save yourself a lot of trouble.

Is there something you need to pray about and seek God's guidance on today before taking action?

Let's Not Be Guilty of Being a Heartbreaker

"Now as He drew near, He saw the city and wept over it."

– Luke 19:41

One time a young man met me at the church office to talk about his plans to get married. However, this wasn't the typical pastoral session where someone comes to me asking about the possibility of my presiding over a wedding ceremony. This meeting was much more personal. This particular guy was wanting to marry my daughter. And he was coming to me not because I was a pastor but due to my being her father, to ask for my blessing.

I was pleased to hear all the things he had to say that day about my daughter, as well as the deep emotion he expressed, indicating that he realizes what a special person she is. I already had a good idea that he, too, was a special young man and our conversation confirmed that truth. So I had no reservations about letting him know that my wife and I fully supported his plans to propose to our daughter.

I thought one statement he made was especially significant. He not only suggested that he could not see his life without our daughter, but since he believed she felt similarly toward him, he couldn't bear the thought of ever breaking her heart. I really appreciate such a guy who so loves my daughter that he would seek to avoid doing anything which might cause her heartache and pain.

Do we love God similarly? Are we careful to refrain from doing anything that would break His heart?

Too often we simply think about our need to do what's right and to obey God's commands in order to avoid making Him mad. We rightly don't want to get on the Almighty's bad side. We don't want to experience some form of judgment or punishment because of our wrongdoing. But hopefully our motivation goes beyond trying to avoid God's wrath. Out of love, we should want to please Him. And the other side of that truth means we shouldn't want to do anything that would cause Him pain and heartache.

I believe the various pictures of God given to us in the Bible—such as of Him being like a husband, a father, and a mother hen to us—all indicate the truth that He loves us so much that we can break His heart through our unfaithfulness, disobedience, and lack of love for Him. We see this spirit in the very embodiment of God—in Jesus Himself. As He drew near the city of Jerusalem whose inhabitants were rejecting Him, He didn't just angrily pronounce judgment on them. The Bible tells us Jesus wept over the city as He thought about their hardened attitude and the terrible things they were going to suffer as a result of it (Luke 19:41–44). The Son of God was heartbroken.

This incident reminds us how we can cause God pain. His heart breaks not over anything we're doing to Him, but rather over what we're doing to ourselves. He sees the blessings we're missing out on because we don't follow His will. He knows the consequences of sin which we'll have to face. He sees the ways we're hurting ourselves by insisting on following our way instead of His. And it truly does break His heart.

The next time you're tempted to choose some other path than the one God wants for you, remember the extent of His love for you and think about how your wrong choice could bring further pain to the One who has already sacrificed so greatly for you. Let's be thankful God loves us so much. And let's be committed to doing nothing that would break our Father's heart.

How should it affect you to know that you can break your Father's heart?

We Shouldn't Be Afraid to Draw Nearer to God

"The fear of the Lord is the beginning of knowledge."

– Proverbs 1:7

I was taking care of the pets at the house of one of my daughters while she and her family were on vacation. Just a couple of days before they left, they welcomed another arrival into that group for whom I would be responsible. Their large Husky had found a small kitten inside its fence. Fortunately they were able to rescue the tiny creature from injury before the dog treated it like a play toy.

Maybe the traumatizing encounter with their canine is part of the reason for it, but so far this kitten lives up to the title "scaredy cat." It acts like it wants to be loving and friendly—meowing and rubbing up against objects as someone talks to it and puts out its food, but it backs away from letting anyone get too close, especially shying away from any attempts to reach out to touch or pet it. My guess is that over time this feline will warm up to people. With a little patient love and care, I think my daughter's family will help the kitten learn there are humans it can trust.

Some people have a similarly hard time trusting God. They want to get to know Him, but they're afraid to do so. This big, Almighty God can seem so overwhelming at times, as well He should. Or maybe His holiness reminds us of how unholy we are, causing us to back away in fear that such a God can't tolerate impure, sinful creatures like us.

Peter seems to have expressed such feelings when he got one of his first glimpses at Jesus' greatness. After an unsuccessful night of fishing, Peter was instructed by Jesus to let down his nets again. And when he did, they caught so many fish that their nets were breaking. The Bible records Peter falling down before Jesus at that point and saying, "Depart from me, for I am a sinful man, O Lord!" (Luke 5:8).

Any of us may rightly feel a sense of inadequacy and unworthiness in the presence of God. The Bible talks about us fearing the Lord. However, it isn't advocating for us to be scared to draw close to Him but rather to respect Him, His holiness, His power, and His authority as the Ruler of the universe.

Some of us may have a desire to draw nearer to God and to let Him touch us with His love, but whenever He reaches out toward us, we pull back. We're not sure we can truly trust Him. We may be afraid that if we get closer He might call us to do something we don't really want to do. Or we might be scared that He will want us to give up something we don't want to forsake. So we purr our spiritual sentiments and go through some religious motions, but we shy away from a total commitment of letting Him have His way in our lives.

What we need to remember is that God loves us. Yes, He's powerful, holy, and worthy of the greatest respect—but He's our Father who loves us more than we could ever imagine. And however He wants to touch our lives, it's going to be for our good. He wants to draw near to us in order to bless us. And anything He takes away from us or anything He tells us to do will be for our benefit.

So let's not shy away from drawing closer to God. As He reaches out to us, we can be assured that it will be with a loving touch.

Are you hesitant or afraid when it comes to drawing closer to God? Why is that? Remind yourself of His goodness and of His great love for you. Seek a closer relationship with Him.

Keep Being the Salt
in Your World

"You are the salt of the earth; but if the salt loses its flavor, how shall it be seasoned?"

– Matthew 5:13

Several times within a few weeks I happened upon a particular type of small creature. It seemed like it had been a long time since I had seen one, so I especially took note of these various recurring encounters. I'm certain that the soggy conditions in our area from all the rain we had received at the time contributed to their more frequent appearance. I'm referring to slugs—those slimy, slithering, slow-moving members of the snail family.

Whenever I see one of those creatures, my mind goes back to when I was a kid. I suppose it's safe for me to confess what I and other children commonly did to slugs back then. We used to pour salt on those poor slugs in order to watch them slowly leave a slimy trail culminating in their death. At the time, I didn't know why it happened. But now I understand that it has something to do with the high moisture content in those creatures—the salt causes them basically to die from severe dehydration.

It's interesting that the same substance we humans look upon favorably and intentionally sprinkle on our food to add flavor results in death for those slugs. Of course doctors remind us that too much of that mineral isn't good for our health either.

Jesus declared that we as His followers would be the salt of the earth

(Matthew 5:13). In other words, we should be impacting the world in which we live and the people whom we are around. Through our actions, words, and character, we should be exerting an influence for Christ.

However, just like with salt, not everyone reacts to that impact in the same way. The Apostle Paul stated such a principle, only using a slightly different analogy. He described us as "the fragrance of Christ among those who are being saved and among those who are perishing. To the one we are the aroma of death leading to death, and to the other the aroma of life leading to life" (II Corinthians 2:15–16).

Some people will be drawn to our saltiness. They will view it as a positive additive to the world which lends hope, faith, comfort, and joy. But others will see it as a negative, even harmful, force. To them it's a revealer of sin, a producer of guilt, and a reminder of coming judgment before God. To one, it's a source of life and flavor. To the other, it's a reminder of the sliminess of their sin that leads to death.

It's no wonder that those for whom such saltiness causes inward pain would tend to lash out at the purveyors of their discomfort. They want to silence the words of truth, twist the motives behind their actions, and malign their character.

While believers should take no pleasure in the conviction and guilt their witness might cause others, neither should we seek to tone down our saltiness in order to lessen that effect. We have to guard against the tendency to be less vocal, to compromise our beliefs, to hide our faith and the actions which spring from it. If we try to diminish our saltiness, it will be at the cost of a close relationship with Christ.

Some people are going to appreciate your life of faith while others won't. But regardless of whether your influence is welcomed or despised, you need to keep being the salt of the earth which Jesus has called you to be.

In what ways are you being salt in your world? Is anything tempting you to lose your flavor or tone down your saltiness? Pray for the Lord to help you have even more of a saltlike impact.

JULY 16

Trust God to Enable You to Fulfill His Calling

"And I thank Christ Jesus our Lord who has enabled me, because He counted me faithful, putting me into the ministry."

– I Timothy 1:12

Right foot blue. Left hand green. Left foot red. No, I'm not describing the appearance of my grandchildren after they've been allowed to use paint or markers, although such a portrayal is not out of the realm of possibility. Those aforementioned phrases are actually a few of the instructions which could be given to players in the game of Twister.

I was reminded of that pastime from my youth a while back when I heard that the inventor of Twister had died. Do you remember the game? The players had to place their hands and feet on various colored circles on a mat. Sometimes you had to stretch and twist to conform to the instructions. And when you had several participants doing so on the same small mat, it might result in some close and awkward encounters, possibly even one player falling down on top of another.

Sometimes life can resemble a game of Twister. We can feel like human pretzels as we get pulled in different directions. We stretch as far as we can and precariously balance ourselves on the tips of our fingers or toes. We try to keep from falling, knowing how such a setback will not only affect us, but how it might drag down the people around us.

In some cases it might be the desire to meet the unrealistic expectations of society, friends, or ourselves that get us so tied up in knots.

Sometimes it may be our unwillingness to say no to someone or to an opportunity. It might even be that we find ourselves being stretched to our limits as we seek to follow what we believe to be God's will for our lives. As we hear some of His commands, they may seem almost impossible for us to attain or to live up to.

Concerning that last situation, we ought to remember that the Lord will enable us to do whatever it is He calls us to do. He won't tell us to put our left foot on the red circle if we're unable to reach it. He doesn't ask us to do the impossible in order to watch us fall as we attempt to do so. "He who calls you is faithful, who also will do it" (I Thessalonians 5:24).

That doesn't mean the Lord won't call us to do some difficult things. It doesn't mean He won't stretch us. Neither does it mean that what He asks us to do might not seem virtually impossible to us, and may even be something we cannot do in our own strength and ability. But no matter how hard or impossible a task may appear, if God is telling us to do it, we can rely on His power to help us fulfill His calling. The Apostle Paul testified, "And I thank Christ Jesus our Lord who has enabled me, because He counted me faithful, putting me into the ministry" (I Timothy 1:12). We can depend on the same God to enable us.

It's also helpful to remember that our Lord isn't just standing off to the side, twirling a spinner and calling out arbitrary instructions to us. He's actually right there in the game with us, upholding us and strengthening us so we can do whatever He calls us to do. When He tells us to step here or to put our hand to a particular task, we know He is with us to empower us to follow through.

So whenever you're feeling all "twisted," make sure what God's calling you to do and then trust Him to enable you to do it.

Are you feeling pulled in all different directions today? Look to the Lord for discernment to know what He wants you to do (and not do) and the ability to do it.

There's a Rainbow
after the Storm

*"I set My rainbow in the cloud, and it will be for a sign of the cove-
nant between Me and the earth."*

– Genesis 9:13

One time I found myself uncomfortably close to some powerful storms that came through our area. On a couple of occasions shortly after the tempest had passed, I drove down roads covered by debris, along with fallen trees intruding into the lanes of traffic. Our neighborhood was a target of one such storm, leaving my yard strewn with a few large limbs, numerous smaller twigs, and enough pine cones to fill up my wheelbarrow several times over.

The following morning, I surveyed the damage as I walked out to retrieve my newspaper. I was surprised to discover that instead of receiving the local edition of that publication, I had been given the neighboring county's version. When I returned to the house, I informed my wife that the previous night's storm was worse than we had realized. Apparently it had blown us into the next county!

One of the positive notes to the rough weather other than the needed rainfall was the sight of a beautiful double rainbow. By the way, did you know that the colors on the second rainbow are inverted—the color which is normally on the top is on the bottom? Check it out the next time you see one.

While I'm familiar with the science behind what causes a rainbow to appear in the sky, I also keep in mind what the Bible says about its origin and purpose. It was a sign of God's promise to Noah that the earth would never again be destroyed by a universal flood. For us that colorful phenomenon not only assures us of the same divine covenant, but it also reminds us of other truths in the face of storms—whether the weather kind or other types of upheavals in our lives.

For one thing it serves as reminder that God is here. He hasn't forsaken us or forgotten us in the midst of the storm. He knows all about our situation.

Secondly it assures us that God is still in control. Do you recall how amazed the disciples were when Jesus calmed the wind and the waves on the Sea of Galilee? They asked, "Who can this be, that even the winds and the sea obey Him?" (Matthew 8:27) As powerful as nature can be through such forces as lightning, tornadoes, wildfires, droughts, and floods, God is greater. And He's mightier than those other stormy situations we have to deal with in life. He can calm our seas too.

The rainbow also reminds us that God's promises are still holding true. Whether it's the pledge not to send another great flood or any other promise He has made in His Word, we can trust its dependability today just as much as when God first said it.

Finally the rainbow reminds us that our storms will eventually pass— they don't continue forever. There is hope for better days and bluer skies ahead.

What storms are you facing? As the winds howl and the thunder rumbles, the rainbow may not be visible. Even in the aftermath, that sign in the sky doesn't accompany every storm. But we can always depend on what it represents. There's a great God who sees us and loves us. And no storms can blow away His promises to us.

So the next time you get to see a rainbow, in addition to being awed by the beauty of its colors, let it remind you of the faithful God who put it there. Be assured that He will see you through the storm.

In middle of your storm, remember the truth of God's faithfulness and love.

What Kind of Clothes Are We Wearing?

"Therefore...put on tender mercies, kindness, humility, meekness, longsuffering."

– Colossians 3:12

It seems that every set of Olympic Games has its controversies or scandals. They may be centered around questionable judging, the behavior of athletes, problems with the venue, or a variety of other issues. One year there was a sizable uproar about the team from the United States. And of all things, it was about their clothing for the opening ceremonies.

There was a public outcry which arose from the revelation that the apparel of our delegation for that initial event was manufactured in China. That fact really shouldn't have surprised us, considering all the other items we use that are made outside our own country. Yet it's understandable to expect that on such an occasion of national pride and international competition that our athletes would be clothed in garments reflecting the creativity and capabilities of our own citizens.

Similarly, shouldn't it be expected that those who are followers of Christ would be clothed in attire which reflects a divine origin and is appropriate for those whose citizenship resides in heaven? No, I'm not talking about long dresses and black suits—not even about white robes and halos.

The Bible refers to our putting off and putting on certain characteristics, attitudes, and behaviors much like a person would do with clothes.

For example, Colossians 3:8 tells us to put off such things as anger, wrath, malice, blasphemy, and filthy language. In contrast, a few verses later it issues the command to "clothe yourselves with compassion, kindness, humility, gentleness, and patience" (3:12).

Such opposing qualities are sometimes described in scripture as being either "of the flesh" or "of the Spirit." The components of one group are produced by the sinful condition of human beings apart from God. They are common qualities which fit right in with this fallen world in which we presently live. However, the characteristics listed in the other category are the result of individuals being transformed through a divine act, resulting in the Spirit of God coming to live within them. Those who possess those qualities will often find themselves out-of-place in this world and more in harmony with their future heavenly home.

Did you ever watched that TV show, *What Not to Wear*? It's the one where someone whose wardrobe needs drastically improving gets a makeover. The hosts assist the person in realizing the flaws in her usual manner of dressing, while discarding most of her old clothes. Then they provide the means and expertise for that individual to find better outfits to wear.

I'm afraid there are too many Christians who need such makeovers when it comes to their spiritual attire. We're still wearing the wrong clothes. We look and act like people who don't know the Lord. We're not listening to the guidance of the Holy Spirit as He tries to cleanse us of the old ways and supply us with a whole new set of clothes.

During one of the news programs examining this controversy about the Olympic uniforms, the reporter kept revealing the tags on the jackets, shirts, and berets reading "Made in China." If someone could pull out and read the tags of our hearts and lives, what would they say—"Made of the Flesh" or "Made of the Spirit"?

Let's cooperate with God as He seeks to clothe us with those Christlike qualities which are appropriate for the citizens of heaven.

Are your wearing qualities "made of the flesh" or "made of the Spirit"?

LET'S OBEY ALL GOD'S COMMANDS WITH EQUAL PLEASURE

"If anyone loves Me, he will keep My word."
– JOHN 14:23

It happened one morning in those predawn hours when a person often finds himself tottering on the brink between sleep and consciousness. I distinctly heard a mysterious voice penetrate the darkness of my bedroom. Was this some sort of divine vision? Was God trying to tell me something? The message the voice communicated was clear—I should eat some Blue Bell ice cream before the day was over.

Well, maybe that voice wasn't so mysterious after all. Admittedly it did sound similar to a commercial I've seen on TV. And the next thing I knew my clock radio was delivering the morning news, letting me know that it was time for me to get up. But was it just a coincidence that I had bought a half-gallon—yes, still a half-gallon rather than one of those 1 ½ pint imposters—of that brand of ice cream a few days before? So just in case it was God speaking rather than a radio advertisement, I made sure to indulge in a bowl of the delicious treat later that afternoon—although my wife reminded me that I had eaten some of it the day before without the incentive of divine guidance.

If God really were to instruct me to eat ice cream, it would be a relatively easy and pleasurable command to follow. But sometimes the things

God asks of us can be a little tougher or less enjoyable. "Deny yourself, take up your cross, and follow Me" (Matthew 16:24). "Bring all the tithes into the storehouse" (Malachi 3:10). "Glory in tribulations" (Romans 5:3). "Lay aside every weight, and the sin which so easily ensnares us" (Hebrews 12:1). "Trust in the Lord with all your heart, and lean not on your own understanding" (Proverbs 3:5). "Be holy in all your conduct" (I Peter 1:15). And the list could go on.

It's interesting how we can be quick to attribute an easy or pleasurable command to God's voice, but tend to hesitate to recognize His guidance when it comes to those tougher areas. Or maybe we make excuses for not obeying right away. *Did I hear correctly? Is that what the Bible really says—maybe I had better wait until I check out a few hundred commentaries before obeying that command, just to make sure.*

It reminds me of the closing remark in one of my favorite movies—the classic tale of *The Adventures of Robin Hood* starring Errol Flynn. At the end of the film, as King Richard bestows favors upon the men of Sherwood for their loyalty, he commands Robin to take the maid Marion's hand in marriage. As the love-struck couple exits the palace hand-in-hand, Robin responds, "May I obey all your commands with equal pleasure, Sire."

That should be our goal in relation to God's commands to us, whether He's telling us to eat a bowl of ice cream or to fast and pray—whether to rise and be healed or to endure hardship and suffering—whether to receive the promise now or wait and trust Him to fulfill it later. No matter how tough or easy, how pleasurable or not, we should seek readily and gladly to obey all of God's commands. After all, we can be confident that whatever God tells us to do comes from His infinite wisdom and His loving heart, and will ultimately be what's best for us.

I just hope that the next time my radio wakes me up with some mistakenly perceived divine announcement, it's not a commercial for Brussels sprouts.

Is God asking something "tough" of you today? Don't put it off or make excuses—obey Him with full confidence in His wisdom and love.

We Need the Spirit's Help to See

"However, when He, the Spirit of truth, has come, He will guide you into all truth."

– John 16:13

A t an out-of-town conference, I had the opportunity to become better acquainted with one fellow pastor in particular. Since he had traveled by plane and I had driven, I provided a ride for him back and forth from the hotel to the church where the conference was taking place. One morning at our meeting, he confided in me that he was having a tough time functioning because he wasn't wearing his glasses. He was afraid he had lost them. Actually he was certain they were somewhere in his hotel room, but he had misplaced them. And since his vision was so poor without his glasses, it was difficult for him to adequately search for them. That can be quite a predicament, leaving a person with a great sense of helplessness. You need your glasses in order to be able to see, but you can't see well enough to be able to find your glasses.

Later that day when we returned to our hotel, I accompanied him to his room to aid in the search. At least I had a good pair of eyes to use (as long as I was wearing my own glasses). The fellow pastor showed me the chair he was sitting in when he last remembered possessing the valuable object of our hunt. It didn't take me but a few seconds before I thought I spied something on the floor between a nearby end table and the sofa. Sure enough, it was his glasses. They were hiding in the shadows not easy for me to spot, much less for someone suffering from poor vision. Later in the conference when we said our goodbyes, this new friend said that he'd always remember me as the one who found his glasses.

That incident reminds me of how helpless we are to see the truth and to overcome our spiritual blindness on our own. We need someone to stand beside us to help us. And fortunately the Lord has provided such a person in the Holy Spirit. He is referred to in the Bible as our "paraclete," the English version of a Greek word which indicates, among other things, someone who will stand beside us. He is our helper in many ways, including in this area of being able to see properly.

First of all, those who have not received Christ into their hearts are spiritually blind. They are as helpless, or even more so, as my fellow-pastor without his glasses. They can't understand the truths of the gospel by themselves. People like you and me can assist by sharing God's Word or our testimony with such individuals. However, even then they will only be able to see and believe if the Holy Spirit is working to open their blinded eyes and to draw them to God. That's why prayer should be such an important part of any effort to reach the lost. We can proclaim the truth, but we can't make people see it or receive it.

Additionally, we as believers are dependent on the Holy Spirit to be our teacher. We need Him to guide us into all truth (John 16:13). Relying on His leadership can keep us from falling into error or from being led astray by false doctrine. And He can continually enlighten us as we study God's Word, enabling us to grow in both the grace and knowledge of the Lord.

We would all be spiritually blind and helpless to do anything about it if not for the ministry of the Holy Spirit to us. Let's be grateful that we have been given this special helper. And let's endeavor to be good students as He teaches us.

Be open to what the Holy Spirit wants you to see today. Listen as He teaches and guides you into the truth.

GOD IS GREATER THAN
ANY OF OUR IDOLS

"To whom will you liken Me, and make Me equal and compare Me, that we should be alike?"

– ISAIAH 46:5

O n one occasion my wife and I attended a church association meeting in Nashville, Tennessee. During some free time one afternoon, we visited the city's full-scale replica of the Greek Parthenon. I have to confess that we didn't originally start out for that attraction. We actually targeted the local Cheesecake Factory for lunch and realized the Parthenon was close by. So we let our stomachs guide us to our destination.

This impressive structure had been originally built for the 1897 Tennessee Centennial Exposition, although it's been reconstructed and renovated since that time. While this building houses a nice art museum, the focal point of the Parthenon is a huge gilded statue of the Greek goddess, Athena. This mythical figure towers 42 feet high. Even the tallest of human beings who stand beside her are dwarfed by her size. When you first walk into the room which houses this statue, you can't help but feel somewhat overwhelmed.

However, the more I pondered this statue, the less impressed I was. Yes, it's a beautiful piece of artwork, but as far as gods go, it seemed rather lowly, finite, and earthly. It was a wonderful sight to behold, but not really anything I would be tempted to worship.

I'm thankful that the one true God, the God we know and serve, is much bigger than that. He cannot be contained in any building—no, not even in the finest Christian sanctuary or cathedral. No image man could create is adequate to express His being or character. He is infinite Spirit. He is more than simply a bigger or more powerful human being. He is not just one of many gods. He is God—the God. He is the Holy One, the Almighty, the Creator of heaven and earth, and the Ruler of the universe.

In several consecutive chapters of the book of Isaiah, the greatness and uniqueness of God is especially emphasized. Over and over some form of the statement is made: "I am the Lord, and there is no other; there is no God besides me" (45:5). It further asks, "To whom will you liken Me, and make me equal and compare Me, that we should be alike?" (46:5).

Few of us today would probably be tempted to worship a statue of Athena or any other so-called god, no matter how huge or lavish it might be. Yet we set up other gods in our lives before whom we bow. Some pay homage to the gods of materialism, money, fame, power, politics, entertainment, pleasure, sex, family, or especially ourselves. Anything can become a god in our lives when we give it the loyalty, service, and honor that is only due the one true God.

None of those substitutes measure up to the real thing. As Isaiah goes on to point out, those idols in our lives can't carry us through the tough times, save us from our troubles, or respond to our prayers. We're facing some big problems in our world today. We need to be looking to the one God who is up to the challenge. Anything else we depend on will fail us sooner or later.

Don't deceive yourself by trusting in some false deity of your own making. There is a God who is bigger than anything we can create or imagine. And thankfully He's bigger than our personal problems and our societal challenges.

Let's put our faith in Someone real and powerful, as well as Someone who fervently loves us. We need such a great God today—one much bigger than 42 feet tall. Fortunately we have one, if we'll just turn our hearts toward Him.

Have you set up any idols in your life? Realize how little and useless they are in comparison to the Almighty God.

Holiness, Not Sin, Should Be the Norm for Believers

"Reckon yourselves to be dead indeed to sin, but alive to God in Christ Jesus our Lord."

– ROMANS 6:11

One day I heard it was National Ice Cream Day. So I "forced" myself to celebrate with a bowl of my favorite treat that afternoon. If you research the subject, you'll discover that every day has been designated as a national observance of something, many of which are little-known or even rather odd. For example, July 22 is National Rat Catcher's Day. I don't know about you, but don't expect me to go chasing down any rodents today.

It reminds me of an episode of the *Andy Griffith Show* on TV. A couple of sweet old ladies were brewing their own moonshine. They thought they were selling it to people only for holidays and special observances, but deceptive customers were coming to them claiming to be observing all sorts of occasions which they had concocted, just so they could receive another bottle of the ladies' creation. As I look down the list of some of the recognized observances on our calendar, I feel like those fictionalized accounts have become a reality.

Unfortunately, some of us have accepted the idea that every day is to be observed as National Sin Day. We've succumbed to the idea that we can't help but do something wrong and offensive to God on a daily basis, maybe even on an hourly basis. For some people it stems from the way they define sin as anything that falls short of the absolute perfection of a holy God. As fallen, finite human beings, none of us can live up to that standard.

However, some still hold to this idea even when thinking of sin more in terms of words, thoughts, or actions in which we are willingly making choices that we know are not pleasing to God or in line with His will for us. I'm afraid some are using this idea that we have to sin each day as a means of justifying their making poor choices, yielding to the temptations they encounter, and indulging their selfish, sinful appetites. If we're not careful we'll find ourselves not even trying to put up much of a fight in the face of such encounters, all too ready to chalk it up to the fact that "we can't help it" and to presume again on God's graciousness to forgive us.

Thankfully we do have a merciful God who is ready to forgive our repentant hearts for those many times we falter and fail. But we also serve a powerful God who gives us spiritual resources to enable us to live some degree of holy lives and to experience a great measure of victory over sin and temptation.

I don't find the Bible picturing the normal Christian life as being one of daily habitual sin. As a matter of fact, God's Word condemns such a notion. Just check out the sixth chapter of Romans. Paul makes it clear that believers should not be continuing in sin. We have been freed from sin's slavery and can live a life characterized by righteousness and holiness. With God's help and by the power of the Holy Spirit living within you, you can choose to do right, to say no to temptation, and to pursue godly desires. "Reckon yourselves to be dead indeed to sin, but alive to God in Christ Jesus our Lord. Therefore do not let sin reign in your mortal body, that you should obey it in its lusts" (Romans 6:11–12).

Seek to honor the Lord in word, thought, and deed today. As a matter of fact, let's determine to make every day National Holiness Day rather than National Sin Day.

Lord, help me to do what's right and to live a holy life—today and every day.

BE WILLING TO ACCEPT YOUR PART OF THE BLAME

"For I acknowledge my transgressions, and my sin is always before me."

– PSALM 51:3

While babysitting three of my grandchildren one evening, I introduced them to the *Andy Griffith Show*. I handpicked an episode I thought they would enjoy—the one in which little Opie Taylor gets careless with his new slingshot and unintentionally kills a mother bird. He learns the tough lesson that sometimes saying "I'm sorry" doesn't undo the consequences of our actions, such as those baby birds no longer having a mother to care for them. However, Opie decided that since it was his fault, he would try to take on the responsibility of feeding and protecting those hatchlings until they were big enough to fly off on their own.

The prevalent attitude in our day seems to be quite different from those values taught in Mayberry. Many in our society would tend to exonerate Opie of any guilt, and instead would affix the blame on his dad for letting him have a slingshot, Barney Fife for glorifying the use of such a weapon, and maybe even the momma bird for being in the wrong place at the wrong time. And the fact that Andy and Barney were in law enforcement would make them even more likely to be targets for blame.

The Bible teaches us to own up to our wrongs and to take responsibility for our sins. The way to find forgiveness and cleansing is through confession and repentance, not by making excuses or by blaming others.

We need to have the attitude of the Psalmist who declared, "Have mercy upon me, O God...For I acknowledge my transgressions" (Psalm 51).

Even if others may have played a role in our wrongdoing and even if they should bear part of the blame, we should not overlook out own guiltiness. Opie may not have meant to kill that mother bird, but he failed to heed his father's warning about being careful with his slingshot. In a sense, it was an accident. However, Opie still bore some responsibility for that accident.

In mankind's initial sin, the serpent was largely to blame for lying to Eve and seducing her into disobeying God's clear command. But that didn't relieve Eve of any responsibility for her actions. Neither did it absolve Adam of the guilt from his subsequent act of disobedience. On that occasion, Adam and Eve did what we human beings still have a tendency to do—try to blame others for our wrongdoing. But as God's resulting judgment revealed, they were all to blame and they all rightly faced the consequences for their actions (see Genesis 3).

In our day, others who are at fault should be held accountable, including those in positions of authority. But we also ought to admit the role we or the person we want to defend may have played in that incident. If we were doing something illegal or being disrespectful or uncooperative with those in authority, or were acting carelessly or in some other way played a role which contributed to what happened, we need to take responsibility for it.

And sometimes, as Opie teaches us, taking responsibility may mean more than just admitting our wrongdoing. It may mean doing whatever we can to make amends for it. We can't change the consequences, but we may be able to make restitution or in some way ease the pain we've caused.

In a society that is often too quick to file lawsuits and point the finger of blame at others, let's have the courage to acknowledge our own wrongdoing and to be willing to face the consequences.

Is there some wrongdoing for which you need to take responsibility before God and man?

Our Impact May Be Greater than We Expect

"Do you not know that a little leaven leavens the whole lump?"
– I Corinthians 5:6

I remember when I took my first Duck Ride. For those not familiar with this mode of transportation, please don't picture me trying to straddle some water fowl. Rather, I'm referring to one of those amphibious vehicles which can travel both on land and in water. They've become fairly popular attractions in tourist areas.

On this occasion we were in Chattanooga for the Annual Meeting of our church association. One afternoon we had some free time to enjoy the sites of the city, so a small group of us decided to go on this Duck tour. We rode in the vehicle down to the river where we stopped at the top of the steep ramp leading into the water below. Our driver asked if we wanted to experience a small splash or a big one. Our adventurous group was united in its call for the bigger version, so the driver put the vehicle in neutral, letting it coast rapidly down the ramp until it hit the water. We got soaked!

Apparently the splash was bigger than even the driver had expected. We learned that he had only been doing this job for a few weeks. He expressed surprise at the extent of its impact, made sure everyone was okay, and that we weren't upset about getting so wet. Maybe he was also concerned that his tip might be diminished if his customers weren't happy. But we just laughingly accepted it as part of the adventure, as well as the opportunity to cool off on a hot day.

Sometimes the splashes we make in life turn out to be much bigger than we expected. On the positive side, what we might consider to be a small act on our part can often turn out to have a huge impact on someone. A word of encouragement, a kind deed, a smile, the sharing of a Bible verse, and other such expressions to which we may give little thought at the time could actually make a tremendous difference. People have discovered later that some small, maybe even long-forgotten action on their part was instrumental in changing someone's life. We don't know how those little things we do today might be used of God to help another person, so let's keep showing His love and sharing His Word each day. Don't forget the parable in which Jesus commended the servant who was faithful in the little things.

But on the negative side, our sins and spiritual failings can also have a more far-reaching effect than we expect. We might think that choosing a path which takes us away from God and His will is something which will only affect us, but more often than not, such actions splash out onto our families, friends, and churches. Or we consider it to be just a small matter or a tiny sin—nothing to get worked-up over. However, those so-called little sins have a way of growing into big obstacles in our relationship with the Lord. We often end up going deeper than we had intended and getting more soaked by those filthy waters than we had planned. Sin is like the leaven or yeast to which the Bible refers—it only takes a little to permeate the whole lump of dough.

So let's not just seek to do right when it comes to the big areas in our lives. Let's pay attention to the little things too. Your small actions of doing good, as well as your response to the little temptations, can create a bigger splash than you might realize.

Pay attention to the little things you do today. They can have a bigger impact than you might think.

Celebrate Your Family Connection with Other Believers

"There is neither Jew nor Greek, there is neither slave nor free, there is neither male nor female; for you are all one in Christ Jesus."

– Galatians 3:28

One time I was reading an engagement announcement in the newspaper, primarily due to some familiarity I had with the local family of the bride-to-be. However as I read the information about her fiancé who is not from this community, I suddenly realized that I knew his family too. His father and I were childhood friends. We attended school together and played on the same Little League baseball team. However, we had no contact with one another since a class reunion many years ago. After coming to this realization, I looked again at the picture of the happy couple and could clearly see the resemblance of the groom-to-be to my childhood buddy. The whole situation made me sit back in my chair and marvel at the truth we often describe with the phrase, "It's a small world."

I'm grateful that we as believers in Christ can experience that phenomena in an even greater way. It's not unusual for us to meet strangers, only to realize shortly afterwards that we know their Father. More than that, we share the same Heavenly Father. We recognize that we are brothers or sisters in Christ—part of the same closely-connected family.

A group from our church went on a missions trip to Mexico some years ago. When we were at the Texas/Mexico border filling out some paperwork, we struck up a conversation with someone else doing the same thing. As we talked, we soon discovered to our mutual amazement that this other individual knew my sister. We had traveled hundreds of miles away from home only to discover the smallness of the world.

After we arrived at our destination in Mexico, we found ourselves not only among strangers, but people from a different culture—people who didn't look like us and who spoke another language. But as we met some of the people in the churches where we ministered, we clearly recognized that we knew one another's Father—that we were members of the family of God. You could see the resemblance—not in the outward appearance, although there was often a joyful smile which served as an outward indication of that family relationship. But you could see the qualities of Christ and His character shining through the lives of those persons as evidence of their connection to Him.

It's wonderful to know that no matter where we travel around the world, we can often encounter people who know the same God and serve the same Lord whom we know and serve. And that makes us more than acquaintances. It makes us family.

And the same holds true in our own communities, even as many of them become more diverse. All of us as human beings share certain connections with one another, but we have an even greater bond with our fellow believers in Christ. We may look differently, follow different traditions, prefer different political parties, have different styles of worship, and a host of other distinctions, but hopefully we can recognize the Spirit of Christ in one another and celebrate the kinship we enjoy.

So while others may choose to focus on the differences which divide us, let's seek to strengthen the bonds we have with one another as members of the family of God. You may look a little different from me, but I know your Father. And we have a connection that we shouldn't ignore or allow others to disrupt. If we both resemble Jesus, then we're family.

So let's support one another and rejoice in the fact that it truly is a small world after all.

Choose to focus on your special connection with fellow believers in spite of other differences.

GOD WILL UPHOLD US
IN DEEP WATERS

*"And when Peter had come down out of the boat, he walked on the
water to go to Jesus"*

– MATTHEW 14:29

I recall when one of our daughters and her family were able to squeeze
in a vacation at the beach before school started up again. Upon their
return, we got to hear from our grandchildren about all the fun activities
they enjoyed on the beautiful gulf coast of Florida. But our daughter also
informed us of a couple of potentially hazardous moments they experienced. On separate occasions it seems that two of our younger grandkids
jumped into the pool or ventured out into deep water without wearing
their flotation devices. They had taken off their "water wings" and had
forgotten to put them back on before taking the plunge. Fortunately
adults were nearby to help them after their unexpected submergence
into the deep. And it didn't seem to leave them with any ill-effects, either
physically or in the sense of an exaggerated fear of the water, although
hopefully it did instill a little more caution into the minds of these young
nonswimmers about the need of wearing the proper gear to help them
stay afloat.

As we plunge into the deep waters of life, we always need to keep in
mind our dependence on God to keep us from sinking. Sometimes we
forget that He is our "water wings" and mistakenly think we can handle
the situation in our own strength. Other times we simply presume that

God is with us and will uphold us, although we haven't taken the time to seek His will and pleasure about the matter. We may be venturing into waters in which God didn't intend for us to go.

Remember Peter who experienced the ultimate sensation of divinely enabled flotation. In other words, he walked on water. I wonder if it felt like having invisible "water wings" on his feet or if the surface of the sea simply felt like solid ground. At any rate, under normal circumstances Peter would not have even stepped out of that boat. Why did he do it this time? Because not only had he witnessed Jesus walking on the water, but he had also heard Jesus invite him to do the same. And as long as Peter kept his eyes on Jesus and trusted Him, he was fine. But when he let his faith turn into fear, he began to sink.

If we plunge into the deep water of tackling difficult challenges or battling strong opposition with the assurance that Jesus is with us and is calling us to that task, we can do so with faith that He can enable us to accomplish His will, even walk on water. But if we simply jump in on our own, we may be in danger of sinking.

There's another account in the Bible of some men who "took it upon themselves" to cast out evil spirits in Jesus' name as they had seen Paul do (Acts 19:13–16). The spirit responded, "Jesus I know and Paul I know; but who are you?" It then proceeded to attack the men. Those would-be exorcists had gotten into deep water over their heads. They had presumed they could handle it. The problem was that they didn't have the same relationship with Jesus that Paul had.

And that's what it comes down to in our case as well. It's not about reciting a certain prayer or going through some other action before we venture out. It's about a right relationship with Jesus. If we're abiding in Him and Him in us, then we can be assured that He will hold us up in the deep water.

So let's not forget our dependence on the Lord and make sure we're always wearing the "water wings" of close fellowship with Him.

Depend on the Lord to keep you from sinking in deep waters of life.

LET'S MAKE USE OF THE
ARSENAL GOD HAS GIVEN US

*"Taking the shield of faith with which you will be able to quench all
the fiery darts of the wicked one."*

– EPHESIANS 6:16

I was watching and listening to my young grandsons playing, pretending they were shooting cannons. I was somewhat surprised that they were imagining using that kind of weaponry as opposed to more modern or even futuristic instruments of battle that many kids have become familiar with through TV and movies. I asked them if they had ever seen any real cannons. When they responded that they hadn't, I told them about a place we needed to go sometime where they could see examples of such weapons.

Due to their enthusiastic response to that suggestion, my wife and I ended up taking the boys over to a nearby national battlefield. While they were thrilled to get to see the cannons at the visitor's center, they were somewhat disappointed when we read them the signs stating that no children should be allowed to climb or sit on those particular objects. And for some reason, that's exactly what kids want to do when they see one.

We tried to explain that the cannons were old and if everybody climbed on them, they might break or wear out. However before the day was over, in a more remote area of the park, we found a couple of cannons free from such restrictions. So we allowed the boys to sit on them long enough to get their picture made.

We also had to squelch their dreams to shoot the cannons, letting them know that those cannons might not function anymore or, even if they did, firing one off might do some damage or hurt someone. We explained that those cannons were just for display, not for shooting.

I think our grandsons had a good time, even though they had to settle for seeing cannons that were more like museum relics than fully functioning weapons.

Let's make sure that our faith and the spiritual weaponry God has provided for us don't fit that description. Our faith shouldn't just be a relic from the past. Neither should it be something that we simply pull out of a closet and dust off every once in a while. It's not meant to be merely a museum piece that we put on display for others to see.

Our faith is intended to be a fully functioning part of our daily lives. The Bible describes faith as a shield by which we can quench the fiery darts of the enemy of our souls (Ephesians 6:16). It protects us as we battle the everyday temptations, trials, and challenges of life. Faith isn't just something we possess; it's something we use to live victoriously.

The same holds true for other parts of our spiritual arsenal. For example, the Bible isn't meant to be relegated to a shelf only to have a verse pulled out occasionally for a word of inspiration or wisdom, like consulting a fortune cookie. It's our authoritative guidebook on the journey of life. As a matter of fact, that same passage in Ephesians describes the Word of God as "the sword of the Spirit." As we believe it and stand upon its promises, we are empowered to fight against Satan and to make headway in the work of God's kingdom.

And don't forget about prayer. And that's the problem—too often we do forget about it. What a privilege we have to bring our requests to a great God who loves us and who can do what we can't do. He tells us to ask and He'll answer, but so often we fail to ask.

God has provided us with our spiritual cannons. Let's quit treating them like historical relics and start using them as the powerful instruments they are to help us win the battles of life.

What spiritual weapons do you need to dust off and start making better use of?

GOD GIVES US A REAL CHOICE

"If you remain completely silent at this time, relief and deliverance will arise for the Jews from another place, but you and your father's house will perish."

– ESTHER 4:14

I watched a movie one time in which God and angels played a significant role. While the film was interesting, it's theology was way out of kilter. For one thing, like so many Hollywood attempts to portray divinity, God and his heavenly messengers were characterized as being merely greater or more powerful versions of human beings. They possessed and exhibited many of the same moral faults and weaknesses we find in ourselves. But the prominent theological problem was in how the movie dealt with the subjects of God's sovereignty and man's free will. The central premise of the movie focused on the idea that angels are around us making adjustments in our lives in order to keep us in line with God's perfect plan. God is pictured as the Chairman of the Board who is only concerned about His plans for the world being carried out. And the angels are portrayed almost as gangsterlike characters who are busy making sure that everything goes according to the Master's plan, even if it means "roughing up" some people or negatively altering their circumstances in order to accomplish that goal.

At issue is humanity's free will. Do we have any real choice, or are our lives being precisely directed by fate or by some all-powerful God? In the movie, it was suggested that we only have "the appearance of free will"—that if we were truly free to decide for ourselves, we would make a mess of things.

The issue of God's sovereignty and man's free will is one that has been debated over the centuries. I certainly can't even begin to touch the depths of that subject in this brief writing. However, let's make sure that we don't acknowledge one biblical truth to the exclusion of the other. Yes, there is an all-knowing and all-powerful God who is ultimately in control of the universe. But He also decided to create mankind with the freedom to make real choices, opening the door to the possibility that man would choose something other than God's will, thus making a mess of things. God isn't primarily a CEO concerned about His plan getting accomplished. He's more like the Heavenly Father who is concerned about what's best for His children. And He knows that if we would choose His way, it would be the most beneficial course of action we could take.

I don't believe human beings can thwart the overarching plans of God for the world, but we can certainly hinder what God hopes to accomplish in our own lives. Think about Queen Esther in the Bible. She faced the choice of whether or not to risk her life in order to speak up in defense of her people. She was told, "If you remain completely silent at this time, relief and deliverance will arise for the Jews from another place, but you and your father's house will perish. Yet who knows whether you have come to the kingdom for such a time as this" (Esther 4:14).

God may have put Esther in that situation in order for her to help the Jews, but she could still choose. And if she chose not to defend them, she would face the consequences. But God's plan to deliver the Jews would still be accomplished, only by some other person or means.

God does have wonderful plans for our lives. He wants us to follow His will for our own good. But we can choose whether or not to do His will. If we exercise that freedom to do what we want instead of what He wants, we won't frustrate God's plans. But sooner or later we will have to face the consequences of that poor choice. So let's be sure that we choose wisely.

Seek to make good choices today. Choose to follow God's will for you.

ARE WE THE REAL THING?

"He who has the Son has life; he who does not have the Son of God does not have life."

– I JOHN 5:12

D id you hear about the guy who received a citation for having livestock in his yard? The only problem is that the livestock turned out not to be so lively after all. The chickens scattered across his yard were all made of ceramic. The official who issued the citation, only to later tear it up, insisted that he was told that there were genuine versions of those critters in the man's backyard. However, none were found. Some people concluded that a neighbor must have mistaken the ceramic birds for the real thing.

I can understand the confusion. There have been numerous times when driving down the road that I thought I spotted a deer, dog, or other creature in a yard, only to realize with a second look that I was viewing some inanimate imitation. Some of them are obvious fakes, while others are very good replicas that from a distance can easily fool someone.

Are we genuine followers of Christ, or are we similar to those ceramic replicas? Some pretenders don't fool anyone, except maybe themselves. They may like to consider themselves to be Christians, but their lives are so tarnished by the works of the flesh (Galatians 5:19–21) that no one takes them seriously.

However, other imitators can do a very good job of looking like a follower of Jesus, talking like one and acting like one. The Bible tells us of Judas who was one of the twelve apostles and someone who outwardly seemed to care about the poor. But we know of his ultimate betrayal of Christ. And then there was a guy named Ananias who brought a certain amount of money to the apostles, only to be exposed as a pretender who was lying to God.

In our day, skillful imitators know how to use those catchphrases such as "God bless you"—"I'll pray for you"—"Praise the Lord"—"Thank you, Jesus." They attend church with Bible in hand. They know what Christians are supposed to do and not do, and outwardly appear to live up to the standard.

But something is still missing. It's the same thing that's missing in those well-sculpted and nicely-painted ceramic chickens. Life. Only in this case we're talking about spiritual life. "He who has the Son has life; he who does not have the Son of God does not have life" (I John 5:12). That's what makes the difference. It's whether or not we have a life-giving relationship with Jesus Himself.

That is something only we can know as we allow God to examine our own hearts. Are those good actions the fruit of the Spirit that is springing up as a natural result of my relationship with the Lord, or are they simply acts painted on my exterior for others to see and admire? Am I going to church and being involved in other good activities out of my love for the Lord and a desire to please Him, or am I simply going through the motions I know are expected of me? Is my spirit alive through daily trusting Jesus, or am I cold and lifeless in my soul?

We may fool others at times. We may even deceive ourselves. But we won't fool the One who is our final Judge.

Let's make sure that we're not simply some stained-glass or ceramic version of a real follower of Jesus. We need to do more than look like a Christian, talk like a Christian, and act like a Christian. We need the life of Christ within us that makes us the real thing.

Do you simply look alive or is the life of Christ truly within you?

It Isn't My World Anymore

"They are not of the world, just as I am not of the world."

– John 17:16

In one of the Sunday comics in the newspaper, an elderly lady was watching her favorite show on TV when her adult son suggested that she switch to one of the news channels instead. He asked her, "Aren't you interested in what's going on in the world?" His mom replied, "I used to be, but it's not my world anymore."

Can you relate to that? Do you ever feel like this isn't your world anymore? It's difficult when you're the new person or the stranger in a group, a neighborhood, or a church. But in some ways it's even harder when you become the outsider not because you moved or changed, but because everything around you has changed. You didn't move into a new neighborhood, but the one in which you've resided for thirty years is no longer the friendly and safe place that it once was. You didn't change churches, but your church has changed—a new pastor, new people, and worship services in which they don't sing the songs you know.

Maybe that's the way we feel about the world in general at times. When I see shows on TV that are supposed to be entertaining and funny but are full of crude humor and vulgarity—it's not my world anymore. When I see what's happening in our nation with the government intruding into more of our private lives and businesses—it's not the free world I know. When young adults would rather send text messages than talk to someone, or when they want to watch a movie on a tiny screen on a phone instead of on a big screen at the theater—it's not my world anymore.

I'm sure such feelings arise partly from getting older. Maybe it's God's way to get us ready to leave this place and move on to the better home He has prepared for us. However, it's also something we should all sense as Christians, no matter how old or young we might be. If we're following God's Word, our values are going to be different from those of a world that doesn't know Christ. What we consider to be important will be different from those who don't share our faith. Some of the popular activities of this world will hold no attraction for us. Actually, we should detest some of the things that are going on. If we're following Jesus, we're going to have a hard time relating to certain aspects of this world and sometimes this world will have a hard time understanding us.

That fact shouldn't surprise us. You may remember when Jesus prayed for His disciples, He said, "They are not of the world, just as I am not of the world" (John 17:16). The Bible also talks about how people who live by faith in God are like strangers or foreigners on this earth (Hebrews 11:13).

So how should we react to this increasing feeling that this isn't our world anymore? Should we become cranky old people who are always complaining about things being different, or should we isolate ourselves from the world? I don't believe either of those is a very good solution. Maybe instead of getting discouraged by this development, we can rejoice in the differences and use them to point people to Christ. Jesus said that we're to be a light in the darkness. That means we've got to be different from the darkness, doesn't it? He also said we should be the salt of the earth. If salt didn't have a different flavor, why would you sprinkle it on your food?

It's okay that this isn't our world anymore. In a way, it never was. Let's be encouraged by the opportunity this gives us to let our lights shine more brightly for Christ.

Resist the temptation to isolate yourself from the changing world. Be a light for Jesus.

JULY 31

THE CHURCH IS BIGGER
THAN IT LOOKS

"You are of God, little children, and have overcome them, because
He who is in you is greater than he who is in the world."

– I JOHN 4:4

There is an antique store that has a sign out front declaring, "We are bigger than we look." Why did the proprietors feel the need to post that statement? It's probably due to the impression a person can get from just looking at the front of the store from the road. It doesn't look like it would be a very big place or would have a large selection of items, but when you go inside you find that not to be true. I've explored the narrow aisles of that establishment on several occasions, and it is packed full of antiques. I think the deceptive appearance comes from the building not being very wide, yet extending back quite far in depth.

I've heard first-time visitors make similar comments about our church building. There's more to it than what they were led to believe from its outside appearance. It's bigger than it looks.

I believe that phrase is also a good description of the church of Jesus Christ as a whole, as well as every individual believer. We are part of the church universal, the Body of Christ. We have a common bond with believers in other churches, no matter what denominational title under which they are organized. We do not stand alone. There are others who are standing beside us in the battle against evil and sin. There are others who are joining us in prayers for the lost and for revival. There are others whose strengths help make up for our weaknesses. We are part of one body with many different members, all working together to do God's work and to bring honor to His name.

And let's not forget that the head of the body is Christ Himself. It's the head that gives the church its size, strength, and importance. Without Him, the church would be nothing. Christ fills His church with Himself and with everything we need to accomplish the work He gives us to do. Sometimes this world just sees the body of the church with all its faults and weaknesses, concluding that it isn't very powerful or significant. But it doesn't take into consideration our head, Jesus Christ, the Son of God. Because of Him, the church is bigger than we look.

The same can be said about us individually. You may not look very big when it comes to power and influence. This world may not consider you a VIP. You may not even appear to be someone who packs much spiritual punch. You may not look like someone who can stand against the forces of evil and temptation and stay true to Christ. But if you have Christ in your heart, you are bigger than you look. I John 4:4 states, "You are of God, little children, and have overcome them, because He who is in you is greater than he who is in the world." That's the key: it's not about who we are but about who lives within us. We may not look like much on the surface, but there is a depth and a power present due to Christ living within us.

Sometimes we can find ourselves feeling small and inadequate. It may result from the way others look at us or from our own renewed awareness of our weaknesses and frailties. We may get discouraged as problems and challenges seem insurmountable, but let's not lose sight of whose we are—we are "of God." You are part of a body with Christ as its head. You have the Spirit of Christ living within you, so that He who is in you is greater than he who is in the world. You are bigger than you look.

Is something or someone making you feel small or inadequate? Remind yourself of who you are in Christ and as a member of His body.

It's Still Important to Obey God's Commands

"You are My friends if you do whatever I command you."

– John 15:14

I hope I'm not becoming just a grumpy old man. However, it seems to me that an increasing number of drivers are ignoring the rules of the road. In this case I'm not simply referring to lack of courtesy, aggressive driving, or being distracted by one's cell phone, although those are all common problems as well. I'm talking about a blatant disregard for the law.

The latest incident I encountered is when I was driving down a two-lane road and started slowing down because the second car in front of me was preparing to make a right-hand turn. However, I noticed a vehicle coming up behind me rather rapidly. After initially slowing down himself, the driver decided to get over in the left lane and pass my car, along with the two in front of me. The double yellow line and the prospect that another vehicle traveling in the opposite direction could have rounded a nearby curve didn't deter this impatient driver from making the illegal maneuver.

Rules seem to mean less and less to people these days. I believe much of it has to do with our attitude toward authority. We think we're the exception, we're above the law, or we can safely ignore that regulation without facing the consequences. It doesn't matter if it's a good or helpful rule or not. If it gets in the way of our agenda or slows us down from achieving our goal, we think it's acceptable to disregard it.

I'm afraid some of us have allowed that attitude to creep into our view of God's rules, or the commands He's given us to live by. There are those who have concluded that those divine laws are not important—all that matters is our relationship with Him. Granted, our salvation is dependent on a personal relationship with the Lord, not with our adhering to a bunch of religious rules, keeping the Ten Commandments, or being obedient to the numerous other directives given to us in scripture. I have joined others in proclaiming the truth that it's all about a relationship, not rules. But does that mean God's commands aren't important? Does it mean that we can simply ignore His rules and live however we want?

Jesus revealed that relationship and rules are connected. What we do with His commands indicates something about the reality and depth of our relationship with Him. Here are a few of His key comments on the subject. "If you love Me, keep My commandments" (John 14:15). "If you keep My commandments, you will abide in My love" (John 15:10). You are My friends if you do whatever I command you (John 15:14). Keeping the rules isn't what gets us or keeps us in good standing with the Lord. However, if we are in a right relationship with Him, we're going to want to obey His commands. It's a sign of our love for Him, our submission to His authority, and our desire to please Him. It also shows our recognition of the fact that His rules are not meant to be burdens but are actually guidelines to help us discover the best way to live our lives.

I'm disturbed by those who profess to be believers but who seem to have no problem disregarding God's commands about how we should live. What you do or refuse to do with God's commands says something about your relationship with Him. So don't ignore God's rules of the road. They are there for your good and the good of others.

Are you disregarding any of God's rules? Recommit yourself to a life of obedience out of love for the Lord.

Let's Not Forsake the Message of the Cross

"But we preach Christ crucified."
– I Corinthians 1:23

Normally in our church we have a small cross displayed on the wall behind the pulpit. However, on a recent Sunday it was missing. No, no one stole it. Neither was it intentionally removed as an indication of some kind of doctrinal change in our congregation. The simple reason for its absence was that the cross had accidentally got knocked off the wall and broken by someone who was cleaning the sanctuary. I'm glad to report that it has since been repaired and returned to its usual prominent location.

On that particular Sunday, I thought I should inform the other congregation which uses our sanctuary after us about the reason for the missing cross, just in case they wondered about it. When I told one of their early-arriving members, she expressed curiosity as to how many people might even notice its absence. But she assured me that if they did, she would let them know why.

Her response got me thinking about how the cross seems to be missing in a number of churches these days. I'm not referring to the object itself—the fact that some churches may choose not to display a cross anywhere. I'm referring more to the message of the cross, the reality which that object represents. It points us back to the crucifixion of Christ and what that event signifies. It's that message which I'm afraid is missing in a lot of Christianity today, and some people don't even notice. Heartwarming stories are being told. Principles are being shared about how we can be better people. Injustices in our world are condemned. Social and political issues are discussed. In many cases, Jesus is mentioned and scriptures are read. However, the message of the cross is still missing, and hardly anybody notices or cares.

I don't believe it's necessary to display a cross on a wall in order to be a Christian church. However, we can't afford to do without the message which that cross represents. Its primary significance is that it's the means by which God provided salvation for lost humanity. It reminds us of our sin and guilt before a holy God, along with His gracious remedy of sending His Son to be the sacrifice for our sin. The cross is the way we can find forgiveness and peace with God. It's what gives us the hope of heaven. Without the cross we would still be hopelessly lost in our sins with the dreadful prospect of hell ahead of us.

So the message of the cross is missing when churches refuse to talk about sin or the sinfulness of humanity, because mankind's fallen condition is what made the cross necessary. The message of the cross is missing in churches which teach that everyone is going to be saved, because it's only those who put their trust in what Jesus accomplished through His suffering and death who receive eternal life. The message of the cross is missing in churches which only proclaim God's love while leaving out His wrath on sin. While the cross does indeed show us the depths of God's love for us, it also shows how much His holy character cannot tolerate that which is unholy.

Let's not forget about or intentionally forsake the message of the cross. Let's not replace it with feel-good stories, self-help philosophies, positive thinking, or calls for social justice. There is no substitute for the cross and what it represents. When it's not present, we had better notice.

"For I determined not to know anything among you except Jesus Christ and Him crucified" (I Corinthians 2:2).

Is the message of the cross still a central part of your life and testimony?

Watch Out for the Unseen Enemy

"For we do not wrestle against flesh and blood, but against principalities, against powers, against the rulers of the darkness of this age, against spiritual hosts of wickedness in the heavenly places."
– Ephesians 6:12

If you had been driving by our church at just the right time one Saturday, you might have witnessed an interesting sight. There was a moment in which I was dancing around on the porch of the church wildly flailing my arms. No, I wasn't having some kind of ecstatic, spiritual experience. I was battling an enemy.

I had been mowing a small stretch of grass in front of our church building when I unknowingly ran over the entrance to a nest of yellow jackets. As you probably know, those bees make their home in the ground. So unless you see those insects flying in and out of the little hole they've made in the soil, you don't know that the nest is there.

However on this occasion I discovered their presence the hard way. After feeling a sharp sting on my leg, I realized what had happened. After running up on the porch to try to escape my attackers, I was still slapping them away and trying to brush off a few stubborn combatants which were angrily clinging to my shoes. I'm fortunate and thankful that I came away from the experience with only the one sting.

I don't know whom you might consider to be your enemy as a follower of Christ. It might be anyone from a terrorist group to our own government to the guy in your office who constantly ridicules you for your faith. But let's never lose sight of the fact that our real enemy is an unseen one. Satan is working underground or behind the scenes to accomplish his purposes of hindering God's work and seeking to hurt and destroy God's people.

The Bible reminds us, "For we do not wrestle against flesh and blood, but against principalities, against powers, against the rulers of the darkness of this age, against spiritual hosts of wickedness in the heavenly places" (Ephesians 6:12). It's easy to focus on the enemies we can see. If I had seen a bear standing on that spot of ground in front of the church, I wouldn't have ventured anywhere close to it. Or if I had spotted a snake slithering along the ground, I could have grabbed a tool to chase it off or kill it. But it's the unseen enemy that got me.

Similarly it's the invisible, spiritual enemy who often sneaks up on us and does us the most harm. Certainly he can use some of the people and organizations we might consider to be enemies as agencies to do his bidding. But even more dangerously, he can attack us in the realm of our own thoughts, desires, and attitudes. Even while we're dealing with the more visible opposition, we have to beware of the unseen enemy tempting our hearts with bitterness, hatred, prejudice, fear, and despair. It's not those who can harm our bodies or take away our rights with whom we should be most concerned. It's the one who can tempt us to get sidetracked from faithfully following Christ and from being His shining lights in the world.

Thankfully the Lord has not left us without adequate defense against our spiritual foes. In that same chapter in Ephesians, it reminds us that He has given us His armor to help us withstand those attacks and to be victorious. This arsenal includes truth, righteousness, faith, salvation, the word of God, and prayer.

So let's keep our armor on and not get so focused on the enemies we can see that we ignore the unseen enemy who can hurt us the most.

Look past your visible enemies today and battle the real enemy of your soul.

SEEK THE REFRESHING WIND OF GOD'S SPIRIT

"And they were all filled with the Holy Spirit."
– ACTS 2:4

On a hot summer day, my wife and I arrived a few minutes early at the restaurant where we were meeting one of our daughters and her family for lunch. So we decided to sit outside on a bench to wait for them. The temperature was high enough to have normally caused us to become uncomfortable and sweaty, but not this time. Not only were we situated in the shade, but more importantly a nice breeze was blowing.

It's amazing the difference a little wind can make. It can transform an otherwise hot and stuffy atmosphere into one that is pleasant and refreshing.

I find it interesting that the same word which is translated "spirit" in the Bible is also used to refer to the wind. Jesus even compared the work of the Holy Spirit to that weather phenomenon. "The wind blows where it wishes, and you hear the sound of it, but cannot tell where it comes from and where it goes. So is everyone who is born of the Spirit" (John 3:8). Like the wind, the Spirit of God is an unseen force that can have a huge impact. We can't control Him anymore than we can harness the wind. There may be much about the way He operates which we can't fully comprehend. However, we recognize and appreciate His refreshing presence when we experience it.

Are we allowing the Holy Spirit to live in us? Are we welcoming

His presence and power to operate in us individually as well as in our churches? Do we encourage and cultivate the blowing of this divine wind in our midst, or do we try to close the windows and stifle the influence He wants to have over us?

Some people and churches are afraid to open themselves up to the Holy Spirit and submit themselves completely to Him. After all, He is the wind who "blows where it wishes," as Jesus suggested. He might get us out of our "comfort zones" or otherwise lead us in new directions, but can't we trust that whatever He wants to do in us will be what's right and best?

Some of us should admit that we need a fresh wind from God to blow into our lives and into our churches. It's so easy to settle into what can become a hot and stuffy atmosphere of merely observing religious practices or getting caught up in our routines and traditions. We need the Spirit of God to blow, infusing those practices with His power and those routines with fresh meaning. We need to let Him bring us back to where it's more about our relationship with God than about organized religion.

No matter who you are or what church you belong to, it's the presence of the Holy Spirit that makes all the difference. No matter how doctrinally sound we may be or how much religious activity may be taking place, we're lacking a vital component if the Holy Spirit is not present and working. He can transform the mundane into the meaningful. He can revive the lifeless. He can refresh the stale.

We need an outpouring of the Spirit similar to what the disciples experienced on the Day of Pentecost—an event accompanied, appropriately enough, by "a sound from heaven, as of a rushing mighty wind" (Acts 2:2). We not only need Him to fill our own hearts, but also to blow through us to impact others.

So may this be our prayer today: "Lord, send the powerful and refreshing breeze of Your Spirit into my life and into Your church."

Let's Be a Beautiful
Bride for Christ

"Pure and undefiled religion before God and the Father is this:…to keep oneself unspotted from the world"

– JAMES 1:27

I remember when our daughter was looking for a wedding dress. Such a search can be full of excitement and joy. However, as my wife has watched the TV show, *Say Yes to the Dress*, I've seen enough of it myself to know that the experience can be a frustrating ordeal at times as well.

Brides often take a few other family members or friends along to help them find a dress in which they will look beautiful on their special day. They appreciate and value the input of these trusted advisors, even though there can be varied opinions. However, more than anything else, these brides are often most concerned about what the groom will like. A woman tends to want her husband-to-be to see her walking down the aisle on their wedding day thinking, *Wow! What a beautiful bride I have!*

The Bible pictures the church as being the Bride of Christ. Each of us who know Jesus as our Savior are included in that imagery. It should be our desire to appear before Him in such a way that He will be pleased, seeing the purity and spiritual beauty of His bride. Yet we know that in ourselves we fall short of that ideal. So what can we do?

The good news is Christ has taken it upon Himself to clothe us with His own righteousness. Through His sacrifice on the cross, He has made a way for us to become spiritually clean and beautiful. The Apostle Paul describes it this way: "Husbands, love your wives, just as Christ also loved the church and gave Himself for her, that He might sanctify and cleanse her with the washing of water by the word, that He might present her to Himself a glorious church, not having spot or wrinkle or any such thing, but that she should be holy and without blemish" (Ephesians 5:25–27). No matter how we may have dirtied up our lives from past sin, the grace of Jesus can forgive us and clean us up.

But this truth about the righteousness of Christ doesn't absolve us of our responsibility concerning this matter. We aren't to live just any old way, getting as filthy as we want and trusting Christ to cover it all up. The Bible teaches that we are to seek to be a holy, pure, and godly people. We are to seek to keep ourselves unspotted from the world (James 1:27). And we're not to make any provision for the flesh, to fulfill its lusts, but rather put on the Lord Jesus Christ (Romans 13:14).

Many believers show too little concern for actually trying to be the kind of bride our Groom wants us to be. We don't think anything about it if we happen to indulge in some sin and get ourselves a little dirty. But can you imagine a bride not caring if she spilled something on her dress, or if she had some big blemish pop up on her face before the wedding?

We should also keep in mind that the goal of Christ isn't just to make us appear to be righteous, but to actually transform us into godly people. He wants to purify our hearts and empower us to have victory over temptation and sin. He wants to impart more of His pure character and qualities into our lives.

So let's say yes to the clothing of Christ's righteousness. Let's say yes to keeping ourselves unspotted from the things of this world that would soil our souls. And let's seek to be the spiritually beautiful bride our Savior calls us to be.

Commit yourself to being a holy and beautiful Bride for Christ.

Rough Roads Can
Be Exciting Times

"And we know that all things work together for good to those who love God, to those who are the called according to His purpose."
– Romans 8:28

"Papaw, can we ride on a bumpy road?" Such was the strange request coming from the backseat of my car. It originated with my three-year-old granddaughter whom we were babysitting one Saturday. She asked that question as we were going to pick up a pizza for our lunch. I tried to explain to her that there weren't any especially bumpy roads between our house and the pizza restaurant. With great disappointment in her voice, she responded, "But I like to ride on bumpy roads."

As I explored the subject further with my granddaughter, and later with her mother, I began to understand the reason for her request. It seems there is a rather rough road that my daughter often uses as a cut-through route when she travels a certain direction. And our grandkids look forward to riding over that stretch of bumpy road. They open their mouths, vocalizing some sort of monotone humming sound. But as they hit those bumps in the road, their voices vacillate in what they find to be a humorous manner. So for our grandkids, a bumpy road is viewed as an opportunity to enjoy this game they play with their voices.

I'll confess that I don't share my granddaughter's affection for bumpy roads. I would rather avoid them. Not only are they physically uncomfortable for us sojourners, but they aren't very good for our vehicles too.

So normally I avoid rough roads and am pleased to see when one gets repaved into a smoother surface.

We tend to look at bumpy roads in life the same way. We don't like them and we avoid them as much as possible. However, we all inevitably encounter those rough patches at times as we journey through life. You know the kind of bumps and potholes I'm talking about—financial hardships, physical problems, family difficulties, along with a host of other challenges that can make life uncomfortable and tough.

I'm not going to suggest to you that we should seek out such bumps in life. I don't know about you, but they seem to find me just fine on a fairly regular basis without my having to go looking for them. However, we could probably have a better attitude about those bumpy roads when we do find ourselves on one. Instead of constantly emphasizing the negative aspects of the experience and complaining about the discomfort, what if we focused more on the opportunity for adventure and the excitement of it all? After all, some of the same people who complain about driving on a bumpy road pay good money to ride a rollercoaster that jerks them all over creation. Sometimes it's just a matter of perspective.

When we encounter one of those rough patches in life, let's joyfully anticipate the prospect of how God is going to see us through it. It's going to be exciting to experience God's help, protection, and grace as we travel this way. Let's be ready to watch with wonder at how God fulfills His promise to work all things together for good to those who love Him (Romans 8:28). Let's look ahead for those new doors He's going to open as those old ones have closed behind us.

I'm not ignoring the fact that those bumpy roads can be hard, painful, and full of sorrow. But neither should we overlook the truth that those same roads can be a source of stronger faith, fresh manifestations of God's power and love, and new adventures in walking with God. So when the road gets rough, let's hang on and look forward to a thrilling ride with the Lord.

Lord, help me view my "bumpy road" as an adventure and opportunity.

Let God's Spirit Show You the Condition of Your Heart

"He will convict the world of sin, and of righteousness, and of judgment."

– John 16:8

Around this time of year, we always open up our home to an exterminator for our annual termite inspection. If you're a responsible homeowner in our part of the country, you know the importance of this regular ritual. Those particular pests, if left unchecked, can do significant and costly damage when they decide to make a meal out of the wood in your house.

So this is the one time each year we not only allow but encourage someone to go into several areas of our home that are usually closed off to guests. Some of us have that one closet or utility room in which all the junk gets thrown in order to keep the rest of the rooms uncluttered. Or there's the basement or garage crowded with enough old stuff to get us an appearance on that TV show about hoarders.

At termite inspection time, I even open up the deepest, darkest recess of our house where we ourselves don't ever venture. I have to go into a basement closet where I loosen the bolts and remove the board covering the entrance to the crawl space under our kitchen and garage. I always do so with great trepidation, not knowing what spiders or other creepy crawlers might be lurking on the other side.

As necessary as those termite inspections are, it's even more important that we allow the Holy Spirit to regularly inspect our hearts and lives. Certain bad attitudes, ungodly desires, erroneous ways of thinking, and other harmful spiritual pests can sneak into our lives virtually unnoticed. Those issues need to be addressed before they do damage to our relationship with the Lord and hinder our effectiveness in serving Him.

Why do we need the Holy Spirit to be involved in these self-examinations? It's the same reason I use a termite inspector. I may recognize some signs of termites being present, but a professional has the expertise to see what I may miss. And he may do a much more thorough examination than I would do myself. Similarly the Spirit of God can see into our hearts and minds to a degree that even we can't match. He knows us better than we know ourselves. And He is ready to point out potentially dangerous aspects of our lives that we might tend to overlook, excuse, or gloss over.

But in order for Him to do a thorough job, we have to open up the darkest recesses of our hearts and minds to Him. We must remove any "off-limits" signs and allow Him full access. He knows all about our deepest secrets, the spiders crawling around in our hearts, and the things we've allowed to clutter our minds. We simply need to let Him shine His light on them so that we can see them and receive His remedy for them. I'm not advocating some kind of obsession with self-examination that leads to constant guilt and always being critical of oneself. I'm talking about a healthy introspection directed by the Holy Spirit that keeps us from letting any sin or other harmful attitude get a foothold in our lives.

If we're believers in Christ, the Holy Spirit is always present as our Guide, Comforter, and, when necessary, Inspector and Corrector. He is ever-faithful to show us our true condition if we're attentive to Him. But occasionally we deliberately need to stop and say with the Psalmist, "Search me, O God, and know my heart…see if there is any wicked way in me" (Psalm 139:23–24).

How long has it been since you've invited the Holy Spirit to do a thorough inspection of your heart and life?

Is there some "closet" you're trying to keep away from the Spirit's inspection? Open it up!

You Can Be Someone's Inspiration

"Imitate me, just as I also imitate Christ."
– I Corinthians 11:1

One time I was driving through a neighborhood when I noticed a couple of kids playing outdoors. That unusual sight in itself made me wonder if the electricity had gone out in that area or what other dire circumstance had pulled those youngsters away from their air-conditioned confines in front of television sets, computers, and video games. And no, they weren't simply standing outside talking, texting, or playing games on a cell phone.

What really got my attention in that passing moment was the boy who was posed on the driveway like a sprinter on his mark getting ready to run a race. Since this took place in the middle of the airing of the Olympic Games, I assume that the boy was emulating what he had seen on TV. Maybe he had been inspired to dream of becoming a track and field star himself one day by watching some of the great runners at that event.

It took me back to my own boyhood aspirations of wanting to be like Dave Wottle after watching his performance in the 1972 Olympics. I could envision myself similarly clad in a golf cap staying near the back of the pack before coming from behind at the last moment to win the race for the United States. Needless to say, I didn't follow through on that dream and never did any serious running.

But it reminds us that we all need people we can look to as a source of inspiration, not just in athletics but in all aspects of life. And that includes people who inspire us to faithfully follow God. It's helpful to see people who exemplify what it means to be a Christian—individuals who show us the possibilities and heights we can reach if we will truly seek the Lord and let Him have His way in our lives.

While we might want to take a moment to give thanks for those folks who have been such an inspiration to us over the years, let me ask a more challenging question: are we living in such a way as to inspire the people who are watching us?

We don't have to be spiritual superstars up on a worldwide public stage in order to fulfill that role. We can be just what most of us are—ordinary guys and gals wearing our golf caps and trying to keep pace in this race toward godliness and heaven. We can inspire others by being faithful to keep running when so many around us are dropping out of the race. We can be an example not by achieving a perfect score but by getting back up after we fall, by not giving up when we seem to be lagging behind, and by steadily following our Savior day after day no matter what hurdles we face or how tired we get.

We can show others that it's possible to courageously stay true to God's Word and our convictions in an ever-changing and sometimes hostile world. We can exemplify a spirit of love and compassion for those around us who are in need and neglected by much of the rest of society. We can model what it means to live a holy life in spite of all the temptations and pressures to do otherwise.

However, our focus doesn't need to be on trying to make ourselves an inspiration to others. It will just happen if we'll be faithful to follow the Lord wholeheartedly and let Him keep working in our lives. So let's continue to run the race and maybe we'll inspire others to join in and meet us at the finish line.

Is anything hindering your life from being a godly inspiration to others?

Wherever We Are,
Let's Live for the Lord

"You comprehend my path and my lying down, and are acquainted with all my ways."

– Psalm 139:3

One year my wife went out of town for an annual national convention in connection with her work. That year's gathering took her to a city that neither she nor I had visited before—Las Vegas. Before she left, as she spoke about her trip, it seemed to engender envy and excitement in some people. But I must confess that Vegas has never been high on my list of vacation destinations. It might be nice to drive through to see the sights, but that would probably be more than enough to satisfy my curiosity about the place. Maybe it has something to do with its reputation of being a "sin city."

Some of us had joked with my wife about behaving herself while she's there, although my mother wasn't exactly being helpful when she gave her $1.25 to play the slot machines in her behalf. Inevitably whenever the conversation turned toward what my wife might or might not do on her trip, someone would bring up the well-worn motto, "What happens in Vegas stays in Vegas."

While that may be an interesting saying to promote the idea that people can indulge guilt-free in the various vices that are offered in that place, I'm afraid it gives a false assurance. No matter where we've gone or what we've done, if we did something we shouldn't have done, we know it, God knows about it, and it will often adversely affect the people around us.

Think about one of the most infamous "sin cities" in the Bible—Sodom. I wonder if the people there had a similar attitude, that "whatever happened in Sodom stayed in Sodom"? If they did, they certainly found out differently. God showed in a dramatic manner that He knew about the wickedness of that place, sending fire and brimstone to destroy it. That divine destruction not only affected Sodom but many of the surrounding cities.

I wonder if King David thought, *Whatever happens in the privacy of my home stays in the privacy of my home*? Such a concept might have especially seemed true for a ruler in the royal residence. So when David took another man's wife there and committed adultery with her, he may have thought that was the end of the matter. But it wasn't long before God's prophet confronted him with his sin. And on top of that, the innocent child who was conceived through that union ended up dying as one of the results of this immoral act. David discovered that there is no hidden and guilt-free immorality. Sinful acts have their consequences.

Let's make sure that we aren't deceiving ourselves with a similar notion. Maybe we think that whatever we do outside of church or out of the sight of the preacher is somehow acceptable. Maybe we think it's OK to "let loose" and do whatever we want to do when we're out of town and in a place where no one knows us. Or maybe we think that what we do when the doors are shut and the blinds are closed goes unseen or doesn't impact anyone but ourselves. Or maybe we adhere to the motto, "Whatever happens on the internet stays on the internet."

God's standards don't change simply because we're in Vegas or because no one else is around to see what we're doing. God knows about it. We know about it. And any immoral behavior in our lives does carry consequences that can affect the people around us.

So let's be committed to godly living no matter where we are—even in Las Vegas, Sodom, or our own living rooms.

Always keep in mind that God is with you and knows what you're doing.

BE CAREFUL TRAVELING ALONG THE EDGE

"Therefore let him who thinks he stands take heed lest he fall."
– I CORINTHIANS 10:12

I was driving along one of the state highways in our area when I came upon a couple of teenage boys. One of them was walking in the grass along the roadway, while the other was riding his skateboard. As I got closer, I could see that the daring one, or should I say the foolish one, was attempting to maneuver his skateboard along a very narrow stretch of pavement between the white line marking the outside of the right lane and the drop-off onto the shoulder of the road. I would doubt the wisdom of such an action anywhere, but especially along a busy highway where the speed limit is fifty-five.

As I passed the young men I naturally moved closer to the center of the road, as did other motorists, in order to give them extra room. I marveled both at the skill of the skateboarder to keep control on what appeared to be only a couple of inches of blacktop and at his foolishness for attempting the feat. I glanced back at them in my rearview mirror just in time to see the young daredevil take a spill. I assume his wheel dropped off the edge causing him to go sprawling partially across the white line into the lane of traffic. Fortunately no car was coming at the moment. As the scene faded out of my sight, the young man appeared to be without serious injury as he slowly picked himself up.

I can only imagine what such a person was thinking, if he was thinking at all. *I'm skillful enough to do this. I'll be able to stop before getting into any real danger. I want to show my friend how good I am. Nothing bad is going to happen to me.* Yet he was very fortunate that he wasn't seriously injured or killed as a result of his daring trip along the edge.

While we may be quick to pass harsh judgment on that skateboarder, let's be sure that we're not acting similarly ourselves. Some people will see how close they can get to the edge of the straight and narrow road of following God without falling off. They think they're strong enough to get close to temptation without actually giving in to it. They tell themselves that they can stop before they go too far or get into any serious danger. They've seen others get hurt, but they foolishly believe the lie that it can't happen to them.

Maybe some adventurous souls like to travel along the edge because it's exciting, risky, and daring. May I suggest an alternative that is even more challenging? See how close you can get to the center of the road. Try to get as far as possible away from sin and temptation in your life. Try to draw as near to God as you can. Try to learn as much as possible about Him. Dare to seek to live in the very center of His will for you. Surrender yourself completely to Him and let Him use you to do His work. If you'll follow that path, I believe you'll find it to be not only adventurous and daring but also wise.

If a parent with a teenage skateboarder is reading this, maybe you need to have another safety chat with your son. And maybe we as God's children need to be reminded of our Father's warnings as well. Flee temptation. Resist the devil. Let him who thinks he stands take heed lest he fall.

Let's all seek to draw nearer to God rather than skate along the edge.

Are you trying to walk too close to the edge in some area of your life? What step can you take to move away from the edge and closer to the Lord?

Live Your Life with a Sense of Expectancy

"These all died in faith, not having received the promises, but having them afar off were assured of them, embraced them...."

– Hebrews 11:13

We're expecting. No, my wife and I aren't aiming to be another Sarah and Abraham, although we're still decades away from the late age at which God blessed them with Isaac. We're actually expectant grandparents again. Our younger daughter and her husband have announced that their first child is on the way. So there will be a lot of excited anticipation in our family over the next months as we look ahead to this new arrival.

In another sense, the statement "We're expecting" should be true of all of us as followers of Christ. It shouldn't be a strange declaration to make about ourselves. A sense of expectancy should characterize our lives as believers. God has given us certain things which we should be excitedly anticipating.

For example, we should be journeying through life with the expectation of Jesus' return. We may not know exactly when it's going to happen, but based on what God's Word reveals, we know He is coming back to take His people home and to judge the world. Just because 2,000 years has passed and it hasn't happened yet doesn't mean we should stop anticipating it. Jesus warned us about that very thing in some of His parables. Let's not lose our sense of expectancy and as a result not be ready when He comes.

Likewise we should be anticipating heaven. We may not be anxious to hop on the bus to that destination today, but we're looking forward to that eternal home once this life is over. We can go through life with a peaceful assurance about what awaits us after death. We're anticipating seeing Jesus, being reunited with loved ones, and experiencing the glorious blessings of that existence.

As a matter of fact, we can be expectant concerning everything God has promised us, both in relation to this life and the life to come. Whether it's His promise of providing for our needs, of helping us through tough times, of comfort, of healing, or whatever else He has said He would do, we can live with the assurance and anticipation of it happening. If God said it, it's a certainty which we can look forward to.

After my sweet little granddaughter found out about her new cousin being on the way, she went up to her aunt and gave her a big hug around the waist. Then she commented, "When I hug you now, I'm also hugging the baby." The Bible talks about those who have faith in God as being those who saw the fulfillment of His promises "afar off" and "embraced them" (Hebrews 11:13). If we're going to embrace God, then we're going to embrace His promises too. We're going to believe what He says and we're going to be anticipating the fulfillment of His words.

Does that spirit characterize you? I'm afraid many of us today are living in expectation of doom and gloom as we look at the world around us. And there's good reason for some of it. God's promises about judgment, sin, and its consequences are true too. But let's not lose sight of all the positive promises of God we can yet anticipate. No matter what happens in the world we live in, we have much to look forward to as followers of Christ. We can still expect His presence with us, His provision for us, and His power to enable us to live for Him. And we can expect a glorious future with Him in heaven.

Don't let anything rob you of the assurance and excitement of the fulfillment of God's promises. Keep expecting!

Live today in anticipation of the fulfillment of God's wonderful promises.

Get Inspired Again to Run Your Race Heartily

"Do you not know that those who run in a race all run, but one receives the prize? Run in such a way that you may obtain it."

– I Corinthians 9:24

D o you watch the Summer Olympics? No matter how uninterested I may feel as these games approach every four years, I inevitably get drawn into it by my competitive and sports-loving nature. However as I've gotten older, I don't often choose to stay up past my bedtime to catch all the action as I once did. If I'm really interested in an event, I can usually go online to find out the results instead of staying up to view the late-night tape-delayed broadcast.

We tend to admire the Olympic athletes not only for their honed skills but also for their drive and hard work which got them there. They not only elicit our admiration, but they also inspire us. They inspire young people who are interested in those particular sports to work hard and pursue their own dream of excelling in them. And they inspire many of the rest of us to give our best efforts in whatever our endeavors may be.

And keep in mind that the efforts of these athletes don't stop once they get chosen to compete in the Olympics. It's not enough simply to be in the race. They keep pushing themselves to do well enough in order to win. Yes, it's wonderful just to be there for the Olympic experience. But the greatest competitors are those who keep striving to win one of those prized medals.

Apparently the Apostle Paul had an affinity for sports too. He sometimes used analogies related to the ancient Olympic Games to convey certain truths. To one church he wrote: "Do you not know that those who run in a race all run, but one receives the prize? Run in such a way that you may obtain it" (I Corinthians 9:24).

Paul wasn't talking to track stars giving them running advice. He was addressing followers of Christ about their journey of faith. He was indicating that we shouldn't allow the fact that we are on the pathway to heaven cause us to become complacent. We shouldn't ease up in our efforts to know Christ better, to serve Him fully, and to seek to bring others into a saving relationship with Him.

We can thank the Lord that we are in the race. We're on the right track. But let's keep running to win. Let's not let up now.

There may be various reasons why we would be tempted not to run this race as heartily as we have in the past. In some cases we may just be weary and unable to physically do everything we once did. Thankfully this isn't a physical race. We can still pursue a close relationship with Jesus. Even though our bodies are weaker, our spirits can still be strong and growing. We can also make use of the opportunities we still have to serve Him, even if they're limited or different from what we were able to do in the past.

In other cases we may feel emotionally weary or discouraged from battling difficult circumstances or from not seeing as many positive results as we would have hoped. At those times we need to get our eyes refocused on the One who called us into this race. The Lord is still right there with us, both cheering us on and helping us. And the prize of His "well done, good and faithful servant" is awaiting us at the finish line if we will keep going.

So whenever you watch the Olympics, get inspired again—maybe not inspired to go out and run a marathon, but inspired to give it all you've got in following Jesus and serving Him.

How have you eased up in the race? Ask the Lord to renew your strength and motivation to run more heartily.

Remember Who Is in Charge

"Therefore submit to God."
– James 4:7

One time my four-year-old grandson got to spend part of a day with my wife's parents while his older siblings were in school. At one point my mother-in-law took the little guy out to the dollar store to pick out a few small gifts, not only for himself but also for his brothers and sister. She told him that when he returned home he was to be the one in charge to distribute those presents.

Due to the fact that I had been asked to meet the other children when they got off the school bus that day, I was present to witness firsthand what happened when my daughter and grandson returned from their trip. When the other children realized there were presents from great-grandmother, they started crowding around and grabbing at the shopping bag. But my littlest grandson waved them aside with the bold announcement, "I am in charge!" To their credit, and with a little encouragement from their mother, the other kids backed off and allowed their little brother to have his moment of being the one to hand out the gifts. Being the youngest in the family, he probably didn't get such an opportunity very often to be "the one in charge."

God has given us the privilege and responsibility of being in charge of certain aspects of our lives. He gave mankind the authority to have dominion over the rest of creation. He puts some of us in positions of authority in our families, on our jobs, and in other spheres of life. He gives His followers some degree of authority over sin and spiritual evil forces in this world. Additionally, He has given us all the free will to make our own choices in life. We can even choose whether or not we're going to obey Him. In many ways, we are in charge.

However, there are some pitfalls that accompany this privilege which we would do well to avoid. For one thing, let's not lose sight of the fact that although we may be in charge of some things, we're not in charge of everything. There are aspects of life over which we have no control or authority. Thankfully we can rest in the assurance that God is still in control over it all, even when events appear to be chaotic or when we can't understand their purpose. No matter what is happening, God is still in charge.

Secondly, we need to be careful that we don't get so caught up in being in charge ourselves that we refuse to submit to God's authority. We may be the boss over certain aspects of our lives, but we still have a bigger boss over us to whom we must answer. He's going to hold us accountable for how we managed the authority He gave to us. Were we good stewards over His creation? Did we properly lead our families, our employees, and others who were under our charge? Did we exercise the authority of Christ over sin and evil in order to live holy lives? Did we use our free will to serve God and to be a blessing to the people around us?

Sometimes we can get so caught up in the fact that we're in charge that we think we know better than God. We claim to be the boss of our lives rather than submitting to and following God's will for us. Don't make the mistake of waving God aside and telling Him you're in charge. Rather, let's choose to back off and let God have His way in our lives.

In what areas do you tend to take charge rather than listen to what God says? Remember who the boss is and submit to Him.

Don't Be a Truth-Twister

"There are some who trouble you and want to pervert the gospel of Christ."

– Galatians 1:7

One day I watched a video someone had posted on Facebook. It included a few short clips from the old TV show *Hee Haw*. Do you remember that program in which Buck Owens and Roy Clark did some "pickin' and grinnin'"? I guess you could call it a hillbilly variety show with a combination of country singing, corny comedy, and even some gospel singing occasionally added to the mix.

In this particular video, one of the clips featured Archie Campbell telling what he called a backwards fairy tale. I think "twisted" would be a better description. Instead of Cinderella, he told about Rindecella. All throughout the story he would switch around the initial letters in words to make them sound different, and sometimes rather funny. My favorite modified phrase in his account was, instead of Cinderella dropping her slipper, she "slopped her dripper."

Thinking my grandchildren would like such an odd retelling of this familiar tale, I made the effort to come up with my own twisted version of the story using some of Archie Campbell's words along with creating a few of my own. And the grandkids did seem to thoroughly enjoy it.

While it can be rather humorous to twist around the words of a fairy tale, it's not so funny when we start twisting the truth, the gospel, and the Word of God. Yet that's what some are guilty of doing today. It's not a new problem. If you look closely at the conversation between the serpent and

Eve in the Garden of Eden, it seems there was some twisting going on already. And in the New Testament the Apostle Paul used a similar word to describe some people who were troubling the churches in Galatia, saying they were wanting "to pervert the gospel of Christ" (Galatians 1:7).

It's one thing to flatly deny God's Word. Such a position is often clear and easily recognizable. However, it's another thing to twist the truth or pervert what the Bible says, which is sometimes more dangerous and more difficult to discern. It can sound good on the surface, but if you listen closely you can hear that it's wrought with errors which can lead people away from the right path.

So what are some examples of such twisting? Claiming that Jesus is the Savior but suggesting He isn't the only way for a person to find salvation. Emphasizing the idea of a loving God to the point that sin, judgment, and hell are downplayed or discarded altogether. Making God's promises to bless His people into some kind of guarantee of great wealth, good health, and worldly success. Transforming faith and prayer into a means of manipulating God into giving us whatever we want. Even making God's grace and forgiveness an excuse for people not to live godly lives or not to believe in the possibility of experiencing a great degree of victory over sin and temptation in their lives.

Some such twisting may be done intentionally by people who know it's not the truth. But in other cases it's the unintentional actions of people who are simply accepting what others tell them or who aren't as familiar with God's Word as they could be. We all have to guard against the temptation to take certain verses out of context, to stake our beliefs on one or two verses while ignoring other passages of scripture, or interpreting verses to say what we want them to say or what would make them more palatable to today's world.

Let's be honest seekers of the truth and diligent students of God's Word. Let's not be guilty of "bisting the Twible."

Are you being honest in your interpretation of scripture?

Uphold the Standards
of God's Word

*"If the Lord delights in us, then He will bring us into this land...
only do not rebel against the Lord"*

– Numbers 14:8–9

In accordance with one of my hobbies, I've been reading another old
book recently. It's the classic novel *The Deerslayer* by James Fenimore
Cooper, first published in 1841. You may have read at least some excerpts
from this work in a high school literature class. The story is set in the wilderness of the early American frontier.

One of the aspects of the book which has captured my interest is
the efforts of the main character to maintain high morals in spite of his
primitive surroundings and the lack of such morals in most of the people
around him. For example, it is portrayed as a time when many people
didn't value or treat American Indians as fellow human beings. The story
also shows that the practice of scalping was not confined to the Indians.
A frontiersman might have been equally tempted to scalp an Indian without provocation simply to receive the money offered for such a prize. So
the main character would often "go against the flow" concerning such
matters in order to do what he believed was right and what he believed
would be most pleasing to God. Not only did he seek to live his life in that
manner, but also encouraged others to live by those higher standards.

Our world has changed quite a bit since those days. Not only has the
landscape of our nation been drastically altered by advances in science,

462

industry, and technology, but many would declare that we now live in a more civilized society. However, the nature of man hasn't seen as great a transformation. People still tend to demean those who look different from them or who are part of another culture. There is still conflict, deception, dishonesty, and violence between the various nations and tribes of this world. Human life is often not valued as highly as it should be. And while scalping may not be a common practice, many people will still do unscrupulous and even inhumane acts in order to gain some money. Morals are still lacking in our day, and in some areas maybe more so than in those frontier times.

So in this moral and spiritual wilderness in which we live today, there is still a need for people who will take a stand for what is right. We need to seek to live in accordance with God's standards and inspire others to do the same.

I heard someone preach a sermon recently about the twelve spies who were sent into the Promised Land to check it out. As you may recall, although Joshua and Caleb were outnumbered ten to two, these courageous men were willing to take a stand for doing the right thing in obeying God and taking possession of the land. They didn't back down even when almost the entire nation sided with the opposing viewpoint and were calling for the execution of these two godly men (see Numbers 14:1–10).

No matter whether you lived in Bible times, in the early American frontier, or in today's spiritual wilderness, heroes are always needed who will bravely seek to live in accordance to the higher standard of God's will, even when the majority around them disagree and may even become hostile toward them. Are you willing to stand against the crowd in order to do the right thing and to uphold the morals taught in the Bible? Will you seek to be a person of integrity who practices what he preaches even when it means "going against the flow"? Will you be such a Joshua and a Caleb in your family, in your community, and in your nation?

In what ways are God and His standards calling you to "go against the flow" today?

WE ARE NEVER TRULY ALONE

"Fear not, for I am with you; be not dismayed, for I am your God."
— ISAIAH 41:10

I remember an occasion some years ago when I wasn't looking forward to my wife going out of town. Over those past few months our house had become increasingly empty. First our son had relocated to Orlando to begin a new job. One of our daughters had returned home for a while to fill the gap. But after accepting a teaching position, she had moved into her own apartment about an hour away from us. And even our beloved basset hound was no longer in residence as she had recently passed away. Therefore when I thought about my wife going out of town for a few days, I dreaded the idea of being alone in a house that would be so quiet. Although I normally enjoy a little solitude, I was concerned that this time things around home might be a little too quiet.

Thankfully the week zipped by relatively speedily. I enjoyed a little time to "be still and know that the Lord is God." But I also kept busy between fulfilling pastoral duties, working on some long-neglected projects around the house, and reading a Christian novel. I really didn't feel the loneliness I had dreaded. However, when the time came, I was very glad to welcome my wife back home.

One of the great things about being a follower of Christ is that we are never really alone. One of the most comforting promises in the Bible is the oft-repeated assurance from God that "I will be with you." That declaration gives us confidence that no matter where we are or what circumstances we're facing, we can rely on the presence of the Lord.

However, the promise is not merely about God being there, as wonderful as that truth is. It's also about the fact that He is Someone who cares about us and can help us. "Fear not, for I am with you; be not dismayed, for I am your God. I will strengthen you, yes, I will help you, I will uphold you with My righteous right hand" (Isaiah 41:10).

Human companionship can be a wonderful blessing of life. But there are times when, for various reasons, we will find it lacking. We can try to fill the void with everything from busyness to the companionship of pets. But the primary comfort in times of loneliness is the knowledge that a caring God is with us—Someone who can be the help, strength, and support that we need to make it through.

Life is full of opportunities to feel like we're all alone: your young child going off to school for the first time; your older child moving away to attend college; the consequences of divorce; broken relationships with other members of the family or with close friends; the death of a loved one; poor physical health that leaves you unable to get out and be in touch with others as in past years.

While our circumstances may change in those ways, the promise of God's presence doesn't change. Although our contact with other people may diminish, our fellowship with the Lord can grow day by day. So whether you're dealing with being an empty nester or a widow or a resident of a nursing home or simply having a spouse go out of town for a few days—remember that if you know Christ, you don't have to fear being alone. You can rely on your Lord to be your ever-present companion and helper.

So in those lonely moments, listen for that same divine voice that has spoken to others through the ages as it reminds you, "I am with you."

Feeling lonely? Seek solace in the fact that God is with you. Use this time to draw closer to Him.

AUGUST 17

THE LORD WILL CARRY YOU

"Even to your old age, I am He, and even to gray hairs I will carry you!"

– ISAIAH 46:4

I babysat our three grandkids one evening while my daughter and son-in-law attended one of those school curriculum meetings for parents. As usual I enjoyed the opportunity to spend some time with those children, but by the time their van pulled back into our driveway, I let out that sigh of relief with which grandparents are familiar—the sigh of a weary survivor that says, *It was a lot of fun, but I think I'm ready for you to go home now.*

As that beloved crew headed out the door, all three kids had gravitated to their father. On his back with arms wrapped around his neck was the oldest child. And in each arm were nestled the two younger siblings. Those grandchildren were still relatively young, but they made for quite a load for one person to carry. I couldn't help but smile as I watched my son-in-law slowly but successfully plod out to the car with his precious cargo. I'm sure if I had tried that task, I would have been down in my back for a week.

The Bible reminds us that our Heavenly Father can and does carry us. In the middle of a passage declaring how manmade idols have to be carried around by people, the prophet Isaiah draws this contrast with the one true living God: "Listen to Me, O house of Jacob, and all the remnant of the house of Israel, who have been upheld by Me from birth, who have been carried from the womb; even to your old age, I am He, and even to

466

gray hairs I will carry you! I have made, and I will bear; even I will carry, and will deliver you" (Isaiah 46:3–4).

We aren't dealing with a god who has to be supported and carried by us. On the contrary, we serve a great God who helps and carries us. And that's a world of difference, isn't it?

Think about those occasions when we tend to pick up and carry our kids—when they're tired, when we're in a hurry and their little legs can't keep up with us, when the path is rough or there is some obstacle or danger. Likewise God carries us when we're weary. He carries us when our efforts and strength can't keep up with the challenges and opportunities before us. He picks us up when dangers and obstacles threaten us. We have a caring God who has upheld us from birth and who continues to do so today.

God can handle carrying us no matter how heavy the load may seem at times between us and all our baggage of afflictions, difficulties, and challenges. And it's no problem for Him to carry the weight of all His many children at the same time.

There's a song that suggests if Jesus could carry the weight of the world on His shoulders, then we should know that He can carry us. The Bible talks about how the Son of God bore the sins of the whole world as He went to the cross. If He could support that unimaginable weight, then certainly He can carry you and me.

So when you don't think you can take another step, put your arms around the neck of Jesus and hang on. When the road is too rough or you don't know which way to turn, rest in His strong arms. Let Him carry you.

In my older age I may not be capable of carrying all of my grandchildren at the same time, but I'm grateful that there is a God who can carry me and you and anyone else who will trust Him—"even to your old age."

In what area of your life do you need to rest in the assurance that God is carrying you?

Don't Let Fear Cause You to Lose Perspective

"The Lord is the strength of my life; of whom shall I be afraid?"

– Psalm 27:1

I'm beginning to wonder if I should be concerned about myself. It seems that I've been finding considerable inspiration from a different source in recent days—the Sunday comics in the newspaper. Well, at least it's the Sunday version, so maybe that makes it more acceptable.

The one that got my attention this time was about a little girl who had called her dad for help because she claimed that a gigantic spider had attacked her. As the father came to the rescue, his daughter told him how the big hairy creature with pointy fangs and evil red eyes had swooped down and knocked her off the couch. However, her dad had a hard time finding this awful beast. As it turned out, the spider was so tiny that he had to look very closely to even see it. When he questioned his daughter about her description of it as being gigantic, she responded, "They're a lot bigger when you're scared of them."

That's true not just of spiders but about most things, isn't it? Fear tends to magnify our problems and challenges. It makes them seem a lot bigger and more formidable than they really are. Fear can transform the proverbial molehills in our lives into mountains. A person, difficulty, or circumstance can grow to gigantic proportions simply due to fear, worry, and an active imagination.

I recall as a child spending the night with my grandparents. They resided in one of those old houses that came alive with strange noises in the dark of night. On a few of those occasions, I remember letting fear creep in as I lay in bed. It wasn't long before every creaking floorboard or each brush of a limb against a window grew in my mind to be the sounds made by some horrible intruder or ghastly ghoul.

We smile at those childish fears, but too often we're guilty of letting adult fears act similarly upon our minds. "But these are real problems, not imaginary ones," we might argue. We may be facing valid concerns about the possibility of losing our jobs, making ends meet financially, resolving serious relationship issues, physical illnesses, and a host of other spiders trying to swoop down on us.

Yes, they may be real, but when we choose the pathway of fear instead of faith, we tend to magnify the size and difficulty of the problem. And as we distort its proportions, we lose sight of how much greater our God is in comparison to that spider. In our minds, it becomes a huge, hairy beast that is not only too hard for us to tame, but is even too big for God to handle.

When facing such circumstances, the Psalmist asked, "The Lord is my light and my salvation; whom shall I fear? The Lord is the strength of my life; of whom shall I be afraid?" (Psalm 27:1). In those situations, if we can remember who God is, along with how big and powerful He is, we can keep a more realistic perspective about our problems and about God's ability to help us overcome them.

We make the choice between fear and faith. In another Psalm (56:3), David declares to God, "Whenever I am afraid, I will trust in You." Will you commit yourself to doing that, too? The spider may be real, but let's not allow fear to make him look bigger than he is. Let's put our trust in a God whose infinity-sized shoes are well able to squash any fearsome spiderlike situation that swoops into our lives.

Has fear over something caused you to lose sight of the greatness of God? Trust Him to handle that matter as well as to take care of you.

HERE COMES THE GROOM

"Those who were ready went in with him to the wedding; and the door was shut."

– MATTHEW 25:10

I was talking to a mom whose daughter was planning on having her wedding in our church building. Although the date for this joyous occasion had been set, there seemed to be some question about the time. The bride-to-be was yielding to the wishes of her groom regarding this matter. Apparently he didn't care what hour the ceremony took place, but for some reason he was insisting that it begin at exactly seventeen minutes past the hour. The wedding was eventually scheduled for 3:17 in the afternoon.

While such a request might appear a little unusual to many of us, the marriage customs in Jesus' day would seem even stranger. In one of his parables (Matthew 25:1–13), Jesus referred to how the groom in that day also had a lot to say about the time of the wedding. Not only could he choose seventeen minutes past the hour for the big moment, but he might not even tell the bride when it was going to happen. He might suddenly show up anytime during the designated day, or even week, of the wedding, ready to whisk his bride off to his house for the festivities. And often it happened in the middle of the night.

Could you imagine such a scenario today? I don't think too many brides would appreciate it. Forget about spending the morning at the hairstylist, last-minute primping, and not sitting down getting the dress all wrinkled. If the groom makes her wait too long, she might get all hot and sweaty, messing up her makeup. And what if he comes in the middle of the night, finding her asleep? She'll have to rush off to her wedding with sleep-filled eyes and messed-up hair! No, it just wouldn't work. Too many grooms would end up with irritable brides and unpleasant honeymoons on their hands if they tried any of that business.

Jesus compared that custom to His coming—not the first one we celebrate at Christmas, but the second one when He'll return to gather His people and judge the ungodly. He plainly states that no one will know the day or the hour when it will occur. Too many of us miss the point of Jesus' parables about His Second Coming. We tend to hear Jesus saying, "Try to figure out when I'm coming." But what He actually taught was, "Watch and be ready, because you don't know exactly when I'm coming."

In this particular parable, Jesus focused on the bride's companions. Some of them weren't ready when the announcement came that the groom was on his way. Because he had delayed his coming, some of those attendants were running out of oil for their lamps. That's part of our problem. Christ's followers have had to wait longer on his arrival than many expected.

From the early days of the church until now, believers have thought it was drawing near. I grew up hearing sermons about how Jesus will certainly come in the 1970s—or how He'll return within forty years of 1948, the year when Israel was reestablished as a nation in their homeland. It didn't happen. But we have to guard against getting discouraged, doubting His promise, or simply losing our sense of expectancy and failing to be prepared. The groom is still coming and He's right on time as far as our Heavenly Father and His plans are concerned.

Our responsibility is to be ready. Being spiritually prepared means that we have a personal, up-to-date relationship with Christ. Jesus commanded us to watch—not just for the signs of His coming but watching after our own souls. Let's not forget that we could face our Lord at any time. Let's watch with oil in our lamps, with the Holy Spirit in our hearts, and with the peace that comes from knowing all is well with our souls.

Would you be ready if Jesus were to come back today?

AUGUST 20

There Is More to Learn
in the School of Faith

"Finally then, brethren, we urge and exhort in the Lord Jesus that you should abound more and more."

– I Thessalonians 4:1

Imagine with me one of the many kindergartners who may have recently started school. This particular child had not learned how to write any of his letters yet. So that first day of school, his teacher informs him that he needs to learn how to write the capital letter A. I don't know how they do it these days—years ago they used these papers which had the letter written on it, then several dotted outlines of that figure for the student to trace over. Finally there were blank spaces where the student could practice forming that letter numerous times until he could consistently get it correct. So after much practice and effort, the aforementioned student finally achieves success at his task, earning the approval of his teacher. Afterwards he naively puts down his pencil, thinking that he's learned all that he needs to know.

He receives a mild shock when his teacher tells him that there is a smaller version of that letter he now must master. Then he notices a long poster plastered along the top of one classroom wall showing that there are twenty-six such letters that he must learn to write. Soon he discovers a similar truth about all his subjects. In math, just when he gets the hang of addition, he finds out about subtraction. Then they move on to bigger and bigger numbers—then multiplication and division. It seems that there's always more to learn. When do we get it all? When we graduate from high school or receive that college diploma? No—we keep learning all of our lives. There are always more facts to know and more skills to master.

Why do we think our walk with God is any different? I'm afraid that sometimes we kick back thinking that we're finished simply because we are familiar with some Bible stories, can quote a few verses, and attend church regularly. Whenever such a thought crosses our minds, let's hear our Heavenly Teacher remind us that although we've done well in learning those ABCs, it's time to move on to deeper things. We may have mastered the addition of Christianity, but it's time to progress to spiritual algebra.

There will always be more to discover about God, who He is, and His will for us. There is more to be learned in mastering the skills of studying the Bible, praying, having right relationships with people, sharing our faith, and ministering to others. The apostle Paul was a good teacher. He commended the Thessalonian Christians for their love, but then encourages them to "increase more and more" (I Thessalonians 4:9–10). No matter how loving we may be, we'll never outlove God. There will always be more people to love, better ways to do it, more ways to express it, and greater sacrifices we can make in behalf of others.

Paul also commanded these same people to "abound more and more" in how they walk and please God (4:1). There is always more to learn in living in accordance with God's will for us. About the time we start gaining ground in our outward actions, the Lord shows us that our thoughts and attitudes need to be improved as well. Our desires and motives come into play. We find out that doing God's will involves not only what we do but how we do it, why we do it, and much more. There are always going to be greater heights to climb in that journey toward holiness.

So the next time we sense that "know it all" or "got it all" attitude creeping in, let's remind ourselves that there are so many ways we can yet improve in loving people and in living out God's will for our lives.

What step can you take today to go deeper with God?

Today Can Be a Meaningful and Joyful Day

"This is the day the Lord has made; we will rejoice and be glad in it."

– Psalm 118:24

As I finished conducting my business inside the bank, the friendly teller concluded our conversation by saying, "Have a nice weekend." As I walked away from the counter, it suddenly struck me: this was Wednesday—around lunchtime in the middle of the week. Yet she was already wishing me a good weekend. If my brain had worked a little faster, I might have responded by saying, "Thank you. And I also plan to have a good Wednesday, Thursday, and Friday before the weekend arrives."

I realize she was possibly simply repeating a phrase out of habit from her constant interaction with customers. However, maybe like so many people these days, she was already focused on the upcoming weekend. Even the local TV news station I often watch has begun to do that with their weather forecast. They call it having the weekend "always in view." Even on Monday morning when they show the forecast, they take a moment to highlight the projected weather for the next weekend.

I understand the tendency to anticipate the weekends, to look forward to the time off work, and to able to involve ourselves in more enjoyable activities. But maybe that says something about our perspective concerning the rest of the week. Maybe it suggests that we view our weekdays as being rather mundane at best, lacking in meaning, purpose, and joy.

As followers of Christ, we have a special day set aside for worship and refreshment. Hopefully we look forward to that time when we gather with other believers for fellowship and inspiration. However, we shouldn't be anticipating Sunday to the point that we miss out on all the opportunities to worship and serve Christ the rest of the week. Every day, even a Monday, can be filled with joyful purpose as we live for the Lord.

There are other special events or experiences we look forward to as Christians—such as the return of Christ and our enjoying the glories of heaven once this life is over. There is a sense in which we should be living while having those future events "always in view." We should be making sure we're spiritually prepared for that time. Likewise we shouldn't forget that we're sojourners in this life and our citizenship lies in a heavenly country.

However, let's not get so focused on what's ahead of us that we miss out on what the Lord wants us to do and experience today. The Bible reminds us, "This is the day the Lord has made; we will rejoice and be glad in it" (Psalm 118:24). This day—today—has been given to us by God. Today can be full of purpose and meaning. Today can be a joyful experience. Today can be a wonderful day to live for God, to serve Him, to love others, to experience His presence, to worship Him, and to enjoy life.

Some of us need to recapture the concept in that Latin phrase, *carpe diem* or "seize the day." No, we don't just live for today with no thought of tomorrow. We do have a wonderful future to anticipate—one which affects how we live now. But at the same time let's make the most of today. Let's seize the opportunities of today. Let's tackle the challenges of today. Let's honor God through what we do and how we live today.

Be thankful for all you have to look forward to as a believer. But at the same time, don't neglect or disparage today. Whether it's a Friday afternoon or a Monday morning, seek to fulfill God's purpose in it. Rejoice and be glad in it.

Rejoice in today. Make the most of its opportunities.

Be Open to Change and Innovation in the Church

"Thus you have made the commandment of God of no effect by your tradition."

– Matthew 15:6

One year around this time in August, we noticed an oddity about one of the large trees on the church property. While most of the tree was sporting its usual green foliage for the middle of summer, the leaves of one small limb were already exhibiting the bright red and orange colors of the autumn season. I've found it not to be uncommon to spot a patch of brown leaves on an otherwise green tree, marking a diseased or broken branch. But this seemed to be a limb that was actually moving forward faster than the rest of the tree, already jumping ahead into the next season.

The Christian church, along with many of its individual members, has been notorious for exhibiting the opposite quality. It's often more like the limb that is just starting to sprout its spring foliage while the rest of the tree is living in late summer or early fall. We tend to be slow to change, to keep up with the latest technology, or to make use of innovative methods. The rest of society seems to be moving forward into the next season while the church appears to be stuck in the past.

One reason for that perception is due to a factor of which the church should not be ashamed nor seek to alter. We are sometimes viewed as being outdated because we still believe in and live by eternal, divine truths.

We still believe certain actions and attitudes are either right or wrong based upon what God has declared, not because of man's ever-changing ideas about those issues. We still hold to some "old-fashioned" principles, while the rest of the world is moving in a different direction. In this case, the church is not being slow to catch on to something new or better—it's refusing to follow society down a harmful and ungodly path.

However in other areas, the church does tend to be guilty of dragging its feet. If I may switch the analogy, we're not quick to jump on the train of change and opportunity when it comes along. I'm not suggesting that we take hold of every fad or trend which temporarily pops up onto the scene. Such a practice can be harmful in itself. But too often we sit around and watch innovations, critique those who do hop aboard, and keep debating whether or not it's a good idea until that train is well down the track. We end up grabbing hold of the rail on the caboose at the last moment, or more often we're the ones pumping the arm on the handcar trying to catch up with the train that left us behind. At that point, we're so far behind that others are already boarding a new train of opportunity or change, while we're still trying to catch the old one. By the time we do catch it, it has lost much of its momentum and influence.

Granted, some churches today seem to go overboard in their attempts to be relevant and innovative. However, many of us suffer from an unfounded aversion to change and creativity. Reaching lost souls should be more important to us than maintaining our traditions or staying with what makes us most comfortable. We don't have to walk away from those eternal truths which have formed the foundation of our faith. We should steadfastly refuse to do so. However, we should be willing to embrace different ways of ministering to people if they will be more effective in reaching today's world with the gospel.

We don't always have to be on the "cutting edge," but let's not spend our days chasing trains that have left us behind.

In what ways do you or your church need to change in order to better fulfill God's purposes for you? Act on it before you miss the opportunity.

Consider the Consequences of Your Actions

"Your sins have withheld good from you."
– Jeremiah 5:25

My dad was having surgery at the hospital in order to replace his pacemaker. Not long after my mom, sister, and I had settled into the waiting room, I heard one of the staff members mention the words "lockdown" and "drill." We also began to notice how quiet the hallway of this normally-busy medical facility had become. We soon discovered that someone had called in a bomb threat to the hospital. No one was being allowed to enter or exit the buildings. And my dad's procedure was put on hold until the "all-clear" signal was given, which didn't occur until three hours later.

I have no idea who would have made such a call or why. Maybe it was just a prank perpetrated by someone who thought it would be funny. Or possibly it was a more sinister act of vengeance from a person who was upset with this particular hospital. I don't know. But I do know that this one foolish act had a ripple effect that impacted a great number of people.

Individuals, including doctors who had responsibilities to carry out, couldn't leave or enter the hospital. A huge traffic jam ensued on the surrounding streets. Police and hospital personnel were having to go around looking for suspicious items instead of fulfilling their normal duties. It wasn't just a matter of inconveniencing some people, but lives of patients could have been put at risk as their procedures were postponed. I wonder if the person who made that threatening call thought about all those repercussions.

Do we consider the consequences of our actions, especially when facing a temptation to do something we know would not be pleasing to the Lord? Maybe we don't take sin seriously enough. It not only impacts our relationship with God, but it also sets into motion a ripple effect that carries over into many areas of our lives as well as the lives of others. Regardless of whether we were just seeking to have a little fun or were intentionally rebelling against our Father's will, such actions can have wide-ranging consequences.

Unconfessed sin can put our spiritual lives in lockdown, hindering us from moving forward in following and serving the Lord. It's only as we confess and repent of those actions that God gives us the "all-clear" to progress in our walk with Him.

Additionally, I don't think we often consider the negative impact those actions have on those around us. We all know what the act of adultery can do to a family. We've seen how an angry word can hurt people. But do we also realize that other sins, even those hidden within the recesses of our hearts and minds, can cause significant ripples which spread out to affect other people? When your heart and life isn't in tune with God, it not only opens the door for you doing and saying things which can have a hurtful influence on others, but you're also not being the positive influence you could be. It's not just about what that sin is making you do, but also what it's keeping you from doing. You're not being the light, the witness, the good ambassador for Christ as effectively as you could be. And others are missing out. Souls might even be put at risk.

Don't take sin lightly. That one little wrong act or attitude might not seem like a big deal, but it can have long tentacles which can reach into other areas of your life as well as into the lives of the people around you.

Lord, forgive me for those times when I didn't consider the consequences of my wrong actions. Help me not to take lightly any sin in my life.

It's Wise to Listen to the Counsel of God

"The way of a fool is right in his own eyes, but he who heeds counsel is wise."

– Proverbs 12:15

One time we had a large tree next to our church removed. I had been pastor of this congregation long enough to remember when the building was being constructed and the decision which was made at that time about this particular tree. We had tried to keep as many trees on our property as possible, not wanting to be one of those owners who clear-cuts the land before making use of it. But this one small oak was fairly close to the porch leading into our sanctuary. If I recall correctly, our builder suggested we might want to take it down. He thought it would probably cause problems years down the road. But we decided to let it stay.

The builder was right. I don't think any of us regret the choice we made at the time. We had enjoyed that tree and its shade for over twenty years. But the builder had a better vision of how big that tree would eventually get and the issues it would raise. It started with frequently clogged gutters, but in recent years had led to limbs rubbing against the roof, protruding toward the steeple, and obstructing the view of the front of the building.

Sometimes other people can see things we can't in certain situations. The Bible says, "The way of a fool is right in his own eyes, but he who heeds counsel is wise" (Proverbs 12:15). Other people's ideas may not always be better than our own, but we shouldn't easily dismiss or disregard the advice of others. Most of us have a tendency to think we know best, especially when it comes to how we live our lives. But sometimes we're not as smart as we think. We can be blinded by our own desires and biases. And other people may have experienced similar circumstances from which they've gained wisdom. "Where there is no counsel, the people fall; but in the multitude of counselors there is safety" (Proverbs 11:14).

While the Bible recommends the idea of considering counsel from other people, how much more should we take into account the counsel of God. He can really see the big picture. He knows how the choice we make today will eventually affect us and others. He can see exactly how big that matter is going to grow and how it will affect our lives next month, ten years from now, and even how it might affect our children and future generations.

Yet how quickly some of us dismiss what God says as being irrelevant and outdated. Or we think for some reason we're the exception to the general rule God has given. "Well, maybe that's true for most people, but my situation is different."

How many problems have sprung up in our lives because we failed to listen to the wise counsel of our Creator? We knew what the Bible said about that issue, but we thought we knew better. We felt the quiet nudging of the Holy Spirit, but we brushed it off and went ahead and did what we wanted to do. And sooner or later, we reaped the consequences of our actions. It may have taken years for the problems to fully blossom—and the consequences may not be fully evident this side of eternity. But now, or one day in the future, we will look back and wish we had listened to God and done things His way.

What is God saying to you today? Listen to His all-wise counsel. It will save you from a lot of headaches down the road.

Be open to the advice of others. And especially pay attention to what God says.

ALWAYS KEEP IN MIND THAT YOU ARE REPRESENTING JESUS

"Now then, we are ambassadors for Christ, as though God were pleading through us."

– II CORINTHIANS 5:20

A few years ago the association to which our church belongs did a rather strange thing—they elected me as their executive director. Some people have suggested that I did an even crazier thing accepting that role in addition to my current pastoral responsibilities. However, I've enjoyed serving in this capacity in spite of the busyness it has added to my life.

Shortly after that election, I took my first road trip to officially represent the association at a church. I had been invited to participate in the celebration of the pastor's recent ordination as well as to deliver the message in the morning service. As I did so, I was somewhat overcome by the sense that I was not there just for myself, or even as a guest minister, but as an emissary of the association. Part of my purpose was to faithfully represent that organization through my words and actions, reflecting its spirit of support and helpfulness. I felt a desire and responsibility to seek to be a blessing to that church, as well as to leave a positive impression of our association.

As believers, we should have a similar sense of purpose and mission. We are responsible to represent Jesus wherever we go. The Bible declares that we are ambassadors for Christ (II Corinthians 5:20), therefore our words and actions should reflect His character. We should seek to faithfully represent Him in such a way that others will want to know Him too.

Around that same time, I was traveling down the road when I noticed the driver in front of me getting impatient with the car ahead of him. He was making various gestures expressing his frustration and even began to drive somewhat aggressively. I couldn't see any cause for his overwhelming displeasure other than traffic moving slower than what he wanted. Then as I looked down at his license plate, my heart sank. It was one on which the owner had chosen to place the sticker which read "In God We Trust."

I thought about what a poor representative this driver was being of someone who was relying on God. If an unbeliever had witnessed his behavior, what would that person have thought about the God whom this man professed to trust?

No doubt we would all have to confess to having been less than stellar representatives of Jesus at times. Under pressure we may have angrily lashed out at someone. While experiencing hardships we may have exhibited a lack of faith. When in a hurry we may have ignored someone in need. And the list could go on.

Maybe we should try to live each day with a greater sense that we are representing Jesus wherever we are and with whomever we come in contact. What I do today isn't just about me. Driving down the road isn't simply about me trying to get somewhere as quickly as I can. Interacting with that server at the restaurant isn't just about me getting my food the way I want it. My interactions with people on the phone and on the computer aren't only about me and my agenda.

I'm an ambassador for Christ. That means I need to think about His purposes and plans. I need to speak, act, and treat people the way that would please Him. I need to be the kind of person whose life will draw others to my Savior, not turn people off from Him.

If you're a believer, you are an ambassador for Jesus whether you like it or not. Others are watching you. So let's each seek to be someone who faithfully represents our Lord.

As you go about your activities today, intentionally remind yourself that you are Christ's ambassador and seek to represent Him well.

DARE TO BELIEVE JESUS CAN DO SOMETHING GREAT

"'Do you believe that I am able to do this?' They said to Him, 'Yes, Lord.'"

– MATTHEW 9:28

It was Irish dramatist George Bernard Shaw who is credited with originally saying these inspirational words: "Some men see things as they are and say 'Why?' I dream things that never were and say 'Why not?'" I've decided that I need to become more of a "Why not?" kind of a person. I should look less at the downside of problems and focus more on the possibilities of what Jesus can do in those situations.

After a certain discovery I made a few years ago, I've concluded it's only right that I of all people should be that kind of an individual. It took me over fifty years to recognize it, but it's right there in my name. Tony spelled backwards is "Y-not." OK, maybe that's stretching things a little, but does your name spelled backwards result in anything interesting? But maybe the fact that you have to turn my name around in order to find that concept is an indication that it's not something that comes naturally for me. I'm going to have to change a little in order to fit the description.

The Bible tells us about a couple of blind men who made such a change (Matthew 9:27–31). I imagine they had often thought of their situation, their disability, their blindness, and wondered "Why?" Why did such blindness overtake them? Why did their dreams of what they had planned to do in life get dashed to the ground and broken? Why were they relegated in that time and culture to standing on street corners begging others for help?

But then Jesus came by. Apparently they had heard about Him because they called out to Him using the title "Son of David," a designation commonly used in reference to the Messiah. They had probably heard about how Jesus had healed others of various physical ailments. So now they dreamed of a new possibility—the prospect of having their sight restored. And they dared to say "Why not?" They believed that Jesus could do something great in their lives.

There may be situations in our lives which we've often pondered, asking that question "Why?" "Why did this happen?" "Why did it happen to me?" Or we may have concerns about our families, our nation, or simply about trying to live for God in this ungodly world in which we find ourselves in today which engender such questions. We can either sit around discouraged and frustrated as we ask "Why?" or we can do as those blind men. We can cry out to Jesus, follow Him, and put our trust in the One for whom nothing is impossible. We can dream of what He might want to do in that situation and say, "Why not?"

Jesus asked those blind men, "Do you believe that I am able to do this?" To their credit, they responded, "Yes, Lord." Then Jesus said, "According to your faith let it be to you." And then their eyes were opened. Jesus is the One who can do great things in our particular situations too. But it's our faith that opens the door for Him to work.

So as we deal with difficulties, challenges, and opportunities today or in the future, let's face them with faith in Jesus as Someone who is able to do great things. Let's confront them with a "why not?" attitude. Let's seek His will with the door wide open to all the possibilities. And then let's dare to say, "Yes, Lord, I believe You can do it."

I'm going to try to be more like that. Y-not you?

Face today's challenges with a "why not" attitude.

Some Things Are Clearly Right or Wrong

"Abhor what is evil. Cling to what is good."
– Romans 12:9

One of our daughters used to teach second graders at a Christian school. During one class session, they were discussing a combination of nutrition and creation. They talked about how God made good foods for us to eat. The class delved into such subjects as the benefits of natural sugars versus the processed sweeteners man has made and often adds to the items he eats. Of course, they also discussed the principle of moderation when it comes to eating all kinds of food. At one point the textbook showed a picture of a variety of fruits on one page and a picture of a bowl of ice cream on the opposite page. My daughter noted how God had made the fruit with its natural nutrients that are good for us. Then she proceeded to point to the other image and ask, "And who made the ice cream?" She called upon one boy whose arm had quickly shot up in the air. That student enthusiastically answered, "Satan!"

My daughter was amused by that unexpected answer, although she could imagine her students returning home that day reporting to their parents that the teacher had declared ice cream to be the devil's creation. So she quickly explained that it was manmade, which she discovered was the answer most of the other students had been ready to give.

As for me, being the ice cream lover which I am, I am rather appalled at the thought of attributing that treat to the devil. However, I do admire the first student's response as revealing his young and still-developing understanding that some things are clearly defined as being either good or evil. If fruit is good, God must have made it. And if ice cream isn't so good for us, then Satan must have been its creator.

I'm afraid that too many people are losing any sense of a clear demarcation between right and wrong. Everything is viewed as relative. What may be right in one situation might be considered wrong in another. What may be good for one person might be evil for someone else. So-called "black and white" issues are becoming harder and harder to pinpoint in the eyes of a vast portion of our society. Fewer people are willing to label anything as absolutely right or as absolutely wrong. They especially avoid calling anything a sin.

On the other hand, as that second grader gets older, he will no doubt discover that there are also gray areas in life—matters in which the boundaries between right and wrong, good and evil are not so plainly drawn. While there are things that can be clearly labeled as one or the other, as being from God or being from Satan, there are other things in which what's right and wrong is not so easily discerned. Therefore we also have to be careful not to dogmatically declare things to be good or evil which may fit more in the gray areas of personal conviction and individual preferences.

So how do we discern the difference between the "black and white" and the gray areas? I believe we have to look to God's Word as our primary guide. And we must accept its declarations as truth regardless of our feelings about the matter and regardless of what society currently deems to be acceptable. If God says something is sin, we had best believe it. And if He doesn't, then we ought to be very careful about making that judgment on our own.

Now, if you don't mind, I think this preacher is going to saunter into the kitchen to get a little bowl of that stuff the devil supposedly made— although it sure tastes heavenly to me.

Are you looking to God's Word as your guide in discerning what is right and what is wrong?

Don't Lose Heart over Physical Limitations

"But we have this treasure in earthen vessels that the excellence of the power may be of God and not of us."

– II Corinthians 4:7

It was so frustrating! I was trying to accomplish a needed job at the church, only to run into one roadblock after another. The grass was getting high and I knew that the person who normally does the mowing was busy. So I thought I could help him out. When I finally found a time I could set aside for that purpose, I went out to crank the mower only to have it slowly turn over once and then remain silent. The battery was dead and I had no means for jumping it off.

A few days later I was able to return to the task with jumper cables in hand. I got the mower running, but had cut only a couple of small sections of the yard when a belt came off. Not being very mechanical, I couldn't overcome that roadblock by myself either. Later, even after someone else put the belt back on and started mowing, before he could finish the job a different belt broke. The next day, with a new belt in place, the job finally got accomplished.

It's frustrating when you want to do something but can't—when you schedule your time, change into work clothes, and make other preparations only to have a mechanical breakdown. Sometimes we face similar frustrations as we try to serve the Lord and the church in other ways. It's not just mowers or other machinery or electronics that let us down. At times it's our own bodies. We want to serve, but we find that our batteries just don't provide us with the energy we once had. And it seems that some part of our physical machinery is always groaning, aching, or breaking, resulting in frequent trips to the medical mechanic for repairs. We may be able to buy a new mower, but we're basically stuck with this body we've been given.

When facing such frustrations, there are several factors we ought to remember. Of course, there's the obvious truth that God can heal our bodies and provide strength and enablement for the tasks He calls us to do. But beyond that, I found several other truths in a section of scripture in which Paul repeatedly encourages some Christians not to get frustrated and lose heart.

First of all, he tells us that "we have this treasure in earthen vessels, that the excellence of the power may be of God and not of us" (II Corinthians 4:7). Those bodily limitations remind us of our inadequacies to do these God-given tasks on our own. They point us, as well as other people, to the recognition that anything we accomplish is due to the Lord and His power. Therefore He deserves the credit and praise, not us.

Secondly, Paul declares that "even though our outward man is perishing, yet the inward man is being renewed day by day" (II Corinthians 4:16). Our bodies may be starting to get a little rusty and dented, but our motors can still be running smoothly. The anointing and power of the Holy Spirit that comes from someone walking close to the Lord can more than make up for any hindrances resulting from our physical maladies.

Finally Paul reminds us that "if our earthly house, this tent, is destroyed, we have a building from God, a house not made with hands, eternal in the heavens" (II Corinthians 5:1). We can comfort ourselves in the knowledge that although this physical body is faltering, we can look forward to something better in eternity. That heavenly housing for our souls will be free of these earthly limitations and hindrances, and will be ours permanently.

So let's not get frustrated and lose heart when our bodies fail us as we try to serve the Lord. Let's have faith that in our weakness, God can show Himself to be strong and can still use us for His purposes.

Are you frustrated over a physical limitation? Trust God to show His strength and glory in it.

LET'S LOOK AT TIME
IN LIGHT OF ETERNITY

"So teach us to number our days, that we may gain a heart of wisdom."

– PSALM 90:12

It was Buzz Lightyear in the Disney movie *Toy Story* who proclaimed as his motto, "to infinity and beyond." That phrase could also be a good description of our eternal God. In a psalm attributed to Moses, it declares, "Even from everlasting to everlasting, You are God" (Psalm 90:2). If you go as far back as you can into history and then keep going, God is there. If you let your imagination look ahead into the future as far as you possibly can and then beyond that, God is there. Whether in reference to the past or the future, God truly is "to infinity and beyond."

He was the same loving, powerful, merciful, holy God one billion years ago as He is today. And He will be the same trillions of years into the future. (If you have a hard time grasping that concept of trillions, just think about all the money our government has been spending in recent years.) This truth about God's eternal nature should give us a better perspective of time, both in relation to God and to ourselves.

I don't have to tell you that we live in a busy world in which we're often hurrying around and trying to meet deadlines. Sometimes we try to fit God into that mold or fashion Him into our image. However we've got to remember that God is beyond time. He is never in any hurry. Neither does He have to meet any deadlines.

There are times when we try to rush God or wonder why He's not doing things as quickly as we think they should be done. But we need to remember who God is and how He views time. We need to trust His timetable. In that same psalm it shows us how differently God looks at time. It says, "For a thousand years in Your sight are like yesterday when it is past" (Psalm 90:4). Four weeks without a job and without a paycheck coming in may seem like an eternity to us, but it's just a fraction of a second to the everlasting God. Thirty years without finding a marriage partner can seem like forever, but to God it's nothing. He sees the bigger picture, the right time to bring two people together, or maybe even an alternative purpose and plan for your life altogether. Instead of attempting to hurry God and give Him deadlines, let's trust Him, resting in the knowledge that He is working everything out in His time and in His way.

In verse 12 of that psalm, it says, "So teach us to number our days, that we may gain a heart of wisdom." There is wisdom in keeping a proper view of time and eternity, especially in relation to our own lives. It's helpful to remember that we are here on this earth for a relatively short span of time, especially when compared to eternity and an everlasting God.

One of the most foolish things we can do is to live strictly for the here and now, rather than living with eternity in mind. We are not being wise if we fail to make preparation for the unending existence that awaits us once our few years here are gone.

We can't number our days by marking them off on a calendar, counting down until the day we die. We don't know exactly when that will be, But we can keep in mind how short our time here is and how long eternity is going to be. And we can get our priorities lined up accordingly. Let's make sure that we're ready to live with God "to infinity and beyond."

Are your priorities in line with a proper view of time and eternity?

God's Presence and Purpose Dispel Loneliness

"I will not leave you nor forsake you."

– Joshua 1: 5

I remember when my wife and I became empty nesters. At first the house seemed too quiet. However, I soon began to recognize and enjoy some of the benefits of the new arrangement, such as consistently getting to bed at a decent time rather than occasionally waiting up for someone to come home after a late night at work or having been out with friends. I've also noticed reductions in the grocery bill and the amount of trash produced by our household.

I thought I was doing well handling the new situation until my wife had to go out of town for a few days. That was when I really began to feel alone. It wasn't just the quietness, but a coinciding struggle over maintaining a sense of purpose. Why cook a meal just for me? Is there still good reason for me to get my work done early in the day so that I have evenings free for the family? After years of my children and their activities taking up much of my time and attention, what constitutes meaningful activity for my life now?

This experience has given me greater appreciation and concern for those who find themselves in some degree of aloneness. Granted, the Bible reminds us that no one who is trusting Jesus as their Savior is ever alone. The Lord has promised always to be with us. And in those times of solitude, we need to encourage ourselves with the assurance of divine companionship. However, the answer for loneliness goes beyond simply the recognition of God's presence with us, as wonderful as that truth is. There must also be a sense of His purpose in our lives.

When children move out, a spouse dies, retirement comes, or other such significant changes occur in life, it often requires a refocusing on the question of why we're here and what it is that God has for us to do. It may mean shifting gears in some aspects of our lives. There are those who choose to respond by some degree of isolating themselves or by idling their time away in front of a television. But others wisely see an opportunity to accomplish things that they couldn't previously because of those work or family restraints. Now they can get some of those special projects around the house completed. They can read and study the Bible more thoroughly or spend more time in prayer. They can cultivate a closer relationship with their Heavenly Father. They can volunteer to help out at church or in other good community organizations.

A nursing home is often a setting ripe for loneliness. Residents have left their own homes, may have less contact with family and friends, and are usually elderly or otherwise limited by physical ailments. I often try to encourage the people I know in those situations with the reminder that they are not alone—that God is with them. But the ones who truly seem to overcome the enemy of loneliness are those who find purpose in their lives within that setting. I think of a dear lady who goes around to the rooms of bedridden fellow patients to read to them. Or another friend who finds fulfillment as other residents or staff members come to her to share their concerns and to ask her to pray for them. Such individuals know not only that God is with them, but that He still has a reason for them being here.

Loneliness can present some real temptations, among which are discouragement, frivolous use of time, and isolation. But those lonely circumstances can also present us with new opportunities to draw close to God and to find fresh purpose in our lives. If you feel alone, remember that God is with you and He has something meaningful for you to do.

When you're feeling lonely, look for fresh purpose from the Lord.

LET'S MAKE SURE GOD IS OUR BUILDING PROJECT FOREMAN

"Unless the Lord builds the house, they labor in vain who build it."
– PSALM 127:1

When my grandson went to his open house for preschool, I'm told that he was acting uncharacteristically shy until he found some cardboard blocks and started building something with them. Many of us also began early in our lives to enjoy the art of building. When I was a small child, I had some wooden blocks with letters and numbers painted on the sides as my primary construction materials. Of course, we also had tinker toys for more complex projects. And don't forget those old Lincoln logs with which you could try to build a house or cabin. At some point during my youth, a new option became popular—something called Legos. And we all know how those blossomed. All those objects from simple square blocks to more versatile Legos fulfilled that desire within us to build.

I believe many of us are still trying to build today—and not just those who are in the construction business. We're trying to build a life for ourselves, along with everything we picture as being included in it. We may be seeking to build a career and financial stability. Some might be focused on building a family with a marriage, kids, and a comfortable home. Some may be looking to build a church, ministry, or some other project for God.

Whatever it is we're building, we need to hear and recognize the truth of Psalm 127:1—"Unless the Lord builds the house, they labor in vain who build it." There may be nothing wrong with what we are attempting to build, but are we doing it God's way? Can we affirm that the Lord is with us? Are we building what He wants us to build and according to His instructions? Are we paying attention to whether He gives us the green light to move ahead or puts up a stop sign in front of us?

I'm concerned that families, careers, houses, and churches are being built without God's presence, power, and blessing. Sometimes this is due to people building in their own strength rather than depending on God. Those who are smart, talented, capable, and gifted need to especially guard against that temptation.

We need to follow the example of Nehemiah in the Bible. He was a very skilled leader. When he led the rebuilding of the walls of Jerusalem, he showed how to go about a building project. He's an example of how to survey a situation, organize people, work hard to get the job done, and how to overcome obstacles and opposition. But Nehemiah didn't attempt to do it in his own strength. His words and actions, especially his frequent prayers, reflected the fact that he was leaning upon God. In the book that bears his name, in the middle of the narrative, Nehemiah suddenly whispers a prayer or cries out to God for help.

As Labor Day approaches, it reminds us of the value of hard work. Yet this psalm balances that truth with the reminder that no matter how hard you work at something, it can be fruitless if God's not in it. Verse 3 suggests that you can get up early, stay up late, sacrifice meals, and put much time and effort into whatever you're building, but all that labor is vain if your life, career, family, church, or ministry is empty of God's glory, power, and blessing.

What are you building today? Let's make sure that our actions and attitudes reflect a spirit of dependence on God. Let's interrupt the narrative of our building project with regular prayers to God for help, strength, and wisdom—because unless the Lord builds the house, all our efforts are in vain.

Are you letting God be in charge of your building project?

ORDINARY PEOPLE CAN BE EFFECTIVE RESCUERS

"Now when they saw the boldness of Peter and John, and perceived
that they were uneducated and untrained men, they marveled."

– ACTS 4:13

When some devastating floods hit Texas, one of the headline stories was how ordinary people became heroes as they joined the rescue effort. Along with the professional first responders who were overwhelmed by the great need, average citizens, especially those with boats, made a significant impact in helping many people make their way to safety. They weren't paid for doing this. They hadn't undergone extensive training, yet they responded to this urgent need. They used the means and abilities at their disposal to rescue people from danger.

Maybe we as followers of Christ need to recapture that spirit. It can be easy to fall into the mindset of letting the professionals help those in the world with spiritual needs. We encounter those folks who are being engulfed by the rising waters of a life lived apart from God—flooded by guilt, meaninglessness, fear, and all the other effects of sin which rain down on their lives. We know they're in peril of being swept away at any time into an eternity without hope and without God. What do we do? We might tell them how great our pastor is. We might invite them to church where hopefully the experts can take over and do the job of saving them. But do we ever consider that maybe God has put us there to be the rescuers?

Maybe we raise our objections at that point: "But I'm not very good at doing that. I might not do it right. I might make some mistakes, I might forget one of the steps they taught me in our church's evangelism class. There are others who could do it so much better." And yet you're the one there with the boat and the opportunity. And the person you're encountering desperately needs to be rescued.

God specializes in using ordinary people to do His work. When we think of the outreach of the early church in the book of Acts, we tend to think of the apostles as being the professionals. But they didn't start out that way. When the religious leaders first encountered these guys who were out boldly proclaiming the gospel and rescuing souls from spiritual danger, they marveled at the fact that these were uneducated and untrained men (Acts 4:13). They hadn't gone through seminary or the expected formal training of that day. They were just some guys out in a boat. But they were being effective in saving people.

When I was in college, I sometimes worshiped at a rather large church. I remember a couple of occasions when they would be stressing the need for personal evangelism and would bring up to the platform one of their members to share about his successful experiences in such spiritual rescues. This particular person had a great passion for those who needed Christ, along with quite an effective track record. Who was he? The church janitor. He was just an ordinary guy. He wasn't one of the best-dressed or most articulate members of the church. He wasn't the church's paid pastor of evangelism. However, he saw people around him in need and he helped rescue them. He became their hero.

What about you and me? If you've experienced the saving grace of God and have had your life changed by Christ, you've got a boat. You've got a testimony and the means to help others find what you've found. No doubt there are people around you who are caught up in the flood of sin and selfishness, along with all its muddy debris in their lives. Let's be willing to reach out to those who need the Lord. Ordinary people can often make the best rescuers.

Who has God put in your pathway who needs to be rescued?

Loving Those Who Hurt You

"Beloved, do not avenge yourselves, but rather give place to wrath."
– Romans 12:19

Did you know grasshoppers can bite? I spotted a rather large specimen of that insect in my garage one time. It wasn't moving well for some reason. I didn't know if it was injured or if it was simply being hampered by what appeared to be some cobwebs or other debris stuck to its legs. So I attempted to help by removing that impediment. However as I was completing that task, the grasshopper turned and bit my finger. It didn't bring blood, but I was surprised at the rather painful pinch the creature delivered.

While I didn't appreciate its rude reaction to my good deed, I still made sure to relocate the grasshopper to a spot outside the garage and away from the pathway of my car. I didn't give it much further thought until a day later. At that time I noticed what remained of that insect not far from where I had left it. It had wandered back into the travel lane of my car and I had unknowingly run over it. I'll admit I didn't shed any tears over its demise. As I thought about the pain it had inflicted on my finger, part of me felt that it had gotten what it deserved. I even thought of a fitting epitaph for the little guy: *Thus it happens to the grasshopper who bites the finger of a preacher.*

We've all been bitten at times. We've been hurt by other people, maybe even by those we thought were incapable or unwilling to ever do so. Maybe it was someone to whom we had lent a helping hand. In some cases we considered them friends, which caused the bite to hurt even worse. You can hear the pain in David's words when he was praying about enemies who were out to do him harm, mentioning that one of them was his "own familiar friend in whom I trusted, who ate my bread" (Psalm 41:9). Jesus referred to the same scripture when He informed His disciples that one of them would betray Him, possibly expressing His own heartache over Judas' actions.

It's tempting to want to strike back when others hurt us, or at least to hold back our kindness toward that person. However, the Bible reminds us to "repay no one evil for evil...do not avenge yourselves, but rather give place to wrath; for it is written, 'Vengeance is Mine, I will repay,' says the Lord" (Romans 12:17–19). We leave that person in God's hands, as well as any retribution. And if God sees fit to inflict payback at some point, we shouldn't rejoice over it. This isn't a grasshopper—it's a valuable soul for whom Christ died.

Jesus took it further than just the command not to seek revenge. He instructed us, "Love your enemies, bless those who curse you, do good to those who hate you, and pray for those who spitefully use you and persecute you" (Matthew 5:44). Even when others hurt us, we should keep making an effort to show them love and kindness. Maybe they don't deserve it. But neither did we when God showed His mercy and grace to us.

Having a loving spirit toward those who hurt us goes against our nature. That's why we need the Lord's help to be able to follow His challenging directions in such situations. Let's pray for God to fill our hearts with His Spirit and with His kind of love.

As followers of Christ in today's world, we're probably going to get bit even more often in the days ahead. When it happens, let's seek God's grace to react in such a way that will identify us with our gracious and loving Lord.

By whom have you been "bitten"? How can you resist the temptation for vengeance and instead show love for that person?

STEP UP AGAIN TO
THE BATTLEFRONT

"This charge I commit to you...that by them you may wage the good warfare"

– I TIMOTHY 1:18

Recently I tuned in to a classic movie channel in time to catch the second half of what is generally considered to be one of the greatest films ever made. As you try to figure out which movie I'm referring to, no doubt your mind will *round up the usual suspects*, everything from *Gone with the Wind* to *The Wizard of Oz*. However, in this case I'm talking about *Casablanca*.

As you hopefully know, it's a story about a man who had once fought for noble causes, but after being deeply hurt by someone he loved, he had retreated into a form of personal isolationism. In the midst of World War II, he tried to remain completely neutral as he ran an American café in the North African city of Casablanca. He had become something of a cynic, not fighting for anything anymore. He occasionally expressed his attitude of self-protection by declaring, "I stick my neck out for nobody."

If we're not careful, *as time goes by* many of us can retreat into a similar state of mind. As a result of being hurt, disappointed, or simply worn out, we try to pull ourselves away from the battles raging in our day. This condition may manifest itself in various ways. Maybe we haven't forsaken our faith, but we tell ourselves it's a personal matter and try to keep a low profile when it comes to the subject of religion. Or we attempt to be neutral when it comes to some of these current societal debates over controversial moral issues. Or we simply refuse to get heavily involved in church activities, opting to take a backseat merely as an interested observer rather than a committed participant.

It can take many forms, but in some way we've chosen to step back from the forefront of the battle. We'll let others take the hurtful blows. We'll let others put forth the backbreaking effort. We'll let others take the risks. We'll let others agonize in prayer over the burdens they carry. We'll just safely and comfortably sit back and watch what happens.

Jesus didn't call His followers to such a noncommitted life. He said that we must be willing to bear our crosses for Him. He called us to a life, witness, and mission which would often result in our being opposed and hated. The Bible often reminds us that we are involved in a spiritual war and we should conduct ourselves as good soldiers of Christ.

By the end of *Casablanca*, the main character had been reminded that there are people and causes worth fighting for. He was moved by love and inspired by the example of others to rejoin the battle. As someone said in response to his eventual courageous actions, "Welcome back to the fight."

Maybe some of us need to rejoin the battle today. In spite of having been hurt, discouraged, or weary from past experiences, we need to be reminded that there are souls for whom we should stick our necks out and a divine cause worth fighting for. Some of us need to recommit ourselves to getting involved again in the work of Christ in the world. No, it isn't easy. It will be painful and tiresome at times—but it's worth it!

Take a stand again for what's right and true regardless of what others think. Volunteer to lead that ministry. Be more of a real warrior in prayer. Burst out of your isolated bubble and hear Christ say, "Welcome back to the fight." And to all who accept that challenge, may I salute you by saying, "*Here's looking at you, kid.*"

In what ways have you withdrawn from the fight? What step do you need to take today to get back into it?

Jesus Can Satisfy Your Thirst

"Whoever drinks of the water that I shall give him will never thirst."
– John 4:14

My grandsons and I went to a local park to walk its circular trail. One of the boys remembered there was a water dispenser at one point along the path. Therefore they decided which direction we should go based on where the water was located. The plan was to walk the trail in such a way that we would end up at the water dispenser ready for a nice refreshing drink as we came near the end of our journey.

It was a nice plan, but like so many of our plans in life, it didn't work out quite the way we thought it would. Several times along the way as we started working up a sweat, one of the boys would longingly wish for us to arrive at that thirst-quenching station. Finally it came within sight. However as the boys ran up to it, they faced nothing but disappointment. First, they saw there were no paper cups to use. However, such a technicality by itself wouldn't necessarily stop some resourceful youngsters from getting a drink. But then when they pushed the button on the dispenser, they discovered there was no water either. Fortunately we knew there was a water fountain in a nearby building, so we eventually were still able to satisfy our desire for something cool to drink.

Have you ever been disappointed when seeking to satisfy your spiritual thirst? We sense a need in our souls that causes us to long for something which will provide peace, meaning, purpose, or some quality we can't exactly put our finger on but which we know is missing from our lives. Someone has described it as a God-shaped void.

There are numerous things in life which look as if they would satisfy our thirst, some which may even advertise themselves as such—wealth, fame, power, and pleasure, just to name a few. However as we finally reach those promised dispensers, they inevitably fail to deliver.

Jesus once claimed that He was a dispenser of living water. He declared, "Whoever drinks of the water that I shall give him will never thirst. But the water that I shall give him will become to him a fountain of water springing up into everlasting life" (John 4:14). Many have come to Jesus looking for the answer to their thirsty soul. And in Him they've found what they were seeking.

There are some who might claim, "Well, I tried Jesus and it didn't work." You may have tried Christianity or a religion. You may have tried going to church. You may have tried some form of spirituality, but did you really try a personal relationship with Christ? It's one thing to learn about a religion, to follow its rules, to participate in its practices, and to officially join as one of its members, but it's another thing to truly put your trust in Christ and to submit your heart and life to Him. I believe those who do so will not be disappointed. Churches may fail us. People who profess to be Christians will let us down. A religious system may not live up to our expectations, but Jesus will not fail us. If we open our hearts to Him in faith, He will satisfy our souls.

If you've been looking for some of these other things in life to quench your thirsty soul, maybe it's time to look to Jesus. Do as the Psalmist suggested: "Oh, taste and see that the Lord is good; blessed is the man who trusts in Him!" (Psalm 34:8). Go ahead. Give Jesus a taste. You won't be disappointed.

Make sure you're not simply delving into religion or spirituality. Take a full, unrestrained drink of the living water of a relationship with Jesus.

Through Christ We Can Live Harmoniously with Those Different from Us

"The wolf also shall dwell with the lamb."
– Isaiah 11:6

One of my daughters has several pets, including a small dog which is part Chihuahua and a young cat about the same size. One day when we were over at her house, I witnessed these two animals playfully interacting with each other. The cat would often initiate the action by swatting at the little dog's tail or reaching out to grab her leg as the canine walked by. The encounter would often escalate into a series of mutual, good-natured sparring and snipping, sometimes culminating in what could only be described as a full-fledged wrestling match. While these sportive incidents are mostly amicable, I'm told there are times when their play gets a little too rough and one or the other can express her displeasure.

While it would be amusing to see two cats or two dogs interacting in such a manner, it's more notable when it's two species who are normally considered to be hostile toward one another. We're more accustomed to dogs chasing cats, cats hissing at dogs, and both biting or clawing with the intent to inflict pain. It's interesting to see examples of what are usually enemies not only getting along or tolerating each other's presence, but actually playing with each other.

The prophet Isaiah described some other members of the animal kingdom surprisingly getting along with each other. "The wolf also shall dwell with the lamb, the leopard shall lie down with the young goat, the calf and the young lion and the fatling together.... The cow and the bear shall graze" (Isaiah 11:6–7).

Some of us may interpret this scripture literally as referring to a time in the future when the nature of animals will be changed in such a way that they will peacefully coexist, such as during the millennial reign of Christ. Others of us can also see in this description a more figurative picture of the Church—how different people, even those who are commonly at odds with one another, can amicably live and serve together as members of the family of God.

We see such a peaceful cohabitation of "cats and dogs" even among the apostles of Jesus. There was Matthew, a man who had been employed by the Romans to collect taxes, serving side-by-side with Simon the Zealot, possibly part of a group who encouraged rebellion against the Romans. And in the book of Acts, we see the normally hostile Jews and Gentiles uniting as members of the one body of Christ.

Is the church today a model of such amicable relationships between those who are often hostile toward one another? Hopefully we experience such peaceful fellowship among our brothers and sisters in Christ. However, I believe the church in general could do a much better job of living out this reality pictured by Isaiah.

In a world that often emphasizes our differences and seeks to divide, the church should represent a contrasting possibility. We should be a witness to the fact that people of different races, cultures, and politics can still harmoniously live together through their mutual faith in Christ. And since we naturally tend to gravitate toward people who are similar to us, we may have to be more intentional in cultivating and exhibiting those more uncommon relationships.

The world needs to see a church where black and white, Republican and Democrat, and any other "dog and cat" relationships you might think of can not only tolerate each other but joyfully live and serve together under the lordship of Christ.

Do we need to let God change us or our attitude in any way in order to accomplish that goal?

A LIFE OF FOLLOWING JESUS
DOESN'T HAVE TO BE BORING

"Then the seventy returned with joy, saying, 'Lord, even the demons are subject to us in Your name.'"

– LUKE 10:17

Road trip! What kind of a picture does that phrase bring to mind? Maybe you think of a family heading out for a week of fun at the beach. Or if you're single, you might think of a wild and crazy adventure with several of your best friends. Whatever the specific situation may be, we tend to envision the concept of a road trip as including some degree of excitement and fun.

What if I told you that I took a road trip one time with three other conservative ministers, two of whom are past retirement age? Some of you might consider the prospect of such a journey to be a nightmare. To be stuck in a car for five hours with such a group would certainly be boring and dull. Think again. Actually I've known some fairly rowdy preachers. Would you believe that before we even had the car loaded, one of those ministers dropped his pants right there in the middle of my driveway? Of course, it wasn't the pants he was wearing at the time, but rather a pair he was carrying on a hanger.

So maybe our group wasn't wild and crazy, but it was a very enjoyable trip. I would even describe it as fun as we ministered at a church, fellowshipped together, and ate some delicious food.

Some people envision the idea of following Jesus in a similar fashion.

They think traveling with Him through life would be too restrictive and dull. Who would be able to have any fun on a road trip with Mr. Pure-and-Holy Himself, as well as the One who will pass final judgment on us one day?

Maybe we should ask His disciples. During those three years of following Jesus when He was on earth, I don't think they were bored. As a matter of fact they seemed to enjoy being able to partner with Jesus in healing the sick and casting out evil spirits. I believe it would've been fun to have gone around filling up those baskets with the leftovers after Jesus had miraculously multiplied the bread and fish. How great it must have been to have seen Jesus raise Lazarus from the dead or to have been on that mountain when Jesus began to glow in His heavenly glory. I'm sure the disciples enjoyed entering Jerusalem with Jesus as the crowds shouted "Hosanna!" And can you imagine being in Peter's sandals, walking on the water without a board or a paddle? Until he got his eyes on the wind and waves, I wouldn't be surprised if he were having fun.

However, don't misunderstand what I'm saying. A life of following Jesus isn't a constant vacation at the beach. It has its share of agonizing Gethsemanes to endure and painful crosses to bear. And there will always be some Pharisees around ready to criticize us for whatever we do. But it's not a life void of excitement and fun.

It may not include all the so-called fun in which the world indulges. But neither do you have to suffer through the hangovers, withdrawals, sexually-transmitted diseases, broken relationships, and other consequences of such activities. As many of us know all too well, the world's kind of fun often comes at a steep price.

Don't resist Jesus' call to follow Him out of fear of missing out on all the fun in life. Taking a road trip with Jesus can be the most rewarding, exciting, and enjoyable experience possible. So put your trust in Him, begin that journey of discipleship, and discover a joy you can't find any other way.

Look for the adventure and fun in walking with Jesus today.

GOD'S INSTRUCTIONS
ARE NOT COMPLICATED

*"But what does the Lord require of you but to do justly, to love
mercy, and to walk humbly with your God?"*

– MICAH 6:8

I remember when my daughter's former bedroom in our house was slowly being transformed into a study for my wife. It provided a quiet space for Cheryl to work as she pursued her further education by taking some online classes. Part of that room makeover involved the purchase of a desk chair. And to my chagrin, Cheryl brought it home in a box emblazoned with one of those stickers reading "some assembly required." As I've previously confessed, I'm far from being the most mechanically-minded person around.

However, as I unpacked the box and looked over its contents, I was pleasantly surprised to discover that this company had prepared its instructions for someone exactly like me. Not only did the paperwork include accurate and detailed pictures showing every step to be taken, but even the bolts and other hardware were enclosed in separate packets. And I don't mean that you had a little bag with twenty of the same kind of bolts in it, some to be used in various steps along the way. No, they had a packet labeled "step one" with just the hardware needed for that initial procedure, and so on throughout the whole process. It was some of the simplest instructions I've ever encountered. Even I would've had a hard time getting confused. And apparently I assembled the chair correctly, because it hasn't fallen apart...so far.

In spite of the way some people view them or try to make them out to be, God's instructions to us are rather simple too. Our Creator knew who was going to be opening up that Bible and reading His directions. He knew that it would be fallible human beings who tended to be rather self-centered, rebellious, and hardheaded. On their own, they would be totally incompetent in spiritual matters and incapable of putting together the kind of holy life that God intended for them.

I didn't have to be an architect or an engineer in order to put that chair together. And you and I don't have to possess seminary degrees in theology in order to live the kind of life that pleases God. It's not about following a bunch of complicated rules that are hard to understand and even more difficult to live by. The prophet Micah narrowed down the Lord's requirements to these: "to do justly, to love mercy, and to walk humbly with your God" (Micah 6:8).

At the risk of oversimplifying matters, I suggest that in light of the rest of scripture, God's instructions are basically summarized in several basic concepts. The first is "believe." Believe in Him and believe what He says. The second concept is "trust." This goes a step further than acknowledging something to be true or factual. We need to actually step out and show that we believe by trusting God to do as He promises. We rely on Him to be our Savior, our Refuge, our Guide, our Strength, and everything else He says He will be to those who follow Him. The third concept is "love." Jesus Himself said that God's law or instructions could be summarized by these commands: to love the Lord with all our heart, soul, mind, and strength; and to love our neighbor as ourselves.

Certainly the picture of the Christian life is full of many more details of how our faith and obedience specifically play out in daily living. But if we're believing in Jesus, trusting in God and His Word, and are loving Him and other people, we're well on our way toward experiencing God assembling the kind of holy life He intended for us. And such a life built according to God's instructions won't easily fall apart.

How are you doing at the basics of believing, trusting, and loving?

LET'S WELCOME GOD'S PRESENCE, NOT RUN FROM IT

"Adam and his wife hid themselves from the presence of the Lord God."

– GENESIS 3:8

Back when our first grandson, Joshua, was little, when he visited us he liked to go outside to see our pets. There was Dorothy, our basset hound, and Chucky, the former stray cat who had taken up residence with us for a number of years. Joshua hadn't learned to say the words "dog" or "cat" at that point, but he would make sounds similar to a dog barking or a cat meowing when he spied those two members of our household. He always expressed his excitement at the prospect of interacting with either one of those animals.

However, our pets had very different reactions when they saw our grandson heading their direction. If our dog heard Joshua's voice or caught a glimpse of him toddling her way, she immediately began to wag her tail. If she was lying in her doghouse, you could hear the loud thumping sound of her tail beating against the sides of that structure. She might have started barking in excited anticipation of his arrival. When he drew near, she would get up as close to him as she could, smell of him, and yearn for him to touch her. She was simply thrilled to have him come out and give her some attention.

But the cat was a different story. Chucky spied Joshua coming toward him and you could see the fear in his eyes. He purposefully started walking off in the other direction. If Joshua continued the pursuit, as he often wanted to do, the cat got panicky and moved a little faster to try to keep out of his reach. As a last resort, he would seek refuge on our deck, knowing that our grandson hadn't infiltrated that safe refuge, at least not to that point. Joshua hadn't ever done anything to the cat to evoke such a response—he hadn't pulled his tail or in some other way hurt the cat. That may be true simply because the cat had never let him close enough to do anything. I don't know if Joshua would have unintentionally inflicted pain on our feline or not, but Chucky didn't even give him the opportunity, sensing danger whenever he got close.

It's interesting to observe two very different reactions to the same person drawing near. Dorothy loved Joshua, while Chucky was afraid of him. It reminds me of how people sometimes react to God's presence. How do we respond when we sense God drawing near to us? Do we enjoy those personal encounters with God? Are we happy to see Him and look forward to the fellowship that we can experience with Him? Do we reach out to Him as He reaches out to us? Or is our reaction more of a fearful one?

We should all have a sense of awe and respect in the presence of the Lord—that "fear of the Lord" attitude which the Bible commends. However, we shouldn't be afraid of getting close to God. If we are, it may be because we're aware that there's something in our heart which isn't right with Him. And we're afraid if God gets close and speaks to us, that He's going to bring up that particular subject again. Maybe we're scared that if God draws near, He might speak to us about doing some things with which we would be uncomfortable. He might insist on changes that run counter to our current plans. We may not mind God being in the neighborhood, but we want to keep Him at a safe distance, just far enough away that His words can't convict us and His touch can't change us.

Let's remember that the only danger God represents is to any sin, selfishness, and other hurtful things in our lives that are contrary to His will for us. He loves us and wants what's best for us. Let's not be afraid of His presence, but rather welcome Him to draw near.

Don't be afraid to draw nearer to the Lord.

Let's Respond to God's Wake-up Call

"But Jonah had gone down into the lowest part of the ship, had lain down, and was fast asleep."

– JONAH 1:5

The two stories in the Bible share some obvious similarities: a boat sailing on the sea; a terrible storm arises; the vessel is in jeopardy of sinking; almost everyone on board is afraid; but one person is fast asleep through it all. In the account recorded in the New Testament, it's Jesus who is found napping while His disciples are terrified that they are about to drown. In the Old Testament story, it's Jonah who is snoozing away in the bottom of the ship.

Regardless of all the common factors on the surface of these accounts, there was a stark difference between the two situations. Jesus was God's own Son who was busy faithfully fulfilling His Father's will for Him. Jonah was God's prophet who was refusing to obey God's call and was attempting to run away from God's presence.

Jesus was a picture of someone experiencing peace in the midst of the storm. We can possess such peace through the storms of life if we know that everything is well with our soul. We can be assured that God is with us and will see us through those turbulent times. But it's another story if we're like Jonah, knowing that we've disobeyed God and are trying to avoid doing His will. If we're sleeping through a storm that God has sent to get our attention—that's not peace. That's a false sense of security.

When someone is running away from God or refusing to do His will, God sometimes allows storms or hard times to come in order to get that person's attention. But too often people are blind to God's efforts, sleeping with a false sense of security. They may deny that the storm has anything to do with them or God. They declare it to be simply Mother Nature or the natural course of life as they curl back up in the bottom of their boat.

Nations can do the same thing. Some of the other Old Testament prophets pointed out how God brought various kinds of storms to Israel—droughts, hunger, enemy attacks—but they still refused to recognize God's hand and weren't willing to turn back to Him.

I wonder sometimes if our nation is in that same boat—Jonah's boat. Many of us know that our country is not where it should be in relation to God. We see our society blatantly accepting and promoting practices that God calls sin. We witness people turning further away from what God says and instead following the dictates of their own hearts. And those who do stand for God's will are being labeled as bigots and people full of hatred.

I'm not one to declare every bad thing that happens as being a judgment from God. But sometimes you wonder if God is trying to wake us up through sending the earthquakes, hurricanes, droughts, wildfires, tornadoes, and other destructive forces we've seemed to increasingly experience in recent times. Whether those events are God's judgment or not, they ought to cause us to wake up, call on God, and turn back to Him. Unfortunately, I haven't seen that happening so far in our nation. Jonah is still sleeping in the bottom of the boat.

Individually, let's pay attention when God tries to send us a wake-up call. And let's pray for our nation that we as a people would arouse from our spiritual slumber, humble ourselves before God, call on Him, and turn from our wicked ways so that He can heal our land.

Are you paying attention to God's wake-up call?

BE A PERSON OF FAITH IN TIMES OF SUFFERING

"Others were tortured, not accepting deliverance, that they might obtain a better resurrection."

– HEBREWS 11:35

Not long ago I received notice of my high school class's fortieth reunion. Forty years? Wow! It's hard to believe. That sounds like a reunion of old folks.

I actually debated on whether or not I wanted to participate in this event. I wasn't part of the "in-crowd" in high school. I wasn't one of the popular athletes or an outgoing "Mr. Personality" or one of the fun-loving partygoers. I didn't fit into any of the social cliques which tend to form among young people in those memorable years. So within the social framework of my graduating class, I could probably best be classified as one of the "others." However, I decided it would still be interesting to attend and see some of those friends and acquaintances from years gone by. And I'm glad to report that it was.

Are you familiar with Hebrews 11 in the Bible? In a sense it's a reunion of a lot of people we meet back in the Old Testament. And we're talking about some big names here—Noah, Abraham, Moses, and David. This chapter emphasizes that the common characteristic which tied them all together was their faith. As they trusted God, He delivered them from tough situations.

However as you get toward the end of this passage of scripture, you run into another group of people we tend to forget about or neglect to mention. They're not named. They're simply referred to as the "others." These people didn't have the great success stories to share about how God gave them victory against an enemy, parted waters so they could escape, or stopped the mouths of lions in order that they not be eaten. No, these folks are described as "destitute, afflicted, tormented"—they suffered, were persecuted, and many of them faced violent deaths (Hebrews 11:35–38).

So why are these "others" included in this chapter which catalogues such great heroes of faith? It's because they belong there. They're part of the class. The Bible testifies that all of these, including the "others," obtained a good testimony through faith (11:39). Instead of experiencing a faith that delivered them from their hardships, they exhibited a faith that enabled them to endure the tough times and the persecution. Their faith was just as real and strong as those who were mentioned earlier. Some of them didn't have to suffer, but it was a consequence of their faithfulness to God and to His Word. They were willing to face adversity rather than turn their backs on God.

The "others" aren't the black sheep of Hebrews 11 whom we should try to hide and not talk about. They're the ones most worthy of being included in this list of people of faith. These were people whom the world despised, hurt, and killed. Yet they're the ones who sacrificed, suffered, and found a faith to help them endure right up to the end. Suffering isn't a dunce cap we wear as believers suggesting that we lack faith or are out of favor with God. Sometimes, especially when it's suffering for our faith, it can be a badge of honor.

If we had our choice, we'd probably prefer to be included in the list of those who experienced great deliverances from God. We don't like to suffer, but sometimes we're faced with the inevitable trials and difficulties of life. Other times we have to suffer as a result of our choosing to stay true to God in the midst of an ungodly world. When those times come, let's pray that God will help us to be one of the "others" who will endure the suffering with a steadfast faith in Him.

Facing some tough times? Be one of the "others" who endures by faith.

HAVE YOU EXPERIENCED
A DEFINING MOMENT
WITH CHRIST?

"And you He made alive, who were dead in trespasses and sins."
– EPHESIANS 2:1

Recently I was reading something I had written years ago. I don't remember the exact situation I was relating, but it made me think, *This must have been before 9/11.* Sometimes a similar thought will pop into my head while watching an old movie. I'm not just referring to the wonderful black and white films, but even some made as recently as the 1980s or 1990s. Maybe it's a scene at an airport or some other location where security is much tighter these days. It reminds me of how many aspects of our lives have changed since that infamous day in September of 2001.

For many in our generation, 9/11 was a defining moment. It altered the way we viewed the world, our enemies, and our safety on our own soil. It significantly changed some of the ways we live our lives. We can see a clear distinction between a pre-9/11 world and the world we have lived in since that day.

There have been other defining moments for generations, nations, and even the entire world. One, of course, is the life of Christ. It was such a defining moment that our calendar was changed to reflect this significant event. Everything in the history of the world is divided into happening either before Christ or after His incarnation.

As individuals, we can also experience such impactful points in time—an event that changes everything. It could be a joyful occurrence, such as a wedding or the birth of a child. Or it could be a tragic event, such as an accident resulting in serious injury or the death of a loved one. We can almost divide the calendar of our lives by that moment—the before and the after.

The Bible indicates that one of the most important defining moments we can experience in life has to do with putting our trust in Jesus as our Savior. The Apostle Paul refers in one place to those "who were dead in trespasses and sins," but whom God made alive together with Christ (see Ephesians 2:1–7). Experiencing such a spiritual rebirth or resurrection can drastically affect the course of our lives here on earth, not to mention the destination of our souls for eternity.

In another letter, Paul wrote about the unrighteous who would not inherit the kingdom of God. He told his readers, "And such were some of you. But you were washed, but you were sanctified, but you were justified in the name of the Lord Jesus and by the Spirit of our God" (I Corinthians 6:11). In other words, they had experienced a defining moment which had changed everything. Their lives could be clearly divided between what they had been and what they were now.

We all need to experience such a transformational moment in our lives. Hopefully we can point to a time, whether or not we can remember the specific day on the calendar, when we put our faith in Jesus and went from being spiritually dead to being spiritually alive. We should know that at some point we have experienced the forgiveness and cleansing that Christ has made available to us.

Such an event divides our lives into a before and after. For some, the difference will be more dramatic than for others. However, for all of us it marks a drastic change in our relationship with God. We go from being lost to being found, from being enemies of God to being friends of God, from being under condemnation to being forgiven, and so much more.

Make sure you've got a defining moment of salvation somewhere in the history of your life. And if you don't, make today that day.

Give God thanks for your defining moment.

FOLLOW GOD'S WAY TO GET THROUGH TODAY'S CHALLENGES

"How shall we escape if we neglect so great a salvation...?"

– HEBREWS 2:3

I remember the first time my wife and I participated in one of those "escape room" adventures. In case you're not familiar with the concept, it's a rather challenging form of entertainment. A group of people get locked in a small room with the mission of finding their way out within the one hour time limit. In conjunction with some storyline, there are various puzzles to be solved and clues to find within the confines of those four walls. You often must come up with the right combination to certain locks or discover hidden keys to open others. You may end up uncovering secret doors to other rooms as you make your way through the maze of mysteries toward the final passageway of escape.

My wife and I faced an additional challenge in our case. Not only was it our first time to try such a venture, but we were the only ones signed up for that time slot. Instead of doing it in the usual manner as a group of up to twelve people, it was just the two of us. We quickly found out the disadvantage of not having more people involved who could be working on various puzzles at the same time. Although we didn't make it all the way to the end within the time limit, we did make good progress. The ones overseeing the activity told us we did very well under the circumstances.

Are you looking for a way of escape? Sometimes we may be looking for ways out of difficult personal situations. Other times we're just trying to find our way through the maze of challenging issues many of us face in today's world. We struggle to get through, looking for some kind of resolution, and believing that somewhere ahead is a door which will open up to a better place.

Some believe the keys to getting there involve some combination of working harder, electing the right leaders, educating people, protesting, or various superficial remedies. However as has been proven throughout history, the underlying issue that keeps getting in the way is the sinful human heart. Unless we deal with that problem, we may make our rooms look better or make our confinement more tolerable, but we're not going to find the way of escape.

The signs are all around us if we'll pay attention and be willing to receive them. One of our problems is that we're ignoring one of the main sources of clues as to how to escape. We're pushing God's Word farther away from our hearts and minds. It lets us know that revival is needed more than merely reform. Repentance is what will get us on the right pathway rather than reeducation. Submission to God will help us find the way rather than a spirit of rebellion against authority. We need God's grace more than we need a greater degree of self-effort.

The good news is that there is a way of escape. Not only is there a better place at the end of the journey, but we would be better off in relation to many of the issues we're struggling with right now if we would be willing to follow God's way. Another bit of good news—we're not having to make this journey alone. Jesus is with us to help us make it through.

The Bible asks, "How shall we escape if we neglect so great a salvation?" (Hebrews 2:3). There is a way out for us, for our nation, and for our world. As individuals and as a society, let's not ignore it or refuse to accept it. Time is running out.

When it comes to the issues you're struggling with today, are you following God's way to get through it?

WATCH OUT FOR SUPERSTITION MIXED IN WITH YOUR FAITH

"Let no one cheat you of your reward, taking delight in false humility and worship of angels, intruding into those things which he has not seen."

— COLOSSIANS 2:18

Occasionally this day will fall on the calendar in such a way as for some people to take special notice—a Friday the thirteenth. Does that fact cause you to look at the day any differently? Do you face life today with a little more fear or caution? Do you find yourself taking special notice of any bad things that happen and chalking them up to the bad luck associated with these infamous days? Or do you simply ignore the date, go about business as usual, or maybe even face it with a determination to go against the flow of superstition and to make it a great day?

I'm reminded of an episode of the *Andy Griffith Show* in which the superstitious nature of Deputy Barney Fife was revealed. However, he steadfastly refused to admit that he possessed such a tendency. He would vehemently declare, "I'm not superstitious! I'm just cautious!" However, it was a caution that caused him to avoid black cats, carry a rabbit's foot, and pass along chain letters, among other such behaviors.

Many of us would probably refuse to classify ourselves as being superstitious people as well. We can see where it doesn't fit in with our claim to be a follower of Christ. We believe God is in control, not some intangible force people call "luck." We recognize that trusting in the Lord to protect us isn't compatible with many of the fear-motivated actions taken by those given to superstition. However, we might be surprised at the number of professing Christians who seek out good luck, who give serious consideration to their daily horoscope, and who pay close attention to bad omens or things like a Friday the thirteenth.

Even though we might not consider ourselves to be someone who falls into that category, we also have to watch out for superstition getting mixed in with our Christian faith and practices. For example, any time we start looking at some physical object as possessing supernatural powers, or using it almost like a magic charm, we should realize that we are straying closer to pagan religion and farther away from faith in Christ. And it doesn't just have to be the religious relics, holy water, or statues of saints which we associate with certain sectors of Christianity. We have to be careful or we can treat in a similar fashion those crosses we wear, those Holy Bibles we carry, or those church buildings in which we meet.

Likewise, we can allow some of our good religious practices to degenerate into activities more akin to a magician reciting an incantation and waving his magic wand rather than acts of meaningful worship. We think if we say the right words or perform a certain ritual in a particular way that it will bring the results we want. Even prayer can become more of a superstitious act if we're using it primarily to try to manipulate God into giving us what we want instead of as a means of seeking Him and His will.

Superstition may also be coming into play when we start overemphasizing the role of angelic beings, either the good ones who minister to God's people or the fallen ones who oppose us. Let's not fall into the worship of such beings—a practice the Bible warns against (Colossians 2:18).

So let's be careful not to deny or excuse any kind of superstition that we've allowed to get mixed in with our lives or our faith. Let's confess it and replace it with a steadfast trust in the Lord.

Have you allowed any form of superstition to infiltrate the practice of your faith in Christ?

Your Good Actions Don't Go Unnoticed by God

"Take heed that you do not do your charitable deeds before men, to be seen by them."

— MATTHEW 6:1

I usually carry a Fitbit in my pocket—one of those activity trackers which keeps up with how many steps you take during a day, along with several other related measurements. When my wife and I went to the beach for a few days, I thought I would easily reach my daily goal of steps. After all, in that seaside setting I usually enjoy taking long walks along the sandy shore in the early mornings and late evenings. However, reaching that desired target turned out not to be as easy as I had figured.

There were times when I intentionally left my Fitbit behind, because I was afraid I would forget about it, get in the water, and either lose or damage the small device. Therefore, many of the steps I took those days were not registered on my tracker. So officially I only reached my goal one of the days we were at the beach, although I knew I was being considerably more active than the device was giving me credit for.

Sometimes our good activities don't get credited to us by other people. Our commendable deeds are done when nobody is around, or they simply go unnoticed and unappreciated. Does that mean they don't count? Does the fact that we don't get man's applause, a pat on the back, or a citizenship award mean those good actions aren't worthwhile? Of course not.

Concerning my physical activity, the goal isn't just to register a certain number of steps on my Fitbit. It's to seek to be more active and to enjoy better health as a result. And I was accomplishing that at the beach, whether or not my tracker was recording it.

And our goal in doing good shouldn't be to have our deeds noted and approved by other people. Jesus clearly warned about such a motive. "Take heed that you do not do your charitable deeds before men, to be seen by them. Otherwise you have no reward from your Father in heaven... But when you do a charitable deed, do not let your left hand know what your right hand is doing, that your charitable deed may be in secret; and your Father who sees in secret will Himself reward you openly" (Matthew 6:1–4).

It's not important that we get the credit with others for what we do. What's important is that we know and God knows what we've done. Our deeds may not register with other people, but they always register with God. He will reward us for our faithful actions, sometimes in this life but certainly once we get to heaven.

However, even with that truth in mind, the reward shouldn't be our main motivation. We shouldn't be doing good deeds just to try to chalk up as many points with God as we can. We can never be good enough to be worthy of His love, favor, and blessings.

Our main motivation should come from our love for the Lord, not from what we may get out of it. Through dying on the cross for our sins, He's already done more for us than we could ever repay. Out of love for Him, we should be seeking to be active in serving Him, aiming toward better spiritual health, and pointing others toward Him by letting His light shine through us.

So whatever you do for the Lord and in serving others in His name, remember that it counts. It matters. Maybe nobody knows about it except you and God—but that's enough.

Make sure the attention and approval of others isn't what's driving you. When it seems what you're doing is going unnoticed and unappreciated, remember that God sees it.

GOD WANTS TO DO SOMETHING
NEW IN YOUR LIFE

"And be renewed in the spirit of your mind, and that you put on the new man which was created according to God, in true righteousness and holiness."

– EPHESIANS 4:23–24

My wife and I were traveling to the Gulf coast when we passed near the little town of Newville, Alabama. I got to thinking how it would be hard to live up to such a name. It wouldn't have been a problem when the town was first established, but what about a year later or twenty years later? Does the place look the same as it did when it first took on that name? Or does it look old now?

In order to truly live up to its name, it seems there would need to be something new going on there all the time—new or remodeled buildings, new people, new activities. As we know, new things don't stay new. They quickly become old things. Apple announces a new version of its iPhone, meaning that the former version isn't new anymore. Not just in technology, but in other areas of life, new has to keep changing in order to stay new.

As followers of Christ, we need to seek to live in Newville. There should be new things going on in our relationship with God, as well as in our lives generally as we seek to live for Him. We know there is a newness about us when we first come to put our faith in Christ. The Bible says, "If anyone is in Christ, he is a new creation; old things have passed away; behold, all things have become new" (II Corinthians 5:17).

But is that the extent of our living in Newville? Did the Lord do something new in our lives ten years ago, twenty years ago, or however long it's been, but hasn't done anything new since that time? God's Word also exhorts us to "be renewed in the spirit of your mind, and that you put on the new man which was created according to God, in true righteousness and holiness" (Ephesians 4:23–24). We were made new when we received Christ, but we also need to be renewed on a regular basis in our hearts, minds, and spirits.

Some things don't change. Concerning Jesus Himself, the Bible declares He is "the same yesterday, today, and forever" (Hebrews 13:8). Although Jesus' character remains the same, I don't believe it takes away from the newness associated with Him and with following Him. When Jesus was on earth, I don't think anyone could claim that He was boring or that following Him was a mundane routine.

I can imagine the discussions His disciples may have had in the mornings as they got ready for their day. *I wonder what new thing Jesus is going to do today. I wonder what disease He's going to heal—what kind of evil spirit He's going to cast out—what new teaching He's going to share today.*

We should have a similar sense of expectation as we walk with the Lord. Let's start our days with a similar hope. *I wonder what new thing Jesus is going to do in my life today.*

There's a place for both the old and the new in our lives. One time Jesus referred to the homeowner who took out his box of valued possessions. He pulled out of it treasures both old and new. There are old things we ought to treasure—wonderful answers to prayer, great things we've witnessed God do for us and others, and ways God has used us in the past. But we ought to be pulling out some new treasures too—fresh answers to prayer and new ways God is using us.

If all we've got to pull out are old treasures, then something is missing. What new thing does God want to do in and through you today?

Look for the Lord to do a new thing in your life today.

SEPTEMBER 16

God's Danger Signs Are There for a Reason

"But of the tree of the knowledge of good and evil you shall not eat."
— Genesis 2:17

I'll admit that I'm not someone who often pays close attention to what people wear or their accessories. But recently I couldn't help but notice the distinctive purse and shoulder strap of a lady I encountered. The strap was deep red with big black letters which repeatedly spelled the word "danger." To be honest with you, it reminded me of the tape you might see around a crime scene, construction zone, or other hazard. It wasn't what I would call attractive. The purse also had a short strip on it with the same design. Does anyone know if that is actually some brand of purse?

I wondered why someone would wear something communicating so vividly that idea of danger. It would seem to be telling people to leave her alone. Was she warning people about what she was carrying in that purse? Was she letting people know that she was a tough person or dangerous in some other way, possibly in a provocative way? Or maybe she was simply in a foul mood and was telling people, *You don't want to mess with me today!* I don't know, and frankly I was afraid to ask.

It would be nice if those things which are dangerous to our souls would display such warnings. What if every temptation toward sin was wrapped in red tape with the word "danger" displayed on it? Maybe we'd think twice before heading that direction.

However, those spiritual hazards often appear exactly the opposite, don't they? They come wrapped up in pretty bows and bright colors. They might even carry deceptive signs encouraging people to "Open me" or "Try it you'll like it" or "This is good."

The Bible tries to warn us of the dangers, but we're often guilty of ignoring its declarations of "Caution," "Don't go there," "Run in the other direction," and "This won't end well." We're blinded by the attractiveness and the promises of momentary pleasure. Or even though we see the warning signs, we sometimes are fooled by such thoughts as *It won't hurt anything* or *I can always turn right around and ask forgiveness for it.*

God didn't wrap red danger tape around the tree of the knowledge of good and evil in the Garden of Eden in order to remind man that it was off-limits. He simply but clearly told Adam not to eat of its fruit, warning him of the fatal consequences of such action. But Eve listened to the serpent's lies instead of to God. She "saw that the tree was good for food, that it was pleasant to the eyes, and a tree desirable to make one wise" (Genesis 3:6). So she took the fruit and ate it, in spite of God's previous warnings.

Mankind's original sin has played out over and over again in various versions in people's lives. Instead of fruit, it may have been any number of things which they knew were not in harmony with God's will for their lives. And just as there were painful consequences to mankind's original sin, we face similar results when we ignore God's warnings. Sin always has its cost. God warns us about those dangers because He's looking out for what's best for us.

There may not be red tape and danger signs around each thing that can hurt us spiritually, but God's Word and the Holy Spirit will be faithful to warn us about them if we'll just pay attention. So let's be watchful and stay clear of anything that poses a danger to our relationship with the Lord.

Pay attention to any "danger signs" from God today.

Your Creator Cares about You

"But the very hairs of your head are all numbered."
– Matthew 10:30

A few years ago someone introduced me to a new world—the world of electric trains. Although I knew there were hobbyists who enjoyed that pursuit, I didn't realize the extent of their efforts. I had pictured a simple little train chugging around an oval track, like the one I had received at Christmas when I was a youngster. It was fun, but it only held a kid's attention for so long.

But on this day, I discovered how creativity has taken that hobby to a different level. I saw tracks of various shapes, with numerous electrical switches to alter how and where the train would run. I was shown multi-level tracks. But what surprised me most was the vast variety of villages and landscapes that can be built all around those tracks. There are kits from which all kinds of buildings can be constructed. And you don't just have to purchase ready-made figures to populate your village. You can build your own people—including painting them and putting certain arms on them, depending on what task you want them to be doing. Some of those figures that accompany smaller trains were so miniscule that a person has to paint them under a magnifying glass! I was amazed at such detailed work that went along with this hobby.

That encounter with the world of electric trains reminded me of our Creator and His interest in the world in which we live. No, we're not just playthings for Him to toy with. Neither are we a hobby that He only pays attention to in His spare time, but we are part of a world that He has created. And His concern for us goes beyond that of a master-builder to the deep love of a Father.

In one sense, we are very tiny and insignificant compared to the One who has made us. It's no wonder the Psalmist asked the Creator, "What is man that You are mindful of Him?" But God does indeed consider us. We're a special creation to Him. He has made us in His own image, "a little lower than the angels," and has crowned us with glory and honor (Psalm 8:4–5).

Furthermore, God isn't just concerned about the train of His overall purposes for this world as it barrels along on its track day after day toward its God-ordained destination. He cares about all the details in His design too. He is concerned about each individual person who populates this world He has made. He not only brought us into existence, but He is also interested in working on us to make us into the unique individual He has envisioned us to be. He doesn't just paint us with one big blob of Christlikeness, He puts each of us under the magnifying glass and works on the various areas of our lives which need to be cleaned up in order for us to become the holy person He has called us to be. He dabs a little love and kindness here, and a little patience and perseverance there. And He molds us and empowers us to serve Him and to fulfill His particular purpose for us in this world.

We are so small compared to the One who is running this place, but we are important to Him—every one of us. And He is intent on loving us and doing a work of transformation in us according to His good purposes.

My old electric train is stored away somewhere in our basement. I think I'll go find it. It may not run, but if nothing else it can serve as a reminder that God cares about us and every aspect of our lives.

Take a few moments to meditate on the fact that the great Creator of the universe cares about you and wants to transform your life.

GET MORE INVOLVED IN
THE MINISTRY OF PRAYER

"But you are a chosen generation, a royal priesthood."

– I PETER 2:9

O ne of the longtime members of our church was facing the prospect of being without a job. She actually worked for a company similar to a temp agency, although some of her positions had turned out to be far from temporary. After seven years at the same place, her agency's relationship with that particular business was coming to a close, leaving her without a job. So as that time drew near, she asked the church to be praying about her upcoming unemployed status.

The Sunday following her final day at work, she reported in our worship service that a new position had already opened up which she would begin within a few days. While she thanked God for answering prayer, she joked that she should have been more specific when requesting prayer from our congregation. In a way our prayers were too effective and the answer came a little too quickly. She had figured on having at least a couple of weeks off from work and had already made some plans.

Isn't it wonderful that God hears and answers prayer! It's rare that He responds more quickly than we would have preferred. More often we find ourselves having to ask, seek, and knock for an extended period of time, impatiently wondering what's taking the Lord so long to give us the answer. For example, earlier that same year someone else in our church was looking for a job and it didn't materialize until after months of praying and searching. But when God did move, she received three job offers in one week!

Sometimes I'm afraid we lose sight of the great privilege God gives us to help other people by praying for them. Certainly there are situations in which we should do more than pray—when we have the ability to assist the person in a tangible way ourselves. But at the same time, let's not downplay the value of interceding for people before a powerful and caring God. In some circumstances, there is nothing else we are able to do to help the person other than pray. And we are bringing their need to a God who can see the whole picture and can work in ways that we can't.

We don't even have to be physically present with people in order to pray for them. You can minister to people who may be hundreds of miles away or clear across the other side of the world. Through interceding for them, you can have an important impact on their lives.

Prayer is more than our way of fellowshipping with God, talking to Him, and bringing our own needs to Him. Prayer is also a ministry. It's a way to serve others. And it's not just a special gift or function for a few select individuals in the church. It's something we all can do and are called to do as believers. The Bible refers to all followers of Christ as priests. One of the truths that title suggests is that we each have been given the privilege and responsibility to use our access to God to intercede for other people and their needs.

A ministry of prayer is something any of us can do. Some of us may not have the talents or resources to serve in other areas, some may be physically unable to get out and do other forms of ministry, but we can all pray for other people.

Will you commit yourself to becoming more involved in interceding for others? Who needs you to pray for them?

LET'S TAKE RESPONSIBILITY FOR OUR BAD ACTIONS

"So they gave it to me, and I cast it into the fire, and this calf came out."

– EXODUS 32:24

My wife told me about an incident that took place one day while she was over at our daughter's house. Our then four-year-old grandson, Joshua, was busying himself playing with a Disney action figure (at least that's what I'll call it—it just sounds better to me than saying that my grandson was playing with a doll). It was Woody, the cowboy character from the *Toy Story* movies.

At one point, Joshua had Woody positioned on the banister at the top of some stairs when he threw the cowboy off and onto the floor below. My daughter warned him not to throw Woody off like that or he might get broken. Without hesitation, my grandson replied, "I didn't throw him. Woody jumped."

Maybe in a little boy's imagination his doll, or rather his action figure, might have jumped from that lofty height, but in reality we know that wasn't the case, unless you happen to accept the premise of those Disney movies that toys really are alive. Or maybe he was just quick to think of an excuse that he hoped might keep him out of trouble with his mother.

It reminds me of what happened when Moses came down from his encounter with God on Mount Sinai to find the people of Israel worshiping a golden calf. He was so angry that he broke the tablets on which the Ten Commandments had been written. Then he confronted his brother, Aaron, whom the Bible says had molded the calf and fashioned it with an engraving tool (Exodus 32:4). Moses asked his brother, "What did this people do to you that you have brought so great a sin upon them." At first Aaron blamed the people for having their hearts set on evil and for asking him to make them gods. Then Aaron admitted to taking gold from the people and putting it in the fire. But then he said, "And this calf came out." In other words, the gold just formed itself into a calf and jumped out of the fire. Right. Such an excuse might be cute coming from a four-year-old in relation to his toy, but it's not acceptable when dealing with sin before a holy God. Aaron wasn't just expressing an active imagination. He was obviously trying to avoid taking full responsibility for his wrong actions.

Let's be careful that we don't try similar excuses in relation to some of our actions. "The mouse on my computer just clicked on that link and took me to that web site." "The accelerator in my car must have gotten stuck and caused me to go so fast over the speed limit." "For some reason my alarm clock doesn't work as good on Sunday mornings as it does on the mornings I have to go to work." "The television just comes on and forces me to spend so much of my time watching it." "That other person forced her affections on me and I couldn't resist." "I didn't spread any gossip—that rumor just grew legs and took off on its own." "All that fattening food just jumped down my throat."

We may not be quite that blatant about it, but we still tend to follow Aaron's example of making excuses and shifting the blame either to other people or even to inanimate objects if we think we can get away with doing so. However God knows the truth, whether anyone else does or not. And He's certainly not fooled by our false claims of innocence or our lame excuses.

So let's own up to our wrongdoings. God knows that computers, cars, alarm clocks, and other people aren't to blame for our sins. And we know that Woody can't choose to jump on his own. But I'm kind of glad that my grandson could imagine it to be so.

Are you making excuses for any wrongdoing in your life?

Trust God to Give You Guidance

"In all your ways acknowledge Him, and He shall direct your paths."
— PROVERBS 3:6

Normally traffic signals aren't hard to figure out. Even my two-year-old grandson could declare from the confines of his car seat that red means stop and green means go. Unfortunately some people drive as if they lack that basic understanding of the rules of the road, or more likely, choose to ignore them. But on those occasions when a traffic light malfunctions, many drivers don't seem to know what to do. From what I understand, it's actually very simple. If the light is completely out, then everyone should treat the intersection as if it's a four-way stop. But if it's flashing, you handle it differently. If it's flashing red on your side, you stop until it's clear to go. If it's flashing yellow, you slow down and proceed with caution.

Recently I ran upon a unique situation that I have to admit caused me some degree of bewilderment. As I approached a traffic signal it was red. But as I got close, the green light came on. However, the red light kept shining as well. It was red and green at the same time. No, there wasn't any sunlight reflecting off one of them—both bulbs were definitely brightly burning at the same time. Such a mixed signal made me pause to ponder whether I should stop or go. Since it appeared that the cars coming from the other direction were stopping, I assumed that it was safe for to me to proceed, although I did so very cautiously.

As we travel through life, we ought to be looking to God for guidance. As we do, sometimes His signals are very clear. He may put up a red light declaring "thou shalt not" get involved in that activity or go in that direction. Or He may give us the green light to go full speed ahead. Those situations are often easier, or at least they're not confusing. It comes down to either choosing to follow God's guidance or choosing to go against it. But at least we know what it is the Lord wants us to do—and hopefully we will choose to go God's way.

It can be more difficult when His signals aren't so clear. You may be facing a crossroads in which the Bible doesn't give you a definite command to stop or to go. You're not trying to decide between a sinful path and a righteous road, but rather between two seemingly good alternatives. And as you pray, sometimes the light may look red and green at the same time. I'm not suggesting that God's guidance is malfunctioning, but simply pointing out the difficulty we sometimes experience in discerning it. In the midst of such confusing mixed signals, which way do you go?

Sometimes we pray for God to make it obvious by throwing up a stop sign, a roadblock, or by closing or opening the door. And that can be a valid request to which we may receive the anticipated answer. However, there are times when the Lord doesn't block one of the optional ways. Instead, we have to wait or proceed prayerfully, always looking for signs of His guidance and listening for the sound of His voice. Some of the tools He may use to direct our path include His written word, the Holy Spirit, other people, our reasoning abilities, our desires, and the changing course of our circumstances.

When God's guidance isn't clear, don't give in to the temptation to doubt that He cares or to think that He takes pleasure in your confusion. Keep praying, keep looking, and keep trusting that He wants to show you the way and in His time will lead you in the right direction.

In what area do you need God's guidance? Keep praying, trusting, and expecting Him to lead you.

LET GO AND TRUST GOD TO TAKE YOU HIGHER

"And when Peter had come down out of the boat, he walked on the water to go to Jesus."

– MATTHEW 14:29

One time my daughter and her family drove over to well-known tourist spot in our state where they enjoyed activities such as the butterfly exhibit and the beach. But their main reason for making the journey on this occasion was a hot air balloon festival. Their hope was to be able to travel heavenward in one of those unusual and magnificent modes of transportation.

They quickly discovered that it would be quite costly for a family of four to take the hour ride that was being offered. So instead they decided to settle for simply getting in one of those baskets and being taken up into the sky for a brief taste of such an excursion while the balloon remained tethered to the ground. Even the prospect of that adventure looked dim at times due to long lines, a lunch break for the crews, and some unco-operative winds. But late in the day they finally got their opportunity and thoroughly enjoyed it.

I've been thinking about the difference in those two ride options. They both took people up in the air to some degree. But the one my daughter and her family experienced was more controlled and less risky than the one where there is no line securing it to the earth. And that's perfectly fine in Papaw's opinion, since my young grandchildren were involved. Yet in the tethered ride the scenery is very limited, the potential for excitement and adventure is less, and the participants don't get to enjoy the experience for as long a period of time. And I imagine that considerably greater heights are attained by those other free-flying balloons.

It reminds me of how some of us try to handle a different kind of heavenward journey. We like the idea of following God, of climbing higher in our spiritual journey, and of reaching a glorious and heavenly destination one day. However, we also like to maintain some degree of control. We want to get in the basket with God, but we don't want to completely let go to allow Him to take us wherever He chooses or wherever the wind of His Spirit takes us. We want a taste of the adventure, but without the risk or without the need to exercise much faith in the Lord.

The life of a follower of Christ doesn't just consist in a one-time decision to believe in Jesus. It involves an ongoing life of faith day by day. And sooner or later we're going to hear the Savior calling for us to go higher than our rope will reach. When that happens, we're going to have to let go and trust the Lord to be our faithful and skillful pilot. We're going to need to allow Him to have full control over every aspect of our lives.

When we insist on staying tethered to the ground, we miss out on so much of the joys and blessings that God intends for us to experience. We can only climb so high when we're holding back from a total surrender of ourselves to the Lord. We can only draw so close to Him when we refuse to fully trust Him as He calls us to do.

What if Abraham had held back when God called him to leave his homeland to go to another land? What if Peter, instead of stepping out and walking on the water when Christ told him to come, had tried to hold onto the boat? Let's not miss out on all the wonderful things God has in store for us as we live and serve Him. Get in that balloon, loose that tether, and trust God to take you to new heights in your adventure of faith.

What would it mean for you to let go and let God have full control of your life?

HABITUAL ACTIONS DON'T HAVE TO BE MEANINGLESS

"So He Himself often withdrew into the wilderness and prayed."

– LUKE 5:16

As we were dealing with a power outage due to a storm, I walked into a darkened room in my home and automatically reached over to flip the light switch. I knew we had no electricity. I was well aware of the futility of my actions. However, I acted by way of habit without really thinking. It's what I'm accustomed to doing when entering a dimly lit room—I turn on the light switch. In later conversations with others in similar circumstances, I had people confessing to doing the same thing numerous times almost every time they would walk into a room. No doubt we are creatures of habit.

This should remind us of the importance of developing good habits in our lives, as well as the dangers of falling into bad ones. Whatever we're accustomed to doing tends to dictate our actions when we're not consciously thinking about it otherwise. We gravitate toward our routines. We're pulled toward doing at this particular moment the very thing we're used to doing at this same time or under similar circumstances. Certainly we're not slaves to those habits, or at least we don't have to be. We can choose a different course. However, in the spur of the moment when our minds are running on autopilot, we tend to flip that light switch or follow whatever other course of action to which we're accustomed. Therefore we need to develop better habits in our lives.

I know some people who despise the idea of doing anything by way of habit. They would suggest that we should always be thinking about what we're doing and why we're doing it. And they definitely have a point. But we all develop habits of one sort or another, whether we like it or not. Isn't it better to cultivate the positive habits that will help us draw closer to God and become the kind of people He calls us to be rather than those which might pull us in the other direction?

For example, we can develop the habit of prayer in our lives. The Bible says that Jesus often withdrew into the wilderness to pray (Luke 5:16). "Often"—that sounds like a habit. We're also exhorted to "pray without ceasing" (I Thessalonians 5:17), which sounds beyond habitual and almost like an obsession. Prayer can become a regular part of our lives, both at particular times in our normal routines and as a practice we almost automatically pursue when storms come, when we walk into dark situations, or under other such circumstances. At those moments our first inclination can be to reach out to our Heavenly Father to talk to Him, to present our need, or to give Him thanks.

But although the practice of prayer can become a habit, we should not pray without engaging our minds and thoughts. Many of us have likely caught ourselves in the middle of praying just repeating the same familiar words and phrases without thinking about what we're saying. Our prayers themselves should not be the products of habit. They should be fresh, sincere, and from our hearts. We should be expressing today's praise, concerns, and intercessions before God. Habit may sometimes bring us to the throne of God, but our prayers should not just be a meaningless routine of repeating the same religious jargon we said the last time we prayed.

So whether it involves prayer, Bible reading, relating to people around us, or countless other areas of life, let's develop good habits to replace bad ones. And just because those practices become habitual, it doesn't mean we have to let them become meaningless.

What good habit do you need to develop? Is there some spiritual habit in your life that has lost some of its meaning? How can you correct that?

Don't Lose Sight of What's More Important

"What will a man give in exchange for his soul?"
– MATTHEW 16:26

One year my wife gave me an early birthday present by taking me to our first Braves' game at the new SunTrust Park. She got us great seats, on the front row of a section above the first base dugout. Not only did we get a good view of the game and the players, but I almost came away with one of those elusive foul balls.

In the bottom of the fifth inning, a batter popped up a ball in our general direction but below us. However, it hit the dugout and took a big bounce up our way. There was a small guardrail in front of us but I reached over it, trying to stretch out to get my hand on that little white sphere. Unfortunately it fell just inches short of my grasp and onto the walkway below where other fans chased it down.

Afterwards I felt badly that I didn't move slightly closer, lean a little further over the railing, and make a more gallant effort to retrieve the foul ball. However, I also was thankful that I didn't foolishly value that prize to the point that I would go tumbling over the rail and get seriously injured as others have done. I'm grateful that in the heat of the moment I didn't lose sight of what was more important.

Isn't that how we sometimes get into trouble in connection with our spiritual wellbeing? We place too much value on some possession or pleasure this world hits our way. We think it would bring us great joy and satisfaction to get our hands on it. After all, it's what many others around us are clamoring after. And in the process we forget about the harm it could do to our souls. We don't think about the consequences of putting that objective ahead of God's will for us. We let our desire for that thing eclipse our love for the Lord. We overvalue it, much like we do with those foul balls. After all, a baseball can be purchased for a relatively cheap price. Yet we consider those balls flying into the stands at major league parks to be prizes worth pursuing with great effort and sacrifice.

Temptations are tempting because of the value we place on that which entices us. One of the ways to overcome those seductions is to always keep in mind what's more important. Nothing is worth the sacrificing of your relationship with the Lord. Nothing is more valuable than your spiritual health. Nothing can take the place of being able to say, "It is well with my soul" and knowing where you're going to spend eternity.

Jesus asked the questions: "For what profit is it to a man if he gains the whole world, and loses his own soul? Or what will a man give in exchange for his soul?" (Matthew 16:26). Even if you gain that foul ball, what do you profit if you fall over the guardrail and break your neck? Likewise, what does obtaining some momentary pleasure matter if it costs you your peace with God and your fellowship with Him for eternity?

One of the problems is that we can get caught up in the heat of a moment and act without taking time to consider the consequences. That's why it's important for us to make these value judgments before that moment comes. Settle in your heart now that nothing is more valuable to you than your relationship with the Lord. Then you'll be ready to act responsibly when that temptation is hit in your direction and not take a spiritual tumble.

Keep reminding yourself that nothing is more important than your relationship with the Lord.

Don't Stay a Baby Believer—Keep Growing

"For everyone who partakes only of milk is unskilled in the word of righteousness, for he is a babe."

– Hebrews 5:13

One of our daughters has a cat which gave birth to kittens a while back. Her family ended up keeping two of the offspring, while homes were found for the rest of the litter. Recently when I was visiting my daughter, I noticed that although those two young cats are getting almost as big as their mother, because she's readily available to them, they still try at times to nurse and obtain the milk which sustained them as kittens. The momma would often growl at their attempts, but would sometimes allow them to have what they wanted in spite of their being too old to need it anymore.

Maybe we've witnessed comparable human behavior when children were allowed to still act like babies when they were old enough to have grown beyond that stage. It not only seems odd and inappropriate, but you wonder if it's hindering the physical, mental, and social development of the child. Babies are cute, but when they should be beyond the baby stage it isn't so cute anymore. If carried out too far, it can even reach a point where it becomes disturbing and a concern.

The same can be said about our spiritual growth. The Bible likens the transformation of our hearts when we put our faith in Christ to a birth. It's wonderful to witness the newness, the enthusiasm, the childlike wonder, and all the other qualities of a recently born-again believer. It's encouraging to see how that babe in Christ hungers for more of God and His Word. The spirit of such individuals often challenges more mature Christians to recapture some of those same attitudes which they may have allowed to fade away over time.

However, as much as we enjoy the positive aspects of new believers, we also hope and expect to see them grow. They shouldn't remain at that new-born stage of development. The writer of the book of Hebrews took to task some believers who had remained baby Christians much longer than was appropriate. "For though by this time you ought to be teachers, you need someone to teach you again the first principles of the oracles of God; and you have come to need milk and not solid food. For everyone who partakes only of milk is unskilled in the word of righteousness, for he is a babe. But solid food belongs to those who are of full age..." (Hebrews 5:12–14).

Apparently God does a little growling at His children who refuse to press on to a deeper faith. It may be easy to say "Amen" at this point as we think about some other believers we know who need to start acting more maturely. But let's be willing to challenge ourselves to keep growing too. Whatever stage we may be at in our relationship with the Lord, it can be easy to get comfortable or complacent and to fail to move forward in our spiritual development.

The milk of the basics of our faith is as awe-inspiring as ever. However, there is so much more to know and to experience about God if we'll pursue it. The emotional highs as we sense God's presence in our lives are exhilarating, but we also need to get grounded in a stable faith that will carry us through when times are tough and the emotions die down.

Challenge yourself to continue to go deeper in Christ—to keep growing in grace and knowledge of Him. Don't live exclusively on the milk when God has more solid food for you to digest. It's time for some of us to start growing up spiritually.

What step can you take today in developing greater spiritual growth in your life?

In the Midst of the Flood, You Are Safe in Jesus

"The Lord knows how to deliver the godly out of temptations and to reserve the unjust under punishment for the day of judgment."

– II Peter 2:9

One time I received a rather unique gift for my birthday. One of my daughters and her husband presented me with a "certificate of authenticity." It confirmed the fact that they had made a donation in my name toward the building of the full-scale replica of Noah's ark which had recently opened to the public in northern Kentucky. So as I understand it, somewhere in the ark is a peg with my name or identification number on it.

My daughter and son-in-law have actually traveled up there to visit that impressive structure. I had already thought I would like to check it out myself sometime. Now I have even more reason to do so. Along with enjoying the exhibits, I'll have a mission—to search for my particular peg within the ark.

In addition to its historical significance, Noah's ark represents God's grace and protection for His people in the midst of judgment on a sinful world. In one passage in the Bible it is cited, along with the sparing of Lot from the destruction of Sodom and Gomorrah, as an example that "the Lord knows how to deliver the godly out of temptations and to reserve the unjust under punishment for the day of judgment" (II Peter 2:4–9). Many people have drawn comparisons between the ark and Christ Himself.

The Bible alludes to this idea when it compares the saving of those eight souls in the ark to our salvation through Christ's death and resurrection (I Peter 3:20–22).

In these turbulent times in which we're living, we might sometimes wish we had an ark to run into, shut the door, and be safe from all the turmoil. The Bible promises that we don't have to worry about there being another literal flood to destroy the earth, but our ungodly world certainly seems to be opening itself up to and inviting the judgment of a holy God in some form or fashion. There seem to be tough times looming on the horizon, including increased lawlessness, violence, and persecution of believers.

The good news is that we do have an ark in Jesus. He is our refuge of safety and protection. Whether God chooses to spare us from having to face those trials or if He gives us the strength to endure them, our souls are safe within the shelter of our relationship with Christ. When the floods come, we can rest in Him. We can be assured that our Lord is with us. Likewise we know He will bring us through the flood to a better place, either in this life or in heaven.

God's judgment may be coming or it may already be here. It's a scary prospect, especially for those who don't know the Lord. And while believers may not look forward to the hardships involved, we still have hope and refuge in Christ. Let's not allow the prospect of judgment on this world to rob us of our joy and contentment in knowing that our souls are right with God.

Noah found favor with God in the midst of judgment, and we can too. However, we need to follow His example of having faith in God and living a godly life in spite of how those around us are failing to do so.

So if you're putting your trust in Jesus as your Savior, be assured that you have a special place in Him. There's a spot with your name on it. No matter how hard it rains or how high the floodwaters rise, you are safe in the ark of Christ.

In times of tribulation and judgment, keep trusting the Lord to be your ark of safety.

CAN THE IMAGE OF JESUS BE SEEN IN YOU?

"For whom He foreknew, He also predestined to be conformed to the image of His Son."

– ROMANS 8:29

Years ago the most frequent method I used for making toast was to put buttered bread under the oven's broiler. There were times when, either for my own entertainment or for that of my young children, I would place the dabs of butter in such a way as to try to create something similar to a smiley face on the finished product.

I understand that now there are toasters which can brown the bread in such a way as to make a face or other designs. You can submit a picture of yourself and end up with an appliance which will produce toast with your own image on it. They also have one popular model that makes toast which looks like Jesus, or at least our perception of what He may have looked like.

Of course people have claimed to see the image of Jesus in some odd places over the years—clouds, stone walls, the grain of wooden objects, liquid spatters, and even in a sock. And if you care to do some research, you'll find even stranger claims of such sightings.

However there is one place in particular where we should hope Jesus' image can be found. And that is in us as His followers. I'm not talking about seeing Jesus' face in some weird configuration of moles on our backs. I'm not even referring to that shining face we often connect with people who have the light of Christ living within. I'm referring more to a likeness in our spirit rather than in any kind of a physical sense.

For example, the love of Jesus should be seen in our lives. Christ loved the unlovable. He showed compassion to those who were in need. He reached out to people whom society had neglected and abandoned. Does the world see that image of a loving Jesus in His followers today? No matter how orthodox we might be in our beliefs and no matter how much religious activity we're involved in, if we don't express this primary characteristic of our Savior, we don't look anything like Him. As I Corinthians 13:1–3 reminds us, if I "have not love, I am nothing."

But the image of Jesus also reflects purity. I know—we're all human, we've all sinned, and none of us are perfect. And we're not going to fully be like Jesus in His purity until we shed these bodies and meet Him in heaven (I John 3:2–3). But we can both seek purity and also attain a measure of that quality in this life through the cleansing power of Jesus' blood. The Bible tells us to keep ourselves pure (I Timothy 5:22), and testifies to the fact that Jesus' followers can experience having their hearts purified by faith (Acts 15:9). If our hearts are marred with impure attitudes and our minds are spending too much time in the gutter, the image of a holy Jesus won't be very recognizable in us.

Let's not forget that any picture of Jesus also includes truth and integrity. Jesus didn't deny eternal realities in order to appease people or to avoid rejection and opposition. He lived by those principles regardless of the personal cost. And He was faithful to share the truth with people even when it wasn't what they wanted to hear. Therefore we can't water down God's Word, seek to be men-pleasers, and back down from living by divine standards without distorting the image of Jesus in us.

Some of us may not care anything about having Jesus' face burned into a slice of our bread, but let's be sure to allow Him to burn His image on our hearts and souls.

Father, make me more like Jesus.

ARE YOU HINDERING YOURSELF FROM RECEIVING GOD'S PROMISED BLESSINGS?

"By which have been given to us exceedingly great and precious promises."

– II PETER 1:4

I remember when a couple of spare keys were made for the lock on the door of our church building. But when those new keys were tested, they didn't open the door. Blame for this failure was naturally ascribed to the keys and to the individual who had cut them out. So those keys were discarded and we tried again by having someone else create two more. However, when those were inserted in the lock, one worked and the other one didn't. But even the one which opened the lock didn't seem to do so very easily.

That's when we wondered if the fault might be with the lock rather than with those keys. So we got a can of that wonderful, all-purpose lubricant, WD-40 (the mechanic's version of duct tape—it can be used for everything) and sprayed it in the lock. And sure enough, after several applications and a little key jiggling, one of those spare keys began to work. And in the process, I noticed a gray film on the key, indicating that the lubricant was working to clean out the gunk which had kept the lock from functioning well.

Similarly, God has given His children some wonderful keys to living a life of blessing in relationship with Him. He has provided us with some precious assurances and glorious promises which offer the hope of opening the door to a joyous and meaningful existence. We like to quote those scriptures, claim those promises, and expectantly watch for God to do as He has said.

How often do we insert these keys into our situation, depending on them to be effective? "We know that all things work together for good…" (Romans 8:28). "He shall direct your paths" (Proverbs 3:6). "You will keep him in perfect peace…" (Isaiah 26:3). "All these things (food, clothing, and other necessities) shall be added to you" (Matthew 6:33). And there are so many more of God's promises we rely on.

But what about when it doesn't seem to be working? What about those times when things don't seem to be working out for good, when God doesn't appear to be directing us, when we aren't experiencing peace in our hearts, when we are lacking some of those necessities in life, and when other assurances seem to be falling short of what they promise? Our tendency is to blame the promise or the One who made it. "Why aren't You doing what You said, Lord? What's wrong with You? What's wrong with Your promise or with Your power?"

Hopefully we all know in our hearts that there's never anything wrong with the Lord or with His faithfulness to fulfill His promises. In some cases we may have misunderstood what He said. In other situations, He may be working to fulfill His Word and we just can't see it. And other times we may need to wait and keep trusting until the right time for God to answer.

But we also need to check out our end of the deal. The key of God's promises is good, but what about our lock? Have we allowed it to get grimy with sin, rusty from complacency, or hardened from lack of use? Most of those promises of God come with conditions. God will do His part if our side is in order.

If you go back and read those full verses mentioned above, you'll see that we must keep our lock lubricated with loving God, trusting Him with all our hearts, and putting Him first in order to be able to receive those wonderful keys God has for us.

So if those keys aren't working for you, don't discard them or blame God. Maybe you just need a little spiritual cleansing in order to experience His promised blessings.

Lord, show me anything in my heart and life which might be keeping me from experiencing Your blessings.

LET'S BE REMINDED OF
WHAT LIFE IS ALL ABOUT

"Let us hear the conclusion of the whole matter: fear God and keep His commandments, for this is man's all."

– ECCLESIASTES 12:13

Today is my birthday. I've sometimes approached this occasion with mixed feelings, especially when it's one of those landmark years—you know, one that ends in a zero. When I was turning fifty, I had already received my official invitation to join the AARP. Additionally, some kind doctor in the area sent me information about a program to "slow the aging of your body and your brain." I'm still not convinced that my wife with her medical connections didn't arrange that mailing. She certainly enjoyed the fact that, whether by accident or by design, I got it as that significant birthday drew close. And there are always a few cards and gifts coming my way that in various ways indicate that I am now undoubtedly over-the-hill.

One of the positive results of facing those milestones in my life is that it has helped me unlock one of the great mysteries of biblical interpretation. The book of Ecclesiastes has always seemed quite different from most of the other writings in scripture. The viewpoint comes across as somewhat pessimistic and melancholic at times. It could actually be considered a rather depressing outlook on life if you stopped short of reading its conclusion.

But now I think I understand. Solomon, if you accept the common view that he is indeed the author of this work, must have penned these words as one of his landmark birthdays approached. That would explain so much about its content. It would account for the attention given to the concept of time in that famous passage about there being "a time for every purpose under heaven." As Solomon wrote about "a time to be born, and a time to die," he may have realized that he was now closer to the latter than to the former.

It would also explain the author reflecting over the past years of his life, thinking about what he had done and wondering about its impact. He spends much of the book in contemplation about the purpose of life while bemoaning many pursuits that in the end turn out to be empty and meaningless. And he looks ahead to the aging of his physical body with a little dread and apprehension, describing in figurative terms the lessening of the senses and the weakening of one's health. But Solomon works his way through to a positive conclusion. He decides that the best course of action is to enjoy life, fear God, and keep His commandments.

I don't really know whether or not Solomon wrote this as he faced another birthday, but I can relate to some of his thinking. There are times in life when we look back and evaluate what we've done. There are moments when we look ahead and wonder what the future holds. And there are pivotal occasions when we need to be reminded of what life is all about and what truly gives it meaning.

Life isn't about work, fame, wealth, pleasure, or even family. It finds its true purpose in having a right relationship with God. Then all those other aspects of life will fall into their proper place.

I think I'll take Solomon's advice and enjoy life. I'll enjoy some birthday cake, time with friends, and playing with my grandchildren. And I'll look ahead to whatever God has in store for me in the years to come. But above all, I'll keep pursuing a life of faith in the One who created me and brought me into this world those many years ago. Landmark birthdays aren't so bad. As Solomon wrote elsewhere, "The silver-haired head is a crown of glory, if it is found in the way of righteousness" (Proverbs 16:31). I just hope I have some hair left to turn silver.

Reflect over your life and consider what is most important. Is that what you're pursuing?

Jesus Calls Us to a Higher Standard of Godliness

"But I say to you that whoever is angry with his brother without a cause shall be in danger of the judgment."

– MATTHEW 5:22

At our church picnic, a game of horseshoes was being set up. You can tell that some of us are getting older when we prefer the competition of tossing horseshoes at a stake over running around playing a game of baseball or kickball as was common in past years at these gatherings. However, no one present was sure how far apart to place the stakes. So after several people offered the same estimation, we decided to use their suggestion as our standard. Some of us went on to play the game at that distance, although our efforts often indicated that we might have been better off sticking with kickball.

Later someone researched the regulations of horseshoes, discovering that our stakes had been considerably closer than the official standard. I halfway joked that if we moved the target that far apart next time, I might have to build up my arm muscles before playing.

I wonder if some of the people in Jesus' day may have felt similarly when they listened to some of His teachings, such as what we have recorded as being part of His Sermon on the Mount. They had been playing the game of life by one standard that a consensus of upstanding religious leaders had spelled out for them when Jesus came along and moved the stakes farther apart. He declared that God's true standard was even more stringent than what they had been previously taught.

For example, Jesus pointed out that while they had been playing by the rule that you love your friends and hate your enemies, God actually wants us to love our enemies and show kindness to them as well. He also declared that while they had been aiming at the stake of not committing such acts as murder and adultery, God's target was for them not even to possess the attitudes, thoughts, and desires that underlie those actions. Additionally, Jesus countered the vengeful personal practice of "an eye for an eye and a tooth for a tooth" with those familiar declarations that individuals should turn the other cheek and be willing to walk a second mile in their relationships with others.

Many of those people who heard Jesus were probably already having a tough enough time trying to live by the old standard. Like me tossing the horseshoes a greater distance, they may have thought that they would have to become considerably stronger to reach this new target. Maybe some of them even thought it impossible.

But the good news is that we don't have to reach God's higher standard in our own strength. As a matter of fact, it would be hopeless for us to try to do it on our own. But if we've received Christ as Savior, we have His Spirit living within us. He can change us and enable us to live in such a way that would please God.

The Holy Spirit can fill our hearts with God's love to the extent that we can actually be kind to the very people who have mistreated us. He can not only change our actions, but also transform our desires, thoughts, and attitudes. And He can empower us to overcome the temptations toward being less than what God calls us to be.

Let's not settle for a false standard of godliness that the world has concocted or a low standard that seems more reachable within our own means. Let's keep pressing toward the goal Jesus has set before us—a high standard of holiness that is possible to reach through the power of the Holy Spirit working within us.

Don't lower the bar. Trust the Lord to help you be a holy person.

BE READY FOR JESUS'
REENTRY INTO THIS WORLD

"The Lord Jesus Christ, who will judge the living and the dead at His appearing."

– II TIMOTHY 4:1

Were you keeping an eye on the sky a few years ago as a satellite fell out of its orbit and reentered the earth's atmosphere? It would have been hard not to have known about it with all the news coverage given to this event in the days preceding its occurrence. The media warned us of the potential danger if some of these larger pieces of metal failed to burn up and actually hit our planet somewhere over a land mass. It was estimated that some twenty-seven chunks of that satellite in various sizes might survive reentry. The countdown to impact was one of the top stories on many newscasts, although they couldn't pinpoint the time or even the day with much degree of accuracy. In spite of all our technology, it seems that the scientists couldn't even figure out what area of earth would be the target of this potential missile from outer space.

Due to the overwhelming odds against any of that space debris hitting one particular human being, we were encouraged not to be concerned. I'm not sure what you could do anyway to avoid a ton of metal raining down on you at high speed. I'm not even sure that hiding in a basement would protect you. I saw one woman interviewed who had been struck by a small piece of a satellite years ago. Her only advice was to look up, and if you see something coming…run! I'm afraid that by then, it might have been too late.

The Bible tells us that Jesus is going to reenter this world one day. Although we know it's going to happen, we don't know when. We have some signs to look for as an indication that this event is drawing near, but none of us can pinpoint the exact date or time, regardless of what some well-meaning people have predicted over the years. Jesus clearly declared that only His Father knows the day and the hour of His return.

Jesus' stated that His first visit to this earth was not for the purpose of bringing condemnation or judgment, but in order to bring salvation (John 3:17). However, His reentry will be a different story. There may be varying interpretations regarding the timeline of those events, but basically Jesus will be returning to gather His followers home and bring judgment on those who have rejected Him. By the time we see Him and realize what's happening, it will be too late for any change in course. For those who aren't trusting Him as Savior, there will be no place to run and hide from the consequences of their sin and guilt.

The wise advice the Bible gives us in light of Christ's coming is to watch and be ready. Such spiritual preparedness centers around an attitude of repentance and faith—an admission of our need, a commitment to turn away from anything in our life that isn't in keeping with God's will, and the placing of our trust in Jesus as the only One who can save us from sin.

If we're ready, the return of Jesus isn't something to be feared or dreaded, but rather an event to look forward to with a spirit of calm assurance. Jesus encouraged His followers to keep their eyes upon the sky as they saw the signs indicating that His coming was getting closer. He said, "Look up and lift up your heads, because your redemption draws near" (Luke 21:28).

Apparently that satellite fizzled out somewhere over the ocean and quickly faded from the headlines. But Jesus' reentry is a certainty that could have a huge impact on each one of us for eternity. Don't ignore His imminent return. Let's make sure that we're ready.

Is there anything you need to take care of today in order to be better ready for the return of Christ?

OCTOBER 1

Quit Swatting Webs
and Go after the Spider

"For out of the heart proceed evil thoughts, murders, adulteries, fornications, thefts, false witness, blasphemies. These are the things which defile a man."

– Matthew 15:19–20

As I was walking around my yard picking up pine cones before mowing, I was reminded that this is the time of year when the webs of a certain kind of spider seem to become more prominent. The numerous trees with their low-hanging limbs in our landscape apparently provide prime locations for those creatures to spin their elaborate traps. So I had to watch out for those sticky webs so as not to get tangled up in them myself. When I spotted one, I had to choose either to avoid it or to remove it.

Knocking down those webs might have solved my problem for that day, but unless I got rid of the spider itself, it was likely that another web would show up in the near future in the same proximity. The webs were the more immediate and recognizable irritant, but it was the spider that was creating those webs and which would continue to do so unless it was dealt with in some way.

In a similar way, it's easy for us to focus most of our time and energy in clearing out the webs which crop up in our lives. We lost our temper again and now we have to clean up the mess. We gave in to that temptation again, so now we've got to spend countless hours, days, maybe even years unwinding from the threads of its consequences. Once again we engaged our mouths before our brains, resulting in a tangled mass of hurt feelings and confusion. The webs keep showing up day after day no matter how many times we knock them down.

It's simpler for us to settle for being web-fighters, waiting for the next one inevitably to show up at which time we'll face it. However, wouldn't it be more productive to go after the spider itself? It might be more difficult, it may even be more painful at the moment, but if we can remove the source of all those irritating webs in our lives, we can focus more time and energy on the main work God has called us to do.

So what's the spider? Is it the devil? Or how about this ungodly world that keeps having its negative impact on us? No, I believe we have to come to terms with the fact that the real source of our problem is within ourselves. It's a heart issue. Jesus said, "For out of the heart proceed evil thoughts, murders, adulteries, fornications, thefts, false witnesses, blasphemies" (Matthew 15:19). The spider in our lives is our own hearts—hearts that tend to be proud, selfish, rebellious, wanting to be in control, unwilling to yield to what God says, and wanting to have its own way.

The good news is that the Lord is able to change our hearts. He doesn't just help us as we deal with all the outcroppings of the spider lurking within. He can give us new hearts, pure hearts, hearts desiring to do God's will above our own will. He can enable us to unselfishly "love one another fervently with a pure heart" (I Peter 1:22).

Will you commit to going after the real source of many of the issues in your life? Instead of just swatting webs, will you deal with the spider? Surrender your will completely to the Lord. Ask Him to cleanse you on the inside from a proud and selfish heart. Trust Him to do it.

Let's aspire with Charles Wesley, "O for a heart to praise my God, a heart from sin set free.... A heart in every thought renewed and full of love divine; perfect and right and pure and good, a copy, Lord, of Thine."

What webs in your life are you continually knocking down? Trust the Lord to help you deal with the spider in your heart.

REGULARLY SEEK GOD'S
CLEANSING IN YOUR LIFE

"Seek the Lord while He may be found, call upon Him while He is near. Let the wicked forsake his way."

– ISAIAH 55:6–7

A s I was driving around last weekend, I noticed the smoke rising from several different fires in various yards along the way. No doubt these were the work of homeowners who were taking advantage of the lifting of our annual burning ban at the start of October. Many of them had probably done as I had over the past months, at least those who tried to abide by the local regulations. They had accumulated quite a pile of yard debris from picking up sticks and pine cones prior to mowing the grass since last spring. Or they had the clippings from bushes which had been trimmed or trees having been pruned which needed to be eliminated from their landscape. So as soon as it was legally permissible, they were outside disposing of the mess which had been building up for quite some time.

Due to the burning ban, many of us let the debris from our yards accumulate over time before getting rid of it. Even during the season of the year when we are allowed to build such fires, we don't do it every time we pick up a few sticks. We often wait until we have a nice stack of kindling before we deal with it.

While that may be a common and recommended method when it comes to disposing of our yard debris, it isn't a very good way to handle the spiritual debris in our lives. Yet that's often what we tend to do. We let those unrepentant sins build up over time. We ignore those little twigs of rebellion and disobedience which have shown up. We make excuses for the bad attitudes that litter the landscape of our lives. We let those weeds of bad habits grow and push aside some of the more godly habits or spiritual disciplines which we used to faithfully practice.

We go about our daily activities trying not to pay much attention to that messy pile in the back corner of our lives. We sometimes wait until the next series of revival services or the annual spiritual life conference or some other special event in which we try to bring all that debris to God for Him to handle in one big cleansing blaze.

Don't get me wrong. God can handle such messes no matter how large they are or how long they've been allowed to accumulate. However, it's so much better for us, our relationship with the Lord, and our own spiritual development if we take care of such matters on a regular basis, not waiting for them to grow into such a stack of debris. We don't even have to wait until the next time we go to church to hear a sermon or to respond to an altar call in order to handle such issues. We can daily seek God's cleansing and enablement to keep our hearts and lives free from those things which would mar the beauty of Christ's righteousness in us.

There are no good reasons to wait for some future time to deal with those spiritual issues. There is every reason to go ahead and let God take care of them today. We may not realize how that debris is hindering our walk with God or our witness to the world around us. It needs to be eliminated now. Let's make it a daily practice to invite the Lord to search our hearts, to reveal any debris which is present, and to purge us of it through the power of His cleansing fire. God has no burning bans when it comes to keeping the spiritual debris out of our lives.

Is there any spiritual debris you need to take care of today?

Courage and Kindness Are a Powerful Combination

"Father, forgive them, for they do not know what they do."

– Luke 23:34

O ne evening my wife and I invited our young granddaughter over to the house to watch a movie version of the classic tale, *Cinderella*. It was a very enjoyable film. And unlike most offerings in theaters or on television these days, there was nothing in it to make us feel uncomfortable about a five-year-old viewing it.

While I tend to prefer superheroes over princesses, Cinderella has always been my favorite among the various fairy tale heroines. And it's not just because of the outward beauty given to her by the animators or by the actresses who portrayed her. I think it's because she showed such sweetness and good character in the face of adversity and abuse.

In this particular version, Cinderella sought to live her entire life in accordance with the exhortation given to her by her dying mother—"Have courage and be kind." Even as she had been discovered by her prince and was walking out the door to begin her "happily ever after," Cinderella's parting words to her abusive stepmother were, "I forgive you."

This combination of courage and kindness seems to be both biblical and Christlike. Throughout scripture we find various individuals being exhorted to be strong and courageous as they encountered opposition, obstacles, and challenges. Likewise there is the ever-present command to love one's neighbor as oneself. The Bible directs us not only to "be kindly affectionate to one another with brotherly love" (Romans 12:10), but even to "love your enemies, bless those who curse you, do good to those who hate you, and pray for those who spitefully use you and persecute you" (Matthew 5:44).

Jesus exhibited both of these characteristics. It's not unusual to hear people today commend His compassion and kindness in how He ministered to the sick and reached out to the social outcasts of His day. However, we shouldn't forget that Jesus also showed courage in holding firm to the truth, pointing out evil, and steadfastly fulfilling His Father's purposes for Him.

I believe Jesus' followers today would do well to follow the advice of Cinderella's mother. We need courage in these changing times. Christians are quickly becoming the unfavored stepchild of our society. Those who hold firm to biblical teachings and values are being marginalized, ridiculed, and even persecuted. We will need courage to faithfully follow Christ in an increasingly hostile environment.

However, we need to be careful as we face these battles that we don't become uncompassionate, hardhearted, vengeful warriors. As tough as it may be, we should still seek to be kind as well. For some of us, this will be the more challenging task. When we're relegated to the lowliest places of service and status in society, can we still have a smile on our face, a song in our heart, and compassion for our fellow man? When we're mistreated, can we still pray as Jesus did, "Father, forgive them"? Can we offer to our abusers those powerful words of Cinderella to her stepmother—"I forgive you"?

It takes courage to survive trying times. But if we can still be kind through it all and in spite of it all, that's being Christlike. May God give all of us this wonderful combination of qualities in our character as we face today's world and tomorrow's uncertainties—"Have courage and be kind."

In what way do you need to be more courageous? To whom do you need to be more kind?

ASK THE LORD FOR DIRECTIONS

"There is a way that seems right to a man, but its end is the way of death."

– PROVERBS 14:12

I was taking a long trip up north to visit a church and some ministerial colleagues in the region. One evening, I went out to eat with a friend who has a reputation for being severely "directionally challenged." My anxiety arose when I discovered his wife was going to be unable to accompany us to our destination. Being in rural Indiana, there weren't many nearby options for restaurants. So the plan was to travel to a town several miles away in order to have dinner.

Shortly after our journey began, my friend suggested that we turn down a side road so he could show me a unique barn. After doing so, he insisted that we should be able to keep following that same road to get to the restaurant. As we drove the next untold number of miles surrounded by cornfields, my friend offered numerous comments expressing a mixture of doubts and confidence. "That house looks familiar." "I don't remember seeing that before." "I think we could turn at this road." "We should at least be heading in the right direction."

After making a phone call to his wife, we discovered, as I feared, that we were nowhere near where we were supposed to be. We ended up having to turn around and retrace our path for quite a few miles before getting back on track. I am glad to report that we finally made it to our destination. And before we left the restaurant to head back, I made sure to ask someone there for directions.

We all have to guard against being "directionally challenged" when it comes to navigating our way through life. The book of Proverbs reminds us twice—maybe for emphasis—"There is a way that seems right to a man, but its end is the way of death" (Proverbs 14:12; 16:25).

How often have we been guilty of turning off onto a side road in life as some unique or attractive object got our attention? We may have done so with every intention of not proceeding very far or for very long, only to lose track of where we were and having a hard time finding our way back.

When we do choose our own alternate route instead of staying on the course God has directed, it's easy to deceive ourselves into thinking we're all right. After all, we hate to admit to being wrong. We don't want to think that we've wasted time and energy going all this way, only to have to turn around. So we grasp for signs of false hope. We encourage ourselves with the idea that others are travelling this same road. Or we otherwise try to make ourselves feel better about having lost our way.

The best course of action to take when we realize we have chosen a wrong road is to turn around. The Bible calls it repentance. We change direction and get back on the pathway of God's choosing.

However, it's even better not to take those wrong turns in the first place. We can often avoid those miscues if we will diligently seek to follow God's directions for our lives. We need to read and study His Word. It's our map revealing God's will for us. We also ought to constantly and prayerfully seek God's guidance, especially when we're facing forks in the road. And we always need to try to keep a submissive spirit, ready to follow whatever direction God leads, even if it's not the one we would have preferred.

Don't wander off in your own direction, no matter how right it may seem. Always seek and follow the Lord's guidance for your life.

Seek God's direction today.

REDISCOVER THOSE CHILDHOOD SPIRITUAL PRACTICES

"Your word have I hidden in my heart, that I might not sin against You."

– PSALM 119:11

As I've gotten older, I sometimes suffer from pain and discomfort in my lower back. Therefore I find it helpful to avoid certain activities, limit how often I give grandkids rides on my back, as well as be careful about how I pick up heavy objects—bend those knees and lift with the legs.

But recently I have rediscovered something which seems to be very effective in keeping me from experiencing such frequent back incidents. Early in the day, or anytime I start feeling a twinge of weakness or pain in my back, I merely do a few simple stretching exercises, like those we did as kids in elementary school. Do you remember those? The teacher would tell us to stand beside our desks and spread out so as not to accidentally, or purposefully, hit each other. Then we'd do those stretching exercises, along with a few jumping jacks. Being a fairly active and agile kid, rotating my arms in circles or reaching down to touch my toes wasn't very challenging. Those activities seemed rather useless to me at the time. However today I'm certainly finding them to be helpful.

I wonder if some of us might likewise benefit from rediscovering a few other activities from our childhood—maybe some of those things we did in Sunday school. How long has it been since you've memorized a Bible verse? I know—it becomes a lot tougher to remember things as we get older. But just because it's hard doesn't mean it isn't worthwhile. Having God's Word tucked away in our hearts and minds where we can refer to it in sudden times of temptation, crisis, witnessing, or other situations is so helpful. And just going through the discipline of memorizing scripture can keep our minds sharp and help us focus on what God is saying to us in that verse. Rediscover the joy and blessing of hiding God's Word in your heart.

Maybe some of us also need to get reacquainted with those great stories in the Bible, the ones our Sunday School lessons often focused on. It's great to dive into the depths of Paul's teachings in the New Testament, along with other doctrinal sections of the Bible, but don't forget those stories from which we can learn from history and from the examples of others. We still need to have faith like David to battle the giants. We still need to be reminded that God can break down the walls of Jericho we're facing. We still need to guard against running away from God's will for us like Jonah did. And we need to have faith like Peter to get out of the boat and walk toward Jesus on the water. Don't think you've outgrown those stories or that you're so familiar with them that there's nothing else for you to learn from them.

And as you're singing all those contemporary songs and traditional hymns, don't forget the simple truths in some of those songs you learned as a child. "Jesus loves me, this I know." "This little light of mine, I'm gonna let it shine." "The B-I-B-L-E, yes, that's the book for me. I stand alone on the Word of God."

We might also do well to remember the truths in some of those prayers we learned as children. "God is great. God is good. Let us thank Him...." "Now I lay me down to sleep; I pray the Lord my soul to keep."

Rediscover some of those activities and timeless truths you may have learned in your youth. Maybe you'll find them to be helpful spiritual exercises which can still stretch your soul today.

Is there some childhood spiritual practice you need to introduce or reinstate in your life?

LISTEN TO THE PROMPTINGS
OF THE HOLY SPIRIT

"Do not quench the Spirit."
– I THESSALONIANS 5:19

I remember back when activity trackers were just coming out. At the time I had told someone in my church that I was thinking about getting a pedometer to measure the amount of walking I did. He told me about those new devices both he and his wife used—something that went far beyond old-fashioned pedometers. He told me how it not only kept up with the number of steps you take each day, but how many stairs you climb and how many calories you burn. It could do much more, even monitoring your activity overnight in order to assess how well you slept.

Someone suggested to me that it would be nice if there were such devices which could track our spiritual activity. I wonder how that would work. Maybe it would count how many times we prayed each day, along with the total minutes we spent talking to God. Or it might count how long we read our Bibles, how many times we thanked God for His blessings, how often we had a song of praise and worship on our lips or simply in our hearts. It might count how many hours we spend in church, how often we witness to someone, or how many steps we take in obedience to God.

But in a sense don't we as believers already have a spiritual activity tracker? I'm referring to the Holy Spirit. He's not a device we stick in our pockets, hook on our belts, or wear on a wristband. He actually lives in our hearts. He is with us at all times and wherever we go.

He is faithful to assure us when we're walking on the right path and lets us know that all is well with our souls. But He's just as faithful to prick our hearts when we take a wrong step, when we're neglecting those valuable spiritual disciplines, and when we've just generally become a little lazy in cultivating our relationship with the Lord.

However, the Holy Spirit doesn't force us to be spiritually healthy. Those activity trackers don't make us physically fit. They simply reveal to us what we are doing or failing to do. They don't zap us with an electric shock to get us out of our recliners and onto a walking trail. They create a report of our activity, if we're interested enough to push a button to see it. And even then, we have a choice to either use that information to set goals and to motivate us to do better, or we can ignore it and remain the way we are. Likewise the Holy Spirit will convict us of sin, guide us into truth, and show us the right pathways to travel. But we have to be willing to listen with an attitude that is eager to become a more spiritually healthy follower of Christ. Too often we fail to pay attention to the Holy Spirit's assessment, or we try to make excuses for ourselves rather than change our behavior. We have to want a closer walk with the Lord and we must choose to submit to His will for us.

Wouldn't it be nice if those activity trackers could give us a boost of energy to take more steps when we're falling short of our goal? The Holy Spirit can do that. He can not only search our hearts and give us His report, but He can also enable us to do what we need to do.

That nice couple in my church graciously gave me one of those activity trackers for my birthday that year. And I've been using it ever since. Are you making use of the Holy Spirit as the One who can show us where we stand spiritually and who can help us take more steps toward a better walk with God?

Listen to the promptings of the Holy Spirit in your life. Accept His assessments and let Him help you make improvements.

YOUR REAL PURPOSE IN LIFE CAN ONLY BE FOUND IN JESUS

"All things were created through Him and for Him."

– COLOSSIANS 1:16

Imagine that a Louisville Slugger baseball bat found itself being shipped from its factory where it had been made to a small town. It was received by an older couple who proceeded to set it aside in a corner of a closet. As the bat stayed there, it began to wonder if it had any real purpose in existing.

But one day the couple removed that uniquely-crafted piece of wood from its isolation and began to use it…to prop open a door. The bat actually started feeling useful. It wasn't long before the older gentleman began to grab the bat and take it with him on walks through the neighborhood—using it to threaten and ward off barking dogs. With that additional daily job, the bat felt a greater sense of purpose.

Then the elderly lady of the household grew more feeble. So she sometimes took the bat and used it almost like a walking cane around the house, to help her maintain her balance and keep herself from falling. The bat was especially pleased to find itself being of such assistance to this kind lady.

This relationship continued until the couple's teenage grandson visited one day. He noticed the bat, grabbed it around its handle, and swung it a few times in an exhilarating way it had never experienced before. His grandparents ended up giving him the bat to take home with him. A few days later, the bat found itself on a field being used to hit baseballs. When it hit a ball in its "sweet spot" sending the sphere screaming into the outfield, the bat knew that for the first time it was fulfilling its real purpose. It realized it wasn't meant to merely prop open doors, scare away dogs, or be used as a walking stick, as useful as some of those activities may have been. It was meant to hit baseballs. That's what the Louisville Slugger company had made it for. And it was only when it was being used for what it was created to do that it found its true purpose and meaning.

The same could be said of us. The Bible declares that all things were created through Jesus and for Him (Colossians 1:16). And that includes us. We have been created by Jesus and for Jesus. Our lives aren't all about us—they're about fulfilling the purpose for which Jesus has created us.

There are many good things we can do with our lives, some of which will give us a sense of meaning and usefulness. But we aren't going to discover the true and greatest purposes of our lives apart from Jesus. We aren't going to discover what we were made to do until we get our lives in line with the One who made us. We were created to know Him, to do His will, and to glorify Him. It's when we put our trust in Him as Savior, surrender our lives to Him, and seek to fulfill His plan and purposes for us that we find true meaning in life.

The Lord has many different specific plans and purposes for each one of us—creating us with our own unique qualities and abilities. But we were all made to live a life that will bring honor and glory to Him.

So don't settle for being a door prop when the Lord has made you to hit baseballs. You're only going to find your greatest joy and meaning as you seek to fulfill your Creator's purpose for your life.

Are you living your life for Jesus and to fulfill His purposes?

LET'S MAINTAIN OUR AWE OF THE MIRACLES OF CHRIST

"Who can this be, that even the winds and the sea obey Him?"

– MATTHEW 8:27

During a trip to the beach some years ago, I saw many of the usual sights as I looked out over the ocean. There were a few heads and shoulders sticking out of the water from those people wading off shore. There were several bodies restfully sprawled horizontally on floats bobbing along with the movement of the waves. An occasional kayaker would paddle past. And in the mornings you might be fortunate enough to see a few dolphins go gliding by.

But there was one sight I had a hard time getting accustomed to. It was seeing someone who, from a certain angle and distance, appeared to be standing on the surface of the water. At times you could see the thin board underneath the person's feet, but other times it was hidden. Paddleboards have since become more popular and common, so you probably know that they allow someone to paddle himself along in an upright position—that is, once he's learned to maintain his balance. I watched one young guy work hard at doing so for quite a while, but the last time I saw him he was still frequently making a splash as he fell off the board into the water.

Viewing someone who appeared to be standing on the top of the sea caused me to think how seeing Jesus walk on water must have looked to His disciples. He wasn't just standing upright. He was taking steps. And there was no board underneath him and no paddle in his hands. He didn't just appear to be walking on water from a particular angle, He was actually doing it. The closer He approached, the clearer it became that this was no clever stunt—this was a miracle.

Some of us may have become so accustomed to reading about the miracles of Christ that they've lost some of their wonder in our eyes. My experience at the beach gave me a fresh sense of awe at the thought of someone actually walking on the surface of the sea. Or imagine someone being raised from the dead as Jesus raised up Lazarus. Think about attending a friend's funeral, viewing the dead body, and witnessing it being lowered into the grave. And then Someone comes along a couple of days later instructing the grave to be dug up and the casket to be opened. And when it is, your friend pops up alive and well.

Or imagine being in the middle of a storm, the setting for another of Jesus' miracles. The local meteorologist interrupts your TV program to show you the nasty red blob on the radar heading your direction. The wind begins to howl and the torrent of rain begins to fall. But then Someone interrupts the weatherman saying "Peace, be still." And suddenly the weather outside is calm and that red blob totally disappears from the radar.

Let's not lose sight of how great it was when Jesus caused the blind to see, the deaf to hear, the lame to walk, and all the other miracles He did.

Likewise let's not get too accustomed to the great things He still does today. Let's not take for granted the miracle of a soul saved and a life transformed through faith in Jesus. Let's not downplay the answers to our prayers. Let's not overlook how the Lord has helped us through those impossible-looking circumstances of our lives—opening the door to a better job, providing for our financial needs, healing our bodies, and restoring a broken relationship.

During my few days at the beach, I never got used to that sight of someone seemingly standing on the water. Similarly let's never lose our wonder at the miracles Jesus did and the great things He's still doing in our lives today.

Think about the great things the Lord has done in your life. Be amazed and give Him thanks.

Be Prepared to Keep
Going to the End

*"For your faithfulness is like a morning cloud, and like the early
dew it goes away."*

– Hosea 6:4

One weekend I ended up watching a little more football than I usually do. That was due in part to getting much of my work finished
beforehand, along with the fact that there were some interesting games
being played. But admittedly the greatest factor was probably that my
wife was out of town for the weekend attending a wedding, leaving me in
the position of not needing to give consideration to her alternate preferences for TV viewing.

Since I watched portions of several different games, a common factor
jumped out at me. I know that teams tend to come out of the locker room
all fired up with energy and enthusiasm to play the game. But it seems
that some take it to a different level—one that's hard to maintain for any
length of time. Early in the game, a player might make a decent routine
play and jump around celebrating as if it was the greatest accomplishment
since Franco Harris' "immaculate reception." Or after a team makes a first
down or stops the other team from doing so, they act as if they had just
won the Super Bowl.

I noticed that some of those teams that were so pumped up and
performed so well early in the contest eventually lost their initial energy
and enthusiasm, allowing their opponent to gain the momentum and,

in some cases, even win the game. It served as a reminder that a football team has to be prepared to play all four quarters. An enthusiastic start is good, but there also needs to be a mindset of enduring till the end of the game.

In His parable of the sower, Jesus compared some people to seed that falls on stony ground. They immediately spring up, initially receiving God's Word with enthusiastic joy. But because their roots don't go deep, they only endure for a while, inevitably withering away in the heat of hard times. The Bible also compares the Christian life to a race—not a sprint but a marathon—encouraging us to "run with endurance the race that is set before us" (Hebrews 12:1).

I'm not suggesting that there's anything wrong with spirited enthusiasm or with us trying to give 100 percent effort in our walk with God, but we need to remember that we can't survive simply by focusing on superficial emotions—we've got to get our spiritual roots down too. And while we seek to run hard at the moment, we've also got to realize that we need to run in such a way as to finish the race well.

The Apostle Peter reminds me of one of those football players. He often came out with an unbridled outburst of energy and enthusiasm. He boldly proclaimed that Jesus was the Son of the living God, he bravely jumped out of the boat to go to Jesus walking on the water, and he enthusiastically declared that he would never forsake Jesus—but before the game was over in those situations, he was being rebuked for letting Satan use him, he was fearfully sinking amid the waves, and he was denying that he ever knew Jesus.

Some of us may need more of the enthusiasm and energy of a Peter. But we also need the stability that he was lacking at that point. We need to remain faithful in the long run. One time God told Israel and Judah, "Your faithfulness is like a morning cloud, and like the early dew it goes away" (Hosea 6:4). Does that describe our lives in relation to God?

Let's not shy away from getting fired up for God, but at the same time let's not mistake one victory or one setback as the end of the game. We need to keep running and remain faithful for the full four quarters.

In what ways do you need to do better at running the race with endurance in order to finish well?

APPRECIATE YOUR PASTOR BUT DON'T WORSHIP HIM

"Let the elders who rule well be counted worthy of double honor, especially those who labor in the word and doctrine."

– I TIMOTHY 5:17

I grew up in a church in which the "Doxology" was sung every Sunday. I hope you know the words to that short hymn of praise: "Praise God from whom all blessings flow. Praise Him, all creatures here below. Praise Him above, ye heavenly hosts. Praise Father, Son and Holy Ghost. Amen."

No one in my church opened up their hymnals to read the words of that particular song. And, of course, back then projecting those words on a screen would have been unheard of. It was just assumed that everyone knew the "Doxology." However, as a child it took me a while to decipher parts of it. I especially remember a point where I was questioning whether to sing "Praise Him, all creatures here below" or "Praise Him, all preachers here below." I guess it made sense to a young boy that preachers in particular would be directed to praise God. So I just mumbled my way through that part, listened closely as others sang, and finally figured it out.

In other ways, I think some of us still struggle with those concepts of "preacher" and "creature." There are those who exalt their pastors to the point that he is viewed as someone who can say or do no wrong and, in some cases, is looked upon almost like the Creator instead of one of

God's human creations. The fault in those cases can lie both with the pastor and the congregation. Some church members have a tendency to put their pastor on a pedestal as a spiritual celebrity or a supersaint. And unfortunately some pastors not only enjoy such status, but also let pride and arrogance gain such a foothold that they may begin to believe it themselves.

Overexalting a pastor will inevitably lead to disappointment and confusion when that preacher lets us down in some way, bringing us to the realization that he's not the god we thought he was. Such a letdown may cause us to question our faith, if indeed we've been putting our faith more in that pastor than in the one God who is truly holy, faithful, and worthy of our worship.

Such a perspective is hard for others of us to imagine, because we preachers, as well as our congregations, know all too well our faults and weaknesses. But maybe we have to guard against the other extreme, viewing our preachers as so "creaturely" that we don't expect them to exhibit a high standard of morality and holiness in their lives. Some of us may like the idea that our preacher is just as bad or sinful as we are, relieving us of some feelings of guilt and condemnation over our own attitudes and behavior.

We need to find the proper balance between those two extremes. While congregations should love and respect their pastors, they should remember that he's only human and should keep their faith focused on Jesus. And we pastors need to heed the biblical warning "not to think of himself more highly than he ought to think" (Romans 12:3). At the same time, people should expect their pastors to be genuine in their relationship with God and pursuing a holy life. We pastors should seek, as Paul instructed Timothy, to "be an example to the believers in word, in conduct, in love, in spirit, in faith, in purity" (I Timothy 4:12).

In recent years, October has become designated as Pastor Appreciation Month. I hope you'll take the opportunity to encourage your pastor by rightfully expressing your love, respect, and appreciation for him. But do him and yourself a favor: don't overexalt him. Remember that your preacher is merely a creature, just like you.

What can you do this week to show proper respect and appreciation for your pastor?

Don't Forget about the Threat of Evil

"Be vigilant; because your adversary the devil walks about like a roaring lion, seeking whom he may devour."

– I Peter 5:8

I played golf with a bear—well, almost. My wife, our oldest grandson, and I stopped for a day in Gatlinburg, Tennessee, while on our way to visit a church. That evening we decided to play a round of miniature golf on a course that was set on a hillside behind the main row of businesses. In the middle of our game, our grandson spotted a big black bear lumbering down the hill and proceeding to walk through the course ahead of us. We excitedly but cautiously watched the intruder until he moved out of sight. Subsequently we continued to play with a nervous, vigilant eye on our surroundings until some other players informed us that they had seen the bear return up the hill and leave the course.

If you've ever been to Gatlinburg, you know that the main road is lined with all sorts of restaurants, souvenir shops, and attractions. As you're walking along that busy tourist district, it's easy to lose sight of the fact that you're actually in the middle of a wilderness area, just a very short distance from the habitat of wild animals and the potential risk of dangerous encounters with those creatures. However on this occasion, we received a memorable reminder of that fact.

Likewise it's often easy to forget about the evil and spiritual dangers lurking in our world. We go about our business as usual with little thought to the risks we face until incidents occur such as the mass shooting of concertgoers in Las Vegas a while back. No doubt most people were caught up in the glitz, glamor, and bright lights of that city with no idea of the evil nearby. When such incidents occur, suddenly we're given a stark reminder of the depths of darkness to which a soul can reach when God is forsaken. We look around us a little more cautiously for a while, but eventually as time passes we tend to forget again…until the next time it erupts.

However, it's not just the evil which humans can inflict on one another that we tend to lose sight of, but also the spiritual forces of wickedness that surround us. The Bible warns us to "be vigilant; because your adversary the devil walks about like a roaring lion, seeking whom he may devour" (I Peter 5:8). I don't think that bear we encountered was looking to harm anyone. He was probably just looking for a bite to eat. But we have a spiritual foe who is actively seeking to hurt and destroy us. He wants to hinder our relationship with God. He wants to keep us from doing good and serving the Lord. If possible, he wants to stop us from getting to heaven one day. We can't afford to lose sight of the reality of his presence or to be ignorant of his tactics (II Corinthians 2:11).

Not only do we need to be aware of such evil around us, but we also need to be prepared. God has provided us with the means to stand up against it. "Put on the whole armor of God, that you may be able to stand against the wiles of the devil.… Therefore take up the whole armor of God, that you may be able to withstand in the evil day, and having done all, to stand" (Ephesians 6:11–13). Take another look in that passage of scripture at the specific equipment God gives us to face our adversary. Let's make sure we're making use of it.

There's a lot of good and godly aspects of this life which we can enjoy. But in the process don't lose sight of the evil lurking nearby. Always be vigilant and keep your armor on.

Be watchful for the devil and his tactics today.

Don't Let Your Fears Hinder Your Walk with Christ

"Do not fear, nor be afraid."
– ISAIAH 44:8

When my grandkids come over for a visit, sometimes we'll pull out an episode of the *Andy Griffith Show* from my DVD collection to watch. They're at the age now where they appreciate the down-home humor from this classic television series. And that especially pleases their Papaw, since it's one of my favorites. A number of those episodes also open the door for our briefly discussing some moral lesson in the storyline after we enjoy the show.

Recently we watched the one in which little Opie was having his milk money taken away from him every morning by a bully. It gave us the chance to talk about the important subject of bullying and what to do about those situations. However, another point we noted was that often what we fear isn't as bad as we think it's going to be. Opie was so afraid of getting a threatened "knuckle sandwich" from his adversary that it caused him to act in ways in which he was ashamed of himself. When he finally worked up the courage to stand up to that bully, he received the promised punch in the face, but it didn't hurt like he thought it would. He realized that what he had been so scared of wasn't nearly as bad as he had imagined.

Fear can be a powerful force in our lives. Sometimes it can be helpful as it keeps us from pursuing perilous paths or avoiding behaviors which could prove to be harmful to us. However it can also hinder us from being willing to travel different roads, try new things, and stand up against the evil and injustices in our world. As followers of Christ, fear can be an obstacle in our efforts to be fully obedient to the Lord and to fulfill the work He's given us to do in this world.

What are some of the specific fears which might hinder our walk with Christ?

The fear of what the Lord might ask me to do or where He might call me to go if I yield completely to His control over my life.

The fear of what other people will think of me or say about me if I let my faith be known or if I become totally committed to Jesus.

The fear of failure—I know my weaknesses, what if I blow it?

The fear of success—if the Lord blesses me in that way, how will it alter my life?

The fear of change in any form or fashion.

The fear of the unknown—having to live by faith.

These are just a few of the fears which we might face as we seek to follow the Lord. Some of them can seem overwhelming. They make us hesitant to be all that God calls us to be. They may cause us to keep silent instead of being bold witnesses for Christ. They can result in our trying to do as Jesus warned about in His Sermon on the Mount—hide our lamps under a basket rather than letting our lights shine for the glory of God. These fears can cause us to do things which make us hang our heads in shame before our Heavenly Father.

Let's learn the lesson Opie Taylor discovered. What we fear often isn't as bad as we picture it to be. And even if it does hurt, that pain pales in comparison to the joy and benefits we'll receive as a result of standing up for what's right and doing what pleases the Lord.

"For God has not given us a spirit of fear, but of power and of love and of a sound mind" (II Timothy 1:7).

Is there some particular fear you need to face?

What Kind of Revival Are We Seeking?

"Revive me according to Your word."
– Psalm 119:25

One day a couple of my grandchildren informed me that one of the toys they enjoy playing with at our house needed new batteries. I checked it out and concluded they were right. The toy sometimes failed to work at all, but even when it did it moved very sluggishly.

The reason I didn't simply accept my grandchildren's diagnosis of the problem is that I've witnessed a certain tendency they've all exhibited at some point in their early years. When something wasn't working properly, they automatically assumed that putting in new batteries was the answer. Sometimes they might have been right, but other times the problem required more than a battery change. And in some cases, unbeknownst to their young minds, the objects in question didn't even use batteries.

Sometimes we tend to do the same thing. When we start getting a little sluggish spiritually or when our church doesn't seem to be functioning very effectively, we automatically assume we need a revival. Some of us can tend to throw the idea of revival around as the solution for every problem, much like young children think new batteries will fix whatever may be broken.

Don't get me wrong. Revival is always appropriate and needed. We never reach a point where we don't need to draw closer to God.

No matter how brightly our passion for the Lord may burn, it could always burn a little brighter and a little hotter. And there are times when we allow our devotion to the Lord to grow dim and we need it to be rekindled.

But let's make sure our idea of revival isn't just about getting our emotions recharged. Let's not confine the concept of revival to simply getting stirred up or feeling better. There's nothing wrong with our emotions being touched—when we encounter God it can often be a very emotional experience. But revival should include more than a good feeling. It involves humbling ourselves before God, letting Him reveal changes needed in our lives, and allowing Him to make those changes. Revival shouldn't just result in a short-term spiritual high, but also in a long-term transformation.

Sometimes the answer to our problems may involve a renewing of our minds, not just a fresh burst of energy. We may need to gain a better understanding of what we as believers need to be doing to be more effective in our day, rather than just seeking a greater passion to keep doing the same things we've been doing. Sometimes the problem can be just as much in our heads as in our hearts.

Additionally, there may be times when what we need is not greater introspection into what's going on in the depth of our hearts in relation to God, but rather more interaction with the people around us who need to hear the gospel and come into a saving knowledge of the Lord. Instead of isolating ourselves to spend more "quiet time" with God, the Lord might be wanting us to get out into the world where our lights can shine and have an impact on others. In other words, true revival for us might not just involve a better devotional life, but more emphasis on serving the Lord and reaching out to other people.

I don't think we can deny that we, our churches, and certainly our nation need revival. It really is one of the primary answers to today's problems. But as we talk about and seek revival, let's remember that we need more than an occasional, superficial spiritual boost. We need a long-lasting Spirit-led transformation of our hearts, lives, minds, and ministries.

Lord, revive my spirit, renew my mind, and move me to serve you better in this world.

WE OWE OUR
SALVATION TO JESUS

"He has…conveyed us into the kingdom of the Son of His love, in whom we have redemption through His blood"

– COLOSSIANS 1:13–14

Do you remember the family that was hiking in Colorado a few years ago when there was a sudden landslide? Huge rocks came tumbling down the side of the hill, killing five or six members of the family. The only person to survive was a teenage daughter. Based on the girl's account of what happened, along with what investigators could uncover about the incident, there is one reason and only one reason why she survived this ordeal. It was because her father had tried to protect her as the landslide hit by putting himself between his daughter and the boulders. He covered her, giving his life in order for her to have a better chance at living.

In the years to come, as this girl looks back and tells others what happened on that fateful day, I doubt if she'll tell about how lucky she was to have survived the landslide when everyone else was killed. I don't think she'll credit her toughness or her own strength for not being crushed by those huge rocks. I'm fairly certain she won't attribute her deliverance to some scientific explanation about the trajectory of the rocks in relation to where she was standing on the hiking trail in comparison to where all the other people were standing.

I'm confident that she'll always tell people, "The only reason I survived is because of my dad and what he did for me at that moment. My deliverance—my living instead of dying—is all about my father. It's about his sacrificial act of love on my behalf."

We can testify to the same truth about Jesus. Our being delivered from spiritual and eternal death is due completely to Him and what He did for us. It's all about Him and His sacrificial act of love on our behalf.

The Bible says God "has delivered us from the power of darkness and conveyed us into the kingdom of the Son of His love, in whom we have redemption through His blood, the forgiveness of sins" (Colossians 1:13–14). The "in whom" refers to Jesus. He's the only reason we can have redemption and can experience the forgiveness of our sins. And notice also that it's "through His blood."

Jesus didn't save us simply by means of His inspiring teachings about how to love others and live right. Neither did He redeem us by setting a wonderful example for us to follow. What saved us was Jesus putting Himself between us and the boulders of sin, death, and hell which were threatening to crush us. And He did it by shedding His own blood—by dying on the cross as the sacrifice for our sins.

Sometimes we get to focusing so much on what we need to do to continue to faithfully follow the Lord that we lose sight of what Jesus has done for us. If we're not careful, we can start associating our salvation more with what we do or don't do instead of keeping the focus on Jesus, the One whom our salvation is all about.

Or sometimes we so emphasize the teachings and example of Jesus that we neglect what He did for us on the cross. Let's never forget that it was through His death that Jesus saved us. Therefore He's the One who deserves our praise and gratitude. Jesus is our Rescuer to whom we should give our utmost love and loyalty.

Let's always remember that the only reason we're not perishing but have eternal life is because of Jesus giving His life out of love for us.

Take time today to give thanks for your Redeemer.

BE AN EFFECTIVE DEFENDER
OF THE FAITH

"Contend earnestly for the faith which was once for all delivered to the saints."

– JUDE 3

On several occasions, I have attended a Christian Apologetics Conference. That doesn't mean that I came back having learned a hundred different ways to say "I'm sorry" or "forgive me" with a more sincere, Christlike spirit. As many of you know, apologetics has to do with defending the faith. But don't picture that idea in the wrong way either. There were no classes training people in martial arts. And Don Rickles wasn't one of the featured speakers teaching Christians how to hurl biting insults back at the people who oppose them.

Christian apologetics is a branch of theology dealing with the defense and proofs of Christianity. Many of the sessions at this conference were intended to equip believers to be able to share their faith better and to be able to knowledgeably and effectively answer the honest questions people might have about the Christian faith. Therefore it dealt with such issues as the biblical account of creation, evidences for Jesus' resurrection, other religions, the belief that Jesus is the only way, the reliability of the Bible, and even such hot topics as same-sex marriage.

But does the average follower of Christ really need to know all that intellectual stuff? Can't we just preach Jesus and share our testimony about what the Lord has done for us? Undoubtedly the account of our spiritual journey and personal experience with Christ can be one of our most potent tools in witnessing to others. However, that doesn't excuse us from being able to intelligently answer the questions people raise concerning these other topics.

But can't we leave the defending of the faith up to the likes of Josh McDowell and Ravi Zacharias and our pastor—those who are better trained for it? While there may be times when we might need to refer people to those who can give them more information than we're able to supply, we should still be able to provide basic answers to those questions. Peter was speaking to average believers when he instructed them to "always be ready to give a defense to everyone who asks you a reason for the hope that is in you" (I Peter 3:15).

We find a similar exhortation in the little book of Jude. The writer explained that he had planned to write to these believers about the subject of salvation, but found it necessary to change direction. Because of false teaching and teachers who had arisen among them, he was now exhorting them "to contend earnestly for the faith which was once for all delivered to the saints" (Jude 3).

We live in similar circumstances today. Christianity and its teachings are being challenged in many different ways. And we have a responsibility to stand up for the truth. As believers, we need to contend for the faith.

However how we do it is also important. At times well-meaning Christians have done more harm than good by the manner in which they attempted to defend their faith. We don't have to attack with guns blazing, with a harsh spirit, and with words aimed at destroying our opposition. That verse in I Peter goes on to say that we are to give a defense "with meekness and fear." We can faithfully share the truth, but we can do it lovingly and respectfully.

The times we live in demand that we become what could be called "thinking Christians." Know what you believe and why you believe it.

Explore the biblical answers to those tough questions people raise. Let's seek to be more effective witnesses for Christ.

Don't find yourself having to apologize for not being a Christian apologist.

What can you do to become a better defender of the faith?

THE CROSS PROVES
WE CAN TRUST JESUS

*"For even the Son of Man did not come to be served, but to serve,
and to give His life a ransom for many."*

– MARK 10:45

O ne of the questions that usually comes up in an election season is, "Who can you trust?" Some of us might believe that we can't trust any of the politicians, at least not completely. But we still might inquire as to which one is the most trustworthy.

I would suggest that this is a more important question than many others which the pollsters ask, such as "Which candidate would you rather have dinner with?" The question of trust focuses on the idea of which person we believe will be more likely to do as he says. In other words, which one will follow through on those promises and nice-sounding plans proposed during the campaign. And which candidate will we be able to depend on to do what's best for our nation rather than simply what's good for himself and his own political future. This question also addresses the issue as to which one we believe will stand by his convictions and principles when lobbyists and others pressure him to do otherwise.

I'll leave it up to you to try to figure out which political candidate may be the most deserving of your trust, but I will endorse Someone else I believe we can all trust completely—and that's Jesus. He is trustworthy because He is Someone who will always do what He says, He will always act in our best interests, and He will always do what is right regardless of the pressures or circumstances.

How do we know? It's not just because He says so—it's because He's proven it. The greatest indicator that we can trust Jesus is the cross.

At the cross, Jesus did what He had said He came to do—give His life a ransom for many (Mark 10:45). He didn't come back later claiming that He had been misquoted or misunderstood. He didn't claim that "is" didn't mean "is," or that "give His life" didn't mean "to die." As unpleasant as it was to do so, He kept that most significant of promises: to give His life so that we could have eternal life.

The cross also shows how much Jesus cares for us. If Jesus had been thinking about Himself or seeking self-promotion, He wouldn't have suffered and died, especially not in such a demeaning manner. But He went to the cross because He was focused on helping us. He didn't run away from the prospect of suffering and death. He marched steadfastly toward it out of love for us. We can trust Somebody who will give His life for us in the way that Jesus did.

Through the cross we can also see the trustworthiness of Jesus in how He did what was right in spite of tremendous pressure to do otherwise. Satan lobbied hard for Jesus to take another pathway. He tempted Jesus with everything this world could offer—fame, fortune, and power. But Jesus refused them all, because it wasn't the right thing to do. He felt the pressure in the Garden of Gethsemane, agonizing over the prospect of His suffering. But in the end He submitted Himself to the will of His Father. He was committed to doing the right thing no matter how high the personal price. That's Someone we can trust.

So whether or not you believe you can trust any political candidates, the cross shouts out loud and clear that we can trust this One who loves us and gave His life for us. Will you put your trust in Him today?

Does your life show that you believe Jesus is completely worthy of your trust? Is anything in your attitude or actions revealing a lack of trust in Him?

The Last Miles of Life's Journey Mean We're Almost Home

As I was returning from a meeting in middle Tennessee, I came upon a familiar stretch of interstate. It's a beautiful few miles of road that includes traveling over part of Nickajack Lake, maneuvering between high walls of rock, and going under a large railroad trestle. Maybe some of you who have occasionally travelled that route can picture the exact spot to which I'm referring.

That area often brings back memories of my trips home from college many, many years ago. I was attending a school which was some 900 miles away from my family and friends in Georgia. Due to the distance, I was only able to make that long drive home once or twice during the school year. As I did, there was always something about that scenic stretch of road north of Chattanooga that stood out to me. Whenever I arrived there, I got a sudden warm feeling that I was almost home. I knew in my mind that I still had a couple of hours of driving to endure, but the sight of that particular scenery would brighten my tired eyes, invigorate my weary body, and encourage my spirit with the idea that I was getting close to my desired destination.

As we take our journey through life and get older, there will be some indications that we are much closer to the end of our long trip than we are to the beginning. The top of our heads begin to look more like snowcapped mountains unless we make an effort to hide that natural transformation.

Or for others of us it might be better described as the forest not being as thick as it used to be.

We often find new roads of wrinkles being cut into the formerly smooth landscape of our skin. And younger drivers, some of whom may be our grandchildren or great-grandchildren, are zooming past us at speeds that make our heads spin. Our vehicles sputter and often need to go into the shop for repairs. And our GPS often forgets where we are and what it is we're supposed to be doing.

Some of our experiences as we near the closing miles of our journey aren't pleasant. But there are others, such as seeing those grandchildren enjoying life, which are as beautiful in our eyes as the scenery in those Tennessee hills.

How do we handle those reminders that we're getting older and that we're nearing the latter stretch of life's journey? We could get discouraged and let that revelation transform us into the proverbial grouchy old man or woman. Or as those who are putting their faith in Christ, we can recognize the wonderful truth that we're almost home. We're drawing nearer to the time when we will be with our Savior for eternity. It won't be long before we'll be reunited with other beloved believers who have made this journey ahead of us. Soon we won't have to experience the physical hardships of this life nor the heartaches that come from living in a spiritually-fallen world.

In spite of those indications that we're well along in our journey, we may yet have many miles to go before we arrive. However, we may be increasingly encountering more of the signs that we're getting closer. Although we'll be tempted to do otherwise, let's allow those landmarks to encourage us rather than dishearten us. Let their reminder put a twinkle in your eye and fresh energy in your soul. Our earthly journey may be drawing nearer to its end, but followers of Christ can rejoice in the truth that we're almost home.

When you think about getting older, try to focus more on the positive fact that you're getting closer to your heavenly home.

LET'S REMEMBER WHO WE ARE

"So God created man in His own image; in the image of God He created him; male and female He created them."

– GENESIS 1:27

For my birthday one year, my wife gave me a choice of presents. She said that I could either choose the practical gift of a new suit or something more pleasurable. Although I tend to be a practical person, on this occasion I selected the pleasurable option. Therefore we headed over to the fabulous Fox Theater in Atlanta to see the show entitled *Wicked*.

If you're not familiar with this production, its title might cause you to question my desire to see it. As a matter of fact, when we were waiting in the lobby my wife jokingly offered to buy me one of the T-shirts they were selling. However, we didn't think it would be appropriate for a pastor to go around wearing a shirt that simply said "wicked" on the front of it.

As you probably know, the show is actually intended to be sort of a prequel to *The Wizard of Oz*. And that film being one of my favorites since childhood is what led us to the Fox on this occasion. The show supposedly provides the backstory for the witches in that classic tale, especially the wicked witch of the west. Seeing where she presumably came from would help people better understand this witch and give them insight into who she truly was.

Sometimes we need to remember our backstory and be reminded of who we are, not just individually but as human beings. And you can't go much farther back than those first two chapters of Genesis having to do with the creation of mankind.

One of the truths that emerge from that account is that God has created us as living souls. Our physical being isn't who we are and shouldn't be the main thing that defines us or controls us. We are more than what we see when we look in the mirror every morning—and aren't we thankful for that? Therefore we need to cultivate that which will make us healthy and beautiful on the inside.

It also means that we will continue to exist as souls once this body dies. Death is not the end of us. We are souls who can have a relationship with God and who are going to live on in one condition or another forever. So instead of simply living for the here and now, shouldn't we be preparing for eternity?

The second main truth brought out in Genesis about human beings is that we were created in the image of God. This doesn't mean that we look like God physically, because the Bible tells us that God is spirit. But our souls possess some of the qualities and abilities found in God—morally, ethically, and intellectually.

It's true that much of that image has been marred by sin. Yet it's still there to some extent. So as we think about who we are as human beings, we ought to see both sides of the same coin. On the one side we are all sinners, part of a fallen human race whose hearts can be "desperately wicked" (Jeremiah 17:9). But on the other side, we should recognize that we are among those who were made in the image of God and that He can restore a great degree of that image in us if we'll let Him do a transforming work in our lives.

So our backstory not only shows who we were originally and what we're like today, but it also reveals what we were meant to be and can become through God's grace and the work of the Holy Spirit in our lives. We don't have to be wicked. We as human beings made in the image of God have a unique opportunity to reflect God's glory to the rest of creation. Are we doing so?

How are you reflecting God's image and glory in your life?

Join with Another Believer in Prayer

"If two of you agree on earth concerning anything that they ask, it will be done for them by My Father in heaven."

– Matthew 18:19

In recent years maybe you've noticed a few small businesses that have chosen similar names for themselves. The first one I heard of was "Two Guys and a Truck"—a moving company. I don't know if they started this trend that others have picked up on, but if you scan a local business directory, as I did, you'll find a number of comparable titles: "Two Guys and a Mop"—"Two Ladies and a Mop"—"Two Ladies and a Vacuum." I assume those are all cleaning services. I also found a listing for "Three Chicks and a Mower" for those who need lawn care.

And then there's the one that had a billboard advertisement right off the local interstate—"Three Girls and a Needle." I'll admit that one scared me a little as my mind went first in the direction of hypodermic needles. But then I saw that it was actually referring to a hair-weaving business.

It started me wondering what those establishments are trying to convey about themselves by using one of those types of names. I think they're hoping to impress upon consumers that they aren't some huge corporation but rather a smaller business. They're just regular people who have the skill and equipment to do the job, and probably do it much cheaper than one of those bigger companies.

I believe Jesus indicates that His followers can claim a similar title. He gives us ordinary believers the equipment to do great things. We could call it "Two Believers and a Prayer." In Matthew 18:19, Jesus declares, "Again I say to you that if two of you agree on earth concerning anything that they ask, it will be done for them by My Father in heaven." Two believers who come together in agreement, with one heart and mind, can accomplish mighty things through prayer.

It's talking about ordinary followers of Jesus. You don't have to belong to a huge church. You don't have to be well known in Christian circles. You don't have to be an author whose books are selling at the local Christian bookstore or an artist who has recorded a praise and worship song. You're not required to be a bishop, a preacher, or even a Sunday School teacher. Just two common people who know and follow Jesus as their Savior can agree and pray and see God answer.

That truth should encourage us. It should excite us to know that God has given us such a privilege. But maybe it should also convict us if we haven't been making good use of this equipment God has given us and haven't been doing our job very well. The needs are all around us. The opportunity is tremendous. But are we joining with other believers in agreement, asking God for those things He wants us to be concerned about?

Too often we try to carry the burden by ourselves. But Jesus' words indicate that prayer can be more effective when we are willing to share our concern with others and let them join us in bringing that need to our Heavenly Father. Look through the book of Acts and notice what God does as a relatively small group of believers pray. Souls are saved. Christians are filled with the Spirit. Boldness and courage are granted in the face of opposition. Prisoners are set free.

God can do similar things in our world and in our lives today. What difficulties are you facing? What burdens are you carrying? Find one or two other believers who will commit to agreeing with you in prayer. Then watch and see what God does.

Who can you approach today about partnering with you in prayer?

The Things of This
World Won't Last

"Therefore, since all these things will be dissolved, what manner of persons ought you to be in holy conduct and godliness?"

– II Peter 3:11

One year for my birthday I received the gift of a book—the full collection of *Peanuts* comic strips from the years 1959 and 1960. It was an especially appropriate present for two reasons. For one thing, 1959 was the year I was born. Secondly, I've always been a fan of Charlie Brown, Snoopy, and the gang. Not only have I followed their adventures in the Sunday "funnies," but I also grew up faithfully watching the classic animated TV specials where Charlie Brown searched for the meaning of Christmas and Linus sat in a field waiting for the arrival of the Great Pumpkin on Halloween.

In one of the comics from this book, it shows Linus building a sandcastle. It was an expansive structure with many towers and other intricate features associated with castles. Linus obviously spent much time constructing this creation. But as he continued to work, a few drops of rain began to fall. The precipitation came down harder and harder until it was a huge downpour. When it was over a few minutes later, the sandcastle had been completely washed away. Linus commented, "There's a lesson to be learned here somewhere, but I don't know what it is."

Since Charles Schultz left it open to interpretation, I'd like to take a stab at what that lesson might be. We spend our lives building our sandcastles, putting much time and effort into doing so. Some of us build different kinds of castles than others, or we may each construct various types at different points in our lives. We build careers, houses, and families. We pursue ambitions, fame, pleasure, riches, power, and other things of this world.

Although some of those pursuits are more worthy than others, we should realize that they're all sandcastles. Anything having to do with this world can be taken away in a moment. A flood, an earthquake, a car accident, a serious disease, an economic collapse, or a pink slip from your employer can quickly result in a downpour that washes away everything you've built. Additionally, the Bible teaches that one day the earth and the things in this world are going to dissolve and pass away altogether (II Peter 3:10).

We tend not to take seriously the street corner prophet holding his sign declaring that the end of the world is near, but let's not lose sight of the truth that one day this world is going to end. It may not be tomorrow, but there is an end to this world and we are moving closer to it every day. So let's guard against viewing our sandcastles as being permanent. We can enjoy them. We can put time and effort into them. They can hold value. But they are not what life is all about. One day those things will be gone and what will we have left?

I John 2:17 puts it in proper perspective. "And the world is passing away, and the lust of it; but he who does the will of God abides forever." II Peter 3:11 phrases it in the form of a question: "Therefore, since all these things will be dissolved, what manner of persons ought you to be in holy conduct and godliness…?" When the sandcastles of this world are all washed away, what will matter is whether or not we did God's will. What will matter is our relationship with Christ.

I don't know if this is the specific lesson Mr. Shultz had in mind or not, but it's certainly a valid one. If this world is temporal and the person who does God's will abides forever, shouldn't we be living our lives the way God wants?

Are you pursuing those things that will matter for eternity?

Avoid Temptations
that Can Trap You

"Flee also youthful lusts…avoid foolish and ignorant disputes"
— II Timothy 2:22–23

One day we went with several members of our family to a farm where a fall festival was being held. Along with the many fun activities offered, there were several areas set up for photo opportunities. At one of those, our grandchildren placed their faces through cutouts in a wooden frame, making themselves all appear to have the bodies of farm animals. Then one of my sons-in-law decided he would do the same. However instead of simply placing his face up against the opening, he stuck his head all the way through the hole. It made for a good picture, but then he discovered he couldn't get his head back through the opening. He struggled with it for several minutes while the rest of us enjoyed a good laugh at his expense. I was beginning to think we might have to find someone with a chainsaw or else my son-in-law was going to go through the rest of life with the body of a horse. However with a little assistance from someone tucking in his ears, he finally escaped his trap.

This incident reminds us that sometimes it's much more difficult to get out of a situation than it was to get into it. We may have intended just to stick our head through the hole to get a peek at what others had been talking about, but then we find ourselves being tempted, pulled in, and struggling to find a way back out. We didn't intend to stay there or to follow that pathway, but often one small step can get us going down that proverbial slippery slope from which it's hard to recover.

The Bible not only teaches that the Lord can give us strength to overcome temptations and deliver us from sin's traps, but it also teaches us the wisdom of avoidance—not going that direction in the first place. Paul instructed his young protégé, Timothy, to "Flee also youthful lusts…avoid foolish and ignorant disputes" (II Timothy 2:22–23). In other words, "Don't even stick your head through those holes. Turn and go the other way." Paul knew how easy it was to get trapped by such things. Many have experienced spiritual downfalls by not running in the other direction when enticements came their way.

However, if we've already taken that first step and find ourselves in such a spiritual predicament, rest assured that help is still available. God can deliver those who have gotten themselves trapped. But we've got to be willing to admit our need for help, quit struggling to try to free ourselves, and submit to His will and His ways.

One of the problems is that sometimes even though we're trapped, we don't really want to let go of what we were reaching for in the first place. You've probably heard about one way monkeys are trapped. A hole is bored out in a gourd just large enough for the monkey's hand to squeeze through. Then some kind of attractive bait is placed inside. When the monkey reaches inside and grabs the bait, his closed fist is too big to fit back through the hole. He refuses to open his hand and to let go of his prize. He's trapped because of his own insistence of hanging on to the bait.

Let's make sure that's not part of our problem. Sometimes we can't get out of our predicament simply because we refuse to release that which attracted us. We won't let go and surrender to God's will.

So think before you stick your head in the hole. And if you do get stuck, make sure you're not still hanging on to something that's keeping you from experiencing God's deliverance.

What temptation could you avoid today if you were really committed to doing so?

OCTOBER 22

Jesus Gets Us through the Maze of Life

"And indeed all was vanity and grasping for the wind."

– Ecclesiastes 2:11

On another occasion when we went to one of these farms which offers a variety of family activities this time of year, it included a corn maze. Our trek through the winding paths cut into the cornfield was made even more challenging by our waiting until after dark to begin our journey. We steadily made our way through the maze, although we sometimes found ourselves traveling in circles or having to retrace our steps after reaching a dead end.

There were signposts along the way at certain intersections. If you could answer a question correctly, you would be pointed in the right direction to take in order to continue toward your desired destination. There were also a few workers stationed along the path who might encourage you with affirmations that you were doing well, that you were going the right way, or that you didn't have too much farther to go. It was an interesting and fun experience. However, we were glad when we finally emerged from that cornfield and were back in the open spaces.

Sometimes life can seem like a maze. We keep moving forward, but it's not always easy to discern if we're going in the right direction. We can't see the bigger picture of the designer of it all. So sometimes we take wrong turns. We end up going in circles or wandering along some side path that leads us to a dead end. There are times when such mistakes cost us years of retracing our steps until we get back on the right path.

The author of the book of Ecclesiastes penned his experiences of attempting to make his way through that maze. He tried all kinds of promising pathways in life—pleasure, riches, work, fame—you name it. However, he discovered that none of those routes got him through the maze. He kept going in circles or hitting dead ends. It all seemed empty, random, and meaningless. But he finally discovered the secret to the riddle of life. He concluded, "Fear God and keep His commandments, for this is man's all" (Ecclesiastes 12:13).

This life does have a design. The One who made it often points us in the right direction if we would pay attention and be willing to follow His leading. He's given us a guidebook in the Bible. He's provided us with others who have successfully navigated this course and can point out the way to us. He often encounters us with His signposts at various pivotal points along the way. But it's up to us to decide if we will seek Him and submit to His way, or if we will ignore His guidance and stubbornly chose our own path instead.

Many of these corn mazes aren't simply cut out into random pathways, but rather if viewed from above they can be seen to form some kind of design. The one we visited was supposed to look like a scene from the *Peanuts* comic strip. If we could see the maze of life from a higher perspective, there's a sense in which it would look like Jesus. He is the only way for us to successfully make our way through this maze. He declared that He was the only way to God and to heaven. We can only get there through following the pathway of faith in Him. It's through loving Jesus and living for Him that life makes sense. It's only in Jesus that we can live life in the best and most meaningful way. And only He gets us through to the desired destination.

Life doesn't have to be a puzzling maze. It can be an a-maze-ing experience if we're living it for the Lord.

Trust Jesus to help you through the maze of life. Start by following His guidance today.

MAKE SURE YOU ARE TRULY
SPIRITUALLY ALIVE

"He who has the Son has life; he who does not have the Son of God does not have life."

– I JOHN 5:12

You may recall a mass shooting which took place a few years ago. While these terrible incidents are becoming all too frequent, this particular one especially stood out because of the unusual event where it occurred. It happened at a gathering called ZombiCon, a convention for fans of those gory, undead creatures from horror shows.

The unique setting for this act of violence reportedly resulted in some understandable confusion. With so many people dressed up as bloody and disfigured zombies, it was difficult in the aftermath to distinguish the victims who were truly injured from those convention-goers who were simply in costume.

Sometimes the church faces an opposite dilemma. When we gather for our Sunday morning conventions, most people who attend appear to be spiritually alive. They've put on their best holy face for the occasion, along with their most moral behavior. Yet we know that for the most part there's a mixture of true believers with those who just appear to be part of the flock. How do you distinguish between the two? Thankfully, we don't have to do so. The final call on who is truly spiritually alive and who is dead isn't ours to make. God is the One who will make that ultimate judgment. We can observe the outward evidences of spiritual life in others, but only God can see the heart.

However, we do need to examine our own hearts and lives. Let's not deceive ourselves into thinking we're spiritually alive simply because we hang around with those who are or because we put on a costume of holiness.

So how do we know if we're spiritually alive or dead? First of all, if you're looking for or depending on such life from any other source than Jesus Christ, you're missing out. The Bible clearly says, "And this is the testimony: that God has given us eternal life, and this life is in His Son. He who has the Son has life; he who does not have the Son of God does not have life" (I John 5:11–12).

Secondly, we need to make sure that we don't just know about Jesus, but also that we have a personal relationship with Him. Have we repented of our sins and put our faith in Jesus as the Savior who came, died, and was resurrected in order to give us eternal life?

If we've done so, then there should also be evidence of such a relationship in our lives. We may not have become instantaneous "saints"—at least not in the way our world usually uses that word—but we should have experienced some kind of positive change in our lives. And we should be seeing an ongoing transformation where we are becoming more like Jesus and are exhibiting an increasing amount of the fruit of the Spirit in our lives—love, joy, peace, longsuffering, kindness, goodness, faithfulness, gentleness, and self-control (see Galatians 5:22).

If we're truly alive in Christ, we should also have some sense of the Holy Spirit living in us and assuring us of our salvation. And finally, those who are spiritually alive are going to be seeking to serve Christ and to help others find life in Him as well.

Let's make sure that we're not just putting on the appearance of spiritual life while lacking the reality of it. While other people might not be able to tell the difference, God can. And He's the only One who really matters.

What signs of spiritual life are present in you?

Watch for Signs That the Groom Is Coming

"Where is the promise of His coming?"
– II Peter 3:4

A few years ago, I had the privilege of presiding over my son's wedding. The ceremony took place outdoors at a beautiful location alongside a creek on our daughter-in-law's parents' farm. I've found that most weddings have their unplanned memorable moments. On this occasion, one of those occurred during the procession. After the mother of the bride entered to take her seat, the big lovable family dog decided it was his turn. At just the right interval ahead of the bridesmaids, and at a perfect, steady pace, the canine unexpectedly sauntered along the path being used by the other members of the wedding party and sat down near the front row.

However as a grandfather, I have to suggest that the cutest participants in that part of the ceremony were two of my grandchildren. My granddaughter was the "leaf girl," tossing colorful fall leaves into the air as she walked along. Beside her came my youngest grandson wearing a sign which announced "Here Comes the Bride."

Hopefully we are all recognizing the signs around us today which seem to be announcing "Here Comes the Groom." The Bible depicts those who follow Jesus as the Bride of Christ. And it tells us that our Groom is coming for us one day.

Some people want to relegate such an idea to the realm of fairy tales and legends. After all, they might suggest, Christians have been claiming Jesus is coming back for centuries and it hasn't happened yet. But that's exactly what the Bible declares would happen. "Scoffers will come in the last days, walking according to their own lusts, and saying, 'Where is the promise of His coming? For since the fathers fell asleep, all things continue as they were from the beginning of creation'" (II Peter 3:4).

This passage goes on to remind us that God's view of time is different from ours. And He is mercifully giving people every opportunity to get ready for that event and the judgment to follow because He doesn't want people to perish. But it also assures us that the promise of Christ's return is certain.

The Bible provides us with numerous signs to watch for as indications that Jesus is coming soon. Admittedly, over the years many people have thought they were witnessing these signs and were expecting the imminent return of Christ only to be disappointed. But as time passes on, these indicators seem to be increasing rather than diminishing.

The threat of pestilences seems to be growing greater. The situation in the Middle East appears to be getting riper for the fulfilling of certain prophesies. The technology is available and the mindset of the people is such as could lead to the rise of a world leader like the Antichrist. An anti-Christian sentiment seems to be growing as a possible precursor of greater persecution of believers. And the barbaric practice of beheading has become the preferred means of execution among certain groups, which sets the stage for the fulfillment of a scripture in the book of Revelation which many had found rather odd until now—"Then I saw the souls of those who had been beheaded for their witness to Jesus and for the word of God" (20:4).

We shouldn't need a cute little kid holding a sign reading "Here Comes the Groom" as our warning. We should be recognizing the signs all around us that Jesus is coming. I don't know if He will come today or if it might not happen for many years yet, but I do know we should make sure our hearts are right with God and that we're doing our part to remind others of His return.

What signs do you see that Jesus' coming is drawing near? How should that affect you?

WE NEED TO BE
SEEKING THE LOST

"I did not come to call the righteous, but sinners, to repentance."

– MARK 2:17

I drove by a church with this message on its sign: "Wanted: Good People for Jesus." Many of us can understand that sentiment. We would be thrilled to see more good Christian people who are dedicated to the Lord come and join our churches. But is that primarily whom we should be seeking?

While it would be great to have a mature believer walk through our church doors and become part of our fellowship, our main desire should be to have a messed-up, lost sinner come to know Christ and then to see that person become "a good person for Jesus." Our mission isn't primarily to bring in the saints—it's to reach out to the sinners.

That's what Jesus did. His most controversial pick to be one of His disciples was probably not His choice of rash Peter or Judas the betrayer. The choice which likely raised the most eyebrows at the time was Matthew. Why? Because Matthew was a tax collector—one of those no-good spineless traitors who was letting himself be used by the Jews' oppressors as a pawn to do their dirty work. Additionally, many of those tax collectors were known for pocketing some of the money for themselves. So they did not win any popularity contests among the Jewish people.

Yet Jesus calls such a person to be one of His twelve closest followers. If Jesus reached out to a tax collector, whom should we be reaching out to? That rough-looking guy with his body covered in tattoos? The young lady who is confused about her sexual identity? The intellectual guy whose hero is Stephen Hawkins? The young person trying to hide under a hoodie? The Muslim? The illegal immigrant? The person who just got out of prison? The neighbor whose language and lifestyle makes us uncomfortable? Or are we just looking for "good people for Jesus"?

When Jesus was confronted about the fact that He was hanging out with "tax collectors and sinners," He responded with that classic statement: "Those who are well have no need of a physician, but those who are sick. I did not come to call the righteous, but sinners, to repentance" (Mark 2:17).

Jesus didn't walk around holding up a sign saying, "Wanted: Good People." If He had carried any sign it would've been one which read: "Wanted: Sinners." He came to minister to those who were spiritually sick. But He didn't just come to make friends with them and to tell them they were fine the way they were. He came to call them to repentance—to turn around and go a different direction. He called them to leave their sin and sinful lifestyles, and to go a better way—God's way.

We don't reach out to sinners with a so-called "love" that accepts their sin. Neither do we try to heal them with a watered-down version of the gospel which they can find acceptable and entertaining. We reach out to them with the medicine that will bring true healing to their ailing souls. And like much medicine, it might not taste very good. It might sting a little as it cleanses their spiritual wounds. But it's the remedy they need—repentance and faith in Christ.

Our task isn't to attract disciples of Christ—it's to make disciples of Christ. In order to do that, we often have to start out with tax collectors, criminals, drug addicts, the worldly, the selfish, or the atheist. Let's be like Jesus and be the doctors who are reaching out to the spiritually sick, calling them to repentance and to a new life in right relationship with the Lord.

Reach out to a lost person today with love and truth.

LIVING BY FAITH WILL PREPARE US FOR DYING WELL

"Yea, though I walk through the valley of the shadow of death, I will fear no evil; for You are with me; Your rod and Your staff, they comfort me."

– PSALM 23:4

One time my wife and I made use of a unique birthday present our children had given me—reservations at a murder mystery dinner theater in Atlanta. One of the reasons my family thought I would especially enjoy this experience is because the current show is based on one of my favorite movies—*The Wizard of Oz*. And they were right. We had a wonderful time.

When we arrived at the theater, I discovered that I had been chosen to have one of the solo speaking parts in the production. And it turned out to be a rather significant role. I was going to play the part of the Wizard himself. And not only that, but as I looked over my lines I found out I would also become the murder victim. I was going to die.

My moment in the spotlight came near the end of Act One. After it was over and we were enjoying the next course in our meal, some of the other guests around me complimented me on the good job I had done. Several of them specifically commented that I had "died well."

That phrase reminds me of what I've often heard people say about themselves in connection with the end of life. They've expressed their hope that when they arrive at that inevitable moment, they will die well.

In doing so, they weren't referring to the means by which they would go out from this life. They weren't expressing a desire to go out in a blaze of glory through some unusual or spectacular event. They were referring more to the manner in which they would pass from this life into the next. And even then, they weren't talking about dying with a dramatic flair—such as putting one's hand to one's brow and gracefully swooning into a neatly crumpled heap on the floor. Neither were they hoping to recite some touching, memorable last words as they drifted off into eternity.

What these people were actually expressing was the desire to exhibit such qualities as faith and courage as they faced the specter of death. They wanted to die well, with a spirit consistent with being a believer in Christ, as opposed to manifesting a spirit of fear, doubt, and panicked agitation in their final moments. I can understand and agree with such a sentiment.

However, we don't know what our circumstances may be when we die. We don't know if we'll come to that moment in a sudden accident or at the end of a prolonged illness. We don't know if it will happen in a flash of violence or during a night of peaceful sleep. So not knowing when or how we'll die makes preparation for it difficult.

I believe one of the best ways we can prepare for dying well is by living well. Are we facing today's challenges with the same spirit of faith and courage we hope to have when we come to that final test? If we will deal with our everyday problems by trusting the Lord and relying on His grace to see us through, we will be more apt to do so when we find ourselves walking through the valley of the shadow of death. We should live by the kind of faith the Psalmist expressed, and then we'll be ready to face death with the same spirit—"I will fear no evil, for You are with me; Your rod and Your staff, they comfort me" (Psalm 23:4).

Let's seek to be people who live well, and then I believe God will give us the grace we need at the appointed time to die well too.

And it doesn't take a wizard to figure that out.

Live well today—live with faith and courage.

Don't Substitute Your Idea of God for the Real Thing

"You shall have no other gods before Me."
– Exodus 20:3

One October, I did something I hadn't done in years: I purchased and put up a Halloween decoration. I didn't want anything ghoulish or gory—just something to get a little reaction from my grandchildren and others as they came to our door looking for treats. So my wife found a rather hideous-looking spider for us to hang up on our porch. Nearby movement or sound will cause the creature's eyes to light up as it slowly descends on its web while eerie noises fill the background.

When I first took a look as to where we might hang our new creepy crawler, I discovered that a real spider had already spun its good-sized web in that prime location near our front door. Not only did it interfere with where I was thinking about placing our decoration, but I was afraid it was so close that its presence might be a little too realistic for anyone who stepped up on our porch. I decided that if this creature hung around, I was going to have to remove it in order to make way for its mechanical cousin. Fortunately it chose to move its web to the far end of the porch a few days later, and then it disappeared altogether.

Let's make sure that we don't try to treat God in a similar manner. We sometimes concoct our own manmade version of God—an image of Him that doesn't line up with what He has revealed about Himself in the Scriptures. Maybe it's the image of a frightening God with wrathful eyes blazing who is always looking for an opportunity to descend on us in order to do us harm. Or maybe it's the opposite picture of a tame God who is as cute and harmless as a little kitten. It's an image that only emphasizes the loving nature of God, seeing Him more like a doting grandfather or a gift-providing Santa Claus.

There are numerous other models of God which people have built, overemphasizing some of His characteristics while completely ignoring others. It should serve as a reminder to us all that we need to know what the Bible tells us about God—not just one or two verses, but the whole of Scripture.

As in the case of the spider, we are sometimes guilty of pushing the real God out of the way in order to make room for our alternate version. When the reality of what He is truly like ventures into our living space and interferes with what we want to do or what we prefer to think, we try to get rid of Him. Some people might rather have an angry God they can curse and fight against rather than to have to come to terms with a God who actually loves them—a God who loves them more than any-one else—a God who loved them so much that He gave His Son to die for them.

Others would rather have a God who loves everybody so much that nothing anybody could do would make Him mad or cause Him to allow anyone to suffer punishment. When they encounter the God of the Bible who labels certain actions and attitudes as sin, or One who warns people of judgment and hell, they quickly want to relegate Him to a museum of antiquities. They prefer to substitute their modern, more docile, more politically-correct version in His place.

So let's be sure to look at our Bibles and at Christ and accept the real God for who He is. And if your kids stop by my house on Halloween, watch out for the spider. It might be the real thing.

Have you substituted some alternate image of God in place of the God of the Bible? Commit to studying God's Word and reminding yourself what He is truly like.

WE WIN WHETHER
WE LIVE OR DIE

"For to me, to live is Christ, and to die is gain."
– PHILIPPIANS 1:21

Do you know what a wishbone is? I'm not referring to the football formation, but rather to the forked bone in front of the breastbone of many birds. I can remember as a kid when my mother would often cook fried chicken for Sunday dinner. If someone found the wishbone, our meal would suddenly get interrupted by a brief competition. Two of us would each grab an end of that wishbone and pull until it snapped into two pieces. The goal was to be the person who came away with the longer piece, because that supposedly meant that your wish would come true. It's been a long time since I've been in a wishbone-pulling battle with anyone but that's OK, because as the youngest in the family, I tended to lose most of the time anyway.

In Philippians 1:19–26, Paul's description of himself reminds me of a wishbone—being pulled in two different directions. It was his own desires that were in conflict. On the one hand, he wished to depart this life and be with Christ. On the other hand, he wished to keep on living. Don't mistake Paul's battle as one of trying to choose whether to live or die. He knew, as we should, that such a decision is in God's hands. He wasn't presuming to take the responsibility of life or death on himself, he was just expressing his wishes about what he preferred God to do.

Why did Paul have a desire to die? It was because he saw all that he would gain from the experience. We usually think of dying in terms of loss. We contemplate on what we're going to leave behind such as family, friends, possessions, and activities that we enjoy, but Paul focused on what he would gain through death. It will mean no more sorrow, sickness, pain, or death. It will result in being with Jesus and with other believers, living in heaven, and all that goes along with our glorious inheritance as children of God. If we know the Lord as our Savior, death is about gain, not loss.

But Paul also possessed a competing desire to keep living. That wish didn't center on not wanting to leave family or the things of this world behind. It was based on God's purpose for Paul and how he could continue to be a help to others in this life. He said "to live is Christ." To keep on living would give Jesus an opportunity to live in Paul, shining His light and showing His love through him. The desire to keep living isn't so much about us as it is about others. It's about how God may want to use us to touch the lives of those around us. So until God decides to take us home, we should want to fulfill His purpose for us and let Christ be magnified in us.

Paul is describing a win-win situation. If he lived, he would win—he would be able to continue to minister to people and share the gospel. And if he died, he would win—he would get to be with Jesus and enjoy all the blessings of heaven.

It's like pulling on that wishbone we mentioned earlier and no matter which piece you get, you win—you get your wish! If you're a follower of Christ, you can't lose when it comes to the matter of living or dying. So there's no need for us to worry about when we're going to die or if we're going to live. That's all in God's hands. The main thing is that we put our trust in Jesus as the One who can save our soul. If we do that, whether we live or die, it's all good.

Affirm that your life, and one day your death, are in God's hands. Remind yourself that whichever God chooses for you at whatever time is a good thing.

HELP OTHERS GET
TO A BETTER PLACE

"Go therefore and make disciples of all the nations."

– MATTHEW 28:19

There was a mortgage company that advertised on TV with the slogan, "Get to a better place." The obvious interpretation of that message is that they're trying to help you purchase the home that you want. When I looked at their company web site, I saw that it also meant that they want to assist you in getting to a better place financially in your life, through refinancing and other such services which they offer.

I was thinking about what a fitting description that motto is of what God is trying to do in our lives. Of course He wants to get us to a better home in heaven one day—a place where there is no more sorrow, sickness, pain, and death—a place of continually being with the Lord and living in the light of His glory. But He also desires to get us to a better place in our lives right now, especially in our relationship with Him. He wants us to know Him, to draw close to Him, and to fellowship with Him. He wishes for us to have meaning and purpose in life through living for Him and serving Him.

But that phrase about getting someone to a better place should also be an appropriate characterization of the mission of the church, as well as each one of us as followers of Christ. We shouldn't only be concerned about ourselves getting to heaven, but we also need to be trying to help others reach that goal. If someone doesn't know the Lord, we ought to be praying for that person and doing whatever else we can to help him reach that better place of faith in Christ. If someone is saved, we should be trying to help that person grow in his faith. We can encourage others in the hope not only that they will enjoy a better place in this life but will also reach that better home in heaven once this life is over.

The amazing rescue of the miners in Chile some years ago took place because a number of people stayed focused on getting those miners out and getting them to a better place. Workers drilled through rock equal in length to two Empire State buildings. Families prayed. And in the end it all paid off. As I watched a few of those miners being rescued, I imagined some parallels to what heaven will be like. When a believer emerges from this earthly life to enter heaven, I can picture similar celebrations taking place. There will be reunions with loved ones. There will be joy in the person arriving, as well as among the angels and saints who have been pulling for, praying for, and waiting for that person to get there.

I don't think we'll need the sunglasses those miners were forced to wear while their eyes adjusted to natural light again, but I imagine we will have to adjust to the brightness of the glory of God that will fill that place. I understand that the president of Chile was present to greet each miner, saluting at least one of them with the phrase, "Welcome to life!" Likewise, I can picture the King of Kings being there to greet His people with a similar salutation as they enter His kingdom.

As those workers and families stayed focused on getting those miners out, we need to keep focused on getting others to that better place. Let's not forget about those around us who are living in darkness. Let's not ignore those who are trapped in sin and need a way out. Let's keep praying, witnessing, working, loving, and doing whatever we can to help them find their way.

What can you do today to help someone make strides toward getting to a better place?

THE DEVIL IS REAL, BUT ALSO DEFEATED

"Resist the devil and he will flee from you."
– JAMES 4:7

This is the week when society typically inundates us with scary images, horror movies, and other depictions of evil as we approach Halloween. Much of this emphasis is intended as nothing more than harmless fun. We recognize that the gruesome characters being portrayed aren't real, so we tend to take the scariness lightly, maybe even with some degree of amusement.

However, let's not make the mistake of ignoring the reality of evil altogether, particularly the reality of the devil. Many recognize the presence of evil in the world as far as its manifestation in certain people is concerned. But some dismiss the idea of supernatural evil and a personal devil as merely a superstition or legend.

Yet the Bible indicates the existence of such forces. "Put on the whole armor of God, that you may able to stand against the wiles of the devil. For we do not wrestle against flesh and blood, but against principalities, against powers, against the rulers of the darkness of this age, against spiritual hosts of wickedness in the heavenly places" (Ephesians 6:11–12).

Why is it important for us to know that the devil is real? One of my grandsons and I were throwing a football around. Like a receiver and quarterback, one of us would run a route while the other threw the ball to him. But if someone else joined us in order to defend against the pass, we would have to be more careful. We couldn't have just thrown the football casually—we would've had to guard against the pass being intercepted. It makes a big difference when you've got someone opposing you. In the same way we need to realize we have a spiritual enemy who opposes us, hates us, and wants to destroy us. Therefore we can't afford to live casually. We've got to guard against our efforts being intercepted. We need to be watchful, take precautions, and be prepared for his attempts to attack us.

The Bible also suggests we should not to be ignorant of the devil's devices (II Corinthians 2:11). If we view evil as simply an impersonal force, we may lose sight of the fact that there is intelligence involved, strategic moves being played, and deceptive practices being employed. If we're not knowledgeable of Satan's tactics, we may get deceived and suffer some losses we might not have experienced if we had been more vigilant.

Additionally, the Bible tells us to "resist the devil and he will flee from you" (James 4:7). We're not called simply to ignore the devil, but to take positive action against him. We need to resist him, his temptations, and his efforts to draw us away from God. We also need to resist his efforts to promote sin, violence, and hatred in our world.

While we need to be aware of the devil and his tactics, we don't need to fear him. Martin Luther wrote, "The prince of darkness grim, we tremble not for him—his rage we can endure, for lo, his doom is sure." Yes, the devil is real, powerful, crafty, and full of hate. None of us in ourselves are a match for him. But Christ has defeated the devil. His ultimate doom is certain. Through Christ we can be victorious, in spite of the devil's efforts.

So don't forget about the existence of supernatural evil. The devil is real and we have to watch out for his tricks and attacks. But we don't have to be scared of him. We can resist him and make him flee through the power of Christ.

Watch out for the devil and his tactics today. Resist his attempts to attack you.

REFORMATION CAN BE SCARY

"But grow in the grace and knowledge of our Lord and Savior Jesus Christ."

– II Peter 3:18

Would you like to scare somebody at church this weekend? You don't have to wear a Halloween costume to the service in order to do it. Simply sneak up behind someone—or better yet, suddenly jump out in front of them—and utter one word. No, it's not "Boo!" The one word that can send shivers down the spine of many believers is "change." Start talking about change or encouraging people to make some changes and you'll likely raise their fear and anxiety levels to greater heights than if they had encountered Frankenstein's monster. Some folks in my church still refer back to the Sunday morning years ago when I put a fright in them simply by directing everyone to change seats and to move to the other side of the sanctuary from their usual spot.

Many of you know that Christianity commemorates a significant event in its history on this day. It's the anniversary of Martin Luther posting his "Ninety-Five Theses" on the door of the church—an act considered by many to mark the beginning of the Protestant Reformation. Keep in mind that Luther was calling for change. This movement was a "reformation." It was an attempt to correct some abuses in the church, to improve some practices, or in other words, to make some changes. And as you might imagine, it was not welcomed by many but rather met with strong resistance.

Many of us still tend to resist the call for change today. Certainly we should evaluate such efforts to determine if they are needed and would lead to improvement. We should guard against the instability of constant change and hold firm to principles and practices which should not be altered. We need to be careful about seeking to change simply for the sake of doing something different whether it would be an improvement or not. Change isn't always a good thing. However when it is needed, we have to be careful about allowing our fears to keep us from embracing it.

Change is not only a big part of life in general, but it's a huge factor in our walk with Christ. When we first come to Christ, we are called to repent—to turn around, to change our minds, to forsake our sins, and to begin to live for the Lord. However, it doesn't end there. The life of a Christian is one of ongoing change. We are to be growing in the grace and knowledge of the Lord (II Peter 3:18), and growth requires change. The Bible tells us that God is working in us to conform us to the image of His Son (Romans 8:29). He is constantly chipping away those aspects of our lives and character that are not like Jesus, while molding us more into His image. That involves change. Moreover, I believe the Lord wants us to have an expanding influence on our world as the light and salt He calls us to be. That may mean making some changes.

Yes, change can be scary. Our first inclination may be to draw back from it. But if it's a change God is wanting, then we need to obey Him and embrace it. It may be the next step in our spiritual growth, the next landmark on our journey to Christlikeness, or the next way of expanding our witness and influence in serving the Lord.

Reformation isn't easy. Just ask Luther. However, let's try to be open to the changes God may be wanting to make today, not only in our churches but in our own lives.

"CHANGE!"—did I scare you?

What changes might the Lord want you to make in your life? Don't draw back from them—embrace them!

Does Your Heart Match Your Appearance?

"Even so you also outwardly appear righteous to men, but inside you are full of hypocrisy."

– Matthew 23:28

My wife usually accompanies our daughter and her family when they go out trick-or-treating on Halloween. So a few days prior to that occasion, she was talking with our young granddaughter about the costumes they were going to be wearing. My wife detailed how she was going to be dressed up as a rather mean and scary character in order to coincide with the theme the rest of the family was following with their outfits. As she finished describing her menacing appearance, our granddaughter tenderly looked at her and commented, "But you'll still be Nana."

I'm not sure if she wanted to comfort my wife with that truth or if she may have been looking for some reassurance in her own mind. But she knew, or at least hoped, she would be able to see beyond the mean-looking exterior on that occasion and know that this person was still the kind and caring Nana whom she dearly loved.

It's a good reminder to us that no matter how we appear on the outside, it's what's on the inside that matters. Unless it's Halloween, it's unusual for people to make themselves appear meaner or more evil than what they really are. More often it's the opposite situation. We try to dress up in the costumes of goodness and holiness when our hearts are far from those actual conditions.

It's reminiscent of Jesus' description of the scribes and Pharisees of His day. He declared to them, "For you are like whitewashed tombs which indeed appear beautiful outwardly, but inside are full of dead men's bones and all uncleanness. Even so you also appear righteous to men, but inside you are full of hypocrisy and lawlessness" (Matthew 23:27–28). Those religious leaders were dressing up like perfect little angels, but in reality they were more like graveyards. Underneath their righteous costumes, they were hypocrites who were full of sin and moral filth. Not only were they spiritually dead, but they were also dragging others down with them.

Sometimes we today are guilty of a similar deception. We try to be good. We make an effort to do the right thing. We may even seek to live outwardly by the commands God gives us in the Bible. But when we look beyond those surface actions, we know we're the same unrighteous person on the inside.

We might do a kind deed to help someone, but in our hearts we know we're actually full of selfishness. We outwardly conform to one of God's commands, but inwardly we know we would do differently if we could get away with it. No matter how godly our costume, we know we're still a sinner whose heart is far from the purity and love which God expects.

The good news is that we don't have to remain in that condition. The Bible tells us that God can change our hearts. Through faith in Christ we can receive more than a better outward appearance—we can get a new and clean heart. "Therefore, if anyone is in Christ, he is a new creation; old things have passed away; behold, all things have become new" (II Corinthians 5:17).

God can so work in us that those outward acts of righteousness become more than a costume hiding what's underneath. They become the true expression of what's in our hearts. God can go beyond making us appear loving, kind, and unselfish—He can transform us inwardly into that type of person.

So don't just wear a costume of godliness. Surrender your heart to the Lord and let Him change you on the inside.

Are you letting the Lord change you from the inside out?

ATTITUDE CAN MAKE
ALL THE DIFFERENCE

"But at midnight Paul and Silas were praying and singing hymns to God, and the prisoners were listening to them."

– ACTS 16:25

It was a Monday and one of the coldest mornings we had experienced in months. You could tell that many people were trying to spend as little time as possible out in the elements. When they had to be outside they were moving quickly to get to a warmer destination, many of them wearing a look of discomfort on their faces as they briskly walked along. However on that same morning, group after group of second-graders marched out of their school bundled up and prepared to take a ride in an open trailer where the cold wind would assault them to an even greater degree. No, they weren't being punished. It was actually just the opposite. They were being rewarded with a hayride. And in contrast to so many others I had witnessed that morning, they were excited about being out there. They were experiencing the same bitter temperatures as everyone else, but their attitude was different. As I rode in the trailer with those kids, there was a spirit of adventure and enthusiasm. To them the frost-covered ground was not something to despise, but a wonder to admire for its snowlike appearance. There was singing, waving at passersby and the occasional declaration, "This is fun!"

Attitude can make a huge difference. We all face the cold winds of adversity blowing into our lives at times. We have to deal with tough situations that we just want to get through as quickly as possible and move on to more comfortable circumstances. But let's not simply endure those Monday mornings of life with a frown on our face, a complaint on our lips, and an eye looking forward to something better down the road. Let's seek to have an attitude expressive of our faith and joy even as we go through the tough times.

"But at midnight Paul and Silas were praying and singing hymns to God…" (Acts 16:25). Many centuries ago a cold, dark prison would not have been a pleasant place to be. No doubt it was an atmosphere full of the sounds of complaining, cursing, and cries of pain. The attitudes being manifested probably ranged from violent anger and bitterness to hope-lessness and despair. No one wanted to be there.

But in the midst of that harsh environment came the sound of Paul and Silas praying and singing praises to God. Not only were these two men in the same setting as the others, but unlike many of them they had been imprisoned unjustly. In a sense, they had even more reason to complain and be bitter. Yet in their cold dungeon, they manifested a different spirit. Their faith moved them to pray instead of cast blame, to sing praises rather than rant and rave.

Don't overlook the rest of that verse. It says, "And the prisoners were listening to them." Others will notice your different spirit. It can be a powerful witness for the Lord. People who are facing the same circumstances as you are will often wonder why you can handle it better. They will question why you can be so upbeat, positive, and hopeful. They might even think you're a little strange for singing in that prison. But they'll listen. And you might have an opportunity to share with them about "the hope that is within you."

Attitude makes a difference. And faith makes a difference in our atti-tude. So when the cold winds blow in your life, your legs may quiver and your teeth might chatter, but you can still have an attitude that will show-case your faith in the Lord.

Seek to have an attitude today that is an appropriate expression of your faith and joy.

Take Advantage of the Darkness to Shine for Jesus

"You are the light of the world.... Let your light shine before men"
– Matthew 5:14–16

I was driving along the interstate towards home one night when I commented to my wife in the passenger seat, "There's something I haven't seen in a while." Off in the distance were a couple of those spotlights which are used to draw people's attention to some special event, like the grand opening of a business. I remember when I was a kid similar beams would flash across the sky signaling that the annual fair was going on in our town.

I suppose my failure to spot those lights as often could be simply due to the fact that as I get older I don't get out as much at night. But I don't think that's the only reason. I wondered if maybe government regulations had made it more difficult or costly to use that equipment. However, my wife noted that the beams from those lights aren't as noticeable anymore due to the brighter night sky—the result of all the lights shining from the businesses and developments which have increased in our area in recent years. Maybe that's why those lights aren't used as often. They simply aren't as effective in drawing attention because the sky isn't as dark as it used to be.

Many of us recognize that we are living in darker times morally and spiritually. We are rightfully concerned about the condition of our society as it turns further away from God and the principles of His Word.

We lament the lack of goodness and godliness in our world. We pray for revival and for a reversal of this trend toward spiritual darkness. We guard against letting the darkness overwhelm us, plunging us into doubt, despair, and a sense of hopelessness.

However at the same time we should see these dark times as an opportunity. It gives us a chance to shine brighter for Jesus. The darkness can make our light more noticeable and more effective as its beams pierce through the cold, harsh, immoral atmosphere of our times. Love stands out in a society filled with hatred, division, and selfishness. Integrity is more conspicuous when it seems so many people can't be trusted. A holy life is hard to miss in a world full of examples of impurity, perversion, and wickedness.

The deeper darkness of our days is not something to rejoice over. However, let's not miss the opportunity it presents to us as followers of Jesus. Our Lord said, "You are the light of the world. A city that is set on a hill cannot be hidden. Nor do they light a lamp and put it under a basket, but on a lampstand, and it gives light to all who are in the house. Let your light so shine before men, that they may see your good works and glorify your Father in heaven" (Matthew 5:14–16).

Jesus has given to us the great privilege and responsibility of being reflectors of His light in this dark world. Sometimes it may mean simply smiling and being pleasant to people. Other times it might mean firmly standing up for what's right and true. Under other circumstances it might mean helping out someone in need. In another case it might mean sharing God's Word with someone. Our light may shine in various ways, but in all situations it means reflecting Jesus and His character in our lives.

Let's not just complain and get discouraged about how dark things are getting around us. Let's go out into that darkness and let the light of Christ shine forth like the bright, steady beam from one of those spotlights.

How can you let your light shine in the darkness today?

BE WILLING TO WARN OTHERS

"Therefore hear a word from My mouth, and give them warning from Me."

– EZEKIEL 3:17

I was driving along with my three-year-old grandson in the backseat when he asked, "Papaw, can you honk?" Although I thought I heard him correctly, the request seemed so unusual that I asked him to repeat the question just to make sure. As he did, I realized to my relief that I wasn't being asked to make a noise like a goose, but rather to blow the horn on my car.

Like many grandparents, I enjoy fulfilling the requests of my grandchildren as much as possible. However, I briefly explained to my grandson that horns are used to get the attention of other drivers, especially as a warning. Since we were in quite a bit of traffic at the time, I told him I would blow my horn once we got to a spot where there weren't any other cars around. It was just a few moments later when I was in the clear and able to delight the little guy by showing him that Papaw could indeed honk.

This incident is a reminder that we need to be careful not to sound a warning when it's not necessary. We all know what happened to "the boy who cried wolf." And in our day you never know how someone may react, or overreact, to having a horn honked at them.

However the Bible points out another problem we may be more likely to face—not warning someone when it really is needed. God told the prophet Ezekiel that He was making him a watchman for Israel. He wasn't referring to someone who repaired clocks, but a person who would stand guard on the city walls to sound the alarm when there was any kind of threat or danger.

The responsibility of such a spiritual watchman was "to warn the wicked from his wicked way" (Ezekiel 3:18). If he failed to do so, he would be held accountable for it by God. In that same verse, the somber consequences of such inaction are declared—"his blood I will require at your hand."

I don't believe it's solely the preachers and prophets of our day who are called to serve as watchmen. All believers have some degree of responsibility to warn those who are in danger. At times we may need to join others in sounding the alarm for our society in general. Other times we may be called to warn specific people within our sphere of influence. From knowing what God's Word says and from looking at their lives, we recognize the threats and dangers. We can see the awful consequences of sin creeping up on them, as well as the eventual judgment of God perched on the horizon. Is it right for us to ignore it and to keep silent?

Sometimes people might need a loud trumpet blast to wake them up. Other times they might simply require a slight beep of the horn as a loving reminder. Whatever we do in warning others, we need to do it prayerfully and under the guidance of the Holy Spirit. Maybe some of us are hesitant because we're afraid of how others might respond to our honking horn. However, we should be more concerned about the consequences that person will face if he keeps going along his current path.

I'm usually not quick to use the horn on my car. There have been times when an incident occurred in which afterwards I regretted not honking. Let's not look back with any regrets about not warning others who need it. Be a faithful watchman, both for their sake and for yours.

Is there someone to whom you need to pass along a warning from God's Word? Pray for the Holy Spirit to guide you in how you can do it truthfully and lovingly.

LET'S NOT TAKE GOD'S GIFTS FOR GRANTED

"In everything by prayer and supplication, with thanksgiving, let your requests be made known to God."

– PHILIPPIANS 4:6

I'm still munching on leftover Halloween candy from not having as many trick-or-treaters as expected stop by our house. I'm not complaining. I learned a long time ago to be sure to buy the kind of candy I enjoy in preparation for such a circumstance as this. So it's not as if I'm having to force myself to eat these delicious goodies.

Of the kids who did come to our door to receive a treat this year, almost all of them were adorable, pleasant, and polite. But you did notice that word "almost," didn't you? One older boy, probably getting a little too old to participate in this activity, was obviously trying to impress the young ladies who accompanied him. First he loudly feigned being frightened of our modest Halloween decoration. Then as I was giving out the candy—which consisted of two of those fun-size candy bars—instead of responding with the typical "Thank you," he tersely quipped, "Another Milky Way, please."

I ignored his comment as I continued to distribute candy to the rest of the small group. When he repeated his request, one of the other kids apologized for his behavior. The youngster was fortunate he didn't receive a lecture about showing gratitude for what others freely and generously give him. It's not that I didn't have another piece of candy to give—as

I've stated, I had plenty to spare—but I didn't appreciate this youngster's ungrateful attitude.

However, this incident caused me to examine my attitude when I go knocking on God's door with another of my requests. Don't get me wrong—I'm not suggesting that God doesn't want us to come to Him or that He is in any way bothered by our asking for His help. On the contrary, the Bible indicates that our Heavenly Father wants us to look to Him as the One who can supply our needs. He delights in our depending on Him and bringing our concerns to Him in prayer. Much like I enjoy giving out candy to those children who stop by my house, God enjoys reaching into the abundant riches of His grace and pouring out His blessings upon us.

But do I really appreciate what God is doing for me? Or am I sometimes guilty of taking His grace for granted? Have I ever received God's gracious gifts, only to turn around without so much as a "Thank You," and suggest to Him, "Another miracle, please"—"Another healing, please"—"Provide for my financial need again this month"—"Protect me as I make another trip"—"Give me guidance about this other tough decision." Again, it's not that God doesn't want us to ask. Let's just make sure we continue to recognize that He's doing this out of His goodness and love for us. He doesn't owe us anything. We don't deserve it. And we should be grateful for any "treat" He sees fit to bestow on us.

We're in November already—this month when we're going to be celebrating a holiday about thankfulness. Let's use this occasion to take stock of our attitude toward the One who has blessed us with so much. No, don't stop knocking on God's door. Don't quit praying, asking, or bringing your needs to your Father. He would be heartbroken if you didn't come to Him. He wants us to rely on Him.

But let's be sure to come with a humble spirit and a grateful heart. Let's try to say "Thank You" to the One who is the Giver of all good things and the Fount of every blessing at least as often as we cry out for His help.

Lord, forgive me for the times when I've taken your gracious gifts for granted.

Let's Use Our Time Wisely

"Walk circumspectly, not as fools but as wise, redeeming the time."
– Ephesians 5:15–16

This is around the time when we perform our yearly autumn ritual of turning our clocks back one hour as we return to Standard Time. Many of us like to think of it as gaining an hour. It's certainly more pleasant than the coinciding activity in the spring when we set our clocks ahead, losing an hour of sleep.

Actually one year I found myself in the unique position of gaining two hours that weekend. Earlier in the day my wife and I had traveled into the Central Time Zone as I prepared to preach at a church in western Tennessee. So after setting our clocks back again that night, the time at which we woke up on Sunday morning was actually two hours different from what we had been used to. Sometimes I find it hard just getting accustomed to the regular time change. But I have to confess I had unusual difficulty adjusting to this doubled-up change. It resulted in my sleeping schedule really getting messed up for those two nights we were there—waking up at 3:30 a.m. feeling like it was time to start the day.

So what do you do with your additional hour on those weekends? Do you simply take advantage of the opportunity for some extra sleep? Or do you stay up later doing something you enjoy, knowing you will still be able to get your usual amount of rest? The idea of extra time is attractive, especially when time is such a precious commodity to us.

It makes me think of the account of King Hezekiah as recorded in II Kings 20. When he became sick, the prophet Isaiah informed him that he was going to die. But in response to Hezekiah's subsequent weeping and praying over the matter, God chose to heal the king, adding fifteen years to his life.

However, it doesn't seem Hezekiah made good use of his extra time in life. One of the most notable events during that era was when the Babylonians came to visit. Hezekiah unwisely showed off all the wealth of the kingdom to his guests. Later he was rebuked by Isaiah and informed that these same people would return one day to conquer and loot the land.

Extra hours in a day or extra years added to our lives sounds like a wonderful gift, but it's only a good thing if we use it wisely. What makes us think we're going to use any extra time better than those everyday hours and years we currently are living in? The Bible reminds us that life is short. That truth is valid whether we live to be thirty years of age or ninety. Let's make good use of these hours, days, and years which we've been given.

The Bible exhorts us to "walk circumspectly, not as fools but as wise, redeeming the time, because the days are evil" (Ephesians 5:15–16). Wise use of our time doesn't just mean being more faithful church attenders or spending more time in prayer or other religious activities, although it certainly may include those things. But it means seeking to live all aspects of our lives in accordance with God's will and purposes. It means making use of opportunities to serve the Lord and to positively impact the lives of people around us. It involves resetting priorities and guarding against ways we may be wasting that precious, fleeting commodity of time.

So instead of wishing for extra hours in our day or additional years to our lives, maybe we should simply seek to do a better job of making use of the time we've already been given.

How could you make better use of your time?

How Do We React to the Hurts of Others?

"Rejoice with those who rejoice, and weep with those who weep."
– Romans 12:15

One Sunday following the morning worship service, my two young grandsons ventured outside to the porch and front yard of the church while waiting for their parents and grandparents. We kept an eye on them as they explored the area doing their boyish things, such as picking fallen acorns off the ground and seeing how far they could throw them. But then my daughter noticed the two-year-old with blood on his hand, although he was paying no attention to it nor acting like he was experiencing any pain.

As his father brought him into the building to assess the extent of his injury and take him to a sink to get washed up, my daughter proclaimed, "His whole finger is bloody!" Upon hearing that declaration, his four-year-old brother got a gleeful look on his face and repeated his mother's words in an excited tone of inquiry—"His whole finger is bloody?" He went rushing after his father and brother to try to get a better look at that awful-sounding sight.

I'm glad to report that it was only a very small cut on my grandson's finger. It just happened to be in such a spot around the knuckle that it exuded an unusual amount of blood for a minor injury. But it's the atti-tude of my other grandson that got my attention—the combination of curiosity and excitement over his little brother's bloody finger.

I'm afraid that many of us tend to get strangely curious and excited about the hurts and injuries of others, sometimes even to the point of gleeful delight. Just notice all the rubberneckers the next time you pass by an accident on the highway, that is if you're not too busy peering over at the crash yourself.

When we hear about someone facing an injury, a loss, a hurtful situation (and it doesn't have to be a physical hurt), what is our attitude? The Bible instructs us to weep with those who weep (Romans 12:15), but too often we feel more curiosity, excitement, and maybe even a relishing of the fact that it happened to them rather than to us. Instead of an attitude that leads to weeping, there's a spirit that leads to a delight in trying to find out all the details and share them with as many others as we can.

That seems to be especially true when churches get their bloody fingers. Do we take secret delight in hearing about the downfall or a nationally well-known megachurch or its pastor? What about some of the injuries churches in our own local areas are facing, from financial hardships to so-called scandals over certain accusations against or revelations about their pastors? Do we inwardly smile at their difficulties and downfalls because we think they're getting what they deserve, or because it may indirectly benefit our own congregation? Or do we feel compassion and pain over the many souls being adversely affected by it all? Do we excitedly chase down the latest tidbits of information in order to gossip, or do we sadly bring that situation before God in prayer? No matter what one might think of that particular church, many of these negative circumstances will ultimately reflect upon the reputation of God Himself.

It's understandable that a four-year-old might get gleefully excited about his brother's bloody finger, but we should exhibit more spiritual maturity when our brethren are hurting. Whether it's an individual or an entire church going through hard times, we need to respond with less of a spirit of smug satisfaction or misguided exuberance, and more with a heart of loving concern.

Lord, give me a greater heart of compassion for others—to weep with those who are hurting.

LET THE LORD BE IN CONTROL OF YOUR LIFE

"Therefore submit to God."

– JAMES 4:7

When one of our grandsons was two years old, he went through the phase of peppering us with the question, "What's this?" His inquiry usually resulted from his watchful eye falling upon some unfamiliar object and was accompanied simultaneously by his finger pointing at it. Normally it was not a tough question to answer. However, I have to admit that sometimes it could be a little challenging to try to explain the function and purpose of certain objects in simple enough language for him to understand. I'm not sure he always comprehended my explanation, but he would faithfully wrinkle his forehead and say "Oh," as if he understood completely.

One day during that time we were drawing. Sometimes he would put the pen in my hand and ask me to draw particular figures—anything from a simple circle to a person or animal. But I also encouraged him to take the pen and put it to creative use. On this occasion he was doing so, when he made a few marks forming a small figure on the page. Then he pointed to it, looked up at me, and asked that perpetual question, "What's this?" I wanted to say, *How should I know? You're the one who drew it. And honestly, it doesn't look like much of anything.* Fortunately, my wife was nearby to suggest that it looked like a banana. "Oh," came the satisfied response from our grandson. As he continued to scribble, point, and ask the same question, either my wife or I would try to come up with some reasonable answer as to what his drawing resembled—a triangle, a car, a bowl. But I must confess that there was a time or two when I simply had to say, "I don't know."

Don't we do that to God at times? We try to take control, grab the pen away from the Creator, and attempt to draw the picture of our lives by ourselves. And after we've managed to form some kind of scribbled mess, we turn to God and ask Him to explain it to us, to help us make sense of it, or to bless it. "Lord, what's this? What's going on? Why is this happening to me?" Sometimes if we don't like the way our picture turned out, we even try to blame Him for the results. And of course, we expect Him to fix what we've created or deliver us from our self-generated predicament.

Under those circumstances the Lord would have every right to think, *Why do you come to Me now? You're the one who created the mess. You insisted on drawing it your way. You're the one who made the choices which led to this result.* But fortunately for us, God has shown Himself to be longsuffering and gracious. Often during the account of the history of the people of Israel in the Old Testament, we see them acting in a similar manner. Although God allowed them to suffer some of the consequences for a period of time, He eventually responded to them with mercy when they sought Him with repentant hearts.

We can count on God to be just as merciful with us. But we should also recognize that the best course of action isn't simply to seek God for forgiveness and assistance after we've tried to take control and made a mess of things. It's to let God be the One to lead our lives and let His hand make the strokes of the pen in the first place. It's to make ourselves yielded instruments who are guided by His Spirit and His Word so that we can draw the picture of our lives in accordance with His plan and purposes for us.

So instead of trying to do it our way and then looking to God for the explanations and quick fixes for all the problems we create, let's allow Him be the master-artist of our lives.

Put the pen of your life completely in God's hand today.

When You Encounter Spiritual Danger, Know What to Do

"He who is in you is greater than he who is in the world."

– I John 4:4

One time I had the privilege of attending a men's retreat at a conference center situated in the beautiful mountains of North Carolina. As our group checked in at the front desk, I found the information on a nearby flyer somewhat disconcerting. It read in big, bold letters, "Notice!! Bear Alert! Black bears have been seen in this area recently." It went on to give some warnings and instructions about what to do if you were to encounter one of those potentially dangerous inhabitants of the region. I've heard varying information about the best course of action under those circumstances, including the concept of playing dead. But apparently that behavior is appropriate only if you're actually being attacked by a bear. If you just happen to come up on one, this flyer explained what to do.

The first commandment was "Do not run." It sounds good, but I'm not sure that message would get from my brain to my legs quick enough in order to stop them from churning into action. I might be halfway down the mountain before stopping to think. Those instructions then declared that a person should remain calm. You should continue to face the bear, slowly back away, and make a lot of noise. It also suggested that you wave your arms or a jacket. Another "thou shalt not" had to do with bending over or kneeling. A person should keep standing upright. So although I would consider it a good idea to say a prayer at that moment, just don't kneel down to do it.

Gratefully, I didn't face the situation where I had to put any of those instructions to use. However, many of us often encounter potential spiritual dangers and various manifestations of the enemy of our soul. We may be walking down our daily path in life, turn a corner, and suddenly find ourselves facing a temptation, challenge, or vicious attack. What do we do?

I'm not sure that the Bible gives us one rule that will fit every situation. There are times when we need to run, as Joseph fled the temptation that confronted him regarding his master's wife. But there are also occasions when we need to move forward, ready to do battle in the name of the Lord. In other cases, we may be called upon to "stand still and see the salvation of the Lord" (Exodus 14:13). Rather than running or fighting, we simply wait, trust, and watch God handle the matter without our help. In each situation, we need to be attentive and obedient to what the Lord wants us to do. And although kneeling may not be a good idea when you encounter a bear, nothing will put more fear into our spiritual enemy than for us to bow before God in prayer.

One thing we don't need to do is to roll over and play dead. Yet that's the course of action too many people take when confronted by evil. We act like we have no life and power in us to resist or to overcome. We forget the biblical truth that "He who is in you is greater than he who is in the world" (I John 4:4). We also neglect the command and promise which says, "Resist the devil and he will flee from you" (James 4:7).

So let this be your warning notice: Be alert! Temptation, evil, and even Satan himself have been spotted in your area! Be prepared and know what to do when the enemy shows up.

When you encounter temptation or evil today, don't just give in to it. Face it from the perspective that your God is greater than the enemy and seek His guidance in how to handle it.

THERE ARE TRUTHS AND STANDARDS WHICH DON'T CHANGE

"Forever, O Lord, Your word is settled in heaven."
– PSALM 119:89

A few years ago I met someone who was telling me about the church he attended. At first he described it as a small church, but a moment later he went even further to say, "Actually, it's a very small church." I was somewhat surprised when he then revealed that the congregation consisted of about 250 people. I suppose such a church is considered tiny when compared to the so-called megachurches with memberships into the thousands. But others of us wouldn't describe a congregation of that size as "very small."

It reminds me of the relative views we have of the outdoor temperature, depending on the season of the year in which we happen to be. In Georgia early in the month of November, we might talk about a temperature of 65 degrees as being warm. But just a few months ago, the exact same temperature would have been described as cool.

I'm not suggesting that truth is relative. On the contrary, I believe there are standards which hold true regardless of how we happen to feel about them. A group of 250 people is the same number of individuals whether you happen to consider it as being small or large. And 65 degrees is the same temperature regardless of whether you feel like it's warm or cool at the time. And there are truths which continue to be valid and relevant regardless of how we view them.

It's not the truth itself that has changed. It's our perspective of it which tends to be altered by the changing seasons of our society or by changes in our own relationship with God. There are standards which God has set which have not changed even though they might make more people uncomfortable these days. The Bible still states the eternal truths which it has proclaimed for many centuries, but we live in a season in which many view those truths with colder hearts or from the standpoint of a society that has replaced them with their own values.

For example, Jesus spoke repeatedly about the eternal punishment and destruction of those who refused to believe in Him. Yet it seems that I'm encountering more and more people, even professing Christians, who don't believe in a hell or in a God who would condemn anyone to such a punishment.

And then there's Jesus' clear statement, "I am the way, the truth, and the life. No one comes to the Father except through Me" (John 14:6). That scripture is an indication that only those who believe in Christ will go to heaven. Yet many people seem to think that all good, moral, or religious people will be there, even those whose religion doesn't acknowledge Jesus as the unique Son of God and Savior.

What God says about sexuality, the value of life, along with many other truths declared in scripture have not changed. But the way they are viewed is changing as these declarations are considered outdated, narrow-minded, and even offensive to a growing number in our day.

Let's not condemn the truth of God's Word because it makes us uncomfortable, or because we know it's not the popular view, or because it runs counter to our society's evolving standards and values. Let's remember that there are truths which remain true no matter how we or others feel about them.

Are you basing your view of truth on what you think, what society says, or on the Word of God?

Lean on the Lord in Your Time of Need

"Because you say, 'I am rich, have become wealthy, and have need of nothing'—and do not know that you are wretched, miserable, poor, blind, and naked."

– REVELATION 3:17

One time we got a small home improvement job done at our house. We were having some wooden handrails built and installed along our front steps. It's not that my wife and I are getting old and feeble, at least not yet—we rarely use that entrance ourselves. But for general safety reasons, we felt it would be helpful for people to have a rail to hold onto when they're approaching or leaving our porch.

What do you lean on for support as you walk through life? What do you grab onto to hold you up when you're weak, when you're weary of the journey, when the stormy winds threaten to blow you away, or when your tough circumstances push against you with such force as to knock you off balance?

Some people depend on their bank accounts to get them through whatever crisis arises. Others look to the government as their main support in time of need. Many are blessed to have family, friends, and fellow believers they can lean on in those moments. Some of those may be more dependable supports than others, but they're all liable to let us down at some point. No matter what other helpful "handrails" we may have available to us in life, the Lord wants us primarily to lean on Him. All those other supports we tend to rely on can disappear, deteriorate, or not be strong enough to hold us up in certain situations. But God will never leave us or forsake us. And He is strong enough to uphold us no matter how heavy the weight of the burden we're carrying.

At times in the Old Testament God condemned Israel for relying on their political alliances rather than on Him. He described their allies as a bruised reed which would not only fail to hold them up, but would also break and pierce their hand with its jagged, sharp edge. God wanted His people to look to Him for help, strength, and deliverance in their time of need. And He still wants us to lean on Him today.

Admittedly, there are some among us who don't see their need for any kind of support. They view themselves as being self-sufficient and able to stand up to whatever life throws at them by means of their own wits, strength, and resourcefulness. It reminds me of a festival we attended a few weeks ago. There was one attraction in which you could walk through this room where the lights were spinning and everything moving in such a way as to make a person dizzy. I depended heavily on the available rails as I slowly staggered through that room. One of my grandsons went through that attraction several times, proudly announcing after his third or fourth trip that he had accomplished it without even touching the handrail.

Sometimes that's how we tend to look at life. We exalt our self-sufficiency. We boast about not having had to depend on anyone else. We did it all ourselves, or so we think. God condemned a church for that kind of attitude. They claimed "We have need of nothing." Yet God revealed that they were actually blind, poor, and miserable (Revelation 3:17). We're fooling ourselves if we think we can handle or are handling the challenges of life all on our own. Without God, we wouldn't make it.

The Lord wants us to recognize our dependence on Him. You don't have to go it alone and you shouldn't try to do so. Cast your care upon the Lord. Lean on Him in your time of need. He's strong enough to hold you up.

Lean on the Lord today. Trust Him to hold you up.

LOOK FOR GOD TO
CONFIRM HIS GUIDANCE

"The Lord will guide you continually."
– ISAIAH 58:11

One weekend I took a trip to eastern Kentucky to attend a leadership conference. This event was being held at a small Bible college in the rural mountains of that region. I had heard its location described as being "in the middle of nowhere," so I took extra precautions to make sure I could find my destination. However as I drove down the road and looked over at what I had amassed in the passenger seat to guide me, I couldn't help but chuckle at myself and wonder if I had overdone it. There was my GPS with the address logged in. But I also had printed up several pages of directions from MapQuest. And finally I had brought along my old, tried-and-true Rand McNally Road Atlas. I guess I figured if any one of those failed me, I had backup.

I'm glad to report that I made it to the conference with very little problem. There were a couple of times when the GPS made an odd suggestion or didn't recognize a new road, but the other tools at my disposal confirmed my route and helped me stay on the right track.

God has provided us with various means of guidance as we travel through life. We have His written Word, the Bible, as our faithful roadmap. We also have the Holy Spirit to nudge us in the right direction and to break through our confusion with His still small voice whispering to our souls, "This is the way you need to go." We have the providential hand of God we can watch for in our circumstances, opening doors or putting up road-blocks in order to steer us along the best path. In addition, God gives us trusted advisors in family, friends, fellow believers, and pastors to whom we can listen. And of course, prayer should encompass all of the above.

At times we may need more than one of those means to guide us. They will often all work together to confirm that we are going the right way. If we're just depending on one source while ignoring the others, we may make a wrong turn.

For example, I heard about a couple who claimed to have prayed diligently about their relationship and had peace of mind that it was acceptable. However, the Bible clearly stated otherwise. Sometimes we can let our own wants and wishes get in the way of God's guidance. It isn't always easy to discern whether it's the Holy Spirit leading us or simply our own spirit coming through. Those are the times when we need confirmation from other sources, such as the Bible. If what we believe the Holy Spirit is leading us to do is contradictory to what God's Word says, then we must be misreading the Spirit's guidance.

On the other hand, while God's infallible Word is always true, it doesn't speak directly to every situation we might face. We need the Holy Spirit to guide us in applying those principles to our specific circumstances.

We also can't rely solely on the direction of open and closed doors. An open door may be God telling us to move forward or it could be Satan inviting us in. Likewise, a closed door might be the Lord saying, "Don't go that way" or it could be Satan putting an obstacle in our pathway in order to try to keep us from going the right way.

I believe if we truly seek the Lord and want His guidance, He will provide it for us. But let's not rely solely on one source. He's given us several means by which we can confirm His will. And if we'll prayerfully listen and faithfully follow Him, He'll get us to our rightful destination.

Are you paying attention to all the means available to you in seeking God's guidance?

Seek After the True Riches

"That I should preach among the Gentiles the unsearchable riches of Christ."

– Ephesians 3:8

s I was walking out of a store, I encountered a little girl and a man whom I assume was her father. I overheard her enthusiastically exclaiming to her dad, "I'm rich!" Then she continued her statement, "I have eighteen cents!" I don't know if this girl had just found that money in the parking lot or what her situation may have been. She sounded genuinely excited about her "riches." I don't think she was being sarcastic at all, unlike the attitude some other youngsters today might have about that same amount of cash.

I certainly didn't say anything to spoil this child's moment, but I couldn't help but smile at her naïve view about what constituted being rich. I couldn't think of anything in the store she was about to enter which she could purchase for eighteen cents. I could envision her soon-to-be disillusionment about her perceived wealth once she found out how much it would actually cost to buy something.

The Bible records Jesus' message to a church which proclaimed to be rich. He informed them that they were actually poor and didn't know it (Revelation 3:17). "Rich" is a rather relative term many people would not claim for themselves. Yet many of us enjoy a level of prosperity and comfort which would lead a lot of people in the world to view us as fitting that description.

What would cause you to proclaim "I'm rich"? Winning the lottery or the Publisher's Clearing House Sweepstakes? Being able to live in a certain size house or drive a particular make of car? Having a bank account containing a certain amount of money? Being financially able to quit your job and take numerous vacations? Or maybe it would be the ability to follow more noble pursuits and start a charitable foundation or donate great sums of money to help others.

Many people have discovered such attainments do not necessarily make them rich. They find out they were as naïve as that little girl who thought she was rich with her eighteen cents. "I'm rich; I live in a mansion." "I'm rich; I have a million dollars." Yet they are soon disillusioned when they realize that such riches aren't as valuable as they had thought.

At some point many of us discover that true riches don't consist of those material things which so many treasure and which they spend their lives striving for. The greater treasures are found in areas that can't be bought in stores or measured by bank statements. Many such riches are found in relationships, not only with family and friends, but most of all with Jesus Christ.

The Bible makes reference to "the unsearchable riches of Christ" which can be ours as believers (Ephesians 3:8). If we know Jesus as our personal Savior, we are truly rich. We have peace with God—if you think that's not valuable, just try living with guilt and under divine condemnation. We can have joy, even in the midst of troubling times. We have a source of love, grace, forgiveness, and strength that helps us get through life, as well as enabling us to be a channel through which God can pour out those blessings on others. We have hope, no matter how bleak this world gets. And we have eternal life and a heavenly inheritance once our time on this earth is completed.

Don't fool yourself into believing that your eighteen cents of this life's "riches" is something to treasure. It won't take you very far and it won't last. But if you know Christ, you can rejoice in the fact that you possess an abundance of riches which are eternal.

What do you consider to be your riches? Are you seeking the riches in Christ?

Be Concerned about Fellow Believers around You

"Let each of us please his neighbor for his good, leading to edification."

– ROMANS 15:2

One Sunday I had the opportunity to visit and preach at another church. During their testimony and prayer time, one man expressed his thankfulness that he was doing better after having been struck in the face by a tree branch earlier in the week.

Not knowing the specific circumstances, I assumed this guy was probably cutting down a tree when one of the large limbs fell on him. But as I spoke to the man after the service, I found out it wasn't anything like that at all. While taking care of a job-related matter, he and another man had simply been walking through a wooded area. As the other fellow who was leading the way brushed by a small tree, one of its branches flipped back and hit his companion just as he was turning around from looking in the other direction. It caught him in the eye, seriously impairing his vision for a few days.

No doubt the other person had no intention of hurting this man. Maybe he didn't realize he was causing those small branches to flip back or possibly he thought the other guy was watching out for them. However, it still resulted in an incident that caused an injury. Maybe the man who got hurt should have been paying better attention. But at the same time, if the guy in the lead would've kept a closer eye on the person behind him and made sure to hold back any such branches until they had both safely passed through, this accident may have been avoided.

We have to watch out for a similar tendency. Sometimes we can be so intent on our own spiritual journey and focusing on the path ahead of us as we seek to follow Christ that we don't pay as close attention as we should to those around us. We plow through those obstacles and challenges, not letting them deter us from moving forward in our walk with God, but without realizing we may be slinging some of those branches right into the pathway of someone else who might have a tougher time dealing with them. We may be running along enjoying our freedom in Christ, while someone behind us is getting all hung up in a briar patch of self-effort, religious rules, and spiritual confusion.

Let's not forget that we have a degree of responsibility towards our brothers and sisters in Christ. We are supposed to be careful not to put any kind of a stumbling block before them—nothing that might be a hindrance to their faith and their spiritual journey. In chapters 14 and 15 of Romans, it emphasizes our need to be concerned about others, even to the point of giving up some of our own rights or wishes. "We then who are strong ought to bear with the scruples of the weak, and not to please ourselves. Let each of us please his neighbor for his good, leading to edification" (Romans 15:1–2).

For example, maybe you think you can handle watching those R-rated movies, having social drinks, and other such activities without it hindering your relationship with the Lord. But what about those who are around you, watching you, and even following your example? Those little branches you brush aside could end up being a big problem for some of them.

Like it or not, we can't just focus on our own pathway. The love of Christ compels us to think about our brothers and sisters in Christ. Are you willing to give up some of your freedom in order to help someone else find their way? Don't let anything in your life be a problem or road-block for that person coming along behind you.

Is some area of your freedom in Christ being a stumbling block to others? What do you need to do about it?

WE NEED TO BE A LITTLE OLD-FASHIONED

"Ask for the old paths, where the good way is, and walk in it."

– JEREMIAH 6:16

If you heard something described as "old-fashioned," would you consider it to be a positive or negative characteristic? Some companies intentionally use that term to describe their hamburgers, ice cream, or other products. By doing so they hope to suggest that their product is of better quality than many of its modern counterparts. During the holidays we may hear various celebrations described as old-fashioned, indicating that they embrace certain long-held traditions which some people find meaningful.

On the other hand, "old fashioned' can be used to describe people or organizations who are living in the past, who aren't willing to give up their old ways for better ways of doing things, or whose styles and methods are outdated. The term can be used in a derogatory way to characterize those who are out of touch with today's world.

When it comes to churches and individual Christians, there are those who proudly claim the title "old-fashioned" and others who try to distance themselves as far away from that idea as possible. Some cling to tradition while others pursue the latest trends. Some see modern technology as tools of the devil to be shunned while others endeavor to use every gadget available in ministry. While we may need to avoid extremes, I believe there's room for a wide variety of expression in these matters, depending on our preferences, purposes, and the people to whom we're ministering.

On the negative side of being old-fashioned, I believe we need to be careful that we aren't holding on to styles and traditions which no longer have meaning or relevance to people today. We ought to be willing to adjust and change, to be willing to put "new wine into new wineskins," in order to effectively minister to our present generation.

But on the positive side of being old-fashioned, there are truths, values, and meaningful traditions which should not be abandoned no matter how much society changes. Regardless of how others may look down upon us as being relics or unintellectual, we should adhere to the belief that the Bible is the uniquely inspired word of God. We should uphold its eternal truths, even when our world is moving away from those long-held concepts, thinking that it knows better today. We need to be old-fashioned enough to believe what God has declared to be right and holy, or wrong and sinful, is still valid. Public opinion, majority votes, legislative decrees, or court decisions cannot alter God's unchanging truth.

I also believe we should seek to maintain old-fashioned personal relationships with people. While current technology allows us to stay in contact electronically with more people in more frequent ways, it can also isolate us from actual face-to-face encounters. Just look around you the next time you're sitting in a waiting room and notice how many individuals are occupied with their electronic gadgets rather than paying attention to the people surrounding them. I believe people need more than Facebook friends and video pastors. They need flesh-and-blood brothers and sisters in Christ with whom they can talk, pray, cry, shake hands, and hug. No matter how contemporary the styles of our churches may be, they should seek to create an old-fashioned family atmosphere where people can personally interact and express the love of God to one another.

Some things from the past need to be changed or discarded. But let's be old-fashioned enough to cling to the things which are good and unchanging.

In what way do you need to be less old-fashioned? More old-fashioned?

Let's Make Sure We're Following Jesus

"Not everyone who says to Me, 'Lord, Lord,' shall enter the kingdom of heaven."

– MATTHEW 7:21

One day as I left a local business, I noticed an elderly gentleman standing in the parking lot next to his car. As I got closer, someone in another vehicle said something to the first man, indicating that they knew each other and were meeting at this location for some purpose. As I got into my car and drove away, I noticed the elderly man hurrying into his car and doing likewise. As a matter of fact, he pulled out right behind me. For the next two or three miles I watched him in my rearview mirror as he remained behind me, in spite of my making several turns. The further along we went, the more agitated he seemed to become and the more uncomfortable I became as he sometimes drove unusually close to my rear bumper. I finally concluded that for some reason this man was intentionally following me.

After I affirmed with another good look in the mirror that I didn't know the man, my mind raced with questions from a combination of curiosity and caution. Could there be something wrong with my car that he's trying to warn me about? Did he recognize me and doesn't particularly like preachers? Or does he need my help? Should I find a spot to pull over and confront the man?

However as I stopped at the next traffic light, the man beeped his horn and exited his vehicle. As I lowered my window, I heard him asking in an irritating tone as he approached, "Where in the world are you going?" Then I saw the look of shock on his face when he saw me. I suggested, "I think you've got the wrong person, don't you?" The man responded, "You're not who I'm supposed to be following."

Jesus spoke about some people who would be surprised one day to discover that they had not been following Him as they thought they had done. "Many will say to Me in that day, 'Lord, Lord, have we not prophesied in Your name, cast out demons in Your name, and done many wonders in Your name?' And then I will declare to them, 'I never knew you; depart from Me, you who practice lawlessness!'" (Matthew 7:22–23).

This is a rather sobering thought—to know that some of us who may have thought we were following Christ will one day realize we weren't. Some may find they were merely pursuing a pathway of religion and tradition. Others may discover they were following a preacher or some other person they admired as a moral or spiritual example. Others will find they were following their own good works rather than Jesus Himself.

This story should remind us that following Christ is primarily about a relationship. It's not about following the similar-looking vehicles of religion and moral rules. It's about a relationship of love and obedience to Christ Himself. In that passage of scripture in Matthew, Jesus was making a distinction between those who merely did good works and those who truly did His will. Good works are certainly part of Jesus' will for our lives. But those actions should spring from a personal relationship with Christ Himself through faith, not through our efforts to be "good enough" to be acceptable to God or to impress other people with our Christianity. Let's not become so focused on the outward vehicles of our faith that we lose sight of the Person we're supposed to be following.

It might be momentarily embarrassing to follow the wrong car, as it was for that elderly gentleman, but it would be eternally tragic to come to the end of the road of life and to realize we haven't been following Jesus.

Are you following Jesus or just something connected to Him?

GOD KNOWS ALL
ABOUT YOUR PAST

"And I thank Christ Jesus…because He counted me faithful, putting me into the ministry, although I was formerly a blasphemer, a persecutor, and an insolent man."

– I TIMOTHY 1:12–13

At various times during an election season, the concept of vetting candidates gains attention. Vetting refers to closely examining and investigating the backgrounds of those who are running for office. I find it interesting that the word itself originated from the idea of a veterinarian examination. I'll leave it to others to speculate as to whether or not that may indicate what we think of our politicians. Such investigations are often used to screen out unfit prospects or to discover issues that might come up and need to be addressed. Opponents may use that process to dig up dirt on someone in order to use it against him or her.

By today's standards, some might suggest that Jesus didn't do a very good job of vetting the Apostle Paul before calling him into an influential position of ministry. He had a huge stain on his résumé. For a while he had become obsessed with persecuting the followers of Christ, sending them to prison, and had even consented to the wrongful execution of their first martyr, Stephen. That would be a huge black mark on anyone's record who was applying for a position in Christian ministry. It caused some people to be scared of Paul and to be skeptical of this flip-flopper's supposed change of heart.

But don't we all have black marks on our records? We've all done things in our past that would disqualify us from going to heaven, from being part of God's family, and from serving the Lord. Maybe we didn't chase down Christians and throw them into prison, but we've all sinned against a holy God.

As we consider our stained pasts, let's remember several things. We need to acknowledge and confess those skeletons in the closet, not try to cover them up. Over the years political candidates have gotten into trouble not just from what they did in the past but also over their attempts to hide it through denials, lies, and excuses. Similarly, in order for us to make things right with God, we need to come to terms with the fact that we've done wrong and are sinners. And we need to confess those matters to God with an attitude of repentance so that we can find forgiveness. Too many people ignore those stains, letting them lie there under the surface as an unseen negative influence on their present lives.

The recognition of our past sinful lives should also give us a greater appreciation for God's mercy and grace. It reminds us of how unworthy we are to receive the wonderful gift of eternal life. And it stirs up a greater love in our hearts for the God who would love us and save us in spite of who we were and what we had done.

We also need to realize that God can use us in some form of ministry regardless of our past sins. Our past doesn't disqualify us from present service. It might even direct us toward a particular ministry—like the woman who reaches out to help prostitutes as a result of her having come out of that situation herself. In other cases our past may restrict us from certain areas of ministries—such as youth ministry not being an option for a former child molester. But whoever we are and whatever our past, God can use us in some kind of service for Him.

Jesus knew everything about Paul's past, and He knows everything about our previous sins, too. But He loves us anyway, is willing to forgive us, and has a place of ministry for each of us. So don't let your past drag you down. Rather, let it remind you to be thankful for the amazing grace of God.

Be grateful that God has saved you and can use you in spite of your past.

THERE'S A WAY BACK WHEN WE TAKE A WRONG TURN

"Remember therefore from where you have fallen; repent and do the first works."

– REVELATION 2:5

O ne weekend my oldest daughter and her family traveled down to Savannah for a combination birthday getaway and a visit with her younger sister. That other daughter of mine was nearing the end of her studies in that beautiful, historic Georgia city where she earned her masters degree in teaching. Unfortunately during that visit she also earned some notoriety for becoming guilty of being able to say, "I took a wrong turn and ended up in another state."

Such a statement might normally be applied to someone directionally challenged, or who was not paying attention to her surroundings, or who refused to stop and ask for directions. But that was not the case in this instance. In parts of Savannah, you're just a few short miles from crossing the river and being in another state. So it's not as bad as it sounds. However, it still makes for a good story and a fun reason to give my daughter a hard time (with her permission).

Apparently she was going to meet my other daughter and her family for lunch when she misunderstood which direction the restaurant was located. So she went one way on I-95 for several miles before realizing that her destination must have been the opposite direction. But then she discovered there were no exits available for her to turn around until, to her chagrin, she found herself having to cross the river and enter South Carolina. She did get turned around at that point and made it to her lunch appointment, only a little later than planned.

We all have to admit that as we've journeyed through life, we've made some wrong turns. In some cases it might be that we just weren't sure which way to go. Other times we may not have asked God for directions. But there may have also been instances when we were guilty of being careless about our journey or when we got distracted by other things. And of course there are those all-too frequent times when we just insisted on going our own way instead of listening to the Lord and following what we knew to be His will for us.

When we make a wrong turn, we often find out that it's not always easy to get turned around and going back in the right direction. Sometimes we get deceived by our surroundings and don't realize that we're off course for a while. And even when we do come to recognize that fact, pride can get in the way of our admitting the error and can hinder our willingness to correct our course. And sometimes those exits can simply be hard to find. The circumstances keep drawing us further in that direction, we gain more baggage from our mistake, and it gets harder and harder to turn around.

Yes, we may take a wrong turn and if we keep going can find ourselves in another state—a state of disobedience to God—a state of hardheartedness and stubbornness—a state of rebellion against the Lord's will for us—maybe even a state of putting our relationship with God in jeopardy.

The good news is that it is possible for us to turn around. The Bible calls it repentance. There is an exit ramp there if we'll truly seek it. If we will confess the error of our ways, be willing to change course, and submit ourselves to going God's way, then I believe He'll help us to get turned around.

So if you've taken a turn away from God's will for your life, stop right now and start seeking the way back.

Have you taken a wrong turn? Confess, repent, and let God help you find your way back.

Let's Be Thankful
for Our Redeemer

"Knowing that you were not redeemed with corruptible things...
but with the precious blood of Christ."

– I Peter 1:18–19

Imagine being trapped in a burning building. The smoke and flames are surrounding you. The whole structure is rapidly becoming engulfed in the fire. As you feel yourself succumbing to the smoke and the intense heat, you realize that you have no means of escape and are facing certain death.

But suddenly you hear a voice yelling from outside the building. "It's a bird! It's a plane! No, it's Superman!" A nearby window shatters as a muscular guy in blue tights and a red cape bursts through and into the room. Although the flames whip all around him, Superman is unaffected by their red-hot sting. He walks right through the fire without experiencing any pain and without one hair of his head getting singed. He comes over to you, pulls his cape around you for protection, lifts you up in his powerful arms, and flies you through the window to safety. You would be grateful for such a hero rescuing you, wouldn't you?

However, what if you're in that situation and instead of a superhero showing up, a firefighter bursts through the door? As he makes his way toward you, you hear him coughing and struggling to survive the blaze himself. When he reaches you, he removes his protective jacket, wrapping it around you instead. Then he walks you through the flames to safety.

But in doing so, although you come away fairly unscathed since you were wearing that protective gear, the firefighter ends up with some severe burns on his face and body that will scar him for life.

In a way, don't you feel more gratitude for that second hero due to what it cost him to come into such a perilous situation to rescue you? Superman wasn't really risking anything—he knew that fire couldn't harm him. But the firefighter paid a hefty price in order to pull you from death and destruction. Yet he was willing to do so.

Let's remember that Jesus isn't just our Superman-Savior or rescuer. The Bible refers to Him as our Redeemer. The word "redeem" means to buy back. It reminds us that it cost Jesus something to save us. He's our firefighter who paid a great price in order to deliver us from destruction. It cost more than simply money, time, or effort. It cost Him his life.

Our hero led us away from the fires of sin and hell even though the flames of ridicule and insults lashed out at Him, even as the whip of a scourging tore the flesh off his back, and even as nails were driven into His hands and feet. He could've called for backup and have been whisked safely out of that painful situation by a host of angels, but then we would have been left behind to our doom. So Jesus kept going, through the agony of crucifixion and of bearing the weight of our sins, in order to lead us away from death and destruction. He paid the price and got us out. When He saw that we were safe, He declared, "It is finished," and He took His last breath.

When you read that word "redeemed" in the Bible or when you sing those hymns about Jesus being our Redeemer, let it remind you of what it cost the Lord to save you. "Knowing that you were not redeemed with corruptible things, like silver or gold, from your aimless conduct...but with the precious blood of Christ" (I Peter 1:18–19). Let's be sure to express our gratitude, in both words and actions, for such a Hero-Redeemer as ours.

Lord, thank You for the price you paid to be my Redeemer.

"DOING WITHOUT" TENDS TO MAKE ONE THANKFUL

"Bless the Lord, O my soul, and forget not all His benefits."

– PSALM 103:2

The lights in our house dimmed, flickered, and then went out altogether. In the middle of a drought, there was certainly no storm in the area to cause such an outage. The news grew potentially worse as I looked outside to see lights shining through the windows of my neighbors' homes. Whatever the problem was, it was affecting only us. The power company quickly responded to our call, coming out and tracing the source to one of the underground lines leading up to our house. While they were busy digging their way through hard, parched ground and tree roots trying to reach that wire, my wife and I enjoyed a romantic candlelight dinner, consisting of McDonald's quarter pounders with cheese and French fries.

As the dark evening wore on, the sounds of digging from outdoors suddenly ceased. Not because they had reached their goal, but because they had accidentally hit a water line. Now we were without both power and water. The electricity was finally restored around 1:15 a.m., but we remained without water until well into the next day. But I have no complaints about the workers or companies involved. They were persistent, helpful, and considerate through the whole ordeal.

The following afternoon when everything was back to normal and I was able to take a nice, hot shower again, I found myself giving thanks for that water flowing out of the faucets. I use it every day, but I couldn't think of the last time I had consciously felt grateful for that valuable resource and had expressed those feelings to God. There are many other things in our lives like that as well. We don't give them much thought until we're forced to make do without them. It may be the electricity or water. Or it may be food or good health. It may be a job, family, or friends. We often don't appreciate them until we find ourselves trying to live without them.

I was visiting with someone in prison around that same time when I mentioned having eaten at a certain pizza restaurant. This man who has been incarcerated for a couple of years got a longing look in his eyes as he commented on how nice it would be to get to go to that place or several other food establishments he named. Being able to stop at one of the local fast food joints is something we take for granted. We may even make fun of their cuisine at times. But what if we had to do without it and live on prison food for a few years?

Maybe it would help us to be more thankful if we thought about what life would be like if we had to do without some of our many blessings. We might be able to remember times in our lives when that was the case—times in the past when we didn't possess some of those blessings. Let's not forget those experiences. And we can think about people today, like my acquaintance in prison or people living in certain other countries or the less fortunate in our own communities, who don't get to enjoy some of the aspects of life that we benefit from every day. We ought to remember the plight of others, not only to stir up our own gratitude but also to remind ourselves to share our blessings with those in need.

And I don't ever want to forget what life was like without Christ in my heart. Let's not take for granted the peace, joy, love, strength, and all the other blessings that come from having eternal life in Jesus. And let's share that gift with those around us who are still facing life without it.

Consider what life would be like without some of your blessings. Let those thoughts stir up a fresh sense of gratitude in your heart.

Approaching Thanksgiving from a Different Side

"Enter into His gates with thanksgiving, and into His courts with praise."

– Psalm 100:4

"Well, at least it can't get any worse." As soon as you hear those fateful words uttered by a character in a TV show or movie, you know what's coming. Something is about to happen that will make the situation even more dire. It's just a reminder to us that no matter how bad circumstances may seem, it could always be worse.

Sometimes we comfort ourselves or others with that proven principle. We may not see any good in a situation. We may be tempted to complain and feel sorry for ourselves. We feel overwhelmed by the inconvenience, pain, challenge, or obstacle we're facing. Then we realize that there are others who are having to deal with much worse—maybe making our problem look miniscule in comparison. Or we recognize that as difficult as our circumstances may be, we're still blessed that we're not suffering something even worse.

As another Thanksgiving approaches, maybe you're having a hard time facing it from the perspective of counting your blessings. However, it's possible we can arrive at that destination by coming at it from a different angle. You may not be able to see the blessings at this point, but you can recognize that things could be worse. And the fact that they're not is reason to be grateful.

The Bible is full of examples from which we can learn life lessons. Some of the situations of people recorded within its pages remind us that things could be worse.

Facing storm damage? It could be worse. You could be one of those in Noah's day dealing with forty days and nights of rain, with enough flooding to wipe out all of mankind. Plus the only boat available has shut its door and left without you.

Concerned about the moral and spiritual condition of our nation, along with its future? It could be worse. Unlike Sodom and Gomorrah, God hasn't rained down fire and brimstone from heaven to completely destroy us...at least not yet.

Got family issues? David's own beloved son not only turned against him, seeking to dethrone his father, but he sought to take David's life. So it could be worse.

Feeling like the government is turning more hostile toward you because of your faith and values? You haven't been thrown in a fiery furnace, cast into a den of lions, or lowered down into a deep, miry pit like some of God's faithful followers had to experience. Yes, it could be worse.

Facing loss? Job lost it all in one sudden swoop—his possessions, his children, and his health. So it could be worse.

In a tight spot? It could be worse. You could find yourself like Jonah, alive and conscious in the belly of a large fish after having gotten kicked off a boat in the middle of a stormy sea.

Got spiritual concerns? It could be worse. You could be like the rich man who found himself in a place of eternal torment begging for a drop of cool water. At least you've still got an opportunity to get right with God before it's too late.

I prefer coming at Thanksgiving head-on with a positive recognition of our many blessings. But sometimes our situations are such as to make it more difficult for us to embrace that truth. So if you need to enter into the spirit of Thanksgiving through the side door this year, that's okay. The main thing is to get there. Whether from counting your blessings or realizing things could be worse, know that there's reason to be grateful to God. So give Him thanks.

Consider how your situation could be worse and give God thanks that it isn't.

TRUST THE LORD TO PROVIDE FOR YOUR NEEDS

"Do not worry about your life, what you will eat; nor about the body, what you will put on."

– LUKE 12:22

I felt like I was watching an episode of the old TV show *Wild Kingdom*. As I was sitting in my living room, my attention suddenly was drawn from the television screen to the window revealing a real-life drama playing out in the front yard. A large bird had swooped down to the base of our cherry tree with wings spread wide as it seemed to be attacking something on the ground. In a moment it went flying off to sit in my neighbor's tree with a squirrel firmly in its deadly grasp. At first I thought the predator was a hawk, but upon closer observation of the fowl as it sat on that limb with its prize, I realized it was actually a large owl.

I knew there was an owl in our neighborhood. We can often hear its distinct and eerie hooting in the early evenings or early morning hours. And although you know in the back of your mind that it must be sustaining itself by preying on small creatures in the area, you don't think much about it until you actually witness the spectacle firsthand as I did that evening.

While this event reminded me of the wonders of nature and the circle of life playing out around us, it also brought to mind the truth about how God provides for us. Jesus used a similar situation to illustrate that truth. He said, "Do not worry about your life, what you will eat; nor about the

673

body, what you will put on. Life is more than food, and the body is more than clothing. Consider the ravens, for they nether sow nor reap, which have neither storehouse nor barn; and God feeds them. Of how much more value are you than the birds?" (Luke 12:22–24).

God takes care of His creatures. He provides nuts for the squirrels and squirrels for the owls. I know some people who wish He would send an owl over their way to help rid them of some pesky squirrels, but the point is: God provides what is needed. And as Jesus suggested, how much more is that true regarding us? If God cares enough to take care of the ravens, the squirrels, and the owls, how much more will He provide what we need?

As we celebrate this time of Thanksgiving, let's remember that the celebration of God's provision is how this holiday started and is the prime subject for our expressions of gratitude. It was the fact that God had supplied the basic needs for the early settlers of this country which led to their wanting to observe a day of thanksgiving. God had provided food, shelter, clothing, and the other necessities to sustain their lives. He had shown His care and His ability to provide, just as Jesus had indicated in this scripture.

And we can still trust the Lord to provide for us today. As we look back over the past year, we can thank Him for taking care of us. As we look ahead to the coming year, we don't have to worry. God still cares about us. We're still of great value to Him. And He'll supply our needs.

But remember, that owl didn't just sit back in the tree and wait for God to hand-feed it. It had to go do the hunting. And God expects us to do our part. But if we do what we can, we can trust that the Lord will make a way for there to be food on our table, along with everything else we truly need. You matter to God. Trust Him to provide.

How does the promise of God's provision give you assurance and peace today?

LIVE LIKE YOU'RE GRATEFUL

One time we went to the theater to watch a new *Peanuts* movie. I was so glad to discover that the film stayed in keeping with the spirit of those original adventures of Charlie Brown and the gang which many of us remember. It was an enjoyable view for the little kids in the audience like my grandchildren, as well as for those of us older kids who still treasure the antics of Snoopy and the other *Peanuts* characters.

As I was leaving the theater that evening, I heard one mom dealing with her misbehaving little boy. After several attempts to get him to stop what he was doing, she finally blurted out in her frustration, "You are so ungrateful!" From her subsequent statements, she was apparently referring to the fact that she had done something nice for her son in bringing him to this movie he wanted to see, but now he was not behaving well. Unfortunately she continued to berate the child in a way and with such harsh language that, in my opinion, is liable to do more harm than good.

In spite of this mom letting her frustrations take her too far in the public scolding of her son, her claim about her child being ungrateful is a valid reminder to us. Gratitude isn't just expressed in our verbal attempts to say "Thank you." It also reveals itself in our actions. This mom probably didn't expect her little boy to come right out and say, "Thank you, Mom, for taking me to the movie." However she did hope that he would show his gratitude by behaving in a way that would please his mother, or at least refraining from actions which would upset her.

There are many thankless jobs around. Parenting is often one of those. Kids don't always stop and express their gratitude for all their parents do for them. Teachers, police officers, and numerous others could also be included among those who don't receive enough expressions of appreciation for what they do. And the ultimate thankless job must be God's. He does so much for us, yet how often we fail to thank Him, except maybe during a short time period in late November. And even then many people simply express gratitude for what they have without directing it specifically toward God.

Let's remember that God wants more than our words of thanks around this holiday. He desires for us to act like people who are grateful to Him. He wants us to show our gratitude by living in ways we know brings Him pleasure and by refraining from such behavior which grieves Him. When we misbehave, God must often be tempted to exclaim to us, "You are so ungrateful!" He has done so much for us, yet we persist in acting in disobedience to His will for us.

So as another Thanksgiving Day approaches, let's not only verbalize our thanks to God, but let's also think about what else we can do to show our gratitude. What actions can we take to bring pleasure to our Heavenly Father? How can we behave ourselves in such a way as to show how thankful we truly are?

Is there something we're doing that we know is grieving the heart of God? Wouldn't this be a great time to change our behavior and attitude into one that would put a smile on God's face instead? God likes to hear us say "Thank you" but even more, He is pleased to see us doing His will and living like people who love Him and love others. Let's strive to act like grateful kids of our Heavenly Father.

What can you do today to show your Heavenly Father how grateful you are?

BE THANKFUL FOR THE PEOPLE IN YOUR LIFE

"I thank my God upon every remembrance of you."

– PHILIPPIANS 1:3

Thanksgiving always falls around the time of my mom's birthday, sometimes on the very day itself. This combination of special occasions reminds me how blessed I am still to have both my parents around at the time of my writing this. And I'm thankful they are doing as well as they are at this stage of their lives.

I hope we've all been taking some time this season to focus on the many ways God has blessed us. As we've done so, I also trust that we didn't simply express our thanks for the "things" of life. They're important, and we should give thanks to the Lord for providing us with a roof over our heads, a car to drive, food on the table, a regular paycheck we can take to the bank, and all the other material blessings. But let's not forget that one of our greatest blessings in life involves the people whom God has given us.

Some of our greatest treasures are the family, friends, and fellow believers in our lives. Their love, support, and friendship are more valuable and meaningful than all the mansions, luxury vehicles, priceless jewelry, latest electronics, and whatever other physical possessions we tend to value. If those people weren't around, we'd miss them so much more than those prized material things.

In the classic holiday movie, *It's a Wonderful Life*, George Bailey finds himself in a world where he had never been born. Certainly he notices the absence of his greatest possessions—his clunker of a car not being where he had left it, the family building and loan business having long ago closed down, and his house being nothing more than a dilapidated, vacant shell.

But what disturbed George most was that his family and friends didn't know who he was. His best friends viewed him as a lunatic stranger. He was tossed out of a place where he was usually welcomed and treated with respect. His wife screamed in fear when he reached out to her. And his own mother failed to recognize him, closing the door in his face. That was when George got the most terrified look on his face. He realized how awful it is to suddenly lose all the people in your life.

It's bad enough to take for granted the material blessings God has given us, but it's even worse when we lose sight of how grateful we should be for the friends and family around us. Those people in our lives have their faults just like we do, by the way. They can sometimes make life difficult and complicated, but our lives would be so much emptier if those individuals weren't around.

Do you remember what happened to George Bailey? When he got back to his real world in which everyone knew him, all his previously overwhelming problems paled in comparison to the gratitude he had for the people around him. As his guardian angel reminded him through a little inscription he wrote in a book, "No man is a failure who has friends."

Some of us may be richer in family and friends than others, some of us may be missing loved ones who are no longer here, but we all have people around us for whom we can be grateful. And if we know Christ as our Savior, we're part of a wonderful family of believers that we can enjoy both now and throughout eternity.

Don't take the people around you for granted. Be thankful for them. It would be a much different world without them.

Give thanks to God for your family, friends, and fellow believers.

Keep Trusting God in Tough Times

"The Lord gave, and the Lord has taken away; blessed be the name of the Lord."

– Job 1:21

I remember the comment made by the mayor of a city hit hard by a typhoon in the Philippines a few years ago. Concerning this devastating event, he suggested, "God must have been someplace else." Logically and theologically, we recognize there are problems with that statement. We know that the God revealed in the Bible is present everywhere and is aware of all that goes on in this world.

However, I think the mayor was speaking less from his head and more from his heart, expressing the question so many others have asked in the aftermath of tragic events—"How could a great and loving God have allowed such a thing to happen?" In other words, if a good and powerful God had been there, He would've stopped it—therefore He must have been someplace else.

A few examples the Bible gives us of others who experienced difficult, life-changing events might shed a little light on this subject. There was Joseph, sold into slavery and later wrongfully imprisoned. Yet many years afterwards he looked back and said to his brothers who instigated it all, "You meant evil against me, but God meant it for good" (Genesis 50:20). I'm not saying everything that happens to us is a good thing. I'm not suggesting that there are not bad events or tragedies. I don't believe we can call it a good thing for several thousand people to lose their lives in a typhoon. But often we may be able to look back and see how God brought something good out of those bad events. We believe He is working to make that new path we're being forced to travel on a good one and a blessing in our lives.

But sometimes we can't see any good in such a tragedy, which takes us to the example of Job. He lost everything in a short time and had no idea why. Although he struggled with it, from the outset Job declared his continued faith in God. He said, "The Lord gave, and the Lord has taken away; blessed be the name of the Lord" (Job 1:21). Along with Job we can affirm that no matter what comes our way, we know God is in control and we can trust Him. We may not see any good coming out of it nor understand why it happened, but we keep trusting the God who loves us and who knows what He's doing.

Another example could be the disciples immediately after Jesus' crucifixion. Certainly they didn't understand why God allowed Jesus to be put to death on the cross. But they soon found out His death was all part of God's plan to bring salvation to mankind. That's the other factor we need to keep in mind about such events in our lives. God tells us, "For my thoughts are not your thoughts, nor are your ways My ways, says the Lord; for as the heavens are higher than the earth, so are My ways higher than your ways, and My thoughts than your thoughts" (Isaiah 55:8–9).

Sometimes in those tough events which come into our lives, God is working out His greater plans and purposes—things we can't understand simply because we can't see the whole picture as God does. At those moments we simply need to have faith that God is fulfilling His purposes through it all.

So no matter what difficulties we may have to face, let's not despair and think God must have been someplace else. Instead let's affirm our trust in Him and declare "Blessed be the name of the Lord."

Concerning what difficult experience in your life do you need to apply these truths?

SOME LESSONS FROM
SAYING GRACE

"For every creature of God is good, and nothing is to be refused if it is received with thanksgiving."

– I TIMOTHY 4:4

O ne of the most common prayers of thankfulness some of us offer up is that of "saying grace," or the blessing, or the giving of thanks before we eat our meals. It has been a joy at times to hear my grandchildren recite such a prayer as the family has prepared to eat together. There's nothing quite like a sweet innocent voice lifting up those simple expressions of gratitude to God—"God is great; God is good; let us thank Him for our food" or "God our Father, once again we just want to thank You."

However as time has gone on, I've also noticed some not-so-pleasing trends that have developed in those same kids concerning those premeal prayers. Sometimes they will recite the prayer so fast that I can hardly make out the words, leaving in doubt whether the one praying is sincere or is merely hurrying through a meaningless ritual. It's also interesting that there were once conflicts over who would get to say the blessing for the food, sometimes resulting in our sitting patiently through the process of each child saying a prayer. But now it seems that there is often more of a reluctance to be the one to volunteer to give thanks. And of course there's that perennial issue of some child going ahead and sneaking some bites of food while someone else is leading the prayer.

While some of those issues simply reflect the humorous immaturity of childhood, they also remind us of attitudes that we all may need to guard against—not just when expressing gratitude for our food, but in connection with our general spirit and practice of giving thanks to God.

Let's be careful that we don't allow our expressions of "Thank God," "Praise the Lord," and "Thank You, Jesus" to become simply habitual phrases which have lost their meaning to us. It's good for us to acknowledge the role of God in bestowing His favor on us, but we need to be sure that behind those spiritually-sounding exclamations is a heart that is truly grateful for what a gracious God has done for us. Let's not lose or lessen our expressions of thanks in our conversations with others and in our prayers, but let's also keep an eye on our hearts to make sure those statements and prayers aren't just empty words.

Another lesson we might learn from those children's prayers is the necessity of maintaining a right attitude about thankfulness. Giving thanks to God should be something we are anxious to do, not words which have to be pried from our lips. Sometimes it's easier to focus on the negative side of our lives. We can always find something to complain about. But no matter what is happening in our personal lives or in the world around us, there are many good reasons to give thanks to the Lord. We need to practice what a beloved song says and count our blessings.

I'm afraid too many of us are like those kids who can't wait to eat their food or who can't pause for a moment in order to express gratitude to God for what He has set before us. We're so busy enjoying and devouring God's provision and gifts that we fail to return thanks to the One who has given them to us.

So let's take time to say thanks to God, and to do so willingly and sincerely. God is great; God is good, let us thank Him for our food...and for all His other wonderful blessings.

Give thanks today—readily and from the heart.

Trust that God Knows What He's Doing

"The Lord has established His throne in heaven, and His kingdom rules over all."

– Psalm 103:19

O ne year our church was helping out a couple of families with groceries for Thanksgiving. As the Sunday which we had set as the deadline to receive all food items drew near, I had a couple of people inquiring as to what was lacking in our collection and seeking suggestions on what they could bring. So I took a few minutes to search through those plastic bags full of cans, jars, and boxes to take stock of those donations. I was able to come up with a few ideas that I could relay back to those who had asked. But while involved in that investigation, I also noticed that there seemed to be one item of which we had an abundance—green beans.

I like green beans. When I go out to eat at certain restaurants, I often order that dish as one of my side items. And that simple casserole made out of green beans, cream of mushroom soup, and French fried onions has become a holiday staple. That was what some folks who donated those beans obviously had in mind, because the other ingredients for that casserole were included, too. However, I know that there are some people who don't like green beans, including a couple of them in my own family. Some kids in particular seem to turn up their noses at the sight of that food. So I was afraid that we had too many green beans for these families we were helping out. Hence, I not only told people what else might be needed, but also informed them that we had enough canned vegetables. But when that last Sunday for collecting food rolled around, along with everything else which came in, sure enough, there were a few more cans of green beans.

The next day as I delivered the groceries to one of those families, I was glad to hear their words of appreciation, along with the exclamation, "Wow! That's a big turkey!" But what pleased me the most was when one of the boys asked me, "Are there any green beans?" That was the only specific food anyone in that family inquired about. I cautiously smiled and assured him that there were quite a few of them included. His face brightened as he declared, "Good. I love green beans."

As I returned to my car to drive back home, I couldn't help but laugh. As usual, God knew exactly what He was doing. I had been trying to balance the menu, fill the gaps, guard against having too much of one item or something people might not like. Yet God knew that there was a boy in that family who loved green beans. And He made sure that there would be plenty of them for him to enjoy this Thanksgiving.

Let's trust that God knows what He's doing in our lives, too. We can prepare, plan, and work, yet the Lord is the One who is in control. When we think things aren't going right, we may be tempted to get frustrated or to try to do it all on our own, relying completely on our own wisdom and strength. Let's remember that God sees the bigger picture much better than we are able to do. And He cares about us and is seeking what is good for us. When we think things are out of balance, God may know that they're progressing just as they should be. He'll take care of us, just as He took care of a boy who loves green beans.

Is there something in your life that seems out of balance or messed up? Remind yourself that God is still in control.

Take a Fresh Look at God's Greatness

"Oh, the depths of the riches both of the wisdom and knowledge of God!"

– ROMANS 11:33

I've always enjoyed hiking in wooded areas, especially during the fall when the changing leaves make those surroundings more colorful. While the paved walking trails are nice especially as we get older, I still prefer the more natural paths where you have to step over roots, around muddy spots, and use rocks as steppingstones.

Whenever I'm hiking in such a setting, I try to make it a point not just to focus on the trail, but occasionally to stop and turn my attention to the beauty around me. I like to pause to take in the sight of the mountain, the canyon, or those secluded woods. It's nice to pause to listen to the quietness, or to the soothing sound of a nearby stream or the scurrying of a squirrel through the leaves. I stop to breathe in the deep woods smell before continuing on my journey. It's refreshing to pause and be reminded of the beauty and greatness of those surroundings.

As we journey through our busy lives, hopefully walking along the trail of following God and His will for our lives, I believe we need to regularly pause along the way. We need to stop and take another good look at the God whom we serve. We need to get our eyes off ourselves and all the challenges on the path before us, and focus on God as a reminder of how great and wonderful He is. Let's turn our attention to

Him and praise Him, not just for what He has done for us but simply for who He is.

I'm not talking about reaffirming in our minds some cold, hard fact about God, His existence, or His character. It should be more than just reciting the words of a creed—"I believe in God the Father Almighty, Maker of heaven and earth." We need to see God afresh in a way that leaves us in awe and wonder. We need an encounter that will make a deep impression on us, positively impacting us as we continue on our journey.

The Apostle Paul seems to express such a moment as he was writing his letter to the Romans. At the end of chapter 11, he stops along the trail of salvation, doctrine, and practical holiness to gaze around him at the greatness of God. He pauses to remind himself and us who are following along that trail of how beautiful, expansive, and incomprehensible is the God behind all these wonderful truths. "Oh, the depth of the riches both of the wisdom and knowledge of God! How unsearchable are His judgments and His ways past finding out!"(Romans 11:33). Paul wasn't just communicating a fact he knew in his head—he was expressing something he deeply sensed in his heart.

It's like being out on a hike when you turn a corner in the path and come upon a breathtaking sight, such as a waterfall or a beautiful view of the valley below. It stirs something in your soul. You don't just think, *There's a waterfall*—you say, "Oh, what a beautiful sight!"

We need occasional "oh" moments with God—times when we don't just affirm the truth "God is great," but when we're also compelled to cry out, "Oh, how great is our God!" Or times when we don't just flippantly say, "God is good," but out of our hearts we feel, *Oh, how good You are to me, God!*

How long has it been since some fresh vision of God or encounter with Him has deeply affected you in some way? If it's been a while, maybe you need to pause in the midst of your busy journey and take a better look at Him today to be reminded of how great He is.

Take time today to meditate on God's greatness and to seek to renew your sense of awe of Him.

Don't Allow Anything to Rival God in Your Life

"For I am God and there is no other; I am God, and there is none like Me."

– Isaiah 46:9

Usually there is a Saturday around this time of year which is a big day for college football. It is what has come to be called "rivalry day." It's the occasion when many schools which consider themselves to be rivals face off on the football field. In our area, that big rivalry consists of the University of Georgia versus Georgia Tech. Similar scenarios play out across the country, often among schools located in the same state, competing to recruit the same players and vying for the affections of the same fans.

So let's consider this question: who or what is God's rival? If God and His team went onto the football field on rivalry day, who would come out of the opposing locker room? Our first thought might be Satan, but consider the way the dictionary defines a rival. It says that a rival is a person or thing that can equal or surpass another in some way. Can Satan, or anyone else for that matter, equal or surpass God? Not according to the Bible. In the book of Isaiah God asks the question, "To whom will you liken Me, and make Me equal, and compare Me, that we should be alike? (Isaiah 46:5). Shortly afterwards the answer is given: "For I am God, and there is no other; I am God, and there is none like Me" (Isaiah 46:9).

God is declaring that He has no rivals. No one can compete on the same field with Him. No one can measure up to Him. No matter who goes out there to play against God, it's a blowout. The game would be called even before it got started, because it would be no contest. When God shows up, there's no competition—no one can compete against Him.

This doesn't mean there aren't those who try to compete against God anyway. Maybe that's where Satan comes in. Apparently he had the audacity to leave God's team, form his own, and think they could beat God. But Satan got trounced, reaffirming the truth that there is none like God.

But we can also be guilty of creating rivals to God in our own lives. Nothing equals God, yet sometimes we let something into our lives which we start putting on an equal basis with Him. Nothing compares to God, yet sometimes we start comparing things to Him, thinking they're just as important or valuable. We allow certain things to compete against God for our love, loyalty, and service. We expend our time, energy, and resources serving those things instead of serving the one true God. It could be almost anything—work, money, family, pastimes—just to name a few of the many possibilities.

If we've been guilty of allowing such a rival in our lives, we need to put it back in its proper place while at the same time reaffirming our love and commitment to the Lord. Let's remind ourselves that there really isn't anyone like Him. Whatever that rival is, it doesn't compare to the Almighty God who created us. It doesn't measure up to our Heavenly Father who loved us so much that He sent His Son to be the sacrifice for our sins. No one compares to the Father who cares for us, protects us, guides us, and helps us through each and every day. No one equals the God who promises never to leave us or forsake us. Those other things come and go, but God sticks with us through thick and thin. There is no one like Him.

So let's recommit our love and loyalty to the Lord today. Reaffirm that in your heart and mind, He truly has no rivals.

Are you allowing anything in your life to be a rival of God?

Let's Stay Focused on the Main Character of the Season

"For unto us a Child is born, unto us a Son is given."
– Isaiah 9:6

One year we tuned in to the Hallmark Channel in order to watch one of its new Christmas movies. For several reasons, we had a special interest in this particular production. For one thing, we knew parts of it had been filmed in the quaint north Georgia town of Dahlonega. Secondly, we were told that one of the prime locations used in the film was the building in which one of our daughters had her wedding a couple of years earlier. However, the most intriguing feature was the possibility that our son-in-law, along with other members of his family who live in that area, might show up in the background of some of the scenes of the movie. They were present at the filming and were used as "extras" in the cast.

In light of those factors, I found myself viewing this film very differently from the way I normally watch a movie. Instead of keeping my eye on the main characters, I was always noticing the background, trying to pinpoint recognizable locations or people. I spotted familiar shops on the square in Dahlonega. I saw rooms we used at the wedding. Our first time through the movie, my wife and I failed to see the recognizable faces for which we were searching. But after receiving more information about the specific scenes involved, as we rewatched our recording of it, we were able to recognize the back of our son-in-law at one point and spied his mother in another scene.

Because of those unique factors, it was different, fun, and interesting watching this particular movie. However, it would have been easy to miss some of the main action due to my attention being given to the secondary scenery and background characters.

As we go through another Christmas season, let's be careful not to do something similar in how we view and experience the holidays. It's so easy to get our eyes on the "extras" that we lose sight of the main character. We can get so wrapped up in what's happening in the background that we miss out on the main storyline.

Many of those secondary things add fun and excitement to our celebrations. And there's nothing wrong with most of them, as long as we don't let them distract us from what's most important.

What is it that tends to draw your attention away from the primary person and message of the season? Maybe it's the jolly old guy in the red suit along with his reindeer, gift-giving, and all the other fun things we associate with him. Maybe for you it's more nostalgic aspects of the holidays—from Charlie Brown's scraggly Christmas tree to a favorite Christmas carol you sing along with on the radio. Others focus on the brightly-lit decorations, the delicious food, the church programs, the big sales at the store, or the fun parties. Many of us can easily come to focus our main attention on family—the joy of seeing excited children talking to Santa or opening gifts—the thankfulness for loved ones being together again for another special occasion.

All those things can be wonderful aspects of the season. However, let's keep in mind that they're extras. They should take a backseat to the main story—that God so loved the world that He sent His Son to be our Savior. Let's not forget that Jesus is the star of this show.

I hope you enjoy many of these various aspects of the holidays, but through it all let's be sure to keep our focus on Jesus and to make sure the meaning of His birth is at the forefront of our celebration.

What can you do to try to maintain your focus on Jesus during the holiday season?

TRUST GOD IN THE FACE OF TERROR

"I will say of the Lord, 'He is my refuge and my fortress; my God, in Him I will trust.'"

– PSALM 91:2

As the holiday season gets into full swing, much of our attention turns to those meaningful, traditional, and fun activities we associate with this time of year. However in recent years we are also confronted with more reminders of the reality of terrorism in our world. Even as people plan to "go over the river and through the woods" to grandmother's house, they're often faced with a global travel alert. As they gather for parades, festivals, and ballgames, they are confronted with an increased police presence and added security. And as they watch the TV news and find the usual holiday stories which warm their hearts, they also see the latest reports on terrorism which can send chills down their spines.

So how do we react to these threats from those who not only seek to instill fear, but who also can actually blow up planes, shoot into crowds, and otherwise injure and kill? And it can be especially disconcerting that some of them seem to be targeting followers of Christ. Does this leave us locked up in our homes, refusing to get out in large crowds, and afraid to go to church? Does it relegate us to living in a state of fear and panic?

Psalm 91:5–6 declares, "You shall not be afraid of the terror by night, nor of the arrow that flies by day, nor of the pestilence that walks in darkness, nor of the destruction that lays waste at noonday." I don't believe this is suggesting that we go around unaware of potential dangers and living recklessly. I don't think this precludes us from taking wise precautions. I don't believe this means we let those terrors strike us without seeking to protect ourselves. What it says is, "You shall not be afraid." Even then, I don't think this is talking about the sudden fright we can experience when someone attacks us, a bomb goes off nearby, or some other sudden event threatens our well-being. We have an instinct of self-preservation that can cause us to be startled by something or someone who puts us in danger.

I believe this is talking about the general spirit and attitude with which we live our lives. In the face of the threat of terrorists, even the possibility of us being targeted as followers of Christ, we should be determined that we're not going to let fear and panic rule our lives. We can still have peace in our hearts from a steadfast trust in the Lord. That's what the rest of this psalm talks about—that God is our refuge and we believe in His ability to protect us. Yes, the threats are real. In some cases, we have enemies who want to either convert us or kill us. But we have a God who is bigger and greater. He can either protect us from those dangers or help us face them with grace and courage. And if anything does harm us, we have the assurance of God's presence through it all, as well as of something better waiting for us once this life is over. In the meantime, we can still go about doing whatever God calls us to do while trusting Him to take care of us.

Maybe some of us need to cut back on listening to those voices in the world which stir up panic and fear of what man might do to us and pay greater attention to the voice of God which engenders peace and trust in Him. Let's keep our eyes on the Lord and strengthen our faith in Him in spite of the terrors in our world today.

How can you balance being wise and cautious with maintaining a calm sense of peace and trust in the Lord?

DECEMBER 2

Recapture the Joy and Meaning of the Season

"And suddenly there was with the angel a multitude of the heavenly host praising God and saying: 'Glory to God in the highest, and on earth peace, goodwill toward men!'"

– LUKE 2:13–14

My wife and I had put up our Christmas tree, along with our other indoor decorations, shortly after Thanksgiving. When our grandchildren came over the next day, it was interesting to watch their reactions to all the new and different items adorning our living room. They enthusiastically explored the plethora of ornaments hanging on the tree. They excitedly pointed out certain ones which, unbeknownst to them, had intentionally been put low on the tree for their eyes to view—such as familiar cartoon characters, frames with their pictures in them, and ornaments they had made for us in years past.

The grandkids also enjoyed going around the room winding up all the musical snow-globes, making the nutcracker disguised as a toy soldier open and close his mouth, and pushing the button to cause a mechanical Santa to dance...over and over and over again. Many of those familiar decorations which we had quickly unpacked without giving them much attention found new life in the eyes of our grandchildren.

As we go through this Christmas season, maybe we should pray for God to give us such childlike eyes to see things in a fresh way. Sometimes I'm afraid we've become so familiar with the account of Jesus' birth, the truths connected to this glorious event, and the various ways we commemorate it that we lose some of the joy and excitement it should stir up within us.

For example, let's look at that traditional Nativity scene with fresh eyes. As you view those figures at the manger, admire Mary's courageous willingness to be used in such a unique way as God's instrument. Be thankful for Joseph's faith and understanding. And when you look at that baby, be amazed at the thought of Him being God in the flesh.

When we sing those familiar Christmas carols, let's pay attention to those words we can unthinkingly recite by heart. Let's feel some of that "joy to the world" because "the Lord is come." Let's remember the impact this event has had on our own lives—this child was "born that men no more may die, born to raise the sons of earth, born to give them second birth." Let's be thankful for that "silent night, holy night" in which "Christ the Savior is born."

When we hear someone read that account from the Gospel of Luke about the trip to Bethlehem, no room in the inn, and the baby laid in a manger, let's be amazed at how God worked things out in accordance with His plan and purposes. And let's hear afresh the message of the angels— the tidings of great joy—the announcement of the birth of a Savior—the proclamation of "Glory to God in the highest, and on earth peace, goodwill toward men!"

Unfortunately, it's all too easy for us to unpack our decorations, perform our holiday programs, sing our carols, and attend all the annual gatherings without any excitement or enthusiasm for the meaning of it all. Yes, it's an old familiar story, but it's just as important today as ever. And to think that it was all done out of love for you. Yes, your picture is hanging on Jesus' tree as one of those for whom He came and died.

May this be our prayer: "Lord, help us see the events and truths of Christmas in a fresh way this year."

Will you pray for the Lord to give you "fresh eyes" to see the wonderful truths of Christmas?

COUNT THE COST AND COMMIT TO CHRIST

"For which of you, intending to build a tower, does not sit down first and count the cost, whether he has enough to finish it"

– LUKE 14:28

One of my sons-in-law came over to our house to help me assemble the wooden structure we use to represent the stable in our outdoor Nativity scene. Actually the more proper description of what took place is that I gave him a hand while he did most of the work. I did help him carry and lift the heavy roof into place. And I was able to find the box of screws we needed for the job. But my son-in-law did the actual assembling.

After all, he's the one who originally created this stable out of wooden pallets and a few other small pieces of lumber as a Christmas gift for us a few years ago. So he knows exactly how it all should fit together. Once the job was completed, I thanked him and commented, "You didn't know when you first gave us this present that you were giving yourself so much work to do to help put it up each year." But my son-in-law graciously responded that he did know what he was getting into at the time. He had figured I would need his help to reconstruct the stable every Christmas season.

I was glad to know that my son-in-law had "counted the cost" before he presented us with this gift. I would hate to think that it had become an unexpected, dreaded job or burden on him. His gift wasn't just a one-time act but an ongoing commitment for years to come.

When we give ourselves to Christ to be His followers, it's a similar proposition. It's more than a one-time decision. It also involves a continuing commitment. I'm concerned that some people think once they've knelt at an altar, said a certain prayer, and been baptized that their spiritual journey is complete. In reality it's just the beginning.

And the pathway we walk in following Jesus isn't always the easiest. As a matter of fact, it rarely is. We will be called upon many times along the way to reaffirm that initial offering of ourselves to the Lord.

In Luke 14:25–33, Jesus encouraged all aspiring disciples of His to count the cost before taking the plunge. He compared it to a man making sure he has enough money to complete the construction of a tower before he starts building it—or like a king who makes sure he possesses the resources to win the war before he goes out to do battle. Likewise, we should make sure we're committed fully and for the long haul when we initially give ourselves to the Lord.

Jesus indicated that there will be times when it will mean putting Him ahead of those who are nearest and dearest to us. He stated that it would involve bearing a cross and being willing to suffer hardship for His sake. He suggested that such a commitment would mean being willing to forsake anything that threatened to come between us and our Savior.

We should know that following Jesus will sometimes be costly. It will mean having to deny ourselves and sacrifice some things. However, the positive side of it all is the fact that whatever we may have to give up, it will be worth it. Having a right relationship with the Lord and receiving the gift of eternal life is the "pearl of great price" which is worth selling everything we own in order to possess.

So let's count the cost and be prepared for whatever may come our way as followers of Jesus. Let's make sure our commitment to Him isn't simply a past event but a daily, ongoing journey.

Are you still counting the cost of a daily, ongoing commitment to Christ? Be assured that it's worth any sacrifice.

LET'S BUILD OUR
LIVES GOD'S WAY

"The living God...allowed all nations to walk in their own ways.
Nevertheless He did not leave Himself without witness."

– ACTS 14:15–17

We have a set of toy building blocks at our house that the grandkids often enjoy when they come over. On such an occasion, one of our grandsons asked me to build a robot out of those interlocking pieces. I gladly complied, having constructed a variety of such figures in the past for their pleasure. However, I didn't get far into the project when my grandson started helping me by adding his own blocks to my creation. He wanted to put some pieces in certain places that I knew would cause the "robot" to be lopsided and unable to stand up properly. I tried to tell my young building partner not to put the blocks there, but he insisted on doing it anyway, in spite of several warnings. Certainly I could've forced the issue—after all, I am quite bigger than he is. Or I could've simply used my serious, authoritative adult voice to overrule his wishes. But I didn't. I allowed him to put the blocks where he insisted. And sure enough, it wasn't long before our creation tumbled over and fell apart.

God is certainly bigger and more powerful than us. He could easily force us to do His will. Or He could boom His instructions down to us in such a thunderous voice that it would make us quiver in fear at the thought of failing to do whatever He said. However, God doesn't force anyone to acknowledge Him, worship Him, or follow His will. In Acts

14:16, Paul is talking about nations who refused to recognize and glorify God, instead choosing to make idols and worship them. The apostle says that God allowed those nations "to walk in their own ways." God allowed them to go the way they had chosen.

God still allows us to walk in our own ways. He shows us the truth, but it's up to us to acknowledge it. He offers us the opportunity to receive the gift of eternal life, but we have to reach out and receive it. In various aspects of our lives, God will show us the best way to build if we'll listen. He'll direct us in the way we should go. But if we insist on doing things our way, in the end He'll let us, although it will be to our detriment. Sooner or later that structure or life that we've built apart from Him will tumble over and fall apart.

However, Paul continues in that passage to say, "Nevertheless God did not leave Himself without witness." Although God didn't force those nations to obey Him, out of love for them He left a witness or reminder to testify as to who He is. It says that He did good to them, giving them needed rain, fruitful crops, and filling them with food and gladness.

When we choose to walk in our own ways, God still leaves us a witness by showing His goodness and love to us in various ways. Those acts testify that there is a God who loves us—a Father who wants us to come home to Him. They're like little post-it notes from God. When we sit down to a table full of food, when we arrive safely at our destination on a trip, when we see the needed rain falling, those notes testify to the reality and goodness of God, in spite of our blindness or rebellion toward Him.

If we're insisting on walking in our own ways instead of following God's direction, let's respond to those ever-present reminders that our loving Father is calling us to turn back to Him. He won't make us do it His way, but there's no doubt that His way is best.

Is there some area of your life in which you've insisted on "walking in your own way" instead of listening to the Lord? What witness has God still left you reminding you of His love and encouraging you to change your course?

The Countdown
to Christ's Coming

"He who testifies to these things says, 'Surely I am coming quickly.'
Amen. Even so, come, Lord Jesus!"

– REVELATION 22:20

As I was driving along noticing the Christmas decorations exhibited outside various homes, one not far from my neighborhood especially grabbed my attention. I couldn't recall having seen a display quite like this one. Underneath a portrayal of Santa Claus was an electronic readout of lighted red numbers, reminiscent of an old basketball scoreboard. Several of the numbers were constant, while the ones on the end flashed a changing procession of descending numerals—seventeen, sixteen, fifteen, fourteen, etc. It didn't take long for me to figure out what that digital clock was doing. It wasn't just counting down the days, but also the hours, minutes, and even seconds until the arrival of old St. Nick on Christmas Day.

Of course, there was no such countdown when Christ came into the world, at least not among the inhabitants of earth. Maybe the angels in heaven were counting the moments to that wonderful event. And when they reached the end of their countdown, they let loose with their well-known "Glory to God in the highest" that was overheard by the shepherds.

Although some people on earth were living in expectation of Christ coming, no one knew exactly when it might be—whether it would be months, years, or decades yet before those Messianic prophecies were fulfilled. Certainly there was no clock counting down to the exact moment.

Even after it happened, very few people were aware that something so significant had occurred.

We find ourselves in a similar situation with regard to Jesus' promise to come again. There are signs to watch for which indicate that this next earth-shattering event is drawing near. However, Jesus declared that none of us can know the exact hour when it will occur. We have to watch, be ready, and stay busy faithfully doing the work God has given us.

As people ride by that display of the countdown to Christmas, I wonder how seeing it makes them feel. How does it make you feel to know that there are only nineteen more days and so many hours until Christmas Day? For some of us, such a thought might cause an emotional swell of panic to rise up within us as we realize that we have shopping to finish (or to start?), decorating to do, cards to send, cookies to bake, and travel plans to complete. But then there are others of us, especially the children or young at heart, who will feel a sense of excitement as we wish that those next nineteen or twenty days would fly by in an instant. We're ready for Christmas to come, and the sooner the better.

How do we feel about Christ's return? Does the thought of Jesus coming back cause us anxiety, panic, or dread? Do we know that we're not ready for that event and wish for more time to prepare ourselves spiritually? Or does the thought of Jesus' return stir up excitement as we look forward to being with our Savior for eternity? Do we have the assurance that we're ready to meet the Lord and that our hearts and lives are in such a condition that we can stand before Him without fear of condemnation? In response to Jesus' claim that He is coming quickly, would we dare exclaim with the apostle John, "Even so, come, Lord Jesus"?

We may not be able to see the clock counting down the days, hours, minutes, and seconds to the return of Christ, but there's no doubt that it's ticking. His coming is certain. And it's drawing nearer every moment. Whether or not we're ready for Christmas, let's always make sure that we're prepared for Christ's second coming.

Are you ready and excited about the prospect of Jesus' return? If not, why?

CHRISTMAS REMINDS US WHY JESUS IS OUR BEST REPRESENTATIVE

"He always lives to make intercession for them."
– HEBREWS 7:25

It's no secret that my wife and I usually give a new pair of cowboy boots to each of our grandchildren at Christmas. They all, including our one granddaughter, enjoy donning that type of footwear. By the time Christmas rolls around they're ready for a new pair, as they've usually either worn out or outgrown last year's edition.

So recently my wife had gone online, placed our order, and two pairs of the boots shortly arrived at our house. But the other two didn't show up for several days, causing us to call the company to check on our order. As my wife waited on hold to speak to a representative, the usual message came up apologizing for the wait and assuring that someone would be with us shortly. However, the recording was not offered in the proper businesslike voice you typically hear on such occasions. It sounded like the person had just stepped out of an old TV western. The twang in his voice and the phrases he used made it sound like he was a true cowboy. I guess the company wanted its customers to feel like this was someone who could relate to those people who like to buy their western wear. It wouldn't surprise me if the person behind the recording was actually wearing a business suit and sitting at a desk in Manhattan, but the company certainly portrayed the idea that there were authentic westerners taking care of their business.

One of the truths this season of the year reminds us of is that we have someone taking care of our business with God who can authentically relate to us. Of course, I'm referring to Jesus. The Bible tells us that since He has been resurrected and ascended to heaven, He now "always lives to make intercession" for us (Hebrews 7:25). He is our great High Priest who not only offered Himself as the sacrifice for our sins, but who also continues to be our Mediator before God the Father.

So when we call on God, Jesus is there to intercede on our behalf. And because Jesus came to this earth as a man, we can have no better representative. Although He is the Son of God with all the power and authority that goes with being at the top of God's kingdom, He has also walked in our shoes, boots, or sandals. He clothed Himself with what we wear, a real flesh-and-blood body. He talks our language, although maybe not with a Southern accent. He can identify with our concerns, our joys, and our struggles, because He's been here Himself as a human being.

When we're weary, we have someone standing in our corner before God who understands. When we're suffering, we know that our representative before God experienced affliction to an even greater degree. When we're brokenhearted about the pain those around us are enduring, when we're discouraged about the direction society is going, when we're dealing with people who oppose us, when we come face-to-face with temptation, when we have huge obstacles blocking out pathway—whatever situation we may encounter in life, whatever concern we bring to the Father in prayer, Jesus can relate to it because in some way He has been there.

Hearing that "cowboy" on the other end of the phone line didn't necessarily inspire me to have greater confidence in the company from which we ordered those boots. However, knowing Jesus, the

One who came to this earth as one of us, is interceding in our behalf before the Father should give us greater assurance and confidence as we pray.

As you pray today, remember that Jesus, the One who has walked in your shoes, is interceding for you.

OUR CHRISTLIKE SPIRIT
SHOULD MAKE US STAND
OUT FROM THE CROWD

"For we are to God the fragrance of Christ among those who are being saved and among those who are perishing."

– II CORINTHIANS 2:15

One weekend we enjoyed some of the holiday festivities being offered in our town, including the annual parade. It was fun helping our grandchildren chase down the pieces of candy thrown their way by the parade's participants. We saw familiar faces walking or riding down the street, greeting them with shouts and vigorous waves. And of course there were some nicely decorated floats.

My family's favorite entry in that year's event had to be the group from a local restaurant. Their ride was equipped with a snow-making machine. There were Christmas songs being sung—granted, it wasn't exactly the quality of the Mormon Tabernacle Choir, but it was loud and enthusiastic. As that float passed by with the "snowflakes" falling and the fervent spirit being exhibited, it just seemed to amp up the atmosphere to a higher level of excitement.

The Apostle Paul compared followers of Christ to a parade. It was a little different celebration from the one we enjoyed last weekend. He seems to be referring to a Roman victory parade when one of their generals had triumphantly returned from war. He, his army, and his captives would march down the street. I also understand that there were often a group of priests who followed along while burning incense. Paul wrote, "Now thanks be to God who always leads us in triumph in Christ, and through us diffuses the fragrance of His knowledge in every place. For we are to God the fragrance of Christ among those who are being saved and among those who are perishing. To the one we are the aroma of death leading to death, and to the other the aroma of life leading to life. And who is sufficient for these things?" (II Corinthians 2:14–16)

As we march through life, we are representing Jesus. We should be giving off the fragrance of Christ wherever we go. Our spirit should be the one which stands out as we pass by those whom we encounter each day. They should see something different about us because of our relationship with the Lord.

Sometimes it should be a spirit of joy and passion, kind of like the atmosphere around that group from the restaurant. Followers of Jesus shouldn't be best known for their sour looks, their negativity, and their lack of enthusiasm. However, other times that spirit will manifest itself as a somber, peaceful, calm presence in the midst of turbulent situations. And through it all, the message of the gospel should be heard through our words and seen through the kind of lives we lead.

I appreciate Paul's question at the end of that challenging comparison—"Who is sufficient for these things?" Who is able to successfully emit such a Christlike fragrance wherever they go? Who can bring that kind of atmosphere with them as they journey through life? I'm certainly not sufficient for it. As someone who tends to be more of an introvert, I can too easily be content with quietly hiding in the background rather than having a prominent place in the parade. Others may struggle more often with keeping their passionate spirits calm and under control.

None of us regardless of our natural temperament are sufficient in ourselves to fulfill this task. The good news is that we don't do it alone.

God is leading our parade. The Spirit of Christ is living in us. Jesus can change us and make us more like Him. Let's allow Him to so work in us that we will stand out as different, as Christlike, in the parade of life.

Lord, work in me that I might emit a Christlike fragrance wherever I go.

GOD IS OUR ROCK OF STABILITY

"For He Himself has said, 'I will never leave you nor forsake you'"
— HEBREWS 13:5

A s I was driving along one of our local roads, I came to a spot where my eyes shifted to the northwest horizon. There in the distance was the top of Stone Mountain, a well-known large outcropping of granite in our area. It was not a sight that surprised me. I knew that this particular location, along with a few other high spots in our area with unobscured views in that direction, offered a glimpse at one of our most recognizable landmarks, except on overcast or exceptionally smoggy days. I just didn't realize how automatic it had become for me to look that way every time I traveled that route.

As I thought more about it, I remembered that I did the same thing as a boy. Although I grew up on the other side of Atlanta, my family often traveled around the interstate on our way to visit relatives. There was a certain stretch of that highway when you would come over a hill and would be able to see that mountain of granite off in the distance. And in all those trips, I don't believe I ever failed to look for it.

I wonder why. I think it may go beyond the fact that Stone Mountain is such an unusual sight in contrast to the surrounding landscape. I believe its magnetic draw even goes beyond the beauty of this natural wonder of creation—a beauty especially displayed when it sits with a blue sky as its backdrop. I wonder if I might be drawn to look in its direction because it's a comforting sign of stability. When so many other things in the world are changing, it's nice to have something you can count on. Although the communities, people, and culture around it have undergone various transformations over the years, including the very park immediately surrounding it, the mountain itself still looks much as it did when I was a child. Somehow it's reassuring to be able to look that direction and to know that it's still there.

It's even more comforting for us to look to God and to know that He is always there. In the midst of an ever-changing world, He is our rock, our mountain, and our landmark of stability. As we journey through life, we can count on His presence and we can rest upon His promises.

When the economy does a nosedive, we lose our jobs, or suffer other financial hardships, we can look to the God who promises to supply all our needs according to His riches in glory by Christ Jesus (Philippians 4:19).

When our health takes a turn for the worse, we can look to the Great Physician who can heal, strengthen, and comfort us (Psalm 103:3).

When we walk through the valley of the shadow of death, we don't have to fear any evil, because we can depend on our Shepherd to be right there with us (Psalm 23:4).

When we find ourselves on a lonely road, separated from family and friends, we can turn our eyes toward the One who promises, "I will never leave you nor forsake you" (Hebrews 13:5).

When we stumble and fall, we will still find the same merciful God who assures us that if we confess our sins, He will be faithful to forgive us and cleanse us (I John 1:9).

So as the landscape of our world, our circumstances, and even ourselves go through changes, let's keep our eyes of faith focused on the One who is like a mountain of granite in our lives. Be assured that He is still there and always will be.

How does it comfort you to know that God is always there?

GOD IS IN THE AUDIENCE SUPPORTING YOU

"For we are God's fellow workers."
– I CORINTHIANS 3:9

One time a young man who was pursuing a calling of God in his life preached his first sermon at our church. That initial step into a pulpit can be rather nerve-racking. I remember when I faced that milestone on an Easter Sunday evening many years ago. Due to the combination of inexperience and jitters, within ten minutes I found myself at the end of what I had planned on being a thirty-minute message. Afterwards everyone was kind and supportive, or maybe they were just pleased at getting out of church so early that night.

The one who was preaching at our church was also a little nervous. The congregation had turned out in good numbers to support him. Some of his own family members from out-of-town were in attendance to encourage him as well. But just a few minutes prior to the beginning of that service, I looked outside to see our district superintendent driving into the parking lot. In the denomination we belonged to at the time, this is a church official who has some authority and supervision over a number of churches in an area. It was not unusual for him to drop by unannounced once or twice a year to sit in on our morning worship. I walked over to our first-time preacher with the news, "Don't let it make you more nervous, but our district superintendent just drove up." His animated response was, "You're kidding!"

We do tend to pay special attention when someone with authority or to whom we are accountable shows up, whether a boss, a government official, or a district superintendent. I'm glad to report that this young man handled the situation well, and we enjoyed a good worship experience together. He also didn't have any problem outdistancing my first ten-minute effort.

We would do well to remember that the One to whom we are ultimately accountable is always part of our audience as we go through life. But the Lord's presence really shouldn't make us nervous, unless we know that we are involved in something that isn't pleasing to Him. My district superintendent downplayed his presence at our service that morning as not being any reason for additional anxiety. It's easier for me to view him that way than it probably was for the one who was delivering his first sermon, because I've known this superintendent for many years. I see him as my friend, supporter, and helper, not as someone who's there to try to find something to criticize.

Can't we look at God in a similar way? It's true that He is our Judge to whom we will give an account. If we're knowingly rebelling against His will for us, we ought to be concerned about the consequences. But when we're trying to live for Him and serve Him, He's not there to nitpick every little thing we do or to try to seek something He can condemn. He's also our friend who wants to support us. He's our Heavenly Father who is there to encourage us. He wants us to succeed. He's pulling for us. But even more than that, He's our partner who is there to work with us and to help us. I couldn't have made it through that first sermon I preached or any others over the years if not for the Lord being there to guide my thoughts and speech, as well as to enable the listeners to receive those words.

So let's remember that whether we're standing in a pulpit, sitting at a desk, driving a car, or relaxing in our homes, the Lord is there as part of the audience. But He's not just there as your King and Judge. He's also there as your Father, friend, supporter, and helper.

As you go through your activities today, remember that God is there to cheer you on and to help you.

In Search of a Silent Night

"But Mary kept all these things and pondered them in her heart."

– Luke 2:19

A s I've begun to listen to a little Christmas music on the radio, one song I've heard on several occasions has stood out to me. I'm not sure of the name of the tune. There are no words accompanying this particular version I've been hearing. It's a jazzed-up instrumental arrangement of a Christmas song with such a rapid tempo that it makes "Sleigh Ride" seem like a casual stroll in the park. It sounds like something you might hear at a sporting event or as the background music for a video of an exciting race. As I listen to it, I picture busyness, hustling and bustling, confusion, and mad dashes toward a goal. And when it reaches its climatic completion, I feel almost like I should be out of breath.

I've concluded that this song would be a fitting theme for our modern celebration of Christmas. I can hear it playing in the background as cars dart in and out of traffic trying to get their passengers to important holiday destinations. I hear it coming over the speakers at the store as impatient shoppers desperately search for those perfect gifts. I sense its notes in the air as people stand in line at the Post Office to mail those packages and cards. I can even hear it being played in our churches as we try to fit in all of the many special activities before a majority of our congregations evacuate to various parts of the country for their family Christmas gatherings.

That tune embodies the spirit I sense as I listen to people describing their busy schedules during these weeks in December, especially those who have young children. Don't misunderstand me. Many of those activities are good and meaningful. Through those times families bond, memories are built, and people are touched by the generosity of others. But in the midst of all the busyness, we need to make some time for contemplation.

Whatever happened to "silent night, holy night, all is calm"? Come to think of it, I'm not sure that first Christmas was all that calm. There was probably a lot of hustling and bustling going on in Bethlehem. Remember, all the hotels were full. There was an unusually large crowd in that little town. And I haven't known too many births of babies that were serene events. They are normally exciting times. The mothers aren't usually quiet as they experience the pains of childbirth. I don't think Mary got an epidural. And in spite of what some of our traditional songs indicate, I would be greatly surprised to discover that baby Jesus didn't make any sounds that night. My guess is that He cried like any other baby would do. Yet in spite of the crowds, the angels, the shepherds, and childbirth, the Bible tells us that Mary took time to ponder the meaning of all these things in her heart. She found some moments for contemplation.

During the busyness of our modern Christmas celebration, let's try to find some moments of "all is calm" and "heavenly peace." Maybe we'll discover it as we curl up in a chair with a cup of hot chocolate, with the TV turned off, watching the lights blinking on the Christmas tree. Maybe we'll find it as we open our Bibles and read through the account of Jesus' birth. It will take some effort, but try to leave behind the tumultuous race embodied in that one tune and return to the theme of "Silent Night." Seek some prayerful moments to refresh your soul and to ponder in your heart the true meaning of the season.

Make some time today to be still and contemplate the wonderful truths surrounding the birth of Christ.

SEEK A PERFECT HEART MORE THAN A FLAWLESS PERFORMANCE

"And whatever you do, do it heartily, as to the Lord."

– COLOSSIANS 3:23

It's that time of the year for children's Christmas programs at churches. I can remember participating in those as a youngster myself, usually dressed up as either a shepherd or a wise man. Our acting generally consisted of trying to look scared at the appearance of the angels, or pointing at and following after a tinfoil-covered star being propelled ahead of us on some kind of makeshift pulley system.

I attended such a program at another church a few years ago. It had its shepherds and wise men too, along with the other cast of the Nativity scene. But it was primarily a singing program. And the children did a wonderful job. While they mainly sang as a group, there were a few solo parts, including one by a boy. I don't know if he volunteered or was recruited for this assignment. Girls always seem to be more willing to sing by themselves than the guys.

The boy who sang didn't have the greatest voice. I noticed a lady in front of me wincing as the youngster's voice cracked on a few occasions. But I enjoyed it. He knew the words and sang his part in a heartfelt manner. As I watched that young man throughout the rest of the program, compared to all the other boys he seemed to be the most passionate singer. He belted out all the words and his face portrayed his enthusiasm as he sang.

It reminds me of how God looks at us. We have to admit that as we seek to live for the Lord and serve Him, often our performance falls short of excellence. We may have good intentions, but sometimes our human limitations get in the way of our doing as well as we would like. Maybe we simply don't have the voice, talent, or skill to excel at that task. Or maybe we're hindered by a lack of physical strength, or shortness of time, or our minds not being as sharp as they used to be.

Don't get me wrong—we should strive to be the best we can be for the Lord. And that may mean trying to sharpen our tools, learn some new skills, and improve our performance in whatever ways we can. This truth we're focusing on here is not to be used as an excuse for laziness, half-efforts, and complacency.

But it's nice to know that God is more concerned about perfect hearts than about perfect performances. Others around us may wince at our mistakes and shortcomings—we may even be disappointed in ourselves at those moments. But God sees our hearts. He's less concerned about our having perfect pitch as we sing our songs for Him as He is about our singing and serving with a passion to please Him. God is looking for us to do whatever we do out of love for Him and love for others. And He likes for us to do it passionately from our hearts. "And whatever you do, do it heartily, as to the Lord" (Colossians 3:23). Earlier in that same epistle, it talks about singing psalms and spiritual songs. It says to do so "singing with grace in your hearts to the Lord. And whatever you do in word or deed, do all in the name of the Lord Jesus, giving thanks to God the Father through Him" (3:16–17).

While we want to strive to do things well, let's be more concerned that we do them from the heart with the right motives. Even our cracking voices and feeble actions will put a smile on God's face if we're using them to glorify Him.

Be less concerned today about trying to have a perfect performance and focus more on having a loving, pure, passionate heart.

We Should Bear the Image of Jesus All the Time

"Let your light so shine before men, that they may see your good works and glorify your Father in heaven."

– MATTHEW 5:16

I've always enjoyed Christmas decorations. When I was a child, it was a regular activity this time of year for our family to hop in the car in the evening to ride around and see the lights. As far as I know, there weren't any of the extensive professional productions you can find today—the ones you often have to pay per carload in order to ride through and view. We simply drove through certain neighborhoods where we hoped, and sometimes knew from past years, that there would be a few houses and yards brightly illuminated.

However, I must confess that I don't care much for a certain type of outdoor decoration that has become popular in recent years. I'm talking about those inflatable characters. I guess they're OK during the prime viewing time after dark—they're certainly big and gaudy enough to be easily seen. But most people don't keep their inflatables operating during the daytime hours. So all you see as you ride by in the morning are what look like some colored tarps littering the yard. It's like looking at the remnants of the wicked witch of the west after Dorothy threw water on her. I keep visualizing this awful picture of Santa slowly deflating while wailing, "I'm melting! I'm melting!"

Even the characters which are kept off the ground by being hung up lose their form when deprived of air. I've seen a few such Santas hanging down from branches in the middle of the day who look like they've been on a forty-day fast. By the way, most of those inflatables seem to be of Santa, polar bears, snowmen, and other such cute characters. I don't recall having seen any of them portraying the Nativity scene. Have you?

I hope that we're not like those inflatables—shining our light and taking the shape of a follower of Christ only during those peak times when we know others are watching. We know how to outwardly make ourselves resemble the form of Jesus. We know how to appear to be inflated with the Spirit of God. But it shouldn't just be something we turn on when we go to church on Sunday or when we're around certain other people. We need to seek to be like Christ all the time, even at work or at home. We should be filled with the Spirit and living like it even when we're completely alone with no one watching.

The Bible does say that we should let our lights shine before men that they may see our good works and glorify God (Matthew 5:16). But that doesn't mean that we're only to turn those lights on at certain times in order for others to see them. We're not decorations who are meant solely for show or characters to be inflated to look like Jesus only when we know others are around. That light of Christ needs to be burning in us all the time. The Spirit of God should be filling us and making us more like the image of Christ in those off-season moments as well as when we're in the spotlight of prime time.

What do we look like when no one else is around? Does our light grow dim? Do we maintain our Christlike shape or do we deflate into something that bears no resemblance to the love, purity, and holiness reflected in the character of the Lord?

It's fine if you choose to have a deflated Santa in your yard most of the day, but as followers of Christ, let's seek to be like Him and to shine for Him at all times.

Let your light shine brightly today, whether anyone else is around to see it or not.

REAL PEACE COMES
THROUGH VICTORY

"For this purpose the Son of God was manifested, that He might destroy the works of the devil."

– I JOHN 3:8

Peace is one of those concepts we hear emphasized during the Christmas season. This is partly due to the announcement of the angels of "peace on earth." But it also comes from the title given to Jesus as being the Prince of Peace.

If you heard someone referred to as a man of peace, you wouldn't expect him to pull out a gun and shoot someone, would you? If he's a man of peace, then you might interpret that to mean that he isn't going to use weapons, force, or violence against others. You might assume such a person would go to great lengths to avoid conflict. A man of peace might be expected to turn the other cheek when someone strikes out at him. He might use words, diplomacy, compromise, and kindness as his weapons.

So when we think of the Son of God as the Prince of Peace, we tend to think in similar terms. We think of the One who loves the world, who promotes unity, and who tells people to be kind to each other, even to do good to their enemies.

However, notice these words from Romans 16:20: "And the God of peace will crush Satan under your feet shortly." It doesn't say that the God of wrath, or the God of judgment, or the God of power is going to crush Satan, but rather the God of peace. Crushing someone is not something you normally associate with a person of peace. Maybe this reminds us that peace doesn't just come through avoiding conflict, or through being kind, or by means of compromise or diplomacy. But there are times when peace is achieved only through victory over the enemy—through crushing the one who is intent on destroying the peace.

I've been in church services where a wasp got inside and was flying around the sanctuary. It can be distracting and can disrupt the service as people focus on that intruder, duck out of its way, and maybe even let out a little exclamation. I've found out that the best thing to do in that situation is simply to stop and get somebody to swat that wasp to the floor and step on it. Crush it. Why? Because I'm a violent person? No—you do it in order to restore the peace that the wasp had disrupted.

And that's what Romans 16:20 indicates. The God who desires peace was going to crush Satan, because he was disrupting the peace and needed to be dealt with like a wasp in a worship service. And that's what Jesus, the Prince of Peace, came to do. He didn't come to make a deal with the devil, but rather to destroy him. He didn't come to compromise with the enemy, but to crush him through His death and resurrection. In Hebrews 2, it says that Christ died so that He "might destroy him who had the power of death, that is, the devil...." I John 3:8 says, "For this purpose the Son of God was manifested, that He might destroy the works of the devil."

Jesus came to swat that wasp that's been flying around us keeping us from focusing on God and yielding ourselves to Him. He came to crush the adversary who has disrupted our peace with God. He came to give us peace through victory—victory over Satan and over sin in our lives.

So as you think about that concept of peace this Christmas, remember how Jesus achieved it. He brought peace not by submitting to sin, evil, and an ungodly world, but by triumphing over them. And we will experience His peace in our lives through that same means—not by compromising with sin and evil, but by overcoming them through the power of Christ.

Don't compromise with any sin or evil in your life. Find peace by overcoming it through Christ.

GOD'S GIFT IS BOTH PRACTICAL AND PERSONAL

"For God so loved the world that He gave His only begotten Son."
— JOHN 3:16

It was one of those unexpected expenses during the Christmas season: our refrigerator died. So as we were out shopping for a new one, my wife and I mutually agreed that we would make this new appliance our Christmas gift to each other for this year. I've been married long enough to know that on certain occasions, such as Valentine's Day and our wedding anniversary, it's best not to give any kind of a present with an electrical cord attached to it. Those items fail to effectively communicate the concept of love. But it's not unusual at Christmas for my wife and I to agree to buy something needed for the house in lieu of personal gifts for each other.

I suppose that most Christmas presents could be placed in one of those two categories. They are either practical gifts such as the socks, shirt, or new toaster that is needed, or they are the personal items that may reflect the person's wants more than his or her needs. If you believe the TV commercials, the special women in our lives tend to prize jewelry in particular as expressions of our love and devotion, getting all excited when they realize that "he went to Jared's." I guess I'm not going to deliver that kind of a thrill this year. Somehow, "he went to Home Depot" just doesn't have the same ring to it.

God's great Christmas gift to us encompasses both of those aspects.

Sending His Son into the world to be our Savior was truly a practical present for the world. It was the very thing we needed the most. Humanity, because of its sin, was at odds with a holy God. So God Himself gave the gift of His Son to bring reconciliation. At the time, many of the people to whom Jesus came thought that they needed something else. They believed that their greatest problem was the fact that the Romans had conquered them. Deliverance from foreign rule was seen as their most pressing need. That's why they rejected Christ, realizing that the freedom He was offering them was not political in nature. However, Christ gave them what they really needed—freedom from sin's bondage.

But God's gift to us wasn't just practical. It was also a very personal and extravagant expression of His love for us. He gave us a gift more priceless than the most exquisite piece of jewelry. He gave sacrificially in leaving the glory of heaven and eventually laying down His own life. And He did it with love for each one of us individually as His motivation. As one of the most familiar verses in the Bible reminds us, "For God so loved the world that He gave His only begotten Son, that whoever believes in Him should not perish but have everlasting life" (John 3:16).

We may think that we have many pressing needs this Christmas. It might be anything from replacing a worn-out appliance to finding a job. Or it might be necessities of a different sort, such as recovering from an illness or keeping a family together. But as important as everything else might be, our greatest need is to have a right relationship with God. And He still offers that very practical gift to us through faith in His Son.

And if you want something extravagant—something that really shows how much you are loved—then unwrap God's gift of salvation that was paid for through Jesus' own blood. He didn't go to a jewelry store to show His love for you—He went to the cross instead.

God's gift is more practical than a refrigerator and more thrilling than a diamond necklace. It's exactly what we need and it expresses His immeasurable love for us.

Father, thank You for the perfect gift of Your Son.

LET'S MAKE ROOM IN OUR HEARTS FOR JESUS

"There was no room for them in the inn."
– LUKE 2:7

We do it without fail every year around this time. We allow an invader into our home. No, I'm not referring to my mother-in-law coming over for a Christmas visit. Actually, she would be welcome—I'm one of those husbands blessed with a wonderful mother-in-law. She's also very generous with her Christmas gifts and I wouldn't do anything to jeopardize my standing with her right before the holiday. The invader I'm talking about is that huge, green one. Again, it's not my mother-in-law (oops, there went my gift!). I'm referring to the Christmas tree.

The remainder of the year we tend to show our displeasure if someone walks through our door with a wet leaf or a few pine needles adhering to their shoes. But let Christmas come around and we bring a whole tree into the house. Then we don't stick it in a basement, or a closet, or an obscure corner in a back room. We place it in a prime location. We even move furniture around to accommodate this guest. How many other times during the year do you rearrange your living room for a visitor? And if that's not enough, we put it by the window, so that this invader can show off its ornaments and lights not only to those inside the house, but also to any passersby. If we procure a real tree, we also commit ourselves to a certain degree of care. There's the effort involved in keeping it watered. Then there's the constant battle to keep the fallen needles off the carpet. Most of the Christmas trees we've had were so proficient at shedding that they would make a long-haired cat jealous.

We're willing to go to a lot of trouble to open up our homes to this annual invader. How does that compare to our willingness to open up the homes of our hearts to the One whom Christmas is all about? There are some who aren't even willing to let Jesus in the door. They'll allow almost anyone or anything else into their lives, but not Him. Others let Him inside, only to relegate Him to a far corner where He's rarely seen. He's there as a resource to be pulled out when needed, especially when there's trouble. But He certainly has no prominent place in the home. To them, He's kind of like my home repair and improvement book. I don't keep it on my coffee table for everyday reading but I know which bookshelf it's on, so I can resort to it the next time the toilet breaks or a light switch starts going bad.

Some are only willing to accommodate this guest named Jesus if they don't have to get rid of anything to make room for Him. It's acceptable to talk about receiving Jesus into your heart—just don't mention repentance or forsaking any of the things in one's life of which He might not approve. Some people aren't willing to rearrange anything in their lives for His sake. They'll receive Jesus, as long as His presence doesn't inconvenience them in any way. Then there are those who gladly make room for Jesus but try to keep His light and glory all to themselves. I believe the biblical analogy is that they try to hide it under a basket. They don't let His light shine through their windows to touch the people around them.

If we're willing to disrupt our homes for a Christmas tree and give it such attention and prominence, can't we do even more for the One who was born in a manger to be the Savior of the world?

Are you letting Jesus have a prominent place in your life? Is there some "furniture" he wants you to rearrange or to get rid of in order to make more room for Him?

CHRISTMAS CAUSES OUR SOUL TO FEEL ITS WORTH

"God sent forth His Son...to redeem those who were under the law, that we might receive the adoption as sons."

— GALATIANS 4:4–5

One of my favorite Christmas songs is "O Holy Night." Its meaningful words and majestic tune combine to create an inspirational piece of music, especially when it's sung by someone who can hit those high notes. However, there's a phrase in this song which can be easily overlooked. At one point it says, "till He (Christ) appeared and the soul felt its worth." What does the birth of Jesus have to do with us feeling our worth or with us recognizing our value?

Sometimes we can think we're not worth very much. Maybe we listen to a world that suggests we're not of much value because of the way we look, because we don't measure up to some of its social or financial standards, because of the type of work we do, or simply because of our age. Or maybe we begin to tell ourselves we're not worth much because of the sins we've committed or the poor choices we've made.

But the coming of Christ into the world sends us a different message. It gives us significance. The Bible tells us that God sent His Son into this world to redeem us (see Galatians 4:4-5). He saw us as something of value, something for which He was willing to pay a price.

If you go to a garage sale, most of the items you see there are probably things you don't value—other people's junk which you wouldn't want if they gave it to you for free. However when you find that particular item you typically search for or collect—a Precious Moments figurine, a certain tool or piece of equipment you like to tinker with, an old book, or a cute outfit for your grandchild—you see some value in it and are willing to redeem that item.

God saw us on the junk table of life with all our problems and faults. He saw how messed up we were. He saw us all tangled up in our sins. Yet He still saw value in us. He was willing to pay a price to redeem us. And He didn't just offer a few pennies or dollars for our redemption. He paid a huge price for our freedom. He gave His precious Son for us.

I was speaking with someone recently about a collection of old coins I have. Whether its coins, baseball cards, electric trains, or ceramic dolls, what they're worth isn't based on the manufacturer's suggested retail price. What such collectibles are worth is basically determined by what someone is willing to pay for them. If there are collectors who are willing to pay $150 for your old Roberto Clemente baseball card, then that's what it's worth. But if they're only willing to pay $10 for it, then that's its value.

What is our soul worth? What kind of price was God willing to pay for us? He didn't send $100 or even $1,000 into the world to buy us back. What He gave up for us was priceless—the life of His Son. We're that valuable to God.

Furthermore, let's not forget why He paid that price. It wasn't simply as a good investment or in order to add us to His collection of souls. "For God so loved the world that He gave His only begotten Son" (John 3:16). God paid that price because out of His great love for us He wanted to set us free and give us eternal life.

So let the birth of Christ cause you to feel your soul's worth. God loves you and He considered you worth the price of His own Son.

Don't lose sight of your value and significance to your Heavenly Father. Rejoice that He sent His Son to redeem you—yes, even you!

WHEN TROUBLES INVADE
YOUR IDEAL CHRISTMAS

"Do not be afraid, for behold, I bring you good tidings of great joy."
— LUKE 2:10

As part of our Christmas decorations, I converted our dining room table into the small town of Bedford Falls, the setting for my favorite movie, *It's a Wonderful Life*. Our display consists of numerous buildings and figurines of characters from the film, along with a train that encircles the entire village. However, I must report that one year quiet, idealistic Bedford Falls experienced its share of trials and tribulation.

First of all, war hero Harry Bailey and his wife experienced a terrible fall, resulting in both of them suffering severely broken legs. Fortunately my wife is a nurse. She was able to mend their injuries to the point that you can't even tell there was a problem. I just hope she uses better means than glue to treat her regular patients.

Then there was the train. At first it didn't work, leaving all the residents of Bedford Falls stranded for the holidays. New batteries didn't solve the issue. Later when one of my grandchildren tried to help out by manually forcing the train around the tracks, she drove it so fast that there was a serious derailment. Thankfully no one was hurt. But the next day all of a sudden a Christmas miracle occurred—the train regained power. Maybe the accident corrected some flaw. Or there's also the possibility that I didn't have the screw on the battery cover tightened enough for there to be a good connection. But I think I'll just chalk it up to a miracle and leave it at that.

Many of us have our idealistic pictures in our minds of how we think the Christmas season should go. It may include pleasant family gatherings, cozily sitting by warm fires with cups of delicious hot chocolate, watching children excitedly open gifts, singing our favorite Christmas songs, enjoying the lighted decorations, and other traditional activities. However, in real life it rarely plays out that way. Our journey through this season is often full of bumps in the road.

My experiences within the span of a few days that year reminded me of that truth. I attended a funeral—death doesn't take a holiday, as some of us know all too well. I visited a neighbor who was battling cancer. One of my grandchildren got sick as we were driving down the road, making a mess all over himself and in my car. A friend was informed that she would no longer have her long-held job. One of my daughters called looking for a ride because her car wouldn't start. Sometimes the season itself creates more trials simply by there being more traffic, busier schedules, and all the additional hustle and bustle of this time of year.

But through it all we still have the message of the angel, "Do not be afraid, for behold, I bring you good tidings of great joy which will be to all people. For there is born to you this day in the city of David a Savior, who is Christ the Lord" (Luke 2:10–11). We don't have to be afraid, because the same Christ who entered the world promises to be with us through all the ups and downs of life. He can give us peace when our plans derail. He can bring us healing and comfort when we're sick. He can give us hope both for this life and for what lies beyond it. He can even do some Christmas miracles in our lives, either through changing our circumstances or transforming us.

So when your Christmas isn't going picture-perfect, look to the One born in Bethlehem to be your source of inspiration and help.

Lord, give me peace, hope, and a trusting spirit when trials invade my Christmas plans.

You Could Be an Elf This Christmas

"Remember the words of the Lord Jesus....' It is more blessed to give than to receive."

– ACTS 20:35

One year around Christmas, I was working on a project of copying and rewording some rather lengthy Articles of Faith. I confess that I'm not much of a typist. I often have to correct many mistakes along the way as my spell-checker program points them out to me. However, I still find that it's important to proofread those documents myself, as the spell-checker doesn't catch every type of error.

I found such a mistake as I reread this particular document I had been creating. It was the kind of error that made me laugh, especially since I caught it before producing the final draft. I guess it wasn't as bad as the church bulletin that encouraged the people to "sin" rather than to "sing," but my error also showed how significant it can be to leave out one little letter. At one point in this serious doctrinal statement of faith, instead of typing the word "self," I had ended up with the word "elf." Needless to say, it didn't exactly fit in with the subject matter. Then again, maybe I was just feeling an extra measure of the Christmas spirit that day.

I've never really thought of myself as an elf. While I'm not among the tallest people around, I don't think I could quite be described as elfish in stature either. And I'm also fairly certain that my ears aren't pointed enough for the job. However, during this season of the year we think of elves as those who help to produce and give away gifts. When you look at it that way, it would be nice if more of us did turn ourselves into elves.

When we were kids, we probably thought of Christmas more in terms of getting presents. However as we become adults, hopefully we find ourselves more wrapped up in the giving of gifts rather than the receiving. But even then, it's easy to fall into the attitude of seeing giving as a burdensome chore that we're obligated to carry out rather than as a privilege and a joy.

As a pastor, I have the opportunity not only to give personally but also to represent a church full of people as they exercise this privilege of showing generosity. I often get to be the one there to see the look of appreciation on the face of the person who comes to collect the Christmas donations for the soldiers serving overseas. Or I get the privilege of handing out the gift cards to the teary-eyed grandparents of some children who wouldn't otherwise have many presents under the tree on Christmas Day due to how a job loss had affected their family. I get to play Santa and give some money to help out the family who is suffering hardship due to a physical injury that is keeping one of them out of work.

The words of Jesus as quoted by the Apostle Paul certainly ring true— "It is more blessed to give than to receive" (Acts 20:35). How can we better experience the joy and blessing of being a giver, not just at Christmas but throughout the year? Let's keep our eyes open to those around us who may be in need. Maybe we can do something to help. Or give to someone who's not expecting to receive something from you. It doesn't have to be a gift you buy at the store. An act of kindness or service might be even more valuable to that person. Or is there someone who would greatly appreciate a visit from you—where your presence would be more treasured than your presents?

Seek to be a blessing to others through giving and you will find yourself being blessed by the Lord.

How could you be a special helper from the Lord? To whom might the Lord want you to give of your resources, time, or service?

WE CAN ALL TELL
THE GOOD NEWS

"Now when they had seen Him, they made widely known the saying which was told them concerning this Child."

– LUKE 2:17

One Sunday night, our church had its annual Christmas program. It was an enjoyable evening full of the music of the season, wonderful fellowship, and delicious refreshments. One of the highlights of the service was when the children of the church sang "Go Tell It on the Mountain." While it may not have been the type of performance that would win a Grammy, it certainly was one that would win a grandma's heart, along with that of grandpas, parents, and any others who sat in the congregation.

Although most of the kids in the small group of singers belted out the words in a spirited fashion, there were a couple of very young children who couldn't be expected to join in the singing. However, those toddlers participated by standing there with the older children and enthusiastically ringing some bells every time the song arrived at the chorus—and sometimes during the verses or whenever else they wanted to do it. I think I even saw a little swaying to the music by those youngest participants—I won't call it "dancing" for the sake of the more conservative church folks among us.

That particular song encourages us to proclaim the good news that Jesus Christ is born—to "go, tell it on the mountain, over the hills and everywhere." Some of us have pulpits or blogs as mountains from which we can shout that important announcement. Others may wonder about their ability or opportunity to participate in that activity of telling others about the birth of Christ, but I believe all of us can do something to communicate that news to the world.

We don't have to preach a Christmas sermon to everyone we meet. But in the normal course of our conversations at this time of year, we can look for opportunities to mention some aspect of the holy event that the holiday is all about. Instead of just talking about shopping, Santa Claus, the prospects for a white Christmas, or some of the other common topics of the season, let's put out a few reminders that we're celebrating the birth of our Savior.

Instead of a generic Christmas card, why not pick one that portrays the Nativity or that contains a message about Jesus? Or you could always write in a few words yourself that point people to the real reason for this annual observance. In our day, simply wishing someone a "Merry Christmas" instead of a "Happy Holiday" can remind people of the person at the center of our celebration. Maybe a prayer of thanks for the food at a family gathering on Christmas Day could include a reference to Christ's birth.

But not all reminders have to be verbal. A smile, a joyful spirit, a generous attitude, or a kind deed can communicate in tangible terms the message of love and giving that were typified by God's gift of His Son. An attempt to be a peacemaker among family can exhibit the qualities of peace and goodwill mentioned by the angels at Jesus' birth.

We may not all be able to sing with a beautiful voice resounding from a mountaintop about the birth of Christ but, like those toddlers, we can ring our bells or we can sway to the music as we show the spirit of the season through whatever means we possess. We can all do something to share the good news with the world around us that a Savior is born.

What can you do to share the good news with others today?

WHY WOULD ANYONE EVER CHOOSE TO LEAVE HEAVEN?

"Christ Jesus, who being in the form of God...made Himself of no reputation, taking the form of a bondservant, and coming in the likeness of men."

– PHILIPPIANS 2:5–7

I was asked to speak at a funeral. What is already a difficult situation for a family often isn't made any easier by it happening during the Christmas season. However, there was comfort in the fact that this man had been blessed to live a long life, and more importantly that he had shown a steadfast faith in the Lord. Therefore his family found consolation in some of those truths we often hear at funerals—that he was in a better place, that he would not have to suffer any more pain or sorrow, and that he was enjoying the presence of God and a reunion with loved ones who had gone on before him. At those times we also like to be reminded of the image of heaven as a place with pearly gates, golden streets, and the river of life. We relish the thought of discarding these old bodies and being fitted with new, improved glorified ones. Heaven sounds like a wonderful place to spend eternity.

Do you think anyone would ever choose to return from that place? There have been books and movies suggesting such a scenario, but it would be hard to imagine that kind of a decision actually being made. I think heaven will be so wonderful and such an improvement over our earthly existence that no one would ever consider the possibility of leaving it.

And yet there was one occasion when someone did choose to travel the opposite direction from the norm. Someone was actually willing to give up the glories of heaven and come to earth. This person knew that it would mean having to trade eternity for a calendar. It would mean giving up unlimited access to the universe and being confined to one little section of one small planet. It would mean forsaking an unimaginable existence as an infinite spirit in order to take up residence in flesh and blood that could suffer and feel pain. It would mean exchanging regal glory and splendor for a very humble lifestyle. It would mean leaving a throne and being born in a manger. And yet Jesus chose to take that journey.

As the Bible states, He "being in the form of God, did not consider it robbery to be equal with God, but made Himself of no reputation, taking the form of a bondservant, and coming in the likeness of men. And being found in appearance as a man, He humbled Himself and became obedient to the point of death, even the death of the cross" (Philippians 2:6–8).

Why did Jesus take such a unique and unfathomable step? Why was He willing to give up so much? It was because He knew that it was the only way anyone else would be able to make that journey in the other direction. If He didn't come to be our Savior, then no one else would be able to find his or her way to heaven.

That's what we're celebrating at Christmas. And although a funeral may be difficult during this season of the year, it also serves as a good reminder to us. The only reason we can have hope and peace about a loved one's "home-going" is because Jesus was first willing to leave His home to come here. Out of love for us, He gave up more than we can imagine. But because He did, one day we will no longer have to try to imagine it. If we know Him as our Savior, we'll get to see it firsthand. And maybe then, when we experience that glory and splendor of heaven for ourselves, we'll fully appreciate what Jesus gave up and what Christmas truly means.

Lord, thank You for being willing to leave the splendor of heaven to come to this earth so that I can go to heaven one day.

What Would Jesus Want?

"And when they had come into the house, they saw the young Child with Mary His mother, and fell down and worshiped Him."

– MATTHEW 2:11

One of the local nursing homes had a Christmas tree in its lobby. I understand that there were some tags hanging on that tree listing the name of a resident along with one gift that person would like to receive. Family, friends, or other visitors could pick one of those names and bring that gift for the appropriate person. It's a nice idea that reminds us not to forget some folks who are too often overlooked as we busy ourselves with all our other Christmas activities and gatherings.

If Jesus' name was on such a tree, I wonder what gift He would want? I don't see Jesus asking for some of the gifts we might request—an item of clothing, some cologne, or the latest electronic gadget. I know it involves some degree of speculation on our part, but based on what the Bible says, I believe there are three main gifts Jesus would want from us.

One would be our worship. The wise men brought Jesus those well-known gifts of gold, frankincense, and myrrh. I guess frankincense is almost like a gift of cologne. Could it have been Old Spice frankincense? Or maybe it was so many years ago that it was actually New Spice at the time. At any rate I don't think the Lord was as pleased with those gifts as He was with the other gift those kings gave Him—they worshiped Him. That gift still pleases the Lord when we offer it to Him. He wants us to recognize Him for who He is and give Him the adoration of which He is worthy.

Have you ever worshiped a baby or small child as those wise men did? Maybe we haven't literally bowed down to one, but the way we look at some of our precious children or grandchildren can sometimes approach an attitude of worship. That baby in Bethlehem deserves such praise. He was the Son of God who had come in the flesh to be our Savior. He wants our gift of worship and is worthy to receive it.

A second main gift I believe Jesus would want is our trust or faith in Him. Jesus didn't come into the world just so people would bow down before Him. He was born so that we might believe in Him and be restored into a right relationship with our Heavenly Father. Jesus knows how important it is for us to do that. He doesn't want us to face God's wrath one day, but rather desires for us to go to heaven to be with Him. So the best gift we could give Him would be to put our trust in Him and as a result allow Him to give us the best gift we could ever receive—that gift of forgiveness and eternal life.

But I can think of one other main gift I believe Jesus would want— the gift of ourselves. One of the families in our church received a special gift one Christmas. Their son who was serving in the Navy and whom they haven't seen in quite a while was home for Christmas. Although he may have brought his family members some other presents, the main gift he brought them was himself. That's the main gift Jesus wants from us. Nothing would please Him more than for each of us to come to Him in the spirit of a familiar hymn that says "Take myself, and I will be ever, only, all for Thee."

So as we give and receive our various other gifts over these next few days, let's not overlook what Jesus truly wants from us. Let's seek to give Him those gifts of our worship, our trust, and ourselves.

What do you need to give Jesus as Christmas approaches?

A Grinch Didn't Steal Our Christmas Spirit

"Arise, take the young Child and his mother, flee to Egypt, and stay there until I bring you word; for Herod will seek the young Child to destroy Him."

– Matthew 2:13

Kidnapped! That was the startling truth I discovered a few days before Christmas as I drove in front of our house to turn into the driveway. Baby Jesus was missing from our outdoor Nativity scene. I stopped the car to check out the situation more closely, making sure that the child hadn't simply fallen off his makeshift manger. I found everything else in its proper place, but the baby was nowhere to be found. There was no doubt that someone had absconded with the lighted figurine of the Savior.

With a mixture of anger and sadness, I wondered why anyone would resort to such a crime. A prank? Pure meanness? Some kind of message about an empty manger or a Christless Christmas? I don't know, but I decided to go ahead and report the incident to the local authorities. After all, the many clones of that child in other people's yards might be in danger of the same fate. I felt that I should at least let someone know about it.

The deputy was very kind and helpful, but I was somewhat disappointed when she didn't offer to put out an Amber Alert for the missing child. I gave a perfect description of the victim—tiny, with a plastic peaceful smile on his face, last seen wrapped up in swaddling clothes—and oh, he still had the cord attached. Maybe the problem was that our only witnesses weren't talking. I suppose the parents were too traumatized by the occurrence. Mary and Joseph could still be found kneeling beside the place where the child lay, staring in paralyzed silence at the empty hay. You would have thought some of the other figures in the scene would have been more helpful, especially those we refer to as wise men. But as much as we give them credit for their smarts, they couldn't offer up even a vague description of the perpetrators. Likewise, the shepherd seemed to bow his head in silent shame, knowing that he was the only one present with a weapon, yet had failed to use that staff to protect the child. The only one who was talking was the sheep. And he kept repeating the same thing we already knew—"It was a baa-aa-aad, baa-aa-aad person."

I guess there are a lot of ways certain people try to remove Christ from Christmas these days. However, the good news is that they will always be unsuccessful. They can steal figurines or do away with nativity scenes altogether, but it doesn't change the truth about a baby born in Bethlehem. They can substitute the word "holiday" for "Christmas" or refuse to utter the name of Christ at all, but one day every knee will bow before Him and every tongue will confess that Jesus Christ is Lord. They may be able to take away some of the outward signs of the real Christmas story, but they can't steal Jesus from our hearts.

This incident reminded me of the story about the Grinch who tried to steal Christmas. He took all the presents, expecting it to ruin the holiday for the residents of Whoville. However when Christmas morning came, those folks still gathered, held hands, and joyfully sang their tune of cele-bration. Although the disappearance of our baby Jesus initially disturbed me, I was determined not to let any Grinches rob us of the true Christmas spirit. I'm glad to report that although our manger was still empty on Christmas morning, we were still singing. I hope you remember the real reason for joy as that day comes too, regardless of your circumstances—a joy you can continue to experience throughout the year.

Lord, help me not to allow any "Grinches" rob me of the joy of Christmas.

CELEBRATE THE UNIQUENESS
OF CHRIST AT CHRISTMAS

"And the Word became flesh and dwelt among us, and we beheld His glory, the glory as of the only begotten of the Father, full of grace and truth."

– JOHN 1:14

At our worship service one Sunday, our church enjoyed the accompaniment of a musical instrument which I doubt any other congregation in the area experienced—no, not even those who were performing their big Christmas programs with full orchestras. We were privileged to hear a missionary guest play the musical saw. The enchanting, almost haunting, tones of that instrument added a special element to such familiar seasonal tunes as "O Holy Night" and "What Child Is This?"

However, it's not just the unique sound of this instrument which makes it stand out, nor the fact that so few people possess the skill to play it. It's also the idea of beautiful music being produced from an object we normally associate with other purposes. To see a saw being used to play music rather than to trim tree limbs tends to fascinate people. It makes us want to grab our handsaw from the tool shed and see what sounds we can get out of it, as unwise, unproductive, and even hazardous such an impulse could prove to be for us untrained amateurs.

As we approach Christmas Eve and Christmas Day itself, let's make sure we don't miss the opportunity to celebrate Christ as the unique instrument bringing salvation to the world. This isn't just the celebration of a baby's birth, as special as such events can be. And it's more than the recognition of a great person coming into the world. Jesus was one-of-a-kind. In the common phrase used to describe Him in scripture, commonly translated as "the only begotten," there is a clear suggestion of uniqueness.

Christmas isn't simply a commemoration of one of the times recorded when angels appeared and brought messages to mankind. This is a once-in-history event—the time when God took on man's nature and form in order to save us from our sins. "And the Word became flesh and dwelt among us, and we beheld His glory, the glory as of the only begotten of the Father, full of grace and truth" (John 1:14). Only Jesus was capable and qualified to provide for our salvation. No one else could have accomplished it. And certainly we were helpless to save ourselves. We couldn't achieve it by using our own tools of good works and self-effort. Only God Himself could come and be the perfect, sinless, holy sacrifice on our behalf. Only Jesus could exhibit God's amazing love and satisfy His justice at the same time.

But just as a handsaw makes for a strange musical instrument, a baby born in a manger seemed like an odd way for such a Savior to enter the world. Many expected the Messiah to come with resounding trumpets in a palace surrounded by an entourage of royal dignitaries, not in the quiet humbleness of a stable in the presence of lowly shepherds. As one song suggests, what a strange way to save the world.

A handsaw may be a strange way to make music, but in the hands of the right person it can do so beautifully. And a baby in Bethlehem may have been a strange way to save us from our sins, but in the hands of God it was the perfect plan being carried out—a beautiful way to show His love and grace.

So take time over these next few days to recognize and celebrate the uniqueness of Christ and His incarnation. In the midst of all the common music of family gatherings, gift-giving, and good food, don't miss the beautiful, unique melody of the Son of God being born to save His people from their sins.

Father, thank You for the unique gift of Your Son.

The Wonder of
the Incarnation

*"Inasmuch then as the children have partaken of flesh and blood,
He Himself likewise shared the same...."*

– Hebrews 2:14

As Christmas day finally arrives, let's remind ourselves of the wondrous nature of the incarnation—the fact that God chose to become a flesh-and-blood human being. His willingness to take this amazing action communicates something to us about the kind of God He is. It lets us know that He identifies with us and He cares about us. This wasn't just the carrying out of some wise plan or the fulfillment of an eternal purpose. The incarnation was also an expression of divine love.

My grandchildren have seen me preaching from pulpits, presiding over weddings, conducting baptisms, and otherwise performing my sacred duties as a minister of the gospel. As such they have seen me dressed up in coats and ties, as well as behaving with a certain decorum expected at such occasions. There have also been times when they've related to me as the one in authority over them when their parents weren't around. Therefore they've experienced some discipline from me when they have misbehaved—telling them no or making them sit in "timeout" for a few minutes. However those aren't the only ways, and certainly not the main ways, I relate to my grandkids.

More often I get down on the floor with them to play games and to wrestle. I give them piggyback rides. I read books with them. I sometimes get down on their level and act like a little kid myself. And while they've seen me dressed rather formally, they've also seen me purposefully wear my cap crooked, make funny faces, or otherwise change my appearance in order to make them laugh. Some of those actions, if witnessed by others, might be judged to be rather undignified for a pastor. Maybe that's one reason I go hopping behind my granddaughter playing "follow the leader" in the privacy of my own living room. However, there have been times when my neighbors could have looked outside and witnessed me taking some giant steps after asking "Mother, may I?" or otherwise running around publicly with my grandkids as if I were one of them.

When I'm dead and gone, I hope those grandchildren not only remember me as a godly preacher but also as someone who loved them, played with them, and took them to Dairy Queen for ice cream. I don't want them to know me just as a detached preacher-grandfather whom they respect, but as the Papaw whom they loved and enjoyed being with.

That's part of what I believe the incarnation says to us about God. He's the holy Lawgiver whose presence was in the midst of the thunderings on Mount Sinai. He's the Judge who's going to pass final judgment on us one day. He's the God who deserves our fear and respect. But He's also the God who got down on the floor with us. He came down to our level. He became one of us, as small and childlike as we are in comparison to His greatness and majesty. He took off His suit and tie, put on His jeans and T-shirt, and lived in our world for a while.

Why did He do it? Because He loves us. He wants us to know that He's more than just the thundering voice that gives out commands or passes judgment. He's also the tender voice that identifies with us and cares about us.

May this amazing truth of the incarnation fill our hearts with wonder and gratitude this Christmas.

Give thanks for the love of God which is shown in the incarnation.

Make Sure You Have a Savior for Christmas

"For there is born to you this day in the city of David a Savior, who is Christ the Lord."

– Luke 2:11

Have you been watching any of the multitude of Christmas movies that come on TV this time of year? Sometimes you can catch an oldie-but-goodie, such as *It's a Wonderful Life* or *Miracle on 34ᵗʰ Street*. Then there are others that have been made in more recent years, including those made-for-TV Christmas flicks. Unfortunately not all of those possess the good quality. As I've perused the TV listings, I've noticed a number of features with similar titles: *A Mom for Christmas*, *A Dad for Christmas*, *A Boyfriend for Christmas*, and even *A Grandpa for Christmas*. It seems as if whatever relationship a person may be lacking in his or her life, a movie is being made about gaining that missing person at Christmas. I'm beginning to wonder how far they'll take it in the next few years. Will future holiday classics be entitled "An Aunt Martha for Christmas" or "A Second Cousin Joe for Christmas"?

It's interesting that the theme of missing relationships keeps showing up. Maybe it reveals the recognition that there are more important things in life than those which might come wrapped under the tree at Christmas. Possibly more of us are realizing that the latest toy or electronic gadget doesn't compare in value to the relationships in our lives. Our deepest wishes at Christmas may have more to do with people than about something money can buy. Christmas can be a good time to deal with strained or broken relationships. Let's pray that God will bring restoration, forgiveness, and a change of attitude where needed. Maybe at one of those family gatherings we will have an opportunity to show God's love and to experience a healed relationship with someone.

In addition, I would suggest another title which would fit that reoccurring theme in the holiday movies. We could call it, "A Savior for Christmas." Of course, it would be about the birth of Jesus. When you think about it, that event is all about relationships too. It has to do with restoring our broken relationship with God and providing a way for us to become part of His family. God gave us the greatest gift that first Christmas. It was exactly what we needed the most in our lives. More than we needed a big-screen TV, a new car, or the latest game system, we needed a Savior. We needed Someone who could save us from sin and who could help us find peace with God. We needed Someone who could rescue us from the road leading to destruction and allow us to get on the road heading toward heaven. That's what Jesus came to do.

Do you remember the announcement of the angel to the shepherds? If not, find a Bible and read that account in Luke 2. The angel declared to the world that "there is born to you a Savior." What the world needed most wasn't a mom or dad or grandpa, but a Savior. Family is important. It's good to have those people in our lives. But it's even more important that we have a right relationship with God. It's vital to know that we've found forgiveness from Him for all the wrong things we've done in the past. It's essential that we have the assurance and peace in our hearts which come from knowing that all is well between us and the Lord.

So my Christmas prayer for you is that any of those missing or broken relationships in your life will be restored. And I especially pray that you will know the joy and peace of having a Savior for Christmas.

What relationships can God help you restore? How is your relationship with Him? Be thankful today for God sending you a Savior.

CHRISTMAS ISN'T EVER OVER

"As You sent Me into the world, I also have sent them into the world."

– JOHN 17:18

W hat are you doing on this day after Christmas? Did you sleep in to catch up on some of your rest from all the busyness of the past few weeks? Are you taking it slow, spending some quiet time by yourself after hectic, crowded family gatherings over the last couple of days? You might be finding some needed relaxation in sitting in the recliner with a cup of coffee and this book in hand.

The children among us will probably spend the day playing with their new toys. Meanwhile many adults will be having their fun by trying to figure out how to install and use the latest electronic gadget they received for Christmas. Others of us may just be sorting through a few gifts trying to decide whether it's something we're going to use or if it's an item we'll store away in the back corner of a closet.

Or maybe you're feeling a little melancholic this morning as you see the empty space under the Christmas tree or as you say goodbye to family members traveling back to their distant homes. Others may be pumped up as they prepare for the after-Christmas sales at the stores. Or you may already be making your plans for taking down those decorations as soon as possible and trying to get your house back to some state of normalcy. After all, Christmas is over for another year, isn't it?

I doubt if the morning after that first Christmas was a quiet one for Mary and Joseph. Taking care of a newborn baby probably didn't leave much time for rest and reflection. The presence of their special child outweighed any melancholy they may have felt over the departure of the shepherds and angels. There was much to do in carrying out their God-given responsibilities as the parents of the Son of God. His birth, as great and significant as it was, wasn't the end. It was only the beginning.

Neither should Christmas be the end for us. Its implications should follow us throughout the year. Because Christ was born in Bethlehem, there's much for us to ponder and even more for us to do.

Although the space underneath our Christmas trees may be empty, our lives can remain full of the presence of Christ. Even though the radio stations may be back to playing their regular music instead of those holiday classics, we can still have a song in our hearts about our Savior. Although family members may be back on the highways heading home, we can still enjoy the close and constant companionship of Jesus who has promised to be with us always.

While we seek some quiet moments for ourselves to renew our physical bodies, we can also spend some quiet times with the Lord in prayer and Bible reading to renew our spirits and strengthen our souls. And although we may be ready to take down the lights from our Christmas tree or from around the windows of our houses, we should continue to let the light of Christ shine through our lives as a positive influence on a dark world.

The day after Christmas isn't the time for a nostalgic letdown. It's time to get pumped up about the possibilities of going out into the world as representatives of the One who was born in Bethlehem. It's time to faithfully move ahead in fulfilling our responsibilities to practice the faith that Jesus gave to us.

On December 26, Christmas isn't really over. It's just taking on a different form as Christ's followers seek to live out the truths of His holy birth for the remainder of the year.

In what ways do you need to carry the truths of Christmas with you throughout the year?

PURSUE A MORE DISCIPLINED LIFE

"Do you not know that those who run in a race all run, but one receives the prize? Run in such a way that you may obtain it."

– I CORINTHIANS 9:24

I remember when my five-year-old granddaughter was taken to the Fox Theater to experience the Atlanta Ballet's performance of *The Nutcracker*. Considering the fact that she had been involved in a ballet class for the past couple of years, it was a special treat for her. She thoroughly enjoyed it. When the show was over, she didn't want to leave.

I heard about a number of comments she made during the performance. I was especially pleased about one statement she offered as she watched those professional dancers working their magic on the stage: "It takes a lot of practice to do that." My granddaughter had the wisdom to realize that it took a lot of hard work and practice to reach such a level of excellence.

Some of us who are much older can tend to lose sight of that truth. We see people who are excelling and we chalk it up to talent, luck, chance, knowing the right people, or other such explanations. In some cases, there may be other factors involved, but we often overlook the hard work, sacrifice, and hours of practice it took for the person to get to that level.

Maybe we even tend to view people whose spirituality we admire in a similar fashion. We attribute their godliness and seemingly close relationship to the Lord to God's special favor, to their unique character, to certain qualities they possess, or to other factors with which they've been blessed but which we seem to be lacking. We see them as reaching a particular level of holiness that is beyond what we could ever experience.

However, we would do well to remember that those saintly Christians we admire didn't become that way overnight. Yes, it did take the transforming work of the Holy Spirit in their lives—the same Spirit who can work in us. And it probably isn't best to say that "it took a lot of practice" for them to get there. That statement suggests a little too much reliance on our own efforts and could be misunderstood as promoting a religion of simply doing the right things. We can't forget that being a follower of Christ is primarily about a personal relationship.

However, we likewise shouldn't overlook the importance of a disciplined life in building such a relationship. If we want a closer walk with God, are we faithfully practicing those disciplines which help promote such godliness? You wish you had such an intimate connection with God as you sense in some other people, so are you setting aside some time each day to spend cultivating such a relationship through prayer and devotional reading? You wish you knew as much about the Bible and God's will as that other believer, so are you regularly reading God's Word, attending a Bible study, and reading good Christian books?

Becoming a mature, godly Christian doesn't just happen. In a sense, it takes a lot of practice. It involves the hard work of consistently saying no to temptation and yes to the will of God. It means sacrificing some selfish or secondary aspects of life and making the pursuit of God a greater priority. It involves finding ways to use our talents and resources to serve the Lord and to minister to others. It means spending time seeking God, worshiping, praying, reading the Bible, serving, and reaching out to others with God's love.

As a new year approaches, let's resolve to be more disciplined in our pursuit of God and godliness. The Lord must be the One to transform us, but at the same time we need to work hard at those means He gives us to affect such change.

How can you "run better" and be more diligent and disciplined in pursuing God in the upcoming year?

TAKE A SMALL STEP IN THE RIGHT DIRECTION

"Walk as children of light...finding out what is acceptable to the Lord."

– EPHESIANS 5:8–10

One time when I was recovering from surgery, I was reminded of the value of small victories. Sometimes you have to take so-called baby steps before you can make greater strides of progress. In those first few days after my procedure, some of my small steps I rejoiced in included being able to walk without assistance, being able to get up from chairs without much pain, and walking out to the mailbox to get my morning newspaper. Those actions didn't mean I was all better and back to normal, but they were steps in the right direction leading toward that goal.

It reminds me of a song from one of the animated Christmas programs which comes on TV each year. There's a song in the show whose tune always gets caught in my head, but I also like the words and the simple message it conveys. Kris Kringle is telling the evil Winter Warlock that he can change from being bad to good. And the song encourages him to do it one step at a time. It reminded me of my literal postsurgical shaky steps as it says, "Put one foot in front of the other and soon you'll be walking across the floor; put one foot in front of the other and soon you'll be walking out the door."

Sometimes we prefer to take giant leaps rather than small steps. And with some of the needed changes in our lives, the Lord works that way.

We can be forgiven of our sins and free from its guilt in an instant. We can have our hearts cleansed and receive the gift of eternal life in a moment of repentance and faith.

But there are other changes which take time. And if we expect to reach them immediately, we may be frustrated and disappointed. Or if we try to achieve them in one giant leap, we will often fall flat on our faces. For example, the Bible tells us that it's God's goal for us "to be conformed to the image of His Son" (Romans 8:29). However, that transformation isn't accomplished in one big step on one day. It usually requires a lot of little steps over the course of a lifetime.

As we approach the beginning of a new year, maybe you're thinking about some needed changes in your life—especially the kind of changes God may want you to make. In some cases it may involve taking a big stride forward, but in other cases it may simply mean being willing to take a small step in the right direction. You may need to take a few baby steps before you can really start walking.

So instead of making some grandiose resolution for the coming year, maybe you would be wiser to think about what the first small step would be to get you headed the right way and focus more on it. What would be the first small step to get you going toward God and what He wants you to be? For someone it might be to stop doing something you know is wrong. For another it might mean getting back to church or back to times of fellowship with God through prayer and His Word. For another it might mean reaching out to someone with forgiveness or love.

Whatever your small step is, trust God to help you take it. Then look for the next step after that. And keep going until you reach the goal. With God's help, simply putting one foot in front of the other will eventually get you there.

Take a first small step today in the direction God wants you to go.

LET'S NOT RECYCLE THE SAME OLD ATTITUDES THIS YEAR

"And I will give you a new heart and put a new spirit within you."
— EZEKIEL 36:26

I loaded a couple of bundles of old newspapers along with some cardboard and other papers into the trunk of my car. I then made one of my periodic runs to a recycling bin located not far from our house. I'll admit that I don't make that trip as often as I should. Sometimes the newspapers in our rack start stacking up so precariously high that it becomes an art to try to carefully place another one on the pile without making it topple over. Likewise, the other recyclable materials are often allowed to take up far too much space on the floor next to our kitchen garbage before being disposed of.

As I made this particular trip, I wondered if I would ever see any of these papers and boxes again. Sometimes I purchase items that claim to be made out of recycled paper, but I suppose the odds of me buying something that was made out of the specific newspaper that I donated are close to astronomical. And even if I did manage to do it, there is no way I could know about it. However someone, somewhere, should eventually receive a product made from those old papers and boxes. That's what recycling is about.

We're approaching a time of the year when many of us ponder the possibility of discarding other "old stuff" in our lives. We could do it anytime, but there's something about the turning of the calendar to a new year that makes it seem like an especially good time to make a change. It may be a long-held habit that we know isn't good for us or pleasing to God. Or it may be something that isn't necessarily wrong but it's just cluttering up our lives, making us less able or efficient in doing everything the Lord has in mind for us. What are you resolving to get rid of this year?

If you're like me, you've probably found out that such resolutions are often unsuccessful. I believe part of the problem is that we usually don't get to the root of the problem. We try to change the outward actions while not dealing with the underlying attitude from which it grows. It's kind of like recycling. For example, we may get rid of one particular manifestation of laziness in our lives, but that lazy disposition is liable to show up again in some other form. Some of us have been recycling the same attitudes or spirit year after year. We need to seek to discover what the attitude is behind the action we believe needs changing. Is it lack of self-discipline? Or is it selfishness? Look past the action and focus on your heart.

But once we do that, is there any hope for long-lasting change? Isn't what we see in our hearts simply the way we are and we're just going to have to live with it? The good news is that we serve a God who can not only help us alter our actions, but who can also change us on the inside. He can cleanse us of all unrighteousness. He can take away our selfishness and give us a love that will put others ahead of ourselves. He can change us, our desires, and our attitudes. He can dispose of that "old stuff" in our lives so that it doesn't pop up again in a different form in the new year.

So let's look a little deeper within ourselves for change this year. Let God change your heart and then see how your actions will be different as a result.

What is there in your heart, spirit, or attitude that needs to change? Pray and trust the Lord to begin to transform you from the inside out.

A New Year Is a Chance
for a Fresh Start

"Forgetting those things which are behind and reaching forward to those things which are ahead."

— Philippians 3:13

In the past I've mentioned how I have exposed my grandchildren to one of my favorite TV series, the *Andy Griffith Show*. Recently my wife introduced them to one of her beloved programs, the PBS series *Anne of Green Gables*. I'm talking about the classic filmed version of the story, the one starring Megan Follows—not any of the more recent remakes which in our sight can never measure up to the previous Emmy Award-winning edition.

While there are many memorable scenes from the show, it also contains some inspiring ideas and quotes. I like the one that is brought out in the course of Anne's conversation with her teacher. It's the idea that tomorrow is always fresh and new with no mistakes in it. It's a helpful reminder that we don't have to be defined by our past or feel hopelessly trapped in previous habits of harmful behavior. It's possible to make a fresh start.

Maybe that would be a helpful concept for many of us to keep in mind as we begin a new year. This might be a good time for some of us to make a fresh start. As we review the past year in our minds, glaring mistakes jump out at us. We didn't keep those New Year's resolutions we were so committed to back in January. We didn't accomplish many of the tasks on our to-do list for the past twelve months. We made some poor decisions, failed God at times, and let down people who were counting on us. We fell into some bad habits. Maybe we lost some of our passion and drifted into complacency.

However, whatever your mistakes were in last year, the new year offers you a fresh start. No, you can't undo the past. There are consequences of previous choices which you may have to live with. But you can start dealing with that situation and your life in general in a better way beginning now. You can seek God's forgiveness for those past wrongs, as well as forgive yourself. You can endeavor with God's help not to make the same mistakes again. You can lean on the Lord to give you strength to overcome temptations, to give you wisdom in your decisions, and to guide your feet along a better path.

In the new year the Lord can help us overcome long-engrained behaviors which have so often defeated us. He can also rekindle the flame for those things we ought to be passionate about, such as knowing Him better, becoming more like Christ, and ministering to a lost world.

However, we shouldn't forget one little word Anne's teacher added to this concept. She reminded Anne that tomorrow has no mistakes in it… yet. No matter what commitments we make, how determined we are, or even how hard we pray, we'll still make our share of new mistakes in the coming year. We'll use poor judgment at times. There will be occasions when we're liable to choose our way over God's way. We won't be perfect. Let's not use that prognosis as an excuse for our failures. But the recognition of that fact can help keep us from being too hard on ourselves when we do falter. We can still repent, find forgiveness, and with God's help start fresh again. And although we'll still make mistakes, we can do better this year. We can make progress. We can experience victory over some of those behaviors and habits. We can become more like Jesus in certain ways. We can have purer hearts and holier lives.

Look at the new year as an opportunity for a fresh start. And trust the Lord to help you make the most of it.

In what way do you need to put past mistakes behind you and make a fresh start with God's help?

Unwrap God's Gift of a New Year

"This is the day the Lord has made; we will rejoice and be glad in it."

– Psalm 118:24

At some point recently, many of us were given the opportunity to unwrap one or more Christmas presents. How do you go about that task? Do you excitedly rip off the paper to get as quickly as possible to whatever is inside? Or maybe you carefully remove the bow and make an effort not to disturb the beautiful packaging any more than you absolutely must. There are some who take their time lifting the gift to evaluate its weight, or shaking it to listen for any noises which might give a hint of what's inside. They may even sit there for a moment imagining what it might be before finally taking the necessary steps to unlock the mystery of its contents.

As we prepare to face a new year, we should consider it a precious gift from God. There are many who were alive to welcome in the year back in January who are no longer with us as the year draws to a close. We're often moved by viewing those end-of-the-year memorials reminding us of famous individuals who have passed away in the last twelve months. Yet many of us are even more aware of people we know personally, some who were near and dear to us, who are not here to see in the New Year. So the fact that we are still alive and are being given this opportunity is certainly a gift for which to be grateful.

So how do you go about opening this gift? Are you going to enthusiastically jump right into it with a first-of-the-year burst of energy as you try to tackle a host of resolutions and goals? Or will you encounter this gift somewhat more reservedly, with personal introspection, dreams of what the months ahead might hold, and cautiously unwrapping its contents? There are some who may be hesitant to open this gift at all, doing so with dread, fear, and concerns about what it might hold.

So how should it affect us to view this new year as a gift from God? For one thing, it reminds us that an all-wise God has a purpose in letting us live to see another year. We can open this gift knowing that it's meant for us and that there is still a reason for us being here. Secondly we can be confident that it is a good gift. God is good and "every good gift and every perfect gift is from above, and comes down from the Father" (James 1:17). Additionally, receiving this gift from God of a new year should challenge us to use it in the ways that would please Him and bring honor to His name.

Have you ever received one of those presents in which you opened one wrapped box only to find another one in inside, and maybe another inside of it? The anticipation tends to build as you are forced to work your way through to reach the gift at the center of it all. In a sense, that's what God is giving us. We don't get to unwrap this year all at once: God gives it to us one day at a time. We may unwrap one day to find a disappointment, another day confusion—not sure why God gave us that or even what it is, and another day we may joyfully unwrap just what we were hoping for. However, through all those daily packages, we know that God is working to bring about good to those who love Him (Romans 8:28).

This is going to be a good year, because it's a gift from a good God. Look forward to unwrapping it one day at a time.

C year, and each day of this year, is a good gift from God.

BIBLE HIGHLIGHTS
READING SCHEDULE

January

1 - Genesis 1
2 - Genesis 3
3 - Genesis 6
4 - Genesis 7
5 - Genesis 8
6 - Genesis 9
7 - Genesis 11
8 - Genesis 12
9 - Genesis 16
10 - Genesis 17
11 - Genesis 18
12 - Genesis 19
13 - Genesis 21
14 - Genesis 22
15 - Genesis 24
16 - Genesis 25

17 - Genesis 27
18 - Genesis 29
19 - Genesis 30
20 - Genesis 32
21 - Genesis 33
22 - Genesis 37
23 - Genesis 39
24 - Genesis 40
25 - Genesis 41
26 - Genesis 42
27 - Genesis 43
28 - Genesis 44
29 - Genesis 45
30 - Genesis 50
31 - Exodus 1

February

1 - Exodus 2
2 - Exodus 3
3 - Exodus 5
4 - Exodus 7
5 - Exodus 8
6 - Exodus 9
7 - Exodus 10
8 - Exodus 11
9 - Exodus 12

10 - Exodus 14
11 - Exodus 16
12 - Exodus 17
13 - Exodus 19
14 - Exodus 20
15 - Exodus 22
16 - Exodus 25
17 - Exodus 28
18 - Exodus 32

19 - Exodus 33

20 - Exodus 34

21 - Exodus 35

22 - Exodus 40

23 - Leviticus 1

24 - Leviticus 4

25 - Leviticus 10

26 - Leviticus 11

27 - Leviticus 13

28 - Leviticus 16

29 - Leviticus 18

March

1 - Leviticus 23

2 - Leviticus 25

3 - Leviticus 26

4 - Numbers 1

5 - Numbers 6

6 - Numbers 9

7 - Numbers 11

8 - Numbers 12

9 - Numbers 13

10 - Numbers 14

11 - Numbers 16

12 - Numbers 17

13 - Numbers 20

14 - Numbers 21

15 - Numbers 22

16 - Numbers 23

17 - Numbers 24

18 - Numbers 25

19 - Numbers 32

20 - Numbers 35

21 - Deuteronomy 1

22 - Deuteronomy 4

23 - Deuteronomy 6

24 - Deuteronomy 7

25 - Deuteronomy 8

26 - Deuteronomy 11

27 - Deuteronomy 15

28 - Deuteronomy 18

29 - Deuteronomy 24

30 - Deuteronomy 27

31 - Deuteronomy 28

April

1 - Deuteronomy 29

2 - Deuteronomy 30

3 - Deuteronomy 31

4 - Deuteronomy 32

5 - Deuteronomy 34

6 - Joshua 1

7 - Joshua 2

8 - Joshua 3

9 - Joshua 4

10 - Joshua 5

11 - Joshua 6

12 - Joshua 7

13 - Joshua 8

14 - Joshua 9

15 - Joshua 10

16 - Joshua 14

17 - Joshua 22

18 - Joshua 23

19 - Joshua 24

20 - Judges 2

21 - Judges 3

22 - Judges 4

23 - Judges 6

24 - Judges 7

25 - Judges 8

26 - Judges 11

27 - Judges 13   29 - Judges 15
28 - Judges 14   30 - Judges 16

May

1 - Ruth 1   17 - I Samuel 16
2 - Ruth 2   18 - I Samuel 17
3 - Ruth 3   19 - I Samuel 18
4 - Ruth 4   20 - I Samuel 19
5 - I Samuel 1   21 - I Samuel 20
6 - I Samuel 2   22 - I Samuel 23
7 - I Samuel 3   23 - I Samuel 24
8 - I Samuel 4   24 - I Samuel 25
9 - I Samuel 5   25 - I Samuel 26
10 - I Samuel 6   26 - I Samuel 28
11 - I Samuel 7   27 - I Samuel 31
12 - I Samuel 8   28 - II Samuel 1
13 - I Samuel 9   29 - II Samuel 2
14 - I Samuel 10   30 - II Samuel 3
15 - I Samuel 13   31 - II Samuel 4
16 - I Samuel 15

June

1 - II Samuel 5   18 - I Kings 8
2 - II Samuel 6   19 - I Kings 11
3 - II Samuel 7   20 - I Kings 12
4 - II Samuel 11   21 - I Kings 14
5 - II Samuel 12   22 - I Kings 17
6 - II Samuel 13   23 - I Kings 18
7 - II Samuel 14   24 - I Kings 19
8 - II Samuel 15   25 - I Kings 21
9 - II Samuel 16   26 - I Kings 22
10 - II Samuel 17   27 - II Kings 2
11 - II Samuel 18   28 - II Kings 4
12 - II Samuel 19   29 - II Kings 5
13 - II Samuel 23   30 - II Kings 6
14 - II Samuel 24
15 - I Kings 1
16 - I Kings 3
17 - I Kings 6

July

1 -	II Kings 17	17 -	Esther 8
2 -	II Kings 18	18 -	Esther 9
3 -	II Kings 19	19 -	Job 1
4 -	II Kings 20	20 -	Job 2
5 -	II Kings 23	21 -	Job 4
6 -	II Kings 25	22 -	Job 5
7 -	II Chronicles 7	23 -	Job 38
8 -	II Chronicles 36	24 -	Job 40
9 -	Ezra 1	25 -	Job 42
10 -	Ezra 3	26 -	Psalm 1
11 -	Nehemiah 1	27 -	Psalm 23
12 -	Nehemiah 2	28 -	Psalm 42
13 -	Nehemiah 4	29 -	Psalm 46
14 -	Nehemiah 8	30 -	Psalm 51
15 -	Nehemiah 12	31 -	Psalm 103
16 -	Esther 4		

August

1 -	1 -Psalm 119	17 -	Jeremiah 36
2 -	Psalm 121	18 -	Lamentations 3
3 -	Psalm 148	19 -	Ezekiel 1
4 -	Proverbs 1	20 -	Ezekiel 3
5 -	Proverbs 31	21 -	Ezekiel 33
6 -	Ecclesiastes 1	22 -	Ezekiel 37
7 -	Ecclesiastes 12	23 -	Daniel 1
8 -	Song of Solomon 1	24 -	Daniel 3
9 -	Isaiah 6	25 -	Daniel 6
10 -	Isaiah 9	26 -	Hosea 1
11 -	Isaiah 40	27 -	Joel 2
12 -	Isaiah 53	28 -	Amos 5
13 -	Isaiah 55	29 -	Obadiah
14 -	Jeremiah 1	30 -	Jonah 1
15 -	Jeremiah 4	31 -	Jonah 2
16 -	Jeremiah 26		

September

1 -	Micah 6	3 -	Habakkuk 3
2 -	Nahum 1	4 -	Zephaniah 3

5 - Haggai 1	18 - Matthew 28
6 - Zechariah 4	19 - Mark 5
7 - Malachi 1	20 - Luke 1
8 - Malachi 3	21 - Luke 2
9 - Matthew 5	22 - Luke 3
10 - Matthew 6	23 - Luke 4
11 - Matthew 7	24 - Luke 10
12 - Matthew 13	25 - Luke 11
13 - Matthew 16	26 - Luke 15
14 - Matthew 24	27 - Luke 24
15 - Matthew 25	28 - John 1
16 - Matthew 26	29 - John 3
17 - Matthew 27	30 - John 4

October

1 - John 10	17 - Romans 4
2 - John 11	18 - Romans 5
3 - John 14	19 - Romans 6
4 - John 15	20 - Romans 8
5 - John 16	21 - Romans 12
6 - John 17	22 - Romans 13
7 - John 21	23 - I Corinthians 1
8 - Acts 1	24 - I Corinthians 3
9 - Acts 2	25 - I Corinthians 9
10 - Acts 7	26 - I Corinthians 10
11 - Acts 9	27 - I Corinthians 13
12 - Acts 10	28 - I Corinthians 14
13 - Acts 13	29 - I Corinthians 15
14 - Acts 16	30 - II Corinthians 4
15 - Romans1	31 - II Corinthians 5
16 - Romans 3	

November

1 - II Corinthians 6	7 - Ephesians 2
2 - II Corinthians 12	8 - Ephesians 3
3 - Galatians 3	9 - Ephesians 4
4 - Galatians 5	10 - Ephesians 5
5 - Galatians 6	11 - Ephesians 6
6 - Ephesians 1	12 - Philippians 1

13 - Philippians 2
14 - Philippians 3
15 - Philippians 4
16 - Colossians 1
17 - Colossians 3
18 - I Thessalonians 4
19 - I Thessalonians 5
20 - II Thessalonians 2
21 - II Thessalonians 3

22 - I Timothy 1
23 - I Timothy 3
24 - I Timothy 4
25 - I Timothy 6
26 - II Timothy 1
27 - II Timothy 2
28 - II Timothy 3
29 - II Timothy 4
30 - Titus 3

December

1 - Philemon
2 - Hebrews 2
3 - Hebrews 4
4 - Hebrews 6
5 - Hebrews 11
6 - Hebrews 12
7 - James 1
8 - James 2
9 - James 5
10 - I Peter 1
11 - I Peter 4
12 - I Peter 5
13 - II Peter 1
14 - II Peter 3
15 - I John 1
16 - I John 2

17 - I John 3
18 - I John 4
19 - I John 5
20 - II John
21 - III John
22 - Jude
23 - Revelation 1
24 - Revelation 2
25 - Revelation 3
26 - Revelation 4
27 - Revelation 13
28 - Revelation 19
29 - Revelation 20
30 - Revelation 21
31 - Revelation 22